CRIMINAL LAW
IN CANADA

CRIMINAL LAW IN CANADA

CASES, QUESTIONS, AND THE CODE

THIRD EDITION

SIMON VERDUN-JONES
SIMON FRASER UNIVERSITY

Harcourt Canada

Toronto Montreal Fort Worth New York Orlando
Philadelphia San Diego London Sydney Tokyo

Canadian Cataloguing in Publication Data

Verdun-Jones, Simon N. (Simon Nicholas), 1947–
    Criminal law in Canada: cases, questions, and the code

3rd ed.
Includes bibliographical references and index.
ISBN 0-7747-3698-4

1. Criminal law — Canada. 2. Criminal law — Canada — Cases. I. Title.

KE8809.V47 2001   345.71   C00-933139-5
KF9220.ZA2V47 2001

Acquisitions Editors: Megan Mueller / Brad Lambertus
Developmental Editor: Klaus G. Unger
Production Editor: Emily Ferguson
Production Coordinator: Cheri Westra

Copy Editor: Stacey Balakofsky
Permissions Editor: Mary Rose MacLachlan
Cover and Interior Design: Sonya V. Thursby, Opus House Incorporated
Typesetting and Assembly: Carolyn Hutchings Sebestyen
Printing and Binding: Tri-Graphic Printing Limited

Cover Art: *Divisadero at Night* by Veerakeat Tongpaiboon, 1998. Oil on canvas, 36" × 48". Copyright courtesy Veerakeat Tongpaiboon.

Harcourt Canada
55 Horner Avenue, Toronto, ON, Canada M8Z 4X6
Customer Service
Toll-Free Tel.: 1-800-387-7278
Toll-Free Fax: 1-800-665-7307

Printed in Canada.
1 2 3 4 5   05 04 03 02 01

To Philip Bean, a true friend and resolute humanitarian

"A friend may well be reckoned the masterpiece of nature."
Ralph Waldo Emerson (1803-1882)

Both of the previous editions of this book owed a great deal to the author's extensive experience in the challenging task of teaching criminal law to students who, for the most part, did not intend to enter the legal profession. This book meets the very specific needs of these particular students. Law school textbooks were not appropriate because the depth of their coverage went far beyond the requirements of such students. Paradoxically, other criminal law textbooks in Canada, although they were specifically written for nonlawyers, were far too general in their approach and did not provide enough details about the law for these particular students. As a consequence, a different kind of criminal law textbook was needed for non-law students in Canada. Judging by the responses to the two previous editions of *Criminal Law in Canada*, it seems that this book has taken a useful step toward meeting this need.

One of the most effective methods of teaching criminal law to criminology, criminal justice, or law and security students is the *case-oriented approach*, in which the student is encouraged to study not only the general principles of criminal law but also the specific details of decided cases. By combining the study of general principles with a close analysis of specific cases, the student learns to apply these principles of criminal law to concrete factual situations that arise in everyday life or to situations that they may encounter in their professional lives. This book is unequivocally based on the case-oriented approach to the study of criminal law. Individual decided cases are discussed in considerable detail and there are

numerous extracts from the opinions of judges. Hopefully, this approach will more adequately meet the needs of students who seek to acquire a working knowledge of Canadian criminal law.

As part of the case-oriented approach, a number of study questions have been included at the end of each chapter (with the exception of the introductory chapter). These are specifically designed to encourage students to test the extent to which they have absorbed the major principles of law covered in each substantive chapter. However, it is important to recognize that the questions are not intended to be particularly complex or difficult; if they were, they would not serve the function of permitting the average student to test his or her understanding of the major principles covered in the chapter. In the author's experience, answering the study questions is a necessary "first step" in the student's digestion of the principles of criminal law and should be followed by more complex problem-solving exercises that draw together a number of different topics and encourage the student to see the criminal law as a whole rather than as a series of separate compartments. It usually takes a few weeks before students are ready to tackle these more complex exercises; instructors might wish to delay their use until students have completed at least the first three chapters of the book. If instructors indicate a need for such problem-solving exercises, the author would be happy to consider producing an instructor's manual containing a number of them.

In the third edition of this book, the number of references to cases that have been decided in jurisdictions outside of Canada has been reduced. In the past decade or so, Canadian courts have paid considerably less attention to precedents from other common law jurisdictions, such as England and Wales, Australia, New Zealand, and the United States. The author has also made a considerable effort to include the most recent decisions made by Canadian courts and, wherever possible, to remove references to decisions of more ancient vintage. Students appear more directly engaged with the subject matter if they feel that it reflects what is happening today. Similarly, the author has removed most of the references in the previous editions to the work of the Law Reform Commission of Canada during the 1970s and 1980s. While many of the commission's recommendations still represent valuable suggestions for reform of the criminal law, it has become increasingly difficult for today's students to identify with them after the passage of two or more decades.

Readers who are familiar with the second edition of *Criminal Law in Canada* will find a number of significant changes in this edition. For example, Chapter 2 of the second edition has now been split into two separate chapters. The new Chapter 2 deals with the *actus reus* elements of a criminal offence, while the new Chapter 3 addresses the question of causation in criminal law in order to present students with more manageable chapters. Another important addition in this edition is the inclusion of an appendix that introduces students to a number of relevant Web sites that offer them the opportunity to greatly expand the scope of their independent research. For many students, pursuing the study of criminal law through the Internet proves to be an exhilarating experience that encourages them to explore the topic more deeply than they would if they limited themselves to conventional print materials.

Since the second edition was published in 1997, there has been a steady stream of significant developments in the body of Canadian criminal law. The most noteworthy of these developments have been incorporated in the third edition. For example, the present edition contains an analysis of the Supreme Court of Canada's decision in *Stone* (1999), which

has fundamentally changed many aspects of the defence of automatism. Also, the decision of the Supreme Court of Canada in *Latimer* (2001) — a well-publicized and highly controversial case that addresses the immensely difficult problem of so-called "mercy killing." The present edition includes a critical discussion of the following Supreme Court of Canada decisions: *Ewanchuk* (1999), which placed significant restrictions on the use of the defence of honest belief in consent in the context of a charge of sexual assault; and *Cuerrier* (1998), which articulated the principle that failure to disclose one's HIV status may result in the invalidation of any consent that has been given to participation in sexual activity if there is a risk of substantial harm to the other party. Among some of the other noteworthy developments that have been added to this edition are the decision of the Supreme Court of Canada in *Winko* (1999), in which the Court upheld the constitutional validity of the *Criminal Code* provisions concerning the disposition of those accused persons found Not Criminally Responsible on Account of Mental Disorder, and the coming into force of the *Controlled Drugs and Substances Act*, S.C. 1996, c. 6. Finally, some new study questions have been added and the appendices were updated.

The author would be most interested in hearing from instructors how their students react to this book and how it may be improved as a teaching instrument. It is in the nature of both writers and teachers to be always striving for improvement! It is hoped that instructors will consider using the companion volume to this textbook — Simon Verdun-Jones's *Canadian Criminal Cases: Selected Highlights* (1999). The author has found that students' comprehension of the principles discussed in the textbook is greatly enhanced when they read a limited number of edited cases. This casebook contains 42 edited cases, strictly limited in length to maintain student interest and facilitate the process of learning Canadian criminal law.

The Instructor's Manual to Accompany *Criminal Law in Canada* offers stimulating teaching material for instructors, such as class exercises, role-playing and mutiple choice games, and discussion questions.

At the beginning of the movie *The Paper Chase* (1973), Professor Kingsfield (portrayed by the Oscar-winning John Houseman) addresses the first-year class at a distinguished American law school. The imposing professor says something along the following lines: "The study of law is a subject that is new and unfamiliar to most of you. You enter law school with a mind full of mush. However, if successful here, you will leave thinking like a lawyer." No doubt, Professor Kingsfield's homily captures the popular view that the study of law is something completely different from anything the average citizen has ever done before and that only dedicated students of the law can unravel its dark mysteries. The layperson tends to be somewhat intimidated by the abstruse language used by lawyers, and therefore the study of law often assumes the proportions of a herculean task for those who have no ambitions to enter the legal profession. Hopefully, this book will satisfy the reader that such perceptions of the nature of legal studies are greatly exaggerated. There is no reason why the study of law should not be straightforward, rewarding, and even enjoyable.

The book makes considerable use of the *case method* of studying law. In other words, it seeks to discuss the general principles underlying Canadian criminal law in the context of specific cases decided by the courts. Each chapter contains not only a statement of the relevant principles of law but also a discussion of the facts of decided cases and numerous extracts from the judgments of the courts. This case-oriented approach hopes to equip the reader to apply the general principles of Canadian criminal law to the kinds of concrete factual situations one may encounter in everyday life or read about in the newspaper.

Provided the reader progresses, step by step, through the book, there should be no difficulty in understanding the basic concepts that underlie Canadian criminal law. It is hoped that each chapter of the book will gradually increase the reader's knowledge of the basic principles of Canadian criminal law so that, by the end of the book, all the "pieces of the jigsaw" will fit neatly together in the reader's mind. Provided the reader is patient and thorough, the study of criminal law should prove to be a rewarding challenge that need arouse none of the fears so frequently associated with it.

The book includes a number of devices to assist the reader in the "digestion" of the material presented. At the end of each chapter (with the exception of Chapter 1), there is a series of study questions that have been designed to ensure that the reader has absorbed the major points in the author's presentation of the relevant legal principles. It is strongly recommended that the reader attempt to answer these questions before proceeding to a new chapter. There is also an extensive glossary that will facilitate the reader's understanding of the major technical terms used in the book. Furthermore, there are two appendices that provide valuable background information: one appendix presents an overview of the Canadian criminal court system and the other contains a brief introduction to the use of law reports.

An important element in this book is the inclusion of an appendix that identifies, and describes, a number of key Web sites that readers should find of great value as a means of pursuing their own, independent legal research. The availability of legal resources on the Internet has provided every student of the law with remarkable opportunities to explore the original text of important cases decided by the courts; significant legislation enacted by Parliament and other legislative bodies — both in Canada and in other countries; and academic analysis of many issues relating to criminal law.

Finally, readers are strongly urged to supplement their study of this book with an in-depth exploration of some of the leading criminal cases that have been decided by Canadian courts. A closer study of some of the critical cases that have helped to shape the contemporary body of Canadian criminal law will certainly add new — and valuable — dimensions to the task of understanding the vital issues that confront Canadian courts on an ongoing basis. To this end, readers might wish to consider obtaining the companion volume to this book: Simon Verdun-Jones, *Canadian Criminal Cases: Selected Highlights* (1999).

ACKNOWLEDGEMENTS

The first edition of this book was the offspring of a distance education course that I prepared for Simon Fraser University in the mid-1980s. At that time, my colleague, Karlene Faith, strongly encouraged me to write a textbook based on some of the course materials. Karlene kindly gave me the benefit of her invaluable expertise as an effective communicator with students as I attempted to render the criminal law accessible to readers who, for the most part, found law to be a daunting area of study. I gratefully acknowledge her salient role in the genesis of this book.

I owe a tremendous debt to the many students at Simon Fraser University who have studied criminal law with me and have exchanged their views on practically every aspect of the first edition of this book. Their enthusiasm and support have made my role thoroughly worthwhile, and their constructive criticisms have greatly assisted me in the preparation of this book. In addition, I am most grateful to my colleagues at the School of Criminology who have contributed indirectly to so many aspects of this book, particularly Neil Boyd, Joan Brockman, Mark Carter, Tara Chang, Ray Corrado, Liz Elliott, Rob Gordon, Margaret Jackson, John Lowman, Richard Konarski, Janet Palmer, Rick Parent, Adamira Tijerino, and Vincent Cheng Yang. I also wish to acknowledge the valuable technical assistance provided by Chris Giles and Marie Krbavac.

A very special debt is owed to Elizabeth Carefoot, of Simon Fraser University, who created the book's humorous cartoons. Elizabeth's uncanny ability to present a complex idea in the form of a pointed cartoon is a constant source of amazement!

Finally, I wish to express my profound thanks to the accomplished editorial staff at Harcourt Canada for having provided the outstanding support and expertise that should be the envy of every textbook author. I particularly wish to mention the immensely constructive role played by Megan Mueller, who was responsible for overseeing the project, and her successor, Brad Lambertus, for his valuable contributions. I must also express my thanks to Camille Isaacs, the highly accomplished developmental editor in the earlier stages of the development of the manuscript. Furthermore, I wish to acknowledge an eternal debt of gratitude to Klaus Unger, who has worked with tireless efficiency and immensely creative energy as the editor of the manuscript. One cannot envisage a more helpful and supportive editor than Klaus. Finally, I wish to thank Emily Ferguson, the production editor, for her contribution to the publication of this textbook.

PUBLISHER'S NOTE

Thank you for selecting *Criminal Law in Canada: Cases, Questions, and the Code,* Third Edition, by Simon Verdun-Jones.

We want to hear what you think about the third edition of *Criminal Law in Canada.* Please take a few minutes to fill out the stamped reply card at the back of the book. Your comments and suggestions will be valuable to us as we prepare new editions and other books.

BRIEF CONTENTS

CONTENTS

Introduction to Canadian Criminal Law

OVERVIEW

This chapter examines the following:

1. The sources of criminal law in Canada;
2. the exclusive power of the Parliament of Canada to enact criminal law and the limits to that power under the *Constitution Act, 1867*;
3. the difference between substantive criminal law and criminal procedure;
4. the most important federal statutes that have been enacted under the criminal law power;
5. the problem of quasi-criminal law and the creation of regulatory offences under provincial and territorial legislation;
6. the complex jurisdictional problems that arise when provincial or territorial legislation encroaches on the criminal law power of the Parliament of Canada;
7. the importance of judicial decisions as a source of the criminal law;
8. the impact of the *Canadian Charter of Rights and Freedoms* on the development of the criminal law in Canada;
9. the leading case of *Morgentaler, Smolig and Scott* (1988), which demonstrates the power of the courts to declare criminal legislation to be invalid under the *Charter*;
10. the importance of section 1 of the *Charter* as a means of justifying an infringement of a *Charter* right or freedom as being a "reasonable limit in a free and democratic society";
11. the so-called *Oakes* test devised by the Supreme Court of Canada as a means of giving guidance to the courts when they are called upon, under section 1 of the *Charter*, to balance the rights of the individual against those of society as a whole;
12. the modification of the *Oakes* test by the Supreme Court of Canada in the *Dagenais* case (1994);
13. the trend towards placing greater emphasis on the needs and interests of women in the enactment and interpretation of the criminal law in Canada;
14. examples of significant amendments to the *Criminal Code* and five leading Supreme Court of Canada cases that illustrate the above trend (the five cases being *Lavallee* (1990), *Butler* (1992), *Park* (1995), *Ewanchuk* (1999), and *Mills* (1999));
15. the need for a fundamental overhaul of the *Criminal Code*;
16. the proposals of the Law Reform Commission of Canada (1987) and the Government of Canada (1993) to recodify the general principles of the *Criminal Code*.

INTRODUCTION

Before embarking upon a detailed study of the general principles of Canadian criminal law, it is necessary to consider a number of preliminary issues. The particular issues to be considered at this juncture are as follows:

◆ The sources of criminal law in Canada
◆ The impact of the *Canadian Charter of Rights and Freedoms* on the criminal law in Canada
◆ Criminal law and the equality of Canadian women
◆ Reform of the criminal law: a new *Criminal Code* for Canada

Unlike the other chapters in this book, this introductory chapter is not bound together by a single, unifying theme. This means that the the the four sections of this chapter may be read separately as self-contained units. However, an understanding of the basic issues raised in each section is recommended in order to appreciate the major trends that are currently shaping the development of criminal law in Canada.

SOURCES OF CRIMINAL LAW IN CANADA

Perhaps the most basic question we can raise in relation to the criminal law is, Where does it come from? The answer is that there are two primary sources of Canadian criminal law: (i) legislation and (ii) judicial decisions that either interpret such legislation or state the "**common law**."

Federal Legislation

Since Canada is a federal state, legislation may be enacted by both the Parliament of Canada and the provincial or territorial legislatures. However, under the Canadian Constitution, there is a distribution of legislative powers between the federal and provincial or territorial levels of government. Which level of government has the power to enact

criminal law? It is clear that criminal law is a subject that falls within the exclusive jurisdiction of the Parliament of Canada. Indeed, by virtue of section 91(27) of the *British North America Act, 1867* (renamed the *Constitution Act, 1867* in 1982), the federal Parliament has exclusive jurisdiction in the field of "criminal law and the procedures relating to criminal matters."

Just how extensive is the scope of the criminal law power under section 91(27) of the *Constitution Act*? Intuitively, many people would say that criminal law is characterized by the combination of a *prohibition* against certain conduct and an accompanying *penalty* for violating that prohibition. Does that mean that the Canadian Parliament can pass legislation on any issue that it chooses and justify it on the basis that, because it contains both a prohibition and penalty, it must be criminal law? If this were the case, there would be absolutely no limits on the scope of the criminal law power. In fact, the Supreme Court of Canada has stated clearly that there must be a third factor, in addition to a prohibition and a penalty, in order for legislation to be recognized as being a genuine specimen of criminal law. What is this third factor?

In the famous *Margarine Reference* case (1949), Justice Rand, of the Supreme Court of Canada, argued that the additional factor is the requirement that the prohibition and penalty contained in the legislation are directed towards a "public evil" or some behaviour that is having an injurious effect upon the Canadian public:

> A crime is an act which the law, with appropriate penal sanctions, forbids; but as prohibitions are not enacted in a vacuum, we can properly look for *some evil or injurious or undesirable effect upon the public against which the law is directed*. That effect may be in relation to social, economic or political interests; and the legislature has in mind to suppress the evil or to safeguard the interest threatened. [emphasis added]

Justice Rand asserted that if the Parliament of Canada chooses to prohibit certain conduct under the criminal law power, this prohibition must be enacted "with a view to *a public purpose which can support it as being in relation to criminal law.*" The public purposes that would be included in this category are "public peace, order, security, health, [and] morality," although Justice Rand acknowledged that this is not an exclusive list.

For example, in *Hydro-Québec* (1997), the Supreme Court of Canada considered the significant question of whether the federal criminal law power could be used to punish those who engage in serious acts of environmental pollution. The case involved the alleged dumping of highly toxic polychlorinated biphenyls (PCBs) into a Québec river. Charges were laid under the authority of the *Canadian Environmental Protection Act*, R.S.C. 1985, c. 16. However, it was contended by the **accused** that the relevant provisions of the Act were unconstitutional because they did not represent a valid exercise of the federal criminal law power. It is noteworthy that the Supreme Court held that the offences created by the legislation did, indeed, fall within the scope of that power. Indeed, Justice La Forest stated — in dramatic terms — that

> ... pollution is an "evil" that Parliament can legitimately seek to suppress. Indeed ... it is a public purpose of superordinate importance; it constitutes one of the major challenges of our time. It would be surprising indeed if Parliament could not exercise its plenary power over criminal law to protect this interest and to suppress the evils associated with it by way of appropriate penal prohibitions.

It is clear that this legislation was deemed to be "criminal law" because Parliament was unequivocally concerned with the need to safeguard *public health* from the devastating consequences of toxic pollution.

In this context, it is noteworthy that the Supreme Court of Canada has recently upheld the validity of amendments made to the *Criminal Code* by Bill C-68, the *Firearms Act* (S.C. 1995, c. 39). This legislation required all gun owners to obtain licences by the end of 2000 and to register all firearms by the end of 2002. There are approximately two million

gun owners and some seven million guns in Canada; hence, this legislation has far-reaching effects. The Government of Alberta launched a constitutional challenge against Bill C-68, claiming that the new firearms legislation represented an intrusion into the provinces' jurisdiction to regulate private property and that it could not be considered a legitimate exercise of Parliament's criminal law power under the *Constitution Act, 1867*. However, a unanimous Supreme Court of Canada rejected this contention in *Reference re Firearms Act (Canada)* (2000). The Court stated that

> We conclude that the gun control law comes within Parliament's jurisdiction over criminal law. The law in "pith and substance" is directed to enhancing public safety by controlling access to firearms through prohibitions and regulations. This brings it under the federal criminal law power. While the law has regulatory aspects, they are secondary to its primary criminal law purpose. The intrusion of the law into the provincial jurisdiction over property and civil rights is not so excessive as to upset the balance of federalism.

> ...

> By requiring everyone to register their guns, Parliament seeks to reduce misuse by everyone and curtail the ability of criminals to acquire firearms. Where criminals have acquired guns and used them in the commission of offences, the registration system seeks to make those guns more traceable.

Regulation of firearms falls within the federal criminal law power.

What important pieces of legislation (or statutes) has the Canadian Parliament enacted in the field of criminal law? Undoubtedly, the most significant federal statute, dealing with both the substantive criminal law and the procedural law relating to criminal matters, is the *Criminal Code*, R.S.C. 1985, c. C-46 (first enacted in 1892). "Substantive criminal law" refers to legislation that defines the nature of various criminal offences (such as **murder, manslaughter**, and theft) and specifies the various legal elements that must be present before a conviction can be entered against an accused person. Similarly, in this context, the term substantive criminal law refers to legislation that defines the nature and scope of various defences (such as provocation, duress, and self-defence).

The term "criminal procedure" refers to legislation that specifies the procedures to be followed in the prosecution of a criminal case and defines the nature and scope of the powers of criminal justice officials. For example, the procedural provisions of the *Criminal Code* classify offences into three categories: **indictable** offences, offences punishable on summary conviction, and "mixed" or "hybrid" offences. These provisions then specify the manner in which these categories of offences may be tried in court. For example, they specify whether these offences may be tried by a judge sitting alone or by a judge and jury, and indicate whether they may be tried before a judge of the Superior Court or a judge of the Provincial (or Territorial) Court.

The procedural provisions of the *Criminal Code* are also concerned with the powers that are exercised by criminal justice officials. For example, the Code clearly specifies the nature and scope of the powers of the police in relation to the arrest and detention of suspects. Similarly, it also specifies the powers of the courts in relation to such matters as sentencing.

In addition to the *Criminal Code*, there are a number of other federal statutes that undoubtedly create "criminal law." These include the *Controlled Drugs and Substances Act*, S.C. 1996, c.19, and the *Young Offenders Act*, R.S.C. 1985, c. Y-1.

It should be noted that there are two other significant federal statutes that have an indirect impact upon the criminal law. These are the *Canada Evidence Act*, R.S.C. 1985, c. C-50 and the *Constitution Act, 1982*, as enacted by the *Canada Act 1982* (U.K.), c. 11. The *Canada Evidence Act*, as its name would suggest, is concerned with establishing various rules concerning the introduction of evidence before criminal courts. For example, the Act indicates when a wife or husband may be compelled to give evidence against her or his spouse and indicates in what circumstances the evidence of a child under 14 years of age may be admissible in a criminal trial. The *Constitution Act* is of great significance to both the substantive criminal law and the law of criminal procedure, since Part I of the Act contains the *Canadian Charter of Rights and Freedoms*. The *Charter* is of immense importance since, as we shall shortly see, it permits courts to strike down, and declare invalid, any legislative provisions that infringe upon the fundamental rights and freedoms of Canadians.

The Problem of Quasi-Criminal Law

In the preceding section, it was established that the *Constitution Act, 1867*, provided that the federal Parliament has exclusive jurisdiction in the field of criminal law and the procedures relating to criminal matters. At this point, the reader no doubt feels that he or she has a clear grasp of the principle involved. Unfortunately, the situation is rendered considerably more complex by the existence of so-called "quasi-criminal law." What is meant by quasi-criminal law? Under the *Constitution Act, 1867*, the provincial legislatures have been granted the power to enact laws in relation to a number of specific matters. For example, section 92 of the Act indicates, *inter alia*, that "property and civil rights in the province" and "generally all matters of a merely local or private nature in the province" fall within the exclusive jurisdiction of the provincial legislatures. By virtue of judicial interpretation of the various provisions of section 92, it is clear that a number of other critical matters fall within the legislative jurisdiction of the provinces; for example, municipal institutions, health, education, highways, liquor control, and hunting and fishing.

Significantly, section 92 (15) of the *Constitution Act, 1867*, provides that the provincial legislatures may enforce their laws by "the imposition of punishment by fine, penalty or imprisonment." At this point, the reader will immediately exclaim that the imposition of fines, penalties, or imprisonment looks suspiciously like the apparatus of criminal law. One is immediately compelled to ask whether this means that the *Constitution Act, 1867*, is contradicting itself, since criminal law is a matter reserved to the exclusive jurisdiction of the federal Parliament. However, the answer is in the negative because such provincial legislation is not considered to be "real" criminal law. Instead, lawyers have termed it *quasi-criminal law*. (The word "**quasi**" means seeming, not real, or half-way.) Since this type of provincial legislation is considered to be quasi rather than real criminal law, it is possible to argue that it does not impinge upon the federal Parliament's exclusive jurisdiction in the field of (real) criminal law.

Cynics will, no doubt, point to the semantic acrobatics involved in the categorization of the provincial offences as quasi-criminal laws. However, the designation of quasi-criminal law can be very well-justified on a pragmatic basis. It is essential to bear in mind that the offences, which may be committed against provincial statutes, are generally far less serious in nature than the "**true crimes**" that may be committed against the *Criminal Code* or other federal legislation, such as the *Controlled Drugs and Substances Act*. The maximum penalties that may be imposed for violation of quasi-criminal laws are generally no more than a relatively small fine or a maximum term of imprisonment of six months or both; under the *Criminal Code* or the *Controlled Drugs and Substances Act*, on the other hand, penalties may range as high as a life term of imprisonment.

Provincial legislatures may delegate authority to municipalities to enact municipal ordinances or by-laws. This municipal "legislation" may also be enforced by the "big stick" of fines or other penalties. Municipal by-laws or ordinances may be considered to fall within the category of quasi-criminal law.

In general, quasi-criminal offences are part of the enterprise of regulating the activities of business, commerce, and trade in the interests of society as a whole. They may, therefore, be properly described as "**regulatory offences**" rather than true crimes. It is for this reason that they cannot be considered to impinge upon the exclusive jurisdiction of the federal Parliament to enact "real" criminal legislation.

It should be added that regulatory offences may also be found in a broad range of federal statutes (for example, the *Competition Act*, R.S.C. 1985, c. C-34; the *Food and Drugs Act*, R.S.C. 1985, c. F-27; the *Fisheries Act*, R.S.C. 1985, c. F-14; the *Migratory Birds Convention Act*, S.C. 1994, c. 22; and the *Trade-Marks Act*, R.S.C. 1985, c. T-13). Taken together with quasi-criminal offences generated under provincial and municipal legislation, these federal offences contribute to a vast pool of regulatory law that has become increasingly complex as modern society has developed. Some idea of the vast number of regulatory offences that presently exist in Canada, and are technically considered to be crimes, may be gleaned from a report issued by the Federal Law Reform commission in 1976. The commission estimated that each Canadian faced some 20 000 offences under federal statutes and a further 20 000 arising under the legislation of each province; significantly, this estimate does not even attempt to include the large number of municipal offences. However, it is noteworthy that, in the *Wholesale Travel Group Inc.* case (1991), Justice Cory of the Supreme Court of Canada noted that the Law Reform Commission of Canada had estimated that by 1983 the number of regulatory offences, *at the federal level alone*, had climbed to some 97 000! As Justice Cory remarked, "there is every reason to believe that the number of public welfare [or regulatory] offences at both levels of government has continued to increase."

This vast body of regulatory criminal law does not make good bedtime reading for the average citizen. Indeed, even the average lawyer is acquainted with only a fraction of the regulatory offences that currently exist. Nevertheless, as we shall see later in

Chapter 9, it is a firm principle of criminal law that "ignorance of the law is no excuse."

Although there will be some detailed discussion concerning regulatory offences in Chapter 6, this book is predominantly concerned with offences arising under the *Criminal Code*. In essence, the greater portion of this book deals with true crimes rather than regulatory crimes or quasi-criminal law.

Problems of Jurisdiction in the Enactment of Legislation

Before leaving the complex area of quasi-criminal law, it is important to remember that the provincial legislatures are restricted to the enactment of legislation genuinely falling within the heads of jurisdiction assigned to them under the *Constitution Act, 1867*. More specifically, it is clear that they may not encroach upon the exclusive federal jurisdiction to legislate "real" criminal law. Unfortunately, it is often difficult for the courts to determine whether provincial legislation has strayed beyond the boundaries of the jurisdiction assigned to the provinces under the *Constitution Act* and whether such legislation is invalid because it has infringed upon the federal Parliament's exclusive criminal law domain. The immense challenge posed by this task can best be demonstrated by referring to some illustrative cases.

In the *Morgentaler* case (1993), the Supreme Court of Canada was called upon to consider whether the Nova Scotia legislature had encroached upon the federal criminal law power when it enacted legislation that permitted the provincial government to prohibit the provision of certain medical services in premises other than hospitals. As we shall see later in this chapter, the Supreme Court of Canada ruled, in the *Morgentaler, Smolig and Scott* case of 1988, that the abortion provisions of the *Criminal Code* were invalid under the *Charter* and, as a consequence, abortion was no longer prohibited by the criminal law. Dr. Morgentaler subsequently indicated that he intended to establish a free-standing abortion clinic in Halifax. The provincial legislature responded by enacting the *Medical Services Act*, R.S.N.S. 1989,

c. 281, which provided that the government could designate certain medical services that must be performed in a hospital and imposed a penalty of a fine between $10 000 and $50 000 on those individuals who performed such services outside of a hospital. The provincial government designated nine services under this legislation; one of the services was abortion. Dr. Morgentaler was charged, under the *Medical Services Act*, with performing fourteen abortions outside of a hospital. The Supreme Court of Canada ultimately accepted Dr. Morgentaler's contention that the legislation was invalid because it encroached upon the Parliament of Canada's exclusive jurisdiction over criminal law.

In delivering the judgment of the Supreme Court of Canada, Justice Sopinka noted that "it cannot be denied that interdiction of conduct in the interest of public morals was and remains one of the classic ends of our criminal law" and that "it seems clear to me that the present legislation, whose primary purpose is to prohibit abortions except in certain circumstances, treats of a moral issue." He went on to say that the legislation was "in pith and substance" criminal law:

> This legislation deals, by its terms, with a subject historically considered to be part of the criminal law — the prohibition of the performance of abortions with penal consequences. It is thus suspect on its face. Its legal effect partially reproduces that of the now defunct [s. 287] of the *Criminal Code* in so far as both precluded the establishment and operation of free-standing abortion clinics. ... *The primary objective of the legislation was to prohibit abortions outside hospitals as socially undesirable conduct*, and any concern with the safety and security of pregnant women or with health care policy, hospitals or the regulation of the medical profession was merely ancillary. *This legislation involves the regulation of the place where an abortion may be obtained, not from the viewpoint of health care policy, but from the viewpoint of public wrongs or crimes.* ... [emphasis added]

On the other hand, in *Ontario Adult Entertainment Bar Association* (1997), the Ontario Court of

Appeal was faced with the question of whether a municipal by-law (passed under the authority of provincial legislation) was invalid on the basis that it violated the exclusive criminal law jurisdiction of the Parliament of Canada. The by-law, passed by the Municipality of Metropolitan Toronto, prohibited nude (or partially nude) attendants from touching patrons in adult entertainment parlours. The effect of this prohibition was to put an end to the practice of "close contact" (or "lap") dancing, during which there may be physical contact between customers and dancers. **Counsel** for the accused argued that this by-law constituted an infringement of the federal criminal law power because it was really legislating morality "under the guise of regulating adult entertainment parlours." The Court of Appeal disagreed. As Justice Finlayson pointed out, the by-law was enacted to *regulate a business "in the interests of health, safety and the prevention of crime"*—a legislative objective that was clearly within the jurisdiction of the province under section 92 of the *Constitution Act, 1867*. It was emphasized that the by-law did not prohibit "close contact" (or "lap") dancing altogether—it merely prohibited touching of the patrons by nude, or partially nude, attendants in the course of this activity. Justice Finlayson noted that touching can "transmit disease and, in certain circumstances, give rise to safety concerns for the attendants." Overall, it was concluded that the real objectives of the by-law were simply to "prevent the harmful effects of lap dancing, which includes health, safety and crime prevention concerns" and to "prevent the development of a riotous atmosphere within adult entertainment bars."

It is significant that a similar approach was adopted by the Québec Court of Appeal in the case of *Drapeau* (1999), where the accused had been charged under section 77 of the *Loi sur les permis d'alcool*, R.S.Q., c. P-9.1, which stated that it was "forbidden for the members of the personnel of the holder of a bar permit and for every person who participates in a show in a bar to mingle with the patrons, drink or dance with them or sit at the same table or counter with them." The accused claimed that the law was invalid because it constituted an infringement of Parliament's exclusive criminal law power. Their argument was based on the contention that the *real* target of section 77 was the practice of "lap-dancing," or "fraternization for the purpose of prostitution": accordingly, they claimed that the main object of the section was to regulate morality —a criminal law objective, which was beyond the jurisdiction of the National Assembly of Québec. However, the Québec Court of Appeal brushed that argument aside, stating that section 77 was merely part of a *comprehensive scheme to regulate the alcohol trade* in the province (an objective that clearly fell within the boundaries of provincial jurisdiction under the *Constitution Act, 1867*):

> The impugned provision, the state objective of which is consumer protection, is ancillary to this scheme and is safely anchored in a recognized field of provincial competence. It is thus *intra vires* the legislature of Quebec.

An impartial observer may well point out that both of these "lap-dancing" cases illustrate that the line between the legitimate exercise of provincial powers to regulate a trade or business, on the one hand, and the unconstitutional intrusion of a province into the realm of the exclusive federal criminal law power, on the other, may sometimes be very fuzzy indeed. Certainly, a court, which is determined to find that these types of provincial legislation really address questions of *public morality*, could probably find the legal justification to invalidate them on the basis that they impinge on the federal criminal law sphere. Of course, in these particular cases, the appellate courts declined to strike down the legislation, but they could probably have made exactly the opposite decision, had they wished to do so. Deciding whether provincial legislation should be struck down on this constitutional basis clearly involves a considerable degree of judicial discretion and the outcome may be almost impossible to predict with any degree of certainty. Indeed, there may well be some justification for the view that criminal law, like beauty, lies in the eye of the beholder.

On the other side of the constitutional coin, the federal Parliament may not encroach upon the areas of jurisdiction exclusively reserved to the provinces under the *Constitution Act, 1867*, unless the legislation concerned genuinely relates to Parliament's criminal law power. For example, under the provisions of the *Constitution Act*, legislation concerning highways falls within the field of provincial jurisdiction, and therefore federal legislation in this area can only be valid if it is enacted under the auspices of the federal criminal law power. This particular issue was considered in the case of *Boggs* (1981), in which the Supreme Court of Canada ruled that (what was then) section 238(3) of the *Criminal Code*, which established the offence of driving a motor vehicle, while disqualified or prohibited from driving, was beyond the power of Parliament to enact and, therefore, invalid. In the *Boggs* case, the accused's driving licence had been suspended by administrative action taken under the authority of provincial legislation (the *Highway Traffic Act*, R.S.O. 1970, c. 202). The question to be determined by the Supreme Court, therefore, was whether Parliament could create a separate offence of driving while disqualified — under section 238(3) of the *Criminal Code* — even though the licensing of motorists is a matter that falls within the exclusive jurisdiction of the provinces and territories to regulate the use of their highways, and even though each province and territory has established its own offence of driving while disqualified. The answer to this question turns on the nature of the particular disqualification concerned.

In delivering the judgment of the Supreme Court, Justice Estey pointed out that there were two separate situations in which a province may suspend or cancel the licence of an operator. First, a driver's licence may be suspended where that individual has been convicted of a driving offence under the provisions of the *Criminal Code* (see, for example, the *Motor Vehicle Act*, R.S.B.C. 1996, c. 318, s. 234). Second, there are certain situations, that arise under the laws of various provinces and territories, in which individual citizens may face administrative suspension of their licences as a consequence of the breach of a *provincial* or *territorial* statute or regulation. For example, as might be expected, provinces and territories generally impose a licence suspension as a penalty for having accumulated a lengthy record of driving offences (see, for example, the *Motor Vehicle Act*, R.S.B.C. 1996, c. 318, s. 93). However, some provinces and territories also impose a licence suspension as a penalty for such conduct as failing to pay civil judgments relating to motor vehicles; failing to make payments to provincial motor vehicle accident compensation funds; and violating regulations concerning the taxation and licensing of motor vehicles, fuel, oil, etc. (see, for example, the *Motor Vehicle Act*, R.S.B.C. 1996, c. 318, s. 90). It is precisely this type of disqualification that worried the Supreme Court of Canada; indeed, as Justice Estey pointed out,

> It is obvious that a suspension of an owner's license for the nonpayment of a judgment arising out of the driving of an authorized driver, or suspension or revocation by the reason of the nonpayment of a fuel oil bill relating to domestic heating oil, have no relationship in practice or in theory to the owner's ability to drive and hence to public safety of the highways of the nation.

In effect, if section 238(3) had been held valid, there would have been numerous circumstances in which the *Criminal Code* could have been used not to punish the violation of a regulation relating to highway safety but rather to criminalize nonpayment of a provincial tax or fee or a civil judgment. If Parliament had limited the scope of section 238(3) to driving suspensions brought about as a consequence of offences committed against the *Criminal Code*, it would have been acting within the limits of its jurisdiction because there would have been a clear link between the suspensions and "public order and safety." However, Parliament did not limit section 238(3) in this way. Indeed, in the view of Justice Estey,

> In its current condition, this section creates an offence to drive anywhere in Canada during a dis-

qualification of one's driver's license by any province for any reason related or unrelated to the use of highways and streets.

In these circumstances, therefore, the Supreme Court ruled that section 238(3) went beyond Parliament's legislative authority in relation to the field of criminal law. In 1985, Parliament amended the *Criminal Code* in response to the Supreme Court of Canada's decision in the *Boggs* case. The new section 259(4) establishes an offence of driving while disqualified, but section 259(5) ensures that the offence will be considered to fall snugly within Parliament's jurisdiction to enact criminal law because it clearly limits the definition of "disqualification" to situations where the accused person has committed a motor vehicle offence under the *Criminal Code* itself.

Judicial Decisions as a Source of Criminal Law

In addition to legislation, such as the *Criminal Code*, a major source of criminal law is the numerous judicial decisions that either interpret criminal legislation or expound the "common law." A significant proportion of this book is concerned with the interpretation of the provisions of the *Criminal Code* by Canadian courts. However, the common law still plays an important role in Canadian criminal jurisprudence. Essentially, common law refers to that body of judge-made law which evolved in areas that were not covered by legislation.

Historically, a considerable proportion of English criminal law was developed by judges, who were required to deal with a variety of situations that were not governed by any legislation. Indeed, until relatively recently, much of the English law concerning theft and fraud was developed by judges in this way. One common law offence, which is of particular relevance to present day criminal law in Canada, is **contempt of court**. However, the common law not only expanded the number of offences in the criminal law, but also developed special

defences that were not covered by any legislation. For example, the Canadian courts have single-handedly developed the law relating to the defence of necessity (a defence that does not appear in the *Criminal Code*); hence, necessity is known as a common law defence.

It should be noted that, since 1954, *with the single exception of the offence of contempt of court,* it has not been possible for a Canadian to be convicted of a common law offence (see section 9 of the *Criminal Code*). However, section 8(3) of the *Criminal Code* preserves any common law "justification," "excuse," or "defence" to a criminal charge "except in so far as they are altered by or are inconsistent with this act or any other act of the Parliament of Canada." This provision is particularly significant since it means that common law defences such as necessity are still applicable in a Canadian criminal trial. In short, while Canadian judges cannot create any new offences at common law, they may still apply the common law principles relating to certain defences, provided, of course, that these principles are not inconsistent with legislation enacted by the Canadian Parliament.

THE IMPACT OF THE *CANADIAN CHARTER OF RIGHTS AND FREEDOMS* ON THE CRIMINAL LAW IN CANADA

The enactment of the *Canadian Charter of Rights and Freedoms* as part of the *Constitution Act, 1982* heralded a dramatic new era in the relationship between the members of Canada's judiciary, on the one hand, and the elected representatives of Canada's federal Parliament and provincial and territorial legislatures, on the other. As an entrenched bill of rights, the *Charter* empowers judges, in certain circumstances, to declare any piece of legislation to be invalid—and of no force or effect—if the latter infringes upon an individual's protected rights. Canadian judges have demonstrated their willingness to use this awesome power where they believe that it is necessary to do so. Indeed, since 1982, there have been numerous court decisions that have resulted in the judicial nullification of various statutory provisions concerning criminal law.

Perhaps the case that has been most decisive in underlining the potential impact of the *Charter* upon Canadian criminal law is *Morgentaler, Smolig and Scott* (1988), in which the Supreme Court of Canada struck down section 287 of the *Criminal Code*, which regulated the performance of abortions in Canada. Section 287 made abortion a criminal offence unless it was carried out in an accredited hospital and it had been previously approved by a therapeutic abortion committee, which had certified that the continuation of the pregnancy "would or would be likely to endanger" the woman's "life or health." Dr. Morgentaler and his associates were charged with conspiracy to procure the miscarriage of female persons contrary to the provisions of section 287. The charges stemmed from their establishment of a free-standing clinic in Toronto to perform abortions on women who had not obtained a certificate from a therapeutic abortion committee.

The Supreme Court of Canada ultimately ruled that section 287 of the *Criminal Code* infringed section 7 of the *Charter*, which guarantees the "right to life, liberty and security of the person and the right not to be deprived thereof except in accordance with the principles of fundamental justice." Chief Justice Dickson ruled that section 287 clearly violated the security of the person:

> Forcing a woman, by threat of criminal sanction, to carry a foetus to term unless she meets certain criteria unrelated to her own priorities and aspirations, is a profound interference with a woman's body and thus a violation of security of the person.

Such a violation of personal security can not be permitted under the provisions of the *Charter* unless it is undertaken in accordance with the principles of fundamental justice. The Supreme Court held that the violation of personal security, imposed by section 287, did not meet these critical requirements of the *Charter*. In the view of the Court, the system of therapeutic abortion committees was "manifestly unfair" because many Canadian women

did not have access to such a committee unless they were willing to travel great distances at substantial expense and considerable personal inconvenience. It was also pointed out that the delays caused by the committee system actually put women's physical and mental health at greater risk.

The Court also ruled that section 287 of the Code could not be salvaged by section 1 of the *Charter*, which states that the rights and freedoms set out in the *Charter* are guaranteed "subject only to such reasonable limits prescribed by law as can be demonstrably justified in a free and democratic society." Section 287 was not a reasonable limitation on the right to personal security because the administrative structure of the therapeutic abortion committees was both arbitrary and unfair, and certain of the rules governing the access to these committees were unnecessary in light of Parliament's objectives of protecting the foetus and protecting the pregnant woman's life or health. The Supreme Court did not rule that the criminal law cannot be used against the performance of abortions in any circumstances. It merely stated that, if Parliament wishes to infringe upon the right to security of pregnant women, it must do so according to the principles of fundamental justice guaranteed by section 7 of the *Charter*.

In 1992, the Government of Canada did attempt to replace section 287 with new *Criminal Code* provisions dealing with abortion, but this amendment was never enacted. Although the new provisions passed the House of Commons, they failed to gain approval in the Senate, and there has been no subsequent attempt to bring abortions under the purview of the *Criminal Code*. As a consequence, abortions are no longer subject to the criminal law and are treated in the same manner as any other medical procedure in Canada.

The *Morgentaler* case illustrates, in dramatic fashion, the scope of the wide-ranging powers that the *Charter* has placed in the hands of Canadian judges. Indeed, as Chief Dickson pointed out, in the *Morgentaler* case,

> Although it is still fair to say that courts are not the appropriate forum for articulating complex and

controversial programmes of public policy, Canadian courts are now charged with the crucial obligation of ensuring that the legislative initiatives pursued by our Parliament and legislatures conform to the democratic values expressed in the *Canadian Charter of Rights and Freedoms.*

However, it is important to recognize that the *Charter* does not require that the courts strike down *every* legislative provision that is considered to be in violation of an accused person's constitutional rights. Indeed, as we have already seen, section 1 of the *Charter* states that

The *Canadian Charter of Rights and Freedoms* guarantees the rights and freedoms set out in it *subject only to such reasonable limits prescribed by law as can be demonstrably justified in a free and democratic society.* [emphasis added]

Section 1, in effect, requires the courts to engage in an elaborate balancing act in which they must decide whether the infringement of an individual's rights can be justified in the name of some "higher good." In the *Oakes* case (1986), the Supreme Court of Canada devised a specific test for the purpose of identifying the factors that should be considered when the courts attempt to decide whether the violation of a *Charter* right is justifiable as a "reasonable limit" in a "free and democratic society." This test has since become known as the "*Oakes* test."

In delivering the judgment of the majority of the justices of the Supreme Court of Canada in the *Oakes* case (1986), Chief Justice Dickson prefaced his remarks concerning section 1 of the *Charter* by emphasizing that the burden of establishing that an infringement of a *Charter* right is justified as a reasonable limit is on the "party seeking to uphold the limitation"; in a criminal case, this will nearly always be the Crown. In other words, there will have to be very strong grounds for overriding individual rights, guaranteed by the *Charter*. However, the Chief Justice recognized that rights and freedoms guaranteed by the *Charter* "are not absolute"

and that "it may become necessary to limit rights and freedoms in circumstances where their exercise would be inimical to the realization of collective goals of fundamental importance."

What issues should a court address when attempting to decide whether a *Charter* violation is justified under section 1? In the *Oakes* case, Chief Justice Dickson stated that this process should be divided into two separate questions:

To establish that a limit is reasonable and demonstrably justified in a free and democratic society, two central criteria must be satisfied. First, the objective, which the measures responsible for a limit on a *Charter* right or freedom are designed to serve, must be "of sufficient importance to warrant overriding a constitutionally protected right or freedom." ... It is necessary, at a minimum, that an objective relate to concerns which are pressing and substantial in a free and democratic society before it can be characterized as sufficiently important.

Secondly, once a sufficiently significant objective is recognized, then the party invoking s. 1 must show that the means chosen are reasonable and demonstrably justified. This involves "a form of proportionality test." ... Although the nature of the proportionality test will vary depending on the circumstances, in each case courts will be required to balance the interests of society with those of individuals and groups. There are, in my view, three important components of a proportionality test. First, the measures adopted must be carefully designed to achieve the objective in question. They must not be arbitrary, unfair or based on irrational considerations. In short, they must be rationally connected to the objective. Secondly, the means, even if rationally connected to the objective in the first sense, should impair "as little as possible" the right or freedom in question. ... Thirdly, there must be a proportionality between the *effects* of the measures which are responsible for limiting the *Charter* right or freedom, and the objective which has been identified as of "sufficient importance."

With respect to the third component, it is clear that the general effect of any measure impugned under s. 1 will be the infringement of a right or freedom guaranteed by the *Charter*, that is the reason why resort to s. 1 is necessary. ... Even if an objective is of sufficient importance, and the first two elements of the proportionality test are satisfied, it is still possible that, because of the deleterious effects of a measure on individuals or groups, the measure will not be justified by the purposes it intends to serve. The more severe the deleterious effects of a measure, the more important the objective must be if the measure is to be reasonable and demonstrably justified in a free and democratic society.

In the *Oakes* case itself, the Supreme Court of Canada had been faced with the question of whether or not to rule that section 8 of the (now-repealed) *Narcotic Control Act*, R.S.C. 1985, c. N-1, was invalid in light of the *Charter*. Section 8 placed a peculiar burden upon the shoulders of an accused person charged with trafficking in narcotics (contrary to section 4(1) of the Act): specifically, the provision stated that, once the Crown had proved that the accused was in possession of a narcotic, then the **burden of proof** automatically fell on the accused to establish that he or she was *not* in possession for the purpose of trafficking.

The Supreme Court briskly found that section 8 infringed an accused person's right — enshrined in section 11(d) of the *Charter* — "to be presumed innocent until proven guilty." Undoubtedly, section 8 of the *Narcotic Control Act* forced accused persons into the position of having to prove their innocence and, in so doing, it constituted a clear breach of section 11(d) of the *Charter*. However, the critical issue in *Oakes* was whether section 8 of the *Narcotic Control Act* could be "saved," under the terms of section 1 of the *Charter*, as a "reasonable limit" on the presumption of innocence. Ultimately, the Supreme Court took the view that section 8 did not constitute a reasonable limit that could be "demonstrably justified in a free and democratic society" and declared it to be invalid and "of no force and effect."

In applying (what is now known as) the *Oakes* test, Chief Justice Dickson first inquired whether Parliament's objective in enacting section 8 of the *Narcotic Control Act* was sufficiently important to justify overriding a *Charter* right. The Chief Justice noted that Parliament's objective was manifestly that of "curbing drug trafficking" by rendering it easier for the Crown to obtain convictions of those who engaged in such harmful conduct. There was absolutely no doubt that Parliament's objective of reducing the extent of drug trafficking in Canada could be characterized as being "pressing and substantial" in nature and Chief Justice Dickson was clearly convinced that there was a need to protect society "from the grave ills associated with drug trafficking."

Having determined that Parliament's objective in enacting section 8 of the *Narcotic Control Act* was sufficiently important to warrant overriding a *Charter* right, Chief Justice Dickson turned to the second part of the test that he articulated in the *Oakes* case. More specifically, were the means used by Parliament (placing the onus of proof on the shoulders of an accused person found in possession of narcotics to establish that he or she was not in such possession for the purpose of trafficking) *proportional to Parliament's objective*? As we noted, Chief Justice Dickson referred to three different components of the proportionality test. However, in the *Oakes* case itself, he stated that it was only necessary to refer to the first of these components; namely, was there a rational connection between section 8 and Parliament's objective of reducing drug trafficking? Chief Justice Dickson concluded that there was no such rational connection. Possession of a minute amount of narcotics does not automatically warrant drawing the inference that the accused intended to traffic in such drugs. Indeed, he said that it "would be irrational to infer that a person had an intent to traffic on the basis of his or her possession of a very small quantity of narcotics." While section 8 might ensure that more accused persons will be convicted of drug trafficking, a conviction of a person found in possession of only a minimal amount of drugs does nothing to reduce the actual incidence of trafficking in narcotics because such an individual is clearly not involved in such activity in the first place! As Chief Justice remarked,

> The presumption required under s. 8 of the *Narcotic Control Act* is overinclusive and could lead to results in certain cases which would defy both rationality and fairness.

It should be noted that the nature of the third step in the proportionality test articulated in *Oakes* was subsequently clarified by the Supreme Court of Canada in the *Dagenais* case (1994), in which Chief Justice Lamer suggested that it is important for the courts to examine *both the salutary and deleterious effects* of an impugned legislative provision on both individuals and groups in Canadian society. He, therefore, stipulated that the third step in the *Oakes* test should be re-phrased in the following manner:

> ... there must be a proportionality between the deleterious effects of the measures which are responsible for limiting the rights or freedoms in question and the objective, *and there must be a proportionality between the deleterious and the salutary effects of the measures.*

It is possible that a court might find that a particular legislative provision — adopted by Parliament in order to achieve a "pressing and substantial" objective — creates relatively few deleterious effects. However, in Chief Justice Lamer's view, that should not mean that the provision automatically meets the requirements of the third component of the proportionality test. Indeed, it may well be the case that the legislative provision in question, while it does not have any significantly harmful effects, does not produce any significantly salutary effects either! If a court should come to this conclusion, then it should rule that the legislative provision has failed the third component of the proportionality test: after all, any infringement of *Charter* rights is a serious matter and certainly cannot be justified if it does not have any significantly positive effects. Section 1 of the *Charter* should not

be used to "save" legislation from invalidation unless the positive benefits of the legislation substantially outweigh any of its potentially negative impacts upon both individual Canadians and Canadian society as a whole.

The *Oakes* test has been consistently applied by Canadian courts whenever they have been confronted with the arduous task of balancing the *individual* rights of the accused against the *collective* rights of society under section 1 of the *Charter*. (For a detailed example of the application of the *Oakes* test in a case where the Supreme Court of Canada ruled that a violation of a *Charter* right was justifed under section 1 of the *Charter*, the reader may wish to turn to Chapter 6 and peruse the discussion of the *Wholesale Travel Group Inc.* case (1991).)

Before leaving this discussion of the impact of the *Charter* on the fabric of the criminal law in Canada, it should be emphasized that there may well be a tendency to exaggerate the extent to which the courts may use their *Charter* powers to override the will of democratically elected legislators. Indeed, it is highly significant that the Supreme Court of Canada recently stated in the *Mills* case (1999) that, in the context of the application of the *Charter*, it is more useful to view the relationship between Parliament and the courts as being one of *constructive* "*dialogue.*" For example, Justices McLachlin and Iacobucci emphasized the view that the courts must always presume that Parliament intends to enact legislation that meets the requirements of the *Charter* and, therefore, must do all they can to give effect to that intention. What the Supreme Court appears to be suggesting is that the invalidation of legislation enacted by democratically elected representatives is a step that should be undertaken only very reluctantly on the part of the courts. Furthermore, even when legislation is struck down as being of no force or effect, it is always possible for Parliament or the provincial or territorial legislature to enact new statutory provisions that respond to the *Charter* concerns expressed by the courts. The *Mills* case suggests that, ultimately, these new provisions will be upheld if the legislators have "listened" to what has been said by the judges in their ongoing dialogue with Parliament and the provincial and territorial legislatures. In essence, according to the Supreme Court in the *Mills* case, the appropriate role of the courts is to assist legislators to implement the will of the people in a manner that is consistent with the Canadian values expressed in the *Charter*: in this view, legislators and courts are working in a partnership and it would be wrong to suggest that the *Charter* is being used to frustrate decisions made in a democratic manner.

CRIMINAL LAW AND THE EQUALITY OF CANADIAN WOMEN

Over the past two decades or so, there has been increasing recognition that a number of areas of Canadian criminal law traditionally reflect the values of men rather than women, and that there is a pressing need for both the Canadian Parliament and the Canadian judiciary to pay much greater attention to the interests and needs of women in the enactment and interpretation of the criminal law. Indeed, as recently as 1982, it was still possible for a husband to rape his wife without attracting any legal sanction whatsoever. It was not until Parliament passed (in Bill C-127, 1983) a number of major amendments to the *Criminal Code*, including the abolition of the crime of rape and the creation of the new, gender-neutral, offence of sexual assault, that this appalling situation was corrected. However, other spheres of the criminal law remain in which it is necessary that a greater degree of sensitivity be shown by Parliament and the courts towards the specific interests and experience of Canadian women.

In recent years there is no doubt that the Parliament of Canada has, in some measure, attempted to address this need. For example, in 1992 (Bill C-49), Parliament amended the *Criminal Code* so as to increase the degree of protection for victims in sexual assault cases (the vast majority of whom are women). These amendments included an extensive redefinition of the concept of consent in sexual assault cases so as to ensure that an accused person will not gain an **acquittal** unless the **complainant** has given a *genuine consent* to sexual activity; the reformulation of the defence of honest belief in consent so as to place a duty on an accused person to take reasonable steps to ascertain whether consent has been given to sexual activity; and the introduction of a revised "**rape shield**" law that gave judges clear guidance as to the limited circumstances in which a complainant's sexual history may be admitted at trial.

It is noteworthy that, in 1995, Parliament addressed an issue that was perceived to constitute a major threat to the security of Canadian women who had been subjected to the horror of sexual assault — namely, the possibility that a man may escape the consequences of his aggressive conduct by pleading extreme drunkenness as a defence. To avoid this possibility, Parliament enacted section 33.1 of the *Criminal Code*, which effectively prevents the perpetrator of a sexual assault from raising a defence of intoxication — no matter how extreme that intoxication may have been at the time of the offence (S.C. 1995, c. 32, s. 1). Furthermore, in 1997, Parliament enacted Bill C-46 with a view to severely restricting the extent to which legal counsel for accused persons may obtain access to the private therapeutic records of complainants in the trial of sexual assault cases. The practice of attacking complainants — by making use of private information gleaned from their therapeutic records — was considered to be a source of profound distress for those women who had already taken the immensely difficult step of reporting a sexual assault and participating in the trial of the accused person. By amending the law regulating the use of such information by the defence, Parliament was clearly responding in a decisive manner to an issue that was of grave concern to Canadian women. More recently, in 1998, Parliament recognized the need to address the horrendous statistics that indicate that individuals with a disability are more likely to become the victims of sexual aggression: as a consequence, the *Criminal Code* was amended by the creation of a new offence of sexual exploitation of a person with a disability (S.C. 1998, c. 9, s. 2).

Bill C-27 (S.C. 1997, c. 16) also made a number of significant amendments to the *Criminal Code* in relation to provisions dealing with violence against women and children (for example, making it clear that female genital mutilation is a crime, and rendering it easier to apprehend and prosecute individuals who seek the services of child prostitutes, whether they are inside or outside Canada).

A final example of legislative action that represents a serious attempt to respond to the concerns of Canadian women is the enactment, in 1993, of a new crime of criminal harassment (S.C. 1993, c. 45). This offence was designed to provide a more effective method of protecting women, in particular, from the terrifying experience of being stalked —a form of oppressive behaviour that has the potential to escalate into serious violence or, even, into homicide (see section 264 of the *Criminal Code*). Significantly, in June 2000, the Government of Canada responded to continuing public concerns about the scourge of stalking by introducing an Omnibus Bill that would double the maximum sentence for criminal harassment from five to ten years' imprisonment.

Inevitably, there will be a considerable degree of debate as to whether these reforms go far enough in addressing the question of violence against women in Canadian society. However, it is clear that Canadian legislators have taken a number of initial steps that may be said to reflect a greater willingness to respond to the concerns of women who feel that they are not treated fairly by the criminal law and the system of criminal justice.

The Supreme Court of Canada has, in a number of recent cases, demonstrated that it also has a commitment to interpreting the criminal law in a manner that is more reflective of women's interests and experience than has been the case in the past. This is not to say that there have not been instances where a decision of the Supreme Court has been considered by some to be detrimental to the interests of women. Indeed, the Court provoked a storm of criticism from many quarters, when, in 1991, it struck down the "rape shield" law that Parliament had originally enacted in 1982 as being invalid

under the *Charter* (the *Seaboyer* and *Game* cases of 1991). However, the general trend in Supreme Court decisions has been in the direction of setting the stage for a considerably more sympathetic response on the part of the courts to the particular needs and interests of women. This trend is well illustrated by the decisions made by the Supreme Court in five leading cases: *Lavallee* (1990); *Butler* (1992); *Park* (1995); *Ewanchuk* (1999); and *Mills* (1999).

The *Lavallee* case (1990) is of fundamental significance because it reflects a major shift of emphasis in the way in which the courts have applied the defence of self-defence to women. The Supreme Court of Canada unequivocally recognized that, when a woman raises the plea of self-defence in response to an attack by a male aggressor, she is not to be judged by the standards of the "reasonable man," but rather by the standards of the "reasonable woman" who finds herself in the same sitation and shares the same experience as the accused.

In delivering her judgment in *Lavallee*, Justice Wilson made a number of critical comments about the traditional lack of sensitivity shown to women by those who make or apply the criminal law. She noted that

> Far from protecting women from [domestic violence] the law historically sanctioned the abuse of women in marriage as an aspect of the husband's ownership of his wife and his "right" to chastise her. One need only recall the centuries-old law that a man is entitled to beat his wife with a stick "no thicker than his thumb."
>
> Fortunately, there has been a growing awareness in recent years that no man has a right to abuse any woman under any circumstances. ... However, a woman who comes before a judge or jury with the claim that she has been battered and suggest [*sic*] this may be a relevant factor in evaluating her subsequent actions still faces the prospect of being condemned by popular mythology about domestic violence. Either she was not as badly beaten as she claims or she would have left the man long ago. Or, if she was battered that severely, she

must have stayed out of some masochistic enjoyment of it.

Justice Wilson pointed out that, in asking the question whether an accused person acting reasonably in using lethal force against a perceived threat by another person, it makes no sense to talk about "what the 'ordinary man' would do in the position of a battered spouse," because most men do not find themselves in this position. On the other hand, some women do and, as Justice Wilson suggests, our conception of "what is 'reasonable' must be adapted to circumstances which are, by and large, foreign to the world inhabited by the 'reasonable man'."

In light of these considerations, the Supreme Court ruled that expert evidence about the nature and effects of the "battered-wife syndrome" could be placed before a jury in order to assist the jurors in deciding whether the accused woman reasonably believed that her life was in danger and whether she acted reasonably when she used deadly force to alleviate that perceived risk. The Court also held that a battered woman, in such circumstances, does not have to wait until she is actually being attacked before she is justified in using lethal force. As Justice Wilson stated,

> I do not think it is an unwarranted generalization to say that due to their size, strength, socialization and lack of training, women are typically no match for men in hand-to-hand combat. The requirement ... that a battered woman wait until the physical assault is "underway" before her apprehensions can be validated in law would, in the words of an American court, be tantamount to sentencing her to "murder by installment." ...

In the *Butler* case (1992), the Supreme Court of Canada considered a *Charter* challenge to the *Criminal Code* provisions relating to obscenity (section 163). The Court concluded that, while section 163 of the Code did indeed violate the freedom of expression guaranteed by section 2(b) of the *Charter*, it was nevertheless a "reasonable limit" within the meaning of section 1 of the *Charter* and was,

therefore, valid. The Supreme Court placed considerable emphasis on the harmful impact of certain types of pornography on women and children in reaching the conclusion that the interests of Canadian society as a whole should outweigh the individual interest of the accused person in exercising his or her freedom of expression. For example, Justice Sopinka stated that

> While the accuracy of this perception is not susceptible of exact proof, there is a substantial body of opinion that holds that *the portrayal of persons being subjected to degrading or dehumanizing sexual treatment results in harm, particularly to women and therefore to society as a whole*. ... [emphasis added]

In applying the *Oakes* test (discussed earlier) to the question of whether section 1 of the *Charter* saved section 163 of the *Criminal Code* from being declared invalid, Justice Sopinka, speaking on behalf of a majority of his colleagues, ruled that Parliament's objective in enacting the obscenity provisions of the Code was to prevent the harms caused to society by the exposure of obscene materials. He went on to state that

> In the words of Nemetz C.J.B.C. in *R. v. Red Hot Video Ltd.* (1985) ... there is a growing concern that the exploitation of women and children, depicted in publications and films can, in certain circumstances, lead to "abject and servile victimization." As Anderson J.A. also noted in the same case, *if true equality between male and female persons is to be achieved, we cannot ignore the threat to equality resulting from exposure to audiences of certain types of violent and degrading material.* Materials portraying women as a class as objects for sexual exploitation and abuse have a negative impact on the "individual's sense of self-worth and acceptance." [emphasis added]

Justice Sopinka went on to conclude that the "objective of avoiding the harm associated with the dissemination of pornography" was "sufficiently pressing and substantial to warrant some restriction on full exercise of the right to freedom of expression." The Supreme Court also determined that the means of achieving this objective (namely, the obscenity provisions in section 163 of the Code) satisfied the "proportionality" requirement specified in the *Oakes* test.

In the case of *Park* (1995), the Supreme Court of Canada dealt with the question of the extent to which an honest, but mistaken, belief in consent can serve as a valid defence to a charge of sexual assault. The particular provision of the *Criminal Code* that was examined in the *Park* case (section 265(4)) and the associated common law interpretation of that provision have since been significantly modified by amendments made to the Code in 1992 (section 273.2). However, the approach taken by Justice L'Heureux-Dubé to this issue serves as a powerful example of the increasing recognition of the need to take account of women's perspectives in the interpretation of the criminal law. Indeed, speaking on her own behalf, Justice L'Heureux-Dubé emphatically observed that "this court must strive to ensure that criminal law is responsive to women's realities, rather than a vehicle for the perpetuation of historic repression and disadvantage."

Until recently, the common law dictated that a man who honestly believed that his victim was consenting to sexual activity was entitled to be acquitted of a charge of sexual assault even if that honest belief was totally unreasonable in the circumstances. Justice L'Heureux-Dubé, in referring to this situation, asserted that "the common law approach to consent may perpetuate social stereotypes that have historically victimized women and undermined their equal right to bodily integrity and human dignity." She pointed out that there is a definite "communication gap" between the way in which most women actually experience the issue of consent to sexual activity and the way in which most men perceive the question of whether consent has been given. Justice L'Heureux-Dubé discussed the impact of the various myths and stereotypes that many men hold in relation to the matter of consent in the context of sexual relations. She noted that men and women have been socialized to accept

the notion that coercive sexuality is "normal" in society and that many men see aggressive sexual behaviour as being a form of seduction rather than an act of rape—which is how such behaviour is actually experienced by their female partners.

Justice L'Heureux-Dubé took the view that the common law reflected these stereotypical views insofar as it effectively permitted a man to gain an acquittal on a charge of sexual assault whenever he could raise a reasonable doubt as to whether he believed that the partner had not *communicated her lack of consent* to him. Justice L'Heureux-Dubé suggested that the real focus of inquiry in such cases should be on whether or not the partner has *communicated her consent*. In other words, according to Justice L'Heureux-Dubé's approach, if the accused claimed that he was acting under an honest mistake as to consent, it would not be enough for him to say, "She did not do anything to tell me that she was not consenting." On the contrary, according to Justice L'Heureux-Dubé, such an accused should only be entitled to raise a valid defence where he can show that he honestly believed that his partner was *communicating consent* and that he honestly misperceived the contents of that communication.

Justice L'Heureux-Dubé contended that the common law approach to mistaken belief in consent actually reinforced the view held by many men that sexual activity is consensual if their partner has not actually communicated the fact that she does not consent. In her view, as long as this approach continues, "the damaging communication gap between the sexes, and the terrible costs that flow from it, will continue unacknowledged and will be perpetuated rather than narrowed." By requiring men to point to the specific behaviour of their partner that they claim indicated a communication of consent to engage in sexual relations, the criminal law, said Justice L'Heureux-Dubé, would help judges and juries separate "the myth and stereotype from the reality," would lead to "more accurate factual determinations," and would "take women's and men's distinct realities more equitably into account."

The *Park* case, although it was decided in 1995, was concerned with the defence of mistaken belief in consent as it existed prior to 1993, when amendments to the *Criminal Code* (Bill C-49) came into effect. Since this time, section 273.2 of the Code provides that this defence may not be raised if *"the accused did not take reasonable steps, in the circumstances known to the accused at the time, to ascertain that the complainant was consenting."* It could well be argued that this legislative change reflects the view of Justice L'Heureux-Dubé that the focus of inquiry in such cases should be on the *communication of consent* by the complainant. After all, if the accused is under a duty to take reasonable steps to *ascertain whether consent has been given*, then he or she must, of necessity, be required to point to some behaviour on the part of the complainant that suggested a communication of consent. In general, a reasonable person would not assume that a mere failure to say "no" amounts to a genuine consent to engage in sexual relations; there must be some conduct on the part of his or her partner that indicates that the partner is saying "yes."

It is significant that the views, expressed by Justice L'Heureux-Dubé in the *Park* case, were subsequently given a ringing endorsement by the Supreme Court as a whole in *Ewanchuk* (1999) — a case in which the Court reinforced the fundamental message that "No means No" in the context of sexual activity. In the *Ewanchuk* case, Justice Major expressed the view that the "law must afford women and men alike the peace of mind of knowing that their bodily integrity and autonomy in deciding when and whether to participate in sexual activity will be respected." On behalf of the majority of the Court, Justice Major emphasized that a defence of honest belief in consent may only be raised where the accused asserts that he had mistakenly believed that the complainant had communicated by words or conduct her consent to engage in sexual activity with him. Therefore, a mistaken belief that silence, passivity, or ambiguous conduct constitutes consent is irrelevant. Furthermore, the Court emphasized the principle that an accused person cannot raise the defence of honest belief by asserting that he thought a clearly expressed "No" was actually an invitation to the accused to engage

in even more persistent and aggressive attempts to initiate sexual activity. In Justice Major's words,

> Common sense should dictate that, once the complainant has expressed her unwillingness to engage in sexual contact, the accused should make certain that she has truly changed her mind before proceeding with further intimacies. The accused cannot rely on the mere lapse of time or the complainant's silence or equivocal conduct to indicate that there has been a change of heart and that consent now exists, nor can he engage in further sexual touching to "test the waters." Continuing sexual contact after someone has said "No" is, at a minimum, reckless conduct which is not excusable.

The final case to be examined in this context is that of *Mills* (1999). This is a decision of considerable significance because it indicates that the Supreme Court of Canada will be very reluctant to use its power under the *Charter* to invalidate legislation that has been designed to protect the rights of vulnerable groups, such as the victims of sexual assault (who are overwhelmingly female). The Court apparently signaled that it intends to take this approach even if such legislation impinges, to some extent, on the traditional rights of an accused person.

In *Mills*, the Supreme Court rejected a *Charter* challenge to provisions of the *Criminal Code* enacted in 1997 with the objective of restricting the use that may be made by lawyers for the accused of the confidential therapeutic records of complainants in trials involving charges of sexual assault. Such records may have been made by psychiatrists, psychologists, or counselors when a victim of sexual assault has sought assistance and gives intimate information that the victim has every reason to believe will be kept in confidence. In *Mills*, counsel for the defence had claimed that, by restricting access to such records and by limiting the circumstances in which they could be used in evidence, the new provisions of the *Criminal Code* seriously infringed the accused's right to make "full answer and defence" — a right that is enshrined in sections 7 and 11(d) of the *Charter*. However, the Supreme Court firmly rejected this argument and declined to invalidate provisions that represented the will of elected members of Parliament to protect the victims of sexual assault from unconscionable attacks by defence counsel. Justices McLachlin and Iacobucci advanced the view that "constitutionalism can facilitate democracy rather than undermine it" and that "one way in which it does this is by ensuring that fundamental human rights and individual freedoms are given due regard and protection." It is noteworthy that the two justices admitted that "Courts do not hold a monopoly on the protection and promotion of rights and freedoms; Parliament also plays a role in this regard and is often able to act as a significant ally for vulnerable groups." In their view, this principle is of particular importance in the context of sexual violence and they conclude that

> If constitutional democracy is meant to ensure that due regard is given to the voices of those vulnerable to being overlooked by the majority, then this court has an obligation to consider respectfully Parliament's attempt to respond to such voices.

Essentially, the *Mills* decision constitutes a strong affirmation by the highest court in Canada of the need to protect the equality rights of women in the trial of sexual assault cases and a commitment to interpreting the *Charter* in a manner that does not automatically restrict those equality rights merely because Parliament sets some limits on the lengths to which an accused person may go in mounting a defence. As Justices McLachlin and Iacobucci point out, the privacy of complainants in sexual assault cases should only be breached where it is absolutely necessary to do so in the interests of a fair trial:

> The right of the accused to make full answer and defence is a core principle of fundamental justice, but it does not automatically entitle the accused to

gain access to information contained in the private therapeutic records of complainants and witnesses. Rather, the scope of the right to make full answer and defence must be determined in light of privacy and equality rights of complainants and witnesses. It is clear that the right to full answer and defence is not engaged where the accused seeks information that will only serve to distort the truth-seeking purpose of a trial, and in such a situation, privacy and equality rights are paramount. On the other hand, where the information contained in a record directly bears on the right to make full answer and defence, privacy rights must yield to the need to avoid convicting the innocent.

The recognition by Parliament and the Supreme Court of Canada that there is a need to ensure that "the criminal law is responsive to women's realities" constitutes an important trend in the evolution of Canadian criminal law. It remains to be seen what shape this trend will take in the future, but it is beyond question that it has already brought about major changes in the way in which criminal law in Canada is enacted and interpreted.

REFORM OF THE CRIMINAL LAW

Canada's *Criminal Code* was first enacted in 1892. It is important, therefore, to recognize that the Canadian *Criminal Code* was very much the product of Victorian England rather than a document that reflected Canadian experience and conditions. Perhaps this should come as no surprise given Canada's colonial past; however, it is surprising that, more than a century later, the Canadian Parliament still has not replaced it with a Code that more accurately reflects modern Canadian conditions.

The *Criminal Code* still contains many signposts to its Victorian past, including such anachronistic offences as pretending to practice witchcraft and possessing a stink bomb. However, since 1892, there has been only one major legislative effort to reshape the Code. This occurred with the enactment of the 1955 version of the Code, although commentators are generally agreed that the 1955 reform was more

Since 1892, amendment of the Criminal Code *has been conducted on a piecemeal basis, leading to a bloated statute that lacks any sort of logic or coherence in its basic structure.*

a form of "good housekeeping" than a radical attempt to refashion the basic structure of the Code. Ever since the original enactment of the Code, in 1892, Parliament has continually added piecemeal amendments to it in order to enable the criminal law to keep abreast of the momentous changes that have occurred in Canadian society during the past one hundred years or more.

This haphazard pattern of law reform is well illustrated by reviewing just a few of the more significant amendments made to the *Criminal Code* between 1997 and 2000. For example, Bill C-95 (S.C. 1997, c. 23) was designed to respond to increasing public concern about the activities of organized criminals in Canada: it amended the *Criminal Code* to create a new offence of participation in a criminal organization and paved the way

for the implementation of new investigative tools that may be used to target the activities of organized crime. Similarly, the increasing use of sophisticated electronic and computer-assisted techniques for the crime of counterfeiting prompted Parliament to amend the *Criminal Code* in order to close any potential loopholes in the currently existing provisions that had been enacted at a time when counterfeiters used more traditional methods of creating false bank-notes (S.C. 1999, c. 5). Furthermore, in response to continuing public demands that the criminal justice system be more protective of the rights of victims, Parliament enacted legislation to amend the *Criminal Code* (S.C. 1999, c. 5) to enhance the safety, security, and privacy of victims of crime. In the same year, public concern in relation to a perceived increase in the abuse of animals led the Government of Canada to introduce Bill C-17 (December 1999), which contained proposals to amend the *Criminal Code* to increase the penalties for those who are intentionally cruel to animals. In addition, widespread public concern about the fatalities and injuries that occur in the course of high-speed police chases led directly to the enactment of Bill C-202 (S.C. 2000, c. 2), which creates a new offence of using a motor vehicle for the purpose of fleeing and evading the police. Finally, in response to one of the latest flurries of public fear about crime, the Government of Canada introduced legislation in June 2000 to deal with the phenomenon of "home invasions." In order to deal with the brutal force often used in this type of crime, the proposed amendment to the *Criminal Code* requires judges to consider home invasion to be an *aggravating* factor in sentencing: if this amendment is ultimately enacted, it will unequivocally signal to the courts that Parliament intends that the most severe penalties should be imposed upon conviction for a robbery or breaking and entering offence that involves the element of home invasion.

This brief overview of just a few of the most recent changes to the criminal law clearly establishes that the pace at which new provisions are added to the *Criminal Code* is most hectic. However, is this type of piecemeal law reform entirely desirable? It is, of course, inevitable — and entirely appropriate — that, in a democratic society, legislators will tend to respond swiftly to the demands of the electorate concerning the high-profile issue of "what to do about crime": by enacting new legislation, politicians will, at least, be seen to be "doing something about the crime problem." Furthermore, it is clear that the face of crime is changing rapidly, and legislators are duty-bound to try and devise solutions that meet our contemporary needs for safety and security. For example, with the advent of instantaneous electronic communication, it is possible for organized criminals to move money around the globe with a few keystrokes at a terminal or to devise ever more sophisticated methods of defrauding those who rely on such modern conveniences as credit cards and shopping on the Internet. Traditional criminal law is incapable of dealing with challenges of this type, and there is no doubt that Parliament has had no option but to enact an increasingly large body of new legislation in order to ensure the safety and security of Canadians. However, the problem with this method of making criminal law is that one cannot keep adding new provisions haphazardly to a *Criminal Code* that is already bursting at the seams. At some stage, it must surely become necessary to undertake a fundamental overhaul of the basic structure of the *Criminal Code* so that it is based on a reasonable degree of philosophical consistency, is not unnecessarily complex, and is comprehensible to the average Canadian. The reality facing Canadians today is that, as a consequence of the amendments that have taken place over more than a century, the *Criminal Code* has become an incredibly complex document, containing more than a thousand separate sections, and lacking any sort of basic logic and coherence in its essential structure. Furthermore, it contains many elements that are more appropriate to the Victorian era, in which it was first enacted, than to the first decade of the twenty-first century.

In one sense, the term "code" is a somewhat strange nomenclature to apply to Canada's *Criminal Code*. To a lawyer from Continental Europe (and, to

some extent, to a lawyer from the Province of Québec), the term denotes a legislative document that sets out the basic principles of law in any given area. Ideally, such a document is written in language that renders it readily accessible to the average citizen and is constructed in such a manner as to reflect a logical and coherent statement of basic principles. In an ideal world, a code eschews complex details, preferring to leave them to the courts, which are expected to interpret it in accordance with the clearly expressed, underlying intention of the legislative body concerned. Canada's *Criminal Code* bears scarcely a passing resemblance to the ideal form of a code, insofar as that term would be interpreted by lawyers in the so-called "**civil law**" tradition. Indeed, it contains no clear articulation of the basic principles of criminal responsibility, is filled with complex details, and is written in technical language that creates difficulty for specialists in the criminal law, let alone the average layperson. Coupled with its Victorian past, these characteristics of the Canadian *Criminal Code* render it an eminently suitable candidate for replacement by a modern *Criminal Code* that both reflects Canadian society in the twenty-first century and is reasonably accessible to the average Canadian.

Although there is an overwhelming case for reforming the *Criminal Code*, such reform has not yet taken place in Canada. Why has there not been a fundamental overhaul of the *Criminal Code* during the one hundred and five or so years of its existence? At least part of the problem seems to have been that, for much the twentieth century, there was no permanent law reform machinery that was capable of paving the way for a major revamping of criminal law in Canada. This situation was rectified in 1970 with the establishment of the Law Reform Commission of Canada. From its inception until its demise in 1992, the commission produced some 64 working papers, 34 reports to Parliament, and a significant number of study papers on a broad range of topics, most of which fell under the broad heading of "criminal law and procedure." There is no doubt that, at certain times, the commission's work exerted a considerable degree of influence on the course of legislative reform in the federal Parliament. For one example of its influence, one may refer to the commission's working paper and report on sexual offences (1977 and 1978), which played a leading part in the subsequent enactment of major reforms that brought about the abolition of the offence of rape and its replacement by the new offence of sexual assault (sections 271, 272, and 273 of the *Criminal Code*) in 1983.

The commission was subsequently allocated the task of preparing the ground for the enactment of a fundamentally different *Criminal Code* that, it was hoped, would ultimately guide Canadian criminal law into the twenty-first century. In 1979, after extensive consultation with his provincial counterparts, the Minister of Justice at the time, Senator Jacques Flynn, announced the initiation of a process of "criminal law review." The critical tasks of initial research and development of policy were assigned to the Law Reform Commission of Canada.

It had originally been intended that the review process would be complete and a new *Criminal Code* introduced in the federal Parliament by 1986. However, for a number of reasons, this deadline was never met. Nevertheless, in December 1986, the commission did publish a report, entitled *Recodifying Criminal Law, Volume One,* and a revised and enlarged edition of this report was submitted to the Minister of Justice of Canada in June 1987. Both reports contained similar versions of a draft *Criminal Code* that had been prepared by the commission.

What was the purpose of the commission's draft *Criminal Code*? In its 1987 report, *Recodifying Criminal Law, Revised and Enlarged Edition,* the commission stated that it hoped that its draft Code would "stimulate further study and work by Parliament and lead ultimately to the enactment of a new *Criminal Code* for Canada that is modern, logical, clear, comprehensive, restrained where possible and strong where necessary." However, the commission also acknowledged that it recognized that the draft Code "is only a first step in a long process leading ultimately, we hope, to the enactment of a new *Criminal Code* made in Canada, by Canadians, for

Canadians and reflecting more accurately our national identity and our common values."

The commission also asserted that

the Commission has developed a new code which aims to be intelligible to all Canadians. It is drafted in a straightforward manner, with a minimum of technical terms, avoiding complex sentence structure and excess detail. It speaks in terms of general principles instead of needless specifics and *ad hoc* enumerations. ... Our new Code is comprehensive, logical, organized, coherent and consistent. It is in harmony with the *Charter* and responsive to the needs of modern Canada.

Although the commission believed that its draft Code would serve as the starting point for a new *Criminal Code* by 1992, Canada still does not have such legislation on the books. Ironically, the year 1992 saw the abolition of the Law Reform Commission of Canada by the Progressive Conservative government of Brian Mulroney—a step that was justified by referring to the need for the federal government to engage in an extensive program of cost-cutting measures. (In 1996, the Liberal government of Jean Chrétien, which came to power in the general election of 1993, established a new law reform body—known as the Law Commission of Canada—pursuant to the *Law Commission of Canada Act* (S.C. 1996, c. 9). However, to date, the Law Commission has not been particularly active in the field of criminal law reform.)

Although the Law Reform Commission of Canada disappeared from the national stage in 1992, it still appeared at that time that there was a considerable degree of acceptance of the need for the implementation of fundamental criminal law reform in Canada. For example, in 1992, a task force of the Canadian Bar Association strongly recommended that there be a recodification of the *general principles of criminal law*, that are contained in the *Criminal Code*, and a similar call was made by the Parliamentary Sub-Committee on Recodification of the General Part of the *Criminal Code*, which issued a report in February 1993. Essentially, these bodies suggested that the first step in *Criminal Code* reform should be to recodify the basic principles of the criminal law (by clearly articulating the general principles of criminal liability and by precisely defining the nature and scope of the major defences that may be raised in a criminal trial). It was felt that recodification of the law relating to individual offences, such as theft, fraud, and assault, could be undertaken at a later time.

The Progressive Conservative government of the day responded to those who were advocating fundamental reform of the *Criminal Code* by issuing a *White Paper* (June 1993), entitled *Proposals to Amend the Criminal Code (General Principles)*. Unfortunately, these proposals were never enacted owing to the federal election that occurred later in 1993. At first, it seemed as though the incoming Liberal government would carry out the law-reform task that its predecessor had failed to complete. In December 1994, the Department of Justice Canada distributed a consultation paper, entitled *Reforming the General Part of the Criminal Code*, and solicited responses from a broad range of Canadians as to the appropriateness of the various policy options that had been identified by the federal government. However, this process never resulted in legislation and, to date, Canadians are still left with an antiquated *Criminal Code* that is in danger of collapsing under the weight of its own contradictions. Instead of overhauling the *Criminal Code*, the Liberal government devoted its attention to a major reform of the criminal law relating to illegal drugs. Indeed, in 1996, Parliament enacted the *Controlled Drugs and Substances Act*, S.C. 1996, c. 19, which entirely replaced the old *Narcotic Control Act* and those parts of the *Food and Drugs Act* that dealt with controlled and restricted drugs.

As Canada entered a new century, the criminal law reform priority of the federal government appeared to lie in the area of youth justice. Indeed, the Government of Canada has been keen to demonstrate its responsiveness to widespread public criticism of the *Young Offenders Act*, R.S.C. 1985, c. Y-1. Consequently, a major legislative project in 1999 was Bill C-3, the proposed *Youth Criminal Justice Act*, which will replace the *Young Offenders Act* and establish a régime that many would interpret as implementing a "get tough" policy on violent young offenders. Perhaps, once this project is completed, Parliament will finally pick up the torch of fundamental reform of the criminal law and present Canadians with a *Criminal Code* for the twenty-first century. It seems unconscionable that a modern society, such as Canada, is still making do with the basic elements of a *Criminal Code* that was first enacted at the end of the nineteenth century!

FURTHER READING

Acorn, A. 1997. Harm, Community Tolerance, and the Indecent: A Discussion of *R. v. Mara*. 36 *Alberta Law Review*: 258.

Alexander, E.R. 1990. The Supreme Court of Canada and the *Canadian Charter of Rights and Freedoms*. 40 *University of Toronto Law Journal*: 1.

Alexander, M. 1988. Censorship and the Limits of Liberalism. 47 *University of Toronto Faculty Law Review*: 58.

Beaman, L.G. 1998. Women's Defences: Contextualizing Dilemmas of Difference and Power. 9 *Women & Criminal Justice*: 87.

Blache, P. 1991. The Criteria for Justification under *Oakes*: Too Much Severity Generated through Formalism. 20 *Manitoba Law Journal*: 437.

Boyle, C. and M. McCrimmon. 1999. The Constitutionality of Bill C-49: Analyzing Sexual Assault Law as if Equality Really Mattered. 41 *Criminal Law Quarterly*: 198.

Boyle, C., et al. 1985. *A Feminist Review of Criminal Law*. Ottawa: Status of Women, Canada.

Brudner, A. 1997. Guilt under the *Charter*: The Lure of Parliamentary Supremacy. 40 *Criminal Law Quarterly*: 287.

Campbell, M.E. 2000. Politics and Public Servants: Observations on the Current State of Criminal Law Reform. 42 *Canadian Journal of Criminology*: 342.

Canadian Bar Association. 1992. Report of the Canadian Bar Association Criminal Recodification Task Force: *Principles of Criminal Liability, Proposals for a New General Part of the Criminal Code of Canada*. Ottawa: Canadian Bar Association.

Clark, L.M.G. 1989. Feminist Perspectives on Violence against Women and Children: Psychological, Social Service and Criminal Justice Concerns. 3 *Canadian Journal of Women and the Law*: 531.

Cossman, B., et al. 1997. *Bad Attitude/s on Trial: Pornography, Feminism, and the* Butler *Decision.* Toronto: University of Toronto Press.

Crerar, D.A. 1996–97. "The Darker Corners": The Incoherence of 2(b) Obscenity Jurisprudence After *Butler.* 28 *Ottawa Law Review:* 377.

Deimann, S. 1998. *R. v. Hydro-Québec:* Federal Environmental Regulation as Criminal Law. 43 *McGill Law Journal:* 923.

Del Buono, V.M. 1986. Toward a New Criminal Code for Canada. (1986) 28 *Criminal Law Quarterly:* 370.

Department of Justice (Canada). 1987. *The Federal Legislative Process in Canada.* Ottawa: Minister of Supply and Services Canada.

Department of Justice Canada. 1994. *Reforming the General Part of the Criminal Code: A Consultation Paper.* Ottawa: Department of Justice Canada.

———. 1994. *Toward a New General Part of the Criminal Code of Canada.* Ottawa: Department of Justice Canada.

Dershowitz, A.M. 2000. Moral Judgment: Does the Abuse Excuse Threaten Our Legal System? 3 *Buffalo Criminal Law Review:* 775.

Farmer, L. 2000. Reconstructing the English Codification Debate: The Criminal Law Commissioners, 1833–45. 18 *Law & History Review:* 397.

Ferguson, G. 2000. Recent Developments in Canadian Criminal Law. 24 *Criminal Law Journal:* 248.

Friedland, M.L. 1993. Canadian Criminal Justice, 1892–1992. 42 *University of New Brunswick Law Journal:* 175.

Government of Canada. 1982. *The Criminal Law in Canadian Society.* Ottawa: Government of Canada.

Graycar, R. 1998. The Gender of Judgments: Some Reflections on "Bias." 32 *U.B.C. Law Review:* 1.

Griffiths, C.T. and S.N. Verdun-Jones. 1994. *Canadian Criminal Justice.* 2d ed. Toronto: Harcourt Brace. 209–77.

Halewood, M. 1990. Men, Sex and Power. 48 *University of Toronto Faculty Law Review:* 329.

Hatch, D.R. 1999. Culpability and Capitulation: Sexual Assault and Consent in the Wake of *R. v. Ewanchuk.* 43 *Criminal Law Quarterly:* 51.

Healey, P. 1984. The Process of Reform in Canadian Criminal Law. 42 *University of Toronto Faculty Law Review:* 1.

Herland, J. 1998. Sounding the Death Knell for *Butler?* A Review of B. Cossman, S. Bell, L. Gotell, & B.L. Ross, *Bad Attitude/s on Trial: Pornography, Feminism, and the* Butler *Decision.* 43 *McGill Law Journal:* 959.

Hogg, P.W. 1999. *Constitutional Law of Canada.* 1999 Student ed. Toronto: Carswell. Chap.18.

Hogg, P.W. and A.A. Bushell. 1997. The *Charter* Dialogue between Courts and Legislatures (Or Perhaps the *Charter of Rights* Isn't Such A Bad Thing After All). 35 *Osgoode Hall Law Journal:* 75.

Hogg, P.W. and R. Penner. 1991. The Contribution of Chief Justice Dickson to an Interpretative Framework and Value System for Section 1 of the *Charter of Rights.* 20 *Manitoba Law Journal:* 428.

Hubble, G. 1997. Feminism and the Battered Woman: The Limits of Self-Defence in the Context of Domestic Violence. 9 *Current Issues in Criminal Justice:* 113.

Hughes, P. 1999. Recognizing Substantive Equality as a Foundational Constitutional Principle. 22 *Dalhousie Law Journal:* 5.

Hunter, I. 1990. The Canadian Abortion Quagmire: The Way in and a Way Out. 6 *Canadian Family Law Quarterly:* 57.

Hurlburt, W.H. 1999. Fairy Tales and Living Trees: Observations on Some Recent Constitutional Decisions of the Supreme Court of Canada. 26 *Manitoba Law Journal:* 181.

Kaiser, H.A. 1990. Preventing Which Crime? A (Relative) Outsider's Perspective on the Orthodoxy of Criminality in the Canadian Reform Agenda. 33 *Criminal Law Quarterly:* 61.

Kasirer, N. 1990. Canada's Criminal Law Codification Viewed and Reviewed. 35 *McGill Law Journal:* 841.

Kazan, P. 1997. Reasonableness, Gender Difference, and Self-Defense Law. 24 *Manitoba Law Journal:* 549.

Kelly, J.B. 1999. The *Charter of Rights and Freedoms* and the Rebalancing of Liberal Constitutionalism in Canada, 1982-1997. 37 *Osgoode Hall Law Journal:* 625.

Klinck, D. 1993. The *Charter* and Substantive Criminal "Justice." 42 *University of New Brunswick Law Journal:* 191.

Koshan, J. 1998. Aboriginal Women, Justice and the *Charter:* Bridging the Divide? 32 *U.B.C. Law Review:* 23.

Kramer, R. 1992. *R. v. Butler:* A New Approach to Obscenity Law or Return to the Morality Play?" 35 *Criminal Law Quarterly:* 77.

Lacombe, D. 1994. *Blue Politics: Pornography and the Law in the Age of Feminism.* Toronto: University of Toronto Press.

Law Reform Commission of Canada. 1975. *Towards a Codification of Canadian Criminal Law.* Ottawa: Information Canada.

———. 1977. Working Paper No. 22: *Sexual Offences.* Ottawa: Information Canada.

———. 1978. Report No. 10: *Sexual Offences*. Ottawa: Information Canada.

———. 1982. Working Paper No. 29: *Criminal Law; The General Part: Liability and Defences*. Ottawa: Supply and Services Canada.

———. 1986. Report No. 30: *Recodifying Criminal Law*, Vol. 1. Ottawa: L.R.C.C.

———. 1987. Report No. 31: *Recodifying Criminal Law*, Rev. ed. Ottawa: L.R.C.C.

———. 1989. Working Paper No. 58: *Crimes Against the Foetus*. Ottawa: L.R.C.C.

———. 1991. Report No. 33: *Recodifying Criminal Procedure, Volume One: Police Powers*. Ottawa: L.R.C.C.

Leidholdt, D. and J. G. Raymond, eds. 1990. *The Sexual Liberals and the Attack on Feminism*. New York: Pergamon Press.

Leigh, L.H. 1983. The Law Reform Commission of Canada and the Reform of the General Part. (1983) *Criminal Law Review*: 438.

L'Heureux-Dubé, C. 2000. The Search for Equality: A Human Rights Issue. 25 *Queen's Law Journal*: 401.

Linden, A.M. 1989. Recodifying Criminal Law. 14 *Queen's Law Journal*: 3.

Liu, M. 2000. A "Prophet with Honour": An Examination of the Equality Jurisprudence of Madam Justice Claire L'Heureux-Dubé of the Supreme Court of Canada. 25 *Queen's Law Journal*: 417.

McConnell, M. and L. Clark. 1991. Abortion Law in Canada: A Matter of National Concern. 14 *Dalhousie Law Journal*: 81.

McCourt, K.M. and D.J. Love. 1989. Abortion and Section 7 of the Charter: Proposing a Constitutionally Valid Foetal Protection Law. 18 *Manitoba Law Journal*: 365.

McLachlin, B.M. 1991. Crime and Women—Feminine Equality and the Criminal Law. 25 *U.B.C. Law Review*: 1.

———. 1999. *Charter* Myths. 33 *U.B.C. Law Review*: 23.

Macklin, A. 1993. Law Reform Error: Retry or Abort? 16 *Dalhousie Law Journal*: 395.

Martin, D.L. 1998. Retribution Revisited: A Reconsideration of Feminist Criminal Law Reform Strategies. 36 *Osgoode Hall Law Journal*: 151.

Mewett, A.W. 1967. The Criminal Law, 1867–1967. 45 *Canadian Bar Review*: 726.

———. 1993. The Canadian *Criminal Code*, 1892–1992. 72 *Canadian Bar Review*: 1.

Mewett, A.W. and M. Manning. 1994. *Mewett and Manning on Criminal Law*. 3d ed. Toronto: Butterworths. 1–121, 689–99.

Minister of Justice of Canada. 1993. *White Paper: Proposals to Amend the Criminal Code (General Principles)*. Ottawa: Minister of Justice of Canada.

Moon, R. 1993. *R. v. Butler*—The Limits of the Supreme Court's Feminist Re-interpretation of Section 163. 25 *Ottawa Law Review*: 361.

Noonan, S. 1991. What the Court Giveth: Abortion and Bill C-43. 16 *Queen's Law Journal*: 321.

Quistgaard, B. 1993. Pornography, Harm, and Censorship: A Feminist (Re)vision of the Right to Freedom of Expression. 52 *University of Toronto Faculty Law Review*: 73.

Roach, K. 1999. The Effects of the Canadian *Charter of Rights* on Criminal Justice. 33 *Israel Law Review*: 607.

Roach, K.W. 1997. Editorial: Legislative Failure and Law Reform. 40 *Criminal Law Quarterly*: 2.

Roberts, J.V. and R.M. Mohr, eds. 1994. *Confronting Sexual Assault: A Decade of Legal and Social Change*. Toronto: University of Toronto Press.

Shaffer, M. 1997. The Battered Woman Syndrome Revisited: Some Complicating Thoughts Five Years After *R. v. Lavallee*. 47 *University of Toronto Law Journal*: 1.

Stalker, M.A. 1989. The Fault Element in Recodifying Criminal Law; A Critique. 14 *Queen's Law Journal*: 35.

Stribopoulos, J. 1999. The Constitutionalization of "Fault" in Canada: A Normative Critique. 42 *Criminal Law Quarterly*: 227.

Stuart, D. 1995. *Canadian Criminal Law: A Treatise*. 3d ed. Toronto: Carswell. 1–69.

———. 1996. *Charter Justice in Canadian Criminal Law*, 2d ed. Toronto: Carswell.

Stuart, D. and R.J. Delisle. 1997. *Learning Canadian Criminal Law*. 6th ed. Toronto: Carswell. Chap. 1.

Trakman, L.E., W. Cole-Hamilton, and S. Gatien. 1998. *R. v. Oakes* 1986–1997: Back to the Drawing Board. 36 *Osgoode Hall Law Journal*: 83.

Verdun-Jones, S.N. 1999. *Canadian Criminal Cases: Selected Highlights*. Toronto: Harcourt Brace. Chap. 1.

Weinrib, L.E. 1992. The *Morgentaler* Judgment: Constitutional Rights, Legislative Intervention, and Institutional Design. 42 *University of Toronto Law Journal*: 22.

The *Actus Reus* Elements of a Criminal Offence

OVERVIEW

This chapter examines the following:

1. The essential nature of the legal concept of *actus reus*;
2. the three major elements associated with the *actus reus*: conduct, circumstances, and consequences;
3. the exceptions to the general rule that these three elements must be proved before there can be a conviction of a criminal offence;
4. the situations in which omissions (failures to act) can give rise to criminal responsibility;
5. the question of whether there should be a legislated duty to rescue those in urgent need of assistance;
6. the requirement that the *actus reus* and *mens rea* elements of an offence coincide;
7. the element of voluntariness that must exist before an individual may be convicted of a criminal offence;
8. the defence of automatism and the situations in which the defence may be raised successfully;
9. the difficulty of drawing a distinction between the defences of automatism and "not criminally responsible on account of mental disorder" as well as the very different consequences that follow from a successful assertion of these defences;
10. the situations in which the defence of automatism may not be raised because the accused condition was at fault in permitting him or herself to become incapacitated;

11. the imposition of both the *primary* (*persuasional*) and *secondary* (*evidentiary*) burdens of proof on those defendants who raise a defence of automatism.

INTRODUCTION

In general, an **accused** person may not be convicted of a criminal offence unless the prosecution can prove *beyond a reasonable doubt*

a) that a particular event or state of affairs was "caused" by the accused's conduct (***actus reus***) and
b) that this conduct was accompanied by a certain state of mind (***mens rea***).

With their ingrained love of mystification, lawyers have traditionally referred to a famous Latin maxim in order to summarize this critical legal principle: "*Actus non facit reum nisi mens sit rea.*" Translated literally, this means that an act does not render a person guilty of a criminal offence unless his or her mind is also guilty. In legal parlance, the concept of *mens rea* refers to the mental elements of an offence while the term *actus reus* refers to all the other elements of the offence that must be proved by the Crown. As Justice Cory pointed out in delivering the judgment of the majority of the justices of the Supreme Court of Canada in the case of *Daviault* (1994),

Originally a crime was considered to be the commission of a physical act which was specifically prohibited by law. It was the act itself which was the sole element of the crime. If it was established that the act was committed by the accused then a finding of guilt would ensue. However, as early as the 12th century, in large part through the influence of canon law, it was established that there must also be a mental element combined with the prohibited act to constitute a crime. That is to say that the accused must have *meant* or intended to commit the prohibited act. The physical act and the mental element which together constitute a crime came to be known as the *actus reus* denoting the act, and the *mens rea* for the mental element. Like so many maxims they are imprecise and in many instances misleading.

Use of the terms *actus reus* and *mens rea* may be quite misleading, for example, if it is assumed that they represent a sharp distinction between the physical and mental elements of an offence. Indeed, there is an increasing degree of acceptance by Canadian courts of the view that the *actus reus* of a criminal offence includes the element of **voluntariness** (discussed later in this chapter). As Justice McLachlin said in delivering the judgment of the majority of the justices of the Supreme Court of Canada in the case of *Théroux* (1993),

> The term *mens rea*, properly understood, does not encompass all of the mental elements of crime. The *actus reus* has its own mental element; *the act must be the voluntary act of the accused for the* actus reus *to exist.* [emphasis added]

Leaving aside the issue of voluntariness for the moment, why is it important to focus on the *actus reus* elements of criminal offences? In response to this question, Gold (1994), for example, has suggested that it is necessary to undertake this task because the *actus reus* elements "identify a human-oriented act that merits designation as a crime by society and merits society's undertaking to locate and deal with those human actors responsible." In

other words, it is the existence of the *actus reus* elements of an offence that justifies the intervention of the criminal justice system. It is not enough that an individual may be considered dangerous and that he or she *might* commit a crime in the future. On the contrary, before an accused person may be held criminally responsible, the Crown must establish that he or she has engaged in *conduct that is defined as criminal in the sense that all the necessary* actus reus *elements can be proved beyond a reasonable doubt.*

One important legal principle that inevitably flows from the maxim *actus non facit reum nisi mens sit rea* is that, even in situations where the accused person has the necessary *mens rea* for a particular offence, he or she nevertheless may *not* be convicted of that offence unless the *mens rea* coincides with the commission of the *actus reus* of the offence. For example, let us suppose that Casanova becomes disillusioned with his marriage to Emma and commences an affair with Lisa. Casanova then decides to leave his wife and persuades Lisa (who is unaware of Emma's existence) to marry him. Casanova and Lisa subsequently participate in a marriage ceremony. Casanova derives some perverse pleasure from his belief that the marriage to Lisa is bigamous. However, Casanova subsequently receives a telephone call and he is informed that Emma was struck by a car and expired twenty minutes before the marriage ceremony with Lisa. It is clear that Casanova had the necessary *mens rea* for the offence of **bigamy** (section 290 of the *Criminal Code*). However, he cannot be convicted of the offence of bigamy because he did not commit the *actus reus* of the offence. Section 290(1)(a)(i) indicates that the offence of bigamy is committed where, **inter alia**, an accused person "*being married,* goes through a form of marriage with another person." Although Casanova fully *intended* to enter into a bigamous union with Lisa, he was (as a consequence of the fatal mishap that befell Emma) no longer a married person at the time of the wedding ceremony.

This tale represents a clear illustration of an underlying principle of criminal law—namely, that the state should punish citizens for *overt actions* rather than for their "wicked" **intentions**. Canadian criminal law generally requires that, before an individual may be convicted of an offence, the Crown must prove both an element of conduct and an accompanying mental element. As Herbert Packer (1968) said, "the limitation of criminal punishment to conduct constitutes the first and most important line of defense against erosion of the idea of culpability, for it keeps the criminal law from becoming purely the servant of the utilitarian ideal of prevention."

THE *ACTUS REUS* AS A COMBINATION OF CONDUCT, CIRCUMSTANCES, AND CONSEQUENCES

In general, it is possible to identify three separate elements of the *actus reus* of a criminal offence:

(i) *conduct* (a *voluntary* act or omission constituting the central feature of the crime);
(ii) the surrounding and "material" *circumstances*;
(iii) the *consequences* of the voluntary conduct.

As an illustration of the application of this analytical framework, we may turn to the offence of assault causing bodily harm. In order to define the elements of the *actus reus* of this offence, it is necessary to refer to three different sections of the *Criminal Code*. First, section 265 defines the nature of an assault: in particular, section 265(1)(a) states that

A person commits an assault when

(a) without the consent of another person, he applies force intentionally to that other person, directly or indirectly. ...

Second, we must turn to section 267 of the Code in order to find the provision that establishes the offence of assault causing bodily harm. This section proclaims that

(1) Every one who, in committing an assault,

(a) carries, uses or threatens to use a weapon or an imitation thereof, or
(b) *causes bodily harm to the complainant*,

is guilty of an indictable offence. ... [emphasis added]

The third, and final, piece of the definitional jigsaw puzzle is to be found in section 2 of the Code, which stipulates that

"bodily harm" means any hurt or injury to a person that interferes with the health or comfort of the person and that is more than merely transient or trifling in nature.

How can we analyze the offence of assault causing bodily harm in terms of the three elements of conduct, circumstances, and consequences? The element of *conduct* is represented by the application of force to the person of the victim. The most critical of the material *circumstances* is that such force was applied without the consent of the victim. Finally, the *consequence*, which must be proved, is that the victim sustained actual bodily harm. As to this final requirement, it may be noted that in the case of *Petrovic* (1984), the Ontario Court of Appeal held that a swollen face and a bleeding nose, caused by the slapping of the victim by her husband, constituted bodily harm within the meaning of the *Criminal Code* definition because they were injuries that were neither "transient" nor "trifling" in nature. Similarly, in *Welch* (1995), the victim suffered "obvious and extensive bruising" to various parts of her body and bleeding from the rectum as a consequence of violent sex acts; these injuries required treatment over a period of a month. The Ontario Court of Appeal had no difficulty in ruling that these injuries constituted bodily harm and dismissed the accused's **appeal** against a conviction of sexual assault causing bodily harm. However, in *Taylor* (1991), the Appellate Division of the Nova Scotia Supreme Court held that, while throwing beer over someone may amount to an assault under section 265 of the Code, it could not be considered an assault *causing bodily harm* within the meaning of the definition in section 2.

Does the term "bodily harm" include *psychological* harm? In *McCraw* (1991)—a case involving threats of sexual assault—the Supreme Court of Canada answered this question in the affirmative: "there can be no doubt that psychological harm may often be more pervasive and permanent in its effect than any physical harm."

This method of analyzing the basic elements of the *actus reus* may also be profitably applied to the offence of sexual assault. Section 271 of the Code indicates that "every one who commits a sexual assault is guilty of" either an **indictable** or summary conviction offence. The section does not, however, define what a sexual assault is. In order to formulate such a definition, it is necessary to look first at section 265, which defines assault in general:

(1) A person commits an assault when

   (a) without the consent of another person, he applies force intentionally to that other person, directly or indirectly;

   (b) he attempts or threatens, by an act or gesture, to apply force to another person, if he has, or causes that other person to believe upon reasonable grounds that he has, present ability to effect his purpose; or

   (c) while openly wearing or carrying a weapon or an imitation thereof, he accosts or impedes another person or begs.

(2) This section applies to all forms of assault, including sexual assault. ...

Since Parliament has not defined the word "sexual" in the context of the offence of "sexual assault," this task has been left to the courts.

How can the basic elements of sexual assault be identified in terms of the requirements of conduct, circumstances, and consequences? In essence, the element of *conduct* generally consists of the inten-

tional application of force (or the threat of the application of force) to the person of the victim. The *consequences* that must be established are either that the accused actually applied force to the victim or that the accused caused the victim to believe on reasonable grounds that the accused had "the present ability" to apply such force (section 265(1)(b)). The relevant *circumstances* that must be proved are that the application of force or the threat of such force took place without the consent of the victim and that the assault is of a "sexual nature."

The requirement, that the assault be of a "sexual nature," was considered by the Supreme Court of Canada in *Chase* (1987). In this case, Chase took hold of a fifteen-year-old girl around her shoulders and arms and grabbed her breasts. When the girl struggled, Chase said, "Come on dear, don't hit me. I know you want it." According to the victim, he also tried to grab her "private" but she prevented him from doing so. Chase was convicted of sexual assault, but he appealed to the New Brunswick Court of Appeal, which substituted a verdict of guilty of common assault. The Court of Appeal held that, in order for an accused person to be convicted of *sexual* assault, there must be contact with the genitals. The Crown appealed against this decision on the basis that the Court of Appeal's definition of sexual assault was too narrow. The Supreme Court of Canada agreed with the Crown and restored Chase's conviction for sexual assault. In delivering the judgment of the Supreme Court, Justice McIntyre asserted that

Sexual assault is an assault within any one of the definitions of that concept in s. [265(1)] of the *Criminal Code* which is committed in circumstances of a sexual nature, such that the sexual integrity of the victim is violated. *The test to be applied in determining whether the impugned conduct has the requisite sexual nature is an objective one: "Viewed in the light of all the circumstances, is the sexual or carnal context of the assault visible to a reasonable observer."*... The part of the body touched, the nature of the contact, the situation in which it occurred, the words and gestures accom-

panying the act, and all other circumstances surrounding the conduct, including threats which
may or may not be accompanied by force, will be
relevant. ... [emphasis added]

In this particular case, the Supreme Court found no
difficulty in deciding that a reasonable observer, in
light of all the circumstances, would have concluded that Chase's grabbing of the victim's breasts
was of a sexual nature.

In the case of *S. (P.L.)* (1991), the Supreme Court
of Canada emphasized that the test as to whether an
assault is sexual is *objective* in nature. The critical
question is whether the hypothetical "reasonable
observer" would have concluded that the assault was
sexual; if a court feels that the reasonable observer
would come to this conclusion, it does not matter
what the accused's *subjective* **motives** may have been.
In other words, it is possible for a court to hold that
an assault was sexual even if the accused claims that
he or she did not engage in the conduct in question
for the purpose of sexual gratification. Justice Cory
stated that the intent of the person committing the
assault "is only one of the factors to be considered in
determining whether the overall conduct had a sexual content." He went on the say that the "appropriate question" is "whether, notwithstanding the
absence of a proven sexual intent, the touching was
committed in circumstances of a sexual nature." The
application of the objective test is perhaps best illustrated by the case of *V. (K.B.)* (1993), in which the
accused had, on several occasions, violently grabbed
his three-year-old son's genitals in order to deter him
from grasping the genital region of adults. The
accused was charged with *sexual* assault even though
he claimed that his actions were motivated solely by
considerations of discipline. Despite this argument,
the accused was convicted at trial and his conviction
was ultimately upheld by the Supreme Court of
Canada. The majority of the justices of the Supreme
Court held that a reasonable observer would have
concluded that the "sexual integrity" of the victim
had been violated even if the father had not engaged
in this conduct for any sexual purpose. As Justice
Iacobucci said,

Among other things, [the father], on three occasions, violently clutched the little boy's scrotum
and there was evidence of bruising and severe pain.
In my view, it was clearly open to the trial judge to
conclude from all the circumstances that the
assault was one of a sexual nature and that the
assault was such that the sexual integrity of the ...
son was violated.

Similarly, in the *Bernier* case (1998), the
Supreme Court of Canada ruled that the accused,
who worked in a facility providing care for the
developmentally disabled, was guilty of sexual
assault when he touched the breasts and testicles of
both male and female residents — even though the
accused claimed that he had no hostile intent,
sought no sexual gratification, and was only "joking." The Supreme Court agreed with the Québec
Court of Appeal that any reasonable person would
have "perceived the sexual context of the touch-
ings": indeed, the sexual integrity of the victims had
been seriously violated by the accused and it was
irrelevant that he claimed that he was just "having
fun" by "bugging" and "kidding" them.

In the *Ewanchuk* case (1999), the Supreme
Court of Canada made an important point about
the *circumstances* that the Crown has to prove as a
critical component of the *actus reus* of sexual assault.
Specifically, the Supreme Court noted that, whereas
the issue of whether an assault is "sexual" in nature
is decided on an *objective* basis, the decision as to
whether there was a lack of consent to sexual touching must be decided on a purely *subjective* basis. Of
course, in determining whether there was a lack of
consent, the court is concerned with the *subjective
intent of the* **complainant** rather than the accused.
As Justice Major noted,

The *actus reus* of sexual assault is established by
the proof of three elements: (i) touching, (ii) the
sexual nature of the contact, and (iii) the absence
of consent. The first of these two elements are
objective. It is sufficient for the Crown to prove
that the accused's actions were voluntary. The sexual nature of the assault is determined objectively;

the Crown need not prove that the accused had any *mens rea* with respect to the sexual nature of his or her behaviour ...

The absence of consent, however, is subjective and determined by reference to the complainant's subjective internal state of mind towards the touching, at the time it occurred ...

The inclusion of assault and sexual assault in the *Code* expresses society's determination to protect the security of the person from any non-consensual contact or threats of force ... It follows that any intentional but unwanted touching is criminal.

EXCEPTIONS TO THE GENERAL RULE REQUIRING CONDUCT, CIRCUMSTANCES, AND CONSEQUENCES

Offences Where Consequences Are Not a Required Element of the *Actus Reus*

While the three elements of conduct, circumstances, and consequences are usually present in the *actus reus* of a criminal offence, there are, nevertheless, certain exceptions to the general rule. For example, there is a significant number of offences in relation to which the Crown is not required to prove that the accused's conduct caused any particular *consequences*. Illustrative of such offences is the crime of perjury. Section 131(1) of the Code states that

> every one commits perjury who, with intent to mislead, makes before a person who is authorized by law to permit it to be made before him a false statement under oath or solemn affirmation, by affidavit, solemn declaration or deposition or orally, knowing that the statement is false.

It is clear that the offence is complete just as soon as the accused has intentionally uttered the false statement; it is not necessary for the Crown to prove that anyone either believed or was influenced by the false statement. As Justice Lyon stated, in delivering the judgment of the Manitoba Court of Appeal in

Evans (1995), "it is not necessary that the false statement actually mislead the court, but only that the accused intended to mislead the court." In other words, the *actus reus* of perjury lacks the element of consequences since the accused may be convicted of the offence regardless of whether his or her false statement influenced anyone.

However, as one might expect, the element of consequences constitutes an essential feature of the *actus reus* of most criminal offences. Typical of the approach taken by the criminal law is the case of *Winning* (1973), in which the accused was convicted of obtaining credit from Eaton's by false pretences (see section 362(1)(b) of the Code). The accused had applied for credit at Eaton's and, as part of her application, she gave her proper name and address. However, she also included at least two false statements. The Ontario Court of Appeal ultimately quashed Ms. Winning's conviction because it was clear from the evidence that Eaton's had not relied on any of the information, contained in the application form, save only for Ms. Winning's name and address (which were correct). Chief Justice Gale said "the appellant did not obtain credit by a false pretence, because the credit was given not in reliance on her application, but rather in reliance on Eaton's investigation of her." In other words, the entry of false statements in the application form was not sufficient for a conviction in Ms. Winning's case because the Crown was unable to prove that her conduct produced the *consequence* that credit was advanced to her. It is, of course, quite possible that the Crown would have been more successful if the charge laid had been that of *attempting* to obtain credit by false pretences (see Chapter 7).

Offences Where Conduct Is Not a Required Element of the *Actus Reus*

While *conduct* constitutes a vital element of the *actus reus* of the great majority of criminal offences, there is an exceptional group of offences that do not require the proof of any conduct on the part of the **defendant**. In order to obtain a conviction in relation to such an offence, the Crown is merely required to prove that *the accused was discovered in a particular "condition" or "state."* For example, section 351(1) of the Code provides that

> Every one who, without lawful excuse, the proof of which lies on him, has in his possession any instrument suitable for the purpose of breaking into any place, motor vehicle, vault or safe under circumstances that give rise to a reasonable inference that the instrument has been used or is or was intended to be used for any such purpose, is guilty of an indictable offence. ...

A classic example of an individual who would be "caught" by this section is the masked man who is discovered lurking around a house at 2:00 A.M. with a large crowbar in his hand. However, a legitimate tradesperson with a set of professional tools would not be caught under this provision if he or she was arriving at the house in order to carry out repairs at the request of the owner. Clearly, the tradesperson would have a "lawful excuse" for being in possession of the tools concerned whereas the masked man would manifestly not have any such justification.

An instructive application of section 351 occurred in the case of *K. (S.)* (1995), where the accused was charged with possession of instruments suitable for breaking into a motor vehicle. He had been discovered with a knapsack, out of the top of which was sticking an "ignition punch." The arresting police officer searched the knapsack and found "vice grips, gloves, seven assorted screws of different sizes and a slot-head screwdriver." The accused was convicted at his trial and his appeal to the British Columbia Court of Appeal was dismissed. In delivering the judgment of the Court of Appeal, Justice Prowse noted that, although the instruments found in the possession of the accused "can be used for legitimate automotive purposes, they are also well known to police for their use in the breaking into, and theft of, automobiles" and that this "is particularly true of the ignition punch." There was no doubt, therefore, that the tools discovered in the knapsack were suitable for breaking into motor vehicles, and it was perfectly clear that the accused

had no legitimate reason for possessing them. However, the accused asserted that the Crown must prove that he had "targeted" a particular motor vehicle before it could be established that it was reasonable to draw the inference that the tools were intended to be used for the purpose of break-ins. In dismissing this argument, Justice Prowse stated that

> While a nexus in time and place between an accused's possession of the instruments and a particular automobile would be a significant factor in determining whether it was appropriate to draw an inference that the accused intended to use the instruments for the prohibited purpose, the absence of such a nexus would not be fatal to a conviction if the other surrounding circumstances were sufficiently compelling to permit the inference to be drawn.

In other words, accused persons can be convicted of possession under section 351 even if they have not given any thought to the question of which particular house, car, etc. will be the target of their break-in activities. All that the Crown must establish is that the instruments in the accused's possession are suitable for the purpose of breaking into houses or cars in general.

Evidently, the offence of unlawful possession of house-breaking instruments does not involve any *act* on the part of the accused; instead, he or she must merely "be found" in possession of the illicit instruments. A similar example arises under section 335(1) of the *Criminal Code*, which makes it an offence to be "the occupant of a motor vehicle knowing that it was taken without the consent of the owner." It is not necessary that the Crown establish that a person accused of this offence was involved in the *taking* of the vehicle without the owner's consent: indeed, all that has to be proved is that he or she was *found in the vehicle* with the necessary guilty knowledge. Significantly, section 335(1.1) does provide the accused with a defence — namely the accused will be acquitted if it can be shown that "on becoming aware that [the vehicle] was taken without the consent of the owner, [he or

Possession of housebreaking instruments: the Crown does not have to prove any conduct on the part of the accused in order to obtain a conviction under section 351.

she] attempted to leave the motor vehicle, to the extent that it was feasible to do so, or actually left the motor vehicle." In the case of *H. (P.)* (2000), it is noteworthy that the Ontario Court of Appeal soundly rejected the view that section 335(1) imposed liability upon individuals for "morally blameless conduct" and, therefore, refused to find that it violated sections 7 and 11(d) of the *Charter*. Indeed, the court clearly stated that, "by its terms, s. 335 plainly requires the Crown to establish beyond a reasonable doubt that the occupant of the motor vehicle *knows* that the vehicle was taken with the consent of the owner" and this does not consti-tute a "morally blameless state of mind."

Perhaps, the best-known example of an offence that does not require proof of any conduct on the part of the accused is having the "care and control"

of a motor vehicle while one's ability to drive a motor vehicle has been impaired by alcohol or a drug or while one's blood level is above that of 80 milligrams of alcohol in 100 millilitres of blood (section 253 of the *Criminal Code*).

Once again, this offence does not require that the Crown prove that the accused was engaged in any act (such as driving); instead, it must merely be established that the *accused was found to be in the condition of having care and control of a vehicle while his or her ability to drive was impaired or while his or her blood level was above the prescribed level* (often referred to as being "above 80").

The first element of the *actus reus* that the Crown must prove under section 253 is that the accused was "impaired" or "above 80." The latter condition must be proved by submitting the results of tests conducted on samples of the accused's breath or blood (see sections 254 to 258 of the Code). However, the *Criminal Code* does not stipu-late any specific test for determining whether the accused was "impaired." Indeed, in *Stellato* (1993), Justice Labrosse, speaking on behalf of the Alberta Court of Appeal, unequivocally rejected the sugges-tion that the Crown must prove that the accused's conduct "demonstrated a marked departure from that of a normal person." On the contrary, Justice Labrosse held that "impairment is an issue of fact which the trial judge must decide on the evidence" and that,

> before convicting an accused of impaired driving, the trial judge must be satisfied that the accused's ability to operate a motor vehicle was impaired by alcohol or a drug. If the evidence of impairment is so frail as to leave the trial judge with a reasonable doubt as to impairment, the accused must be acquitted. If the evidence establishes *any degree of impairment ranging from slight to great*, the offence has been made out. [emphasis added]

The Supreme Court of Canada later indicated its total agreement with Justice Labrosse's ruling on this issue (see *Stellato* (1994)). However, it is impor-tant to emphasize that the critical issue under section 253 is not whether the accused's *general abilities* are impaired by alcohol or other drugs but rather whether his or her *ability to drive* is impaired. As Justice Conrad said, in delivering the majority judgment of the Alberta Court of Appeal in *Andrews* (1996),

> The courts must not fail to recognize the fine but crucial distinction between "slight impairment" generally, and "slight impairment of one's ability to operate a motor vehicle." Every time a person has a drink, his or her ability to drive is not necessarily impaired. It may well be that one drink would impair one's ability to do brain surgery, or one's ability to thread a needle. *The question is not whether the individual's functional ability is impaired to any degree. The question is whether the person's ability to drive is impaired to any degree by alcohol or a drug.* [emphasis added]

The next element of the *actus reus* that must be established under section 253 of the Code, assuming that the accused was not driving the vehicle concerned, is that he or she was "in care and control" of the vehicle. It is important to recognize that the courts have interpreted the concept of being in care and control of a motor vehicle in an extremely expansive manner. For example, in the case of *Ford* (1982), the defendant had been present at a party. As the night proceeded, he entered his vehicle on a number of occasions and started the engine in order to keep it warm. Ford had made arrangements with another person to drive him home because he was impaired. However, the police found Ford behind the steering wheel of the car, with the engine running. It was accepted that Ford was later going to trade places with his friend and that, therefore, he had *no intention to drive the car himself.* He was acquitted at his trial, but the **acquittal** was set aside by the Prince Edward Island Court of Appeal and the case was sent back to the magistrate on the basis that an intention to drive was *not* an essential element of the offence of being in care and control of a motor vehicle. The Supreme Court of Canada dismissed Ford's appeal against this ruling. Justice Ritchie, speaking for the majority of the Court, said:

> Nor, in my opinion, is it necessary for the Crown to prove an intent to set the vehicle in motion in order to prove a conviction. ... Care or control may be exercised without such intent where an accused performs some act or series of acts involving the use of the car, its fittings or equipment, such as occurred in this case, *whereby the vehicle may unintentionally be set in motion creating the danger the section is designed to prevent.* [emphasis added]

Similarly, in the case of *Pilon* (1998), the accused was found to be "in care and control" of his truck while his ability to operate a motor vehicle was impaired. Two police officers found him asleep in the driver's seat of his truck. His blood-alcohol concentration was 202 milligrams of alcohol per 100 millilitres of blood. There was no question that the accused was severely intoxicated. However, Pilon contended that he had not entered his vehicle with the intention of driving it, but rather with the intention of "sleeping off" his state of intoxication. He had thrown the keys underneath the passenger's seat and placed his feet on the passenger's side. He had then fallen asleep in this reclining position. The trial judge rejected the accused's contention that, given these circumstances, the latter could not be considered to have been in "care and control" of his truck. In the words of the judge, "it is a simple matter to pick keys up off the floor and put the key in the ignition and do something which could set the vehicle in motion." The accused's subsequent appeal was rejected by the Ontario Court of Appeal, which concurred with the trial judge's view that Pilon had engaged in a "course of conduct associated with the vehicle which would involve a risk of putting the vehicle in motion."

On the other hand, in the case of *Toews* (1985), the Supreme Court of Canada ruled that the accused could not be considered to be in care and control of a vehicle where he was merely using his truck as a bedroom. The police had found the accused's truck on private property at 5:15 A.M. He was lying on the front seat, wrapped up in a sleeping bag. The key was in the ignition but the engine was not running. Speaking for the Court, Justice McIntyre stated that *acts of care or control, short of driving, are acts which involve some use of the car or its fittings and equipment, or some course of conduct associated with the vehicle which would involve a risk of putting the vehicle in motion so that it could become dangerous.* Each case will depend on its own facts and the circumstances in which acts or care or control may be found will vary widely. ... In the case at bar the car was on private property and the respondent was not in occupation of the driver's seat. He was unconscious and clearly not in *de facto* control. The fact of his use of a sleeping bag would support his statement that he was merely using the vehicle as a place to sleep. ... It has not been shown then that the respondent performed any acts of care or control and he has therefore not performed the *actus reus*. [emphasis added]

Although it may seem somewhat strange to convict someone of an offence in the absence of any conduct on his or her part, it cannot generally be called unjust since the condition or state in which the accused is found is invariably *preceded* by voluntary conduct that is accompanied by *mens rea* (guilty mind). Would-be housebreakers deliberately arm themselves with the tools of their trade and they do so with the manifest purpose of engaging in nefarious criminal activities. Similarly, impaired drivers drink voluntarily, with the knowledge that drinking may impair their ability to drive, before they ever enter a motor vehicle. As Chief Justice Lamer, of the Supreme Court of Canada, said in the *Penno* case (1990),

Such persons can reasonably be held responsible when they voluntarily consume intoxicating substances and risk putting the public safety in danger by assuming care or control of a motor vehicle, whether they intended to assume care or control or whether intoxication did not allow them to realize what they were doing. By voluntarily taking the first drink, an individual can reasonably be held to have assumed the risk that intoxication would make him or her do what he or she otherwise would not normally do with a clear mind.

In the cases of both the housebreaker and the impaired driver, it is clear that voluntary (and culpable) conduct precedes the discovery of the accused in the prohibited state or condition. On the other hand, where the accused's condition or state has *not* been voluntarily induced, he or she may not reasonably be convicted of a such an offence. For example, in *Butler* (1939), it was suggested in the Alberta Court of Appeal that a highly intoxicated person, who (without his knowledge or consent) is placed in a motor vehicle by his "friends," may *not* be convicted of having care and control of a vehicle while impaired. Clearly, in this situation, the accused did not enter the vehicle voluntarily and, since he could not have foreseen that his friends would place his insensible body in the vehicle, it would be patently unjust to convict him of an offence.

Nevertheless, it is significant that it has been suggested that there are certain elements contained in the offence of "being in care and control" of a motor vehicle while "impaired" or "above 80" that may subject an accused person to the very real threat of unjust treatment. Those who consider the offence created by section 253 to be problematic, in terms of its basic fairness, point to section 258(1)(a) of the Code, which must be read in conjunction with section 253. Section 258(1)(a) provides that

Where it is proved that the accused occupied the seat or position ordinarily occupied by a person who operates a motor vehicle, etc. ... the accused shall be deemed to have had the care and control of the vehicle, etc. ... *unless the accused establishes that the accused did not occupy that seat or position for the purpose of setting the vehicle,* etc. ... in motion. ... [emphasis added]

What this section does is to require trial courts to make the finding that any accused persons, discovered sitting in the driver's seat of a motor vehicle, were in care and control of that vehicle for the purposes of section 253 of the Code *unless* they can establish that they did not occupy the driver's seat for the purpose of setting the vehicle in motion.

Obviously, this places an extremely valuable weapon in the armoury of the prosecution, because the Crown does not have to prove the *actus reus* element of being in care and control once it can demonstrate that the accused was sitting in the driver's seat: he or she will then be *deemed* to have been in care and control. Where the Crown relies on the "presumption of care and control" articulated in section 258(1)(a), the onus shifts to the accused to prove that, although sitting in the driver's seat, he or she did not have any intention of driving the vehicle in question.

The operation of section 258(1)(a) is well-illustrated by the case of *Hatfield* (1997), in which the accused was *sleeping* on the *fully reclined* driver's seat of his car, which had been parked in an industrial parking lot. He was discovered by the police in this position and was charged with being in care or control of a motor vehicle, while impaired or "above 80." Hatfield's defence was that he had been drinking at a restaurant, had driven a short distance, and immediately decided that he was not fit to drive; therefore, he proceeded to the parking lot in order to "sleep it off." The Ontario Court of Appeal was required to determine whether the presumption encapsulated in section 258(1)(a) applied to the particular circumstances of Hatfield's case: it answered this question in the affirmative and upheld Hatfield's conviction of being in care or control while impaired. Speaking for the court, Justice Goudge emphasized that it was irrelevant that the driver's seat was in a fully reclined position at the time of the police intervention. It was indisputable that Hatfield was occupying the seat ordinarily occupied by the operator of the motor vehicle. Therefore, the "plain language of the section" dictated that the presumption of care or control should be triggered in the Crown's favour: "where all that is necessary is for the occupant to bring the driver's seat up to its vertical position, the presumption must apply unless rebutted." The next issue that arose was whether Hatfield could successfully rebut the presumption by claiming that, *at the time that the police officers*

found him in the parking lot, his intention was merely to sleep — not to put the vehicle in motion? The Court of Appeal strongly rejected Hatfield's argument:

> ... to rebut the presumption of care or control the appellant must show that his occupancy began without the purpose of setting the vehicle in motion. The evidence here was entirely to the opposite effect. The appellant occupied the driver's seat in order to drive the vehicle away from the restaurant where he had been drinking. He intended to continue driving when he decided that he was no longer impaired.

Of course, one assumes that a trial judge, in such a case, would take into account the fact that the accused did make a responsible decision to pull off the road until he had sobered up. However, such a consideration would be relevant only in the context of meting out an appropriate *sentence*: it has no bearing on the accused's guilt or innocence in relation to the offence.

Does section 258(1)(a) infringe section 11(d) of the *Charter*, which enshrines the presumption of innocence? Under this provision of the *Charter*, if legislation stipulates that an accused person can be convicted of an offence even though there is a reasonable doubt as to his guilt or innocence, it will be held to be in violation of section 11(d). The question then becomes one of whether it can be saved under section 1 of the *Charter* as a "reasonable limit" on a *Charter* right. When Parliament uses phrases such as "unless the accused establishes," the courts usually interpret this as meaning that the accused must prove the issue (e.g., the absence of an intent to drive a vehicle) "on the balance of probabilities." In this light, it is clear that, under the terms of section 258(1)(a), accused persons can only escape conviction under section 253 by proving that it is more probable than not that they occupied the driver's seat *without entertaining any intention to drive the vehicle in question*. It is not enough for them to raise a reasonable doubt as to their intentions in this respect.

On the face of it, therefore, it would appear that section 258(1)(a) infringes section 11(d) of the *Charter* because an accused person may be convicted of the offence of being in care and control under section 253 even if, at the end of the trial, there is a reasonable doubt as to whether he or she occupied the driver's seat with the intention of setting the vehicle in motion. In the case of *Whyte* (1988), the Supreme Court of Canada held that section 258(1)(a) did indeed infringe section 11(d) of the *Charter*. However, the Court refused to declare section 258(1)(a) invalid because it considered it to be a reasonable limit under section 1 of the *Charter*.

Chief Justice Dickson, in delivering the judgment of the Supreme Court, pointed out that it does not follow, as a matter of inexorable logic, that every one who is found sitting in the driver's seat of a vehicle has care and control of that vehicle for the purposes of the offences under section 253 of the Code. For example, a taxi-driver may enter his or her vehicle and occupy the driver's seat merely in order to use the radio to report an accident; clearly, the taxi-driver has no intention, in these circumstances, of doing anything to the vehicle that might set it in motion. As Chief Justice Dickson stated,

> A person can be seated in the driver's seat without an intention to assume care or control of the vehicle within the meaning of [s. 253]. ... reasonable explanations for sitting in the driver's seat can readily be imagined. It cannot be said that proof of occupancy of the driver's seat leads inexorably to the conclusion that the essential element of care and control exists. ...

The Chief Justice went on to say that

> [Section 258(1)(a)] requires the trier of fact to accept as proven that an accused had care or control of a vehicle, an essential element of the offence, *in spite of a reasonable doubt about the exis-*

tence of that element. The section therefore breaches the presumption of innocence guaranteed by s. 11(d) of the *Charter*. [emphasis added]

In ruling that section 258(1)(a) was "saved" by section 1 of the *Charter*, the Supreme Court noted that it would be impractical to require the Crown to prove that the accused intended to drive the vehicle of which he or she is found to be in care and control. If proof of such an intention were required in order to convict an accused person under section 253 of the Code, it might be possible for extremely intoxicated persons to claim that they were "too drunk" to form the intent to drive, even though their advanced state of intoxication rendered them a serious danger to the public. According to Chief Justice Dickson, the "presumption of care and control" contained in section 258(1)(a) represents a reasonable compromise in attempting to deal with the manifest dangers posed by drunk drivers. On the one hand, the Crown does not have to shoulder the impossible burden of proving that the accused intended to drive his or her vehicle; indeed, the Crown only has to establish that the accused became intoxicated voluntarily. On the other hand, an accused person will not be convicted *automatically* merely because he or she was found sitting in the driver's seat while impaired or "over 80." Section 258(1)(a) does permit such a person to escape conviction by showing that there was some reason (other than driving) for entering the vehicle and occupying the driver's seat. The Supreme Court, therefore, found section 258(1)(a) to be a "restrained parliamentary response to a pressing social problem" and, accordingly, ruled that it was a "reasonable limitation" on the presumption of innocence.

Having examined the difficult exceptions to the general rule that the *actus reus* of an offence consists of conduct, circumstances, and consequences, we now turn our attention to the problems that arise when the Crown claims that the accused's conduct consisted of a "failure to act."

CAN A FAILURE TO ACT CONSTITUTE A CRIMINAL OFFENCE?

The General Principle: No Liability for Omissions Unless There Is a Pre-existing Duty to Act

In the preceding discussion of the essential elements of the *actus reus*, it was pointed out that some conduct on the part of the accused is, generally, a prerequisite for conviction of a criminal offence. In what circumstances may a mere *failure* to act (or an omission) render an accused person liable to conviction of a criminal offence?

Let us suppose that Desmond is walking past a lake. As he goes on his way, he hears some pitiful screams that emanate from Jeremy, a 4-year-old boy who is drowning in the lake. Desmond, who is quite capable of rescuing Jeremy from the relatively shallow water, callously ignores the pleas for help and walks directly to his place of business. Can Desmond be convicted of the offence of **manslaughter** for failing to rescue Jeremy? The simple answer to this blunt question is "no" (except, perhaps, in the Province of Québec, where there is a statutory duty to rescue those in danger where this may be done without undue risk to the rescuer). The principle of law applicable to this situation is that *an accused person may not be convicted on the basis of a mere omission unless he or she is under a prior (legal) duty to act*. For example, if Jeremy had been Desmond's son, the outcome would have been very different because a parent is under a legal duty to preserve the life of his or her child when it is reasonably possible for him or her to do so (see section 215(1)(a) of the Code, which places a parent or guardian under a duty to provide the "necessaries of life" to a child under the age of 16 years).

A valuable illustration of the application by the courts of the general principle just outlined is furnished by the case of *Browne* (1997). Here, Browne (22) and his female friend, Greiner (19), were dealers in crack cocaine. The trial judge noted that they were "at the very least close friends, probably

boyfriend–girlfriend," although they did not live with each other. Both Browne and Greiner had been searched by the police in a drugs "crackdown" and subsequently released. However, in order to avoid detection, Greiner had swallowed a plastic bag containing crack cocaine. Tragically, she could not subsequently throw up the bag and the drug entered her system, causing a highly toxic reaction. By the time Greiner reached the hospital, she had died. Browne was charged with criminal **negligence** causing death on the basis that he had "failed to render assistance to Audrey Greiner by failing to take her immediately to the hospital." The Ontario Court of Appeal noted that the relationship between Greiner and Browne did *not* fall into any of the categories of relationship (such as husband –wife, parent–child or caregiver–dependent) that impose an automatic legal duty to provide care and assistance. Therefore, Browne was under no duty to take care of Greiner: the existence of a "boyfriend–girlfriend" relationship does not *per se* render either of the parties criminally liable for a failure to act.

Voluntarily Assuming a Legal Duty Under Section 217 of the *Criminal Code*

Even though individual citizens in Canada are under no general legal duty to act, it is possible that they may *voluntarily assume responsibility for undertaking a particular service* and, in certain circumstances, they will be required to fulfill that commitment if a failure to do so would be dangerous. This legal principle is enshrined in section 217 of the *Criminal Code*, which states that "every one who undertakes to do an act is under a legal duty to do it if an omission to do the act is or may be dangerous to life." The courts have emphasized that section 217 only applies where the accused makes a serious, conscious undertaking to carry out a certain task and where reliance by another person on this undertaking would be considered reasonable in all of the circumstances. Take, for example, the case of *Browne* (1997), discussed immediately above. The trial judge had found that Browne had given an undertaking to Greiner to render assistance to her and to take her to the hospital as rapidly as possible. This undertaking, which the trial judge ruled fell within the scope of section 217, was made when Browne "took charge" of Greiner, "after he knew that she had ingested crack." The accused was convicted of criminal negligence causing death because, according to the trial judge, his failure to call 911 instead of taking her to hospital in a taxi constituted "wanton and reckless disregard" for Greiner's life. However, the Ontario Court of Appeal unanimously set aside the conviction and acquitted Browne. Justice Abella pointed out that the word "undertaking" in section 217 must be interpreted in light of the fact that an accused person, such as Browne, could be liable to a maximum sentence of life imprisonment if there is a conviction for criminal negligence causing death that is based on a failure to perform such an undertaking:

> The threshold definition must be sufficiently high to justify such serious penal consequences. The mere expression of words indicating a willingness to do an act cannot trigger the legal duty. There must be something in the nature of the commitment, generally, though not necessarily, upon which reliance can reasonably be said to have been placed.

Essentially, the trial judge had found that, because Browne and Greiner were partners in drug dealing, Browne had made an implicit undertaking that he would take Greiner to hospital if she were ever to swallow cocaine. However, the Court of Appeal took the view that there was absolutely no undertaking "in the nature of a binding commitment." As Justice Abella stated, Browne's words to Greiner when he knew she was in a life-threatening situation, "I'll take you to the hospital," "hardly constitute a legal undertaking creating a legal duty under s. 217" and, in the absence of such an undertaking, "there can be no finding of a legal duty." Of course, one can readily think of situations in which courts would almost certainly find that a binding commitment has been made. For example,

a mountain guide is not forced to take a group of climbers into dangerous terrain that is unknown to them. However, once the expedition is underway, the guide cannot suddenly flee the scene if it would create a situation that would be dangerous to the climbers' lives. Under these circumstances, the guide would be considered to have made a solemn undertaking that clearly falls within the purview of section 217. Should one of the climbers fall down a precipice and die, as a direct consequence of the guide's abandonment of his or her duty, then the latter would be liable to conviction for criminal negligence causing death or manslaughter.

SPECIFIC LEGAL DUTIES IMPOSED BY THE *CRIMINAL CODE*

There are a number of statutory provisions that impose a legal duty to act in a variety of situations in Canada; for example, section 129(b) (duty to assist a police officer), sections 215 – 218 of the Code (various "duties tending to the preservation of the lives of children and others who are in a position of dependence on others"), and section 263 (duty to safeguard an opening in ice or an excavation on land so that people do not fall in).

Section 215 is a very significant provision that imposes a duty to act on persons who are, in one way or another, responsible for the welfare of others. Section 215 states that

(1) Every one is under a legal duty

    (a) as a parent, foster parent, guardian or head of a family, to provide necessaries of life for a child under the age of sixteen years;

    (b) as a married person, to provide necessaries of life to his spouse; and

    (c) to provide necessaries of life to a person under his charge if that person

        (i) is unable, by reason of detention, age, illness, mental disorder or other cause, to withdraw himself from that charge, and

(ii) is unable to provide himself with necessaries of life.

(2) Every one commits an offence who, being under a legal duty within the meaning of subsection (1), fails without lawful excuse, the proof of which lies on him, to perform that duty, if

(a) with respect to a duty imposed by paragraph (1)(a) or (b),

    (i) the person to whom the duty is owed is in destitute or necessitous circumstances, or

    (ii) the failure to perform the duty endangers the life of the person to whom the duty is owed, or causes or is likely to cause the health of that person to be endangered permanently; or

(b) with respect to a duty imposed by paragraph (1)(c), the failure to perform the duty endangers the life of the person to whom the duty is owed or causes or is likely to cause the health of that person to be injured permanently. ...

Similarly, section 218 of the Code provides that

Every one who unlawfully abandons or exposes a child who under the age of ten years, so that its life is or is likely to be endangered or its health is or is likely to be permanently injured, is guilty of an indictable offence. ...

An illustration of the application of section 215 may be found in the case of *Degg* (1981), in which the accused was charged with failing to provide the necessaries of life to her infant son who had died in a state of severe malnutrition and dehydration. The mother had failed to keep medical appointments

for the child despite the fact that her son's poor medical condition was obvious. Furthermore, it was established that the accused was well aware of the medical facilities available to her and the child. In these circumstances, the accused was convicted of the offence charged.

The *Degg* case may be usefully compared with *Reedy (No. 2)* (1981), in which the accused was charged with wilful abandonment of a child under the age of ten years and that, by such abandonment, he did thereby endanger the child's life (contrary to section 218 of the Code). Reedy had agreed to baby-sit three children, aged one to three years, while their parents were going to be away for a "short while." Reedy had recently been released from hospital and he informed the parents that he was not feeling well, and, for this reason, he requested that they return early. For their part, the parents promised to return within an hour. After the passage of between two and one-half and three hours, Reedy telephoned the parents and told the mother that, if she was not back within a couple of hours, he was going to leave. After two further phone calls, the parents still had not returned and, almost five hours after starting to baby-sit the children, Reedy felt so sick that he decided to go to the hospital. At this time, the children were asleep and Reedy expected that they would sleep (as they usually did) for another one and one-half to two hours. He shut the door upon leaving, but did not lock it believing that the children would not be able to open it and that the parents would not otherwise be able to gain access. Reedy also assumed that the parents would return before the children awakened.

Tragically, two of the children woke up before their parents' return and left the house. Sherry, a three-year-old girl, was later killed by a car while crossing a highway. It was clear that Reedy had assumed the responsibility of caring for the children (see section 217 of the Code). However, the Court held that the parents were also under a legal duty to return within the promised time—particularly since they were well aware of the accused's condition. Reedy was ultimately acquitted. In the words of Judge Vannini,

In these circumstances, I cannot find that the accused abandoned the children within the meaning thereof in [s. 218] of the Code and, in any event, I do find that he left the children unattended with lawful justification and excuse because of the sickness which came upon him.

An important question that arises under section 215 is whether the accused was aware of the fact that a person, to whom he or she owed a duty to provide the necessaries of life, was actually in need of the accused's assistance. For example, parents may not be convicted of an offence under section 215 for failing to provide medical services to a child if they had no reason to know that their child was suffering from a medical problem. However, does this mean that a parent who has an *unreasonable* belief that a child is not sick is entitled to an acquittal on this basis? An example of an unreasonable belief arises in the situation where a parent knows that a child needs a certain medical treatment to maintain life (e.g., insulin injections for a diabetic child), but withdraws all treatment because an "angel" told the parent that the child was cured. Although the parent in this example may be totally sincere in his or her religious belief, there is no doubt that most people would regard the withdrawal of treatment from a sick child in these circumstances as being unreasonable. Parents do have the absolute right to refuse treatment for themselves, but there is no right to withhold treatment from their children who are too young to make such important decisions for themselves. If the test of criminal responsibility under section 215 is purely *subjective* (based on what the particular accused believed, regardless of the reasonableness of that belief), the accused must be acquitted. However, if the test is *objective* in nature (based on what the *reasonable* parent would have appreciated in the circumstances), the accused must be convicted. What test should be applied by the courts?

In the case of *Naglik* (1993), the Supreme Court of Canada held that the standard to be applied under section 215 of the Code is an objective one. In the words of Chief Justice Lamer,

Naglik was charged under [s. 215(2)(a)(ii) and (3)], which make the failure to to provide necessaries an offence where "the failure to perform the duty endangers the life of the person to whom the duty is owed, or causes or is likely to cause the health of the person to be endangered permanently." I would hold that s. 215(2)(a)(ii) punishes a *marked departure from the conduct of a reasonably prudent parent in circumstances where it is objectively foreseeable that the failure to provide the necessaries of life would lead to a danger to the life, or a risk of permanent endangerment to the health, of the child.* [emphasis added]

It may be noted that section 215 (2) of the *Criminal Code* makes a specific defence available to those individuals who have been charged with failing to provide the necessaries of life: namely, the defence of "lawful excuse." However, section 215(2) states that the burden of proving this defence lies on the shoulders of the accused. In *Curtis* (1998), the Ontario Court of Appeal ruled that placing the onus of proof on the accused in this manner infringed the presumption of innocence that is enshrined in section 11(d) of the *Charter* and could not be justified under section 1. Instead of declaring the whole of section 215 of the *Criminal Code* to be invalid, however, the court held that only the words, "the proof of which lies on him" should be struck down under the *Charter*. Therefore, as a consequence of the *Curtis* decision, the defence of "lawful excuse" continues to exist, under section 215(2); however, at the end of a criminal trial, the Crown will now be required to prove — beyond a reasonable doubt — that the accused did *not* have a "lawful excuse" for the failure to provide necessaries. *Curtis* is a decision of the Ontario Court of Appeal, and it remains to be seen whether the appellate courts in other provinces and territories — and, ultimately, the Supreme Court of Canada — will adopt the same approach. As far as the substance of the "lawful excuse" defence is concerned, one can well imagine circumstances in which parents, for example, might not be aware that their child is in necessitous circumstances: if such parents have acted reasonably, then the absence of any knowledge of the danger threatening their child would constitute a "lawful excuse." Similarly, an individual who sees his or her spouse drowning in a swollen, fast-running, and deep river would be considered to have a "lawful excuse" not to jump in to the rescue if he or she is unable to swim (of course, one would expect the individual concerned, at least, to seek help from other parties and there would generally be no "lawful excuse" for failing to do so).

CRIMINAL NEGLIGENCE, MANSLAUGHTER, AND FAILURE TO ACT

If a failure to perform a legal duty results in death or bodily harm to the person to whom the duty is owed, the accused may be liable to conviction for the more serious offences of *causing death by criminal negligence* (section 220 of the Code) or *causing bodily harm by criminal negligence* (section 221 of the Code). According to section 219(1)(b) of the Code, if an accused person fails to perform a legally imposed duty and, by this failure, "shows wanton or reckless disregard for the lives or safety of other persons," he or she is guilty of criminal negligence causing bodily harm or death (as the case may be). It is also important to bear in mind that the offence of *manslaughter* may be committed where the accused causes the death of his or her victim as a consequence of criminal negligence on the part of the accused (see sections 222(5)(b) and 234 of the Code). The elements that the Crown must prove in order to obtain a conviction both for the offences of criminal negligence causing death and manslaughter (by means of criminal negligence) are identical in each case. Which charge the Crown ultimately chooses to pursue is primarily a matter of prosecutorial tactics.

One possible explanation for the existence of these twin charges is that, historically, Canadian juries were reluctant to convict motorists charged with manslaughter as a consequence of criminally negligent driving conduct. On the other hand, it is contended that juries were more willing to convict

the accused for engaging in such conduct where the charge was that of criminal negligence causing death (despite the fact that conviction of the charge carries exactly the same maximum penalty of life imprisonment), which was generally perceived to bear a lesser degree of stigma than the crime of manslaughter. Apparently for this reason, the offence of criminal negligence causing death was added to the provisions of the *Criminal Code*. However, it seems that even this change did not bring about a satisfactory rate of conviction of motorists who caused death on the roads and, in 1985, Parliament created the new offences of dangerous driving causing death (section 249(4)) and impaired driving causing death (section 255(3)); both of these offences carry a maximum sentence of fourteen years' imprisonment.

Is There a Duty to Act When a Person Creates a Dangerous Situation by Accident?

Should the criminal law impose a duty to act upon an individual who creates a dangerous situation by accident? Needless to say, the nature of the duty would be to take steps to combat the dangerous situation created by the accused's own act. Apparently, there is no Canadian authority on this point; however, this issue was considered by the House of Lords in the English case of *Miller* (1983), in which the accused had been drinking and had subsequently stretched himself out on his mattress and lit a cigarette. He fell asleep while smoking, and awoke to find the mattress on fire. However, instead of dealing with the fire, he just went into another room and went to sleep. He was charged with arson. It was clear that the fire had started through the negligence, rather than the deliberate conduct, of the accused.

In his judgment, Lord Diplock stated that

I see no rational ground for excluding from conduct capable of giving rise to criminal liability conduct which consists of *failing to take measures that lie within one's power to counteract a danger that one has oneself created, if at the time of the conduct one's state of mind is such as constitutes a necessary ingredient of the offence.* I venture to think that the habit of lawyers to talk of "actus reus," suggestive as it is of action rather than inaction, is responsible for any erroneous notion that failure to act cannot give rise to criminal liability in English law. [emphasis added]

In this particular case, the accused should have taken such steps, as he was able, to prevent or minimize the damage to the property at risk. The House of Lords, therefore, upheld his conviction of arson.

The *Miller* case opens the door to a potentially significant expansion of criminal liability in relation to omissions. To date, it is not clear whether it will be adopted as part of the criminal law in Canada.

Should There Be a Duty to Rescue?

There has been a good deal of heated controversy concerning the approach of the criminal law in the area of omissions. More specifically, it has been contended that every citizen should be under a duty to rescue a fellow citizen whose life or safety is in peril, provided, of course, that it is reasonably safe and practical to undertake such a rescue. Proponents of this viewpoint would urge that criminal liability should be imposed on such a person as Desmond who, in the example outlined above, declined to assist a drowning child. However, the present approach of Canadian criminal law is, as we have seen, to impose criminal liability for a failure to act *only* when such an omission occurs in the context of a prior legal duty to act. Among the arguments in support of the *status quo* is the contention that it would be difficult to enforce a "duty to rescue." Just how far are individual citizens expected to go in attempting to save their fellows from danger? This question is almost impossible to answer in the abstract and it has always been felt that the criminal law should set clear standards of liability, so that every citizen knows, ahead of time, exactly what he or she must do to avoid criminal liability. Furthermore, it is suggested that

the criminal law should abstain from trying to force people to live up to a higher standard of morality; this should be a job for organized religion or the schools rather than the blunt instrument of the criminal sanction.

On the other hand, it has been contended that every citizen should be under a duty to rescue a fellow human being whose life or safety is in peril, provided of course that it is reasonably safe and practical to undertake such a rescue. Indeed, the Law Reform Commission of Canada has recommended that the *Criminal Code* impose a general duty on all citizens to render aid in an emergency. The commission points to the single exception to the general legal rule in Canada as a concrete demonstration that their proposal is certainly within the realm of practicality. This exception is contained in legislation passed by the Province of Québec. Section 2 of the *Québec Charter of Human Rights and Freedoms* (R.S.Q., c. C-12) provides that

> Every human being whose life is in peril has a right to assistance. Every person must come to the aid of anyone whose life is in peril, either personally or calling for aid, by giving him the necessary and immediate physical assistance, unless it involves danger to himself or a third person, or he has another valid reason.

The Québec provision does not create a criminal offence *per se*; in other words, there is no offence of failing to rescue a person in danger. However, the Québec provision may play a significant role in leading to the conviction of an accused person under the *Criminal Code* because the Code imposes criminal liability, in certain circumstances, for failure to perform a duty imposed by law. The Québec provision imposes just such a duty. For example, a failure to provide assistance to a victim who subsequently dies, in circumstances indicating a wanton and reckless disregard for the life or safety of the victim, could possibly result in a conviction of manslaughter by criminal negligence or criminal negligence causing death.

When a Failure to Act May Render an Accused Person Liable as a Party to an Offence Committed by Another Person

To this point, we have been discussing the circumstances in which an accused person may be convicted of an offence in which the *actus reus* element of conduct may consist of a failure to act on his or her part. However, there are some situations in which a failure to act may lead to an accused person becoming a party to an offence that is *actually committed by someone else*. This might occur where the accused fails to perform a legal duty and this failure to act is considered to amount to aiding and/or abetting (assisting or encouraging) an offence committed by another party. Paragraphs (b) and (c) of section 21(1) provide that an accused person is a "party to an offence" if he or she "does or omits to do anything for the purpose of aiding any person to commit it" or "abets any person in committing it."

For example, in the case of *Nixon* (1990), the accused was the officer in charge of the lock-up or jail where a prisoner was assaulted. The accused was charged with aggravated assault, but the trial judge was not satisfied that he had actually committed the assault himself. However, the Court of Appeal ruled that the trial judge was correct in convicting the accused on the basis that he aided or abetted the officers who did commit the assault. The accused was unquestionably under a duty to protect the prisoner under both the B.C. *Police Act* and the *Criminal Code*. Nixon's failure to protect the prisoner, when he was under a clear legal duty to do so, therefore constituted aiding or abetting of the assault committed by his fellow officers (assuming that this failure to act was prompted by the *intention* to assist or encourage the other officers in their criminal activities). As Justice Legg stated, in delivering the judgment of the Court of Appeal,

> A person becomes a party under s. 21(1)(b) if he fails to act for the purpose of aiding in the commission of the offence. Where there is a duty to act, and the accused does not act, it is open to the

court to infer that the purpose of the failure to act was to aid in the commission of the offence.

Similarly, under s. 21(1)(c), a person who "abets" the offence becomes a party. The cases show that in some circumstances a failure on the part of the accused to act to prevent the offence may constitute positive encouragement. One situation in which this will be the case is where the accused had a duty to prevent the offence and failed to act. Thus, s. 21(1)(c) also punishes omissions in the sense that it punishes the encouragement of an offence that is provided by the omission.

> ... it is clear from [the trial judge's] judgment that she inferred that [Nixon] had encouraged the commission of the offence by finding that [he] was at the scene when the vicious act occurred and failed to perform his duty as a police officer to protect [the prisoner].

THE NEED FOR THE *ACTUS REUS* AND *MENS REA* TO COINCIDE

The phrase *actus non facit reum nisi mens sit rea* necessarily implies that, before an accused person may be convicted of a crime, the Crown must prove that there was a moment when both the *actus reus* and *mens rea* elements of the offence coincided. In other words, there is a requirement of *simultaneity* between the *actus reus* and *mens rea* elements of an offence.

This requirement of simultaneity is well illustrated by the case of *Poirier* (1989), in which the accused reported an alleged theft to the police, who subsequently started an investigation. A few days later, the accused tried to withdraw his complaint and the police concluded that no theft had ever occurred. He was charged with public mischief, under s. 140 of the Code, on the basis that, "with intent to mislead," he caused a "peace officer to enter on or continue an investigation" by "reporting that an offence has been committed where it has not been committed." The New Brunswick Court of Appeal ruled that the trial judge had been correct to acquit the accused on the basis that there was a reasonable doubt as to whether, *at the time he initially filed the complaint*, he had the intent to mislead the police. The fact that he might have subsequently developed such an intent (for example, at the time he withdrew the complaint) was irrelevant since the Crown had to establish beyond a reasonable doubt that the *actus reus* of the offence (the laying of the complaint) and the necessary *mens rea* (the intent to mislead) did, in fact, occur simultaneously.

The requirement of simultaneity clearly makes excellent sense when applied to the great majority of situations in which it is alleged that the accused has committed a crime. However, there are certain circumstances in which the application of this principle becomes problematic.

In a case of homicide, for example, it may well happen that the victim dies as a consequence of a *series* of violent acts committed by the accused over an extended period of time. In such circumstances, the Crown may not be able to prove that the accused had the necessary *mens rea* for **murder** or manslaughter at the exact moment that the fatal blow was delivered, even though it is clear that the accused did have such *mens rea* at some stage during the series of acts that resulted in the victim's death. Does this mean that the accused must be acquitted of murder or manslaughter because the Crown cannot prove the simultaneity of *actus reus* and *mens rea*? In the case of *Cooper* (1993), the Supreme Court of Canada answered this question in the negative.

Cooper was charged with murder after fatally strangling a young woman. He stated that he became angry with the victim, hit her, grabbed her by the throat and shook her. He claimed that he could not remember anything else until he woke up and discovered the victim's body next to him. Expert evidence established that the victim had died of manual strangulation and that death had occurred between 30 seconds and two minutes after pressure was applied to her neck. Under section 229(a) of the *Criminal Code*, culpable homicide is murder where the accused either intends to kill the victim or "means to cause" the victim "bodily harm that he knows is likely to cause his death, and is reckless whether death ensues or not." Cooper

asserted that he did not have the necessary *mens rea* for murder at the time that the victim was actually killed because he had "blacked out" before her death occurred. Nevertheless, he was convicted at trial and the Supreme Court of Canada ultimately ruled that his conviction was justified.

Speaking on behalf of the majority of the justices of the Supreme Court, Justice Cory pointed out that, where an accused person has committed a series of acts that result in the death of the victim, these acts should be considered as being "all part of the *same transaction*," and that, if the necessary *mens rea* for murder coincides *at any time* with one or more of these separate acts, the accused may be convicted. For example, if the accused repeatedly beats a victim about the head with a baseball bat, he or she could be convicted of murder if, at any time, the necessary *mens rea* for murder coincided with one or more of the blows administered by the accused.

In *Cooper*, the Crown took the view that the accused did, at some point, have the intention to inflict bodily harm that he knew was likely to cause death and was reckless whether death ensued or not (see section 229(a)(ii)). After all, the accused must have been aware that "breathing is essential to life" and that strangulation was likely to cause the victim's death. Justice Cory held that the jury had acted reasonably in concluding that the necessary *mens rea* did exist at some stage, even though it might not have lasted during the whole episode of strangulation. In his view,

> I do not think that it is always necessary that the requisite *mens rea* (the guilty mind, intent or awareness) should continue throughout the commission of the wrongful act.
>
> There is no question that in order to obtain a conviction the Crown must demonstrate that the accused intended to cause bodily harm that he knew was ultimately so dangerous and serious that it was likely to result in the death of a victim. *But that intent need not persist through the entire act of strangulation. ...*
>
> Here the death occurred between 30 seconds and two minutes after he grabbed her by the neck.

It could be reasonably inferred by the jury, that when the accused grabbed the victim by the neck and shook her that there was, at that moment, the necessary coincidence of the wrongful act of strangulation and the requisite intent to do bodily harm that the accused knew was likely to cause death. … *It was sufficient that the intent and the act of strangulation coincided at some point. It was not necessary that the requisite intent continue throughout the entire two minutes required to cause the death of the victim.* [emphasis added]

Another problem arises with the application of the principle of simultaneity of *actus reus* and *mens rea* when the accused commits an initially innocent act but *subsequently* forms the *mens rea* necessary for conviction of a criminal offence. The courts have taken the view that, if the *actus reus* committed by the accused was fully completed before the moment that the necessary *mens rea* was formed in the accused's mind, then there is no criminal offence. This is essentially what happened in the *Poirier* case, discussed earlier in this section. The accused in that case was found not guilty of public mischief because, when he initially made his complaint to the police, he did not know that it was false. The fact that he later realized its falsity is irrelevant, since the *actus reus* was fully completed before the accused acquired his guilty knowledge. However, the courts have also held that *mens rea* can be "superimposed" on an initially innocent act so as to justify convicting the accused of a crime. This situation would arise where the accused has been found to have committed a *continuing actus reus* (such as repeating a false statement) and to have subsequently developed the necessary *mens rea*. Here, the courts would rule that the *actus reus* and *mens rea* elements of the offence did coincide, at some point, and that, therefore, a crime has been committed.

The notion of a continuing *actus reus* was utilized by the Supreme Court of Canada in *Detering* (1982), in which the accused was charged with fraud, contrary to section 380 of the *Criminal Code*. An employee of the Ontario Ministry of Consumer and Commercial Relations had been involved in the monitoring of garage repair businesses. She had taken a "well-used car" to Detering's repair shop. She knew that the transmission had been "slightly tampered with and could be rectified with a few minutes work." She informed Detering that she had transmission trouble. After road-testing the vehicle, Detering informed her that the transmission needed to be rebuilt and that the repair costs would be $189 plus tax. When the ministry employee reclaimed the car, she paid this sum. The bill indicated that the transmission had been rebuilt; however, it was established that this was not true. Detering was convicted, at this trial, and appealed to the Ontario Court of Appeal, which dismissed his appeal but substituted a conviction for *attempt* to commit fraud since the ministry employee had not, in fact, been deceived by Detering's representation. Detering, then, appealed to the Supreme Court of Canada.

One of the arguments advanced by his **counsel** was that there was no concurrence between the *actus reus* of the offence (namely, the representation as to the need for the transmission to be rebuilt) and the requisite *mens rea* (namely, the intent to defraud). In effect, Detering claimed that he made the representation as to the need for the rebuilding of the transmission *before* he knew that it was untrue. Therefore, he asserted that the *actus reus* of the offence was completed before the necessary *mens rea* came into existence. However, the Supreme Court of Canada soundly rejected this contention. In delivering the judgment of the Court, Chief Justice Laskin stated that the accused "renewed" or "continued" his original representation, that the transmission required fixing, *after* he became aware that it was untrue. In this particular case, therefore, there was a concurrence between the *actus reus* (the representation) and the *mens rea* (knowledge that the representation was false).

In light of cases such as *Cooper* and *Detering*, it is clear that the courts may manifest considerable ingenuity in "bending the rules" concerning the requirement of simultaneity in relation to the *actus reus* and *mens rea* elements of criminal offences in order to achieve what they perceive to be a just result.

THE ELEMENT OF VOLUNTARINESS IN THE *ACTUS REUS*

It is a fundamental principle of criminal law that a defendant's conduct cannot render him or her criminally responsible unless it is proved that such conduct was "voluntary." If the accused's conduct is involuntary, he or she cannot be held criminally responsible because the consequences of such conduct did not flow from the exercise of his or her "free will."

As Justice Cory stated, in delivering the judgment of the majority of the justices of the Supreme Court of Canada in *Daviault* (1994),

> unless the legislator provides otherwise, a crime must consist of the following elements. First, a physical element which consists of committing a prohibited act, creating a prohibited state of affairs, or omitting to do that which is required by the law. Secondly, *the conduct must be willed; this is usually referred to as voluntariness.* Some writers classify this as part of the *actus reus*, others prefer to associate it with *mens rea*; however, all seem to agree that it is required. ... If persons other than lawyers were asked what constituted willed or voluntary conduct they would respond that such an act or conduct must involve a mental element. *It is the mental element, that is the act of will which makes the act or conduct willed or voluntary.* [emphasis added]

For example, take the case of (the perhaps inappropriately named) *Lucki* (1955), who negotiated a right-handed turn on an icy street. *Through no fault of his own*, his car skidded on a sheet of ice and came to rest on the wrong side of the street. He was charged with being on the wrong side of the dividing line, but was acquitted on the basis that he had arrived at this position through no *voluntary* act of his own.

In cases such as *Lucki*, the accused persons involved experience normal consciousness and are well aware of what they are doing even though their conduct is involuntary. However, there is another form of involuntary conduct where the accused experiences impaired consciousness. In the criminal law, this condition is known as *automatism,* and it is this form of involuntary conduct that has generated a seemingly endless series of problems for the criminal courts.

AUTOMATISM

Automatism has been defined as "a state of impaired consciousness ... in which an individual, though capable of action, has no voluntary control over that action" (Justice Bastarache, on behalf of the majority of the Supreme Court of Canada in *Stone* (1999)). Provided the state of automatism did not arise because of a **mental disorder** or as a consequence of self-induced intoxication, then the individual affected by it is entitled to be acquitted of a criminal charge.

As Justice La Forest, of the Supreme Court of Canada, noted in the case of *Parks* (1992), the defence of automatism is directly relevant to the question of whether the Crown has established that the accused has committed the *actus reus* elements of a criminal offence:

> Automatism occupies a unique place in our criminal law system. Although spoken of as a "defence," it is conceptually a subset of the *voluntariness requirement* which in turn is part of the *actus reus* component of criminal liability. [emphasis added]

It would be a mistake to confuse automatism with a state of complete unconsciousness. Indeed, as Justice Bastarache pointed out in the *Stone* case (1999), "medically speaking, unconscious means 'flat on the floor,' that is a comatose-type state": clearly a comatose individual is not capable of carrying out any actions at all — let alone a crime! Therefore, it is more accurate, Justice Bastarache said, to define automatism as being a form of "impaired consciousness, rather than unconsciousness." Perhaps, it is most helpful to think of automatism as constituting a state of *severely clouded consciousness that prevents the accused from acting voluntarily.*

Conceptually, there are, at least, five separate categories of automatism: (i) automatism caused by such "normal" conditions as sleep-walking or hypnosis (which are not considered by the courts to be the result of mental disorder); (ii) automatism triggered by an external trauma, such as a blow to the head; (iii) automatism that is *involuntarily* induced by alcohol or other drugs; (iv) automatism that is voluntarily self-induced by the use of alcohol or other drugs; (v) automatism caused by a mental disorder (or a "disease of the mind"). However, only those conditions that fall within categories (i) to (iii) may lead to the acquittal of an accused person on the basis of the legal defence of automatism.

Automatism Caused by Such States as Sleep-Walking or Hypnosis

A person who acts in a state of automatism that is associated with a "normal" condition, such as sleep-walking or hypnosis, is entitled to a complete acquittal of any criminal charge. The use of the adjective *normal* is intended to emphasize that these conditions are not the result of a mental disorder. The commission of criminal offences in such conditions is admittedly rather rare; however, the important case of *Parks* (1992) demonstrates that this category of automatism nevertheless has a great deal of practical significance.

In *Parks* (1992), the evidence indicated that the accused had apparently fallen asleep and then driven some 23 kilometers to the home of his parents-in-law where he stabbed and beat them both. His mother-in-law died from her injuries, while his father-in-law ultimately survived his serious injuries. A number of expert witnesses appeared for the defence and supported a defence based on

sleep-walking; the Crown, however, presented no expert evidence on this issue. Testimony was presented to the effect that Parks had enjoyed "excellent relations" with his parents-in-law prior to the incident in question and that several members of his family had suffered from sleep disorders such as sleep-walking, adult enuresis (bed-wetting), nightmares, and sleep-talking.

Parks was acquitted at his trial on the basis that he was acting in a state of automatism at the time of the attacks on his parents-in-law. The Ontario Court of Appeal affirmed his acquittal on an appeal by the Crown and underscored the view that sleep-walking is a normal condition. In the words of Justice Galligan,

> The thesis of the medical evidence was that the impairment of the respondent's faculties of reason, memory and understanding was caused not by a disorder or abnormal condition but by a natural, normal condition—sleep. ... In a very real sense, sleep impairs the human mind and its functioning. Sleep, however, can hardly be called an illness, disorder or abnormal condition. It is a perfectly normal condition.

The Crown subsequently appealed to the Supreme Court of Canada, but the Supreme Court agreed with the Ontario Court of Appeal and dismissed the appeal. As Chief Justice Lamer pointed out, the medical evidence had been that "a person who is sleep-walking cannot think, reflect or perform voluntary acts." More specifically, there was expert testimony to the effect that "during the slow wave sleep stage the cortex, which is the part of the brain that controls thinking and voluntary movement, is essentially in coma" and that "when a person is sleep-walking, the movements he makes are controlled by other parts of the brain and are more or less reflexive." Since Parks was sleep-walking at the time of the attacks on his parents-in-law, he was not capable of acting voluntarily; therefore, he could not be convicted of a criminal offence.

Automatism Triggered by an External Trauma

Perhaps the classic example of automatism is the situation where an external blow to the head causes an episode of unconsciousness, during which the accused engages in conduct that would otherwise be considered criminal. Even though a person who has suffered such a blow to the head may *appear* to be acting normally, he or she is nevertheless in a state of altered consciousness and is not able to control his or her conduct. Since the accused person, in these circumstances, acts unconsciously, it is clear that he or she will be unable to recall any of the events following the trauma to the head; therefore, an important element of the accused's condition is that he or she suffers from amnesia.

In the case of *Bleta* (1965), for example, the accused and a man called Gafi were fighting in a Toronto street. In the course of the fracas, Bleta fell and hit his head on the pavement. Bleta regained his feet and followed Gafi who had started to walk away. Bleta then drew a knife and fatally stabbed Gafi in the neck area. Two of the bystanders watching the fight, as well as a police officer, commented that Bleta appeared to be in a "dazed condition" at the time of the fatal blow. Bleta's counsel successfully contended that his client was acting unconsciously and with no voluntary control over his actions at the time of the stabbing. The Supreme Court of Canada implicitly accepted the legitimacy of the automatism defence, although it decided the *Bleta* case on other grounds.

Automatism Involuntarily Induced by Alcohol or Other Drugs

Accused persons who, through no voluntary action on their part, become so severely impaired by alcohol or other drugs that they fall into a state of automatism are entitled to be acquitted of a criminal charge because they are incapable of acting voluntarily. For example, suppose that Arthur laces Sally's orange juice with vodka without the latter's knowledge. In these circumstances, if Sally lapses into a state of automatism, she must be acquitted of any criminal charge arising out of her activities while she was in such a condition. Similarly, in the case of *King* (1962), the accused visited a dentist in order to have two teeth extracted. For this purpose, he was injected with sodium pentothal, a quick-acting anaesthetic. The accused claimed that he received no warning that he might subsequently become impaired by the drug and that he was not advised to refrain from driving a motor vehicle. King left the dentist's office, entered his car, and became unconscious while driving it. His car then crashed into a parked vehicle and he was charged with impaired driving. He was subsequently convicted at his trial; however, this conviction was set aside by the Ontario Court of Appeal.

The Supreme Court of Canada affirmed the judgment of the Ontario Court of Appeal. However, the Supreme Court justices appeared to have different reasons for this decision.

For example, Justice Ritchie, with whom Justice Martland agreed, focused on the absence of *mens rea* on the part of the accused. He indicated that, where a driver is found in an impaired condition as a result of taking alcohol or any other drug, a presumption arises that he or she induced this condition voluntarily. However, this presumption can always be "rebutted" (or set aside) if there is evidence that raises a reasonable doubt as to whether, through no fault of his or her own, the accused was disabled and, therefore, unable to appreciate that he or she was (or might become) impaired. In the *King* case, it was concluded that the presumption of voluntariness *was* rebutted because there was evidence that the accused's impairment was caused by a drug, administered by a dentist in the course of a recognized medical procedure, and the effect of the drug was apparently not made known to the accused.

Justice Taschereau, on the other hand, explicitly based his judgment on the view that the prosecution had failed to prove an essential element of the *actus reus* of the offence:

It is my view that there can be no *actus reus* unless it is the result of a willing mind at liberty to make a definite choice or decision, or in other words, there must be a willpower to do an act whether the accused knew or not that it was prohibited by law. ...

> When a doctor has given an injection of a drug to a patient, who is not aware of the state of mind it may produce, there is no volitive act done by the driver and he cannot be convicted. [emphasis added]

It should be mentioned that the defence that was so successfully raised by the accused in the *King* case would be most unlikely to succeed before the courts of today. Hospitals, medical offices, and dentists' surgeries currently require a patient to sign a form prior to any medical procedure that requires the administration of an anaesthetic that might impair consciousness. This form generally notifies patients that they must not drive a vehicle and should arrange for other transportation (e.g., relatives or a taxi) to pick them up after the procedure. Similarly, it is unlikely that accused persons, who have taken prescription drugs, would be able to successfully claim that they became impaired involuntarily because of lack of knowledge of the effects of the drugs in question. Indeed, in most parts of Canada, pharmacists routinely place a red warning label indicating that certain drugs should not be mixed with alcohol or specifically warning patients that they should not operate machinery, in the event of drowsiness. In short, in contemporary times, it would be very difficult for an individual to claim that he or she could not have foreseen that a drug or other intoxicating substance could cause impairment of consciousness. If there is *foresight of impairment* and the drug or substance is *taken of the individual's own accord*, then there is absolutely no basis for claiming that the accused acted involuntarily.

Automatism Voluntarily Self-Induced by Alcohol or Other Drugs

The general rule of Canadian criminal law is that accused persons, who have *voluntarily* ingested alcohol and/or other drugs and have, as a consequence, experienced a state of altered consciousness, are *barred from raising the defence of automatism*. At best, they may be able to raise the **partial defence** *of intoxication* (discussed in Chapter 9) and, if successful, they will be convicted of a less serious offence rather than given an absolute acquittal. For example, a successful defence of intoxication will lead to the accused being acquitted of a charge of murder and convicted, instead, of the less serious offence of manslaughter.

Traditionally, the courts have assumed that those who *voluntarily* ingest intoxicating substances are *at fault* in so doing and are, therefore, not entitled to the absolute acquittal that follows a successful assertion of a defence of automatism. Such people would be considered to be at fault because it may be taken for granted that every citizen is fully aware that the consumption of intoxicating substances can lead to impairment, and that this impairment might cause him or her to act in a way that might infringe the law. When individuals have such substances of their own free will and with an awareness of the potential consequences of their conduct, then, naturally, the courts will consider that they have voluntarily chosen to run the risk that they might commit an offence of some kind.

Take, for example, the case of *Saxon* (1975), in which the defendant was charged with impaired driving. At trial, he was convicted, but the conviction was quashed, on appeal, by the Alberta District Court. The Crown then appealed to the Supreme Court of Alberta. The theory of the defence was that Saxon was acting as an automaton (i.e., unconsciously) at the time he entered his vehicle. Saxon asserted that he had taken some tranquilizers prior to consuming a modest quantity of liquor at a beer parlour and that he did not realize that the interactive effect of the tranquilizers and alcohol (which "potentiate" one another) would render him impaired. The Appellate Division of the Alberta Supreme Court substituted a verdict of guilty on the basis that the average person must be aware that the consumption of drugs and alcohol might cause him or her to become impaired. In the words of Justice Prowse,

By imputing to an accused the teaching of common experience he is taken to know that alcohol weakens the restraints and inhibitions of a reasonable person. One restraint that is weakened is that of limiting the amount consumed in the light of the effects produced by the liquor already consumed, and these effects may well vary depending upon circumstances such as the effect of lack of sleep, food or as in the present case, the consumption of other impairing substances. *The accused's appreciation of the risks of becoming impaired is determined before and not after he has taken alcohol and drugs....* [emphasis added]

The *Saxon* case is useful as an example of the unsympathetic approach taken by the courts toward those who voluntarily consumed intoxicating substances to the point that they entered into a state of altered consciousness. However, an accused person may well say, "if I can establish that I was *acting involuntarily at the specific moment that I committed the conduct* in question, then convicting me of a criminal offence for what took place while I was in this state of automatism violates my rights under section 7 of the *Charter.*" More specifically, the accused might contend that convicting him or her in such circumstances constitutes a deprivation of the "right to liberty and security of the person" in a manner that is not "in accordance with the principles of fundamental justice." Is this a valid constitutional argument against the traditional principle of criminal law that bars the accused from pleading automatism where he or she has voluntarily become intoxicated?

In the *Penno* case (1990), the Supreme Court of Canada was confronted with this constitutional argument in the context of a charge of being impaired while in care and control of a motor vehicle (section 253 of the Code). The accused contended that it was a violation of section 7 to convict him of this charge when he was in such an extreme state of intoxication that he had no awareness of even entering his vehicle. However, the Court firmly ruled that there was no violation of the *Charter* in these circumstances. The Court emphasized

the fact that impaired driving offences are quite distinct from other "**true crimes**" that are to be found in the *Criminal Code*, and that individuals accused of committing these serious offences should not be permitted to raise the defence of automatism. In effect, in order for a person accused of an offence under section 253 to claim the benefit of the defence of automatism, it would have to be shown that he or she were intoxicated to such an extreme degree that they were not aware of what they were doing when they assumed care and control of, or started to drive, a motor vehicle. If such an argument were to lead to an acquittal, it would mean that the more intoxicated such accused persons are, the more likely it is that they would be able to gain a total acquittal on the basis of automatism! Obviously, this would fly in the face of the need to protect Canadians from the very real and immediate dangers posed to them by impaired drivers.

In rejecting the contention that highly intoxicated motorists can plead the defence of automatism, Justice Wilson pointed out, in her judgment in the *Penno* case (1990), that Parliament had made impairment an essential element of the *actus reus* of the offences contained in section 253 of the Code and there is no infringement of the *Charter* when the accused person, in such circumstances, is prevented from raising the defence of automatism. In her view,

the mental element of the offence under [s. 253] includes the voluntary consumption of alcohol but the *actus reus* requires the voluntary consumption of alcohol to *the point of impairment.* The distinction appears to make sense in that alcohol consumption to the point of impairment could well negate the intent to have care or control of the motor vehicle and result in the absence of *mens rea* whereas simple consumption might not. The *actus reus* requires *impairment* by alcohol and not just the prior consumption of alcohol. By making the requirement of impairment an element of the *actus reus* rather than the *mens rea* of the offence, Parliament has avoided the vicious circle which would otherwise be inherent in the offence.

… crimes in which intoxication is made an element of the offence, *i.e.*, part of the *actus reus*, are in a different category from crimes in which intoxication is relevant to the mental element only. I find no unconstitutionality in the creation of the former type of offences. … [emphasis added]

However, when the Supreme Court of Canada addressed a constitutional challenge to the traditional rule excluding self-induced intoxication from the scope of the automatism in a case that fell outside of the specific context of impaired driving charges, it adopted a totally different approach. Indeed, in *Daviault* (1994), the Court held that, if *extreme* — albeit voluntarily induced — intoxication produces a state of mind "akin to automatism or insanity," then the accused is entitled to an outright acquittal. The Court held that it would indeed infringe section 7 of the *Charter* if severely impaired persons could be convicted of criminal offences despite the fact that they lacked even a minimal awareness of what they were doing. Justice Cory, in delivering the majority judgment of the Supreme Court, stated that the "fundamental principles of justice," enshrined in section 7 of the *Charter*, would be infringed in such circumstances because the Crown would not be able to establish the voluntariness component of the *actus reus* of the offence charged. Insofar as the voluntariness requirement is concerned, Justice Cory stated that

> The *actus reus* requires that the prohibited criminal act be performed voluntarily as a willed act. A person in a state of automatism cannot perform a voluntary willed act since the automatism has deprived the person of the ability to carry out such an act. It follows that someone in an extreme state of intoxication akin to automatism must also be deprived of that ability. Thus a fundamental aspect of the *actus reus* is absent. It would equally infringe s. 7 of the *Charter* if an accused who was not acting voluntarily could be convicted of a criminal offence. … to convict in the face of such a fundamental denial of natural justice could not be justified under s. 1 of the *Charter*.

Clearly, the *Daviault* case brought about a sea-change in the Canadian criminal law. Prior to this case, it had always been assumed that those who voluntarily ingested intoxicating substances were at fault for doing so and, therefore, were not entitled to the absolute acquittal that follows a successful assertion of the defence of automatism. The decision in *Daviault* reversed this traditional principle of criminal law and the Supreme Court of Canada, by virtue of its interpretation of the requirements of the *Charter*, held that any person who falls into a state of *extreme* intoxication is entitled to an acquittal *regardless of the fact that this state was voluntarily induced*. The only exception would be offences relating to impaired driving, where Parliament has made impairment a central element of the *actus reus*.

Nevertheless, the impact of the *Daviault* case was remarkably short-lived. In 1995, Parliament decided to "trump" the *Daviault* decision, by amending the *Criminal Code*. This was felt to be necessary because many Canadians had expressed their shock at the implications of the Supreme Court's decision for the prosecution of those who, in a state of intoxication, commit violent acts against women and children. In spite of the Supreme Court's views about the requirements of the *Charter* in such circumstances, Parliament added section 33.1 to the *Criminal Code*. Under the terms of this provision, accused persons cannot gain an acquittal on the basis of intoxication-induced automatism if they have been charged with any offence that "includes as an element *an assault or any other interference or threat of interference by a person with the bodily integrity of another*." In light of section 33.1, individuals who become impaired to the point of automatism and who are charged with offences involving personal violence are clearly precluded from raising the automatism defence and must instead raise the *partial* defence of intoxication, which, as we shall see later, is in any event only available in relation to a limited number of offences, known as "**specific intent**" offences. (A detailed discussion of the defence of intoxication and "specific intent" offences may be found in Chapter 9 of this book.)

Essentially, for any offence involving personal violence, section 33.1 restores the old criminal law principle that applied before the *Daviault* case (1994) was decided. However, in so doing, Parliament has arguably flouted the Supreme Court of Canada's interpretation of the requirements of section 7 of the *Charter* in this particular context. Therefore, it is almost certain that section 33.1 will be challenged under the *Charter* and the Supreme Court will be required to reconsider its ruling in *Daviault*. Undoubtedly, the key question will be whether section 1 of the *Charter* can "save" section 33.1 of the *Criminal Code*. Perhaps the Supreme Court will take the view that Parliament was justified in moving to protect women and children from drunken violence and that section 33.1, therefore, constitutes a "reasonable limitation" on an accused person's rights under section 7 of the *Charter*. On the other hand, the Court may decide to re-assert its views in *Daviault* and declare section 33.1 to be invalid because it will lead to the conviction of individuals who did not act voluntarily. In any event, until the Supreme Court reaches its decision in the appropriate case, there will be considerable uncertainty as to the constitutional validity of section 33.1.

Automatism Distinguished from Amnesia

It is important to distinguish between *automatism* and *amnesia* (loss of memory). The defence of automatism is concerned with the question of whether accused persons acted voluntarily at the time of their alleged offences. The fact that they have no recollection of what happened does not necessarily mean that they acted involuntarily. For example, it is a common consequence of consuming alcohol that individuals may act *voluntarily and in a conscious, purposive manner* but still not have any memory of what happened at a certain point after they started to drink. Clearly, such people should not be absolved of criminal liability simply because they cannot remember the crimes that they committed while under the influence of alcohol that was consumed voluntarily.

Take, for example, the sad case of *Honish* (1991), in which the accused went to a motel and consumed a large quantity of anti-depressant drugs and sleeping pills mixed with alcohol. His intention was to commit suicide. However, one hour later, he was driving his car and was involved in a serious accident; he went through a yield sign and struck another vehicle, causing injuries to three of its occupants, including a small child. Honish drove through the intersection and came to a stop only when he struck a parked vehicle. He was charged with three counts of impaired driving causing bodily harm. However, Honish claimed that he had absolutely no recollection of what had happened between the time that he was lying down on his bed in the motel and the moment when he woke up in hospital after the accident. Was this state of amnesia relevant to Honish's criminal responsibility? A critical finding of fact made by the trial judge was that Honish was *not acting in a state of automatism* at the time of the accident. There were skid marks, indicating that Honish had attempted to take evasive action, and there was evidence that he had initially climbed out of his car and engaged in "sharp verbal exchanges" with one of the wounded passengers in the car that he had struck in the intersection. At that time, Honish also apologized for having hit the people in the other car and admitted he was drunk. The trial judge, therefore, held that Honish had not been in state of automatism at the time of the accident, and this meant that his state of amnesia was irrelevant. The accused was convicted on all three counts and his appeals to both the Alberta Court of Appeal and the Supreme Court of Canada were rejected. (Incidentally, it is important to note that, even if the cocktail of drugs and alcohol ingested by Honish had indeed produced a genuine state of automatism, he would nevertheless still have been prevented from successfully raising a defence based on his extreme state of voluntarily induced intoxication: see the *Penno* case (1990) and section 33.1 of the *Criminal Code*, discussed in the previous section.)

Automatism Caused by a Mental Disorder

Where the accused's condition is caused by a mental disorder, he or she is not entitled to be acquitted by reason of the defence of automatism. Instead, the Court must treat the accused's defence as being that of "not criminally responsible on account of mental disorder" ("**NCRMD**") in accordance with the provisions of section 16 of the Code (the NCRMD defence is fully discussed in Chapter 8). Section 16(1) of the Code provides that

> No person is criminally responsible for an act committed or an omission made while suffering from a mental disorder that rendered the person incapable of appreciating the nature and quality of the act or omission or of knowing that it was wrong.

The courts have drawn a sharp distinction between automatism, which leads to a complete acquittal of the accused, and the NCRMD defence, which leads to a special verdict, under section 672.34, that "the accused committed the act or made the omission but is not criminally responsible on account of mental disorder." This distinction is critical because the special NCRMD verdict may result in the accused being kept in custody in a psychiatric facility or being released into the community under far-reaching conditions (section 672.54). In contrast, those defendants who are acquitted as a consequence of the successful assertion of a defence of automatism immediately leave the courtroom without any restrictions whatsoever on their future freedom of action. As Justice Bastarache, of the Supreme Court of Canada, aptly noted in the case of *Stone* (1999), "the determination of whether mental disorder or non-mental disorder automatism should be left with the **trier of fact** must be taken very carefully since it will have serious ramifications for both the individual and society in general."

The Definition of Mental Disorder: Problems of Judicial Interpretation

Section 2 of the *Criminal Code* defines the term "mental disorder" as a *"disease of the mind"* —a phrase that has been used by the courts for centuries. In the *Stone* case (1999), the Supreme Court of Canada emphasized that the decision as to whether a particular mental condition should be considered a "disease of the mind" is one that is made exclusively by the trial judge, as a *question of law*. It is not an issue that may be determined by the opinions of medical experts, although the courts will certainly take the views of these experts into account in the course of their decision-making process. In the past, the courts have found it extremely difficult to decide whether certain types of mental condition (such as clouded consciousness associated with a sleep-walking episode or extreme psychological shock) should be placed within the category of "disease of the mind," thereby bringing the accused under the provisions of section 16 of the *Criminal Code*, or whether they should be classified as a form of automatism, thereby laying the basis for an unqualified acquittal should the accused's defence prove to be successful at trial.

How have the courts attempted to resolve the question of whether the accused's condition does — or does not — constitute a "disease of the mind"?

One of the more influential cases that addressed this thorny issue was the English case of *Quick* (1973). In this case, which has been frequently cited by Canadian courts, Lord Justice Lawton furnished the following definition of disease of the mind:

> In our judgment the fundamental concept is of a malfunctioning of the mind caused by disease. A malfunctioning of the mind of transitory effect caused by the application to the body of some *external factor* such as violence, drugs, including anaesthetics, alcohol and hypnotic influences cannot fairly be said to be due to disease. [emphasis added]

In the *Quick* case, the accused was a diabetic who was charged in connection with a brutal assault upon a severely disabled patient at the institution where he worked. Quick contended that, at the time of the alleged offence, he was suffering from automatism, induced by a condition of hypogly-caemia; it was contended that this hypoglycaemic condition (very low blood-sugar levels) was caused by Quick's regular injection of insulin. The Court of Appeal ruled that Quick should be acquitted, on the basis of the defence of automatism, because the administration of an insulin injection should be considered an *external* factor within the terms of the test set out above. Quick's hypoglycaemic condition could not be categorized as a disease of the mind, which, of course, can only be regarded as an *internal* factor.

The internal–external test articulated in the *Quick* case tends to create some strange results in certain circumstances. For example, both the English and Canadian courts have consistently held that those suffering from epilepsy are to be considered to be suffering from a disease of the mind, even though few laypersons would consider epilepsy to be a form of mental illness. It is probably difficult for individuals who have epilepsy to accept that, if they commit a crime while in an epileptic fit, they must be found NCRMD and might conceivably be sent to a psychiatric facility or be released into the community only on the basis of restrictive conditions. However, it is surely instructive that, in the English case of *Sullivan* (1983), the House of Lords refused to change the internal–external approach that categorizes epilepsy as a disease of the mind.

The internal–external test also does not work very well when applied to conditions such as sleep-walking. As noted earlier, the Supreme Court of Canada decided, in the *Parks* case (1992), that sleep-walking is not an abnormal condition and that the accused was entitled to an absolute acquittal on the basis of a successful defence of automatism. However, it is clear that the justices of the Supreme Court of Canada had to look beyond the simple internal–external test in order to make the determination that sleep-walking is not a mental disorder.

In the *Parks* case (1992), the justices of the Supreme Court of Canada were of one mind in holding that the expert testimony at the accused's trial was unanimously agreed on three points:

> (1) the respondent was sleep-walking at the time of the incident; (2) sleep-walking is not a neuro-logical, psychiatric or other illness: it is a sleep disorder very common in children and also found in adults; (3) there is no medical treatment as such, apart from good health practices, especially as regards sleep. It is important to note that this expert evidence was not in any way contradicted by the prosecution. ...

In light of this expert evidence, how did the justices of the Supreme Court decide that Parks was not suffering from a mental disorder? Justice La Forest (with whom a majority of the other justices concurred) emphasized that the term "disease of the mind" contains a "legal or policy component" as well as "a substantial medical component." In other words, the courts must reserve to themselves the final decision as to whether a particular mental condition may be properly characterized as a mental disorder, and they must do so in light of the policy that they believe is appropriate. Central to the determination of an appropriate legal policy is the need for the courts to balance the individual interests of the accused with the need to protect society from dangerous persons. This is not a task that can be left to medical or psychiatric experts.

Justice La Forest argued that there are two distinct approaches to the policy component of the inquiry into whether a condition constitutes a disease of the mind. These two approaches have been referred to as the "continuing danger" and "internal cause" theories:

> The "continuing danger theory" holds that any condition likely to present a recurring danger to

the public should be treated as [mental disorder]. The "internal cause" theory suggests that a condition stemming from the psychological or emotional make-up of the accused, rather than from some external factor, should lead to a finding of [mental disorder]. The two theories share a common concern for recurrence, the latter holding that an internal weakness is more likely to lead to recurrent violence than automatism brought on by some intervening external cause.

Justice La Forest pointed out that the "internal cause" theory (as represented by the internal–external test) has acquired a position of dominance in Canadian criminal law. However, he also suggested that the theory does not provide much enlightenment when applied to the issue of sleep-walking. The reason for this "poor fit" lies in the fact that it is possible to characterize certain factors as being either internal or external in origin, depending on one's particular point of view. In *Parks*, the Crown argued that the causes of the accused's violent episode of sleep-walking were internal. That is, they consisted of a combination of genetic susceptibility and the ordinary stresses of everyday life (such as lack of sleep and a high level of personal strain). Since the average person would take such forms of stress in his or her stride, the Crown contended that the fact that the accused went into a state of automatism indicated that he or she was suffering from an (internal) mental disorder. In contrast, Justice La Forest indicated that the defence could just as easily contend that the factors that, *for a person who is awake*, are "mere ordinary stresses can be differently characterized for a person who is asleep, unable to counter with his conscious mind the onslaught of the admittedly ordinary strains of life." In his view, one could "argue that the particular amalgam of stress, excessive exercise, sleep deprivation and sudden noises in the night that causes an incident of somnambulism is, for the sleeping person, analogous to the effect of concussion upon a waking person, which is generally accepted as an external cause of ... automatism." Justice La Forest, therefore, con-

cluded that the internal–external dichotomy becomes so blurred in the context of sleep-walking that is it "not helpful in resolving the inquiry" as to whether the accused's condition should be considered one of automatism or one arising from a mental disorder or disease of the mind.

As far as the "continuing danger" approach is concerned, Justice La Forest concluded that the potential recurrence of the accused's condition is "but one of a number of factors to be considered in the policy phase of the disease of the mind inquiry." In particular, he asserted that the absence of a likelihood of recurrence does not *per se* preclude a finding that the accused was suffering from a disease of the mind. In the case of sleep-walking, he contended that the medical evidence demonstrates that there is little likelihood of recurrence.

In Justice La Forest's view, therefore, neither the recurring danger approach nor the internal cause theory can be readily applied to the phenomenon of sleep-walking. This being the case, it was necessary in his opinion to take into account other *policy* considerations, such as the questions of whether the defence of sleep-walking may be easily feigned and whether the recognition of this condition as a form of automatism will "open the floodgates to a cascade of sleep-walking defence claims." In this respect, Justice La Forest noted that there have been few cases in which **somnambulism** has ever been raised as a defence, even though it has been recognized as a defence for at least a hundred years. It is, therefore, unlikely that the floodgates will be opened by determining that sleep-walking is a form of automatism rather than a mental disorder.

Similarly, in Justice La Forest's view, the medical evidence suggests that it is difficult to feign sleep-walking: "precise symptoms and medical histories beyond the control of the accused must be presented to the trier of fact, and as in this case the accused will be subjected to a battery of tests." In short, Justice La Forest found that there were no compelling policy reasons why Parks's sleep-walking should not be considered as a form of automatism. He concluded his analysis of this issue by stating that "it is for the Crown to prove that somnambulism stems from a disease of the mind; neither the evidence nor the policy considerations in this case overcome the Crown's burden in that regard."

Clearly, considerable concern may be aroused when an individual such as Parks, who has caused serious harm to others (albeit involuntarily), is granted a total acquittal and released unconditionally back into the community. To the layperson, the accused's condition would probably appear to be the result of a sleep disorder and there would most likely be a degree of apprehension that this disorder might recur. The reasoning of the Supreme Court of Canada, that Parks's mental state was caused by the normal condition of sleep and was, therefore, not the product of a disease of the mind, would probably not be particularly convincing from the layperson's point of view. After all, the type of sleep-walking engaged in by Parks (driving 23 kilometres at night and then committing two brutal attacks) is grossly abnormal when considered in the context of the layperson's everyday experience. Similarly, one suspects that the average layperson would not consider Parks's condition to be comparable to that of a person suffering from the effects of a concussion or some other physical injury. However, it is also likely that the average layperson would not consider a person who sleep-walks to be mentally disordered. As we shall see shortly, the answer to this legal conundrum may be to place those who are acquitted on the basis of automatism under a similar regime as those who are acquitted as being NCRMD; in particular, it might be desirable to ensure that someone who is acquitted on the basis of the sleep-walking defence is required to observe certain conditions (such as reporting periodically for medical monitoring) if he or she is to be released immediately back into the community.

In the more recent *Stone* case (1999), the majority of the Supreme Court of Canada expressed agreement with the general approach adopted by Justice La Forest in *Parks*. Indeed, Justice Bastarache suggested that judges should not be restricted to the "internal cause" and "continuing danger" theories

when they are required to determine whether a specific mental condition constitutes a "disease of the mind" for the purposes of section 16 of the *Criminal Code*. Instead, they should adopt, what Justice Bastarache calls, *"a more holistic approach"*—one that explicitly takes into account the types of *policy* factors identified by Justice La Forest in *Parks*. In his view,

> ... the continuing danger factor should not be viewed as an alternative or mutually exclusive approach to the internal cause factor. Although different, both of these approaches are relevant in the disease of the mind inquiry. As such, in any given case, a trial judge may find one, the other or both of these approaches of assistance. To reflect this unified, holistic approach to the disease of the mind question, it is therefore more appropriate to refer to the internal cause factor and the continuing danger factor, rather than the internal cause theory and the continuing danger theory.

However, it is significant that, in the *Stone* case, the majority of the Supreme Court of Canada stated that there should be a *presumption that any state of automatism is the result of a mental disorder.* Justice Bastarache noted that "it will only be in rare cases that automatism is not caused by mental disorder." In his judgment, he suggests that there should be a "rule that trial judges start from the proposition that the condition the accused claims to have suffered from is a disease of the mind":

> They must then determine whether the evidence in the particular case takes the condition out of the disease of the mind category.

Indubitably, the *Stone* case signals an intention on the part of the Supreme Court to reduce the scope of the automatism defence in favour of an approach that results in a finding that the accused is NCRMD — a verdict that leaves the door open for the imposition of post-trial restrictions on the accused's liberty (e.g., the requirement of treatment).

Sleep-walking as the basis for a defence of automatism: the lesson of Parks.

Psychological Blow Automatism

Prior to the decision of the Supreme Court of Canada in *Stone* (1999), Canadian courts had recognized a form of automatism known as a "psychological blow automatism." This version of the automatism defence strongly reflects the influence of the so-called "internal–external test."

In light of the internal–external test, first articulated in the *Quick* case (1973), it is indisputable that a *physical* blow to the head must be considered an *external* factor and that, if it causes a state of unconsciousness, the accused is entitled to an absolute acquittal on the basis of automatism. What is the situation, however, where the accused claims to have been in a state of dissociation (where the mind does not go with the body) as the consequence of a *psychological* blow? More specifically, should such a blow be considered an external or an internal factor? Resolution of this issue created many serious problems for the Canadian courts over a period of several years, during which there were conflicting decisions. However, in the important case of *Rabey* (1980), the Supreme Court of Canada set some definitive guidelines that address the many critical issues raised by the phenomenon of psychological blow automatism.

Rabey had severely assaulted a fellow university student after he had discovered that she had expressed a sexual interest in another man and that she regarded Rabey as a "nothing" who kept bugging her in class. Rabey had been "infatuated" with this female student, and he had discovered her true feelings toward him by reading a private letter that she had written to a friend. Rabey testified that he could not remember striking his victim. A psychiatric expert testified, on behalf of the defence, that the accused had been in a "dissociative state" at the time of the attack. In his view, this dissociative state had been induced by the powerful emotional shock suffered by the accused when his image of the victim was "shattered" by the discovery of her real feelings toward him. The witness proceeded to contend that a conversation the accused had had with the victim on the following day had triggered the dissociative state and that Rabey's condition was comparable to that produced by a physical blow. In the expert's opinion, there was no evidence that the accused suffered from any pathological condition and that it was unlikely that the dissociative state would ever recur.

However, a psychiatric witness appearing for the Crown testified that the accused was not in a dissociative state at the time of the attack on the victim. In his view, the defendant merely went into an "extreme rage" and could probably have formed the specific intent required for the offence charged. The witness also asserted that, if the accused *had* been in a dissociative state, he would have been suffering from a disease of the mind because such a state is a subdivision of hysterical amnesia, which he regarded as mental illness. The trial judge acquitted Rabey on the basis that there was a reasonable doubt as to whether he was in a state of automatism induced by an external cause. In her view, the defendant was, therefore, not mentally disordered within the meaning of section 16 of the Code. However, the Ontario Court of Appeal allowed an appeal by the Crown and ordered a new trial.

In delivering the judgment of the Court in *Rabey* (1977), Justice Martin proceeded to fashion a general test for distinguishing between the NCRMD defence and automatism:

> In general, the distinction to be drawn is between a malfunctioning of the mind arising from some cause that is primarily internal to the accused, having its source in his psychological or emotional make-up, or in some organic pathology, as opposed to a malfunctioning of the mind which is the transient effect produced by some specific external factor such as, for example, concussion. *Any malfunctioning of the mind, or mental disorder having its source primarily in some subjective condition or weakness internal to the accused (whether fully understood or not), may be a "disease of the mind" if it prevents the accused from knowing what he is doing, but transient disturbances of consciousness due to certain specific external factors do not fall within the concept of disease of the mind. …* Particular transient mental disturbances may not, however, be capable of being properly categorized in relation to whether they constitute "disease of the mind," on the basis of a generalized statement, and must be decided on a case by case basis. [emphasis added]

Justice Martin concluded that the dissociative state, alleged by Rabey, could not be categorized as a transient state produced by an external cause. On the contrary, it could only be termed a "disease of the mind":

> *The ordinary stresses and disappointments of life which are the common lot of mankind do not constitute an explanation for a malfunctioning of the mind which takes it out of the category of a "disease of the mind."* … The dissociative state must be considered as having its source primarily in the respondent's psychological or emotional make-up. [emphasis added]

It is important to bear in mind, however, that Justice Martin also accepted the view that there may well be some "extraordinary external events" that might affect even the "average normal person" without any reference whatsoever to the subjective make-up of the person exposed to such events. Justice Martin listed a number of situations in which it might be possible to hold that the dissociative state of mind, which has resulted from an emotional shock, should be classified as arising from an external cause, thereby entitling the accused to an outright acquittal — for example, a situation where the defendant has witnessed the murder of, or a serious assault upon, a loved one. In essence, Justice Martin was prepared to permit an accused person who has suffered from a psychological blow to claim the benefit of the defence of automatism *if a reasonable person might have become dissociated in the same circumstances*. For this reason, the test in the *Rabey* case might well be called the "reasonable dissociation" test.

The Supreme Court of Canada (by a thin four to three majority) affirmed the decision of the Ontario Court of Appeal in *Rabey* (1980). Justice Ritchie, in delivering the brief majority judgment, expressly adopted the critical passages excerpted above from the judgment of Justice Martin in the Ontario Court of Appeal. Justice Ritchie rejected the view that a finding that Rabey was suffering from a mental disorder would be unfair to the accused. He suggested that it would be "unthinkable" that a person found to be NCRMD because of "a transient mental disorder" would be confined in a psychiatric facility if he were not considered to be dangerous.

In the *Stone* case (1999), the Supreme Court of Canada re-affirmed the approach that it had adopted in *Rabey* (1980). Stone was charged with the murder of his wife, whom he had stabbed 47 times. Stone stated that, while travelling with him by car, the victim had insulted and berated him over an extended period. He recounted that he had stopped the vehicle in a parking lot, where the alleged insults continued. According to Stone, the taunts made by his wife included hurtful comments about his lack of sexual prowess. Stone stated that he had suddenly experienced a "whoosh" sensation that "washed over him from his feet to his head." When he was finally able to focus his eyes again, he found that he was standing over his wife's dead body and that he was holding a hunting knife in his hand. At his trial, Stone claimed that he had been in a "dissociative" state at the time of the killing and sought to rely on the defence of psychological blow automatism. The trial judge ruled that, if the accused really had been in a dissociative state, then it had been caused by a "disease of the mind" and the appropriate defence was that of NCRMD under section 16 of the *Criminal Code*. The jury ultimately rejected the NCRMD defence and convicted Stone of manslaughter (accepting the accused's alternative defence of provocation, as defined by section 215 of the Code).

The Supreme Court of Canada subsequently rejected Stone's appeal, ruling that, in the circumstances of this particular case, the trial judge had been perfectly correct to refuse to put a defence of psychological blow automatism to the jury. Justice Bastarache, speaking for the majority of the Court, stated that

> ... the internal cause factor and the continuing danger factor, as well as the other policy factors set out in this Court's decisions in *Rabey* and *Parks* all support the trial judge's finding that the condition the appellant alleges to have suffered from is a disease of the mind in the legal sense. In particular, the trigger in this case was not ... "extraordinary external events" that would amount to an extreme shock or psychological blow that would cause a normal person, in the circumstances of the accused, to suffer a dissociation in the absence of a disease of the mind.

Justice Bastarache emphasized that, where an accused person claims to have been suffering from psychological blow automatism, there must be evidence of "an *extremely shocking trigger*" because only such an overwhelmingly powerful event is likely to cause a "normal person" to react by "entering an automatistic state." In *Stone*, the accused could not point to such a severe trigger; rather, the circumstances of his case suggested that it was more appropriate for Stone to raise the partial defence of provocation (which reduces murder to manslaughter). It is also noteworthy that Justice Bastarache took the view that the "plausibility" of a claim of psychological blow automatism is significantly reduced if a single individual "is both the *trigger* of the alleged automatism and the *victim* of the automatistic violence" (as was the case with Stone's wife); indeed, such a claim should be "considered suspect." This is an important ruling insofar as it ensures that the psychological blow automatism defence may not be raised successfully in cases of alleged provocation. Finally, Justice Bastarache made some interesting observations about the applicability of the "continuing danger factor" in the context of a psychological blow automatism defence. He noted that the courts should really be focusing their attention on whether the alleged trigger of an automatistic episode is likely to recur:

> The greater the anticipated frequency of the trigger in the accused's life, the greater the risk posed to the public and, consequently, the more likely it is that the condition alleged by the accused is a disease of the mind.

In the past, the courts have tended to devote their attention exclusively to the question of whether the defendants are likely to repeat their violent behaviour if they were to be confronted once again by the "alleged trigger of the current automatistic episode." Clearly, public safety is much more likely to be threatened if a triggering event is likely to recur on a regular basis than if it is only a remote possibility that the trigger will ever be encountered again by the accused in the future. Therefore, it constitutes sound judicial policy to investigate the "continuing danger factor" in terms of whether the trigger is likely to recur rather than whether the accused is likely to become violent should he or she be exposed to the trigger again.

All things considered, the combined effect of the *Rabey* and *Stone* cases will render it extremely difficult to successfully raise a defence of psychological blow automatism in the future. Only the most extreme forms of shock will be considered to constitute the kind of psychological blow that might cause an ordinary person to enter into a state of dissociation. In the absence of evidence of such an extreme assault on an individual's mind, the courts will hold that the only defence available to the accused is that of NCRMD under section 16 of the *Criminal Code*.

THE PROBLEM OF RECKLESSLY INDUCED AUTOMATISM

A critical question that must be addressed is whether accused persons who *recklessly* cause their own state of automatism should be entitled to an absolute acquittal. By using the word *recklessly* we mean to say that the accused persons concerned *subjectively* appreciate the fact that their conduct creates a risk of danger, but they deliberately choose to run that risk without any justification for doing so. We have seen that, in the case of intoxication as the result of the voluntary ingestion of alcohol or other drugs, special rules apply and that, in light of an amendment to the *Criminal Code* (section 33.1), defendants are precluded from raising the defence of automatism in such circumstances. What is the situation where individuals recklessly bring about a state of automatism by means other than alcohol and other drugs?

This issue was squarely raised in the English case of *Bailey* (1983), in which the accused was charged with wounding with intent or, alternatively, with unlawful wounding. His defence was that he had been acting in a state of automatism caused by a condition of hypoglycaemia (low blood-sugar levels) that had arisen as a consequence of his failure to take sufficient food after an injection of insulin. The trial judge ruled that the defence of automatism was not open to the accused since his incapac-

ity had been self-induced by his failure to eat properly, as was required after a dose of insulin. As a consequence, the accused was convicted of wounding with intent.

Upon Bailey's appeal, the Court of Appeal ruled that there had been a misdirection to the jury on the issue of self-induced incapacity. Indeed, Lord Justice Griffiths asserted that a defendant does not lose the benefit of the defence of automatism merely because his or her condition was self-induced: the defence would only be lost where the accused was reckless as to the risk that he or she would lapse into state of automatism and engage in dangerous conduct. In the view of Lord Justice Griffiths, it was not common knowledge, even among diabetics, that a failure to eat food, after taking an insulin injection, may result in dangerous conduct. Of course, if a particular defendant did appreciate that such a failure may lead to dangerous conduct and, nevertheless, deliberately "ran that risk," then he or she would clearly have been reckless and would lose the benefit of the defence of automatism. However, in any given case, the Crown would have to establish the accused's subjective awareness of the inherent risks in his or her conduct before a conviction could be entered:

> In our judgment, *self-induced automatism, other than that due to intoxication from alcohol or drugs, may provide a defence to crimes of basic intent. The question in each case will be whether the prosecution has proved the necessary element of recklessness.* In cases of assault, if the accused knows that his actions or inaction are likely to make him aggressive, unpredictable or uncontrolled with the result that he may cause injury to others and he persists in the action or takes no remedial action when he knows it is required, it will be open to the jury to find that he was reckless. [emphasis added]

In other words, the Court of Appeal took the view that the answer to the question of whether a self-induced incapacity will disentitle an accused person from relying on the defence of automatism, will (except in the case of intoxication from alcohol and/or drugs) *depend on the facts of each individual case* and, in particular, on whether the accused was *reckless* as to the risk of danger created by his or her conduct.

It will be remembered that, in the *Quick* case (1973), the accused was acquitted of a charge of assault causing bodily harm because, at the time of the assault, he was in a state of automatism that had been induced by the hypoglycaemia that followed an injection of insulin. Let us suppose, hypothetically, that the facts of the case were that the accused had previously experienced a similar incident in which he had not eaten after giving himself an insulin injection and, after falling into a state of hypoglycaemia, had attacked one of his patients. In these circumstances, the Crown could argue that the accused should not be entitled to plead the defence of automatism. This argument could be made on the basis that, if the very same sequence of events had happened previously, Quick must have been well aware of the risk that was being created by his conduct, and he was, therefore, at fault in continuing with that conduct in the absence of any justification for doing so (that is, he acted recklessly).

Automatism and the Primary or Persuasional Burden of Proof

A golden thread that runs through the fabric of Canadian criminal law is the principle that, at the end of a trial, the *Crown must prove all of the essential* mens rea *and* actus reus *elements of a crime* before a citizen may be convicted of it; furthermore, the Crown is required to prove its case "*beyond any reasonable* doubt." In other words, the *primary* or *persuasional* **burden of proof** is placed on the shoulders of the prosecution and the *standard of proof* that must be met is that of proof beyond a reasonable doubt.

Nevertheless, in the *Stone* case (1999), the Supreme Court of Canada (by a 5 – 4 majority) held that, where the defence of automatism has been raised, the primary — or persuasional — burden of proof must be placed on *the accused*: in other words, the accused has to prove his or her innocence — a

requirement that constitutes a dramatic exception to the general rule that applies to the conduct of criminal trials in Canada. However, the standard of proof is not that of "beyond a reasonable doubt" but rather that of "*on the balance of probabilities*" (the same standard of proof that applies in civil trials in Canada). Put more simply, the accused must prove that it was more probable than not that, at the time of the alleged offence, he or she was in a state of automatism. As Justice Bastarache stated, on behalf of the majority in *Stone*, "the legal burden in cases involving automatism must be on the defence to prove involuntariness on a balance of probabilities to the trier of fact."

Is it justifiable to require an accused person to prove the defence of automatism, rather than leaving it to the Crown to disprove it? Justice Bastarache reasoned that it is necessary for this exception to be made to the general rule. He took the view that genuine cases of automatism are "extremely rare" and the reality is that it is a condition that may be "easily feigned" by those who attempt to avoid all responsibility for their actions by merely saying, "I don't remember anything about it!" In this respect, Justice Bastarache approved the views of Justice Schroeder, of the Ontario Court of Appeal, who had remarked in the case of *Szymusiak* (1972) that automatism is a defence that has been treated with "wholesale skepticism" because while, "in a true and proper case," it may be the only defence open to an honest defendant, "it may just as readily be the last refuge of a scoundrel." Furthermore, Justice Bastarache stated that most, if not all, of the necessary medical information concerning the alleged condition of automatism rests firmly in the control of the accused. Indeed, it would be impossible for the Crown to obtain necessary medical information if the accused should choose to be uncooperative with medical witnesses summoned by the Crown. Therefore, according to Justice Bastarache, it would be totally impractical to "saddle the Crown with the legal burden of proving voluntariness beyond a reasonable doubt." He noted that Parliament had already relieved the Crown of this very burden in relation to the defence of "not criminally responsible on account of mental disorder." Indeed, section 16 of the *Criminal Code* (subsections (2) and (3)) makes it clear that the burden of proof is on the accused to establish the mental disorder defence "on the balance of probablities." Significantly, in *Stone*, Justice Bastarache fully admitted that placing the onus on the accused to prove the defence of automatism constitutes a violation of the presumption of innocence, guaranteed by section 11(d) of the *Charter*; however, he held that this nevertheless constitutes a "reasonable limitation" that is justified under section 1 of the *Charter*.

It is noteworthy that the minority of the justices of the Supreme Court of Canada, in the *Stone* case, strongly disagreed with the decision taken by a majority of their colleagues to impose the primary — or persuasional — burden of proof on those accused persons who raise the defence of automatism. Indeed, Justice Binnie, on behalf of the minority, stated that it was inappropriate for the Court, rather than Parliament, to make such a change in the criminal law. Furthermore, Justice Binnie expressed the view that placing the primary burden of proof on the accused "would create a potential for injustice where a jury entertains a reasonable doubt about the voluntariness of the accused's conduct." In other words, juries would now be required to convict defendants in criminal trials even though there is still a reasonable doubt as to whether they were acting in a state of automatism. After all, it is far easier to raise a reasonable doubt about one's guilt than it is it is to prove one's innocence on the balance of probabilities. Undoubtedly, the dramatic decision to impose the primary burden of proof on the accused was taken because the majority of the Supreme Court in the *Stone* case evidently believed that the automatism defence is susceptible to crafty manipulation by unscrupulous defendants and that the only means of ensuring the integrity of the justice system is to free the Crown from the burden of proving that the accused was not in a state of automatism at the time of his or her alleged offence. One thing is certain: on this point, the decision in *Stone* will continue to be very controversial!

Automatism and the Secondary or Evidentiary Burden of Proof

Automatism is the first defence that we have encountered in this book. It is important to bear in mind that every trial judge has a discretion whether to permit a defence to be considered by the trier of fact at the end of a criminal trial. The trier of fact may be a jury or the trial judge him- or herself if sitting alone. In order to prevent entirely speculative defences from being placed before the trier of fact, the courts have developed the notion that accused persons must jump over an initial hurdle: this is known as the *secondary* or **evidentiary burden of proof**. Essentially, this means that defendants must be able to point to evidence that is sufficient to establish that there is "*an air of reality*" to their defence. For practically all of the defences that may be raised by an accused person in a criminal trial, the evidentiary burden of proof is met where the accused can satisfy the trial judge that there is *evidence which is capable of raising a reasonable doubt in the mind of the trier of fact*. If this burden is not met, then the defence will not be considered at the end of the trial when the judge or jury makes the decision as to whether the accused is innocent or guilty of the charges laid. However, if the evidentiary burden is met, then the defence is placed before the trier of fact and the onus is now placed on the prosecution to prove — beyond a reasonable doubt — every element of the *actus reus* and *mens rea* of the crime charged. It is critical to recognize that the decision as to whether the evidentiary burden of proof has been met is one that is made *exclusively by the trial judge as a matter of law* (hence, where there is a jury, the members of that body have no part to play in making this determination).

Let us suppose that an accused person raises the defence of honest mistake of fact. The accused must satisfy the evidentiary burden of proof if the defence is to be a "live issue" at the end of the trial. However, once this initial hurdle has been surmounted, the ultimate burden of proof is placed squarely on the Crown to prove, at the end of the trial, that the accused was *not* acting under an honest mistake of fact and must do so beyond a reasonable doubt. Put another way, once the accused has satisfied the evidentiary burden, he or she only has to raise a reasonable doubt as to whether he or she was operating under the influence of a mistake of fact in order to gain an acquittal. Clearly, the evidentiary burden of proof is, in general, not particularly onerous and is simply designed to prevent patently thin defences from being placed before the trier of fact. This is an important consideration, of course, where there is a jury that might be easily confused by evidence that is purely speculative in nature.

Where the defendant advances a defence of automatism, he or she is also required to meet the evidentiary burden of proof before it will be considered a "live issue" at the end of the trial. However, in light of the *Stone* case (1999), it is now clear that the evidentiary burden is considerably more onerous for those who raise automatism as a defence. As Justice Bastarache noted, "the defence must satisfy the trial judge that there is evidence upon which a properly instructed jury could find that the accused acted involuntarily *on a balance of probabilities.*" Clearly, this statement reflects the fact that the primary burden of proof in automatism cases is (as we have seen) on the accused, rather than the Crown. In order to meet the evidentiary burden of proof in a case of alleged automatism, it is clearly not enough for the accused to merely claim that "I don't know what happened ... my mind went blank." Indeed, it is absolutely necessary that the accused point to *some expert psychiatric or psychological testimony* that lends support to the defence. Furthermore, it will generally be required that the accused point to some previous history of automatism or dissociative states. For example, in a case such as that of *Parks* (1992), the accused's defence of automatism was considered to be more credible in light of his (documented) history of previous sleep-walking episodes. Justice Bastarache also noted that the accused will be more likely to satisfy the evidentiary burden of proof if there is corroborating evidence from bystanders that "reveals that the accused appeared uncharacteristically glassy-eyed, unresponsive and or distant immediately

before, during or after the alleged involuntary act." Furthermore, Justice Bastarache suggested that a claim of automatism is more likely to be credible if there is no *motive* for the alleged offence: "a motiveless act will generally lend plausibility to an accused's claim of involuntariness." Summing it all up, Justice Bastarache concluded,

> I leave it to the discretion and experiences of trial judges to weigh all of the evidence available on a case-by-case basis and to determine whether a properly instructed jury could find that the accused acted involuntarily on a balance of probabilities.

What we may conclude from the above discussion about the evidentiary and persuasional burdens of proof, that are imposed on an accused person who raises the automatism defence, is that it will be extraordinarily difficult for him or her to gain an acquittal on this basis. There is undoubtedly no need to fear that the automatism defence will be abused on a widespread basis.

STUDY QUESTIONS

1. Jim is a youth worker who is employed by the provincial government. While he was one of the staff members at a custodial institution, some youths complained that he touched them on the arms and legs. Jim is surprised that there have been such complaints, and he says that he only touched the youths as a means of demonstrating his genuine concern for their welfare. Crown counsel is considering laying charges of sexual assault against Jim. Do you think such charges would be likely to succeed at a trial?

2. David lives with his five-year-old son, Nemo, and his wife, Mary, in a third-floor apartment. Since she was severely injured in a motor vehicle accident some time ago, Mary has been confined to a wheelchair and requires constant attention. One night, David goes out to a bar where he indulges in some drinking with a

friend. When he is walking up the street toward his home, he sees both flames and smoke coming out of the apartment building. There are a number of people outside the building but there is no sign of the fire brigade. David refuses to enter the building because he says he is "frightened of fires." A few minutes later, two neighbours emerge from the building and bring out Nemo and Mary, who have been burned and are suffering from smoke inhalation. They subsequently recover in hospital. However, a neighbour reports David's failure to go into the building and the police decide to lay charges against him. What charge(s) (if any) could reasonably be laid against David?

3. Digger is a farmer who owns a big, old barn. Unknown to Digger, Egbert (a vagrant) is sleeping in the barn at night in order to keep warm during the winter months. One night, Digger goes into the barn and accidentally drops a lighted cigarette onto some tinder-dry straw. He leaves the barn and locks the door. However, he soon notices that smoke and flames are pouring from one of the windows in the barn. He then hears Egbert screaming for help. Digger refuses to unlock the door and Egbert is burnt to a cinder. Digger even fails to call the fire brigade because he wants to claim the insurance money for the barn. Is Digger guilty of any criminal offence(s)?

4. Daniel is driving, within the speed limit, on a country road. He suddenly skids on some ice and his car slides into a ditch. He leaves the car, with the keys still in the ignition, and asks for help at a nearby farmhouse. The farmer calls for a tow-truck and he gives Daniel a few whiskeys since the latter looks as though he is in a state of shock. Daniel returns to the car to wait for the tow-truck. However, a police car arrives and Daniel is asked to take a breath test. Daniel is subsequently charged with being in care and control of a motor vehicle while impaired by alcohol (contrary to section 253 of the Code). Is he likely to be found guilty of this offence?

5. Veronica is taking some powerful tranquillizers and is aware that she should not ingest alcohol while she is taking them. Unfortunately, she goes to a party and has a few glasses of wine. Subsequently, she leaves the party and enters her car. The police find her in a state of total unconsciousness, sitting in the driver's seat of her vehicle. Veronica later claims that she has absolutely no memory of leaving the party and was not conscious when she entered her car. However, the police wish to lay a charge of being in care and control of motor vehicle while impaired (section 253 of the Code). Would such a charge be likely to succeed at trial? Would it make a difference to your answer if Veronica's physician had told her that it was safe for her to "drink in moderation" while she was taking the tranquillizers?

6. Donald suddenly attacks his best friend, Vincent. There is apparently no reason for the attack. When charged with assault causing bodily harm, Donald claims that he is a diabetic who was in a hypoglycaemic state (as a consequence of taking his insulin injection without eating any meals). He says that he has never experienced such an episode before. Does Donald have any defence to the charge? Would it make any difference to your answer if Donald knew that he could become violent if he did not eat after taking his insulin injection?

7. Joyce is a single mother who is trying to raise her young daughter, Melody, as best she can. Melody suffers from diabetes and Joyce's physician has told her that Melody will die if she does not have regular injections of insulin. One day, Joyce believes that she has experienced a vision and that an angel has told her that Melody has been cured and no longer needs her injections. Joyce stops giving her daughter the insulin and Melody eventually goes into a coma. By the time Melody is taken to hospital, it is too late to save her and she dies. Joyce claims that she honestly believed that her daughter was cured and that she did

not need any treatment. The police are convinced that Joyce's religious beliefs are sincerely held. Nevertheless, Crown counsel is considering laying criminal charges against Joyce. What charges (if any) would be likely to succeed at trial?

8. Fred is climbing a mountain with his friend, Barney. They enter into a ferocious conflict and Fred knocks Barney unconscious by hitting him on the head with an ice pick. Fred comes to believe that Barney is dead and, four hours later, he throws Barney over a cliff. The body is later recovered by the police. Forensic experts are prepared to testify that Barney was still alive when he was thrown over the cliff and that he would most probably have survived had he not been so gravely wounded by the fall from the top of the cliff. Fred's lawyer claims that her client cannot be convicted of a homicide offence, because when he threw his friend off the cliff, he honestly believed the latter was dead. What charge(s) would you lay (if any) against Fred and what degree of success would the charge(s) be likely to enjoy at trial?

9. Derek is walking towards his home when he sees a gang of armed robbers emerging from his local bank. The robbers brutally kill one of the customers, Charlie, who is standing outside the bank and is accidentally placed between the gang and their getaway car. Upon seeing this distressing scene, Derek goes into a state of shock and attacks George, one of the robbers, who is trying to give himself up to the police because he disapproves of the killing of Charlie by his colleagues. George is quite seriously wounded by this onslaught. After Derek is taken to the police station, he claims that he does not remember anything about the attack on George; all he remembers is the brutal killing by the other bank robbers. Does Derek have any defence to a charge of assault causing bodily harm? Would it make any difference to your answer if Derek was a "highly nervous" individual and was taking tranquillizers on a regular basis?

10. Prospero takes his four-year-old son, Ariel, for a walk in the local park. Once they enter the park, Prospero sits down in a chair and falls fast asleep. Ariel wanders away and is killed by a truck as he is trying to cross a busy road on the outskirts of the park. Prospero later states that he suffers from narcolepsy (a condition characterized by a frequent — and uncontrollable — desire to sleep). What charges might be laid against Prospero and, if such charges are laid, would he have any defence(s) available to him?

FURTHER READING

Ashworth, A. 1995. *Principles of Criminal Law.* 2d ed. Oxford: Oxford University Press. 93 – 111.

Boyle, C. 1984. *Sexual Assault.* Toronto: Carswell.

———. 1994. The Judicial Construction of Sexual Assault Offences. In J.V. Roberts and R.M. Mohr, eds. *Confronting Sexual Assault: A Decade of Legal and Social Change.* Toronto: University of Toronto Press. 136 – 56.

Brahams, D. 1983. *R. v. Sullivan:* Epilepsy, Insanity and the Common Law. 133 *New Law Journal:* 137.

Brudner, A. 2000. Insane Automatism: A Proposal for Reform. 45 *McGill Law Journal:* 66.

Buxton, R. 1984. Circumstances, Consequences and Attempted Rape. (1984) *Criminal Law Review:* 25.

Campbell, I.G. 1991. Dissociative States in Australia. 3(1) *International Bulletin of Law & Mental Health:* 29.

Campbell, K.L. 1981. Psychological Blow Automatism: A Narrow Defence. 23 *Criminal Law Quarterly:* 342.

Clark, R.S. 1972. Overmastering Physical Force 14 *Criminal Law Quarterly:* 413.

Coles, E.M. and D. Jang. 1996. A Psychological Perspective on the Legal Concepts of "Volition" and "Intent." 4 *Journal of Law and Medicine:* 60.

Dagan, H. 1999. In Defense of the Good Samaritan. 97 *Michigan Law Review:* 1152.

Delisle, R.J. 1999. *Stone:* Judicial Activism Gone Awry to Presume Guilt. 24 *Criminal Reports (5th):* 91.

Gold, A.D. 1994. Lessons about *Mens Rea;* Three Recent Cases. 36 *Criminal Law Quarterly:* 157.

Gorsuch, N.M. 2000. The Right to Assisted Suicide and Euthanasia. 23 *Harvard Journal of Law & Public Policy:* 599.

Grant, I., D. Chunn, and C.L.M. Boyle. 1994. *The Law of Homicide.* Toronto: Carswell.

Grant, I. and L. Spitz. 1993. Case Comment: *R. v. Parks.* 72 *Canadian Bar Review:* 224.

Healy, P. 1992. Note on *R. v. Penno.* 71 *Canadian Bar Review:* 143.

———. 2000. Automatism Confined. 45 *McGill Law Journal:* 89.

Holland, W.H. 1982. Automatism and Criminal Responsibility. 25 *Criminal Law Quarterly:* 66.

Josep, R. 1999. The Neurology of Traumatic "Dissociative" Amnesia: Commentary and Literature Review. 23(8) *Child Abuse & Neglect:* 715.

Kelley, D.N. 2000. A Psychological Approach to Understanding the Legal Basis of the No Duty to Rescue Rule. 14 *Brigham Young University Education & Law Journal:* 271.

King, J. 1999. Criminal Law: "Am I my Brother's Keeper?" Sherrice's Law: A Balance of American Notions of Duty and Liberty. 52 *Oklahoma Law Review:* 613.

Law Reform Commission of Canada. 1979. Study Paper: *Consent to Medical Care.* Ottawa: Ministry of Supply and Services Canada.

———. 1980. Working Paper No. 26: *Medical Treatment and Criminal Law.* Ottawa: Minister of Supply and Services Canada.

———. 1982. Working Paper No. 29: *Criminal Law; the General Part—Liability and Defences.* Ottawa: Ministry of Supply and Services Canada.

———. 1984. Working Paper No. 33: *Homicide.* Ottawa: Ministry of Supply and Services Canada.

———. 1985. Working Paper No. 46: *Omissions, Negligence and Endangering.* Ottawa: L.R.C.C.

———. 1987. Report No. 31: *Recodifying Criminal Law.* Rev. ed. Ottawa: L.R.C.C.

Libman, R. 1991. The Defence of Drinking and Driving Offences: Too Drunk to Drive; Too Drunk for a Defence? 3 *Journal of Motor Vehicle Law:* 15.

McInnes, M. 1991. Psychological Perspectives on Rescue: The Behavioral Implications of Using the Law to Increase the Incidence of Emergency Intervention. 20 *Manitoba Law Journal:* 656.

———. 1994. Protecting the Good Samaritan: Defences for the Rescuer in Anglo-Canadian Criminal Law. 36 *Criminal Law Quarterly:* 331.

———. 1994. Restitution and the Rescue of Life. 32 *Alberta Law Review:* 37.

McSherry, B. 1993. Defining What Is a "Disease of the Mind": The Untenability of Current Legal Interpretations. 1 *Journal of Law and Medicine:* 76.

———. 1998. Getting Away with Murder? Dissociative States and Criminal Responsibility, 21 *International Journal of Law and Psychiatry:* 163.

Mewett, A.W. and M. Manning. 1994. *Mewett & Manning on Criminal Law.* 3d ed. Toronto: Butterworths. 125 – 68, 493 – 518.

Ozer, I.J. 1997. The Epilepsy Defence Reconsidered. 33 *Criminal Law Bulletin:* 328.

Packer, H.L. 1968. *The Limits of the Criminal Sanction.* Palo Alto: Stanford University Press.

Stuart, D. 1995. *Canadian Criminal Law.* 3d ed. Toronto: Carswell. 71 – 137.

Stuart, D. and R.J. Delisle. 1995. *Learning Canadian Criminal Law.* 5th ed. Toronto: Carswell. 173 – 282, 667 – 702.

———. 1997. *Learning Canadian Criminal Law.* 6th ed. Toronto: Carswell. 175 – 255.

Swihart, G., J. Yuille, and S. Porter. 1999. The Role of State-Dependent Memory in "Red-Outs," 22 *International Journal of Law and Psychiatry:* 199 – 212.

Usprich, S.J. 1987. A New Crime in Old Battles: Definitional Problems with Sexual Assault. 29 *Criminal Law Quarterly:* 200.

Varn, M. and A. Chandola. 2000. A Cognitive Framework for *Mens Rea* and *Actus Reus:* The Application of Contactics Theory to Criminal Law. 35 *Tulsa Law Journal:* 383.

Verdun-Jones, S.N. 1979. The Evolution of the Defences of Insanity and Automatism in Canada from 1843 – 1979: A Saga of Judicial Reluctance to Sever the Umbilical Chord to the Mother Country? 14 *U.B.C. Law Review:* 1.

———. 1993. The Supreme Court of Canada Examines the Sleep-Walking Defence: *R. v. Parks.* 4 *International Bulletin of Law & Mental Health:* 36.

——— 1999. *Canadian Criminal Cases: Selected Highlights.* Toronto: Harcourt Brace. 27 – 44.

Weinrib, E.J. 1980. The Case for a Duty to Rescue. 90 *Yale Law Journal:* 247.

Yeo, S.M.H. 1991. Recent Australian Pronouncements on the Ordinary Person Test in Provocation and Automatism. 33 *Criminal Law Quarterly:* 280.

Ziegler, M. 2000. Nonfeasance and the Duty to Assist: The American Seinfeld Syndrome. 104 *Dickson Law Review:* 525.

Ziff, B. 1984. A Comment on *R. v. Miller.* 22 *Alberta Law Review:* 281.

Causation in the Criminal Law

OVERVIEW

This chapter examines the following:

1. The fundamental principles of causation that apply in the criminal law, with specific reference to the law of homicide;
2. the requirement that there be a causal connection between the accused's conduct and the consequences prohibited by the criminal law (the "*but for*" test);
3. the requirement of *foreseeability* as a vital element in determining whether an accused should be held accountable for his or her conduct;
4. the legal definition of death and its impact on the situation where the victim is maintained on life-support machinery;
5. the principle that a defendant can be considered to have caused the death of a person, even if the effect of the defendant's actions is only to *accelerate* the victim's death from some other disease or disorder, and the implications of this principle for the medical treatment of terminally ill patients;
6. the criminal responsibility of those who are involved in acts of euthanasia and assisted suicide;
7. the principle that there can be more than one cause of death;
8. the approach adopted by the courts when there is an *intervening act* between the defendant's wounding of a victim and the latter's ultimate demise;

9. the requirement that the defendant's act be a contributing cause to the victim's death "outside the *de minimis* range" (the *Smithers* test of causation);
10. the special rule of causation that applies in relation to first degree murder under section 231(5) of the *Criminal Code* (the *Harbottle* test);
11. the legal principles that are applicable in the situation where a wounded victim is given improper medical treatment and subsequently dies;
12. the problem of determining the cause of death where the victim refuses life-saving medical treatment;
13. the special rules that apply where death has been caused by the impact of the accused's actions upon the *mind* of the victim.

INTRODUCTION

Where an essential element of the **actus reus** of an offence is the occurrence of certain specified consequences, it must be proved that the **defendant's** conduct caused those consequences. In other words, unless the Crown can prove that, *"but for" the accused's conduct the prohibited consequences would never have occurred,* the courts will rule that the accused did not "cause" those consequences and is not criminally responsible for them. As Justice Lambert of the B.C. Court of Appeal put it in *Nette* (1999), a homicide case,

In order for an action or a willed inaction to be a cause of death it must meet the "but for" test, otherwise described as a *causa sine qua non.* If the action or willed inaction does not meet that test then it is not a cause at all of the death.

For example, in the Canadian case of *Cyrenne, Cyrenne and Cramb* (1981), the accused were charged with criminal **negligence** causing death (contrary to section 220 of the Code). Two of the accused were the parents of a twelve-year-old girl, while the third was their religious minister. The girl had become critically ill from a rare blood disease. She was taken to hospital, but when it became clear that the treating physicians intended to give her a blood transfusion, the accused removed her from the hospital. The accused, who were all Jehovah's Witnesses, stated that it was against their religion to permit the giving of blood transfusions and that, in their view, they were of no benefit and possibly harmful from a medical point of view. The trial judge found that the accused were not entitled, as reasonable parents, to deprive their child of emergency medical treatment. In his view, they had acted "in reckless disregard of the life and safety" of the child; in this sense, they had been criminally negligent. However, the charge against the accused was that of criminal negligence *causing death*, and the accused were ultimately acquitted on the ground that the trial judge was not convinced beyond a reasonable doubt that their reckless conduct actually caused the child's death. District Court Judge FitzGerald said in this respect,

> While it is more probable than not that the actions of the three accused persons in preventing Sara Cyrenne from receiving a transfusion caused her death it must also be conceded that it is more than remotely possible that the transfusion might have been ineffective or even fatal. In such circumstances, *I cannot be morally certain that what the accused did or failed to do was what caused the child to die.* There is thus a reasonable doubt and the accused must be acquitted of the charge of criminal negligence. [emphasis added]

Issues of causation generally do not pose major problems for the criminal law since the *mens rea* elements of "**true crimes**" always include the requirement that the accused, or at least a reasonable person in the accused's situation, be able to foresee that their conduct might cause the consequences that are prohibited by law. If the consequences of one's actions are foreseeable, it is relatively simple to conclude that there is a causal link between those actions and their consequences. From another point of view, it might also be pointed out that the requirement of foreseeability ensures that an accused person's criminal responsibility for his or her actions is not unlimited; he or she can only be punished for prohibited consequences that could be foreseen.

The specific nature of the *mens rea* requirement of foreseeability varies with the nature of the offence. Where the offence is one which requires proof of **intention**, the Crown must establish that the accused actually intended to bring about the consequences that are prohibited by law, and an intention to bring about such consequences necessarily implies that they are foreseen by the accused. Similarly, if the offence is one that imposes liability for reckless behaviour, the Crown must prove that the accused foresaw the risk that his or her conduct would cause the prohibited consequences. Finally, where offences that impose liability for criminal negligence are concerned, the Crown must prove that a reasonable person, with the knowledge that the accused had of the relevant circumstances, would have foreseen that his or her conduct would cause the consequences forbidden by the criminal law.

Although the requirement of foreseeability has generally rendered the issue of causation a relatively simple one for the courts to determine, it is nevertheless important to note that there are some instances in the *Criminal Code* where Parliament has given a special meaning to the concept of causation. Take, for example, section 436 of the Code, which creates the offence of "arson by negligence":

(1) Every person who owns, in whole or in part, or controls property is guilty of an indictable

offence and liable to imprisonment for a term not exceeding five years where, as a result of a marked departure from the standard of care that a reasonably prudent person would use to prevent or control the spread of fires or to prevent explosions, *that person is a cause of a fire or explosion in that property* that causes bodily harm to another person or damage to property.

(2) Where a person is charged with an offence under subsection (1), the fact that the person has failed to comply with any law respecting the prevention or control of fires or explosions in the property is a fact from which a marked departure from the standard of care referred to in that subsection may be inferred by the court. [emphasis added]

Clearly, section 436 imposes criminal liability on the basis of a most unusual concept of causation. The layperson would be most unlikely to say that an accused person had "caused" a fire or committed "arson" when, for example, the latter has not started a fire but has failed to install a proper sprinkler system as required by the municipal by-law concerned. However, section 436 does provide that the accused is "a cause" of the fire in such circumstances if the failure to install the sprinkler system *caused the fire to spread.*

The application of section 436 is illustrated by the case of *Harricharan* (1995), in which the accused was charged with arson by negligence following a fire that destroyed his house. There was no evidence whatsoever that the accused started the fire. He woke up in the early hours of the morning to the sound of a loud bang. He ran to a window and observed smoke and flames coming through his garage. He then rushed to the kitchen in order to use the telephone to summon the fire brigade. He, unfortunately, lived in a rural area in which the 911 emergency number was not available, and he could not locate the seven-digit number that he needed to call for assistance. Meanwhile, the kitchen was filling up with smoke, so he ran back upstairs and started to remove var-

ious important items from his home and put them in a nearby barn. The accused was confused and eventually became so tired that he just collapsed in the barn and was lying there when the fire trucks eventually arrived.

The nearest neighbour to the accused's home was about a five-minute run away. It seems that, about 90 minutes after the fire started, a neighbour had seen the flames and smoke and had called the fire brigade. However, by the time the fire fighters arrived, the accused's house had been totally destroyed. The trial judge determined that the accused was not responsible for starting the fire (the cause of which was never identified), but he convicted the accused of the offence under section 436. In the view of the trial judge, this section imposed a duty on the accused to prevent the spread of the fire and the accused had violated this duty by saving personal items from the house rather than running to a neighbour's house to call the fire brigade. According to the trial judge, the accused's conduct amounted to a "marked departure from the standard of the reasonably prudent person" within the meaning of section 436(1).

Significantly, the trial judge ruled that there was no burden on the Crown to prove that the fire would not have spread even if the accused had run to his neighbour's house to seek help and even if the fire brigade had come as quickly as possible. In his view, it was enough for the Crown to establish that the accused was under a duty to prevent the spread of the fire and that he had not shown that he was physically or mentally incapacitated from going to his neighbour's house for help. In essence, the trial judge convicted the accused without requiring the Crown to establish a causal connection between the accused's failure to summon the fire brigade and the spread of the fire.

The Ontario Court of Appeal set aside Harricharan's conviction and entered an **acquittal**. All of the justices of the Court agreed that the trial judge had made a fundamental error of interpretation when he ruled that, under the provisions of section 436, the Crown did not have to establish that the fire would not have spread even if the accused had gone to his neighbour for help. Indeed, according to Associate Chief Justice Morden, section 436 "clearly requires proof of a causal connection between the accused's breach, the resulting spread, and the injury or damage." The Chief Justice made some instructive comments about the nature of an accused person's liability under section 436:

> This provision imposes a duty to prevent or *control the spread* of fires. This carries with it the clear implication that the fire may have been originally caused by some agency other than that of the accused. The act or omission which is part of the *actus reus* must be something that is a breach of this duty. The section provides that where, as a result of the breach of this duty on the part of the accused, the accused is *a cause* of a fire in property owned or controlled by the accused which, in turn, causes bodily harm to another person or damage to property, he or she is guilty of the offence. The section is concerned with "a fire" which, through spreading, causes bodily harm or damage to property. *The term "a cause" is significant. It recognizes that other "causes" may be contributing factors to the origin or spread of the fire.* [emphasis added]

Later on in his judgment, the Associate Chief Justice noted that

> *The accused, as a result of a breach of the duty [under s. 436], may be "a cause" of the spread of a fire that, in turn, causes bodily harm or damage. He is, therefore, "a cause" of a fire that causes injury or damage.* [emphasis added]

Clearly, the *Harricharan* case (1995) illustrates the fact that, although Parliament has the power to expand the concept of causation to include a failure to prevent the spread of a fire, the Crown will, nevertheless, be required to establish some form of causal connection between the accused's failure to act and the prohibited consequences. Insofar as section 436 is concerned, this means that there must

be proof that the accused's negligence actually contributed to the spread of the fire.

SPECIFIC RULES CONCERNING CAUSATION IN HOMICIDE CASES

Perhaps because of the severe nature of the crimes concerned, there are a number of special rules concerning the issue of causation in relation to such offences as **murder**, **manslaughter**, **infanticide**, criminal negligence causing death, dangerous driving causing death, and impaired driving causing death. We shall examine these rules in some depth.

The Definition of Death for the Purposes of the Criminal Law

It almost goes without saying that, in order to convict an accused person of murder, manslaughter, infanticide, or impaired/dangerous driving causing death, the Crown must prove that the victim was, in fact, *dead* after the accused inflicted injuries on him or her. In the vast majority of cases, criminal courts have no difficulty deciding when a human being has died. If an individual has ceased breathing and the heart has stopped beating (and normal resuscitation procedures, if appropriate, fail to work), then it is clear that he or she is dead. However, in today's hospitals, it is possible to use life-support machines that artificially maintain heart and circulatory functions, and the application of this medical technology can potentially create some difficulties for criminal courts that are faced with the problem of pinpointing the moment when a patient can legitimately be considered dead.

Suppose, for example, that Brutus inflicts a severe head injury on Julius in the course of a robbery. When Julius is taken to hospital, the doctors immediately conclude that, without the use of life-support machinery, he will not be able to breathe or maintain the circulation of blood in his body. After Julius is hooked up to a life-support machine, the attending medical practitioners decide that he has suffered such a massive brain injury that he is "clinically dead." Julius's next of kin is consulted and the life-support machine is switched off by his physician. Could Brutus turn around at his trial and claim that, since the life-support machine could have maintained Julius's respiratory and circulatory functions on an indefinite basis, there is no evidence that he killed Julius and that, in fact, it was the physician's act of flicking the switch that was the act that really precipitated death? The answer to Brutus's argument would be that, if the doctors' diagnosis was that Julius had suffered "*total, irreversible brain death*," then he was "*dead*" from the point of view of modern medical science and switching off the life-support machine was merely a recognition of that tragic reality; hence, Brutus could not claim that Julius was still alive when the artificial life support was withdrawn.

Unfortunately, to date, Parliament has not kept pace with modern medical technology and has not defined "death" for the purposes of the criminal law. However, the Law Reform Commission of Canada recommended, some two decades ago, that death should be defined in legislation in a manner that is consistent with modern medical developments. More precisely, the commission advocated the adoption of the following definition: "a person is dead when an irreversible cessation of all that person's brain functions has occurred." In its 1981 report, *Criteria for the Determination of Death*, the commission recommended that the Canadian Parliament amend the *Interpretation Act*, R.S.C. 1985, c. I-21, so as to contain the following provision:

For all purposes within the jurisdiction of the Parliament of Canada,

(1) a person is dead when an irreversible cessation of all that person's brain functions has occurred.

(2) the irreversible cessation of brain functions can be determined by the prolonged absence of spontaneous circulatory and respiratory functions.

 (3) when the determination of the prolonged absence of spontaneous circulatory and respiratory functions is made impossible by the use of artificial means of support, the irreversible cessation of brain functions can be determined *by any means recognized by the ordinary standards of medical practice*. [emphasis added]

Where an individual is *not* connected to a life-support machine, death will be determined on the basis of whether breathing or blood circulation is still taking place. For example, if A and B both shoot C within seconds of each other, there may be a question as to whether C was still alive between the shot by A and the shot by B. If there is some bleeding from the gunshot wound inflicted by B then it is clear that C was still alive at the moment that B pulled the trigger.

A sophisticated medical technology has been developed to determine whether an individual who is on life support has suffered total brain death, and various protocols have been developed to provide guidance to physicians who are called upon to make this determination. However, these protocols usually require that the same medical tests be repeated at an interval of 24 hours or so in order to ensure that the patient really has suffered total brain death rather than, for example, a temporary reaction to a drug that causes a major depression of the nervous system. This means it takes a considerable time before it can be determined beyond question that total brain death has occurred when the patient is being kept artificially alive by life-support machines.

Adoption of the Law Reform Commission's definition of death would clearly resolve any uncertainty that currently exists in Canada.

Until 1999, the *Criminal Code* (section 227) maintained the archaic rule that an accused person could not be convicted of an offence of homicide unless the death of the victim occurred "within one year and one day from the time of the occurrence of the last event by means of which (he/she) caused or contributed to the cause of death." Centuries ago, this old **common law** rule made some sense insofar as the relatively primitive state of medical science rendered it very difficult for the Crown to prove that there was the necessary causal link if a victim were to linger for a long period. However, today, modern medicine is much better equipped to establish such a link and, for this reason, Parliament repealed section 227 in 1999 (S.C., c. 5, s. 9(1)). Furthermore, it may be noted that the repeal of section 227 has the effect of forestalling the creation of a situation in which a court may be compelled to acquit an accused person of a homicide offence simply because the victim had been on life-support machinery for a period that is greater than one year and a day. Under the current law, this issue now becomes utterly irrelevant.

Acceleration of Death

A most significant legal principle relating to causation is enshrined in section 226 of the Code:

> Where a person causes to a human being a bodily injury that results in death, he causes the death of that human being notwithstanding that the effect of the bodily injury is only to *accelerate his death* from a disease or disorder arising from some other cause. [emphasis added]

It is clear that a murderer should not be excused from punishment for his heinous act merely because the victim was, for example, a terminal patient who had only a few more weeks to live. However, the operation of section 226 becomes more problematic when it is considered in the context of the treatment of the terminally ill by legitimate medical practitioners. If a physician administers a lethal dose of a drug with the clear intention of carrying out a so-called "mercy killing," he or she is guilty of murder; **euthanasia** is certainly not permitted under Canadian law (see section 14 of the *Criminal Code*, which clearly states that "no person is entitled to consent to have death inflicted upon

him" and that the criminal liability of the person who inflicts death, in such circumstances, is not affected by the giving of such consent). However, what is the situation where the physician administers a drug with the explicit intention of reducing the agony suffered by a terminal patient but, nevertheless, realizes that this treatment may have the incidental effect of hastening death? This issue was considered in the English case of *Bodkin Adams* (1957). In his summing-up to the jury, Justice Devlin said

> murder was an act or series of acts, done by the prisoner, which were intended to kill, and did in fact kill. It did not matter whether Mrs. Morrell's death was inevitable and that her days were numbered. If her life were cut short by weeks or months it was just as much murder as if it was cut short by years. There had been a good deal of discussion as to the circumstances in which doctors might be justified in administering drugs which would shorten life. Cases of severe pain were suggested and also cases of helpless misery. The law knew of no special defence in this category, but that did not mean that a doctor who was aiding the sick and dying had to calculate in minutes or even hours, perhaps not in days or weeks, the effect on a patient's life of the medicines which he would administer. If the first purpose of medicine—the restoration of health—could no longer be achieved, there was still much for the doctor to do, and *he was entitled to do all that was proper and necessary to relieve pain and suffering even if the measures he took might incidentally shorten life by hours or perhaps even longer.* The doctor who decided whether or not to administer the drug could not do this job if he were thinking in terms of hours or months of life. The defence in the present case was that the treatment given by Dr. Adams was designed to promote comfort, and if it was the right and proper treatment, the fact that it shortened life did not convict him of murder. [emphasis added]

Dr. Adams was subsequently acquitted. It is most likely that a Canadian court, faced with the same circumstances, would adopt the approach taken by Justice Devlin in the *Adams* case. It is particularly noteworthy that Justice Sopinka explicitly approved the principle contained in *Adams*, when he delivered the majority judgment of the Supreme Court of Canada in the *Rodriguez* case (1993):

> The administration of drugs designed for pain control in dosages which the physician knows will hasten death constitutes active contribution to death by any standard. However, *the distinction here is one based on intention—in the case of palliative care the intention is to ease pain, which has the effect of hastening death, while in the case of assisted suicide, the intention is undeniably to cause death ...*
> In my view, distinctions based on intent are important, and in fact form the basis of our criminal law. [emphasis added]

It is important to emphasize that a physician does not commit murder where he or she acts on a request by a competent, adult patient to *withdraw treatment* and death ensues as a consequence. In fact, the physician is required to withdraw treatment in these circumstances since every competent adult has the right to refuse treatment even if such a refusal results in death. For example, in the case of *Nancy B. v. Hôtel-Dieu de Québec* (1992), Nancy B. was a 25-year-old woman who had suffered for two and a half years from an incurable neurological disorder, known as Guillain-Barré syndrome. She was totally paralyzed and depended on a respirator to keep her alive. She knew that her condition could not be reversed and decided that she would rather die than continue her life "literally tied to her hospital bed." She sought a court order directing the hospital and her physician to disconnect the respirator.

Justice Dufour, of the Québec Superior Court, determined that Nancy B. was competent to make decisions for herself and that she, therefore, had a right to refuse treatment. The physician was given permission to disconnect the respirator. Nancy B. later died after the physician carried out her request.

However, a physician may not give assistance to a patient who wishes to commit suicide. Indeed, section 241(b) of the *Criminal Code* states that it is an **indictable** offence to aid or abet a person to commit suicide. Is section 241(b) valid under the *Charter*? The Supreme Court of Canada has answered this question in the affirmative.

In the *Rodriguez* case (1993), a 42-year-old woman who was dying from amyotrophic lateral sclerosis (a degenerative disease of the muscles), sought a declaration that she had a right, under the *Charter*, to have assistance from a physician in committing suicide when her life become no long bearable. Her condition was deteriorating rapidly and, at some point, she would be completely unable to move. Her life expectancy was between two and fourteen months. The Supreme Court of Canada ultimately rejected the assertion that, under the terms of the *Charter*, a terminally ill person has the right to an assisted suicide and upheld the validity of section 241(b).

In the *Rodriguez* case, the Supreme Court recognized that section 241(b) effectively deprived Sue Rodriguez of her autonomy and caused her both physical pain and psychological distress. However, a bare majority of the justices (five to four) held that section 241(b) was nevertheless valid because it reflected the principle of the sanctity of life. More specifically, it did not infringe the rights of Sue Rodriguez under section 7 (right to security of the person), section 12 (right to be free from cruel and unusual punishment), or section 15 (right to equality) of the *Charter*. According to Justice Sopinka, speaking for the majority of the justices,

> Section 241(b) has as its purpose the protection of the vulnerable who might be induced in moments of weakness to commit suicide. This purpose is grounded in the state interest in protecting life and reflects a policy of the state that human life should not be depreciated by allowing life to be taken. This policy finds expression not only in the provisions of our *Criminal Code* which prohibit murder and other violent acts against others notwithstanding the consent of the victim but also in the

policy against capital punishment and, until its repeal, attempted suicide. This is not only a policy of the state, however, but is part of our fundamental conception of the sanctity of human life.

According to Justice Sopinka, a blanket prohibition of suicide (such as that contained in section 241(b)) "is the norm among western democracies, and such a prohibition has never been adjudged to be unconstitutional or contrary to fundamental human rights." In his view, "to permit a physician to lawfully participate in taking life would send a signal that there are circumstances in which the state approves of suicide."

It is not entirely clear that the strong legal distinction that Justice Sopinka draws between the situations that pertained in the cases of *Nancy B.* and *Rodriguez* is quite as logically compelling as he suggests. Nancy B. could only die *with the assistance of her physician,* who ultimately turned off the respirator because her patient was physically incapable of doing it herself. Was this not a case of physician-assisted suicide? It is no doubt true that, in Nancy B.'s case, one can argue that it was her terrible disease that killed her through suffocation, whereas in Sue Rodriguez's case, it would have been the overdose of drugs that would have brought about her death. However, let us suppose entirely by way of hypothesis that another physician switched off the respirator *without Nancy B.'s consent.* Would we not say, in these circumstances, that it was the physician who caused the patient's death? After all, Nancy B. would have survived indefinitely if the machine had continued to operate. Most of us would have little difficulty in determining that the hypothetical, rogue physician committed murder by switching off the machine against the patient's will. In this sense, it was the physician's act that was the immediate cause of death. However, in the real-life case of *Nancy B.,* can one deny that the physician's conduct in turning off the switch was a cause of the patient's death (it, at least, *accelerated* Nancy B.'s death)? If the act of switching off the machine is a contributing cause of death, then one could make the argument that Nancy B. was granted a right to a physician-assisted

suicide. However, Sue Rodriguez was denied the right to a physician-assisted suicide because she was seeking the right to die by means of an overdose of drugs rather than by switching off a respirator. There is clearly a difference between the facts in *Nancy B.* and *Rodriguez,* but does this difference justify granting one patient a right to commit suicide with the assistance of her physician but denying it to another? Ironically, Nancy B. might have survived for many years on the respirator but Sue Rodriguez's days were very limited. This is not to argue that Nancy B. should have been forced to live on, contrary to her wishes. Indeed, it is a fundamental principle of Canadian law that no doctor can continue to administer any form of treatment if a mentally competent patient refuses to give consent. What is being suggested is that Sue Rodriguez should have been granted the same option as Nancy B. and that, perhaps, the justifications for upholding section 241(b) of the Code are not quite as overwhelming as the majority judgment of the Supreme Court of Canada would appear to suggest. Undoubtedly, this whole issue is complex and will remain a source of profound disagreement among many Canadians.

Liability of the Accused Where There Is More Than One Cause of Death

One principle of causation that is frequently misunderstood concerns the proposition that the defendant's act does not have to be the "sole" cause of the victim's death in order to convict him or her of culpable homicide. For example, let us suppose that Desmond strikes and wounds Vincent, who subsequently dies from massive internal hemorrhaging. Medical evidence establishes that Vincent was a hemophiliac and that the wound inflicted by Desmond would not have caused the death of a person who was not suffering from this medical condition. Desmond cannot claim that, because hemophilia was a significant "cause" of death, he should be excused from liability for culpable homicide. In other words, while both Desmond's wounding of Vincent and the latter's hemophilia each contributed to his demise, Desmond is still liable to punishment. Depending on his intention, at the time of the wounding, Desmond will be convicted of murder or manslaughter. This example also illustrates the principle that aggressors must "take their victims as they find them." They cannot point to their victims' physical weaknesses as an excuse for their homicidal acts.

This principle was dramatically illustrated in the tragic case of *Smithers* (1977). In *Smithers*, the accused was charged with manslaughter. He was a member of a "midget hockey" team; the deceased, Cobby, had been a member of an opposing team that had been playing Smithers's team on the day of the incident in question. Smithers had been subjected to racial insults by Cobby and others. Smithers and Cobby were later given game misconducts following a "heated and abusive exchange of profanities." Smithers threatened to "get" Cobby, who was very apprehensive as a consequence. When the latter tried to leave the arena, Smithers pursued him. Cobby hurried towards a waiting car but Smithers caught up with him and "directed one or two punches" to his head. Smithers's team mates intervened and grabbed him. However, he managed to deliver a hard, fast kick to Cobby's stomach (the latter had been making no effort to defend himself). Seconds after this kick, Cobby collapsed, gasping for air. He stopped breathing and was dead upon his arrival in hospital. It was found that Cobby had died as a result of the "aspiration of foreign materials present from vomiting." Normally, when an individual vomits, the epiglottis functions so as to cover the windpipe, thus preventing the stomach contents from entering the air passage. For some reason, this mechanism failed in Cobby's case.

Smithers was convicted of manslaughter and ultimately his **appeal** went to the Supreme Court of Canada, where the central issue was that of causation. Smithers's **counsel** argued that there was insufficient evidence that the accused's kick caused the vomiting. On this issue, Justice Dickson made the observation that

it may be shortly said that there was a very substantial body of evidence, both expert and lay, before the jury indicating that the kick was at least a contributing cause, outside the *de minimis* range, and that is all that the Crown was required to establish. *It is immaterial that the death was in part caused by a malfunctioning epiglottis to which malfunction the appellant may, or may not, have contributed.* [emphasis added]

Later in his judgment, Justice Dickson stated that it is a "well-recognized principle that one who assaults another must take his victim as he finds him." Ultimately, Smithers's appeal was dismissed.

Of course, while the accused's act need not be the "sole" cause of death, it must nevertheless, as the *Smithers* case stipulated, be "outside the *de minimis* range" (i.e., it must be shown to have had more than a *minimal* impact on the events leading to the victim's death). Another way of putting this is that the accused's conduct must make a "more than negligible contribution" to the victim's death. Clearly, if an accused person inflicts a minor wound on a victim, who is subsequently given a grave wound by a third party, the impact of the minor wound would be considered to be within the *de minimis* range and the accused would, therefore, not be held criminally responsible for causing the death of the victim, should the latter die. In these particular circumstances, a court would hold that the sole cause of death was the wound by the third party.

The broad reach of the *Smithers* test is well-illustrated by the extraordinary circumstances that were revealed in the case of *Meiler* (1999). The accused was convinced that his wife, from whom he was separated, was "seeing" a man called Roach and he later admitted that he decided to kill Roach and then commit suicide. He took a loaded shotgun, cocked it, and put his finger on the trigger with the intention of killing Roach. It appeared that one Skrinjaric intercepted Meiler and jumped on his back. There was a struggle for the gun, which tragically discharged and killed Nick Biuk, who was standing close by. Meiler was charged with second-degree murder (on the basis of section 229(c) of the Code—discussed later in Chapter 4). One of the central issues was whether Meiler could be said to have "caused" the victim's death. Applying the *Smithers* test, the Ontario Court of Appeal appears to have experienced no difficulty in answering this particular question in the affirmative. As Justice O'Connor noted, in delivering the judgment of the court:

> Clearly there can be more than one cause of death. The test in *Smithers* does not restrict the test of causation to the most proximate, the primary or the only cause of death. *It simply requires that the act in issue be at least a contributing cause.*
>
> … The appellant was physically linked to the discharge of the gun. He brought it to the scene, loaded it, cocked it, put his finger on the trigger and was holding it at the time it was discharged. There can be no doubt that but for the appellant's acts Biuk would not have been fatally shot. *His acts were a contributing cause of the death.* [emphasis added]

In the case of *Pinske* (1988), the Supreme Court of Canada, not only reaffirmed the authority of the *Smithers* test of causation, but also rejected the suggestion that the Crown must prove that the accused's conduct was a *substantial* cause of death. In a motor vehicle case involving a charge of criminal negligence causing death, the B.C. Court of Appeal ruled that, in line with the rule in the *Smithers* case, there could be a conviction of the accused provided his or her criminally negligent conduct was at least a contributing cause outside the *de minimis* range. Significantly, the Court of Appeal held that there had been a misdirection on the part of the trial judge, who had instructed the jury that the accused's driving behaviour had to be a "substantial cause of the accident and not just a minimal or insignificant cause." The Supreme Court of Canada upheld the judgment of the B.C. Court of Appeal without giving reasons.

The judgments in the *Smithers* and *Pinske* cases are somewhat troublesome, since the rule of causation that they have articulated can result in the conviction of an accused person even where his or her contribution to the death of the victim is comparatively minor. The *Smithers* test, as reaffirmed in *Pinske*, is particularly problematic in cases where driving conduct contributes in some way to the death of a victim. In such cases, charges of criminal negligence causing death, dangerous driving causing death, or impaired driving causing death may be laid, and if the accused person's conduct contributes to the death of someone in even a relatively minor way, there will nevertheless be a conviction, provided that his or her contribution is more than negligible in nature. Such a conviction could be imposed even if there were other—far more serious—causes of the traffic "accident" that led to the victim's death. There is, therefore, a serious question whether the *Smithers* rule is a just one in such circumstances.

Perhaps owing to the growing judicial awareness of the potential injustice of applying the *Smithers* rule to the (often) complex set of factors that may be involved when a traffic accident occurs, provincial courts of appeal in both Alberta and Saskatchewan have insisted that the Crown must always be required to prove that the accused's driving constituted a "real factor" in the chain of causation that led to the death of the victim. For example, in delivering the judgment of the Alberta Court of Appeal in the case of *Ewart* (1990), Justice McClung said that, however broad the *Smithers* test of causation may be, it still requires that the Crown prove that *"the underlying dangerous driving or impaired driving"* was *"a real factor in bringing about any bodily harm or death. … A dangerous or impaired driver in the vicinity without any more is not enough."*

In *Ewart*, the accused was charged with several offences, including impaired driving causing death, dangerous driving causing death, and impaired driving causing bodily harm. The accused attempted to pass a car that he was following. He pulled out, but when he saw that he would not be able to pass in time, he pulled back into his lane. Unfortunately, the driver of a car travelling in the opposite direction misjudged the distance between herself and the accused and applied her brakes. The road was icy and the car swerved onto the shoulder and then into the path of the car that the accused had earlier attempted to pass. In the ensuing accident, one person was killed and two others injured. The trial judge acquitted the accused of all the offences, except that of impaired driving, on the basis that he had not *caused* the accident that led to the death and bodily harm; indeed, in the view of the trial judge, the "driving action of the accused was insignificant" in this respect. The Alberta Court of Appeal subsequently dismissed an appeal by the Crown against the acquittals. Justice McClung asserted that

> I can agree ... that on the evidence the operation of the Ewart vehicle was the traceable origin of Mrs. Rossman's reaction and the ensuing collision. But that does not cast Ewart's attempt to pass as criminal. ... In a court applying criminal sanction [*sic*] it is doubtful whether any driver can become, by operation of law alone, an insurer against extreme and unforeseeable responses of other users of the road.

Given the extremely broad net that is cast by the *Smithers* test, the question arises as to whether it is invalid under the *Charter*. In the case of *Cribbin* (1994), the Ontario Court of Appeal answered this question in the negative. In delivering the judgment of the court, Justice Arbour contended that the *Smithers* test of causation did not infringe the fundamental principles of justice enshrined in section 7 of the *Charter*. It did not set too low a standard of fault, and it was not so vague as to be unconstitutional. In Justice Arbour's view, causation is a concept that is embodied in the fundamental principle of justice that the "morally innocent should not be punished":

> [this principle] requires that the law should refrain from holding a person criminally responsible for consequences that should not be attributed to him or her. This is because criminal causation as a legal rule is based on concepts of moral responsibility, rather than on demonstrable mechanical or scientific formulas. ...

However, Justice Arbour emphasized that the issue of causation cannot be considered in isolation from the requisite elements of *mens rea* that must be proved by the Crown. The *Cribbin* case involved a charge of manslaughter. The *mens rea,* or fault, element that the Crown would have to prove in such a case is *objective* in nature, namely, that the accused "committed an unlawful dangerous act in *circumstances where a reasonable person would have foreseen the risk of bodily harm which is neither trivial nor transitory.*" The causation element of the *actus reus* of manslaughter is that "the unlawful act is at least a contributing cause of the victim's death, outside the *de minimis* range." Justice Arbour went on to say that

> Both causation and the fault element must be proved beyond a reasonable doubt before the prosecution can succeed. *Combined in that fashion, both requirements satisfy the principles of fundamental justice in that any risk that the* de minimis *test could engage the criminal responsibility of the morally innocent is removed by the additional requirement of objective foresight.* [emphasis added]

Although the *Cribbin* case (1994) held that the *Smithers* test of causation is valid under the *Charter* where the accused is charged with manslaughter or other less serious offences, it is highly significant that the Supreme Court of Canada has ruled, in the case of *Harbottle* (1993), that the test is not strict enough when the accused is charged with the offence of **first degree murder** under section 231(5). Normally, the Crown must prove that a murder was "planned and deliberate" if the accused is to be convicted of first degree murder (see section

231(2) of the Code). However, section 231(5) of the Code stipulates that murder will automatically be treated as first degree murder where death occurs in the course of the commission (or attempted commission) of certain (very serious) offences:

Irrespective of whether a murder is planned and deliberate on the part of any person, murder is first degree murder in respect of a person when the death is caused by that person while committing or attempting to commit an offence under one of the following sections:

(a) section 76 (hijacking an aircraft);

(b) section 271 (sexual assault);

(c) section 272 (sexual assault with a weapon, threats to a third party, or causing bodily harm);

(d) section 273 (aggravated sexual assault);

(e) section 279 (kidnapping and forcible confinement);

(f) section 179.1 (hostage taking).

In *Harbottle,* the accused and another man had participated in a sexual assault of a seventeen-year-old woman and then discussed how they could kill her. The other man eventually strangled the victim with her brassière while Harbottle held her legs in order to prevent her from resisting the deadly attack on her. The victim died and Harbottle was charged with first degree murder. The Crown relied on section 231(5) of the Code in light of the fact that the victim had died in the course of a sexual assault. The question arose as to whether the *Smithers* test of causation was adequate in the context of a first degree murder charge. The Supreme Court of Canada ruled that, while the *Smithers* test was adequate for a charge of manslaughter, it was not strict enough for a charge of first degree murder. However, the Court did not rely on the *Charter* in arriving at this conclusion. Rather, it referred to the seriousness of the consequences of a conviction of first degree murder and to the specific wording of section 231(5). In delivering the judgment of the Court, Justice Cory noted that

The consequences of a conviction for first degree murder and the wording of the section are such that the test of causation for [s. 231(5)] must be a strict one. In my view, an accused may only be convicted under the subsection if the Crown establishes that *the accused has committed an act or series of acts which are of such a nature that they must be regarded as a substantial and integral cause of the death....*

The substantial causation test requires that the accused play a very active role—usually a physical role—in the killing. Under [s. 231(5)], the actions of the accused must form an essential, substantial and integral part of the killing of the victim. ...

According to Justice Cory, the evidence in the *Harbottle* case clearly established that the accused "was a substantial and an integral cause of the death" of the victim:

There is every reason to believe that, had it not been for Harbottle's holding of her legs, she would have been able to resist the attempts to strangle her. In those circumstances, it is difficult to believe that Ross could have strangled her in the absence of the assistance of Harbottle.

It is particularly noteworthy that, in referring to the *Smithers* case, Justice Cory openly acknowledged that the test of causation for manslaughter reflected a lower standard than the test for first degree murder. However, he appears to have accepted the view that, in homicide cases, there may be different tests of causation, depending on the seriousness of the charge. Certainly, it remains to be seen whether the Supreme Court of Canada will confine the application of the more rigorous *Harbottle* test of causation solely to *first degree* murder charges that fall within the purview of section 231(5) of the Code. No doubt, some defendants may argue that the *Harbottle* test should be applied to *all* charges of *first degree* murder or even to charges of *second degree* **murder** as well.

...wever, the appellate courts of Ontario ...lumbia have ruled that the more rig-...us *Harbottle* test does *not* apply to charges of *second degree* murder (although neither court settled the question of whether it should be extended to cover all forms of *first degree* murder). For example, in *Meiler* (1999), Justice O'Connor stated, on behalf of the Ontario Court of Appeal, that

> Although *Harbottle* does not specifically say that the causation test for murder under s. 229 is the same as that set out in *Smithers*, the reasoning in *Harbottle* leads towards that conclusion. The court held that the more restrictive test of substantial cause reflects a higher degree of blameworthiness for first degree murder than for murder, thereby implying that there is a less restrictive causation test for murder that is not first degree. Further, the court made the obvious point that the substantial test is higher than the contributing cause test in *Smithers* ...
>
> ... I am of the view that the causation test laid down in *Smithers* is the proper test under s. 229 ...

Similarly, in *Nette* (1999), Justice Lambert, of the B.C. Court of Appeal, held that the *Smithers* test applied to charges of second degree murder. It is particularly noteworthy, however, that Justice Lambert thought that the existing form of the *Smithers* test—namely, "a contributing cause beyond *de minimis*," should be reworded since the Latin terminology might confuse juries. In the view of this appellate judge,

> ... the *Smithers* standard is a "contributing cause that is not trivial or insignificant."... A cause that it not insignificant is a cause that is significant. So I consider it accurate to describe the *Smithers* standard as "a significant contributing cause." However, it is possible that the same standard is more comprehensible when cast in the negative, as "a contributing cause that is not trivial or insignificant."

In Justice Lambert's view, the "significant contributing cause" (or "contributing cause that is not insignificant") standard of causation applies to *both manslaughter and second degree murder charges* in Canada. Furthermore, Justice Lambert rejected the view that the *Smithers* test was unfair to the accused:

> I consider that the significant contributing cause test is legally sound in relation to the offence of murder, and that *it is not inconsistent with the objectives of the criminal law in relation to moral blameworthiness.* [emphasis added]

This final comment would appear to suggest that it would be very difficult for an accused person to successfully launch a *Charter* challenge to the *Smithers* rule—even as it applies to the extremely serious crime of murder (as noted earlier, in the *Cribbin* case (1994), the Ontario Court of Appeal has already held that the *Smithers* test does *not* infringe the *Charter* insofar as it applies to *manslaughter*).

The Problem of Intervening Acts

Some of the most challenging issues of causation in the criminal law relating to homicide undoubtedly arise when there is an *intervening act or event* that occurs between the defendant's original wounding of the victim and the latter's subsequent death. Suppose that Adonis stabs Jason with a pocket knife and that, three minutes later, Hercules arrives on the scene and strangles Jason to death. In terms of the criminal responsibility of Adonis, there is a very real issue of causation: namely, did the intervening act of Hercules sever the chain of causation between the original stab wound inflicted by Adonis and Jason's subsequent death? What principles do the courts turn to when confronted by such difficult questions?

We have seen that the *Smithers* case (1977) established that an accused person generally cannot be convicted of a homicide offence unless his or her conduct made a *more than negligible contribution* to the victim's death. However, in the context of a case involving an intervening act or event, the Crown must also show that the original wound was "operative" (or having some impact) at the time of the victim's death if the accused is to be rendered criminally responsible for homicide. In other words, in the hypothetical case outlined above, the Crown would have to establish that the original stab wound was more than a trivial wound and that it was operative or actually contributing to Jason's death at the time he expired.

The application of these principles is neatly illustrated in Canadian case of *Kitching and Adams* (1976), in which the defendants were charged with causing the death of a man called Junor by an unlawful act, thereby committing manslaughter. At their trial, they were convicted of this offence. They then appealed to the Manitoba Court of Appeal. The defendants had caused the infliction of severe brain injuries upon the victim by dropping him on the sidewalk while he was in a state of extreme intoxication. Junor was taken to hospital and attached to a respirator. A neurologist determined that Junor, who was unable to breathe on his own, had suffered complete brain death. However, the respirator continued to maintain the victim's bodily functions until his kidneys could be removed for transplant purposes. After removal of the kidneys, the respirator was switched off. Upon their appeal, Kitching and Adams contended that the removal of the kidneys caused Junor's death, and that the conduct of the doctors, in effecting this removal, broke the chain of causation between their conduct and Junor's tragic death. However, as one might have expected, this contention was rejected by the Court of Appeal. For example, Justice O'Sullivan said,

> I think that counsel for the accused proceeded on a fundamental misconception of the law. They assumed that, if it could be shown that death resulted in this case from the removal of the kidneys, then the accused should be acquitted because there would be a reasonable doubt that they had been the cause of death.
>
> The assumption underlying counsel's conduct in this case is that there can be only one cause of death. *I think the law is that the conduct of a defendant in a criminal trial need not be shown to be the sole or "the effective" cause of a crime. It is sufficient if it is a cause. ... [emphasis added]*

I think the authorities are clear that there may be two or more independent operative causes of death.

Without in this case criticizing the doctors of Health Sciences Centre or suggesting that they were guilty of any improper conduct, I am of the opinion that their conduct was irrelevant to the questions before the jury. Even if it could be shown that the actions of the doctors constituted an operative cause of Mr. Junor's death—and I emphasize that I do not suggest that the evidence would support such a conclusion—still that would not exonerate the accused unless the evidence left a reasonable doubt that the accused's actions also constituted an operative cause of the deceased's death.

On that question, the evidence was overwhelming. Whether or not the kidneys had been removed, the deceased could not have lasted more than a short period of time even with artificial assistance.

In effect, the court held that, even if the removal of the kidneys did constitute an operative cause of death, *the actions of the doctors had not broken the chain of causation* between the defendant's conduct and Junor's death: the massive brain injury was contributing to Junor's death beyond any reasonable doubt. It was irrelevant that the doctors' conduct might have contributed to Junor's death as well, since there can be more than one legal cause of death.

Of course, there may be situations in which an intervening act does operate to sever the causal chain between the conduct of the accused and the ultimate death of the victim. For example, suppose that Villain poisons his elderly uncle, Moneybags, in order to gain the latter's fortune prematurely. However, before the poison has any serious effect, Moneybags is attacked by his demented butler, Grovel. In the attack, Grovel cuts Moneybags's throat with a sword taken from Moneybags's collection of weapons. Moneybags dies within five minutes of the attack. In these circumstances, it is clear that the intervening act (the attack by Grovel) was so overwhelming in its impact that it broke the causal chain between Villain's poisoning of Moneybags and the latter's untimely demise. Of course, Villain would be guilty instead of *attempted* murder.

Slightly different considerations apply when the victim dies as a result of *some subsequent act or event that would not have occurred but for the accused's action in wounding him or her.* In these circumstances, the liability of the accused will depend upon *whether the victim's death from the subsequent act or event can be viewed as a "natural consequence" of the accused's conduct.* In other words, the question is, Would a reasonable person have foreseen the likelihood of the victim's death from the subsequent act or event? For example, in *Bradley* (1956), the accused attacked his victim, who fell unconscious to the pavement of a city street. Unfortunately for the victim, it was a January night in the city of Winnipeg and the temperature was a bitterly cold $-20°C$. Furthermore, the victim was severely intoxicated. It did not appear that Bradley realized that the victim had suffered a severe head injury, but the Supreme Court of Canada assumed that, given the circumstances, it was a "natural consequence" of the accused's conduct that the victim would die from exposure if left unconscious in such freezing weather. In this situation, therefore, it was reasonably foreseeable that death would ensue from Bradley's attack and subsequent abandonment of the unconscious victim. On the other hand, suppose that Feste stabs Toby, who is taken to hospital for treatment. After two weeks, Toby has made a good recovery, and it is decided to transport him to another medical facility for a special diagnostic test. However, *en route*, Malvolio, the ambulance driver, has a massive heart attack and the ambulance goes over a cliff. Toby dies in the crash. In these circumstances, it is likely that a court would hold that Toby's death in the wreck of the ambulance is not a natural consequence of Feste's original stab wound: *this is*

not an outcome that can reasonably be foreseen and, therefore, Feste would not be convicted of murder or manslaughter (of course, he could be found guilty of an offence such as aggravated assault or attempted murder).

The Impact of Improper Medical Treatment Upon the Chain of Causation

A fascinating area of the law concerns the question of whether *improper medical treatment* administered to the victim may be considered to have broken the chain of causation between the accused's original wounding of the victim and the latter's death. The two leading cases in this area are English, but the principles expressed in them have certainly been approved by Canadian courts. In *Jordan* (1956), the accused had been convicted of the murder of a man called Beaumont and had been sentenced to death. Jordan had stabbed Beaumont in the abdomen in the course of a disturbance at a café. However, upon his appeal to the English Court of Criminal Appeal, new medical evidence was introduced. The evidence tended to establish that Beaumont had been subjected to improper medical treatment. First, he had been administered an antibiotic drug to which he proved to be intolerant. After severe diarrhoea developed, the administration of the drug was discontinued. However, the next day, a different physician recommended therapy with the same drug. Second, in the words of the court,

> Other steps were taken which were also regarded by the doctors as wrong—namely, the intravenous introduction of wholly abnormal quantities of liquid far exceeding the output. As a result the lungs became water-logged and pulmonary oedema was discovered. Mr. Blackburn said that he was not surprised to see that condition after the introduction of so much liquid, and that pulmonary oedema leads to broncho-pneumonia as an inevitable sequel, and it was from bronchopneumonia that Beaumont died.

Another critical element of the medical evidence was the assertion that, while the original stab wound had penetrated the intestine of the victim, it had "mainly healed at the time of death." In these circumstances, the court quashed Jordan's conviction. Clearly, the improper (and grossly negligent) treatment had *broken the chain of causation between the original wounding and Beaumont's tragic death.* Indeed, since the wound was mainly healed, it could not be said that it was an operative cause of death at the time that Beaumont expired. In effect, it was the physicians who effectively killed Beaumont, not the accused.

In stark contrast to *Jordan* is the English case of *Smith* (1959), in which the accused was convicted by a general court-martial of the murder of Private Creed (a soldier in a "rival" regiment). Smith had stabbed Creed with a bayonet in the course of a confrontation between men of two British regiments stationed in Germany. Creed was dropped twice on his way to the first aid station, where the attending medical officer was so busy dealing with other victims of the disturbance that he did not have time to appreciate the seriousness of Creed's medical condition. He was given artificial respiration (which was an inappropriate treatment given the fact that his lung had been punctured) and a transfusion of saline solution, since no facilities for a blood transfusion were available. The unfortunate Private Creed died approximately two hours after the stabbing had occurred. Medical evidence for the defence contended that, had Creed not received such inappropriate treatment and had he been given a blood transfusion, the chances for his recovery would have been "as high as 75 percent."

Defence counsel relied on the *Jordan* case in pressing the Courts-Martial Appeal Court to quash Smith's conviction. Nevertheless, the conviction was upheld. Lord Chief Justice Parker stated that

> It seems to the court that *if at the time of death the original wound is still an operating cause and a substantial cause, then the death can properly be said to be the result of the wound, albeit that some other*

cause of death is also operating. Only if it can be said that the original wounding is merely the setting in which another cause operates can it be said that the death does not result from the wound. Putting it another way, *only if the second cause is so overwhelming as to make the original wound merely part of the history can it be said that the death does not flow from the wound.* [emphasis added]

Since Private Creed died so quickly after the original stab wounds, it was clear that Smith's conduct was "an operating and substantial cause" of death at the time Creed expired. In the *Jordan* case, the victim died a number of days after the original wounding and, furthermore, the stab wounds had mainly healed when the improper treatments were administered. In this sense, the original wound was "merely part of the history" that led to the victim being in the hospital. In the *Smith* case, Lord Chief Justice Parker concluded the judgment of the Court by saying,

> A man is stabbed in the back, his lung is pierced and haemorrhage results; two hours later he dies of haemorrhage from that wound; in the interval there is no time for a careful examination and the treatment given turns out in the light of subsequent knowledge to have been inappropriate and, indeed, harmful. In those circumstances no reasonable jury or court could, properly directed, in our view possibly come to any other conclusion than that the death resulted from the original wound.

The *Smith* case was decided in England, but the legal principle applied is also enshrined in section 225 of the Canadian *Criminal Code*:

> Where a person causes to a human being a bodily injury that is of itself of a dangerous nature and from which death results, he causes the death of that human being notwithstanding that the immediate cause of death is proper or improper treatment that is applied in good faith.

It will be noted that section 225 refers only to treatment "that is applied in good faith." Presumably, improper medical treatment that is administered, for example, by a grossly intoxicated surgeon, would not be considered to have been applied in good faith; therefore, in such a case, the accused might well argue that the chain of causation has been broken by the improper treatment and that, owing to its specific wording, section 225 is not applicable.

Refusal of Treatment by the Victim of an Assault

Another provision of the *Criminal Code* that raises important issues concerning causation in homicide cases is section 224:

> Where a person, by an act or omission, does anything that results in the death of a human being, he causes the death of that human being notwithstanding that death from that cause might have been prevented by resorting to proper means.

One potential application of this section of the Code is to the situation where the victim of a serious wounding refuses to take medical treatment. For example, in the old English case of *Holland* (1841), the accused was charged with the murder of a man called Garland by severely cutting him across one of his fingers with an iron instrument during the course of an ambush. Despite medical advice concerning the very real dangers of infection, Garland refused to have his finger amputated. Two weeks later, Garland contracted lockjaw (tetanus) from the wound and, although the finger was then amputated, it was too late to save his life. Holland was, nevertheless, convicted of murder. Justice Maule said,

> it made no difference whether the wound was in its own nature instantly mortal, or whether it became the cause of death by reason of the deceased not having adopted the best mode of treatment, the real question is, whether in the end

the wound inflicted by the prisoner was the cause of death?

It might well be contended that the victim did not behave unreasonably in this case since the standards of surgical amputation in 1841 might well have given cause for second thoughts even to the bravest of men or women. Today, it is likely that the victim in the *Holland* case would be advised to have an anti-tetanus injection in order to prevent a catastrophic infection of his wound. One wonders if a modern court should convict an accused person of murder if the victim of a finger injury chooses to ignore this medical counsel and subsequently succumbs to a tetanus infection. After all, if the defendant can show that a simple injection could have prevented death from a relatively minor wound, should he or she be convicted of murder or manslaughter if the victim resolutely refused a treatment that would have been highly effective and would have been both safe and relatively painless? Unfortunately, section 224 would appear to require that the accused be convicted in spite of these considerations because it does not require that the original wound be serious in nature.

Even if courts were allowed to take into consideration the question of whether a victim has acted unreasonably in refusing treatment, they would always have to confront a major problem in deciding whether such a refusal has broken the chain of causation between the original wounding and the victim's death. Quite simply, the problem is that it is difficult to decide whether a victim's refusal of treatment is *reasonable or unreasonable*. For example, what is the situation where a victim refuses a potentially life-saving treatment because it offends his or her religious beliefs? Who is to say whether another person's sincerely held religious beliefs are reasonable or unreasonable?

In *Blaue* (1975), the accused attacked an eighteen-year-old woman with a knife, inflicting a serious stab wound that penetrated one of her lungs. At the hospital, it was determined that the victim had lost a considerable amount of blood and she was advised, by the attending surgeon, that she needed a blood transfusion. The victim refused since she was a Jehovah's Witness. She persisted in her refusal despite the clear knowledge that she would die without such a transfusion. The victim later died. On an appeal against his conviction of manslaughter, Blaue contended that the victim's refusal to have a blood transfusion was unreasonable and that, therefore, the chain of causation between the original wounding and the girl's death had been severed. The English Court of Appeal unequivocally rejected this contention. In the words of Lord Justice Lawton,

> The physical cause of death in this case was the bleeding into the pleural cavity arising from the penetration of the lung. This had not been brought about by any decision made by the deceased girl but by the stab wound. ... *It has long been the policy of the law that those who use violence on other people must take their victims as they find them. This in our judgment means the whole man, not just the physical man.* It does not lie in the mouth of the assailant to say that his victim's religious beliefs which inhibited him from accepting certain kinds of treatment were unreasonable. *The question for decision is what caused her death. The answer is the stab wound. The fact that the victim refused to stop this end coming about did not break the causal connection between the act and the death.* [emphasis added]

It is clear that a Canadian court, applying section 224 of the Code, would be compelled to reach exactly the same conclusion as the English Court of Appeal did in *Blaue,* should a similar set of facts arise in Canada. Indeed, given the undoubted severity of the wound to the victim's lung, few would dispute the justice of her assailant's conviction of manslaughter. However, it might well be argued that the *Criminal Code* should be amended so that section 224 only applies to those cases *where the initial injury is serious in nature.* This would mean that Blaue would not be able to contend that the chain of causation was broken by his victim's failure to agree to a blood transfusion, because the stab

wound undoubtedly amounted to an extremely severe injury. On the other hand, Holland (if tried today) would be acquitted under such an amended provision, because the initial injury to the victim's finger was relatively minor and the latter's refusal to take an injection could be considered to have broken the chain of causation. In the *Holland* case, a relatively minor injury led to an infection that killed the victim. In today's setting, he could have avoided this infection very easily by accepting a simple, effective, and (almost) painless injection. To date, no such amendment to the *Criminal Code* has been proposed and, for the present, the courts must continue to convict defendants such as Holland.

Causing Death by Acting on the Victim's Mind

Sections 222(5)(c) and (d) and 228 of the *Criminal Code* establish a number of important principles concerning the causation of death by acting on the victim's mind. Section 222(5)(c) states that a person commits culpable homicide when he or she causes the death of another person "by causing that human being, by threats of fear or violence or by deception, to do anything that causes his death." This section applies in the following situation, for example. David threatens to beat up Goliath, who has no route of escape. Goliath is so terrified by David's extraordinarily violent threats to disfigure him that he jumps to his death from the window of his tenth-storey apartment. In these circumstances, David would be held to have caused Goliath's death and would be criminally liable for the culpable homicide.

Section 222(5)(d) states that culpable homicide is committed when an accused person causes the death of another "by wilfully frightening that human being, in the case of a child or sick person." An illustration of the circumstances, in which this provision might apply, occurred in the old English case of *Towers* (1874), in which the accused violently assaulted a young girl who was holding a four-and-a-half-month-old child. The girl screamed so piercingly that the child was frightened and cried until it became black in the face. From the time of the attack, the child suffered convulsions and died one month later. Justice Denman said

> if the man's act brought on the convulsions or brought them to a more dangerous extent, so that death would not have resulted otherwise, then it would be manslaughter.

Section 228 of the Code indicates that there are strict limitations upon the criminal law's power to punish individuals for homicides caused by an "influence on the mind." This section provides that

> No person commits culpable homicide where he causes the death of a human being
>
> (a) by any influence on the mind alone, or
> (b) by any disorder or disease resulting from influence on the mind alone,
>
> but this section does not apply where a person causes the death of a child or sick person by wilfully frightening him.

This section was relied upon by the Alberta Court of Appeal when it quashed a verdict of manslaughter in the case of *Powder* (1981). It appears that the accused was involved in a break-in when he was confronted by the deceased. There was a struggle and the deceased died as a result of acute heart failure that had been caused by the "fear and emotional stress" generated by the break-in and subsequent conflict. There was no evidence that the physical strain involved in the struggle or any blow struck by the accused contributed in any way to the victim's death. The deceased had a pre-existing heart condition that was precipitated by the fear and emotional stress that engulfed him. In other words, the deceased had died as a consequence of an "influence on his mind alone"; therefore, section 228 was applicable and the accused could not be convicted of homicide.

The *Powder* case can be usefully compared with that of *Rusland* (1992). Here, the accused had physically assaulted a 66-year-old man who had suffered a heart attack a few months prior to the assault and was waiting for by-pass surgery. The victim died as a consequence of the fracas. The trial judge acquitted Rusland and purported to follow the *Powder* decision insofar as he concluded that "the death of the deceased, by reason of his medical history, was not culpable homicide, being caused by stress only in an emotional situation." However, the Crown's appeal against this acquittal was allowed by the Ontario Court of Appeal which ordered a new trial.

The Court of Appeal pointed out that there was evidence that Rusland *actually knew about the dangerous health condition* suffered by the victim:

> Despite that knowledge, there is evidence that [Rusland] placed his hands on the deceased's shoulders and pushed or chucked the deceased who had come to intervene after the respondent had struck his own mother in the face.

If the new trial established that Rusland knew about the victim's perilous state of health and *wilfully frightened him to death,* section 228 would not save him from a conviction of manslaughter even though the deceased died as a consequence of an "influence on the mind alone." Indeed, section 222(5)(d) clearly states that "a person commits culpable homicide when he causes the death of a human being" by "wilfully frightening that human being, in the case of a sick person."

What is the difference between the *Powder* and *Rusland* cases? In the *Powder* case, the accused did not know of his victim's heart disease and thus could not have wilfully (deliberately) frightened him to death. In *Rusland,* there was evidence to suggest that the accused knew about the deceased's cardiac condition and deliberately frightened him to death by pushing him around.

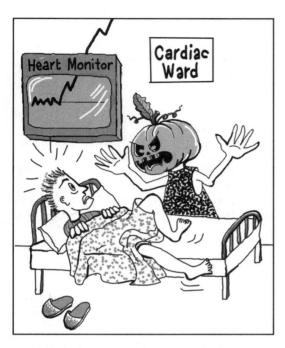

Wilfully frightening a sick person to death.

STUDY QUESTIONS

1. Marlon arrives at his house late at night and discovers that there is an intense fire in his basement. It is clear that he cannot use his own telephone to seek help because it is already engulfed in thick smoke. However, instead of running immediately down the street to ask a neighbour to call the fire brigade, Marlon spends at least four minutes retrieving an original oil painting by Renoir from his living room. By the time that he has completed the rescue of this priceless possession, his neighbour has already called the fire brigade. Although the fire fighters arrive within five minutes, it is too late to save the house from heavy damage. There is evidence that the fire was started accidentally by a burglar. However, the police assert that Marlon should have called the fire brigade earlier and are asking Crown counsel to lay a charge of arson by negligence (under section 436 of the Code). Do you think that such a charge would be successful at Marlon's trial? Would it make any difference to your answer if Marlon had stored inflammable materials in his basement, contary to the provisions of the local fire-prevention by-law?

2. Atila attacks Priscilla with a knife and gravely injures her. He steals her handbag and runs away into the bush. Priscilla is taken to hospital where she is told that she must have a blood transfusion. She refuses this treatment on religious grounds. Priscilla dies a day later and Atila is charged with murder. A doctor says Priscilla would have had a 95 percent chance of survival if she had taken the transfusion. Is Atila guilty of murder?

3. Bill is late for a critical business appointment and he is desperately searching for a taxicab to provide him with swift transportation to his destination. He notices that Mike is just about to enter a taxicab so he violently pushes Mike away and jumps into the backseat of the vehicle. Tragically, Mike falls and his head hits the sidewalk. Mike later dies from his head injuries. The neurological specialist is prepared to testify that Mike had an "eggshell-thin" skull and that, while the fall would not have killed an ordinary person, the combination of the fall and the structural weakness of the skull was the sole cause of death in this particular case. Bill is charged with manslaughter. His counsel argues that Bill did not cause Mike's death; in fact, she argues, it was caused by what amounts to an "act of God." Does Bill have a valid defence?

4. Arthur shoots Cecil in the abdomen and the latter is immediately taken to hospital. An emergency operation is undertaken and the bullet is removed from Cecil's body. At first, Cecil appears to be making excellent progress, but after

about a week, he develops some internal bleeding. Cecil is operated on by Dr. Death, who has taken a large dose of amphetamines. Dr. Death fails to stop the bleeding and Cecil dies the next day. An independent medical specialist states that "any competent surgeon" would have saved Cecil's life. Would Arthur be considered criminally responsible for Cecil's death?

5. Duncan attacks Macbeth who is strolling through a wheat field on the Canadian prairies. Duncan knocks Macbeth unconscious and then leaves him lying on the ground. An hour later, a combine harvester passes over the spot where Macbeth is lying and he is killed. Is Duncan criminally responsible for Macbeth's death?

6. Geraldine knows that her husband, Christopher, has a very serious heart condition. Indeed, his physician has made it clear to Geraldine that excessive exertion and/or fright could kill Christopher. One night, Geraldine turns off all the electrical power in their house and puts on a terrifying mask. She then goes into the room where Christopher is resting on his bed and jumps on him. Christopher believes that Geraldine is an intruder who is trying to kill him. Suddenly, he loses consciousness and expires then and there. A medical expert concludes that Christopher died of a catastrophic heart attack that had probably been caused by fright. Geraldine says that she was only indulging in some fun and that she and Christopher frequently played such games with each other. If Geraldine were to be charged with murder or manslaughter, would she have a defence?

FURTHER READING

Ashworth, A. 1995. *Principles of Criminal Law.* 2d ed. Oxford: Oxford University Press. 93–118.

Bargaric, M. 1999. Euthanasia: Patient Autonomy Versus the Public Good. 18 *University of Tasmania Law Review:* 146.

Bourque, P. 1980. Proof of the Cause of Death in a Prosecution for Criminal Negligence Causing Death. 22 *Criminal Law Quarterly:* 334.

Brock, D.W. 1999. A Critique of Three Objections to Physician-Assisted Suicide. 109 (3) *Ethics:* 519.

Browne, A. 1989. Assisted Suicide and Active Voluntary Euthanasia. 2 *Canadian Journal of Jurisprudence:* 35.

Calandrillo, S.P. 1999. Corralling Kevorkian: Regulating Physician-Assisted Suicide in America. 7 *Virginia Journal of Social Policy & The Law:* 41.

Campbell, T. 1979. Euthanasia and the Law. 17 *Alberta Law Review:* 188.

Coles, E.M. and D. Jang. 1996. A Psychological Perspective on the Legal Concepts of "Volition" and "Intent." 4 *Journal of Law and Medicine:* 60.

Dickens, B.M. 1993. Medically Assisted Death: *Nancy B. v. Hôtel-Dieu de Québec.* 38 *McGill Law Journal:* 1053.

DuVal, G. 1995. Assisted Suicide and the Notion of Autonomy. 27 *Ottawa Law Review:* 1.

Emmanuel, E.J. 1999. What is the Great Benefit of Legalizing Euthanasia or Physician-Assisted Suicide? 109(3) *Ethics:* 629.

Galloway, D. 1989. Causation in Criminal Law: Interventions, Thin Skulls and Lost Chances. 14 *Queen's Law Journal:* 71.

Grant, I., D. Chunn, and C.L.M. Boyle. 1994. *The Law of Homicide.* Toronto: Carswell. Chap 3.

Groot, R. 2000. When Suicide became Felony. 21 *Journal of Legal History:* 1.

Healy, P. 1993. Suicide and Solitude. 24 *Criminal Reports (4th):* 389.

Hoffmaster, B. 1994. Dragons in the Sunset: The Allure of Assisted Death. 14 *Windsor Yearbook of Access to Justice:* 269.

Jones, D.A. 1999. The U.K. Definition of Death. 140/141 *Law & Justice:* 56.

Jones, D.J. 1993. Retrospective on the Future: Brain Death and Evolving Legal Regimes for Tissue Replacement Technology. 38 *McGill Law Journal:* 394.

Kennedy, I.M. 1977. Switching Off Life Support Machines: The Legal Implications. (1977) *Criminal Law Review:* 443.

Kushnir, L. 1976. Bridging the Gap: The Discrepancy Between the Medical and Legal Definitions of Death. 34 *University of Toronto Faculty Law Review:* 199.

Law Reform Commission of Canada. 1979. Study Paper: *Consent to Medical Care.* Ottawa: Ministry of Supply and Services Canada.

———. 1979. Working Paper No. 23: *Criteria for the Determination of Death.* Ottawa: Ministry of Supply and Services Canada.

———. 1980. Working Paper No. 26: *Medical Treatment and Criminal Law*. Ottawa: Minister of Supply and Services Canada.

———. 1981. Report No. 15: *Criteria for the Determination of Death*. Ottawa: Ministry of Supply and Services Canada.

———. 1982. Working Paper No. 28: *Euthanasia, Aiding Suicide and Cessation of Treatment*. Ottawa: Ministry of Supply and Services Canada.

———. 1982. Working Paper No. 29: *Criminal Law; the General Part—Liability and Defences*. Ottawa: Ministry of Supply and Services Canada.

———. 1983. Report No. 20: *Euthanasia, Aiding Suicide and Cessation of Treatment*. Ottawa: Ministry of Supply and Services Canada.

———. 1984. Working Paper No. 33: *Homicide*. Ottawa: Ministry of Supply and Services Canada.

———. 1987. Report No. 31: *Recodifying Criminal Law*. Rev. ed. Ottawa: L.R.C.C.

MacKinnon, P. 1984. Euthanasia and Homicide. 26 *Criminal Law Quarterly*: 483.

Manson, A. 1993. Rethinking Causation: Implications of *Harbottle*. 24 *Criminal Reports (4th)*: 153.

Mewett, A.W. 1994. Editorial: Causation and the Charter. 37 *Criminal Law Quarterly*: 1.

Mewett, A.W. and M. Manning. 1994. *Mewett & Manning on Criminal Law*. 3d ed. Toronto: Butterworths. 145–154.

Meyers, D.W. and J.K. Mason. 1999. Physician-Assisted Suicide: A Second View from Mid-Atlantic. 28(3) *Anglo-American Law Review*: 265.

Montgomery, J.W. 1999. Human Dignity in Birth and Death: A Question of Values. 140/141 *Law & Justice*: 65.

Moore, M.S. 2000. The Metaphysics of Causal Intervention. 88 *California Law Review*: 827.

Morse, S.J. 2000. The Moral Metaphysics of Caustaion and Results. 88 *California Law Review*: 879.

Nuccetelli, S. and G. Seay. 2000. Relieving Pain and Foreseeing Death: A Paradox About Accountability and Blame. 28 *The Journal of Law, Medicine & Ethics*: 19.

Ogden, R. 1994. *Euthanasia and Assisted Suicide in Persons with Acquired Immunodeficiency Syndrome (AIDS) or Human Immunodeficiency Virus (HIV)*. New Westminster, B.C.: Peroglyphics Publishing.

Ogden, R.D. 1995. The Right to Die: A Rejoinder to Bruce Wilkinson's Critique. 21 *Canadian Public Policy*: 456.

Ogden, R.D. and M.G. Young. 1998. Euthanasia and Assisted Suicide: A Survey of Registered Social Workers in British Columbia. 28 *British Journal of Social Work*: 161.

Parks, R.C. 2000. A Right to Die with Dignity: Using International Perspectives to Formulate a Workable U.S. Policy. 8 *Tulane Journal of International & Comparative Law*: 447.

Pratt, D.A. and B. Steinbock. 1997. Death with Dignity or Unlawful Killing: The Ethical and Legal Debate over Physician-Assisted Death. 33 *Criminal Law Bulletin*: 226.

Pullman, D. 1996. Dying with Dignity and the Death of Dignity. 4 *Health Law Review*: 197.

Rodgers, G. 1991. The Test of Causation in Criminal Driving Cases. 3 *Journal of Motor Vehicle Law*: 137.

Rozovsky, L.E. and F.A. Rozovsky. 1990. *The Canadian Law of Consent to Treatment*. Toronto: Butterworths.

Ryan, H.R.S. 1993. Leaving Euthanasia for Parliament. 24 *Criminal Reports (4th)*: 366.

Saunders, M.G. 1975. Determining the Presence of Death; A Medical, Legal and Ethical Problem. 6 *Manitoba Law Journal*: 327.

Schiffer, L. 1984. Euthanasia and the Criminal Law. 42 *University of Toronto Faculty Law Review*: 93.

Searles, N. 1996. Silence Doesn't Obliterate the Assisted Truth: A Manitoba Survey on Physician Assisted Suicides and Euthanasia. 4 *Health Law Review*: 197.

Sneiderman, B. 1993. The Case of Nancy B.: A Criminal Law and Social Policing Perspective. 1 *Health Law Journal*: 25.

———. 1985. Why Not a Limited Defence? A Comment on the Proposals of the Law Reform Commission of Canada on Mercy-Killing. 15 *Manitoba Law Journal*: 85.

———. 1997. A Winnipeg Inquest: A Case of Natural Death or Physician-Assisted Suicide? 24 *Manitoba Law Journal*: 365.

———. 1999. *Latimer, Davis*, and *Doerksen*: Mercy Killing and Assisted Suicide on the Op. Ed. Page. 25 *Manitoba Law Journal*: 449.

Sneiderman, B. and M. Verhoef. 1995. Patient Autonomy and the Defence of Medical Necessity: Five Dutch Euthanasia Cases. 34 *Alberta Law Review*: 374.

Stuart, D. 1995. *Canadian Criminal Law*. 3d ed. Toronto: Carswell. 119–137.

Stuart, D. and R.J. Delisle. 1997. *Learning Canadian Criminal Law*. 6th ed. Toronto: Carswell. 256–288.

Tanovich, D.M. and J. Lockyer. 1996. Revisiting *Harbottle:* Does the "Substantial Cause" Test Apply to All Murder Offences? 38 *Criminal Law Quarterly:* 322.

Van den Hagg, E. 1997. Whose Life Is It: Decriminalize Assisted Suicide and Euthanasia? 33 *Criminal Law Bulletin:* 262.

Verdun-Jones, S.N. 1999. *Canadian Criminal Cases: Selected Highlights.* Toronto: Harcourt Brace. 45–67.

Wilkinson, B. 1995. "The Right to Die" by Russel Ogden: A Commentary. 21 *Canadian Public Policy:* 449.

Yeo, S. 2000. Blamable Causation. 24 *Criminal Law Journal:* 144.

Young, M.G. and R.D. Ogden. 1998. End-of-Life Issues: A Survey of English-speaking Canadian Nurses in AIDS Care. 9 *Journal of the Association of Nurses in AIDS Care:* 18.

Zalman, M. and J. Strate. 1997. Last Rights: Assisted Suicide and the Limits of the Judicial Process. 33 *Criminal Law Bulletin:* 205.

The Mental Element in the Criminal Law: Subjective Liability

OVERVIEW

This chapter examines the following:

1. The nature of the *mens rea* or mental elements that the Crown must prove in order to convict an accused person of a "true crime";
2. the role of the *mens rea* requirements as a means of ensuring that the morally innocent are not punished under the criminal law;
3. the difference between subjective and objective *mens rea* requirements;
4. the particular forms of subjective *mens rea* requirements, namely, intention and knowledge, recklessness, and wilful blindness;
5. the nature of intention and knowledge in Canadian criminal law;
6. examples of special mental elements that must be proved in addition to intention and knowledge ("fraud" in sections 380 and 322 of the Code and "planned and deliberate" in section 231(2));
7. the distinction between direct and indirect intention and knowledge;
8. the distinction between intention and motive;
9. the problems associated with proving intention and the use of the test of the "reasonable person" as a means of assisting in the process of determining whether an accused person possessed the necessary subjective intent;
10. the concept of transferred intent;
11. the nature of specific (or ulterior) intent offences;
12. the *Charter* requirement that conviction of certain offences be based on proof of subjective *mens rea*, with particular reference to the crime of murder;
13. the nature of recklessness as a form of subjective *mens rea*;
14. examples of offences in relation to which an accused person may be convicted on the basis of proof of recklessness (murder under section 229(a)(ii), damage to property etc. under section 429(1), arson under sections 433 and 434; and criminal harassment under section 264);
15. wilful blindness as a form of subjective *mens rea*.

MENS REA: AN INTRODUCTION

In Chapter 2, we saw how the terms **actus reus** and **mens rea** were derived from the latin maxim *"actus non facit reum nisi mens sit rea,"* or "an act does not render a person guilty of a criminal offence unless his or her mind is also guilty." Chapters 4 and 5 turn the spotlight on the principles that apply when a court is required to determine whether an **accused** person's "mind is guilty." In short, these chapters will identify the various *mens rea* elements of a criminal offence that must be established before an individual may be held criminally responsible for his or her conduct.

In Chapter 2, it was pointed out that it would be a mistake to assume that there is a clear-cut distinction between the *physical* and *mental* elements of a criminal offence. Indeed, since an act must be the *voluntary* act of the accused if the *actus reus* elements are to exist, the *actus reus* in essence contains its own mental element. So what is meant by the term *mens rea*?

Basically, *mens rea* refers to all of the mental elements (other than **voluntariness**) that the Crown must prove in order to obtain a conviction of a criminal offence. These mental elements inevitably vary from crime to crime. The *mens rea* for **murder** is obviously very different from that required for theft or arson. In order to ascertain the necessary *mens rea* elements that must be established by the Crown, it is therefore vital to analyze the mental element(s) that are required in relation to each component of the *actus reus* of the specific offence concerned (that is, conduct, circumstances and consequences). As Gold (1994) points out,

> The *mens rea* of an offence consists of the sum total of the mental states required for that offence: the mental state required with regard to the activity (act or comission or status) plus the mental state required with regard to any required circumstances plus the mental state required with regard to any required consequences plus any additional intent or other mental state required by the provisions creating the offence.
>
> Mens rea *is not one mental state: it is a sum or combination of mental states. ...* [emphasis added]

The reason why the *mens rea* elements of an offence are of paramount importance in criminal law is that they operate to ensure that only those who are *morally blameworthy* are convicted of "**true crimes**" under the *Criminal Code*. As Justice McLachlin, of the Supreme Court of Canada, said in the case of *Théroux* (1993),

> Mens rea ... refers to the guilty mind, the wrongful intention, of the accused. *Its function in the criminal law is to prevent the conviction of the morally innocent — those who do not understand or intend the consequences of their acts.* [emphasis added]

Similarly, Justice Lamer, of the Supreme Court of Canada, said in the *Reference Re Section 94(2) of the Motor Vehicle Act* case (1985),

> It has from time immemorial been part of our system of laws that the innocent not be punished. This principle has long been recognized as an essential element of a system of justice which is founded upon a belief in the dignity and worth of the human person and on the rule of law. [emphasis added]

Furthermore, Justice Lamer went on to assert that this principle is one of the "fundamental principles of justice" enshrined in section 7 of the *Charter*.

In essence, the *mens rea* requirements of the criminal law operate to excuse from criminal liability all those accused persons who cannot be considered to be blameworthy for their conduct. For example, an accused person who is under a fundamental mistake of fact as to an essential element of the *actus reus* of an offence must be acquitted of a true crime because he or she would lack the necessary *mens rea* for that offence and would therefore be morally innocent. This is precisely the situation that occurred in the famous English case of *Tolson* (1889), in which the accused had been charged with **bigamy**. In September 1880, she was married to one Tolson. However, in December 1881, the latter deserted his bride. Both the accused and her father made extensive enquiries concerning the whereabouts of Mr. Tolson and, through his elder brother and "general report," they learned that Mr. Tolson had perished on a ship bound for the United States, which had apparently plummeted to the ocean floor with all hands on board. In January 1887, the accused, not unreasonably supposing herself to be a widow, married another man. The second husband was fully informed as to Ms. Tolson's prior marriage, and it was perfectly clear that the wedding ceremony was in no way concealed. Unfortunately, in December 1887, Mr. Tolson re-emerged in England. As a consequence, Ms. Tolson was charged with the by-no-means-minor offence of bigamy. The jury convicted Ms. Tolson but stated that she had, in good faith, believed her husband to be dead at the time of her second marriage. The trial judge sentenced her to one day's imprisonment. The matter was then referred to the Court for Crown Cases Reserved. This court ruled that

Tolson (1889): a case of mistake as to an essential element of the actus reus *of the offence of bigamy.*

Ms. Tolson should be acquitted on the basis that she had operated under a mistake of fact, and therefore lacked the necessary *mens rea* that must be proved by the Crown in relation to a charge of bigamy.

The court clearly ruled that the criminal law is predicated on the notion that the Crown must prove that a certain (culpable) mental state (*mens rea*) exists before an accused person may be convicted of a true crime. In this particular case, Ms. Tolson clearly believed in a state of facts that, if true, would have rendered her second wedding an entirely innocent act. She honestly believed that she was a widow, and therefore the notion that she would become a bigamist never crossed her mind. Putting it another way, she was under a fundamental mistake as to the most critical *actus reus* element of the offence of bigamy (namely, that the accused person or his or her intended spouse was *already married* at the time of the marriage

ceremony that led to the charge of bigamy). Ms. Tolson mistakenly believed that she was not already married, and therefore lacked the *mens rea* required for conviction of the offence of bigamy.

The *Tolson* case (1889) illustrates a situation in which the accused lacked *mens rea* because she was not aware of a critical *circumstance* that constituted an essential component of the *actus reus* of the offence with which she was charged. However, an accused person may also lack the necessary *mens rea* elements for conviction of an offence where he or she does not understand or intend the *consequences* of his or her actions. Indeed, this proposition was underscored by Justice McLachlin, of the Supreme Court of Canada, in the case of *Théroux* (1993):

Typically, *mens rea* is concerned with the consequences of the prohibited *actus reus*. Thus in the crimes of homicide, we speak of the consequence of the voluntary act—intention to cause death, or reckless and wilfully blind persistence in conduct which one knows is likely to cause death. In other offences, such as dangerous driving, the *mens rea* may relate to the failure to consider the consequences of inadvertence.

For example, section 16 of the *Criminal Code* provides that those individuals who are so mentally disordered that they do not appreciate what they are doing should be found not criminally responsible. Clearly, such individuals would not understand the consequences of their actions and are, therefore, lacking in *mens rea* (or, putting it another way, they are not morally blameworthy). Similarly, section 13 of the Code states that children under the age of 12 years cannot be held criminally accountable for their actions. Presumably, Parliament enacted this provision in recognition of the view that young children are not capable of fully understanding the consequences of their conduct, and in this sense, they do not have the necessary *mens rea* for conviction of a criminal offence. Finally, an accused person who absent-mindedly leaves a store with an item that has not been paid for will not be found guilty of theft if there was no intention on his or her part to take the item without purchasing it. Here, the accused lacks the *mens rea* for theft (intentional and fraudulent taking of someone else's property), and it would run contrary to the fundamental principles of justice to convict an innocent person of such a crime.

SUBJECTIVE AND OBJECTIVE MENS REA

Although it is clear that an individual who lacks the necessary *mens rea* for an offence cannot be held criminally responsible because he or she is morally innocent, it is important to recognize that there are two distinct types of *mens rea* requirements in Canadian criminal law. Supreme Court Justice McLachlin, as she then was, stated in the case of *Creighton* (1993),

> The mens rea of a criminal offence may be either subjective or objective, subject to the principle of fundamental justice that the moral fault of the offence must be proportionate to its gravity and penalty. Subjective *mens rea* requires that the accused have intended the consequences of his or her acts, or that, knowing of the probable consequences of those acts, the accused have proceeded recklessly in the face of the risk. The requisite intention or knowledge may be inferred directly from the act and its circumstances. Even in the latter case, however, *it is concerned with "what was actually going on in the mind of this particular accused at the time in question."*…

> Objective *mens rea*, on the other hand, is not concerned with what the accused intended or knew. Rather the mental fault lies in failure to direct the mind to a risk which the reasonable person would have appreciated. *Objective* mens rea *is not concerned with what was actually in the accused's mind, but with what should have been there, had the accused proceeded reasonably.* [emphasis added]

Subjective *mens rea* is based on the notion that accused persons may not be convicted of a criminal offence unless (a) they *deliberately intended* to bring about the consequences prohibited by law or (b) *subjectively realized* that their conduct might produce such prohibited consequences and proceeded with that conduct regardless of their actual knowledge of that risk. Subjective *mens rea*, therefore, requires that the Crown prove that the accused *deliberately chose to do something wrong.*

Objective *mens rea*, in contrast, does not require proof that accused persons deliberately intended to bring about a prohibited consequence or even that they subjectively appreciated the risk that their conduct might produce such a result. Objective *mens rea* is predicated on the principle that *reasonable persons, in the same circumstances as the accused, would have appreciated that their conduct was creating a risk of producing prohibited consequences and would have taken action to avoid doing so.* Here the fault of the accused does not lie in deliberately choosing to do something wrong; instead, the fault is to be found in the fact that the accused had the capacity to live up to the standard of care expected of a reasonable person and failed to do so. As Justice McLachlin said, in the passsage quoted above, "the mental fault lies in failure to direct the mind to a risk which the reasonable person would have appreciated."

It is important to acknowledge that those who have subjective *mens rea* will generally be treated as being more blameworthy than those who are convicted on the basis of objective *mens rea*; after all, the former have deliberately chosen to do something wrong, whereas the latter were not even aware of the risk that their conduct was creating (although a reasonable person would have been). The Supreme Court of Canada has, therefore, ruled that, in order to ensure that the degree of punishment imposed on offenders is commensurate with the extent of their fault, the most serious punishments should be reserved for those who are proved to have possessed subjective *mens rea*. As we shall see, the most important example of the application of this principle is in relation to the offence of murder. The

Supreme Court of Canada has ruled that, since murder carries the most severe penalty in the *Criminal Code* as well as the greatest degree of associated stigma, accused persons may not be convicted of this offence unless they *subjectively* foresaw the risk that their conduct would bring about someone's death (see the *Martineau* case (1990) discussed later in this chapter).

PARTICULAR FORMS OF SUBJECTIVE *MENS REA*

Objective *mens rea* is discussed at length in Chapter 5. In the present chapter, we examine the various forms of subjective *mens rea* that the Crown may be required to prove; these are *intention* and *knowledge, recklessness,* and *wilful blindness.* Furthermore, we shall discuss certain situations in which, in addition to intention and knowledge, the Crown must prove some special mental element that is required by the definition of the particular offence in question (such as "fraud" in the case of a charge of theft under section 322).

The Concepts of Intention and Knowledge

Many of the definitions of criminal offences contained in the *Criminal Code* explicitly require the proof of *mens rea* in the form of an *"intended" consequence or actual "knowledge" of particular circumstances.* For example, section 265(1) of the *Criminal Code* provides that

> a person commits an assault when a) without the consent of another person, he applies force *intentionally* to that other person, directly or indirectly. ... [emphasis added]

Similarly, section 155(1) of the Code provides that

> everyone commits incest who, *knowing* that another person is by blood relationship his or her parent, child, brother, sister, grandparent or grand-

child, as the case may be, has sexual intercourse with that person. [emphasis added]

In other circumstances, the requirement that the accused intend to bring about a certain consequence, or that he or she engage in conduct with knowledge of particular circumstances, may not be expressly stated in the Code; however, the courts may well hold that such a requirement is "implied" by the language used by Parliament. For example, in the case of *Prue and Baril* (1979), the Supreme Court of Canada ruled that the offence of driving while disqualified (contrary to what was then section 238(3) of the *Criminal Code*) required knowledge, on the part of the **defendants**, that their driving licences were suspended, despite the fact that there was no express requirement of knowledge in section 238(3) (the equivalent section is now section 259(4)). Furthermore, it is significant that, whether the requirement of *knowledge* is express or implied, the Crown must prove that the accused had knowledge of *all of the elements of the actus reus* (as Justice Sopinka pointed out, on behalf of the majority of the Supreme Court of Canada in the *Jorgensen* case (1995)).

Sometimes the *Criminal Code* employs other terms to indicate a requirement of intent. For example, section 139(1) states that "everyone who *wilfully* attempts in any manner to obstruct, pervert or defeat the course of justice in a judicial proceeding," in the specified circumstances, is guilty of an offence. Similarly, section 229 of the Code provides that

> culpable homicide is murder
>
> (a) where the person who causes the death of a human being
>
> (i) *means to* cause his death, or
> (ii) *means to* cause him bodily harm that he knows is likely to cause his death, and is reckless whether death ensues or not ...
>
> [emphasis added]

Not surprisingly, Canadian courts have ruled that terms such as "wilfully" and "means to" are merely synonymous for the requirement of "intent."

One final point should be made about the *mens rea* requirement of "knowledge." Where the Crown is required to prove *knowledge* of a particular circumstance, or set of circumstances, it must also prove that that circumstance or set of circumstances did, in fact, exist. As Supreme Court of Canada Justices Cory and Iacobucci stated in the *Dynar* case (1997), *it is not possible to know something that is false.* Put another way, "knowledge implies truth." In *Dynar*, the Supreme Court ruled that an individual may not be convicted of the crime of laundering money "knowing" that the moneys in question are the "proceeds of crime," if the property in question has not, in fact, been obtained or derived as a consequence of criminal activity. This reasoning applies even if the accused mistakenly *believed* that the property in question constituted the proceeds of crime. It is significant that, after the *Dynar* case went to trial, section 462.31 of the *Criminal Code* was amended so that the relevant offence is now one of laundering money "*knowing or believing* that all or a part of (the) property or of those proceeds was obtained or derived directly or indirectly" from the commission of a crime.

Special Mental Elements That Must Be Proved in Addition to Intention and Knowledge

Canadian courts have ruled certain terms in the *Criminal Code* have special, technical meanings. When such technical terms are employed in the Code, the Crown is required to prove a particular mental state *in addition to* intention or knowledge. Conspicuous examples of such special, technical terms are "fraudulently" (in relation to theft, under section 322), "fraudulent" (in relation to the offence of fraud under section 380), and "planned and deliberate" (in relation to the distinction between first and **second degree murder**, under section 231).

THE MEANING OF "FRAUDULENT" IN SECTION 380

As Justice Cory pointed out, on behalf of the majority of the Supreme Court of Canada in the *Cuerrier* case (1998), "the essential elements of fraud are *dishonesty ... and deprivation or risk of deprivation.*" Therefore, in their interpretation of the term "fraudulent" in the specific context of section 380(1) of the *Criminal Code*, the courts have insisted that the Crown prove that the accused acted *dishonestly*. This element of dishonesty is required *in addition* to proof that the accused acted intentionally or with knowledge of the particular circumstances. The judicial interpretation of the concept of fraud has clearly emerged in relation to charges laid under section 380 of the *Criminal Code*. Section 380(1) states that

> everyone who, by *deceit, falsehood or other fraudulent means,* whether or not it is a false pretence within the meaning of this Act, defrauds the public or any person, whether ascertained or not, of any property, money or valuable security [is guilty of an offence] ... [emphasis added]

It is clear that fraud is not confined to the obtaining of property, etc. by deceit or falsehood, which essentially involve lying on the part of the defendant. After all, section 380(1) specifically refers to "*other* fraudulent means," which means that the concept of fraud in the Code extends beyond situations where the defendant deliberately tells a lie. The nature of fraud, as it is defined in section 380(1), was extensively discussed by the Supreme Court of Canada in the case of *Olan, Hudson and Hartnett* (1978).

The facts in the *Olan* case are extremely complicated. However, a highly simplified version will suffice for our purposes. The accused were charged with defrauding a dry-cleaning company, Langley's Limited, of money and valuable securities worth some $1 million. Beauport Holdings Limited, a company controlled by one of the accused, took over Langley's Limited by purchasing a controlling block of its shares; however, it needed a substantial bank loan to do so. Representatives of Beauport Holdings Limited were then placed in control of the board of directors of Langley's Limited. The new directors caused Langley's Limited to divest itself of its holdings in "blue chip" securities (that is, valuable and secure investments) and to purchase shares in another company, Beauport Financial Corporation Limited, which was controlled by two of the accused. Some $790 000, which was acquired by Beauport Financial as a result of the share purchase, was then loaned to Beauport Holdings. This money was used to pay off part of the bank loan that Beauport Holdings had used to purchase the controlling block of Langley's shares. In essence, Langley's had exchanged its secure and valuable investment portfolio for shares in Beauport Financial, whose principal asset was the debt owed to it by Beauport Holdings. In the previous year, Beauport Holdings sustained a net operating loss and its current liabilities exceeded its assets by more than $1 million. Clearly, the value and security of the shares in Beauport Financial were somewhat shaky at best. On these facts, it was contended by the Crown that the sale of Langley's shares had been carried out for the personal interests of the new directors rather than for the *bona fide* business interests of Langley's Limited.

It was clear that the accused had not been deceitful or uttered any falsehood. Indeed, the accused vigorously claimed that their activities had all been "above board." However, the question arose as to whether their conduct nevertheless constituted fraud within the meaning of section 380 of the Code. The Court emphasized that the prosecution was not required to prove any deception on the part of the accused. Indeed, Justice Dickson, in delivering the judgment of the Court, stated that the words "other fraudulent means" in section 380(1) "encompass all other meanings which can properly be stigmatized as dishonest." In the view of the Supreme Court, the prosecution must establish two separate elements in order to prove fraud, namely *dishonesty* (the *mens rea*) and *deprivation* (the *actus reus*). Insofar as this particular case was concerned, Justice Dickson said that

Using the assets of the corporation for personal purposes rather than *bona fide* for the benefit of the corporation can constitute dishonesty in a case of alleged fraud by directors of a corporation ...

The element of deprivation is satisfied on proof of detriment, prejudice, or risk of prejudice to the economic interest of the victim. *It is not essential that there be actual economic loss or the outcome of the fraud.* [emphasis added]

The Court ruled that, while the accused may well have intended to have Beauport Holdings repay the loan to Beauport Financial, this would not prevent them from being found fraudulent if their conduct was otherwise shown to involve dishonest deprivation for their own personal ends. In this particular case, the Supreme Court ordered a new trial, which was to be conducted in accordance with the principles enunciated by Justice Dickson.

In the case of *Théroux* (1993), the Supreme Court of Canada ruled that, in a case of fraud under section 380 of the Code, it is not necessary for the Crown to prove that the accused subjectively appreciated that his or her act was dishonest. Indeed, Justice McLachlin, in delivering the judgment of the majority of the justices of the Supreme Court stated that, in order to establish the *mens rea* elements of fraud, the Crown only has to "prove that the accused knowingly undertook the acts which constitute the falsehood, deceit or other fraudulent means, and that the accused was aware that deprivation could result from such conduct." If these elements are proved, it does not matter if the accused believes that he or she was acting in a perfectly legitimate manner.

In *Théroux*, the accused was a businessman who was involved with a company that was constructing two residential housing projects. Théroux falsely represented to potential buyers that their deposits would be insured by the Fédération de Construction du Québec. The construction company became insolvent and the projects were not finished. As a consequence, most of the potential buyers lost the entire amount of their deposits. At the accused's trial for fraud, the trial judge found that Théroux honestly believed that the housing projects would succeed and that the buyers would not lose their deposits. However, the trial judge stated that this was not a defence to a charge of fraud and convicted Théroux. The accused's **appeals** to both the Québec Court of Appeal and the Supreme Court of Canada were dismissed.

According to Justice McLachlin, the accused's belief that the projects would succeed and that the buyers would not lose any money was irrelevant. In defining the offence of fraud under section 380, she stated that

> The prohibited act is deceit, falsehood, or some other dishonest act. The prohibited consequence is depriving another of what is or should be his, which may, as we have seen, consist in merely placing another's property at risk. The *mens rea* would then consist in the subjective awareness that one was undertaking a prohibited act (the deceit, falsehood or other dishonest act) which could cause deprivation in the sense of depriving another of property or putting that property at risk. If this is shown, the crime is complete. The fact that the accused may have hoped the deprivation would not take place, or may have felt there was nothing wrong with what he or she was doing, provides no defence. ... The personal feeling of the accused about the morality or honesty of the act or its consequences is no more relevant to the analysis than is the accused's awareness that the particular acts constitute a criminal offence.

The "dishonesty" of the means is relevant to the determination whether the conduct falls within the type of conduct caught by the offence of fraud; *what reasonable people consider dishonest assists in the determination whether the* actus reus *of the offence can be made out on particular facts.* That established, it need only be determined that an accused knowingly undertook the acts in question, aware that deprivation, or risk of deprivation, could follow as a likely consequence. [emphasis added]

As far as the facts in *Théroux* were concerned, it was clear that the accused had committed the *actus reus* of fraud. He had deliberately told falsehoods to the potential buyers and those lies caused deprivation in two respects: first, the depositors failed to obtain the insurance that they were promised, and second, their money was placed at risk (a risk which ultimately did materialize since the majority of them lost the entire amount of their deposits).

The critical question, therefore, was whether the *mens rea* elements of fraud had been proved. Justice McLachlin answered this question affirmatively:

> [Théroux] told the depositors they had insurance protection when he knew that they did not have that protection. He knew this to be false. He knew that by this act he was depriving the depositors of something they thought they had, insurance protection. It may also be inferred from his possession of this knowledge that [he] knew that he was placing the depositors' money at risk. That established, his *mens rea*, is proved. The fact that he sincerely believed that in the end the houses would be built and that the risk would not materialize cannot save him.

The outcome in *Théroux* may usefully be compared with that in the *Parisé* case (1996), in which the accused had been charged with welfare fraud under section 380(1)(a) of the *Criminal Code*. Essentially, the Crown contended that Parisé should have reported to the welfare authorities two events that occurred while she and her children were receiving social assistance benefits (namely, the arrival of a male friend in her household and the sale of a small piece of real estate). The Supreme Court of Canada ultimately agreed that Parisé should be acquitted because she honestly believed that these two events had not changed her financial dependency on social assistance benefits and that, therefore, her entitlement to these benefits was not affected. Given this belief, she could not be characterized as having been "fraudulent." Indeed, according to Justice Sopinka, who delivered the judgment of the Supreme Court:

> We are satisfied that the trial judge accepted the evidence of the appellant that she honestly believed that her circumstances had not changed so as to affect her entitlement to income assistance. In view of this finding, *an essential element of the* mens rea *for the offence was negatived.* [emphasis added]

FRAUD IN SECTION 322 OF THE CODE (THEFT)

The interpretation of the word "fraudulently" as meaning *dishonestly* is also illustrated by an interesting series of cases in which some Canadian courts have determined that the offence of theft may not be committed when an accused engages in a "prank" or a "well-intentioned blunder." It has been ruled that the intention to engage in a prank or a well-intentioned blunder negates the element of dishonesty that must be proved in relation to a charge of theft. Section 322 of the *Criminal Code* provides that

(1) everyone commits theft who *fraudulently* and without colour of right takes,* or *fraudulently* and without colour of right converts to his use or to the use of another person anything whether animate or inanimate, with intent,

    (a) to deprive temporarily, or absolutely, the owner of it or a person who has a special property or interest in it, of the thing or of his property or interest in it,

    (b) to pledge it or deposit it as security,

    (c) to part with it under a condition with respect to its return that the person who parts with it may be unable to perform, or

---

*"Without colour of right" means without having a belief that one has a legal right to the property in question; this concept is fully discussed in Chapter 9.

    (d) to deal with it in such a manner that it cannot be restored in the condition in which it was at the time it was taken or converted.

In the case of *Wilkins* (1965), the accused was charged with the theft of a police officer's motorcycle. Nichol, the police officer, was engaged in the act of writing out a parking ticket to place on the windshield of a motorcar, owned by one Mike Borysuik. At this point, the defendant approached Nichol and stated, "If you give Mike a ticket I am going to ride your motorcycle around the parking lot" (referring to a parking lot located at the front of a nearby supermarket). Nichol seemingly could not hear what Wilkins said because his helmet covered his ears and there was a loud noise coming from his motorcycle. Nichol just smiled in response to Wilkins's approach. It appears that both Nichol and Wilkins were reasonably well-acquainted. When Nichol did not cease writing the ticket, Wilkins drove the motorcycle down the street, where he was intercepted by a police cruiser. He was, subsequently, charged with theft. Wilkins stated, most forcefully, that he had no intention of stealing the motorcycle and was merely playing a joke on Nichol. The accused was ultimately acquitted by the Ontario Court of Appeal. In ordering the accused's **acquittal**, Justice Roach stated that

> In the instant case the facts could not possibly justify a conviction of theft. The accused did not intend to steal the vehicle, that is, to convert the property in it to his own use but only to drive it ... his intention was merely to play a joke on Nichol and the Judge so found. *The intention to perpetrate this joke, stupid though it was, is incompatible with the evil intent which is inherent in the crime of theft.* [emphasis added]

It is interesting that the Court pointed out that the police *should* have charged the accused with the offence of taking a motor vehicle without the consent of the owner (section 335 of the Code).

However, the courts have emphasized that the so-called "prank" defence is one that has a very narrow scope. For example, in the case of *Neve* (1999), the accused had been convicted of robbery (an offence that generally requires the Crown to prove *both* an *assault* and a *theft*). Neve believed that the **complainant** in this case had beaten one of her pregnant friends, causing a miscarriage. Neve and a friend took the complainant to a field located near a major highway just outside Edmonton. Neve and her friend tore off the complainant's clothes with a knife and left her standing naked in the field, in a temperature of about five degrees Centigrade. The complainant was later rescued by a passing motorist. The police found one item of the complainant's clothing at the scene of the incident but, owing to the extreme darkness, did not find any of her other clothes in the immediate vicinity. Neve claimed that her sole objective had been to humiliate the complainant to "get even" for what Neve believed the latter had done to a friend. She emphatically denied that she had taken any of the complainant's clothes for the purpose of sale, etc. Indeed, the defence suggested that the missing items of clothing had been thrown out of Neve's car when she was leaving the field.

In order to establish that a theft (and, hence a robbery), had occurred, the Crown was required, under section 322(1), to prove that Neve had acted "fraudulently." However, Neve said that she had not acted dishonestly. Her **counsel** contended that dishonesty necessarily involves "swindling or trickery" and that, in this case, Neve's actions had taken place without any "deceit, falsehood or trickery." Indeed, when the complainant had refused to disrobe herself, then Neve and her friend had "simply removed the complainant's clothes in a straightforward and open manner." Both the trial court and the Alberta Court of Appeal soundly rejected this line of argument and Neve's robbery conviction was ultimately upheld. The Court of Appeal noted that it is irrelevant that the complainant's clothes had been removed in an "open manner":

The reality is that many thefts and robberies are committed openly, without deception or trickery. The fact that an offender openly and blatantly takes property from a victim makes little difference to the victim. The result is the same; the victim's property has been wrongly taken.

… for property to be taken "fraudulently," it is enough that the taking be done *intentionally, under no mistake, and with knowledge that the thing taken is the property of another person*. This will suffice to characterize the taking as fraudulent. [emphasis added]

What was the fate of another argument advanced by defence counsel, namely, that Neve had been engaging in a "prank" and, therefore, could not be considered to have acted "fraudulently"? While the Court of Appeal appeared to be prepared to recognize that certain forms of prank may not amount to theft, it took the view that, in Neve's case, there was absolutely no basis for characterizing her violent act as a "prank":

A prank is a practical joke. What happened here does not fit that description. It was a taking for the purpose of depriving the victim, albeit not for the benefit of the taker. It was not a joke and motive does not change the character of the act if the property was taken for the purpose of depriving the owner. Accordingly, the defence thesis that Neve did not take the complainant's clothing "fraudulently" must fail.

Incidentally, it is important to remember that section 322(1)(a) of the Code provides that, in relation to a charge of theft, the Crown must prove that the accused intended to deprive the victim of his or her property "*temporarily or absolutely*." Therefore, it is of no importance that Neve only intended to keep the complainant's clothes for a short period; as the Court of Appeal noted, "the obvious intent was to deprive the complainant of [her clothes] for a period of time, however brief."

In this context, it is noteworthy that Supreme Court of Canada has emphasized that an accused person can be considered to have acted "fraudulently" even if he or she claims that there was never any intention to cause loss to the victim. For example, in *Skalbania* (1997), the accused had been charged with theft of $100 000. The Crown relied on section 332 of the *Criminal Code*, which specifies that the crime of theft has been committed if the accused, having received money for a specific purpose, "*fraudulently*" applies that money to some other, unauthorized purpose. Skalbania had approached a man called Gooch and encouraged him to participate in a real estate deal that the accused was seeking to make with a third party. Gooch gave Skalbania a cheque for $100 000, with an explicit direction that it was to be kept in a trust account pending the outcome of the business negotiations. Skalbania instructed his bookkeeper to transfer the $100 000 from his company's trust account to the company's current account, and all of the money was spent on matters entirely unrelated to the business deal in which Gooch was planning to participate. The business deal never came off and, more than two months later, Skalbania repaid Gooch his $100 000 together with "a sum by way of compensation for delay and inconvenience."

Had Skalbania committed theft through his deliberate misappropriation of money that had been given to him for one, specific purpose (the proposed joint business venture between Skalbania and Gooch)? It was clear that Skalbania had used the funds in the trust account for unauthorized purposes but had he acted "*fraudulently*"? The accused claimed that he always intended to reimburse Gooch in full, should the business deal fall through, and that he had demonstrated his good faith by returning the money with interest. The Supreme Court of Canada held that Skalbania had, in fact, acted "fraudulently," even though the accused was adamant that he had not intended to *steal* Gooch's money. As Justice McLachlin said, in delivering the judgment of the Court,

> ... an intentional misappropriation, without mistake, suffices to establish the *mens rea* under s. 332(1) ... The word "fraudulently," as used in this section, connotes no more than this. *The dishonesty inherent in the offence lies in the intentional and unmistaken application of funds to an improper purpose.*
>
> ...
>
> In short, the trial judge found: the appellant knew that the money belonged to Mr. Gooch; that the appellant knew the purpose to which the money was supposed to be applied; and that the appellant knowingly, without mistake, applied the money to different purposes. [emphasis added]

THE MEANING OF PLANNED AND DELIBERATE IN SECTION 231(2) (FIRST DEGREE MURDER)

A final example of an important, technical term is contained in section 231(2) of the *Criminal Code*. This provision states that "murder is **first degree murder** when it is *planned* and *deliberate*." In order to convict an accused person of the crime of murder, the Crown is normally required to prove that the accused *intended* to kill his or her victim or meant to cause bodily harm that is likely to cause death and is reckless whether death ensues or not (section 229(a) of the Code).

Once the Crown has established that the accused acted intentionally, the issue then arises as to whether he or she should be found guilty of first *or* second degree murder. Section 235(1) provides that, in either case, the accused will be sentenced to life imprisonment. However, Parliament has drawn a clear distinction between first and second degree murder in relation to the time that individuals must serve before they may be eligible for parole. Section 745 provides that persons convicted of first degree murder will not be eligible for parole until they have served 25 years of their sentence (although they may take advantage of section 745.6, the so-called "faint-hope clause," which allows them to seek a judicial review of the noneligibility period after serving fifteen years of their sentence). Where an individual is convicted of second degree murder, section 745.4 of the Code provides that the trial judge may set a period of noneligibility for parole ranging from a minimum of ten years to a maximum of 25 years; it should be noted that section 745.2

of the Code provides that the jury may make a rec-ommendation to the trial judge as to the noneligi-bility period that should be imposed in relation to an individual convicted of second degree murder.

Clearly, in order to establish first degree murder, the Crown must normally prove not only that the accused intended to kill his or her victim but also that he or she did so in a *planned and deliberate manner*. What do these words mean? In the case of *Widdifield* (1961), the trial judge (Justice Gale of the Ontario High Court) issued the following instructions to the jury in relation to the meaning of the words "planned and deliberate":

> I think that in the Code *"planned" is to be assigned … its natural meaning of a calculated scheme or design which has been carefully thought out, and the nature and consequences of which have been consid-ered and weighed.* But that does not mean, of course, to say that the plan need be a complicated one. It may be a very simple one, and the simpler it is perhaps the easier it is to formulate.
>
> The important element, it seems to me so far as time is concerned, is the time involved in devel-oping the plan, not the time between the develop-ment of the plan and the doing of the act. One can carefully prepare a plan and immediately it is pre-pared set out to do the planned act, or, alterna-tively, you can wait an appreciable time to do it once it has been formed.
>
> *As far as the word "deliberate" is concerned, I think that the Code means that it should also carry its natural meaning of "considered," "not impulsive," "slow in deciding," "cautious," implying that the ac-cused must take time to weigh the advantages and disadvantages of his intended action.* This is what, as it seems to me, "deliberate" means. [emphasis added]

This definition of the words planned and deliberate has been widely cited in subsequent cases.

An example of the application of the principle stated in *Widdifield* is furnished by the later case of *Smith* (1980), in which the accused was charged

with first degree murder in relation to the death of one Skwarchuk. It appears that Smith, Skwarchuk, and a third man, called Massier, went on a hunting trip together. They arrived at an abandoned farm house and stopped there. While Massier was smash-ing the windows of the house, Smith and Skwar-chuk entered into a vigorous argument. Massier heard a shot and saw Smith standing with a shotgun in his hand and Skwarchuk running away. The lat-ter had been shot in the left elbow, his arm was hanging down and blood was squirting on the ground. Massier stated that Skwarchuk was scream-ing and yelling. Smith reloaded his shotgun and shot Skwarchuk, at least twice, from long range. It appeared that some pellets hit Skwarchuk in the back but he continued to run. However, Smith shot Skwarchuk again and he fell down and stayed on the ground.

Smith then approached Skwarchuk who was sit-ting on the ground, and shot him in the back of the head. Skwarchuk fell down dead. Smith was subse-quently arrested by the police and charged. At his trial, he was convicted of first degree murder; how-ever, on appeal, the Saskatchewan Court of Appeal substituted a conviction for second degree murder. The Court of Appeal was not satisfied that the killing was both planned and deliberate. Chief Jus-tice Culliton delivered the judgment of the court. He stated that

> I realize that it is both difficult and unwise to give an exhaustive meaning to the word "planned." It is a common word and to it should be attrib-uted its meaning as understood in everyday life. Clearly, *planning must not be confused with inten-tion as the planning would only occur after the intent to murder had been formed. There must be some evidence the killing was the result of a scheme or design previously formulated or designed by the accused and the killing was the implementation of that scheme or design.* It is obvious a murder com-mitted on a sudden impulse and without prior consideration, even though the intent to kill is clearly proven, would not constitute a planned murder.

In the present case, there is not the slightest evidence the appellant (Smith) had given any consideration to the murder of Skwarchuk until after he and Skwarchuk had left the house ...

I am satisfied that there was no evidence whatever to support the conclusion that the actions of the appellant, cruel and sadistic as they were, in killing Skwarchuk was the implementation of a previously determined design or scheme. I think it is obvious his actions were the result of a sudden impulse. It would be pure speculation to try and determine what triggered that impulse. [emphasis added]

The courts have often recognized that an important factor to take into consideration in determining whether the accused acted in a "planned and deliberate" manner is whether the accused acted in a state of intoxication. As we shall see in Chapter 9, if intoxication prevents the accused person from forming the *specific intent to kill*, it serves as a **partial defence** and reduces the severity of the charge from murder to **manslaughter**. However, it may well be that the accused's state of intoxication was not so serious as to prevent him or her from forming the specific intent to kill. Nevertheless, his or her state of intoxication may still be particularly relevant to the issue of whether the accused acted in a planned and deliberate manner when he or she killed the victim. In the words of Justice Gale in the *Widdifield* case (1961),

The capacity to form the essential intent to kill or to do harm and the capacity to plan and deliberate are not the same. A greater mental capacity is surely required to formulate a plan, even a simple one, and to deliberate upon that plan than is required to form the intent to kill or to do harm. *The Code does not envisage the deliberation, as it seems to me, of a mind which is substantially impaired by alcohol. Conversely, a lesser degree of intoxication will surely interfere with and render impossible a plan or deliberation such as is envisaged by the Code. ...* [emphasis added]

In the case of *Wallen* (1990), the Supreme Court of Canada also considered the question of the impact of intoxication on an accused person's ability to plan and deliberate within the meaning of section 231(2). The Court ruled that a trial judge must always direct the jury to consider the issue of intoxication and its effect on the accused's ability to plan and deliberate *separately* from the issue of intoxication and its effect on the accused's ability to form the intent to kill. Curiously, however, the members of the Court could not agree whether the trial judge must *always* instruct the jury that a *lesser* degree of intoxication may be sufficient to negative the requirement of planning and deliberation than to negative the requirement of intent to kill. All members of the Court, however, appeared to believe that such an instruction would be "helpful" to the jury. The Court ordered a new trial for the accused, who had been convicted of first degree murder, because the trial judge had repeatedly used the phrase "very intoxicated" when referring not only to the question of whether the accused had intended to kill his victim but also to the question of whether he acted in a planned and deliberate manner.

Similarly, the Supreme Court of Canada has clearly acknowledged that mental illness may also have the effect of negativing the element of *planning and deliberation* required for conviction of first degree murder. As Chief Justice Lamer stated in the *Jacquard* case (1997),

It is true that some factor, such as a mental disorder, that is insufficient to negative the charge that the accused *intended* to kill, may nevertheless be sufficient to negative the elements of *planning and deliberation*. This is because one can intend to kill and yet be impulsive rather than considered in doing so. It requires less mental capacity simply to intend than it does to plan and deliberate.

Of course, it must be emphasized that, if an accused person suffered from a particularly severe form of **mental disorder** at the time that the alleged offence was committed, then it is possible that the accused might be able to prove that he or she should be found "not criminally responsible on account of mental disorder" (**NCRMD**) under the terms of section 16 of the *Criminal Code* (a special defence that is fully discussed in Chapter 8). However, an accused person, who is not successful in raising this defence and is instead convicted of murder, may still point to the mental disorder at the time of the killing and claim that it prevented him or her from acting *with planning and deliberation*. If the accused manages to raise a reasonable doubt on this issue, then there must be a conviction of *second degree*, rather than first degree, murder.

The *Allard* case (1990) demonstrates the various stages that must be followed when the issue of mental disorder is raised in relation to a charge of first degree murder. The accused was charged with this offence after she administered a vitamin capsule, laced with a fatal dose of strychnine, to her husband. The accused's defence was that she was not criminally responsible on account of mental disorder and that, in any event, she did not kill her husband intentionally or in a planned and deliberate manner. The trial judge instructed the jury that, if the accused failed to prove that she was not criminally responsible under section 16 of the Code, they must "disregard [the mental disorder] defence completely." Allard was subsequently convicted of first degree murder. However, the Québec Court of Appeal allowed her appeal and ordered a new trial. The court found that the original trial judge should have pointed out to the jury that, even if the accused had not proved that she was not criminally responsible under the terms of section 16 of the Code, she might be able to raise a reasonable doubt as to whether her mental disorder prevented her from forming the intent to kill; if she did raise such a doubt, she would have to be acquitted and convicted of manslaughter instead. However, if the jury is satisfied beyond a reasonable doubt that the accused *did* form the intent to kill her husband, it will still have to consider the totally separate question of whether her mental disorder prevented her from acting in a planned and deliberate manner; if she could raise a reasonable doubt on this score, she would be acquitted of first degree murder and convicted of second degree murder.

Before leaving our discussion of first degree murder, it is important to consider the implications of the decision of the Supreme Court of Canada in *Nygaard and Schimmens* (1989). Prior to this decision, it was generally assumed that where a conviction of first degree murder was based on the allegation that the killing had been planned and deliberate, the Crown would base its case on the contention that the accused met the *mens rea* requirements for murder set out in section 229(a)(i) (namely, the accused *meant to cause the death of the victim*). However, under the provisions of section 229(a)(ii), accused persons who have killed someone may also be found guilty of murder if they meant to inflict bodily harm that they knew was likely to cause death and were reckless whether death actually ensued or not. Are there circumstances in which such persons can be considered to have committed first degree murder, in the sense of having acted with planning and deliberation?

In the *Nygaard and Schimmens* case (1989), the Supreme Court of Canada unanimously held that such individuals could indeed be convicted of first degree murder in certain circumstances. The facts of the case were that the victim had died from multiple skull fractures following a ferocious beating with a baseball bat. The Crown did not rely on section 229(a)(i) of the Code since there may have been a question as to whether the person who wielded the bat actually intended to kill the victim. However, the Crown did contend that this person *meant to cause bodily harm that was likely to cause death and was reckless as to whether death ensued or not* (in other words, he foresaw the risk of death and nevertheless proceeded with the brutal assault). In delivering the judgment of the Supreme Court of Canada, Justice Cory stated that, as far as section 229(a)(ii) is concerned,

> the vital element of the requisite intent is that of causing such bodily harm that the perpetrator knows that it is likely to cause death and yet persists in the assault. *There can be no doubt that*

a person can plan and deliberate to cause terrible bodily harm that he knows is likely to result in death. Nothing is added to the aspect of planning and deliberation by the requirement that the fatal assault be carried out in a reckless manner, that is to say by heedlessly proceeding with the deadly assault in the face of the knowledge of obvious risks. *The planning and deliberation to cause the bodily harm which is likely to be fatal must of necessity include the planning and deliberating to continue and persist in that conduct despite the knowledge of the risk.* The element of recklessness does not exist in a vacuum as a sole *mens rea* requirement, but rather it must act in conjunction with the intentional infliction of terrible bodily harm. I, therefore, conclude that planning and deliberation may well be coupled with the *mens rea* requirement of [s. 229(a)(ii)] and that a first degree murder conviction can be sustained by virtue of the combined operation of [s. 231(2)] and [s. 229(a)(ii)]. [emphasis added]

THE DISTINCTION BETWEEN DIRECT AND INDIRECT INTENTION AND KNOWLEDGE

For the purpose of analysis, it is possible to draw a distinction between **direct** and **indirect intention** and knowledge. The term *direct intention* refers to intention in the popular sense of desire, purpose, aim, objective, or design. In this sense, it clearly reflects the layperson's understanding of the word intention. For example, let us suppose that Pumblechook points a shotgun at Jaggers's head and pulls the trigger. In the absence of exceptional circumstances (such as a mental disorder sufficient to bring the accused within the purview of section 16 of the Code), it is clear that Pumblechook must have intended to kill Jaggers (in the sense that he deliberately sought to bring about this consequence by his conduct). Of course, we would still say that Pumblechook intended to inflict death even if his chances of success, at the time he pulled the trigger, appeared to be quite small. For example, Pumblechook may have aimed his shotgun at a great dis-

tance from Jaggers and therefore needed a great deal of "luck" in order to be successful in hitting and killing him. However, if the evidence establishes that Pumblechook clearly *desired* to bring about this consequence, he must be taken to have *intended* to inflict death.

The term *direct knowledge* reflects the layperson's understanding of the word knowledge. In essence, direct knowledge denotes *actual* knowledge of particular circumstances. For example, suppose that Fagin is given a stolen watch by the Artful Dodger. Fagin clearly knows that the watch is stolen because the Dodger told him that he removed it from the pocket of Mr. Bumble. Obviously, Fagin has direct knowledge that the watch has been stolen and, of course, would be subject to conviction under section 354 of the *Criminal Code* (possession of property obtained by crime).

As we have noted, the popular interpretations of the terms intention and knowledge correspond to the legal terms direct intention and direct knowledge. However, for the purpose of the doctrine of *mens rea*, the scope of the terms intention and knowledge has been expanded by the evolution of the concepts of *indirect* intention and knowledge.

What is meant by *indirect intention*? Let us suppose that Bob does not desire that his conduct produce a certain consequence B but nevertheless knows that such a consequence B is a necessary step on the way to accomplishing the objective that he really does wish to achieve (consequence A). Can we say that Bob "intends" the undesired consequence B? The answer is yes.

Imagine that Bob Cratchitt clearly wishes to wound Scrooge by hurling a rock at him. Scrooge unfortunately happens to be visiting Fezziwig's house. Cratchitt is a close friend of Fezziwig and would certainly not intend to cause him any grief. Nevertheless, the only way in which Cratchitt can accomplish his objective of wounding Scrooge is by hurling the rock through the window (which is closed). There is no doubt that Cratchitt does not *desire* to break the window but, on the other hand, he realizes that he must do so in order to attain his objective of wounding Scrooge. Let us suppose that

Cratchitt throws the rock at Scrooge, *knowing* the window is closed. There is no difficulty in determining that Cratchitt intends to wound Scrooge. However, does he "intend" to break Fezziwig's window? For the purpose of the criminal law, Cratchitt will be held to have *indirectly* intended to break the window and is liable to conviction of wilful damage of property (section 430 of the *Criminal Code*). Putting it in legal terms, Cratchitt is deemed to have intended to break the window because he knew this *undesired* consequence was a condition **precedent** to the attainment of his *desired* objective of wounding Scrooge.

There is another situation in which the concept of indirect intention becomes of critical importance. Let us suppose that Nell wants to achieve a certain objective (consequence A), but she knows that it is probable (although not certain) that her conduct in achieving this objective will produce another consequence B that she does *not* want to happen. Let us also suppose that Nell does, in fact, produce both consequences by her conduct. Can Nell say that she did not really intend consequence B because it was always possible that she could have achieved her desired objective (consequence A) without also causing the undesired consequence B? The answer to this question is an emphatic no and Nell would be considered to have intended both consequences A and B.

Consider the following hypothetical example. Quilp joins a gang of terrorists and is ordered to destroy a shipment of arms destined for the military. To this end, he buries a land-mine under the road. The land-mine is designed to detonate by remote control, and Quilp's plan is to explode the bomb as the truck, carrying the shipment, passes over it. Quilp does not wish to kill the driver of the truck but he necessarily knows that the explosion is "virtually certain" to do so. It is just possible that the driver may escape alive but Quilp knows that this is highly unlikely. When the truck passes over the land-mine, Quilp detonates it and, in the ensuing explosion, the driver (Noggs) is killed instantaneously. Did Quilp "intend" to kill Noggs, assuming that he did not *wish* to cause this consequence?

The answer must be yes. Once again, the accused would be deemed to have *indirectly intended* the death of Noggs and, therefore, would be liable to conviction of murder.

An interesting example of this type of indirect intention is provided by the case of *Buzzanga and Durocher* (1980), in which the two defendants were charged with wilfully promoting hatred against an identifiable group, contrary to section 319(2) of the *Criminal Code*. More specifically, they were charged with promoting hatred against members of the Francophone community in Essex County (Ontario), by communicating statements contained in copies of a handbill entitled "Wake Up Canadians Your Future Is At Stake!" The prosecution of Buzzanga and Durocher was steeped in irony since they both identified themselves strongly with French-speaking Canadians. The prosecution arose as a consequence of the attempt of the defendants to secure the construction of a French-language high school in Essex County, which the Essex County Board of Education had decided not to build. In fact, in December 1976, the majority of candidates elected to the school board were persons who opposed the construction of the French-language high school. It was after this defeat that the accused disseminated the handbill that contained the following inflammatory statements:

Did you know that those of the French minority who support the building of the French-language high school are in fact a subversive group and that most French Canadians of Essex County are opposed to the building of that school?

Who will rid us of this subversive group if not ourselves?

If we give them a school, what will they demand next ... independent city states? Consider the ethnic problem of the United States, and take heed.

We must stamp out the subversive element which uses history to justify its freeloading on the taxpayers of Canada, now.

The British solved this problem once before with the Acadians, what are we waiting for ... ?

Durocher testified that his purpose was to demonstrate the prejudice against French Canadians and to "expose the truth" about the problem with the French-language school, while Buzzanga stated that he intended the pamphlet to be considered merely as a "satire." They both appeared to have believed that the pamphlet would create a "furor" that would provoke a reaction on the part of the Ontario government, who would then put pressure on the school board to build the French-language school. Their evidence, if believed, suggested that neither of them wished to promote hatred against French-speaking people; indeed, as they pointed out, if they *had* nursed such an intention, they would have been promoting hatred against themselves. Nevertheless, at their trial, the defendants were convicted and they appealed to the Ontario Court of Appeal. Their appeal was allowed and a new trial ordered.

The judgment of the Ontario Court of Appeal was delivered by Justice Martin, who held that the word "wilfully," in the context of section 319(2), means "with the intention of promoting hatred." Therefore, the critical issue was clearly whether the defendants could be deemed to have *intended* to promote hatred, when their long-term objective was to obtain what they considered to be a benefit to the French-speaking community—namely, a French-language high school. Justice Martin agreed that

> as a general rule, a person who foresees that a consequence is certain or substantially certain to result from an act which he does in order to achieve some other purposes, intends that consequence. The actor's foresight of the certainty or moral certainty of the consequence resulting from his conduct compels a conclusion that if he, none the less, acted so as to produce it, then he decided to bring it about (albeit regretfully), in order to achieve his ultimate purpose. His intention encompasses the means as well as his ultimate objective.

> I conclude, therefore, that the appellants "wilfully" (intentionally) promoted hatred against the French Canadian community of Essex County

only if: (a) Their conscious purpose in distributing the document was to promote hatred within that group, or (b) They foresaw that the promotion of hatred against that group was certain or morally certain to result from the distribution of the pamphlet, but distributed it as a means of achieving their purpose of obtaining the French-language high school. [emphasis added]

Alternative (b) identified by Justice Martin represents a conspicuous example of the application of the concept of indirect intention. Having established the appropriate principles that should be applied in cases of this nature, the Ontario Court of Appeal ordered a new trial for Buzzanga and Durocher. Significantly, Justice Martin's interpretation of section 319(2) was subsequently affirmed by the Supreme Court of Canada in the cases of *Keegstra* (1990) and *Andrews* (1990).

Direct and Indirect Knowledge

The concepts of *direct* and *indirect knowledge* are closely related to those of direct and indirect intention. *Direct knowledge* exists in the situation where the accused has *actual knowledge* that particular circumstances exist. *Indirect knowledge* exists when the accused, although he or she has no *actual knowledge* that the particular circumstances exist, nevertheless knows that they are "*virtually certain*" to exist. For example, suppose that Barkis purchases two colour television sets from Jorkis. Jorkis does not explicitly inform Barkis that these TV sets are stolen. However, he tells Barkis that they "fell off the back of a truck" and sells them at an extremely low price. In these circumstances, only a naïve simpleton would fail to realize that these goods are stolen. Therefore, given that Barkis is neither naïve nor a simpleton, it should be easy to conclude that Barkis knows that it is virtually certain that the TV sets are stolen and he may be convicted of a charge under section 354(1) of the *Criminal Code* (possession of property obtained by crime). Here, Barkis has *indirect* knowledge that the goods are stolen.

INTENTION AND MOTIVE DISTINGUISHED

In the *Lewis* case (1979), Justice Dickson, while delivering the judgment of the Supreme Court of Canada stated that

> In ordinary parlance, the words "intent" and "motive" are frequently used interchangeably, but in the criminal law they are distinct. In most criminal trials, the mental element, the *mens rea* with which the Court is concerned, relates to "intent," i.e., the exercise of a free will to use particular means to produce a particular result, rather than with "motive," i.e., that which precedes and induces the exercise of the will. The mental element of a crime ordinarily involves no reference to motive. ...

In the case of *Dynar* (1997), Justices Cory and Iacobucci of the Supreme Court of Canada articulated a clear rationale for drawing this distinction between intention and **motive**:

> Society imposes criminal sanctions in order to punish and deter undesirable conduct. *It does not matter to society, in its efforts to secure social peace and order, what an accused's motive was, but only what the accused intended to do.* It is no consolation to one whose car has been stolen that the thief stole the car intending to sell it to purchase food for a food bank. [emphasis added]

The case of *Buzzanga and Durocher* (1980), discussed in the previous section, is an excellent illustration of the need to distinguish between *intention* and *motive*. The defendants' *motive* for issuing the handbill was laudable (namely, the construction of a French-language high school); however, it is quite possible that, in accordance with the second alternative principle identified by Justice Martin, they could be found guilty of *intentionally* promoting hatred against the very group whose interests they wished to advance.

As Justice McLachlin, speaking on behalf of a majority of the justices of the Supreme Court of Canada, said in the *Théroux* case (1993), *an accused person's personal system of values is not a relevant consideration* in determining whether he or she has the necessary *mens rea* for conviction of an offence:

> A person is not saved from conviction because he or she believes that there is nothing wrong with what he or she is doing. *The question is whether the accused subjectively appreciated that certain consequences would follow from his or her acts, not whether the accused believed that the acts or their consequences to be moral.* Just as the pathological killer would not be acquitted on the mere ground that he failed to see his act as morally reprehensible, so the defrauder will not be acquitted because he believed that what he was doing was honest. [emphasis added]

As we noted in Chapter 3, a physician who deliberately injects a massive overdose of drugs in order to terminate the painful existence of a slowly dying patient may be convicted of murder on the basis that he or she *intended* to cause death, despite the fact that his or her *motive* was to relieve the pain and suffering of a futile existence. In short, if defendants cause the *actus reus* of a crime with the necessary *mens rea,* it is entirely irrelevant that they claim to be acting out of what some may consider to be praiseworthy motives.

In the example of the doctor who carries out a mercy killing, we can see that the *mens rea* for murder is, normally, an intention to kill or an intention to inflict bodily harm that is likely to cause death and recklessness as to whether or not death ensues. The doctor clearly intends to bring about the death of the patient and, if the patient does in fact die, the doctor has committed the *actus reus* of murder together with the requisite *mens rea*. The doctor's motive is absolutely irrelevant because it is not part of the definition of the crime of murder. In this particular case, if the doctor was convicted of first degree murder, the judge could not take the motive into account because there is a fixed sentence (life sentence with a minimum nonparole period of 25 years). However, for most other offences, trial judges have considerable discretion in setting the appropriate sentence and it is highly likely that noble (albeit misguided) motives will result in a more lenient sentence being imposed.

The *Latimer* case (1998) illustrates the immense difficulty that may arise when an accused person's motives may not be taken into account because of a *mandatory* sentence that is prescribed in the *Criminal Code*. Robert Latimer asphyxiated his severely disabled, twelve-year-old daughter with carbon monoxide and claimed that he had killed her out of *compassion*—his motive had been to end (what he perceived to be) his daughter's intolerable suffering. Since it was clear that Latimer carried this act out *intentionally*, he was convicted of second degree murder. Both the trial judge and jury appeared to accept that Latimer was telling the truth when he stated that he had engaged in a so-called "mercy killing." However, section 745 of the Code imposes a mandatory sentence for second degree murder. That sentence is one of life imprisonment, with no eligibility for parole for a period of between ten and 25 years (this period to be set by the trial judge, who is required to consult with the jury on this issue). When consulted in relation to the appropriate non-parole–eligibility period, the jury in the *Latimer* case recommended that the accused be eligible for parole after only one year in custody (a sentence that is not permitted, in light of the *mandatory minimum* period of ten years that is imposed by section 745). In a highly unusual move, the trial judge ruled that, in light of the fact that Latimer acted out of compassionate (albeit profoundly misguided) motives, it would constitute cruel and unusual punishment under section 12 of the *Charter* to sentence him to life imprisonment with no eligibility for parole for ten years. Consequently, Justice Noble granted Latimer a **constitutional exemption** from the provisions of section 745 and sentenced him to one year in prison and one year on probation. However, the Crown appealed against this sentence and

the Saskatchewan Court of Appeal set it aside, substituting a sentence of life imprisonment with no eligibility for parole for ten years. The Court of Appeal rejected the notion that Latimer was entitled to a constitutional exemption and stated that it is up to Parliament to deal with the question of whether there should be special sentencing provisions to deal with the issue of so-called "mercy-killing":

> In the meantime is it not for the court to pass on the wisdom of Parliament with respect to the range of penalties to be imposed on those found guilty of murder.

The question of whether those who commit murder from compassionate motives should be treated more leniently than other individuals who perpetrate this crime is highly controversial and has deeply divided Canadians. Some would argue that the justice system is functioning in a profoundly unjust manner if "mercy-killers," such as Latimer, are treated in the same manner as those who kill for motives of which we profoundly disapprove. On the other hand, some would contend that the life of Latimer's daughter was taken *without her consent* and that she was killed because she was severely disabled; therefore, it may be argued, if we grant more lenient sentences to those who kill in such circumstances, we are effectively devaluing the lives of all persons with a disability.

It is significant that, in January 2001, the Supreme Court of Canada unanimously affirmed the position taken by the Court of Appeal. In the words of the Supreme Court,

> … the minimum mandatory sentence is not grossly disproportionate in this case. We cannot find that any aspect of the paticular circumstances of the case or the offender diminishes the degree of criminal responsibility borne by Mr. Latimer.

However, the Supreme Court did emphasize the fact that the Government of Canada has the power to grant clemency in cases such as that of *Latimer*. This power is known as the "royal prerogative of mercy" and, as the Court indicated, "is the only potential remedy for persons who have exhausted their rights of appeal and are unable to show that their sentence fails to accord with the *Charter*."

While the accused's motive is not one of the mental elements that must be established by the Crown in order to establish criminal responsibility, it may, nevertheless, be very relevant to the trial process. More specifically, the presence of motive(s) may well be a critical part of the Crown's case in establishing the guilt of the accused. As Justice Dickson asserted, in delivering the Supreme Court of Canada's judgment in the case of *Lewis* (1979), the prosecution can always introduce evidence that an accused person had a motive for committing the offence because, if it can prove the existence of such a motive, it is more likely that the accused did commit the offence. As Justice Dickson pointed out, "men [*sic*] do not usually act without a motive." Conversely, if the accused can establish that he or she had no motive for committing the crime, this is an important fact in his or her favour when the **trier of fact** comes to consider the question of innocence or guilt.

For example, in the *Stone* case (1999), Justice Bastarache, on behalf of the majority of the Supreme Court of Canada, emphasized that the credibility of a defence of **automatism** is considerably enhanced if there is no apparent motive for the alleged crime:

> ... the plausibility of a claim of automatism will be reduced if the accused had a motive to commit the crime in question ... On the other hand, if the involuntary act is random and lacks motive, the plausibility of the claim of automatism will be increased.

The practical importance of motive in a criminal trial is illustrated by the case of *Monteleone* (1987). The accused had been charged with arson, as a consequence of a fire, which started in his clothing store. The fire was so extensive that it destroyed the whole building in which the store had been located and it was not possible to determine the exact cause of its origins. However, the fire inspector testified that "the fire was of incendiary origin because his investigation revealed no accidental cause." The trial judge directed the jury to acquit the accused because the evidence did not justify drawing an inference that he had deliberately set the fire. However, the Crown successfully appealed to the Ontario Court of Appeal, which ordered a new trial because the trial judge should have allowed the jury to consider evidence of Monteleone's *motive* and *opportunity* to commit the crime of arson. The Supreme Court of Canada subsequently affirmed the Court of Appeal's decision and, on the issue of *motive*, Justice McIntyre noted in his judgment on behalf of the Court,

> There was evidence of some difficulties with the retail sales tax branch regarding tax owing in respect of the business operation and a substantial assessment had been made upon the business for payment of arrears. There was evidence of a substantial indebtedness to the bank and a bank overdraft. There was, as well, evidence of the appellant's indebtedness arising in connection with his sister which involves substantial liability on two mortgages. There was evidence of difficulties he had encountered in dealing with his insurance claim involving varying claims and statements. *This evidence was such that it should have been left to the jury on the issue of motive.* [emphasis added]

Similarly, in *Charemski* (1998), the Supreme Court of Canada held that evidence of motive should be considered by the jury in a case in which the accused had been charged with the murder of his estranged wife, whose dead body had been found in her bathtub. There had been evidence concerning Charemski's "*animus*" (hatred) towards his wife (allegedly arising from his anger concerning her relationships with other men) and a financial *motive* for killing her. Speaking on behalf of the majority of the Supreme Court, Justice Bastarache stated that

> The Crown also led evidence suggesting the appellant may have had a financial motive to kill his wife. The appellant, who receives social assistance, held a life insurance policy on the deceased in the amount of $50,000. The Crown adduced evidence to establish that this represents a great deal of money in Poland, where the appellant (who is Polish) has been living on and off for the past five years. On the basis of these facts, the Crown, in my opinion, adduced sufficient evidence from which a jury, properly instructed, could have inferred the requisite mental state for homicide. That is, *the jury could have inferred from the evidence of the animus and financial motive that the accused intended to kill his wife.* [emphasis added]

PROVING INTENTION

Using the Test of the "Reasonable Person" as a Means of Determining Subjective Intent

One of the more difficult tasks confronting the prosecution in a criminal trial is proving that the defendant had the requisite intention or knowledge. How can these elements be proved? Sometimes, "the facts may speak for themselves." It will be obvious that the accused must have had the necessary intention or knowledge and, unless he or she comes up with an explanation that casts doubt on that conclusion, a judge or jury will have no difficulty in finding the accused guilty. As Justice McLachlin, speaking on behalf of the majority of the Supreme Court of Canada, asserted in the *Théroux* case (1993),

> the Crown need not, in every case, show precisely what thought was in the accused's mind at the time of the criminal act. In certain cases, subjective awareness of the consequences can be inferred

from the act itself, barring some explanation casting doubt on such inference. The fact that such an inference is made does not detract from the subjectivity of the test.

However, the facts will not always speak for themselves, and other methods must be used in order to determine the accused's *subjective* intent or knowledge at the time of the incident in question. Of course, either at the time that the alleged offence was committed or at their trial, accused persons may volunteer a statement as to what their intention or knowledge was at the critical time. Such statements or "confessions" may well be sufficient to ensure a conviction. On the other hand, accused persons may state that they did not possess the requisite intention or knowledge and, therefore, ought to be acquitted. In these circumstances, the judge or jury, as the case may be, could well choose to believe such a statement and acquit them. However, since accused persons have a vested interest in exculpating themselves, there may be a real question as to their credibility.

How can accused persons' credibility be determined? One way in which their credibility may be tested is to ask the question, What would a *reasonable* or *ordinary* person have *intended* or *known* in the particular circumstances in which the accused found themselves? In answering this question, the judge or jury will, no doubt, apply their own experience of everyday life. If there is a great divergence between what the reasonable person would have intended or known and what accused persons state they intended or knew, it is quite likely that the accused's version of events will not be believed. Conversely, if there is a close similarity between the accused's statement of what they intended or knew and what the judge or jury feels a reasonable person would have intended or known in the same circumstances, it is most likely that the judge or jury will consider that the accused are telling the truth.

The willingness of the courts to employ the "common sense" standard of the "reasonable" person is reflected in the ancient **common law** maxim, that people must be taken to have "intended" the natural and probable consequences of their acts. The meaning of this maxim is quite straightforward. As Justice Cory noted, in delivering the judgment of the Supreme Court of Canada in the case of *Seymour* (1996),

> Common sense dictates that people are usually able to foresee the consequences of their actions. Therefore, if a person acts in a manner which is likely to produce a certain result it generally will be reasonable to infer that the person foresaw the probable consequences of the act. In other words, if a person acted so as to produce certain predictable consequences, it may be inferred that the person intended those consequences.

Suppose, for example, that Pecksniff places the barrel of a revolver against Jonas's head and pulls the trigger. What are the natural and probable consequences of pulling the trigger of a revolver in these circumstances? The obvious answer is the death of Jonas. Since it is clear that an ordinary person would have appreciated what the natural and probable consequences of his or her acts would be, in these circumstances, it is surely reasonable to assume that Pecksniff intended to kill Jonas.

However, the courts have emphasized that the "natural and probable consequences" inference only serves as a useful yardstick that may — or may not — be appropriate to use in all the circumstances of an individual case. Certainly, the trier of fact is not bound to draw the inference that a particular accused person had the necessary *mens rea* simply because a reasonable person would have done so. As Justice Cory of the Supreme Court of Canada noted in the *Seymour* case (1996), the "common sense inference that people are usually able to foresee the consequences of their actions" should be considered "a reasonable inference which *may* be drawn but is not required to be drawn by juries." In this respect, Justice Cory expressly approved a statement made in the judgment of Justice Roach of the Ontario Court of Appeal in *Giannotti* (1956),

> ... as a man is usually able to foresee what are the natural consequences of his acts, so it is, as a rule, reasonable to infer that he did foresee and intend them. But, *while that is an inference which may be drawn, it is not one which must be drawn. If on all of the facts of the case it is not the correct inference, then it should not be drawn* ... [emphasis added]

Putting this another way, whenever a criminal offence is defined in terms of *subjective mens rea* requirements, then it is critical to ensure that the "natural and probable consequences test" is only used in a genuine effort to establish what the particular accused person in the case *subjectively knew and intended.* As Justice Cory stated in the *Seymour* case (1996), "the common sense inference as to intention, which may be drawn from the actions of the accused, is simply a method to determine the accused's *actual* intent."

In the majority of cases, no doubt, the judge or jury will tend to disbelieve accused persons who claim that they did not possess the requisite knowledge or intention when the ordinary or reasonable person, in the same circumstances as the accused, would have possessed such knowledge or intention. However, it is important to bear in mind that people do not always act reasonably nor do they always have the same capacities as the hypothetical reasonable person. For example, certain individuals may be so mentally impaired that they are incapable of foreseeing the consequences of their actions even though an ordinary person, in exactly the same circumstances, would have done so. Similarly, even an average person, under stress, may well panic and fail to act as the hypothetical reasonable person would have done in the same circumstances.

If there is a reasonable doubt that the accused possessed the requisite intention or knowledge, he or she must be acquitted despite the fact that the "ordinary" or "reasonable" person would have possessed the necessary *mens rea* in the same circumstances. For example, in *Beyo* (2000), the accused had visited the home of relatives of his estranged wife. Among other acts, he broke the window in a door and he was charged, *inter alia*, with the offence of mischief (wilfully destroying or damaging property, contrary to the provisions of section 430(1)(a) of the *Criminal Code*). The critical issue on this charge was whether Beyo "wilfully" broke the window. There was Crown evidence to the effect that the accused had pounded on the glass with a closed fist in "what seemed to be an attempt to break the glass to gain entry into the house." However, Beyo himself testified that he was merely "banging on the glass to make noise to attract attention": he claimed that he had done this because he believed that his son had been kidnapped and was in the house. Therefore, the accused's version of events was that he had struck the window repeatedly in the hope that the noise would cause the police to intervene and he stated that "*he did not intend to break the glass* and as soon as it broke he immediately offered to pay for the damage."

The trial judge brought to the jury's attention the "old common law rule" that "every man's intention must be presumed from the manner in which he behaves" and stated that

> There is a glass door and Mr. Beyo is an educated man ... *He must know that continued hitting of that glass is likely to break it. Any reasonable person must know that and he would therefore be found guilty of the mischief* with regard to the offence of breaking the window. [emphasis added]

The accused was convicted and he appealed to the Ontario Court of Appeal, which set aside the finding of guilt of mischief. On behalf of the court, Justice Rosenberg noted that the trial judge did not bring to the jury's attention the accused's own evidence as to the state of his mind at the time of the alleged offence. Indeed,

> ... if the appellant's version of events were accepted, a finding of guilt, while possible, was not inevitable. His state of mind had to be determined by a consideration of the evidence including the appellant's testimony, the evidence of others that

he was obviously in an agitated state and concerned for the welfare of his son. *It could not be determined by application of any legal presumption nor solely from a comparison with what a reasonable person would know.* [emphasis added]

Clearly, in *Beyo*, it was not appropriate to draw the "common sense inference" as to intention because there was some credible evidence that was capable of raising a reasonable doubt as to whether the accused did in fact intend to break the window.

Similarly, if an accused person is intoxicated, the trial judge must make it crystal clear that, if the members of the jury harbour any doubts about that person's *actual* intention or knowledge in relation to a crime requiring proof of subjective *mens rea*, then the "common sense inference" may not be applied at all (see the Supreme Court of Canada decisions in *Robinson* (1996) and *Seymour* (1996), which are fully discussed in Chapter 9, under the heading of "Intoxication").

THE CONCEPT OF TRANSFERRED INTENT

Let us suppose that Romulus intends to hit Remus with a belt. Romulus takes aim at Remus, but his belt misses its mark and instead strikes and wounds Cato. It is clear that Romulus "intended" to wound Remus. However, can he be convicted of an assault causing bodily harm to Cato? The answer is that Romulus could, indeed, be convicted under section 267 of the Code because of the operation of the ancient common law principle of *transferred intent*. In essence, this principle provides that Romulus's intention to hit Remus can be *transferred* to the assault actually committed against Cato. Romulus intended to commit the *actus reus* of an assault (albeit the victim was supposed to be Remus) and actually committed the *actus reus* of assault when he hit Cato. Therefore, it seems to be both just and reasonable to convict him of assault causing bodily harm.

The operation of this principle is well illustrated by the case of *Deakin* (1974), in which the accused

A case of tranferred intent.

intended to swing at a man called Pelletier. In swinging at him, Deakin came into contact with some glass ornaments sitting on top of a television set. Unfortunately, the glass shattered into fragments and Mrs. Pelletier (rather than her husband) was injured. The accused was charged with assault causing bodily harm.

At his trial, Deakin was acquitted. However, the Crown appealed and the Manitoba Court of Appeal allowed the appeal and entered a conviction against the defendant. In delivering the judgment of the Court of Appeal, Justice Matas stated

> It is not suggested, in the case at bar, that [Deakin's] act in hitting out at Mr. Pelletier was either an accident or a mistake. The learned trial Judge found that the accused intended to strike Pelletier. ... As a result of accused's commission of an unlawful act in striking at Mr. Pelletier, Mrs. Pelletier was injured; the accused's intention to strike Mr. Pelletier is deemed to have been directed (transferred) to the assault on Mrs. Pelletier. ... Lack of hostility toward Mrs. Pelletier, and lack of a specific intent to harm *her*, are irrelevant. Nor is it of any significance that Deakin struck an object that injured Mrs. Pelletier.

An example of transferred intent in the *Criminal Code* may be found in section 229(b):

> Where a person, meaning to cause death to a human being or meaning to cause him bodily harm that he knows is likely to cause death, and being reckless whether death ensues or not, by accident or mistake causes death to another human being, notwithstanding that he does not mean to cause death or bodily harm to that human being ... [is guilty of murder].

A rather bizarre set of circumstances led to the application of this section by the Supreme Court of Canada in the case of *Droste* (1984). In this case, the defendant was charged with first degree murder. The Crown introduced evidence to the effect that Droste had told his co-workers that he intended to kill his wife. It appeared that he was sexually involved with another woman, and that he wished to recover the proceeds of an insurance policy that had recently been placed on Mrs. Droste's life. He told one of his co-workers that he planned to crash his car, set it on fire, and leave his spouse to perish in the conflagration. On the day of the incident in question, Droste was seen to be applying gasoline to the inside of his car. He later entered the car with his wife and two small children and left for a birthday party. On the way, a fire broke out. His wife stated that Mr. Droste then tried to hit her on the head with a screwdriver and yelled at her to release her grip on the steering wheel. Tragically, the car struck the abutment of a bridge. The parents managed to extricate themselves from the blazing wreck, but they were unable to save the children, who were asphyxiated by the smoke. There was no evidence whatsoever that Mr. Droste harboured any ill will toward his children.

The trial judge instructed the jury that, if they were satisfied beyond a reasonable doubt that Droste's intention to kill his wife was planned and deliberate and that in the course of carrying out that intention he caused the death of his children by accident or mistake, the resulting homicide constituted first degree murder. The jury convicted, and both the Ontario Court of Appeal and the Supreme Court of Canada ultimately upheld the conviction. Justice Dickson noted, in the Supreme Court, that

> The jury found that Mr. Droste, meaning to cause the death of a human being (Mrs. Droste), by accident caused the death of another human being (each of the children). He is therefore guilty of murder pursuant to [s. 229(b)]. ...

A critical component of the doctrine of transferred intent is the requirement that the accused's intent may only be transferred where the *actus reus* and *mens rea* of the same offence coincide. In the *Deakin* case, discussed earlier, the accused clearly intended to commit an assault upon Mr. Pelletier; however, he actually assaulted Mrs. Pelletier. Since he both intended to commit assault (*mens rea*) and actually committed the *actus reus* of assault (albeit upon a different victim), the doctrine of transferred intent was applicable. However, in the case of *Vandergraaf* (1994), the situation was quite different. The accused had intended to throw a small jar of peanut butter onto the ice at a hockey arena. As was the case for many other fans, he was upset that the team he supported had lost a game in overtime. Tragically, his aim was erratic, and the jar hit a woman who was standing in the front row at ice level, causing an injury to her. The accused was charged with assault with a weapon (section 267). The trial judge convicted the accused because he had the "intention to apply force in a general sense."

However, the Manitoba Court of Appeal allowed Vandergraaf's appeal and entered an acquittal. As Justice Philp said,

> Without proof of an intention to apply force to the complainant, *or to another person*, there cannot be a conviction of assault. ... [emphasis added]

Unlike the accused in the *Deakin* case, Vandergraaf never intended to apply force to a human being, and he therefore lacked the *mens rea* for assault even though he accidentally committed the *actus reus* of this offence. Therefore, the doctrine of transferred intent could not apply.

The limitations upon the doctrine of transferred intent may be illustrated by considering the following hypothetical examples:

1. Let us suppose that Sinbad, the knife thrower at the local circus, has a burning desire to kill Hercules (the circus strong man). One evening, as dusk falls, he sees what he thinks is the silhouette of Hercules against the evening sky. He throws a knife at the figure and his aim is true. However, when Sinbad goes to inspect the corpse, he discovers that he has killed Leo (the lion tamer) by mistake. In these circumstances, it is clear that Sinbad is guilty of murder. After all, he killed the person at whom he was aiming his knife, and it is irrelevant that he was mistaken as to the person's identity.

2. Sinbad is walking in the local park when he sees Hercules coming toward him. He decides to seize his chance to kill Hercules and takes aim with one of his knives. Just as he is throwing the knife, he trips and the knife deviates from its course, killing Chuckles, the clown, who was walking unseen in the long grass. Once again, it is clear that Sinbad is guilty of murder under section 229(b). He intended to kill one human being and actually killed another.

3. Sinbad is still desperate to kill Hercules. He sees him walking side-by-side with Jumbo, the circus elephant, in a parade. Once again, he

decides to strike while the iron is hot and aims his knife at Hercules. However, the knife misses its mark and instead kills Jumbo. Unlike examples 1 and 2, the doctrine of transferred intent may not be applied since the *actus reus* and *mens rea* of the same crime do not coincide. Although Sinbad committed the *actus reus* of killing an animal, contrary to section 445 of the Code, he did not intend to commit this offence and his intention to commit murder (in relation to Hercules) cannot be transferred from one type of offence to another. In brief, intention can only be transferred within the limits of the same offence.

4. A dispirited Sinbad decides to kill Bruin, the circus bear. He takes aim with his knife and throws it toward the bear. However, at the last minute the knife deviates from its course and kills Hercules. Sinbad's intent to kill an animal (contrary to section 445 of the Code) cannot be transferred so as to convict him of murder—even though he has committed the *actus reus* of homicide by killing Hercules. Of course, it is probable that Sinbad would be convicted of causing death by criminal **negligence**, contrary to section 220 of the Code. It is also probable that Sinbad could be convicted of an attempt to kill an animal, just as he could have been convicted of attempted murder in example 3. However, liability for these attempted offences would clearly not be based upon the doctrine of transferred intent, but rather on general principles of criminal law.

The doctrine of transferred intent has been criticized because it might lead to a situation in which an individual is punished for what is, at best, an *accident*. The Ontario Court of Appeal expressed some sympathy for this view in *Irwin* (1998). In this case, the accused was fighting a man called Graham on the outdoor patio of a restaurant. As the two men grappled with each other, they fell over the victim, causing him serious injuries. The Crown laid a charge of assault causing bodily harm and relied on the principle of transferred intent,

applied in the *Deakin* case (above). The accused was convicted and appealed to the Ontario Court of Appeal. This court took the view that the doctrine of transferred intent, in the specific context of an *assault* charge, "raises difficult problems." Justice Doherty stated that "these problems could have been avoided had the appellant been charged with unlawfully causing bodily harm to [the victim]" (see section 269 of the *Criminal Code*). The court amended the indictment so as to charge Irwin with unlawfully causing bodily harm and then affirmed his conviction. What the Court of Appeal did in *Irwin* is to signal to Crown counsel that, wherever possible, they should try to avoid using the theory of transferred intent in cases of this type. The offence of unlawfully causing bodily harm was an appropriate charge to lay in the *Irwin* case because the accused's unlawful behaviour had caused injury to the victim, and it was only necessary for the Crown to prove that any reasonable person engaged in fighting in a public place would have foreseen the risk that someone in the vicinity of the fight might be physically injured. This approach neatly avoids the need to rely on the doctrine of transferred intent. Whether *Irwin* heralds a general move away from judicial reliance on the doctrine of transferred intent in cases of this type remains to be seen.

SPECIFIC OR ULTERIOR INTENT

The concept of *specific* or *ulterior intent* is somewhat difficult to understand in the abstract. However, it is important to bear in mind that the concept is primarily relevant to the defence of intoxication, which will be discussed in considerable detail in Chapter 9. Basically, it will be seen that intoxication may be a partial defence to a charge of a crime requiring proof of specific or ulterior intent. In contrast, under section 33.1 of the *Criminal Code*, intoxication can never be a defence to a charge of a so-called *basic intent* (or **general intent**) offence if it involves "an element of assault or any other interference or threat of interference by a person with the bodily integrity of another person."

For most criminal offences, the Crown need only prove that the accused committed the prohibited act intentionally and with the necessary knowledge of the material circumstances. For example, in relation to a charge of assault, the Crown need only prove that the defendant intended to bring about the *actus reus* of assault (either the application of force without the consent of the victim or a threat to use force in the situation where the victim reasonably believes that the accused has the present ability to carry out the threat). Similarly, in relation to a charge of wilful damage to property (section 430(1)), the Crown need only prove that the accused intentionally caused the *actus reus* of the offence (namely, the infliction of actual damage to the property in question). These two offences are called *basic intent* crimes. In each case, the Crown need only prove that the accused intended to commit the *actus reus* of the offence in question.

In contrast, there are a number of offences in relation to which the Crown must prove a *further* mental element in order to obtain a conviction. In relation to these offences, the Crown must prove not only an intention to commit the *actus reus* of the crime in question, but also the intention to produce some further consequence *beyond* the *actus reus*. This additional mental element places such offences within the category of *specific intent* offences contained in the *Criminal Code*. The following are considered to be examples of specific intent offences:

1. Murder—this crime can be defined, in most cases, as an assault committed with the *specific (or ulterior) intent* to kill (section 229(a)).
2. Assault with intent to resist or prevent the lawful arrest or detention of the accused or another person (section 270(1)(b)).
3. Possessing a weapon for a purpose dangerous to the public or for the purpose of committing an offence (section 88).
4. Theft—for example, taking something fraudulently and without **colour of right** with intent to deprive (either temporarily or absolutely) the owner of it or a person who has a special

property or interest in it, of the thing or of his or her property or interest in it (section 322)(1)(a)).
5. Robbery—for example, assaulting a person with intent to steal from her or him (section 343(c)).
6. Breaking and entering with intent to commit an **indictable** offence (section 348(1)(a)).

There have been various attempts to define the elements that separate specific or ulterior intent crimes from basic intent crimes. In Canada, one of the most authoritative attempts to offer such a definition was made in the case of *George* (1960), in which the accused was charged with the offence of robbery. The evidence indicated that the accused had visited the home of an 84-year-old man called Averis, and demanded money from him. He then beat Averis severely with his bare fists, broke his nose and caused numerous other serious bodily injuries to the victim. He then stole the sum of $22. The victim indicated that George had threatened to kill him unless he gave him money.

George's main defence was that he was in a severe state of intoxication at the time of the alleged offence. At his trial, the County Court judge acquitted the accused on the following basis:

> You are being acquitted not because you didn't do it—there is no doubt in my mind that you did do it—you are being acquitted because I have found that you were so drunk on the night in question that you were unable to form an intent to do it.

The Crown appealed the accused's acquittal. The appeal was unsuccessful in the B.C. Court of Appeal but was ultimately successful before the Supreme Court of Canada. Essentially, the Supreme Court affirmed the accused's acquittal on the charge of robbery. Since robbery is a specific or ulterior intent offence, drunkenness may be a partial defence. Therefore, the Court judged that the accused had been rightly acquitted. However, every charge of robbery necessarily includes a charge of assault (in essence, a robbery normally involves both an assault and a theft), and an accused person may always be convicted of any lesser offence that is considered to be included in the charge upon which he or she is tried. The Court pointed out that a simple assault is a crime of basic (or general) intent, and drunkenness can not be a valid defence to such a charge. Therefore, the Supreme Court of Canada entered a verdict of guilty of common assault against George. The case is important since at least two justices of the Supreme Court of Canada endeavoured to define the concept of specific or ulterior intent. Justice Fauteux provided the following definition:

> In considering the question of *mens rea* a distinction is to be made between (1) intention as applied to acts considered in relation to their purposes and (2) intention as applied to acts considered apart from their purposes. *A general intent attending the commission of an act is, in some cases, the only intent required to constitute the crime while, in others, there must be, in addition to that general intent, a specific intent attending the purpose for the commission of the act.* [emphasis added]

Justice Ritchie furnished an alternative explanation for the distinction between basic (or general) and specific (or ulterior) intent offences:

> *In considering the question of* mens rea, *a distinction is to be drawn between "intention" as applied to acts done to achieve an immediate end on the one hand and acts done with a specific and ulterior motive and intention of furthering or achieving an illegal object on the other hand.* Illegal acts of the former kind are done "intentionally" in the sense that they are not done by accident or through honest mistake, but acts of the latter kind are the product of preconception and are deliberate steps taken towards an illegal goal. The former acts may be purely physical products of momentary passion, whereas the latter involve the mental process of formulating a

specific intent. A man, far advanced in drink, may intentionally strike his fellow in the former sense at a time when his mind is so befogged with liquor as to be unable to formulate a specific intent in the latter sense. ... [emphasis added]

In his *dissenting* judgment in the *Bernard* case (1988), Chief Justice Dickson strongly — albeit unsuccessfully — contended that the distinction between specific and general intent was "artificial" and should be eliminated. However, it is significant that, in the more recent *Daviault* case (1994), the Supreme Court of Canada unequivocally reaffirmed the existence of this distinction as a fundamental element of Canadian criminal law. As Justice Cory stated, in *Daviault*,

> The distinction between crimes of specific and general intent has been acknowledged and approved by this court on numerous occasions ... The categorization of crimes as being either specific or general intent offences and the consequences that flow from that categorization are now well established in this court.

SUBJECTIVE *MENS REA* AS A *CHARTER* REQUIREMENT: THE CASE OF MURDER

Impact of the *Charter* on the Doctrine of *Mens Rea*

We have seen that the *mens rea* elements of a criminal offence may be based on subjective or objective liability. However, Parliament does not have a totally free hand in making this decision. Indeed, the Supreme Court of Canada has ruled that the *Charter* demands that there be a minimum requirement of subjective *mens rea* for "very few" offences, such as murder. Indeed, in the case of *Vaillancourt* (1987), Justice Lamer stated that

> there are, though very few in number, certain crimes where, because of the special nature of the

stigma attached to a conviction therefor or the available penalties, the principles of fundamental justice require a *mens rea* reflecting the particular nature of that crime. Such is theft, where, in my view, a conviction requires proof of some dishonesty. Murder is another such offence. The punishment for murder is the most severe in our society and the stigma that attaches to a conviction for murder is similarly extreme. In addition, murder is distinguished from manslaughter only by the mental element with respect to the death. It is thus clear that there must be some special mental element with respect to the death before a culpable homicide can be treated as murder. That special mental element gives rise to the moral blameworthiness which justifies the stigma and sentence attached to a murder conviction.

The Supreme Court of Canada decided in the subsequent case of *Martineau* (1990) that, while Parliament may impose objective liability in relation to certain *Criminal Code* offences, such as dangerous driving or manslaughter, the crime of murder is so serious that the *Charter* requires that the Crown prove that the accused *either deliberately intended to kill or, at the very least, subjectively foresaw the risk that his or her conduct was likely to cause death*. To convict an accused person, in the absence of these subjective elements, would amount to depriving him or her of "the right to life, liberty and security of the person" in a manner that contravened the "fundamental principles of justice" enshrined in section 7 of the *Canadian Charter of Rights and Freedoms*. As Chief Justice Lamer contended, on behalf of the majority of the Supreme Court of Canada,

> In my view, in a free and democratic society that values the autonomy and free will of the individual, the stigma and punishment attaching to the most serious of crimes, murder, should be reserved for those who choose to intentionally cause death or who choose to inflict bodily harm that they know is likely to cause death. *The essential role of requiring subjec-*

tive foresight of death in the context of murder is to maintain a proportionality between the stigma and punishment attached to a murder conviction and the moral blameworthiness of the offender. Murder has long been recognized as the "worst" and most heinous of peace-time crimes. It is, therefore, essential that to satisfy the principles of fundamental justice, *the stigma and punishment attaching to a murder conviction must be reserved for those who either intend to cause death or to cause bodily harm that they know will likely cause death.* [emphasis added]

In *Vaillancourt* (1987), *Martineau* (1990), and *Sit* (1991), the Supreme Court of Canada declared the various parts of section 230 of the *Criminal Code* to be invalid under the *Charter*. Section 230 had made it possible to convict accused persons of murder even though they did not subjectively foresee the likelihood that their conduct would cause death. Since this section is now totally invalid, it will not be discussed further. However, the constitutional requirement — that *subjective foresight must be proved before an individual may be convicted of murder* — is clearly of vital significance to the development of Canadian criminal law. What remains to be seen is the extent to which the Supreme Court of Canada may be willing to expand the category of offences for which proof of subjective *mens rea* is a *Charter* requirement.

The *Charter* Requirement of Subjective *Mens Rea* and Section 229(c) of the *Criminal Code*

Section 229 of the *Criminal Code* defines the circumstances in which culpable homicide will be categorized as murder. Section 229(a) states that

Culpable homicide is murder

(a) where the person who causes the death of a human being

    (i) means to cause his death, or

(ii) means to cause him bodily harm that he knows is likely to cause his death, and is reckless whether death ensues or not.

The vast majority of murder charges fall within the scope of section 229(a) of the Code and it is clear that both of the *mens rea* requirements under subsections (i) and (ii) are based on the accused's *subjective foresight of the likelihood of death*. Therefore, section 229(a) clearly meets the constitutional standard prescribed by the Supreme Court of Canada in the *Martineau* case (1990). However, section 229(c) of the Code expands the scope of the crime of murder to cover another set of circumstances and, in so doing, it raises certain doubts concerning its constitutional validity.

Section 229(c) states that murder has been committed

(c) where a person, for an unlawful object, does anything that he knows *or ought to know* is likely to cause death, and thereby causes death to a human being, notwithstanding that he desires to effect his object without causing death or bodily harm to any human being. [emphasis added]

In essence, section 229(c) states that accused persons may be convicted of murder provided that they caused the death of the victim with the purpose of effecting an "unlawful object" and that they did so either

1. with actual knowledge that they were doing something that was "likely" to cause death to someone, or
2. in the situation where they "ought" to have known that the death of someone was a "likely" consequence of their conduct.

The use of the words "ought to know" in section 229(c) clearly indicates that Parliament intended to impose an *objective* test of criminal responsibility in

these circumstances. In other words, the court is directed to consider what *reasonable* persons would have contemplated, had they been confronted by the same set of circumstances as the accused. This means that an accused person may be convicted of murder, under the provisions of section 229(c), even if he or she did not *subjectively* foresee the likelihood of death ensuing from their conduct: all that the Crown needs to prove is that *a reasonable person would have done so*. In this sense, the use of the words "ought to know" undoubtedly infringes the *Charter* requirement that an individual may only be convicted of the extraordinarily serious crime of murder where the Crown can prove *subjective* foresight of death.

In *Martineau* (1990) (a case that actually dealt with the constitutional validity of section 230 of the Code), Chief Justice Lamer expressed the view that the requirement of subjective foresight as a precondition for conviction of murder "casts serious if not fatal doubt on the constitutionality of part of (s. 229(c)) of the Code, specifically the words "'ought to know is likely to cause death.'" He went on to state that

In my view, subjective foresight of death must be proven beyond a reasonable doubt before a conviction of murder can be sustained and, as a result, it is obvious the part of [s. 229(c)] of the Code allowing for a conviction upon proof that the accused ought to have known that death was likely to result violates ss. 7 and 11(d) of the *Charter*.

The Chief Justice also contended that section 229(c) could not be saved by section 1 of the *Charter* as a reasonable limit in a free and democratic society.

Technically, Chief Justice Lamer's views on the validity of section 229(c) of the Code do not represent a definitive ruling by the Supreme Court of Canada on this question (*Martineau* was, after all, concerned with the validity of section 230, rather than section 229(c), of the Code). Nevertheless, there is little doubt that the Chief Justice's analysis of the application of the *Charter* to section 229(c) does constitute an accurate statement of the law. Therefore, the current situation is that the words "ought to know" in section 229(c) have no force and effect and the courts must act as though these words have been expunged from this particular provision of the Code. Basically, section 229(c) now applies only where an accused person engages in a dangerous act, that he or she *subjectively* foresees is likely to cause death, and does so for a *separate, unlawful object.*

What is meant by "unlawful object" in the specific context of section 229(c)? This aspect of the section was interpreted by the Supreme Court of Canada in the case of *Vasil* (1981), in which the accused was charged with the murder of two children, who died as a result of a fire that he had started. Vasil had been living with the mother of the children. The evidence indicated that he was an alcoholic and had been drinking heavily on the day in question. It appears that he accompanied the children's mother (Mrs. Gilchrist) to a party. Following an argument at this event, Vasil returned to the house in a state of anger. He then took the babysitter to her home and returned to the house, where he spread lighter fluid in various parts of the house. He then struck some matches, which started the fire. Vasil claimed that he had spread the lighter fluid around the house only as a means of ruining various household items (such as a rug) and that he had struck the matches for a similar purpose. In any event, the ensuing fire resulted in the death of the two children, who were asleep in the house. The accused made a number of statements to the police. In one of these statements, he indicated that he had soaked various household items with lighter fluid for the following reasons:

> The only way I felt I could get back was to do something physical. I went back to the house from the party and called her (Mrs. Gilchrist) several times. She said she would leave when she felt like it. I figured "you bitch, I would f—g well fix you." I unplugged the fridge and freezer and soaked

them with barbecue fluid. I threw a match on it between the wall and the living-room. I left and drove around. I went back to the house where the party was at and talked to her again. Then I went to the ... police station.

Vasil was convicted at his trial of the murder of the two children. However, for reasons that are not pertinent here, the Supreme Court of Canada ultimately ordered a new trial. One of the other issues that was raised in the case was whether Vasil had set fire to the household items (an obviously dangerous act) for an "unlawful object." In the Supreme Court of Canada, Justice Lamer (speaking for the majority of the justices) articulated the following definition of the words "unlawful object" in section 229(c):

> Under the circumstances I think it not unreasonable to recognize that the intent of Parliament [s. 229(c)] is best respected by circumscribing *the words "unlawful object" when used in that murder section as meaning the object of conduct which, if prosecuted fully, would amount to a serious crime, that is an indictable offence requiring* mens rea.
>
> Applying this interpretation of [s. 229(c)] to the present case, the jury had to be told that, if they believed beyond a reasonable doubt that the accused intended to damage the food and furniture, such an object was an unlawful object; indeed, the fact that Mrs. Gilchrist was sharing in the cost of the furniture is not contested and as a result *the wilful destruction, damaging, obstruction, interference with that property is mischief, an indictable* mens rea *offence.* ... [emphasis added]

An interesting application of Justice Lamer's definition of unlawful object occurred in the case of *Rabishaw* (1983). In the *Vasil* case (1981), the unlawful object required by section 229(c) was the accused's desire to damage property (which is an indictable offence under section 430 of the Code). In the *Rabishaw* case, the New Brunswick Court of Appeal faced another set of circumstances in which the accused was alleged to have set fire to property in a house; the dwelling burned down with the tragic loss of a child's life. The Crown claimed that the unlawful objects, for the purposes of section 229(c), were the accused's desire to "embarrass someone" or his wish to "ingratiate himself with his girlfriend" by setting fire to the house and by subsequently rescuing his small son (presumably so as to appear as some sort of hero). The Court ruled that these were not unlawful objects, within the meaning of section 229(c); clearly, these goals, if achieved, would not amount to the commission of an indictable offence. On the other hand, if the Crown could establish an intent to burn, damage or destroy the house, the unlawful object required by section 229(c) would be clearly established. In this particular case, a new trial was ordered in order to establish whether the accused's object really was unlawful according to the definition presented in the *Vasil* case.

A dramatic illustration of the application of section 229(c) occurred in the extraordinary case of *Meiler* (1999). The accused was convinced that his estranged wife was "seeing" a man called Roach. He later admitted that he decided to kill Roach and then commit suicide. He took a loaded shotgun, cocked it, and put his finger on the trigger with the intention of killing Roach. It appeared that one Skrinjaric intercepted Meiler and jumped on his back. There was a struggle for the gun, which tragically discharged and killed Nick Biuk who was standing close by. Meiler was charged with second degree murder. The Crown relied on the provisions of section 229(c) of the Code to establish the necessary *mens rea* for murder. The trial judge instructed the members of the jury that Meiler could be convicted of murder under section 229(c) if they found that, for the unlawful object of killing Roach, the accused had carried a loaded gun with his finger on the trigger and that he had *known* that what he was doing was *likely to cause the death of a human being*. The trial judge also stated that, if Meiler's conduct had caused the death of Biuk and if he had the necessary *mens rea* under section 229(c), then it was irrelevant that the gun discharged accidentally. Meiler was convicted of sec-

ond degree murder and his subsequent appeal to the Ontario Court of Appeal was dismissed.

In delivering the judgment of the Court of Appeal in *Meiler,* Justice O'Connor held that the Crown had established the necessary *mens rea* requirements for conviction of murder, under the provisions of section 229(c). Furthermore, the court rejected Meiler's argument that it would be unfair to convict him of murder when he did not foresee the *precise circumstances* in which a human being was likely to be killed (Meiler contended that he had intended to kill Roach, not Biuk, and the immediate cause of death had been the *accidental* discharge of the firearm during Meiler's tussle with Skrinjaric). Justice O'Connor stated that,

Section 229(c) applies notwithstanding that the offender may not wish to cause injury or death to anyone. The requirement of a further or other unlawful object does not mean that the offender must have more than one object; it simply requires that there be an unlawful object other than the assault on the deceased for which object the offender did the act or acts that caused death.

The trial judge instructed the jury that the appellant's intent to kill Roach was an unlawful object; about that there can be no dispute. ... (I)n order for the jury to convict they must have found that the acts of the appellant were done for the unlawful object, killing Roach, and that this was a different object than causing harm or death to Biuk ...

...

In my view, s. 229(c) does not require that an offender foresee the precise situation or all of the events that result in the death. It is sufficient if the offender has the subjective foresight that the acts done for the unlawful object are likely to cause death and those acts are sufficiently linked to the death to have caused the death within the meaning of the section.

...

The moral blameworthiness of an offender who does certain acts for an unlawful object knowing that those acts are likely to cause death to someone other

than the subject of the unlawful object is no less seri-
ous because the offender does not foresee the very situ-
ation or the precise circumstances that ultimately lead
to that death. [emphasis added]

As we shall see in Chapter 5, although the Supreme Court of Canada has ruled that the *Char-*
ter dictates that, on a charge of murder, the Crown
must prove that the accused *subjectively foresaw* the
likelihood of death, in the later case of *Creighton*
(1993), it ruled that an *objective test of liability* may
be imposed in relation to the offence of manslaughter (that is, the objective foreseeability of bodily
harm). The Court ruled that the *Charter* does not
require subjective *mens rea* for manslaughter primarily because the stigma and penalty associated
with manslaughter are much less severe than is the
case with murder. However, it is significant that the
Supreme Court of Canada has decided that subjective foresight of death is required by the *Charter* as
a minimum form of *mens rea* in the case of attempted murder (*Logan* (1990)).

RECKLESSNESS AS A FORM OF SUBJECTIVE *MENS REA*

Definition of Recklessness

One form of subjective *mens rea* that may be sufficient for conviction of a criminal offence is *reckless-*
ness. In some instances, Canadian courts have expanded the *mens rea* elements required in relation to
"true crimes" to include recklessness as an alternative to intention or knowledge. For example, when
considering the offence of sexual assault in the
Sansregret case (1985), the Supreme Court of
Canada accepted the view that recklessness as to the
victim's consent was sufficient *mens rea* to sustain a
conviction. In other words, the Court indicated
that either actual knowledge that the victim did not
consent or recklessness as to this matter are both
states of mind that will justify conviction of sexual
assault (Parliament later amended the *Criminal*
Code in order to reflect the Supreme Court's ruling
in this respect; see section 273.2, enacted in 1992).

Similarly, if defendants charged with possession
of stolen goods receive them, knowing that there
is a substantial chance that they may have been
stolen, their recklessness justifies the imposition
of criminal liability despite the fact that the prosecution cannot prove, beyond a reasonable doubt,
that they had actual knowledge that the goods
were stolen.

In addition, the *Criminal Code* specifically states
that recklessness is a form of *mens rea* sufficient to
justify conviction of the accused in relation to a
number of categories of criminal offences. Before
discussing these categories of offences, however, it is
necessary to define the concept of recklessness.

People are reckless, with respect to a *consequence*
of their actions, when they foresee that it *may* occur
but do not *desire* it nor *foresee* it as certain. For
example, Sykes fires a gun into a crowded lecture
hall in order to "scare a few students." Sykes does
not wish to kill anyone, but he necessarily realizes
that someone may be killed. He decides to proceed
with his irresponsible conduct regardless of this
risk. In these circumstances, we would clearly say
that Sykes is reckless as to the consequence that
someone may be killed by his actions. People are
reckless with respect to a *circumstance* when they
realize that it *may* exist but neither know, nor desire,
that it exists. For example, suppose that Wegg points
a revolver at Boffin. Wegg does not know whether
the gun is loaded. He hopes that the gun is not
loaded, but decides to pull the trigger regardless. We
would have little difficulty in branding Wegg as
reckless. It will be noted that, in both the above
examples, the accused undoubtedly foresee the risk
that their conduct creates. They then decide to proceed with their course of conduct regardless of their
appreciation of the inherent risk of so doing.

Professor Glanville Williams has forcefully contended that recklessness, as a form of *mens rea,*
involves two basic elements:

(a) *subjective* foresight of the risk created by the
accused's conduct; and
(b) an *unjustified* assumption of that risk by the
accused (in the sense that a reasonable person

acting prudently would not have assumed the risk).

It will be noted that the first element of recklessness identified by Williams is based upon a subjective test of responsibility. Accused persons must *subjectively* appreciate the nature of the risk created by their conduct. It is for this reason that recklessness is sometimes known as *advertent negligence*. Indeed, where recklessness is the required form of *mens rea*, accused persons must subjectively *advert* (pay attention to) the risk created by their conduct. As Justice McIntyre said, in delivering the judgment of the Supreme Court of Canada in the *Sansregret* case (1985),

> In accordance with well established principles for the determination of criminal liability, recklessness, to form a part of the criminal *mens rea*, must have an element of the subjective. It is found in the attitude of one who, aware that there is danger that his conduct could bring about the result prohibited by the criminal law, nevertheless persists, despite the risk. It is, in other words, *the conduct of one who sees the risk and takes the chance.* [emphasis added]

The second element of recklessness described by Williams refers to the question of whether the assumption of a risk is justified in all the circumstances of the particular case. In determining whether the assumption of risk is justifiable, Williams suggests that the question that must be asked is "would a 'reasonable' or 'ordinary' person have assumed that risk?" In other words, an *objective* test is employed. If accused persons fall below the standard of care expected of reasonable persons facing the same circumstances, the accused are negligent and, if they are *subjectively* aware of the risk that their conduct is creating, they are *advertently negligent* (that is, they are reckless).

It should be pointed out that the criminal law does not penalize all individuals who assume a high degree of risk. It only punishes those individuals who *unjustifiably* assume such a risk. For example, a

surgeon may decide to undertake an operation with a high degree of risk if it is the only option available to save a patient's life; clearly, taking such a risk would be eminently justified provided that a reasonable surgeon would have performed the operation in the same circumstances. On the other hand, a defendant who fires a gun into a crowded lecture hall is clearly not justified in assuming the risk that someone will be killed. No reasonable person would do such a thing.

By way of summary, therefore, it can be stated that reckless people subjectively appreciate the risk that their conduct creates; however, criminal responsibility is only imposed if reasonable persons would not have assumed such a risk in the same circumstances. Since reckless people fully appreciate that their conduct creates a substantial risk and proceed regardless, we may say that they *deliberately* choose to do something wrong. Liability for recklessness, therefore, is clearly based upon the *moral blameworthiness* of the individual defendant.

Examples of *Criminal Code* Offences Requiring Proof of Recklessness

While the courts have themselves expanded the concept of *mens rea* to include recklessness in relation to a number of criminal offences, the *Criminal Code* expressly states that recklessness is sufficient *mens rea* for conviction in relation to the three following categories of offences.

(A) MURDER
Section 229 of the *Criminal Code* provides that

Culpable homicide is murder

(a) Where the person who causes the death of a human being

   (i) means to cause his death, or
   (ii) means to cause him bodily harm that he knows is likely to cause his death, and is

reckless whether death ensues or not. ...
[emphasis added]

Section 229(a)(ii) deals with the situation where an accused person has killed someone and the Crown can prove that he or she intentionally inflicted bodily harm that he or she subjectively realized would be likely to cause death. If the Crown can also establish that the accused continued with the assault on the victim, *regardless of his or her knowledge of that deadly risk*, there will be a conviction of murder. This would be a classic example of recklessness as a form of subjective *mens rea,* because the accused clearly chooses to inflict a degree of injury that he or she *subjectively* realizes is likely to cause the death of the unfortunate victim.

In the case of *Williams* (1995), the B.C. Court of Appeal emphasized that the accused person's knowledge that what he or she was doing was likely to cause death must coincide both with the intention to cause bodily harm and the recklessness as to whether or not death ensued.

(B) DAMAGE TO PROPERTY, ETC.
Section 429(1) of the *Criminal Code* provides that

Every one who causes the occurrence of an event by doing an act or by omitting to do an act that is his duty to do, knowing that the act or omission will probably cause the occurrence of the event and being *reckless* whether the event occurs or not, shall be deemed, for the purposes of this Part, wilfully to have caused the occurrence of the event. [emphasis added]

Parliament has unequivocally chosen to treat reckless defendants in exactly the same manner as those who have acted wilfully (or intentionally) in relation to the various property offences set out in Part XI of the Code. These offences include mischief in the sense of damage to property (section 430), injuring or endangering cattle (section 444), injuring or endangering other animals (section 445), and causing unnecessary suffering to animals or birds (section 446).

(C) ARSON
Sections 433 and 434 of the Code impose criminal liability for both intentional and reckless damage to property that is caused by fire or explosion. Section 433 states that

Every person who intentionally or *recklessly* causes damage by fire or explosion to property, whether or not that person owns the property, is guilty of an indictable offence and liable to imprisonment for life where

(a) the person knows that or is *reckless* with respect to whether the property is inhabitated or occupied; or
(b) the fire or explosion causes bodily harm to another person. [emphasis added]

Section 434 provides that

Every person who intentionally or *recklessly* causes damage by fire or explosion to property that is not wholly owned by that person is guilty of an indictable offence and liable to imprisonment for a term not exceeding fourteen years. [emphasis added]

(D) CRIMINAL HARASSMENT
Section 264(1) of the *Criminal Code* clearly specifies that the necessary *mens rea* for the offence of criminal harassment is either actual knowledge that the victim is being harassed or recklessness as to this circumstance:

No person shall, without lawful authority and knowing that another person is harassed or *recklessly* as to whether the other person is harassed, engage in conduct referred to in subsection (2) that causes that other person reasonably, in all the circumstances, to fear for the safety or the safety of anyone known to them. [emphasis added]

Section 264(2) sets out four types of conduct that may constitute the *actus reus* of criminal harassment: (a) "repeatedly following" someone; (b) "repeatedly communicating" with someone; (c) "besetting or watching the dwelling house" or work place of someone; and (d) "engaging in threatening conduct" directed at someone.

As Justice Berger noted, on behalf of the Alberta Court of Appeal in the case of *Sillipp* (1997),

> A conviction under s. 264 requires the accused have "known" that his subsection (2) conduct was causing the complainant to be harassed, or that he was aware of such risk and was reckless or wilfully blind as to whether or not the person was harassed.

Since criminal harassment is an offence that requires proof of subjective *mens rea*, the accused can successfully raise the defence of honest mistake of fact by raising a reasonable doubt as to whether he or she subjectively realized there was a risk that the complainant was aware of being harassed. For example, if an accused person indicates that he or she honestly believed that, although the accused was frequently standing outside of the complainant's residence, the latter was completely unaware of his or her presence, then the accused must be acquitted of the charge. As Justice Berger noted, a " 'morally innocent accused' who honestly believed that his subsection (2) behaviour was not known to the complainant, and who was not reckless or wilfully blind, would escape criminal liability." It is noteworthy that, in the case of *Krushel* (2000), the Ontario Court of Appeal explicitly approved Justice Berger's analysis of the *mens rea* elements of criminal harassment.

WILFUL BLINDNESS AS A FORM OF SUBJECTIVE *MENS REA*

Canadian courts have expanded the *mens rea* requirement of certain offences to include *wilful blindness*. This form of *mens rea* exists when accused persons are virtually certain that particular circumstances exist (for example, that goods are stolen) but deliberately "shut their eyes" to these circumstances. It does seem reasonable that

accused persons, who suspect that they are involved in criminal activities but deliberately refrain from "asking the final question" that will reveal all, should be treated as though they actually knew the circumstances that rendered conduct criminal. If the law did not adopt this policy, unscrupulous defendants would be permitted to cheat justice with impunity. While wilful blindness is closely related to recklessness, the Supreme Court of Canada has emphasized that the two concepts should, nevertheless, be kept distinct. In delivering the judgment of the Court, in the case of *Sansregret* (1985), Justice McIntyre contended that

> Wilful blindness is distinct from recklessness because, while recklessness involves knowledge of a danger or risk and persistence in a course of conduct which creates a risk that the prohibited result will occur, *wilful blindness arises where a person who has become aware of the need for some inquiry declines to make the inquiry because he does not wish to know the truth.* He would prefer to remain ignorant. The culpability in recklessness is justified by consciousness of the risk and by proceeding in the face of it, while in wilful blindness it is justified by the accused's fault in deliberately failing to inquire when he knows there is reason for inquiry. [emphasis added]

It is significant that Canadian courts have routinely expanded the scope of subjective *mens rea* to include wilful blindness, even when Parliament has only used such words as "knowingly" or "recklessly" in its definition of an offence in the *Criminal Code*. For example, earlier in this chapter, it was pointed out that, in relation to the offence of criminal harassment (section 264), Parliament specified that the accused must either "know" that the victim is being harassed or be "reckless" as to that circumstance. However, in the *Sillipp* case (1997), the Alberta Court of Appeal added, on its own account, that the accused could also be convicted if he or she is "wilfully blind" as to whether the victim is being harassed.

Examples of Wilful Blindness

The doctrine of wilful blindness was applied in the case of *Oluwa* (1996), in which the accused had been charged with importing heroin and possession of heroin for the purpose of trafficking. The circumstances were somewhat bizarre. The accused had been travelling by air from Tokyo to Mexico City. The accused's flight had a short stopover at Vancouver International Airport. He was required to wait in the "Transit Departure Facility," while the plane was being cleaned and refueled. Oluwa's behaviour aroused suspicion and it was discovered that he was carrying heroin packages in his intestinal tract. The accused's defence was that he lacked the *mens rea* for the charge of importing a narcotic because there was no evidence to prove that he actually knew his plane would be stopping in Canada and, therefore, he could not be said to have intended to come to this country. In support of this position, he pointed out that his ticket did not indicate that there would be a stopover. However, this argument was rejected at his trial, and his conviction was subsequently upheld by the B.C. Court of Appeal. On behalf of the majority of the court, Chief Justice McEachern indicated that, even if the Crown could not prove actual knowledge on the part of the accused, proof of recklessness or *wilful blindness* as to the risk that the plane would land in a country, such as Canada, would suffice for a conviction of importing a narcotic. The Chief Justice noted that Oluwa was an experienced international traveller and that "it is common for long-distance flights to make schedule stops." Insofar as the issue of wilful blindness was concerned, Chief Justice McEachern concluded that

> In this case, with respect, I cannot conclude other than that the appellant, if he did not know his flight would stop in Canada, which seems inconceivable, was *wilfully blind to that fact. His lack of knowledge, if any, resulted from his wilful failure to obtain information which was readily available and which was of significant importance to him. Because*

> *of his wilful blindness, the law attributes such knowledge to him.* [emphasis added]

Similarly, in the *Tejani* case (1999), the accused, a Toronto currency exchange dealer, had been charged with attempted money laundering, contrary to the provisions of section 19.2 of the (now-repealed) *Narcotic Control Act*, R.S.C. 1985, c. N-1. A critical element in the *mens rea* for this offence was the accused's *belief* that the funds in question constituted the "proceeds of drug trafficking, importing or exporting." The Ontario Court of Appeal, in upholding the accused's conviction, stated unequivocally that the offence could be proved on the basis of the accused's *wilful blindness* as to the source of the money that was intended to be laundered. Indeed, Justice Laskin stated, in delivering the judgment of the court, that, on a charge of attempting to launder money, the necessary *mens rea* requirements "can be satisfied not only by a finding of belief but also by a finding of wilful blindness." In the view of the Court of Appeal, the trial judge had not erred in finding that Tejani was wilfully blind:

> [The trial judge] ... could reasonably conclude that the appellant *shut his eyes* to the source of Debellis' money because the appellant *knew or strongly suspected that inquiring would fix him with the knowledge the funds were the proceeds of illicit dealing in drugs.* [emphasis added]

The courts have emphasized, however, that wilful blindness exists only when accused persons have every reason to suspect the existence of circumstances that would render their actions criminal, but deliberately shut their eyes because they think it will serve their purposes to plead ignorance to the authorities. It is not enough for the Crown to contend that the accused was negligent in the sense of failing to make the inquiries that a reasonable person would have made in the circumstances. For example, in the case of *Gould* (1990), the accused had been charged with possession of a jade carving, knowing that this artifact had been obtained by the commission of theft (an indictable offence under section 354 of the *Criminal Code*). The jade walrus had been purchased by Gould in a bar, for a price that was about one third of that which might have been charged in a commercial gallery. On this basis, the trial judge convicted Gould, stating that the accused had "turned a blind eye" and that "he made no inquiry where inquiry was called for." The B.C. Court of Appeal later set aside Gould's conviction. One of the reasons for this decision was that the trial judge had made an error when he had ruled that Gould had been "wilfully blind" to the fact that the jade walrus had been stolen. Justice Gibbs stated that

> There is no evidence of facts known to the accused when he purchased the walrus which could lead to a conclusion that he deliberately refrained from making inquiries. Indeed, there is no evidence about whether he made an inquiry, or did not make an inquiry. Neither in my opinion, given that the stolen item was a specialized objet d'art, was there impartial evidence of such a marked and obvious discrepancy between value and price that it would lead to a logical inference that a prospective purchaser would be put on his inquiry.

Clearly, merely neglecting to make inquiries (even those that a "reasonable person" might make) does not *per se* constitute wilful blindness — a considerably more culpable state of mind must be proved by the Crown.

STUDY QUESTIONS

1. Grumpy has a flea-bitten dog, which is always barking at night. Grumpy's neighbour, Patience, cannot sleep as a result. One night, Patience sees the dog in Grumpy's yard. She fires a rifle at the dog in order to kill it. Tragically, the bullet misses the dog and kills Grumpy who is just behind (in the shadows). Is Patience guilty of any offence(s)?

2. Nero sets fire to his petfood store at 2 A.M. on a Sunday morning in order to collect the insurance money. The store is located near to a number of other business premises. There is a major fire and an alert passer-by, seeing the flames, makes a "911" call. Owing to an unfortunate error on the part of the dispatcher, the fire brigade takes some time to arrive. In the meantime, the fire has spread to another building, a photography studio, owned by Claudius. Both Nero's store and Claudius's studio are reduced to mere burnt-out shells. Worse still, the fire fighters discover the charred body of Vincent, a homeless person, who was using Claudius's studio as a place in which to sleep. There is some evidence that Nero knew that Vincent was present in Claudius's studio at nighttime. Nero is charged with murder. Is he guilty of this offence?

3. Ramsbottom is a young law and security student at Valleyview College. On registration day, he goes to a crowded registrar's office and proceeds to a cashier's desk, where he loudly demands "all the cash" and states that he has a gun in his pocket. When the cashier dutifully produces the money, Ramsbottom takes it but, seeing a security guard approaching in the distance, he suddenly scatters the money in the air and shakes the hand of the cashier, saying that, of course, he was "only joking." The police are immediately called to investigate this incident and they ask Ramsbottom to turn out the contents of his pockets. Among the contents is a screwdriver. Ramsbottom claims that he has a reputation for being a practical joker. What charges could reasonably be laid against Ramsbottom? Which (if any) would be most likely to result in conviction?

4. George works for a government agency. His salary has been frozen for three years and he is becoming frustrated with his financial position. He complains to his immediate superior who suggests that George should "inflate" his expense accounts to compensate for his inade-

quate salary. George follows this advice, but an auditor questions him and discovers that George has submitted expense claims that exceed his actual expenditures by some $10 000. George vociferously declares that he thought that he was not doing anything wrong because his superior had encouraged him to follow this course of action and because he had a moral right to rectify the injustice he had suffered as a consequence of the salary freeze maintained by the government. If you were Crown counsel in this case, what charge(s) (if any) would you lay against George?

5. Desmond is sitting at a bar, consuming a considerable quantity of alcohol. He is upset because he has been fired from his job as a security officer. He stands up and shouts, "I'm mad and I'm not going to take it anymore; I think I'm going to kill someone." He rushes out of the bar and makes his way up Main Street. He suddenly goes into a parking lot and decides to steal a car. He is just about to enter a car when he is challenged by Centurion, the night attendant. Without warning, Desmond swings around and shoots Centurion in the chest. Centurion dies before the ambulance arrives. Desmond is arrested and charged with first degree murder. Medical witnesses are agreed that Centurion was not so drunk as to prevent him from forming the intent to kill Centurion. Is he likely to be convicted of first degree murder? Would it make any difference to your answer if there is evidence that Desmond was mentally disordered rather than intoxicated?

6. Henry goes into a bar where he meets Geoffrey, who claims that he is an artist. Geoffrey offers Henry a beautiful painting of a polar bear and says that he can have it for the sum of $100, provided that Henry gives him cash immediately. Henry purchases the painting and displays it in his office. Some days later, the police inform Henry that the painting was stolen from a famous art gallery and that it is actually worth $20 000. If you were Crown counsel would you prosecute Henry even though he loudly proclaims that he did not know the painting was stolen?

7. Fred is very angry with his friend, Jim, because the latter has just given him a cheque, which has been rejected by the bank on the basis of "insufficient funds." Fred decides to teach Jim a lesson by savagely beating him with a crowbar. Jim suffers such ghastly head injuries that he subsequently dies. Fred says that he realized that Jim was "hurting badly," but he claims that he never intended to kill him. Would it be possible to charge Fred with first or second degree murder?

8. Bill Sykes has recently separated from his spouse, Nancy. Sykes knows very well that Nancy does not want to have any form of communication with him and has told him that, if he does not leave her alone, she will summon the police. Sykes makes no effort to communicate with Nancy but he frequently parks his car a few hundred yards up the street from Nancy's house and keeps an eye on who is entering and leaving the residence. Nancy sees Sykes's car on a number of occasions and, fearing for her safety, calls the police. Sykes is arrested and subsequently charged with criminal harassment. Sykes indignantly claims that he had absolutely no intention of harassing Nancy and that he believed that she was entirely unaware of his presence in the street. Would Sykes have any defence against the charge laid against him?

FURTHER READING

Alexander, L. 2000. Insufficient Concern: A Unified Conception of Criminal Culpability. 88 *California Law Review:* 931.

Ashworth, A. 1995. *Principles of Criminal Law.* 2d ed. Oxford: Oxford University Press. 83–84, 151–200.

Binder, G. 2000. Meaning and Motive in the Law of Homicide. 3 *Buffalo Criminal Law Review:* 755.

Brucker, T. 1997. *The Practical Guide to the Controlled Drugs and Substances Act.* Toronto: Carswell. 61–66.

Brudner, A. 1996. Proportionality, Stigma and Discretion. 38 *Criminal Law Quarterly:* 301.

Cairns-Way, R. 1990. Constitutionalizing Subjectivism Another View. 79 *Criminal Reports (3d Series):* 260.

Campbell, K.L. 1993. Contract Killings. 35 *Criminal Law Quarterly:* 305.

Cornish, J.L., K. Murray, and P.I. Collins. 1999. *The Criminal Lawyers' Guide to the Law of Criminal Harassment and Stalking.* Aurora, Ont.: Canada Law Book.

Dressler, J. 2000. Does One *Mens Rea* Fit All?: Thoughts on Alexander's Unified Conception of Criminal Culpability. 88 *California Law Review:* 955.

Enns, R. 1999. *A Voice Unheard: The Latimer Case and People with Disabilities.* Halifax: Fernwood Publishing.

Finkel, N.J. 2000. Commonsense Justice, Culpability, and Punishment. 28 *Hofstra Law Review:* 669.

Finkelstein, C. 2000. The Inefficiency of *Mens Rea.* 88 *California Law Review:* 895.

Fletcher, G.P. 1978. *Rethinking Criminal Law.* Boston: Little, Brown & Company.

———. 2000. The Nature and Function of Criminal Theory. 2000. 88 *California Law Review:* 687.

France, S. 1995. Gains and Lost Opportunities in Canadian Constitutional *Mens Rea.* 20 *Queen's Law Journal:* 533.

Galloway, D. 1992. Criminal Liability and the Centrality of Intention. 5 *Canadian Journal of Jurisprudence:* 57.

Gold, A.D. 1994. Lessons about *Mens Rea:* Three Recent Cases, 36 *Criminal Law Quarterly:* 157–67.

Grant, I. 1990. The Impact of *Vaillancourt v. R.* on Canadian Criminal Law. 28 *Alberta Law Review:* 443.

Grant, I., D. Chunn, and C.L.M. Boyle. 1994. *The Law of Homicide.* Toronto: Carswell.

Hart, H.L.A. 1962. *Punishment and Responsibility.* Oxford: Clarendon Press.

Holland, W.H. 1998. *The Law of Theft and Related Offences.* Toronto: Carswell. 145–199.

Law Reform Commission of Canada. 1984. Working Paper No. 33: *Homicide.* Ottawa: Minister of Supply and Services Canada.

———. 1982. Working Paper No. 29: *Criminal Law: The General Part: Liability and Defences.* Ottawa: Minister of Supply and Services Canada.

———. 1987. Report No. 31: *Recodifying Criminal Law.* Rev. ed. Ottawa: Law Reform Commission of Canada.

Leigh, L.H. 1983. The Law Reform Commission of Canada and Reform of the General Part. [1983] *Criminal Law Review:* 438.

Lindsay, P. 1989. The Implications of *R. v. Vaillancourt:* Much Ado About Nothing? 47 *University of Toronto Faculty Law Review:* 465.

Mewett, A.W. 1996. Editorial: Murder is Murder. 38 *Criminal Law Quarterly:* 257.

Mewett, A.W. and M. Manning. 1994. *Mewett & Manning on Criminal Law.* 3d ed. Toronto: Butterworths. 169–92, 219–22.

Minister of Justice of Canada. 1993. *White Paper: Proposals to Amend the* Criminal Code *(General Principles).* Ottawa: Minister of Justice of Canada (June 28, 1993).

Nightingale, B.L. 1996. *The Law of Fraud and Related Offences.* Toronto: Carswell. Chaps. 7–11.

Odujirin, A. 1998. *The Normative Basis of Fault in Criminal Law: History and Theory.* Toronto: University of Toronto Press.

Paciocco, D.M. 1995. Subjective and Objective Standards of Fault for Offences and Defences, 59 *Saskatchewan Law Review:* 271.

Packer, H.L. 1968. *The Limits of the Criminal Sanction.* Palo Alto: Stanford University Press.

Perell, P.M. 1996. The Fraud Elements of Deceit and Fraudulent Misrepresentation, 18 *Advocates' Quarterly:* 232.

Roach, K. 1996. *Criminal Law.* Concord, Ont.: Irwin Law. 88–110.

Robinson, P.H. and J.M. Darley. 1996. *Justice, Liability and Blame: Community Views about the Criminal Law.* Boulder, Colorado: Westview Press.

Stalker, M.A. 1989. The Fault Element in Recodifying Criminal Law: A Critique. 14 *Queen's Law Journal:* 35.

Stribopoulos, J. 1999. "The Constitutionalization of 'Fault' in Canada: A Normative Critique," 42 *Criminal Law Quarterly:* 227.

Stuart, D. 1995. *Canadian Criminal Law.* 3d ed. Toronto: Carswell. 139–251.

Stuart, D. and R.J. Delisle. 1997. *Learning Canadian Criminal Law.* 6th ed. Toronto: Carswell. 289–301, 370–450.

Thornton, M. 1992. Intention in Criminal Law. 5 *Canadian Journal of Law and Jurisprudence:* 177.

Verdun-Jones, S.N. 1999. *Canadian Criminal Cases: Selected Highlights.* Toronto: Harcourt Brace. Chap. 3.

Wasserstrom, R.A. 1967. H.L.A. Hart and the Doctrines of *Mens Rea* and Criminal Responsibility. 35 *University of Chicago Law Review*: 92.

White, N.R. and J.V. Roberts. 1985. Criminal Intent: The Public's View. 25 *Canadian Journal of Criminology*: 455.

Williams, G. 1965. *The Mental Element in Crime.* Oxford: Oxford University Press.

Wootton, B. 1981. *Crime and the Criminal Law: Reflections of a Magistrate and Social Scientist.* 2d ed. London: Stevens & Sons.

The Mental Element in the Criminal Law: Objective Liability

OVERVIEW

This chapter examines the following:

1. The nature of objective liability as a form of *mens rea* in Canadian criminal law;
2. the principle that it is only the most serious forms of negligence that render an individual guilty of an offence under the *Criminal Code*;
3. the requirement that the Crown must prove a marked departure from the standard of the reasonable person acting prudently in order to gain a conviction in offences that impose objective liability;
4. the difference between mere carelessness and criminal (or "penal") negligence;
5. the principle that objective liability does not take into account the peculiar personal characteristics of the accused except where he or she lacks the capacity to appreciate the nature of the risk which his or her conduct is creating;
6. the *Criminal Code* offences that impose objective liability as the requisite *mens rea* for conviction;
7. the nature and scope of the offence of dangerous driving and the modified objective test of liability;
8. the difference between dangerous driving and careless driving;
9. the nature and scope of the offence of unlawful act manslaughter and the critical impact of the decision of the Supreme Court of Canada in the *Creighton* case (1993);

10. the *mens rea* requirement for unlawful act manslaughter unlawfully causing bodily harm and assault causing bodily harm: namely, objective foreseeability of bodily harm;
11. the nature of offences based on criminal negligence, as defined in section 219 of the *Criminal Code*;
12. the failure of the Supreme Court of Canada to decide in the *Tutton and Tutton* and *Waite* cases (1989) whether the *mens rea* for criminal negligence is based on a subjective or objective test;
13. the view that, in light of subsequent Supreme Court of Canada decisions in *Hundal* (1993) and *Creighton* (1993), it may be expected that the Supreme Court will ultimately adopt an objective test of liability for criminal negligence;
14. *Criminal Code* sections that impose an elevated standard of care for those (such as surgeons) who engage in inherently dangerous activities that require a certain level of training and skill.

INTRODUCTION: WHAT IS OBJECTIVE LIABILITY?

In Chapter 4, we examined the *mens rea* elements of criminal offences that are based on the need for the Crown to prove *intention, knowledge, recklessness, or wilful blindness*. These *mens rea* elements are *subjective* in nature because they require that the particular **accused** be subjectively aware of the risk that his or her conduct will cause certain consequences that are prohibited by law. The present chapter explores the *mens rea* elements of criminal offences that are based on the need for the Crown to prove only that the accused person's conduct fell below the standard of the hypothetical reasonable person, regardless of whether he or she was subjectively aware of the risk that his or her conduct would cause consequences that are prohibited by the law. If the reasonable person, placed in the same circumstances as the accused, would have been aware of the risk and would have avoided taking it, the accused is guilty of the offence. This form of liability is *objective* in nature because it does not take into account what (if anything) actually went on in the accused's mind. As Justice McLachlin stated, in delivering the judgment of the majority of the justices of the Supreme Court of Canada in the *Creighton* case (1993),

> Objective *mens rea*... is not concerned with what the accused intended or knew. Rather the mental fault lies in failure to direct the mind to a risk which the reasonable person would have appreciated. *Objective* mens rea *is not concerned with what was actually in the accused's mind, but with what should have been there, had the accused proceeded reasonably.* [emphasis added]

A person who falls below the standard of the reasonable person is considered to have acted *negligently*. However, it is only the more serious forms of **negligence** that will lead to an individual being convicted of a crime under the *Criminal Code*. Merely being *careless* (that is, falling just a relatively small degree below the standard of the reasonable person) may render one liable, at **civil law**, to pay compensation, but it will not make one a criminal. As Chief Justice Lamer of the Supreme Court of Canada said in the *Gosset* case (1993),

> Negligence in a criminal setting, or what I shall hereinafter refer to as "penal negligence"... subjects those convicted to the possibility of imprisonment. *Unlike negligence under civil law, which is concerned with the apportionment of loss, penal negligence is concerned with the punishment of moral blameworthiness.* [emphasis added]

What Chief Justice Lamer meant is that, if someone carelessly causes injury to another person or damage to that person's property, it is fair to require that the individual who caused the injury or damage should compensate the victim of that carelessness. After all, the party who was careless should be made to shoulder the financial loss rather than the victim. Suppose, for example, that I accidentally break my friend's china teapot by knocking it off a table with my elbow. I am reading a detective mystery and am so absorbed in this pleasant task that I forget where I am and, when the telephone rings, I automatically start to get up from the table, not realizing that my elbow is next to the teapot. I am deeply shocked to find that I have knocked the teapot onto the floor, and I can honestly say that I caused this damage completely inadvertently (i.e., without being at all aware of the risk that my elbow might hit the teapot and cause it to fall on the floor).

However, my friend would justly say that I had been careless because a reasonable person would have been more careful in the circumstances. What I have done would not be considered a serious case of negligence. This is definitely not a situation where there has been a marked departure from the standard of the reasonable person: indeed, it is the kind of accident that could happen to anyone. Clearly, I should not be convicted of an offence under the *Criminal Code* for such simple carelessness. However, in all fairness, I should feel obligated to buy my friend another teapot since I was the one who was careless, and if I were to be so ungenerous as to refuse to pay up, my friend might be able to sue me for damages in a civil court.

However, although mere carelessness may render an individual liable to be sued in a civil court, it is not sufficient to render him or her liable for conviction of an offence under the *Criminal Code*. On the contrary, it is only where there is a *marked departure* from the standard of care expected of a reasonable person that the accused can be convicted of a *Criminal Code* offence. In other words, only the most serious forms of negligent behaviour can lead to a conviction of a **"true crime."**

This principle is extremely important because the Supreme Court of Canada has recognized that section 7 of the *Charter*, which guarantees that no person may be deprived of life, liberty, or security of the person except in accordance with the fundamental principles of justice, dictates that an accused person may not be convicted of an offence under the *Criminal Code* unless he or she is *morally blameworthy*. Is a person whose behaviour constitutes a marked departure from the standard of the reasonable person morally blameworthy? In the *Creighton* case (1993), Justice McLachlin, speaking on behalf of the majority of the justices of the Supreme Court of Canada, answered this question in the affirmative:

> It is now established that a person may be held criminally responsible for negligent conduct on the objective test, and that this alone does not violate the principle of fundamental justice that the moral fault of the accused must be commensurate with the gravity of the offence and its penalty. ...
>
> Moreover, the constitutionality of crimes of negligence is also subject to the caveat that *acts of ordinary negligence may not suffice to justify imprisonment.* ... The negligence must constitute a "marked departure" from the standard of the reasonable person. *The law does not lightly brand a person as criminal.* ... [emphasis added]

Justice McLachlin also made the important point that, in general, a person who commits an offence negligently should receive a less severe sentence than a person who acts with subjective awareness of the risk that his or her conduct creates. This merely reflects the principle that the punishment for an offence should be commensurate with the degree of fault manifested on the part of the offender.

A good example of the application of the principle that a high degree of negligence is required before an individual may be convicted of an offence

under the *Criminal Code* is furnished by the case of *Finlay* (1993), in which the accused was charged with storing firearms and ammunition in a careless manner, contrary to the provisions of (what was then) section 86(2) of the *Criminal Code*. Section 86(2) stated that "every person who, without lawful excuse, uses, carries, handles, ships or stores any firearm or ammunition in a careless manner or without reasonable precautions for the safety of other persons" is guilty of an offence.*

On the face of it, section 86(2) undoubtedly imposed objective liability, but it also seemed to require the conviction of an accused person who has merely been careless in the storage of firearms and ammunition. However, the Supreme Court of Canada, while holding that section 86(2) did indeed impose objective liability, nevertheless stated that the fault requirement consisted of "conduct that is a marked departure from the standard of a reasonable person in the circumstances." If the Court had ruled that section 86(2) required the conviction of individuals who had merely acted carelessly, it would have been obliged to find that it was in violation of section 7 of the *Charter*. However, by interpreting the section as requiring a marked departure from the standard of the reasonable person, the Court was able to find that it met the requirement that a person may not be convicted of a *Criminal Code* offence unless he or she is morally blameworthy. Indeed, as Chief Justice Lamer noted in his judgment, section 86(2) of the Code clearly met the "minimal fault requirement" that is inherent in the principles of fundamental justice enshrined in section 7 of the *Charter*:

---

*Section 86 of the Code was amended in 1995. The current provision, which replaced the subsection discussed in the text above, is section 86(1), which reads as follows:

> Every person commits an offence who, without lawful excuse, uses, carries, handles, ships, transports or stores a firearm, a prohibited weapon, a restricted weapon, a prohibited device or any ammunition in a careless manner or without reasonable precautions for the safety of other persons.

By enacting s. 86(2), Parliament has seen fit to impose on all people owning firearms a specific and rigorous duty of care. It is a basic tenet of the principles of fundamental justice that the state not be permitted to punish and deprive of liberty the morally innocent. Those who have the capacity to live up to a standard of care and fail to do so, in circumstances involving inherently dangerous activities ... cannot be said to have done nothing wrong.

In the *Creighton* case (1993), Justice McLachlin emphasized that the objective test of liability does not take into account the peculiar personal characteristics of the accused person (such as background, education, or psychological disposition) except in the rare circumstance where the accused lacks the capacity to understand the nature and quality or the consequences of his or her acts or to appreciate the risk involved in his or her conduct. For example, a visually impaired person might not have the physical capacity to appreciate a risk that would be obvious to someone who had normal vision and, in this particular circumstance, a court would be obliged to enter an **acquittal** because it would be grossly unjust to hold an accused person to a standard of care that it is physically impossible for him or her to meet. Another example was given by Justice McLachlin in the *Creighton* case. She hypothesized that an illiterate person who mishandles a bottle of nitroglycerine without realizing what it is would not be held to the standard of the reasonable and literate person who would, of course, be able to read the label on the bottle.

In essence, therefore, Justice McLachlin and the majority of the justices of the Supreme Court of Canada emphasized the need for the "maintenance of a single, uniform legal standard of care" for offences imposing objective liability "subject to one exception: incapacity to appreciate the nature of the risk the activity in question entails." She went on to state that

I can find no support in criminal theory for the conclusion that protection of the morally inno-

cent requires a general consideration of individual excusing conditions. The principle comes into play only at the point where the person is shown to lack the capacity to appreciate the nature and quality or the consequences of his or her acts. Apart from this, *we are all, rich and poor, wise and naïve, held to the minimum standards of conduct prescribed by criminal law.* This conclusion is dictated by a fundamental principle of social organization. As Justice Oliver Wendell Holmes wrote "... when men live in society, a certain average of conduct, a sacrifice of individual peculiarities going beyond a certain point, is necessary to the general welfare." [emphasis added]

Why is it necessary to maintain a uniform standard of conduct in the application of the test of objective liability? According to Justice McLachlin,

The purpose of Parliament in creating an offence of objective foresight, as in manslaughter, is to stipulate a minimum standard which people engaged in the activity in question are expected to meet. If the standard is lowered by reason of the lack of experience, education, or the presence of some other "personal characteristic" of the accused, the minimum standard which the law imposes on those engaging in the activity in question will be eroded. The objective test inevitably is transformed into a subjective test, violating the wise admonition ... that there should be a clear distinction in the law between subjective and objective standards, and negating the legislative goal of a minimum standard of care for all those who choose to engage in criminally dangerous conduct. ...

The reasons why people fail to appreciate the risk inherent in their conduct are, according to Justice McLachlin, "legion":

They range from simple absent-mindedness to attributes related to age, education and culture. To permit such a subjective assessment would be "coextensive with the judgment of each individual, which would be as variable as the length of the foot of each individual" leaving "so vague a line as to afford no rule at all, the degree of judgment belonging to each individual being infinitely various."... *Provided the capacity to appreciate the risk is present, lack of education and psychological predispositions serve as no excuse for criminal conduct, although they may be important factors to consider in sentencing.* [emphasis added]

However, although the courts will not take account of personal characteristics of the accused when applying the objective test of liability, it is important to bear in mind that the test is not applied in a total vacuum. The court must take account of the nature of the particular activity in which the accused was engaged and the specific knowledge that he or she had of the relevant circumstances. The question for the court then becomes "would a reasonable person, *having exactly the same knowledge of the relevant circumstances as the accused*, realize that his or her conduct was creating a risk of bringing about consequences that are prohibited by the criminal law?" As Justice McLachlin asserted in the *Creighton* case (1993),

the answer to the question of whether the accused took reasonable care must be founded on a consideration of all the circumstances of the case. *The question is what the reasonably prudent person would have done in all the circumstances.* Thus a welder who lights a torch causing an explosion may be excused if he has made an inquiry and been given advice upon which he was reasonably entitled to rely, that there was no explosive gas in the area. [emphasis added]

OFFENCES IMPOSING OBJECTIVE LIABILITY

Driving Offences and Objective Liability

There are two general offences that may arise from poor driving behaviour on the part of Canadian motorists: dangerous driving and careless driving.

Dangerous driving is an offence that arises under section 249(1) of the *Criminal Code* enacted by the federal Parliament:

Everyone who drives a motor vehicle, on a street, road, highway or other public place in a manner that is dangerous to the public, having regard to all the circumstances including the nature, conditions and use of such place and the amount of traffic that at the time is or might reasonably be, expected to be at such place [is guilty of an offence]. ...

It should be noted that more severe penalties are applicable where the dangerous driving results in bodily harm (section 249(3)) or death (section 249(4)).

Careless driving is an offence that arises under the various provincial statutes that govern the operation of motor vehicles on the highways. In British Columbia, for example, the offence is known as "driving without due care and attention," contrary to section 144 of the *Motor Vehicle Act*, R.S.B.C. 1996, c. 318.

Both of these driving offences involve the imposition of objective liability in the sense that the Crown does not have to prove that the accused was subjectively aware of the risk that his or her driving conduct created for other users of the highway. For each offence, the Crown only has to establish negligence in the sense that the accused's driving conduct fell below the standard of the reasonable driver acting prudently in all of the circumstances. So what is the difference between the offences of dangerous and careless driving?

The critical distinction between two driving offences lies in the *extent* to which the Crown must prove that the accused departed from the standard of the reasonable driver. Conviction of *dangerous driving* can take place only where the accused's driving conduct constitutes a *marked departure from the standard of care expected of the reasonable driver* in the particular circumstances facing the accused. For example, in *Brannan*

(1999), Justice Donald of the B.C. Court of Appeal stated that, while a driver's simple "failure to keep a proper lookout" might amount to "civil negligence," it nevertheless "falls short of the requirement for dangerous driving." Conviction of the offence of *careless driving*, in contrast, may occur *whenever the accused falls below the standard of care expected of a reasonable driver.* Indeed, *any* deviation from that standard of care (no matter how minor it might be) can lead to a conviction of careless driving.

Before embarking on a more detailed discussion of the offence of dangerous driving, it should be pointed out that it would be possible for motorists to be charged with the general offences of **manslaughter**, criminal negligence causing bodily harm, or criminal negligence causing death as a consequence of their driving misconduct. However, it seems that it is somewhat unlikely that prosecutors will turn to these general charges when the specific offences of dangerous driving, dangerous driving causing death and dangerous driving causing bodily harm are now open to them. Indeed, the latter two offences carry maximum penalties of fourteen and ten years' imprisonment respectively. It is significant that an offence of "criminal negligence in the operation of a motor vehicle," which was contained in the *Criminal Code* for many years, was dropped in 1985.

For many years, there was an ongoing controversy as to whether the offence of dangerous driving requires proof of **subjective** *mens rea* on the part of the accused or whether a conviction may be obtained on the basis of an objective standard of liability. The Supreme Court of Canada finally put this controversy to rest when, in the *Hundal* case (1993), it ruled that the appropriate test to apply in determining whether the accused had the necessary *mens rea* for dangerous driving is the "modified objective test."

Justice Cory, in delivering the judgment of a majority of the justices of the Supreme Court, asserted that it would not be practical to require the Crown to prove that the accused subjectively appre-

ciated the risk created by his or her driving conduct. Indeed, in his view,

> to insist on a subjective mental element in connection with driving offences would be to deny reality. It cannot be forgotten that the operation of a motor vehicle is … automatic and with little conscious thought. …

Justice Cory, therefore, articulated an *objective* test in order to determine whether the accused had the necessary *mens rea* for dangerous driving. This test is as follows:

> the trier of fact should be satisfied that the conduct amounted to a marked departure from the standard of care that a reasonable person would observe in the accused's situation.

The provincial offence of careless driving: momentary inattention that falls below the standard of the reasonable driver.

However, Justice Cory also emphasized that the Court, in addressing this issue, must take into account the particular circumstances facing the accused and his or her perception of those circumstances. The question that should be asked is whether a reasonable person, *with the same knowledge of the facts as the accused*, would have appreciated the risk generated by the accused's driving conduct and would have refrained from taking such a risk. In this sense, said Justice Cory, the test can be considered a *modified* objective test:

> Although an objective test must be applied to the offence of dangerous driving, *it will always remain open to the accused to raise a reasonable doubt that a reasonable person would have been aware of the risks in the accused's conduct.* The test must be applied with some measure of flexibility. That is to say the objective test should not be applied in a vacuum but rather in the context of the events surrounding the incident. [emphasis added]

For example, if the accused suffers a totally unexpected heart attack, epileptic seizure, or detached retina, he or she may engage in driving conduct that, from an objective point of view, represents a gross departure from the standard of the reasonable driver; indeed, the accused may, in such cirumstances, become involved in an horrendous accident. However, the accused would be acquitted under the modified objective test because even a reasonable person, with the knowledge that the accused had, could not have foreseen that such a disastrous event might happen. On the other hand, if the accused knew that there was a chance, for example, that he or she was likely to have an epileptic fit, there would be a conviction of dangerous driving because a reasonable person, armed with that knowledge, would have foreseen the risk created by continuing to drive and would have refrained from doing so. As Justice Cory put it,

> if an explanation is offered by the accused, such as a sudden and unexpected onset of illness, then in order to convict, the trier of fact must be satisfied that a reasonable person in similar circumstances ought to have been aware of the risk and of the danger involved in the conduct manifested by the accused.

Justice Cory also stated that the modified objective test satisfied the minimal *mens rea* requirements dictated by the *Charter*. Indeed, he asserted the view that the *mens rea* requirement for dangerous driving that was articulated in the *Hundal* case was particularly appropriate for such an offence:

> the *mens rea* for the offence of dangerous driving should be assessed objectively but in the context of all the events surrounding the incident ... As a general rule, personal factors need not be taken into account. This flows from the licensing requirement for driving which assures that all who drive have a reasonable standard of physical health and capability, mental health, and a knowledge of the reasonable standard required of all licensed drivers.
>
> In light of the licensing requirement and the nature of driving offences, a modified objective test satisfies the constitutional minimum fault requirement for [s. 249] of the *Criminal Code* and is eminently well suited to that offence.

In the *Hundal* case (1993) itself, the accused had driven his overloaded dump truck into an intersection in downtown Vancouver where he collided with another vehicle, killing its driver. The evidence was that Hundal had entered the intersection *after* the relevant traffic light had turned red, while the deceased driver had proceeded into the intersection after receiving a green light. The accused claimed that the traffic light had just turned to amber and that, at this point, it was too late for him to try to stop his vehicle. However, several witnesses stated that the dump trunk drove through the red light and it was estimated that at least one second passed between the end of the amber light and the time when the accused's vehicle proceeded into the intersection. The trial judge, therefore, rejected Hundal's explanation for the accident and convicted him of dangerous driving. The Supreme Court of Canada ultimately upheld the conviction and ruled that the trial judge had been correct to apply a modified objective test in order to determine if Hundal had the necessary *mens rea* for dangerous driving. As Justice Cory noted,

> The trial judge carefully examined the circumstances of the accident. He took into account the busy downtown traffic, the weather conditions, and the mechanical conditions of the accused vehicle. He concluded, in my view very properly, that *[Hundal's] manner of driving represented a gross departure from the standard of a reasonably prudent driver.* No explanation was offered by the accused that could excuse his conduct. ... [emphasis added]

If persons accused of dangerous driving have an excuse that might lead to their acquittal under the "modified objective test," articulated in the *Hundal* case, then there is an onus on them to establish that there is some evidence which gives "an *air of reality*" to such a defence. In other words, they must meet the **evidentiary burden of proof** before their excuse may be considered. In *Reed* (1997), for example, the accused had been charged with three counts of dangerous driving causing death. He had been driving his elevated truck at night and had taken a curve at a speed that was at least 20 km/h in excess of the posted speed limit. Reed lost control of the vehicle and crossed over into one of the oncoming lanes, where he collided with a vehicle carrying three young men, all of whom perished. The trial judge acquitted the accused but the B.C. Court of Appeal allowed the Crown's **appeal** and substituted verdicts of guilty. The Court of Appeal accepted the Crown's argument that, *on its face*, Reed's driving constituted *dangerous driving* and that he was, therefore, under an *evidentiary burden to establish an explanation for his conduct*. Beyond some reference to the claim that "almost all drivers" speed on the highway

in question, there was no explanation on Reed's part that satisfied this evidentiary burden; therefore, the Court of Appeal held that he was guilty of the offence charged. As Justice Cumming noted,

> It cannot be said that the respondent's driving of the type of motor vehicle that he had, at night, at a speed more than 20 kilometers in excess of the speed limit, on a curve and totally on the wrong side of the road, is other than a "marked departure from the norm."

The Supreme Court of Canada subsequently upheld the judgment of the B.C. Court of Appeal (*Reed* (1998)).

On the other hand, in the *Stogdale* case (1995), the accused could offer an explanation for his conduct that led to his ultimate acquittal. The accused was the master of a Coast Guard vessel that was involved in a fatal collision with a fishing vessel on Lake Erie. The conditions were foggy, and Stogdale's vessel was operating at full speed without a foghorn. He was charged with dangerous operation or navigation of a vessel causing death. The trial judge convicted Stogdale, but the Ontario Court of Appeal set aside the conviction and entered an acquittal. Justice Austin stated that the trial judge had "*failed to consider all of the surrounding circumstances and the appellant's perception of those circumstances*," as required by the "modified objective test." Even the expert testimony on behalf of the Crown had been to the effect that, if the visibility at the time of the accident had been "half a mile," then proceeding at full speed without a foghorn would have been "safe," since the vessel was using radar. The Court of Appeal noted that Stogdale had *mistakenly* believed that the visibility was, in fact, at least one-half mile and, therefore, had operated at full speed, *honestly* believing that it was safe to do so. Furthermore, the Court of Appeal considered that Stogdale's estimate of visibility, although it ultimately turned out to be inaccurate, was nevertheless a *reasonable* estimate (indeed, two other officers on his vessel agreed with it). Therefore, the Crown had not established the necessary *mens rea* for dangerous operation or navigation of the vessel. Stogdale had presented an excuse for what, on the face of it, might otherwise have been considered dangerous operation of his vessel. However, he was able to point to evidence that gave an air of reality to his defence that he had acted reasonably; in other words, he had satisfied the evidentiary burden of establishing a valid excuse. The Court of Appeal clearly believed that the Crown had not been able to prove beyond a reasonable doubt that a *reasonable person, on the basis of the facts as Stogdale honestly and reasonably believed them to be, would have appreciated the risk of danger and would have refrained from taking it.*

Dangerous Driving and Criminal Negligence

Later in this chapter, the concept of criminal negligence will be discussed. Sections 220 and 221 of the *Criminal Code* respectively provide for the offences of *criminal negligence causing death* and *criminal negligence causing bodily harm*. It is possible for the Crown to lay either of these charges in situations where an accused's driving behaviour has caused death or bodily harm respectively. This immediately raises the question of how one is to distinguish between the offences of dangerous driving causing death or bodily harm (sections 249(3) and (4)) and the offences of criminal negligence causing death or bodily harm (sections 220 and 221). It appears that *both offences require proof of a "marked departure"* from the standard of the reasonable driver and that *the* mens rea *for both offences is objective in nature.* Therefore, the difference between the two sets of offences lies in *the degree to which the accused's behaviour departs from the standard of the reasonable.* The criminal negligence offences are considered to be more serious in nature and, therefore, a *more marked departure* from the standard of the reasonable driver must be established than is the case for the offences involving dangerous driving.

For example, in the *Palin* case (1999), Justice Deschamps, in delivering the judgment of the Québec Court of Appeal, addressed the nature of the distinction between criminal negligence and dangerous driving in the following manner:

> [O]n a scale of seriousness which goes from civil liability to criminal negligence, *criminal negligence is located higher up the scale than dangerous driving,* that is that *the departure must be more marked,* this norm being present in both the physical and mental elements of the offence. [translation; emphasis added]

In the earlier case of *Fortier* (1998), the Québec Court of Appeal held that the greater degree of "moral blameworthiness" that was associated with the criminal negligence offences is encapsulated in the definition of criminal negligence in section 219 of the *Criminal Code* (which, as will be seen shortly, requires proof that the accused showed "*wanton or reckless disregard* for the lives or safety of other persons"). Justice LeBel, in delivering the judgment of the court, referred to the "necessity of establishing reckless disregard in order to render a verdict of criminal negligence, rather than the marked departure from the standard of reasonable conduct, which is sufficient to find the accused guilty on a charge of dangerous driving."

Unlawful Act Manslaughter

In a following section, we shall see that individuals may be convicted of manslaughter on the basis that they caused the death of a human being (**actus reus**) by criminal negligence (*mens rea*). However, this is not the only basis upon which individuals may be convicted of manslaughter under the *Criminal Code*. Indeed, there is another form of manslaughter that is known, by criminal law commentators, as "unlawful act manslaughter." What is meant by this term? In order to explain the meaning of the term, it is first necessary to examine the Code provisions that deal with culpable homicide.

Section 222(4) of the *Criminal Code* gives the various forms of culpable homicide: **murder**, manslaughter and **infanticide**. Subsection 222(5) indicates four means by which culpable homicide may be committed:

A person commits culpable homicide when he causes the death of a human being,

(a) by means of an unlawful act,

(b) by criminal negligence,

(c) by causing that human being, by threats of fear or violence or by deception, to do anything that causes his death, or

(d) by wilfully frightening that human being in the case of a child or sick person.

What are the distinctions between murder, infanticide, and manslaughter? Section 234 of the *Criminal Code* states that "culpable homicide that is not murder or infanticide is manslaughter." In other words, manslaughter is a *residual* category of culpable homicide because it is defined in terms of what it is not, rather than what it is. If culpable homicide is neither murder nor infanticide, then it must be categorized as manslaughter. Murder (according to section 229) is, in general terms, defined in terms of the accused's intent to kill, while infanticide (according to section 233) is committed where a woman kills her newborn child and her mind is "disturbed" because she has not fully recovered from the effects of giving birth or because of "the effect of lactation consequent on the birth." By a process of elimination, one may draw the conclusion that manslaughter must, generally, be defined as an unintentional form of killing that cannot be excused as an accident or justified in some other manner (such as self-defence). Section 222(5) indicates that, in general, there are two distinct forms of manslaughter: *manslaughter by criminal negligence* and *unlawful act manslaughter.*

As we shall see in the next section, manslaughter by criminal negligence is defined by referring to a combination of sections 222(5)(b) and 234 of the Code. However, another form of manslaughter may arise as a consequence of combining sections 222(5)(a) and 234; this is what has become known as "unlawful act" manslaughter. When the accused commits an unlawful act (usually an assault) that results in death, he or she will be convicted of murder if there is an intent to kill or if there is an intent to inflict bodily harm that the accused knows is likely to cause death and is reckless as to whether death ensues or not (section 229(a)). Indeed, as the *Martineau* case (1990) established, an accused person cannot be convicted of murder in Canada unless he or she *subjectively foresees the likelihood of death* ensuing from his or her conduct.

However, let us suppose that an accused person causes the death of a victim as a consequence of an unlawful act (such as an assault) but does not possess the necessary *mens rea* for murder. In these circumstances, it is likely that the accused will be convicted of unlawful act manslaughter. Unfortunately, while section 222(5)(a) states that culpable homicide may be committed "by means of an unlawful act," it does not define the necessary *mens rea* for conviction of unlawful act manslaughter. As noted above, section 234 merely states that any culpable homicide that is neither murder nor infanticide is manslaughter. Since the Code provides no guidance in this respect, the Supreme Court of Canada has articulated the test that must be used by the courts when determining if the accused had the necessary *mens rea* for unlawful act manslaughter.

In the *Creighton* case (1993), the Supreme Court ruled that the *mens rea* for unlawful act manslaughter is the *objective foresight of the risk of bodily harm that is neither trivial nor transitory in nature.* In other words, in order to convict the accused of unlawful act manslaughter, the Crown must prove that the accused had the necessary *mens rea* for the commission of the unlawful act that resulted in death (e.g., an assault) and that a reasonable person, in the same circumstances as the accused, would have foreseen the risk of bodily harm, given the inherently dangerous nature of the unlawful act.

In the *Creighton* case itself, the accused had been charged with (unlawful act) manslaughter after he had injected a quantity of cocaine into the arm of the deceased. He had not sought to determine the quality or strength of the drug before doing so. After the injection, the deceased went into violent convulsions and appeared to stop breathing. The accused would not permit a friend to call 911 for emergency assistance and the deceased was left on her bed for six to seven hours before such assistance was finally called. At this point, the deceased was pronounced dead.

What was the alleged "unlawful act" in *Creighton?* The Crown successfully argued that the accused had been trafficking in narcotics contrary to section 4 of the (now repealed) *Narcotic Control Act,* R.S.C. 1985, c. N-1. Under that act, the word "traffic" included "giving" or "administering" a narcotic. Granted that Creighton had committed an unlawful act resulting in death (the *actus reus* of manslaughter), what *mens rea* elements must the Crown prove in order to obtain a conviction of manslaughter?

Justice McLachlin, speaking for a majority of the Supreme Court of Canada, stated that

the test for the *mens rea* of unlawful act manslaughter in Canada ... is (in addition to the *mens rea* of the underlying offence) *objective foreseeability of the risk of bodily harm which is neither trivial nor transitory, in the context of a dangerous act. Foreseeability of the death is not required.* [emphasis added]

Justice McLachlin also stated that the "question is what the reasonably prudent person would have done in all the circumstances" and that

the *mens rea* for objective foresight of risking harm is normally inferred from the facts. The standard is that of the reasonable person in the circumstances of the accused. *If a person has committed a manifestly dangerous act, it is reasonable, absent indications to the contrary, to infer that he or she failed to direct his or her mind to the risk and the need to take care. However, the normal inference may be negated by evidence raising a reasonable doubt as to lack of capacity to appreciate the risk.* Thus, if a *prima facie*

case for *actus reus* and *mens rea* is made out, it is necessary to ask a further question: did the accused possess the requisite capacity to appreciate the risk flowing from his conduct? If this further question is answered in the affirmative, the necessary moral fault is established and the accused is properly convicted. If not, the accused must be acquitted. [emphasis added]

As far as the facts in the *Creighton* case (1993) were concerned, Justice McLachlin emphasized that the central issue was "whether the reasonable person in all the circumstances" facing the accused "would have foreseen the risk of bodily harm"? To this question, Justice McLachlin believed there was a simple answer:

At the very least, a person administering a dangerous drug like cocaine to another has a duty to inform himself as to the precise risk the injection entails and to refrain from administering it unless reasonably satisfied that there is no risk of harm. That was not the case here. ...

Not every unlawful act that results in death constitutes unlawful act manslaughter. This proposition is illustrated by the case of *Vaillancourt* (1995), in which the accused and his friend, Palardy, had gone to pick up a video cassette in Vaillancourt's apartment. Palardy noticed a .32 calibre revolver on the accused's night table and asked Vaillancourt how the firearm worked. The accused opened the magazine of the gun and let the bullets slide out into the palm of his hand. Vaillancourt closed the magazine without checking to see if any bullets remained inside it. He then pulled the trigger and, on four occasions, nothing happened. However, by the fifth try, Vaillancourt was pointing the gun at Palardy's head and, when the accused pulled on the trigger, a bullet, which had remained inside the magazine, was discharged and killed Palardy. Vaillancourt was charged with (unlawful act) manslaughter.

There was no doubt that Vaillancourt had engaged in an "unlawful act" because the *Criminal*

Code (section 87) renders it an offence to point a firearm (*whether loaded or unloaded*) at another person if this is done "without lawful excuse." However, the critical issue in the case was whether Vaillancourt had the necessary *mens rea* for manslaughter. The evidence was to the effect that the accused honestly believed that the magazine had been fully emptied because it had an extractor, which was supposed to expel all of the bullets when it was opened. There was no evidence of any animosity between Vaillancourt and Palardy and the latter showed no fear at the time of the shooting because he also believed that the gun was unloaded. Indeed, as the trial judge noted, Vaillancourt was, at Palardy's request, "simply demonstrating the operation of the gun." The trial judge emphasized that the accused had "taken the precaution of emptying the magazine, that he was familiar with the gun and that he had every reason to believe that all of the bullets had fallen out of it." The trial judge, therefore, acquitted the accused because there was *no evidence that a reasonable person, on the facts as the accused perceived them to be, would have foreseen the risk of non-trivial bodily harm* to Palardy. After all, in most circumstances, an unloaded firearm does not *per se* pose a threat of bodily harm and Vaillancourt *honestly* (and *reasonably*) believed that the gun did not contain any bullets. Put another way, the pointing of an unloaded firearm is not a "manifestly dangerous act" (a requirement identified by Justice McLachlin in the *Creighton* case as being an essential element in unlawful act manslaughter), and Vaillancourt believed that he was merely demonstrating the operation of an unloaded revolver at the time of the fatal tragedy.

The Québec Court of Appeal upheld the acquittal of Vaillancourt. As Justice Brossard noted, on behalf of the court, "in so far as the respondent is concerned, he pointed an unloaded gun, in the quite amicable context of demonstrating the handling of the gun, and without any malevolent intention of any nature whatsoever."

Before leaving our discussion of unlawful act manslaughter, it is important to emphasize that not all dangerous acts are unlawful. Take the tragic case of *Davis* (1978), in which the accused was charged with manslaughter after he had intravenously injected into the arm of a girlfriend some pyribenzamine pills he had crushed and dissolved in water. It was clear that this injection was made with the enthusiastic consent of the victim. Unfortunately, immediately after the injection, the victim became unconscious and suffered a number of convulsive spasms. She later died before an ambulance could reach her. Medical evidence indicated that "the fluid and hemorrhage in the lung, which were the cause of death, were consistent with the intravenous injection of a drug." At his trial, the accused was convicted of unlawful act manslaughter. However, the Saskatchewan Court of Appeal allowed his appeal and quashed his conviction. The court pointed out that pyribenzamine could be lawfully purchased at any drug store without a prescription and there was no law regulating its use. Furthermore, Davis did not have any idea that the injection of the drug could be dangerous. Therefore, in the words of Chief Justice Culliton,

> It cannot be said that anything which Davis did … was unlawful. That being so, there is no foundation for any suggestion that [the victim] … died as a result of an unlawful act by Davis. If it were otherwise, there would be a foundation for a manslaughter conviction.

Of course, the *Davis* case (1978) contrasts dramatically with the *Creighton* case (1993), in which the drug injected into the victim was cocaine, the mere possession of which is illegal under (what is now) the *Controlled Drugs and Substances Act*, S.C. 1996, c. 19.

However, it is significant that the Supreme Court of Canada has ruled that engaging in a so-called fair fist fight constitutes an assault, even though both parties may have given their consent to participate in this form of pugilism. Indeed, in the case of *Jobidon* (1991), the Court ruled that no one has the right to consent to the infliction of bodily harm and that, where the accused had struck the victim on the head with his fists thereby causing death, he was guilty of (unlawful act) manslaughter. Jobidon had committed an assault and any reasonable person would have foreseen the risk of some bodily harm when a person is struck on the head by a series of punches.

The Offences of Unlawfully Causing Bodily Harm and Assault Causing Bodily Harm

The offences of *unlawfully causing bodily harm* (section 269 of the Code) and *assault causing bodily harm* (section 267) also provide two significant examples of the imposition of **objective mens rea**. In the *DeSousa* case (1992), the Supreme Court of Canada held that the *mens rea* for unlawfully causing bodily harm is "*objective foresight of bodily harm.*" If an accused person commits an "unlawful act" (an offence under federal or provincial legislation), which is *objectively dangerous*, then, if bodily harm is the consequence of that unlawful act, he or she will be convicted of unlawfully causing bodily harm. Put another way, if a reasonable person would have foreseen the risk of *non-trivial bodily harm*, then it is irrelevant whether this particular accused subjectively foresaw such a consequence. In *DeSousa*, the accused was involved in a fight that resulted in a bystander being injured. The accused had allegedly thrown a bottle against a wall and a fragment of glass had struck the bystander, wounding her in the arm. The accused claimed that section 269 of the *Criminal Code* should be struck down under section 7 of the *Charter* because it contravened the "principles of fundamental justice" insofar as it "put an accused person at risk of imprisonment without the requirement of a blameworthy state of mind." The trial judge agreed with this argument and quashed the indictment against DeSousa. However, the trial judge's decision was later overturned by the Ontario Court of Appeal and the accused's appeal to the Supreme Court of Canada was firmly rejected.

Speaking on behalf of the Supreme Court, Justice Sopinka stated that the principles of fundamental justice, enshrined in section 7 of the *Charter*, were not infringed by the imposition of objective *mens rea* in relation to the offence of unlawfully causing bodily harm:

> One is not morally innocent simply because a particular consequence of an unlawful act was unforeseen by that actor. In punishing for unforeseen consequences the law is not punishing the morally innocent but those who cause injury through avoidable unlawful action. *Neither basic principles of criminal law, nor the dictates of fundamental justice require, by necessity, intention in relation to the consequences of an otherwise blameworthy act.* [emphasis added]

This *mens rea* requirement — of objective foresight of non-trivial bodily harm — also appears in the context of the offence of assault causing bodily harm (section 267). For example, in the case of *Dewey* (1999), the **complainant** had been fighting with another man, when the accused came between them and "forcefully shoved the complainant," whose head then struck a jukebox or a corner of the wall as he was falling to the ground. The complainant suffered very serious injuries. At his trial, the accused was convicted of assault causing bodily harm. Dewey appealed to the Alberta Court of Appeal. He claimed that, while the offence did, indeed, impose objective liability, it was nevertheless necessary for the Crown to prove that a reasonable person would have foreseen *the particular type of bodily harm that ultimately occurred in this case* (namely, that the victim would fall and strike his head on the juke box or the wall). In dismissing Dewey's appeal, the Alberta Court of Appeal stated that the Crown has satisfied the *mens rea* requirements for assault causing bodily harm if it proves that the reasonable person would have foreseen *any sort of non-trivial bodily harm whatsoever*. It is not necessary for the Crown to prove that the *specific type of bodily harm that was inflicted* could have been foreseen by a reasonable person placed in the same circumstances as the accused. As Justice McLung stated on behalf of the Court of Appeal,

The trial judge found that Dewey pushed the complainant more forcefully than would cause a stumble. *It is objectively foreseeable that this action would create a risk of bodily harm which is neither transitory nor trivial.* [emphasis added]

The Offence of Criminal Negligence

Section 219(1) of the Code provides that

Every one is criminally negligent who

(a) in doing anything, or
(b) in omitting to do anything that it is his duty to do,

shows wanton or reckless disregard for the lives or safety of other persons.

This definition of criminal negligence is applicable to the following offences: causing death by criminal negligence (section 220), causing bodily harm by criminal negligence (section 221), and manslaughter by criminal negligence (section 222(5)(b) and section 234).

According to the provisions of section 219(1) of the *Criminal Code*, an accused person may be convicted of an offence, involving criminal negligence, in relation to both *positive acts* and *omissions*. Where the gist of the charges is that the accused *failed* to act, it must first be established that the accused was under a legal *duty* to act (section 219(2) indicates that "duty" means a "duty imposed by law"). It should also be pointed out that section 219 is concerned with the most culpable forms of negligence; indeed, it specifies that, in order to obtain a conviction, the Crown must establish that, in either doing something or failing to do something that it was his or her duty to do, the accused showed "wanton or reckless disregard for the lives or safety of other persons." As we shall see, this has been interpreted as meaning that the accused will be found guilty of criminal negligence where his or her conduct (whether it is an act or an omission) amounts to a

marked departure from the standard of the reasonable person acting prudently in the circumstances facing the accused.

It would be easy to say, without qualification, that the *mens rea* elements of criminal negligence are based on objective liability. Unfortunately, when the Supreme Court of Canada had the opportunity to address this issue in 1989, there was a three to three split between the justices as to whether the appropriate test was objective or whether it required a minimal degree of subjective awareness on the part of the accused of the risk created by his or her conduct. However, the view of most commentators on Canadian criminal law seems to be that, since the Supreme Court of Canada in the subsequent cases of *Creighton* (1993) (unlawful act manslaughter) and *Hundal* (1993) (dangerous driving) unequivocally accepted the view that "penal negligence" is based on an objective test of liability, the Court will almost certainly rule in the future that the *mens rea* of offences involving proof of criminal negligence is also objective in nature. Therefore, this chapter has included criminal negligence as a form of objective *mens rea*.

What did the Supreme Court of Canada actually say in the cases of *Tutton and Tutton* (1989) and *Waite* (1989) when it addressed the issue of the necessary *mens rea* elements that must be proved in a case involving criminal negligence? *Tutton and Tutton* involved charges of manslaughter against the parents of a five-year-old boy who had died after they failed to provide him with necessary medical attention (they had ceased giving their diabetic son his insulin injections because the mother had a vision that the boy had been healed and no longer needed them). The theory of the Crown was that the accused were guilty of manslaughter by criminal negligence. The accused were convicted, but a new trial was ordered by the Ontario Court of Appeal because the trial judge may have caused the jury to believe that the accused were required to prove that they had a lawful excuse for what they did. Placing the burden on an accused to prove his or her innocence would, of course, be inconsistent with the presumption of innocence that is now guaranteed by section 11(d) of the *Charter*. The Supreme Court of Canada agreed with the Ontario Court of Appeal that the trial judge had made a serious error with respect to the **burden of proof** and it upheld the order for a new trial.

For present purposes, the important aspect of the Supreme Court of Canada's decision in *Tutton and Tutton* (1989) is the analysis of the nature of the *mens rea* elements that the Crown must prove in relation to an offence involving criminal negligence. On this issue, the justices divided equally (three to three). One group, led by Justice McIntyre (and including Justices Lamer and L'Heureux-Dubé), took the view that the test was objective in nature:

> The test is that of reasonableness, and proof of conduct which reveals a marked and significant departure from the standard which could be expected of a reasonably prudent person in the circumstances will justify a conviction of criminal negligence.

Significantly, Justice McIntyre emphasized, as the majority of the justices of the Supreme Court of Canada were later to do in *Creighton* and *Hundal*, that the objective test should not be applied in a total vacuum. Indeed, he said that

> Events occur within the framework of other events and actions and when deciding on the nature of the questioned conduct, surrounding circumstances must be considered. *The decision must be made on a consideration of the facts existing at the time and in relation to the accused's perception of those facts.* Since the test is objective, the accused's perception of those facts is not to be considered for the purpose of assessing malice or intention on the accused's part but only to form a basis for a conclusion as to whether or not the accused's conduct, in view of his perception of the facts, was reasonable. This is particularly true where, as here, the accused have raised the defence of mistake of fact. If an accused under s. [219] has an honest and rea-

sonably held belief in the existence of certain facts, it may be a relevant consideration in assessing the reasonableness of the conduct. For example, a welder, who is engaged to work in a confined space believing on the assurance of the owner of the premises that no combustible or explosive material is stored nearby, should be entitled to have his perception, as to the presence or absence of dangerous materials, before the jury on a charge of manslaughter when his welding torch causes an explosion and a consequent death. [emphasis added]

Lining up on the other side in the *Tutton and Tutton* case (1989) were Justices Wilson and La Forest as well as Chief Justice Dickson, who clearly stated that proof of criminal negligence requires some proof of a *subjective awareness* on the part of the accused that his or her conduct presents a risk to the lives and safety of others. In other words, the Crown must prove that the accused was reckless or wilfully blind as to the risk. However, it is interesting that Justice Wilson, in delivering her judgment, can only be said to have "watered down" the subjective test by stating that conduct on the part of the accused that shows a wanton and reckless disregard for the lives and safety of others will constitute *prima facie* evidence of this mental element, and in the absence of evidence to the contrary, the court may conclude that the accused was aware of the risk or was wilfully blind to it. What this means in practice is that, *if the accused's conduct amounts to a marked departure from the standard of the reasonable person, it will normally be assumed that the accused had an awareness of the risk involved.* The assumption will only be set aside if the accused can point to some evidence that would indicate that he or she was not, in fact, aware of this risk. For example, such evidence might show that the accused was developmentally disabled to such an extent that he or she could not foresee the consequences of his or her behaviour even though a person of "normal" mental abilities would have been able to do so.

In the *Waite* case (1989), the Supreme Court of Canada reproduced the same three to three split that occurred in the *Tutton and Tutton* case (1989). The facts in *Waite* were that the accused, after drinking alcohol, had driven his car at high speed on the wrong side of the road and without proper headlights (even though it was late in the evening and the light was poor). There were a number of people on the road, taking part in a church hayride. Most were riding in wagons but some were walking alongside them. The evidence was that Waite decided to "play chicken" with the wagons and that he told his friends, "Let's see how close we can get." Tragically, he struck five people who were walking by the wagons, killing four of them and severely injuring one. Waite was charged, *inter alia*, with four counts of criminal negligence causing death and one of criminal negligence causing bodily harm.

The trial judge instructed the jury that, in order to obtain a conviction of an offence involving criminal negligence, the Crown must prove that there was, on the accused's part, "a deliberate and wilful assumption of the risk involved in the manner in which he was driving." Waite was acquitted of the criminal negligence charges and the Crown appealed to the Ontario Court of Appeal, which allowed the appeal and ordered a new trial because the trial judge had erred in instructing the jury to apply a subjective test in determining whether the accused had been criminally negligent. Waite then appealed to the Supreme Court of Canada, but the appeal was dismissed.

As in the *Tutton and Tutton* case, the Court split into two groups: Justice Wilson (with whom Chief Justice Dickson and Justice La Forest concurred) presented the view that the test of criminal negligence should be subjective in nature, whereas Justice McIntyre (with whom Justices L'Heureux-Dubé and Lamer concurred) contended that the test should be objective. Interestingly enough, both groups agreed that the trial judge's instruction to the jury had been too favourable to the accused. Justice Wilson said that the trial judge had erred when he required the Crown to prove deliberation and wilfulness on the part of the accused. In her view, while the test is subjective, the "mental element in criminal negligence is the minimal intent of aware-

ness of the prohibited risk or wilful blindness to the risk." In contrast, Justice McIntyre repeated the view that the Crown did not have to prove any subjective awareness of the risk on the part of the accused; it was sufficient if it proved that there was a "marked and substantial departure from the standard of behaviour expected of a reasonably prudent person in the circumstances."

In *Anderson* (1990), the Supreme Court of Canada once again avoided making a final decision as to whether the test for criminal negligence is subjective or objective in nature. In this particular case, it was not necessary to choose between the two approaches because the application of either test would result in the same decision. Justice Sopinka noted that, whichever approach is adopted, the Crown is always required to prove that the accused's conduct represented a marked departure from the norm. He also suggested that when dealing with criminal negligence, in which there must be a danger to the lives and safety of others in order to obtain a conviction, the difference between the objective and subjective approaches is relatively small:

> The greater the risk created, the easier it is to conclude that a reasonably prudent person would have foreseen the consequences. Equally, it is easier to conclude that the accused must have foreseen the consequences. It is apparent, therefore, that as the risk of harm increases, the significance of the distinction between the objective and subjective approaches decreases. The ultimate in this process of reasoning is reached when the risk is so high that the consequences are the natural result of the conduct creating the risk. The conduct in such circumstances can be characterized as intentional.

The failure of the Supreme Court of Canada to choose between the objective and subjective tests of criminal negligence has left the criminal law in some degree of uncertainty. However, as noted earlier, the subsequent Supreme Court of Canada decisions in the *Creighton* and *Hundal* cases (1993) unequivocally embraced the objective test of liability for unlawful act manslaughter and dangerous driving, respectively, and it would be extraordinarily surprising if the Supreme Court does not adopt the same approach towards criminal negligence when it is next called upon to confront the issue.

It is significant that, in a series of cases decided after *Tutton and Tutton* and *Waite* (1989), the Ontario Court of Appeal took the view that, until the Supreme Court of Canada decides otherwise, it will continue to apply an objective test of criminal negligence (see, for example, *Nelson* (1990), *Cabral* (1990), and *Gingrich and McLean* (1991)).

The requirement that there be a "marked departure from the standard of the reasonable person" in a case of criminal negligence is well illustrated by the tragic case of *Barron* (1985). The accused was charged with manslaughter after the death of his friend, who had fallen down a steep staircase. Barron, who was only sixteen years old, had been drinking at a party and had given his friend only a "slight push involving minimal force." They were apparently intending to go downstairs and, for a joke, run into a room dressed only in their underpants (in order to shock the young women who were there). The friend was a little reluctant so Barron gave him a nudge to encourage him to proceed down the staircase. Unfortunately, the friend died as a result of the slight push and the ensuing fall from the top of the staircase. The trial judge convicted the accused of manslaughter on the basis of criminal negligence:

> I am satisfied beyond a reasonable doubt that the accused, by *failing to give thought to the obvious and serious risk of severe bodily harm to his friend, showed wanton and reckless disregard for his friend's life and safety.* In not so adverting, he was criminally negligent. [emphasis added]

However, the Ontario Court of Appeal allowed Barron's appeal and entered an acquittal. The court ruled that there had not been a "marked and substantial" departure from the standard of the reasonable person, taking into account the minimal amount of force actually used, the fact that the circumstances that gave rise to the danger occurred suddenly, and that Barron's "behaviour in response thereto was immediate." In the view of the court, Barron's inadvertence had been only "momentary in nature."

It will be remembered that section 219 of the *Criminal Code* indicates that criminal negligence occurs when an individual either *does* anything or *omits* to do "anything that it is his [or her] duty to do" and thereby shows "wanton or reckless disregard for the lives or safety of other persons." Clearly *criminal negligence includes acts of both commission and omission.* Should the required *mens rea* element that the Crown must prove in relation to a charge of criminal negligence be the same, or different, when the accused's conduct consists of an *omission* as opposed to an act of commission? Significantly, in its decision in the *Tutton and Tutton* case (1985), the Ontario Court of Appeal had ruled that an *objective* test should be applied where the accused was charged on the basis of an *act of commission* but that a *subjective* test should be applied where the accused was charged on the basis of an *act of omission.* However, the majority of the justices of the Supreme Court of Canada appeared to reject the contention that the nature of the *mens rea* for criminal negligence may vary in the manner described by the Ontario Court of Appeal. Although the justices of the Supreme Court could not agree as to whether the *mens rea* for criminal negligence is *subjective* or *objective* in nature, they nevertheless appeared to be unanimous in holding the view that the same test (whether it be subjective or objective) applies to both positive acts and omissions.

This principle was applied by the Ontario Court of Appeal in the more recent case of *Canhoto* (1999). Here, the accused had been convicted of manslaughter (by criminal negligence), following the death of her two-year-old daughter,

Kira. A significant part of the Crown's case against Canhoto was based on her *failure to intercede* when Kira's grandmother had forced water down the child's throat as part of a ritual to "expel evil spirits." As a consequence of this violent exorcism, Kira had died from asphyxiation. During her appeal to the Ontario Court of Appeal, Canhoto's **counsel** contended that "the fault component of crimes of criminal negligence must vary depending on whether liability arises out of conduct or an omission" and suggested that a more onerous standard should apply to omissions as opposed to acts of commission. Of course, counsel emphasized that Canhoto's conduct consisted of an *omission* (a failure to intervene during the fatal exorcism of her own daughter). However, the Court of Appeal decisively rejected Canhoto's appeal against her conviction and, in delivering the judgment of the court, Justice Doherty held that the Supreme Court of Canada's decision in *Tutton and Tutton* (1989) had effectively rejected the line of argument advanced by her counsel:

> The determination of fault based on a failure to direct one's mind to a risk can be applied equally to acts and omissions. The need for a uniform standard for the determination of criminal culpability is as important where the law imposes a duty to act and no action is taken, as it is in cases where a person engages in conduct which creates that same risk. It would run contrary to the principle of uniformity and the values underlying that principle if the criminal law were to distinguish between a parent who chooses not to administer a life-saving drug to his child, thereby risking the life of that child, and a parent who actually removes the needle containing the drug from the arm of the child, thereby creating the very same risk.
>
> ... *The fault element for crimes of criminal negligence should be the same, regardless of whether liability arises out of a failure to act where there was a duty to act or out of actions which create a risk.* [emphasis added]

CAUSING DEATH BY CRIMINAL NEGLIGENCE AND MANSLAUGHTER BY CRIMINAL NEGLIGENCE: TWO IDENTICAL TWINS

The reader will, no doubt, have raised the following question while reading the preceding sections: What is the difference between the offences of causing death by criminal negligence (section 220 of the Code) and manslaughter by criminal negligence (sections 222(5)(b) and 234)? The answer is that the elements of each offence are identical. Why, then, are there two separate offences? The answer appears to lie in historical considerations. The offence of causing death by criminal negligence was created in 1955 as a direct consequence of the notorious reluctance of juries to convict motorists who killed others while driving their vehicles of the offence of manslaughter. It was felt that juries would be more willing to convict motorists of an offence that did not bear the heavy stigma of manslaughter. The irony is that the critical elements of the two offences as well as the penalty are the same in all respects. Significantly, in 1985, Parliament later added two new offences that deal with vehicular homicide, namely, dangerous driving causing death (section 149(4)) and impaired driving causing death (section 255(3)).

CRIMINAL CODE SECTIONS IMPOSING A SPECIAL STANDARD OF CARE

Where an individual is engaging in activities that are so inherently dangerous as to pose a serious risk to the safety of others, the *Criminal Code* may require him or her to meet an "elevated standard of care," namely, *the standard of care expected of a reasonable person who has acquired the necessary expertise and training to engage in such activities.* Examples of situations in which the *Criminal Code* imposes such an elevated standard of care are sections 79 (possession of explosives), 86(1) (use and storage of firearms), and 216 (administration of surgical and medical treatment). If there is a marked departure from the elevated standard of care, the accused's negligence will justify conviction of the relevant *Criminal Code* offence.

Clearly, the Code sections mentioned above all deal with situations in which one would expect the responsible citizen to acquire a reasonable degree of expertise *before* engaging in conduct that has the potential to be dangerous to the lives and safety of others. Undoubtedly, those who undertake to deliver medical care, to handle explosives, or make use of firearms, may all be said to be engaging in activities that are inherently fraught with many potential dangers. Therefore, a citizen who, for example, engages in medical treatment is judged by the standard of the reasonable medical practitioner rather than the reasonable person in the street who has no medical training. As Justice McLachlin stated in the *Creighton* case (1993),

> A person may fail to meet an elevated *de facto* standard of care in either of two ways. First, the person may undertake an activity requiring special care when he or she is not qualified to give that care. Absent special excuses like necessity, this may constitute culpable negligence. An untrained person undertaking brain surgery might violate the standard in this way. Secondly, a person who is qualified may negligently fail to exercise the special care required by the activity. A brain surgeon performing surgery in a grossly negligent way might violate the standard in this second way. The standard is the same, although the means by which it is breached may differ.

Reasonable Medical Treatment and Section 216

Section 216 of the *Criminal Code* provides that:

> Everyone who undertakes to administer surgical or medical treatment to another person or to do any other lawful acts that may endanger the life of another person, is, excepting cases of necessity,

under a legal duty to have and to use *reasonable skill and care* in so doing. [emphasis added]

This section clearly imposes an elevated standard of liability on those who administer surgical or medical treatment or engage in other lawful activities that may endanger the lives of others. Such individuals are expected to possess the knowledge and skills of the average, competent medical practitioner etc. This means that, while accused persons who administer such treatment may not subjectively appreciate the risk that their conduct is creating, they may still be convicted of an offence under the *Criminal Code* if the reasonable medical practitioner would have appreciated such a risk.

This principle is illustrated by the tragic case of *Rogers* (1968), in which the accused, a former doctor who had been struck from the rolls, was charged with causing death by criminal negligence. Although prohibited from engaging in medical practice, he continued to pose as a doctor and began to treat a little boy who suffered from a skin disorder. Rogers prescribed such an insufficient diet that the boy ultimately died of gross malnutrition. Rogers claimed that he honestly believed that his diet would be beneficial for the boy and that he did not foresee the risk that it might be dangerous. His counsel, therefore, argued that the Crown must prove that his client was reckless (or subjectively aware of the risk) before a conviction could be entered against him. Rogers was, nevertheless, convicted at trial and his appeal to the B.C. Court of Appeal was dismissed. The Court of Appeal emphasized that section 216 of the *Criminal Code* prescribes an *objective* test of criminal responsibility and that the Crown was, therefore, not obliged to establish that the accused *subjectively* appreciated the risk that his conduct was creating. Since a reasonable doctor would have appreciated the risk created by the inadequate diet, Rogers was correctly convicted. As Justice Nemetz said in relation to this point,

> Once all of the medical witnesses had testified that the possessors of reasonable medical knowledge would foresee that the taking away of pro-

teins and calories (as was in fact done by Rogers) would probably result in death, it became irrelevant for the trial judge to put Rogers' belief to the contrary to the jury. It was Rogers' duty to have the "reasonable knowledge" that was delineated and which represented the advances in scientific and medical knowledge to this day. If he persisted in this treatment notwithstanding that body of reasonable knowledge he ran the risk of bringing about the unwished result, namely, the death of the child.

Similarly, in the case of *Sullivan and Lemay* (1986), Justice Godrey of the B.C. Supreme Court ruled that two midwives, who were serving as birth attendants at a home birth, were covered by the phrase "any other lawful act that may endanger the life of another person" that appears in section 216 of the Code. On this basis, they were considered to be under a "legal duty to have and to use reasonable knowledge, skill and care" in their activities. Therefore, they were required to meet the standard of "a competent childbirth attendant whether the title is midwife, general practitioner or obstetrician" notwithstanding the fact that they had no formal training as midwives.

The Duty to Take Reasonable Care in the Handling of Explosives and Firearms— Sections 79 and 86(1)

The *Criminal Code* also imposes an elevated standard of care in relation to the handling of explosive substances. Section 79 states

> Everyone who has an explosive substance in his possession or under his care or control is under a legal duty to use reasonable care to prevent bodily harm or death to persons or damage to property by that explosive substance.

A similar duty has been imposed on those who handle firearms. Section 86(1) of the Code provides:

> Every person commits an offence who, without lawful excuse, uses, carries, handles, ships, transports or stores a firearm, a prohibited weapon, a restricted weapon, a prohibited device or any ammunition or prohibited ammunition in a careless manner or without reasonable precautions for the safety of other persons.

In each case, these provisions would be interpreted by the courts as requiring that an accused person meet the standard of care expected of a reasonable person who has taken some training in the safe handling of explosives and firearms. The standard is not that of the "reasonable novice" who tries his or her best to cope with explosives or firearms

Handling explosives: the need for an elevated standard of care.

with no knowledge of basic safety precautions. However, as the Supreme Court of Canada said in the *Finlay* case (1993), there can only be a conviction of an offence under the *Criminal Code* if the accused's behaviour can be designated as a marked departure from the standard of care expected of a reasonable person who has the necessary training and skills to deal with explosives and firearms.

Significantly, the Supreme Court of Canada has ruled that the elevated standard of care imposed by provisions of the *Criminal Code*, such as section 86(1), is that of the reasonable person acting prudently. Naturally, the reasonable person will acquire sufficient knowledge about the use, storage, and transportation, etc., of firearms *before* undertaking such activity. As Justice McLachlin said in the *Creighton* case (1993),

> Where individuals engage in activities for which they lack sufficient knowledge, experience, or physical ability, they may be properly found to be at fault, not so much for their inability to properly carry out the activity, but for their decision to attempt the activity without having accounted for their deficiencies. *The law expects people embarking on hazardous activities to ask questions or seek help before they venture beyond their depth.* [emphasis added]

However, it is important to bear in mind that the criminal law only requires the individual who uses firearms to meet the standard of care expected of a reasonable person who is acting prudently and who has acquired the necessary knowledge to engage in this activity safely. *In other words, the law imposes a "single minimum standard" and does not raise it—or lower it—according to the particular expertise of the **defendant** in a specific case.* For example, in the *Gosset* case (1993), Chief Justice Lamer suggested that a "police officer trained and experienced in the use of firearms should be held to a higher standard of care in the handling of firearms than the non-police officer." However, the majority of the Supreme Court of Canada has rejected Chief Justice Lamer's

approach. In *Creighton* (1993) Justice McLachlin clearly articulated the rationale for the position adopted by the majority of the justices of the Supreme Court:

> Just as the adoption of a uniform standard of care which is blind to personal characteristics of the accused short of incapacity precludes lowering the standard for deficiencies of experience and temperament, so it precludes raising the standard for special experience or training. *Since the criminal law is concerned with setting minimum standards for human conduct, it would be inappropriate to hold accused persons to a higher standard of care by reason of the fact that they may be better informed or better qualified than the person of reasonable prudence.* Some activities may impose a higher *de facto* standard than others; brain surgery requires more care than applying an antiseptic. But ... this flows from the circumstances of the activity, not from the expertise of the actor. [emphasis added]

In other words, a police officer who is charged with an offence of criminal negligence as a consequence of his or her use of a firearm will be judged by the standard of the reasonable person who uses firearms prudently, and not by the standard of an expert in the use of firearms. The standard of care under section 86(1) is "elevated" in the sense that an individual must acquire a minimum level of knowledge and skill before embarking on such a manifestly dangerous enterprise as dealing with firearms. However, if that individual attains this minimum level of knowledge and skill and acts prudently, then he or she cannot be found to have been guilty of criminal negligence.

STUDY QUESTIONS

1. Dennis, intending to scare his wife, Veronica, brandishes a sharp knife before her. Unfortunately, their child (Quasimodo) rushes in and

accidentally knocks his mother forward. She falls onto the knife and is killed. Should Dennis be charged with any offence(s)?

2. Nero has a personal grudge against Siegfried, a local farmer. In order to extract revenge, Nero decides to set fire to Siegfried's barn. The barn burns down before the firefighters can arrive to save it. Tragically, Crassus (a vagrant) had been sleeping in the barn at the time and was killed by the fire. Nero says that he honestly believed that there was no one in the barn when he set it alight. What charges might be laid (if any) against Nero?

3. Cecil and his sister, Daphne, are looking through the vast amount of items stored in their grandfather's basement. Daphne finds an old-fashioned revolver, with a rotating cylinder, containing six bullet chambers. She quickly opens the gun and notices that the chamber opposite the firing-pin is empty. She points the gun at Cecil, saying "bang, bang, you're dead," and pulls the trigger. To her surprise, the gun discharges and Cecil is killed. A gun expert tells the police that, when the trigger is pulled on such a revolver, the cylinder containing the bullets rotates. The chamber opposite the firing-pin was empty when Daphne first looked at the gun but, when she pressed the trigger, an adjacent chamber containing a live bullet rotated into a firing position. Daphne claims that she had no idea how revolvers operated and that she honestly believed the gun would not fire when she pulled the trigger; the expert says that this is just the sort of misconception that is quite common among those who are inexperienced with revolvers. The police are thinking of charging Daphne with manslaughter. Would such a charge be likely to succeed in a criminal trial?

4. Hermes, six years old, is taken for walk near a wading pool in Aquamarine Park by Isolde, his nanny. Hermes splashes water on Desmond, a man of 28, who has never seen Hermes before. Desmond has just been dismissed from his job

without cause by his boss and is infuriated by Hermes's behaviour. Desmond pushes the little boy into the pool. Hermes screams and starts to flounder in the water. Desmond believes that Hermes is "crying wolf" because he assumes that the water in a wading pool must be very shallow. However, Henry (the municipal employee responsible for this part of the park) has failed to repair some deep holes that have developed at the bottom of the pool, and at the point where Hermes falls in, the water is more than four feet deep. Hermes cannot swim. Isolde is a former member of the Neptune University swimming team and can easily rescue Hermes. However, Isolde is engaged in conversation with Tristan, a good friend, and does nothing except wave to the struggling Hermes and urge him to stop playing the fool. Tristan is also an excellent swimmer. He goes over to the edge of the pond and reaches out for the boy, but Hermes is too far from the edge and Tristan returns to his intimate conversation with Isolde. Hermes drowns. Desmond, who has already left the scene, does not learn that Hermes was drowned until he is visited by the police.

Consider:

(i) The charges that might be laid in this case.
(ii) The persons against whom the charges might be laid.
(iii) The approach that might be taken by defence counsel.

5. Dagwood drives his truck straight through a stop sign and crashes into a lamppost. Fortunately, no one was injured. Dagwood is charged with dangerous driving. He claims that he momentarily lost attention when he was changing a cassette in his tape deck, and before he realized that he was close to a stop sign, it was too late to bring his truck to a halt. He also claims that the truck was too heavy to

bring to a halt within the few seconds during which he had become aware of the stop sign. Is he guilty of the charge laid against him? Would it make a difference if Dagwood stated that he momentarily fell asleep because the driving conditions had been extremely treacherous (e.g., heavy snow or rain) and he was exhausted?

6. Forsyte is driving his car through a school zone when he suddenly experiences a massive heart attack and loses consciousness. Sadly, his car mounts the sidewalk and strikes a young child, who subsequently dies. Forsyte is charged with dangerous driving causing death. Is he likely to be convicted of this charge? Would it be a relevant consideration that Forsyte had already experienced two heart attacks?

7. Hamlet and Ophelia have a young daughter, Gertrude. They know that Gertrude, who suffers from diabetes, requires regular insulin injections in order to stay alive. Hamlet and Ophelia are members of a society that organizes seances and both of them firmly believe in the existence of a "spirit world." Hamlet tells Ophelia that he has experienced a vision in which he saw his father's ghost, who told him that Gertrude was cured of her diabetes and there was no longer a need for any injections. Ophelia implicitly believes what Hamlet has told her and they cease giving Gertrude her insulin injections. Gertrude lapses into a coma and, by the time she is taken to hospital, it is too late to save her life. Crown counsel wishes to lay charges of manslaughter against Hamlet and Ophelia. Is it likely that such charges would be successful at a trial?

8. Charles is a developmentally disabled adult who functions at the same mental level as an eight-year-old child. He finds a large rock and decides to go to a bridge that spans a highway. He then drops the rock on to a passing truck, killing its driver. The police wish to lay a charge of manslaughter or criminal negligence causing death against Charles. What would you do if you were Crown counsel in this case?

9. Arthur has three rifles and a large supply of ammunition in his residence. The guns are properly registered, as required by the *Criminal Code*. However, one day Arthur leaves one of the rifles in the garage instead of locking it up in a secure cabinet. His ten-year-old nephew, David, finds the gun and points it at his friend, Jonathan. Tragically, the gun is faulty and unexpectedly discharges, wounding Jonathan in the leg. Could Arthur be charged with criminal negligence causing bodily harm?

10. Hippocrates is a plastic surgeon who, for the past 30 years, has specialized in "face lifts" and similar surgical procedures. One day, he is summoned to the emergency room of the hospital and is told that, since no other surgeons are available, he must operate on Traddles, a man who has suffered major internal injuries in a car accident. Hippocrates realizes that Traddles will die without immediate surgery, so he very reluctantly undertakes to perform the operation. Traddles subsequently dies, and it is suggested that Hippocrates was negligent because he did not know the latest surgical techniques that could have saved a patient who had suffered such devastating injuries as had Traddles. If you were Crown counsel, would you charge Hippocrates with manslaughter or criminal negligence causing death?

11. Sabrina is a single mother of very limited means. She lives in a tiny apartment. She has only a living room (where she and her son, Nemo, also sleep), a small kitchen, and a bathroom. Nemo, who is five years old, frequently plays in the bathroom, where he loves to float some plastic toys in the bathtub. One day, Duncan, Sabrina's boyfriend, comes for a visit. Alcohol is consumed and the two adults decide to go to bed. Nemo is placed in the bathroom and told to play with his boats in the bathtub. Sabrina locks the bathroom door from the outside. She then engages in sexual relations with Duncan. After about half an hour, the adults dress themselves and decide to play with Nemo. When they unlock and open the bath-

room door, they discover Nemo floating face down in the water. Despite the application of mouth-to-mouth resuscitation techniques by Duncan and the early arrival of the paramedics (summoned by a distraught Sabrina), Nemo cannot be revived. In light of this tragic drowning, Crown counsel is considering laying charges against Sabrina. What charges might reasonably be laid and what defences might be open to Sabrina in light of these charges?

12. Squeers and Snawley are fighting in a bar. Gride angrily throws a beer glass at them in order to bring the disturbance to an end. The glass unfortunately shatters as it strikes part of the sprinkler system. A large piece of glass is embedded in the arm of Smike, an innocent bystander. Smike is taken to hospital and it requires 47 stitches to close his substantial wound. Gride tearfully tells the police that he never meant to harm anyone and appears to be genuinely contrite. What charge(s) might reasonably be laid against Gride?

FURTHER READING

Archibald, B.P. 1997. Fault, Penalty and Proportionality: Connecting Sentencing to Subjective and Objective Standards of Criminal Liability (with Ruminations on Restorative Justice). 40 *Criminal Law Quarterly:* 263.

Ashworth, A. 1995. *Principles of Criminal Law.* 2d ed. Oxford: Oxford University Press. 175–194.

Baker, B.M. 1987. *Mens Rea,* Negligence and Criminal Law Reform. 6 *Law and Philosophy:* 53.

Cairns, R. 1992. The *Charter,* the Supreme Court and the Invisible Politics of Fault. 12 *Windsor Yearbook of Access to Justice:* 128.

Carlton, T. 1992. A Principled Approach to the Constitutional Requirement of Fault. 24 *Ottawa Law Review:* 613.

Connolly, R. 1994. Dangerous Operation of a Motor Vehicle: More than Careless, But Less than Criminally Negligent? 5 *Journal of Motor Vehicle Law:* 253.

Fruchtman, E. 1987. Recklessness and the Limits of *Mens Rea:* Beyond Orthodox Subjectivism. 29 *Criminal Law Quarterly:* 315.

Gold, A.D. 1989. Note: Criminal Law—Criminal Negligence. 31 *Criminal Law Quarterly:* 405.

———. 1993. Constructive Manslaughter Should Not Have Survived. 23 *Criminal Reports (4th):* 262.

Grant, I. and C. Boyle. 1993. Equality, Harm and Vulnerablility: Homicide and Sexual Assault Post-*Creighton.* 23 *Criminal Reports (4th):* 252.

Grant, I., D. Chunn, and C.L.M. Boyle. 1994. *The Law of Homicide.* Toronto: Carswell. Chap. 6.

Hart, H.L.A. 1962. *Punishment and Responsibility.* Oxford: Clarendon Press.

Healy, P. 1990. *Anderson:* Marking Time or a Step Back on Criminal Negligence? 75 *Criminal Reports (3d):* 58.

———. 1993. The *Creighton* Quartet: Enigma Variations in a Lower Key. 23 *Criminal Reports (4th):* 265.

———. 1995. Repeal Criminal Negligence. 37 *Criminal Law Quarterly:* 205.

Hawke, K. 1991. The *Mens Rea* of Criminal Negligence. 3 *Journal of Motor Vehicle Law:* 1.

Horder, J. 1997. Gross Negligence and Criminal Culpability. 47 *University of Toronto Law Journal:* 495.

Klimchuk, D. 1996. Circumstances and Objectivity. 45 *Criminal Reports (4th):* 24.

Law Reform Commission of Canada. 1982. Working Paper No. 29: *The General Part: Liability and Defences.* Ottawa: Ministry of Supply and Services Canada.

———. 1984. Working Paper No. 33: *Homicide.* Ottawa: Ministry of Supply and Services Canada.

———. 1985. Working Paper No. 46: *Omissions, Negligence and Endangering.* Ottawa: L.R.C.C.

———. 1987. Report No. 31: *Recodifying Criminal Law.* Rev. ed. Ottawa: L.R.C.C.

Lefurgey, J. 1993. Case Comment: *R. v. Hundal* and *R. v. Rajic:* How Bad a Driver Must You Be to Be a Criminal? 5 *Journal of Motor Vehicle Law:* 185.

Leigh, L.H. 1983. The Law Reform Commission of Canada and the Reform of the General Part. [1983] *Criminal Law Review:* 438.

Mackinnon, P. 1990. Note: Criminal Law—Criminal Negligence and Recklessness—Criminal Law Reform: *R. v. Tutton; Waite v. R.* 69 *Canadian Bar Review:* 177.

Marko, J.G. and S.C. Hutchinson. 1990. Ball of Confusion: Criminal Negligence after *Tutton.* 2 *Journal of Motor Vehicle Law:* 59.

Mewett, A.W. 1992. The Enigma of Manslaughter. 34 *Criminal Law Quarterly:* 362.

Mewett, A.W. and M. Manning. 1994. *Mewett & Manning on Criminal Law.* 3d ed. Toronto: Butterworths. 193–219, 915–20.

Minister of Justice of Canada. 1993. *Proposals to Amend the Criminal Code (General Principles).* Ottawa: Minister of Justice of Canada (June 28, 1993).

Mitchell, G.G. 1995. Significant Developments in Criminal *Charter* Jurisprudence. 37 *Criminal Law Quarterly*: 461, 463–73.

Paciocco, D.M. 1995. Subjective and Objective Standards of Fault for Offences and Defences. 59 *Saskatchewan Law Review:* 271.

Rosenberg, M. 1990. The *Mens Rea* Requirements of Criminal Negligence: *R. v. Waite* and *R. v. Tutton.* 2 *Journal of Motor Vehicle Law:* 243.

Stribopoulos, J. 1999. The Constitutionalization of "Fault" in Canada: A Normative Critique. 42 *Criminal Law Quarterly:* 227.

Stuart, D. 1989. Criminal Negligence: Deadlock and Confusion in the Supreme Court. 69 *Criminal Reports (3d Series):* 331.

———. 1993. Fault: Welcome New Directions from the Supreme Court. 19 *Criminal Reports (4th):* 186.

———. 1993. The Implications of *DeSousa* for the Crimes of Aggravated Assault and Dangerous Driving. 16 *Criminal Reports (4th):* 326.

———. 1995. *Canadian Criminal Law.* 3d ed. Toronto: Carswell. 227–41.

———. 1998. Annotation: *R. v. Reed.* 15 *Criminal Reports (5th):* 29.

Stuart, D. and R.J. Delisle. 1997. *Learning Canadian Criminal Law.* 6th ed. Toronto: Carswell. 451–79.

Verdun-Jones, S.N. 1999. *Canadian Criminal Cases: Selected Highlights.* Toronto: Harcourt Brace. Chap. 4.

Yeo, S. 2000. The Fault Elements for Involuntary Manslaughter. 43 *Criminal Law Quarterly:* 291.

The Special Case of Regulatory Offences: Strict and Absolute Liability in Canada

OVERVIEW

This chapter examines the following:

1. The distinction between "true crimes" and regulatory offences;

2. the special status of regulatory offences in Canadian criminal law and the distinction between strict and absolute liability;

3. the critical decision of the Supreme Court of Canada in the *Sault Ste. Marie* case (1978), in which the Court articulated the principles that should be applied in determining whether a regulatory offence imposes strict or absolute liability;

4. the implications of the Supreme Court's ruling that defendants charged with an offence of strict liability are entitled to an acquittal if they prove they were not negligent (or acted with "due diligence");

5. the principles applied by the courts when deciding whether a regulatory offence is one of strict or absolute liability;

6. the decision of the Supreme Court of Canada in the *Wholesale Travel Group Inc.* case (1991) that strict liability is not invalid under the *Charter*;

7. the impact of the *Charter* on absolute liability offences and the presumption that such offences are invalid if combined with the potential penalty of imprisonment.

INTRODUCTION: DEFINING THE NATURE OF CULPABILITY IN THE FIELD OF REGULATORY OFFENCES

The Supreme Court of Canada has recognized that there is a critical distinction to be drawn between **"true crimes"** and **"regulatory offences."** What is the nature of this distinction? As Justice Cory stated in the *Wholesale Travel Group Inc.* case (1991),

Acts or actions are criminal when they constitute conduct that is, in itself, so abhorrent to the basic values of society that it ought to be prohibited completely. Murder, sexual assault, fraud, robbery and theft are all so repugnant to society that they are universally recognized as crimes. At the same time, some conduct is prohibited, not because it is inherently wrongful, but because unregulated activity would result in dangerous conditions being imposed upon members of society, especially those who are particulary vulnerable.

The objective of regulatory legislation is to protect the public or broad segments of the public (such as employees, consumer and motorists, to name but a few) from the potentially adverse effects of otherwise lawful activity. Regulatory legislation involves a shift of emphasis from the protection of individual interests and the deterrence and punishment of acts involving moral fault to the protection of public and societal interests. While criminal offences are usually designed to condemn and punish past, inherently wrongful, conduct, regulatory measures are generally directed to the prevention of future harm through the enforcement of minimum standards of conduct and care.

Today, regulatory offences arise in relation to such diverse matters as the maintenance of the quality of meat sold to the public, the regulation of the packaging of food products, the establishment of rigorous standards concerning the weights and measures used by retailers, the regulation and control of pollution, the control of misleading advertising, and the establishment and maintenance of a regime of traffic regulation. Indeed, as Justice Cory stated in the *Wholesale Travel Group Inc.* case (1991), "regulatory measures are the primary mechanisms employed by governments in Canada to implement public objectives" and "it is through regulatory legislation that the community seeks to implement its larger objectives and to govern itself and the conduct of its members." He went on to say that

It is difficult to think of an aspect of our lives that is not regulated for our benefit and for the protection of society as a whole. From cradle to grave, we are protected by regulations; they apply to the doctors attending our entry into this world and to the morticians present at our departure. Every day, from waking to sleeping, we profit from regulatory measures which we often take for granted. On rising, we use various forms of energy whose safe distribution and use are governed by regulation. The trains, buses and other vehicles that get us to work are regulated for our safety. The food we eat and the beverages we drink are subject to regulation for the protection of our health.

In short, regulation is absolutely essential for our protection and well being as individuals, and for the effective functioning of society. It is properly present throughout our lives. The more complex the activity, the greater the need for and the greater our reliance upon regulation and its

enforcement. ... Of necessity, society relies on government regulation for its safety.

Given the pivotal importance of regulatory legislation, it is scarcely surprising that there is an immense number of different regulatory offences that arise from federal, provincial, and municipal legislation. In 1976, the Law Reform Commission of Canada pointed out that there were some 20 000 *regulatory* offences arising under federal legislation and some 20 000 under the legislation of the average province in Canada. By 1983, the Law Reform Commission of Canada estimated that the number of regulatory offences, at the federal level alone, had climbed to some 97 000!

Perhaps, the most significant aspect of the distinction between true crimes and regulatory offences is to be found in the differing concepts of fault that underlie the two categories of prohibited conduct. Conviction of a true crime (such as robbery) necessarily involves a judgment that the offender has seriously infringed basic community values and is, therefore, considered to be morally culpable—to a high degree—for his or her actions. In contrast, conviction of a regulatory offence (such as accidentally mislabelling a food item) may involve very little (if any) moral culpability on the part of the offender. As Justice Cory said in the *Wholesale Travel Group Inc.* case (1991),

regulatory offences and crimes embody different concepts of fault. Since regulatory offences are directed primarily not to conduct itself, but to the consequences of conduct, conviction of a regulatory offence may be thought to import a significantly lesser degree of culpability than conviction of a true crime. *The concept of fault in regulatory offences is based upon a reasonable care standard and, as such, does not imply moral blameworthiness in the same manner as criminal fault.* Conviction for breach of a regulatory offence suggests nothing more than that the defendant has failed to meet a prescribed standard of care. [emphasis added]

What are the practical consequences of drawing a distinction between true crimes and regulatory offences? Foremost among these consequences is the fact that, whereas the Crown must prove some form of *mens rea* in order to obtain the conviction of an offender for a true crime, it generally does not have to do so in the case of a regulatory offence. As we have seen in Chapters 4 and 5, with true crimes, the Crown normally has to prove — in addition to the *actus reus* requirements — one or more of the following forms of *mens rea*: **intention**, knowledge, **recklessness**, **wilful blindness**, or criminal **negligence** (a marked departure from the standard of the ordinary person). However, in the case of a regulatory offence, all that the Crown normally has to prove are the *actus reus* elements of the offence concerned.

We shall see shortly that an **accused** person may escape incurring liability for most regulatory offences by proving, on the balance of probabilities, that they acted with "due diligence" (i.e., that they were *not* negligent). However, there are some regulatory offences where even this defence is not available to an accused person.

EVOLUTION OF THE JUDICIAL APPROACH TO REGULATORY OFFENCES IN CANADA

In order to understand the present-day status of regulatory offences in Canada, it is necessary to conduct a brief survey of their history. Since the mid-nineteenth century, English courts drew a distinction between "real crimes" and what they called "public welfare" offences, which arose under the various statutes regulating trade, commerce, and industry. Public welfare offences (or, in today's language, regulatory offences) were not considered to be acts that were inherently wrongful (as was the case with real crimes); rather, they were described as acts arising in the course of conducting otherwise lawful activities that were "prohibited in the public interest" under threat of a financial penalty. As we shall see, Canadian courts also adopted this distinc-tion between real crimes (or "true crimes") and pub-lic welfare offences and enshrined it in their own criminal jurisprudence.

Since public welfare offences were not consid-ered to be real crimes, courts in both England and Canada ruled that it was not necessary for the Crown to establish *mens rea* on the part of the **defendant**. Once the Crown had established that the prohibited act had been committed, the accused was automatically liable to conviction. Historically, this somewhat Draconian approach toward so-called public welfare offences was categorized as the imposition of *strict* or *absolute* **liability**. For more than a century, the terms strict and absolute liabil-ity were treated as virtual synonyms by the courts. However, as we shall discuss shortly, now an extremely significant distinction must be drawn between strict and absolute liability. For the pur-pose of the present historical discussion, however, we shall use the term absolute liability.

One of the classic Canadian cases, in which a court imposed absolute liability in relation to a public welfare (or regulatory) offence is that of *Ping Yuen* (1921), in which the accused was a vendor of soft drinks in Moosomin, Saskatchewan. A police officer searched his business premises and removed five bottles of soft drinks from the accused's stock. When these bottles were analyzed, it was found that three of them contained a percentage of alcohol in excess of the amount allowed by the Saskatchewan *Temperance Act, 1917*. The accused was charged with a violation of the Act. Under this statute, sec-tion 35(1) provided that "in case any person engaged in the business of selling soft drinks or nonintoxicating liquors keeps or has with his stocks of such drinks or liquors or on his business premises any liquor as defined by this Act, such person shall be guilty of an offence. ..." At Ping Yuen's trial, the magistrate found that the accused did not know that any of the bottles contained more alcohol than the law permitted. Furthermore, even the prosecu-tion admitted that it was not possible for the accused to test any of the bottles without destroying their contents for sale purposes; in other words, there was no practical way in which Ping Yuen could have avoided breaking the law! The accused was, nevertheless, convicted on the basis that since he was charged with a public welfare offence, the legislature must be taken to have intended to impose absolute liability in relation to the offence. The accused's conviction was subsequently upheld by the Saskatchewan Court of Appeal. In essence, the court ruled that Ping Yuen's offence was not a "true crime," to which any stigma attached. Instead, it was an act prohibited in the public interest under the threat of a financial penalty.

A critical point to bear in mind is the fact that, even though Ping Yuen had acted no differently than the "reasonable" retailer would have done in the circumstances, he was nevertheless convicted of the offence. In other words, Ping Yuen was not blameworthy in any sense whatsoever, but this was not considered relevant by the court; indeed, it is the conviction of a person who is without fault that constitutes the very essence of absolute liability. Interestingly, Ping Yuen was fined 50 dollars, which, in 1921, must have been quite a stiff penalty for a small-scale retailer. In the Court of Appeal, Justice Turgeon said:

> in the case of beer in this province, it seems to me to be the true intent of the Act that persons who deal in the article are made responsible for it being of a certain quality, namely, not more than 1.13% of alcoholic content, and when they have a too strong alcoholic article in their possession they are liable to the penalty. ...

In essence, the court seemed to be saying that, in order to protect the public, the risk of possessing beer with an excessive alcoholic content was placed solely upon the retailer's shoulders. Since the accused was engaged in the retail business, he must accept such a risk as part and parcel of doing business.

If the offence in the *Ping Yuen* case is a classic example of a public welfare (or regulatory) offence, the crime in the case of *Beaver* (1957) is an ideal illustration of a real crime (or "true crime") for

which proof of full *mens rea* is mandatory. The *Beaver* case involved charges of selling and possessing heroin. These charges arose under the old *Opium and Narcotic Drug Act, 1952.*

In the *Beaver* case, the prosecution claimed that Parliament intended to impose absolute liability in relation to the offences of selling and possessing heroin. The Crown pointed out that Parliament did not insert such words as "knowingly" or "wilfully" in relation to these offences and that, therefore, this indicated the intent to impose absolute liability. The majority of the Supreme Court of Canada soundly rejected this argument and ruled that the offences of possessing and selling heroin were clearly real crimes and not mere public welfare offences. Indeed, Justice Cartwright asserted that

> It may be of assistance in examining the problem to use a simple illustration. Suppose X goes to the shop of Y, a druggist, and asks Y to sell him some baking soda. Y hands him a sealed packet which he tells him contains baking soda and charges him a few cents. X honestly believes that the packet contains baking soda, but in fact it contains heroin. X puts the package in his pocket, takes it home and later puts it in the cupboard in his bathroom. There would seem to be no doubt that X has had actual manual and physical possession of the package and that he continues to have possession of the package while it is in his cupboard. The main question raised on this appeal is whether, in the supposed circumstances, X will be guilty of the crime of having heroin in his possession?

Justice Cartwright ruled that the offences charged in the *Beaver* case, bore no resemblance to so-called public welfare offences concerned with the regulation of legitimate trades, industry, etc.

> I can discern little similarity between a statute designed, by forbidding the sale of unsound meat, to ensure that the supply available to the public shall be wholesome, and a statute making it a serious crime to possess or deal in narcotics; the one is

Ping Yuen (1921): making the vendor absolutely liable for the contents of drinks sold in the store.

to ensure that a lawful and necessary trade should be carried on in a manner not to endanger the public health, the other to forbid altogether conduct regarded as harmful in itself. As a necessary feature of his trade, the butcher holds himself out as selling meat fit for consumption; he warrants that quality; and it is part of his duty as trader to see that the merchandise is wholesome. The statute simply converts that civil personal duty into a public duty. ...

It would, of course, be within the power of Parliament to enact that a person who, without any guilty knowledge, had in his physical possession a package which he honestly believed to contain a harmless substance such as baking soda but which in fact contained heroin, must on proof of such facts be convicted of a crime and sentenced to at least six months' imprisonment; but I would

refuse to impute such an intention to Parliament unless the words of the statute were clear and admitted of no other interpretation. ...

In the last passage, Justice Cartwright was referring to the fact the offences charged carried a mandatory *minimum* sentence of six months' imprisonment plus a fine of $200. In essence, the *Beaver* case established that, in relation to real crimes, the Crown must prove full *mens rea*. However, cases such as *Ping Yuen* established that, in relation to public welfare (or regulatory) offences, the Crown need only prove that the accused committed the prohibited act and no further consideration need be given to whether the accused was at fault.

THE ARGUMENTS FOR AND AGAINST ABSOLUTE LIABILITY

What were the arguments in favour of imposing absolute liability? A number of arguments were advanced over the years. For example, it was contended that those who engage in activities that may harm the public welfare should be required to meet a high standard of care and attention. Many people believed that, by requiring the Crown to prove *mens rea* in relation to regulatory offences, too many legal loopholes were created for individuals and corporations to evade their responsibilities to the public. It was argued that absolute liability would remove such loopholes and, thus, would act as an "incentive" for such persons to take precautionary measures, *over and above those that would normally be taken*, in order to ensure that mistakes and accidents did not occur. The theory, here, was that if an individual or a corporation realized that there were no legal loopholes to slip through when they were charged with a regulatory offence, they would take an extraordinary degree of care to avoid committing such an offence.

Another argument advanced in favour of absolute liability was that of administrative efficiency. It was alleged that it would be far too great a burden for the Crown to prove mental culpability in relation to the great number of petty regulatory offences that come before the courts. Since there is a need to process a large number of cases involving regulatory offences it has been argued that the Crown must have access to a swift and administratively efficient system of law enforcement. It was contended that, if the Crown were required to establish *mens rea* in relation to regulatory offences, the whole system of justice would rapidly grind to a halt and, as a result, hundreds of thousands of violators would escape conviction. Therefore, it was contended that absolute liability was a pragmatic necessity if there was to be effective regulation of trade, commerce, and industry in the country.

There are, of course, numerous arguments that militate against the imposition of absolute liability. For example, one of the strongest arguments of this nature is that absolute liability contradicts a deeply ingrained sense of justice since it punishes those who lack any moral culpability. It is a basic notion in our society that an individual who lacks moral culpability should not be convicted of a criminal offence. As the great American Justice Oliver Wendell Holmes once said, "Even a dog distinguishes between being kicked and being stumbled over." Another argument against absolute liability is that it destroys the individual citizen's basic freedom of choice. Indeed, traditional legal theorists, such as Professors Hart and Packer, have contended that the doctrine of *mens rea* is designed to maximize personal freedom in that only the individual who deliberately *chooses* to break the law is subject to conviction. Absolute liability, of course, would destroy such freedom since it is not based on individual culpability.

In the *Sault Ste. Marie* case (1978), Justice Dickson, on behalf of the Supreme Court of Canada, presented a number of convincing arguments against the imposition of absolute liability:

> The most telling is that it violates fundamental principles of penal liability. It also rests upon assumptions which have not been, and cannot be, empirically established. There is no evidence that a higher standard of care results from absolute liability. If a person is already taking every reasonable precautionary measure, is he likely to take additional measures, knowing however much care he takes, it will not serve as a defence in the event of breach? If he has exercised care and skill, will conviction have a deterrent effect upon him or others? Will the injustice of conviction lead to cynicism and disrespect for the law, on his part and on the part of others? These are among the questions asked. The argument that no stigma attaches does not withstand analysis, for the accused will have suffered loss of time, legal costs, exposure to the processes of criminal law at trial and, however one may downplay it, the opprobrium of conviction.

THE EMERGENCE OF A NEW APPROACH IN THE COURTS: THE "HALF-WAY HOUSE"

Whatever the arguments for and against absolute liability may be, there is little doubt that Canadian courts became increasingly uncomfortable with the "all-or-nothing" approach that they had embraced in relation to regulatory offences. Under this strategy, courts held either that an offence required that the Crown prove *mens rea* beyond a reasonable doubt or that it imposed absolute liability and, therefore, deprived the defendant of any defence based on his or her lack of fault. There was no half-way position between these two extreme alternatives and, as a consequence, the courts were forced to convict Canadians of regulatory offences in situations where they may have been totally without fault—which is precisely what happened in the case of *Ping Yuen* (1921).

In 1941, the Australian High Court laid the foundations of a legal doctrine that would eventually furnish an answer to the judicial dilemma concerning absolute liability. In the Australian case of *Proudman v. Dayman* (1949), the High Court of Australia suggested that there was a "half-way house" approach that might be adopted in relation to regulatory offences. Basically, the "half-way house" approach permits those defendants who are charged with a regulatory offence to advance the defence that *they were not negligent*. If this defence is sustained, they must be acquitted of the offence. Why is this called a "half-way house" approach? The answer is that it finds a middle ground between, on the one hand, requiring the Crown to prove all the *mens rea* elements of an offence beyond a reasonable doubt and, on the other, automatically convicting an accused person merely because he or she has committed the *actus reus* of a regulatory offence.

When the Crown charges an individual with a true crime, it must establish, beyond a reasonable doubt, all the elements of the *actus reus* and *mens rea* of the offence in question. In other words, the primary or **persuasional burden of proof** in relation to true crimes is nearly always placed upon the shoulders of the Crown. Accused persons are under no obligation to prove their innocence, and it is enough for them to raise a reasonable doubt in order to escape conviction. However, the half-way house approach provides that the Crown merely has to prove that the accused committed the *actus reus* elements of the regulatory offence in question. At that point, the **burden of proof** shifts to the accused to establish his or her innocence by proving on the balance of probabilities that he or she was not negligent.

Placing the onus of establishing their innocence upon accused persons themselves is clearly a fundamental departure from the normal rules of criminal law that apply in relation to real crimes. Indeed, the half-way house approach gives the Crown a significant advantage when prosecuting individuals for regulatory offences. This advantage is based on the fact that the Crown does not have to prove any mental element in relation to such offences. However, unlike the doctrine of absolute liability, the half-way house approach *does* permit defendants to advance a defence, but they must establish this "due diligence" defence on the balance of probabilities in order to escape conviction of a regulatory offence. It is not enough for the accused merely to

raise a reasonable doubt as to whether he or she acted without negligence.

Although the half-way house approach was first articulated in Australia as long ago as 1941, it was not until 1978 that the Supreme Court of Canada decided to adopt it in Canada (albeit in a modified form). An important development that occurred in the years immediately preceding the Supreme Court's decision in 1978 was the enactment of an increasing number of statutes (both at the federal and provincial levels) that made provision for a defence of due diligence in relation to certain regulatory offences. The introduction of this defence was, in essence, a legislative application of the half-way house approach since the onus of proving the defence was placed on the accused.

THE SUPREME COURT OF CANADA ACCEPTS THE HALF-WAY HOUSE APPROACH: THE *SAULT STE. MARIE* CASE

In 1978, the Supreme Court of Canada finally announced a *qualified* acceptance of the half-way house approach in the seminal case of *Sault Ste. Marie* (1978). In his judgment on behalf of the Court, Justice Dickson furnished a strong critique of the various arguments advanced in favour of absolute liability in relation to regulatory offences. He noted that an increasing number of statutes were including a defence of due diligence in the context of regulatory offences, and that some Canadian courts were already attempting to apply the half-way house approach developed by the Australian High Court despite the fact that it had not yet been recognized by the Supreme Court of Canada. Justice Dickson then unequivocally expressed the view of the Supreme Court that the half-way house approach should be adopted as part of the criminal law of Canada:

> The correct approach, in my opinion, is to relieve the Crown of the burden of proving *mens rea*, having regard to ... the virtual impossibility in most

regulatory cases of proving wrongful intention. *In a normal case, the accused alone will have knowledge of what he has done to avoid the breach and it is not improper to expect him to come forward with the evidence of due diligence.* This is particularly so when it is alleged, for example, that pollution was caused by the activities of a large and complex corporation. Equally, there is nothing wrong with rejecting absolute liability and admitting the defence of reasonable care.

In this doctrine it is not up to the prosecution to prove negligence. Instead, it is open to the defendant to prove that all due care has been taken. This burden falls upon the defendant as he is the only one who will generally have the means of proof. This would not seem unfair as the alternative is absolute liability which denies an accused any defence whatsoever. *While the prosecution must prove beyond a reasonable doubt that the defendant committed the prohibited act, the defendant must only establish on the balance of probabilities that he has a defence of reasonable care.* [emphasis added]

THE THREE CATEGORIES OF OFFENCE SINCE THE *SAULT STE. MARIE* CASE

In delivering the judgment of the Supreme Court of Canada, Justice Dickson held that there are three different categories of criminal offences in Canada. These are:

(A) Offences in which the existence of *mens rea* must be proved by the Crown beyond a reasonable doubt.
(B) Strict liability offences, in which there is no necessity for the Crown to prove the existence of *mens rea;* however, defendants may avoid liability by proving that they acted with "due diligence" (in other words, that they were not negligent).
(C) Absolute liability offences, in which there is no necessity for the Crown to prove the existence of *mens rea* and in which it is not open to

defendants to avoid liability by proving that they acted with "due diligence."

True crimes clearly fall within category A. Regulatory offences would *normally* fall within category B (i.e., offences of strict liability) *unless* the legislature uses such words as "wilfully" or "knowingly," which indicate a clear intent to require proof of full *mens rea.* Those regulatory offences that do not fall within categories A or B will be considered offences of "absolute liability" (category C). However, Justice Dickson stressed the point that regulatory offences will only be placed in category C where the legislature has made it perfectly clear that it intends to impose a regime of absolute liability. In this respect, Justice Dickson said that

> The over-all regulatory pattern adopted by the Legislature, the subject-matter of the Legislation, the importance of the penalty, and the precision of the language used will be primary considerations in determining whether the offence falls into the third category.

It is clear that, in the *Sault Ste. Marie* case, the Supreme Court of Canada drew a sharp distinction between "strict" and "absolute" liability offences. By permitting the accused to advance the due diligence defence only in relation to strict, and not absolute, liability offences, the Court in effect indicated that it was willing to acccept only a qualified version of the half-way house approach. Clearly, the Supreme Court was disinclined to make the due diligence defence available in relation to *all* regulatory offences, and this means that there will still be a limited number of regulatory offences that will be considered to impose absolute liability. However, as we shall see shortly, the imposition of absolute liability will, in certain circumstances, be considered invalid under the *Charter.* Therefore, courts will naturally be somewhat reluctant to find that a legislature intended to impose absolute liability if the consequence of that determination is that the offence must be struck down and declared as having "no force and effect."

THE FACTS IN THE *SAULT STE. MARIE* CASE

In the *Sault Ste. Marie* case, the facts were that the accused was a municipal corporation that was charged with the offence of "discharging, causing to be discharged, or permitting to be discharged or deposited materials into a body of water or on the shore or bank thereof, or in such place that might impair the quality of the water," contrary to section 32(1) of the Ontario *Water Resources Act*, R.S.O. 1970, c. 332. The City of Sault Ste. Marie entered into an agreement with a private company for the disposal of all the city's refuse. The company chose to dump garbage on a site that bordered a creek. Garbage was dumped over a number of fresh-water springs that flowed into the creek. After a period, water pollution resulted from this method of garbage disposal. How did the Supreme Court determine into which category the offence charged fell? Was it a true crime requiring proof of full *mens rea* or was it a regulatory offence imposing either strict or absolute liability?

Justice Dickson indicated that "pollution offences are undoubtedly public welfare (regulatory) offences enacted in the interests of public health. There is thus no presumption of a full *mens rea*." Indeed, he said that such a presumption only applies in the case of offences that are "criminal in the true sense." The learned justice then decided that the offence charged fell within the second category of offences—namely, offences of strict liability. The major reason for this decision was that, in the legislation that created the offence with which the defendant was charged, the Ontario legislature had not used words that indicated unequivocally that it intended to impose absolute liability. By placing the offence charged within the category of strict liability offences, the Court, therefore, made available to the defendant a defence of acting with "due diligence." A new trial was ordered in which the City of Sault Ste. Marie would have the opportunity to show that it had acted with such "due diligence."

The *Sault Ste. Marie* case is arguably one of the most significant decisions rendered by the Supreme Court of Canada during the past two decades or so. It clearly set the stage for a radically different approach to the whole issue of regulatory offences. Since this case was decided in 1978, the great majority of regulatory offences have been treated as imposing strict, rather than absolute, liability, and this means that the accused has the benefit of the defence of due diligence. As Justice Cory said in the *Pontes* case (1995):

> The decision in *Sault Ste. Marie* ... established that a person accused of a strict liability offence may avoid conviction by proving, on the balance of probabilities, either that he had an honest but mistaken belief in facts which, if true, would render the act innocent, or that he exercised all reasonable care to avoid committing the offence. That is to say, he did what a reasonable person would have done in the circumstances to avoid the occurrence of the prohibited act. In my view, if neither of these two facets of the defence of due diligence is available to an accused, the offence cannot be said to be one of strict liability. By definition, a strict liability offence requires that the defence of due diligence be available. Put another way, if the offence does not permit a due diligence defence, then it cannot be a strict liability offence.

However, one of the most difficult tasks that the courts have faced since the *Sault Ste. Marie* case was decided is that of determining exactly which regulatory offences should be singled out as imposing absolute liability. Justice Dickson's judgment in *Sault Ste. Marie* indicates that the category of absolute liability offences covers only those regulatory offences where the legislature has made its intention clear to impose such liability. Unfortunately, it is a rare occasion indeed on which the legislature imposes such liability in an *explicit* manner. Therefore, in most cases, it is a matter of judicial interpretation whether a regulatory offence is one of absolute liability. How, then, do the courts determine whether the legislature "intended" to impose absolute, as opposed to strict, liability? Undoubtedly, their starting point is the judgment of Justice Dickson in the *Sault Ste. Marie* case in which he articulated four major criteria that should guide the courts in drawing the distinction between strict and absolute liability offences.

EXAMPLES OF THE APPLICATION OF THE PRINCIPLES ARTICULATED IN THE *SAULT STE. MARIE* CASE

The Importance of Examining the Overall Regulatory Pattern in a Statute

In the judgment of the Supreme Court in *Sault Ste. Marie* (1978), Justice Dickson referred to the "overall regulatory pattern" as being an important criterion in making the decision whether a particular regulatory offence should be considered as being one of strict or absolute liability. By this he meant that, if a legislature expressly included a defence of due diligence for some offences in a regulatory statute but failed to do so for other offences within the same statute, one may normally conclude that the legislature intended to impose absolute liability in relation to the second group of offences.

This principle is illustrated by the case of *Kurtzman* (1991), in which the Ontario Court of Appeal ruled that the offence of failing to stop at a red light, contrary to section 124(16) of the *Highway Traffic Act*, R.S.O. 1980, c. 198, was an offence of absolute, rather than strict, liability. In delivering the judgment of the court, Justice Tarnopolsky stated that

> Section 124 is found in Part IX of the *Highway Traffic Act*. ...
>
> In contradistinction to s. 124(16) other provisions in Part IX of the Act clearly contemplate that a defence of due diligence at least will be available to an accused. Section 114(3), for example, provides that, where traffic control devices are placed

so as to indicate the closure of a highway, "no person shall drive or operate a vehicle on the closed highway or part thereof in *intentional disobedience* of the signs or traffic control devices" (emphasis added). Section 136(1) prohibits a driver from following another vehicle "more closely than is *reasonable and prudent* in the circumstances. ..." If the legislature had intended s. 124(16) to be construed in a similar manner, so as to exculpate an accused who has made a reasonable and prudent efforts to stop his or her vehicle, it could have included similar language.

However, it does not necessarily follow that a court will find a regulatory offence to be one of absolute liability in such circumstances. As we shall see shortly, the fact that absolute liability will be ruled invalid under the *Charter* if it is combined with potential imprisonment means that courts will generally be reluctant to conclude that a legislature intended to rule out a defence of due diligence only by looking at the overall regulatory pattern of the statute. Although this pattern is always a *relevant* factor, it is not decisive *per se* (as can be seen in the *Rube* case (1991 and 1992), discussed below).

The Importance of Examining the Subject Matter of the Regulatory Offence

Justice Dickson indicated, in the Supreme Court of Canada's judgment in *Sault Ste. Marie* (1978), that the "subject matter of the offence" is a critical consideration in determining whether an offence is one of absolute rather than strict liability. In general, it would appear that the greater the threat to the public that is posed by the commission of a regulatory offence, the more likely it is that this offence will be found to impose a regime of absolute liability.

For example, in Ontario, the Court of Appeal has indicated that if public safety is the subject matter of regulatory legislation, offences under that legislation may be considered as offences of absolute liability (if the legislature has not indicated otherwise by, for example, providing for a due diligence defence). In the *Kurtzman* case (1991), by way of example, the Court stated that the subject matter of the offence of failing to stop at a red light under the provisons of the *Highway Traffic Act* was indeed public safety. Justice Tarnopolsky stated that

> The apparent object of the *Highway Traffic Act* is the safe and orderly conduct of traffic on public highways. With respect to s. 124(16) specifically, users of the highways obey traffic signals at intersections in reliance on similar obedience by other users of the highways. *The need for strict regulation for the purposes of safety is thus apparent.* [emphasis added]

For similar reasons, the Ontario Court of Appeal has also ruled that speeding is an offence of absolute liability. Although the case was decided before the *Sault Ste. Marie* case, the court applied the same principles later articulated by the Supreme Court and is, therefore, of considerable significance in illustrating how Canadian courts are likely to draw the distinction between offences of strict and absolute liability.

In *Hickey* (1976), the facts were that the accused was caught in a police radar trap. However, Hickey testified that he honestly believed that, because of the reading of his speedometer, he was not exceeding the speed limit. He was driving a truck owned by his employer. He indicated that his speedometer was not functioning properly, but that he had no reason to suspect that it was defective in any way. At the time, the police officer concerned tested the speedometer and found that it was, in fact, defective. Nevertheless, the police officer charged the accused with speeding. A majority of the Divisional Court of the Ontario High Court of Justice acquitted the accused on the basis that speeding fell within the category of strict liability offences. Since the accused had acted reasonably (that is *without* negligence), he was entitled to be acquitted. However, the Ontario Court of Appeal overruled the Divisional Court and convicted the accused on the basis that speeding, under the Ontario *Highway Traffic Act*, R.S.O. 1970, c. 202, was a regulatory

offence that falls within the third category of absolute liability. In its brief judgment, the Court of Appeal approved the dissenting judgment of Chief Justice Estey in the Divisional Court. The learned Chief Justice had stated,

> the Legislature has evinced a clear intention to absolutely prohibit driving at speeds contrary to those specified. ...
>
> To determine whether the offence created is one of absolute liability ... the Court must examine the precise wording of the offence creating the provision, the contextual matter, the type of conduct regulated, the revealed purpose of the Act, the size, type and nature of penalty imposed, and the stigma, if any, to be attached by the community to conviction. ...
>
> The *Highway Traffic Act* evidences the clearest legislative intent and purpose of establishing a simple code of rules for the conduct of people who by their own volition take recourse to the highways in motor vehicles. The statute imposes precise speed limitations for varying types of highway, road conditions and other express considerations. ... The language could not be more precise or, indeed, more abrupt unless the Legislature, in order to create an offence of the third category, were to go to the extent of adding at the end of such a clause words to the effect "and there shall be no defence available to any person who exceeds the aforementioned speed limit." ...
>
> *Apart from all other considerations this code of conduct for the use of highways reveals a constant realization on the part of the Legislature of the need for strict regulation for the purposes of safety.* ...

Some appellate courts in other provinces have followed the approach taken in *Hickey* (1976) and have declared speeding to be an absolute liability offence; for example, the B.C. Court of Appeal did so in the case of *Harper* (1986). However, other appellate courts have refused to do so. For example, in *Williams* (1992), the Appeal Division of the Nova Scotia Supreme Court held that speeding was an offence of strict liability and that the accused, therefore, has the opportunity to advance a defence of due diligence. However, the court did not treat the subject matter of the offence as being of central importance to its decision. Instead, it focused on another issue that will be discussed more fully later in this chapter, namely, whether the offence of speeding would be considered invalid under the *Charter* if it were to be designated as an offence of absolute liability. Justice Chipman, in delivering the judgment of the court, noted that imprisonment was a potential penalty (if the accused defaulted on a fine). If speeding were to be viewed as an offence of absolute liability, it would be invalid under the *Charter* because it combined absolute liability with imprisonment. Therefore, the court found that the legislature must have intended speeding to be an offence of strict liability.

The Importance of the Penalty in Determining Whether a Regulatory Offence Imposes Strict or Absolute Liability

The Supreme Court of Canada's decision in *Chapin* (1979) illustrates the principle that, if a severe penalty may be imposed upon conviction of a regulatory offence, it is highly unlikely that the courts will consider such an offence to be one of absolute liability.

Ms. Chapin was charged under section 14(1) of the *Migratory Bird Regulations*, which provided that "… no person shall hunt for migratory game birds within one-quarter mile of any place where bait has been deposited." Section 12(1) of the *Migratory Birds Convention Act*, R.S.C. 1970, c. M-12, provided: "Every person who violates this Act or any regulation is, for each offence, liable upon summary conviction to a fine of not more than $300 and not less than $10, or to imprisonment for a term not exceeding six months, or to both fine and imprisonment." Section 22(1) of the Act also provided for a mandatory prohibition, upon conviction, of either holding or applying for a migratory game bird hunting permit for a period of one year from the date of conviction. Clearly, these were relatively severe penalties by any measure that one cares to use.

Ms. Chapin had been duck hunting near Chatham, Ontario, on a windy afternoon in mid-October 1976. She was walking through a marsh with a friend. She was engaged in conversation with this friend and was not paying much attention to anything "except the beautiful day." After she had shot two ducks, Ms. Chapin was arrested by a conservation officer of the Ontario Ministry of Natural Resources. The officer had noticed, on the road that Ms. Chapin had taken on her way to the duck blind from which she had undertaken her shooting, a small pile of "soybeans, weed seeds, and wheat." The officer admitted that it was difficult to notice this small pile of alleged "bait." Nevertheless, a charge was laid against Ms. Chapin. The pile was apparently located some 50 yards from the blind from which Ms. Chapin had been shooting. The officer also suggested that he had seen some grain in the water on either side of the "duck boards," which were placed over the water and led to the duck blind. Ms. Chapin testified that she was completely unaware of the existence of the grain. She indicated that it had been a very windy day and that a number of objects were flying through the air. It seems that everyone accepted that she did not know the grain was there until it was pointed out to her by the officer from the Ministry of Natural Resources. It was not established how the "bait" came to be placed where it was.

Ms. Chapin was convicted at trial but acquitted by the Ontario Court of Appeal. The Crown **appealed** to the Supreme Court of Canada, which ultimately rejected the Crown's appeal. The issue raised before the Supreme Court was clearly whether the offence charged fell within the category of absolute or strict liability offences. In delivering the judgment of the Court, Justice Dickson ruled that the offence was one of strict liability and that the accused, therefore, was entitled to advance a defence of due diligence. What was the reasoning of the Court? Justice Dickson pointed out that the offence charged could hardly be called a true crime. He indicated that the *Migratory Birds Convention Act* is a "*regulatory* statute enacted by the Parliament of Canada for the general welfare of the Canadian public, not to mention the welfare of the ducks." In his view, therefore, this was clearly a public welfare offence. However, the critical issue, of course, was whether it was an offence of absolute or strict liability. Justice Dickson pointed out that the normal presumption was that a regulatory offence imposes strict liability and that the Crown must, therefore, advance strong arguments as to why this presumption should be displaced in any given case. He rejected the argument that difficulties of enforcement justified the imposition of absolute liability and focused his attention on the relatively severe penalties that might be imposed upon conviction:

> *Difficulty of enforcement is hardly enough to dislodge the offence from the category of strict liability, particularly when regard is had to the penalties that may ensue from conviction.* I do not think that the public interest, as expressed in the Convention, requires that s. 14 of the Regulations be interpreted so that an innocent person should be convicted and fined and also suffer the mandatory loss of his hunting permit and the possible forfeiture of his hunting equipment, merely in order to facilitate prosecution. [emphasis added]

In the *Chapin* case (1979), the perceived severity of the penalties that might have been imposed led the Supreme Court to conclude that the regulatory offence in question was one of strict, rather than absolute, liability. The *Kurtzman* case (1991) illustrates the converse proposition that the imposition of a light penalty may be one of the considerations that persuades a court to rule that the legislature intended to render a regulatory offence one of absolute liability. In this case, the Ontario Court of Appeal ruled that the offence of failing to stop at a red light under the provisions of the Ontario *Motor Vehicle Act* should be considered an absolute, rather than strict, liability offence because, among other reasons, the penalties were relatively trivial. Justice Tarnopolsky pointed out that the penalty for conviction of the offence was a minimum fine of $60 and a maximum of $500. He went on to state that

Imprisonment is not a potential penalty except, perhaps, in default of payment. Also, I would agree…that there is today little, if any, stigma attached to the violation of the *Highway Traffic Act* provisions concerning compliance with traffic signal indicators. I note, too, that suspension or revocation of one's driver's licence is not a penalty which may be imposed upon conviction under s. 124(16) alone.

The Importance of Examining the Precise Wording of Regulatory Legislation

The language used by the legislature has been considered an important yardstick in determining whether a regulatory offence is one of absolute, rather than strict, liability. For example, in the *Kurtzman* case (1991), the Ontario Court of Appeal paid close attention to the precise wording of the Ontario *Highway Traffic Act* in drawing the conclusion that failing to stop for a red light was an offence of absolute liability. In this respect, Justice Tarnopolsky noted that the "words used in s. 124(16) are mandatory and clearly do not anticipate a defence of due diligence or reasonable care being raised." He also pointed out that this was particularly significant in light of the fact that other provisions of the same part of the act did explicitly state that a defence of due diligence was available to the accused. Justice Tarnopolsky went on to rule that, since the language used in section 124(16) was "mandatory and absolute," it made no sense to inquire into the "reasonableness of the driver's efforts":

> the driver either stops or he does not. In this case, he did not and, therefore, in my view, he contravened the provision.

The need for the courts to pay close attention to the precise wording of a regulatory statute was also highlighted in the cases of *Dilorenzo and Bancroft* (1984), in which the issue to be decided was the correct interpretation of section 189a of the Ontario *Highway Traffic Act*, R.S.O. 1980, c. 198.

Section 189a(1) required drivers to stop their motor vehicles when requested to do so by a police officer "who is readily identifiable as such." Section 189a(2) provided that a person who fails to obey such a request is liable to a fine of not less than $100 and not more than $2000 or to a prison term of not more than six months, or to both penalties. Section 189a(3), however, also provided that, where a person has been convicted of this offence, the court may make an order suspending the driver's licence to drive for a period of three years where it is "satisfied on the evidence that the person *wilfully* continued to avoid police while a police officer gave pursuit." The Ontario Court of Appeal ruled that the offence, defined in section 189a(1), was an offence of strict liability and that there was no onus on the Crown to prove *mens rea* on the part of the defendants. Of course, this characterization of the nature of the offence left it open to the defendants to establish a valid defence by proving that they had acted with due diligence.

It was contended, however, that once the accused had been convicted under section 189a(1), the Crown did not have to prove *mens rea* in relation to a motion to impose the higher penalty, provided for in section 189a(3). This contention was firmly rejected. On behalf of the court, Justice Robins stated that

> before the order may be made (under s. 189a(3)) the court must be satisfied that the person convicted of contravening s. 189a(1) engaged in a particular type of aggravated conduct, that is, that he "wilfully continued to avoid police while a police officer gave pursuit". The word "wilfully" used in this context means with an intention of avoiding the police and, in my opinion, must be construed so as to import *mens rea*.

The court, therefore, held that the Crown must establish, *beyond a reasonable doubt*, the requisite *mens rea*, as defined in section 189a(3), before the suspension could be imposed. This case illustrates the importance of paying extremely close attention to the actual wording of a section that creates regulatory offences, since the same section of a statute may well contain different types of offences depending on the precise words employed by the legislature concerned. In this case, an offence of "strict liability" (for which the Crown did not have to prove any elements of *mens rea*) was established by a single section that also made provision for a higher penalty to be imposed in certain circumstances (but only where the Crown could prove the necessary *mens rea* requirements). In other words, this single section essentially contained one offence of strict liability and one offence that required proof of *mens rea*.

Raising the Defence of Due Diligence

An excellent example of the application of the due-diligence defence is furnished by the case of *London Excavators & Trucking Ltd.* (1998). The accused company was an excavating subcontractor who had been hired to work on a large construction project at a hospital site. The general contractor told the accused company that the area to be excavated was "clear" of any "gas, electrical and other services." The accused company had worked with the general contractor before and considered it to be "knowledgeable and reliable." During the course of the excavating operations, the accused company's backhoe operator struck some concrete and stopped his machine. The general contractor's assistant supervisor stated that the concrete was just "part of the footing of an old nursing station" and told the backhoe operator to remove it. In fact, the concrete encased a hydro duct and, when it was penetrated by the backhoe, there was an explosion. Neither the accused company's foreman nor its backhoe operator had taken any steps to check the accuracy of the information that had been provided to them by the assistant supervisor of the general contractor. A plan of the construction site that was in the possession of the general contractor showed the existence and exact location of the hydro duct that was struck; however, it had never been shown to the accused company.

Fortunately, there were no injuries as a consequence of this excavating misadventure. However, the accused company was duly charged for having *failed to ensure that the required safety procedures were carried out* in accordance with the provisions of the Ontario *Occupational Health and Safety Act*, R.S.O. 1990, c. O.1. Under the relevant set of regulations, excavation work should not commence until the various services in the area have been "accurately located and marked." The accused company, as an employer, was placed under a statutory duty to "request the owner of the service to locate and mark the service." Section 25(1)(c) of the Act stated that the employer "shall ensure ... that the measures and procedures prescribed are carried out in the work." The Act made clear that a subcontractor will be considered an "employer" for the purposes of these safety provisions. Section 66(3) of the Act also established a due diligence defence: namely, "it shall be a defence for the accused to prove that every precaution reasonable in the circumstances was taken." In light of these statutory provisions, there was no doubt that the accused company had been charged with a strict liability offence and that it was required to prove the defence of due diligence on the balance of probabilities.

The accused company contended that it had honestly believed the information provided to it by the general contractor's supervisors was accurate and had "faithfully passed it on" to the accused company's foreman. However, the accused company was nevertheless convicted because it had not established that it had taken every reasonable precaution. It was just not enough to claim that it had honestly relied on the word of the general contractor's supervisors. The Ontario Court of Appeal upheld the conviction of London Excavators & Trucking Ltd. On behalf of the Court of Appeal, Justice Catzman succinctly indicated why the accused company had failed to establish the due diligence defence:

> *It was not objectively reasonable for the appellant to continue to rely, without further inquiry, upon the direction of the general contractor once an unexpected concrete obstacle had been encountered in a location the general contractor had pronounced safe to excavate.* At that point, it was incumbent on the appellant, in the interest of the safety of its employees and others who might be exposed to the risk of harm, to *ensure that the prescribed measures and procedures designed to protect their safety had been carried out in the workplace ...* the appellant could have done so in a number of ways: it could have insisted on seeing the site plan ... it could have insisted on seeing a locate certificate issued by the utility; if ... there was no such certificate, it could have halted work until the utility's representative had attended at the site and done the locates; or it could itself have ordered hydro locates for the area in which it was expected to excavate. [emphasis added]

Employers are frequently the target of prosecutions under regulatory legislation and, of course, they may raise the defence of due diligence if they are charged with an offence of strict liability. In this respect, it is important to remember that, while an *employee* is usually the individual who commits the act that effectively precipitates a prosecution for a regulatory offence, the trial court must nevertheless focus its attention upon the issue of whether the *employer* acted with due diligence. The court will generally ask whether the employer took *reasonable steps to ensure that his or her employees carried out their jobs in accordance with the standards set by the regulatory legislation concerned.* For example, did the employer institute an adequate training program for employees, and did the employer maintain an adequate system for monitoring employee performance?

Take, by way of example, the Nova Scotia case of *Sobey's Inc.* (1998), where the employer, a corporation, had been charged with the sale of tobacco or a tobacco product to a person under the age of nineteen years (contrary to section 5(1) of the *Tobacco Access Act*, S.N.S. 1993, c. 14). The Nova Scotia Court of Appeal emphasized that the central issue in the case was not whether the employee, who allegedly sold the tobacco, was "duly diligent," but rather whether Sobey's Inc. acted with due diligence in all of the circumstances. In delivering the judgment of the Court of Appeal, Justice Cromwell quoted the words of Justice Dickson, in the *Sault Ste. Marie* case (1978):

> *Where an employer is charged in respect of an act committed by an employee acting in the course of employment, the question will be whether the act took place without the accused's direction or approval ... and whether the accused exercised all reasonable care by taking reasonable steps to ensure the effective operation of the system.* [emphasis added]

IS STRICT LIABILITY A VALID DEVICE UNDER THE *CHARTER*?

The decision in the *Sault Ste. Marie* case (1978) is based on the recognition of a category of regulatory offences that impose strict liability. However, *Sault Ste. Marie* was decided before the enactment of the *Charter*, and a critical question that arises is whether strict liability is constitutionally valid. As we have noted, the very essence of strict liability is the requirement that the accused shoulder the responsibility of proving that he or she acted without negligence (the defence of due diligence). It might well be argued that requiring the accused to establish his or her innocence is an infringement of the presumption of innocence guaranteed by section 11(d) of the *Charter*, and that strict liability is, therefore, an invalid device that should be struck down. Precisely this argument was advanced in the case of *Wholesale Travel Group Inc.* (1991).

It is noteworthy that, in this case, the Ontario Court of Appeal ruled that strict liability did indeed infringe upon the presumption of innocence and was, therefore, invalid under the *Charter*. The Ontario Court of Appeal held that strict liability is only valid as a device if it is interpreted as meaning that accused persons must be acquitted of regulatory offences whenever they raise a reasonable doubt that they acted with due diligence. According to the Court of Appeal, in strict liability situations, the accused is only under an *evidentiary burden* to show some evidence that could *raise a reasonable doubt* on the question of whether he or she acted with due diligence in the particular circumstances of the case; once he or she satisfies this evidentiary burden, the onus is on the Crown to prove beyond a reasonable doubt that the accused was negligent.

If the Ontario Court of Appeal's decision in this case had been upheld by the Supreme Court of Canada, it clearly would have struck at the very foundations of the half-way house approach endorsed in the *Sault Ste. Marie* case (1978). However, a majority of the justices of the Supreme Court of Canada did not agree with the Ontario Court of Appeal and ruled, in the *Wholesale Travel Group Inc.* case (1991), that strict liability is not invalid under the *Charter*.

The *Wholesale Travel Group Inc.* (1989) case was concerned with the offence of false or misleading advertising under the provisions of the federal *Competition Act*, R.S.C. 1970, c. C-23. Under (what was then) s. 37.3(2) of the Act, Parliament made available a defence of due diligence to those charged with false or misleading advertising:

> No person shall be convicted of an offence under section 36 or 36.1, *if he establishes that,*
>
> (a) the act or omission giving rise to the offence with which he was charged was the result of error;
> (b) he took reasonable precautions and exercised due diligence to prevent the occurrence of such error ... [emphasis added]

The Ontario Court of Appeal took the view that the words "if he establishes that" are of no force and effect because placing the burden on the accused to establish the defence of due diligence on the balance of probabilities violated the presumption of innocence enshrined in section 11(d) of the *Charter* and could not be justified as a reasonable limitation under section 1 of the *Charter*.

The majority of the justices of the Supreme Court of Canada, however, took the view that placing the onus on the accused to prove the defence of due diligence was not invalid under the *Charter*. Three of the five justices in the majority took the view that strict liability did infringe section 11(d) of the *Charter* but that it was justified as a reasonable limitation under section 1. The other two justices in the majority contended that, if one looks at strict liability within the specific context of regulatory offences, it does not violate section 11(d) of the *Charter* and that, even if it did, it would be saved by section 1.

Speaking for those justices who believed that strict liability did infringe the *Charter* but was saved by section 1, Justice Iacobucci said that there was no doubt that "the reverse onus on the accused to establish due diligence on a balance of probabilities" violates section 11(d) of the *Charter*. However, the critical issue was whether this infringement of the accused's *Charter* right is "demonstrably justified in a free and democratic society." Justice Iacobucci applied the so-called *Oakes* test and concluded that the infringement was justified.

The first issue under the *Oakes* test is whether Parliament's objective was of "sufficient importance to warrant overriding a constitutionally protected right or freedom." In this particular case, Justice Iacobucci concluded that

> the specific objective of placing a persuasive burden on an accused to prove due diligence is to ensure that all those who are guilty of false or misleading advertising are convicted of these public welfare offences *and to avoid the loss of convictions because of evidentiary problems which arise because the relevant facts are peculiarly in the knowledge of the accused.* The legislative objective is of sufficient importance to warrant overriding the right guaranteed by s. 11(d) of the *Charter*. It relates to concerns which are "pressing and substantial" in Canadian society; especially when one considers the over-all objective of the *Competition Act* which is

to promote vigorous and fair competition throughout Canada. [emphasis in original]

The second issue under the *Oakes* test is whether there is an appropriate degree of *proportionality* between Parliament's legitimate objective and the means used to achieve that objective (namely, placing the onus on the accused to prove the defence of due diligence). Justice Iacobucci asserted that there clearly was a "rational connection between the desired objective and the means chosen to attain the objective." The device of strict liability and the undeniable advantages that it gives to the Crown in prosecuting an individual for having committed a regulatory offence undoubtedly advance the objective of ensuring that there is an increased likelihood of convicting those who have engaged in false or misleading advertising.

However, under the *Oakes* test, it must also be established that placing the onus on the accused to prove the due diligence offence impaired the presumption of innocence "as little as possible" in order to accomplish Parliament's objective. Justice Iacobucci concluded that there was no reasonable alternative device to which Parliament could have turned in order to pursue its objective of effective enforcement of regulatory legislation. In particular, he rejected the suggestion that Parliament could have adopted the alternative of imposing a "mandatory presumption of negligence" in regulatory offences. Adoption of this approach would mean that, once the Crown had proved the *actus reus* elements of the offence, there would be a presumption that the accused was negligent and, unless he or she introduces evidence that raises a reasonable doubt about this issue, the trial court must enter a conviction. The problem with this alternative, according to Justice Iacobucci, is that in practice the accused is the only person who is likely to have a detailed knowledge of the steps that he or she has taken to avoid committing a regulatory offence; in other words, the accused will usually be the only party who is in position to bring forward evidence relating to due diligence. If an accused person could escape conviction of a regulatory offence merely by raising a reasonable doubt, it would place the Crown in a thoroughly disadvantageous position because, at the end of the trial, it would have to prove facts that were "largely within the peculiar knowledge of the accused." In the view of Justice Iacobucci, "such an alternative would in practice make it virtually impossible for the Crown to prove public welfare offences such as the one in question and would effectively prevent governments from seeking to implement public policy through prosecution."

Finally, under the *Oakes* test, it must be shown that "the means chosen must be such that their effects on the limitation of rights and freedoms are proportional to the objective." On this topic, Justice Iacobucci stated that

> regulated activity and public welfare offences are a fundamental part of Canadian society. Those who choose to participate in regulated activities must be taken to have accepted the consequential responsibilities and their penal enforcement. One of these consequences is that they should be held responsible for the harm that may result from their lack of due diligence. Unless they can prove on the balance of probabilities that they exercised due diligence, they shall be convicted and in some cases face a possible prison term. These participants are in the best position to prove due diligence since they possess in most cases the required information. Viewed in this context, and taking into account the fundamental importance of the legislative objective as stated and the fact that the means chosen impair the rights guaranteed by s. 11(d) as little as reasonably possible, the effects of the reverse onus on the presumption of innocence are proportional to the objective.

Justice Cory (with whom Justice L'Heureux-Dubé agreed) took the view that strict liability did not infringe section 11(d) of the *Charter* in the first place. In his view, in considering whether section 11(d) was infringed by placing the onus on the accused to prove the defence of due diligence, one must take account of the fact that the context is one of regulatory offences rather than true crimes:

> Criminal offences have always required proof of guilt beyond a reasonable doubt; the accused cannot, therefore, be convicted where there is a reasonable doubt as to guilt. This is not so with regulatory offences, where a conviction will lie if the accused has failed to meet the standard of care required. Thus, the question is not whether the accused exercised *some* care, but whether the degree of care exercised was sufficient to meet the standard imposed. If the false advertiser, the corporate polluter and the manufacturer of noxious goods are to be effectively controlled, it is necessary to require them to show on a balance of probabilities that they took reasonable precautions to avoid the harm which actually resulted. *In the regulatory context, there is nothing unfair about imposing that onus; indeed, it is essential for the protection of our vulnerable society.* [emphasis added]

Indubitably, the *Wholesale Travel Group Inc.* case (1991) has settled an extremely important question of principle under the *Charter* and has placed the half-way house approach, embodied in strict liability, on a firm constitutional basis. Unfortunately, many other questions still have to be answered in the area of regulatory offences in Canada, particularly insofar as absolute liability offences are concerned.

IS THERE ANY ROOM FOR STRICT LIABILITY IN THE *CRIMINAL CODE*?

In general, it appears to be well established that *strict liability is a concept that is not applicable to the "real crimes,"* that are encapsulated in the *Criminal Code.* However, in the *Smillie* case (1998), the B.C. Court of Appeal suggested that there may well be *exceptional* circumstances in which it may be appropriate to characterize a *Criminal Code* offence as being one of strict liability. The accused had been charged with three counts of storing a firearm in a manner contrary to a regulation that had been issued under the authority of section 116(1)(g) of the *Criminal Code*. Section 86(3) of the Code provides that

> Every person who stores, displays, handles or transports an firearm in a manner contrary to a regulation made under paragraph 116(1)(g)
>
> > (a) is guilty of an indictable offence and liable to imprisonment for a term not exceeding two years.

The trial judge ruled that the charges against the accused violated section 7 of the *Charter* and quashed all the counts in the indictment. However, the Crown appealed, and the B.C. Court of Appeal ruled that the offence charged did not, after all, violate the provisions of the *Charter*. (A new trial was ordered for Smillie; however, the Crown subsequently entered a stay of proceedings on all counts.)

In delivering the judgment of the Court of Appeal, Justice Ryan noted that Parliament had established a "strict regime with respect to the storage, display, handling and transportation of firearms." *In order to obtain a conviction under section 86(3), the Crown is merely required to establish that the accused did not store firearms in accordance with the provisions of the regulations issued under the authority of section 116(1)(g) of the Code.* In other words, Justice Ryan ruled that the offence under section 86(3) of the Code did not require the proof of any form of *mens rea* on the part of the accused. The Crown does not even have to establish that the accused acted negligently. It will suffice if it proves that the accused failed to abide by the terms of the relevant regulations.

It seems to run contrary to our most basic notions of criminal law that an accused person may be convicted of an **indictable** offence under the *Criminal Code* without the necessity for the proof of any form of *mens rea* whatsoever. However, Justice

Ryan held that the offence under section 86(3) was, in reality, "*quasi-regulatory*" in nature: "although it is found in the *Criminal Code*, it is *essentially a regulatory measure in the interest of public safety.*" Therefore, the Court of Appeal characterized the offence as being one of *strict liability* and noted that the accused could "defend the charge by raising a reasonable doubt with respect to a mistake of fact or by raising a doubt that he or she was duly diligent in his efforts to comply with the regulation in question."

In firmly rejecting the assertion of Smillie's **counsel** that section 86(3) infringes section 7 of the *Charter*, Justice Ryan ruled that the nature of the minimal fault requirements for conviction of an offence "are contextually flexible and will depend on a number of factors":

> "True" criminal offences are presumed to require full *mens rea*, but as the offence moves down the continuum to acquire a regulatory aspect, that is, to impose sanctions for the prevention of harm rather than to punish for past conduct, the requirement for full *mens rea* diminishes.

According to Justice Ryan, any person who enters a manifestly dangerous area of conduct, such as dealing with firearms, must fully expect that there will be government regulation of such activity, and it *must be presumed that he or she will be aware of this regulatory régime*:

> … where a person is voluntarily operating in a regulated area, and therefore deemed to have notice of the standard of care required of him or her, the *mens rea* requirement loses importance and, where the maximum punishment is not high, the necessity for full *mens rea* will not be as great.

The offence under section 86(3), according to the B.C. Court of Appeal, is a "quasi-regulatory" offence, which carries a maximum sentence of imprisonment of two years ("not insignificant, but not high for an indictable offence"). In this sense,

Justice Ryan believed that the offence does not "give rise to a significant degree of stigma." Furthermore, the accused may rely on a defence of due diligence in relation to his or her efforts to meet the standards prescribed by the relevant regulation. In light of all these factors, Justice Ryan took the view that *the offence under section 86(3) does not result in the punishment of individuals who are totally lacking in blameworthiness*: "there is an element of mental fault or moral culpability present (that is) proportionate to the seriousness and consequences of the offence." That being the case, there was no infringement of section 7 of the *Charter*.

The *Smillie* case raises some profoundly disturbing questions concerning the extent to which the courts may be willing to import the concept of strict liability into their application of the *Criminal Code*. One might well ask whether it is appropriate to excuse the Crown from proving any element of *mens rea* (either subjective or objective) when the accused is charged with an indictable offence under the *Criminal Code* (as was the case in *Smillie*). Surely, an integral part of the rationale for the judicial endorsement of strict liability has always been that the concept is *only applicable to regulatory offences* (*viz.*, offences that are not considered "real crimes"). Can we "explain away" the *Smillie* case as being a most unusual exception to the general principles of criminal responsibility under the *Criminal Code*? After all, section 86(3) is an odd creature to find in the *Criminal Code*, since it involves the breach of regulations. Furthermore, it is significant that Justice Ryan stated that the accused need only *raise a reasonable doubt* as to whether he or she acted with due diligence. This means that the type of strict liability referred to by the B.C. Court of Appeal in *Smillie* is significantly different from the type of strict liability with which we are all familiar in the context of federal and provincial regulatory legislation. Indeed, as we have seen, the half-way house approach, that is the characteristic hallmark of strict liability in the context of federal and provincial regulatory legislation, is ultimately based on the requirement that the accused must

prove the defence of due diligence *on the balance of probabilities*. It certainly remains to be seen whether the *Smillie* case will open the door to further use of strict liability in relation to *Criminal Code* offences or whether it will be viewed as a "one-off" case that has no **precedent** value outside of its unique context.

THE *CHARTER* AND ABSOLUTE LIABILITY OFFENCES

The *Wholesale Travel Group Inc.* case (1991) unequivocally established that a regime of strict liability is not invalid under the *Charter*. However, the Supreme Court of Canada has adopted a dramatically different approach vis-à-vis statutes that create offences of absolute liability. Indeed, the Court has held that, as a general rule, absolute liability offences are invalid under the *Charter* if they may be punished by the imposition of a term of imprisonment.

This leading authority on this issue is the landmark decision of the Supreme Court of Canada in *Reference Re Section 94(2) of the Motor Vehicle Act* (1985), which raised the issue of whether section 94(2) of the *Motor Vehicle Act*, R.S.B.C. 1979 was consistent with the requirements of the *Charter*. Section 94(1) of the British Columbia statute provided that it was an offence for a person to drive while prohibited or suspended from driving. The penalty for breaching the provisions of this section was, on first conviction, a fine and imprisonment for not less than seven days and not more than six months (in other words, a mandatory prison sentence). Section 94(2) explicitly stated that the offence created by section 94(1) "creates an absolute liability offence in which guilt is established by proof of driving, whether or not the defendant knew of the prohibition or suspension." Not surprisingly, the Supreme Court of Canada declared this Draconian provision to be contrary to the provisions of the *Charter*.

Justice Lamer stated the issue very simply:

A law that has the potential to convict a person who has not really done anything wrong offends the principles of fundamental justice and, if imprisonment is available as a penalty, such a law then violates a person's right to liberty under s. 7 (of the *Charter*). ...

In other words, *absolute liability and imprisonment cannot be combined.* [emphasis added]

Section 7 of the *Charter*, of course, provides that "everyone has the right to life, liberty and security of the person and the right not to be deprived thereof except in accordance with the principles of fundamental justice."

Significantly, Justice Lamer indicated that it makes no difference whether the imprisonment imposed as a consequence of conviction of an absolute liability offence is *discretionary* or, as in the case of section 94(2), *mandatory:*

Obviously, imprisonment (including probation orders) deprives persons of their liberty. An offence has that potential as of the moment it is open to the judge to impose imprisonment. There is no need that imprisonment, as in section 94(2) be made mandatory.

On the other hand, Justice Lamer did not address the critical issue of whether imprisonment, *as an alternative to the non-payment of a fine*, would contravene section 7 of the *Charter* when an absolute liability offence is concerned. In the later case of *Pontes* (1995), the majority of the Supreme Court of Canada expressly left this issue "up in the air." As Justice Cory stated,

I would leave open for future consideration the situation presented by an absolute liability offence punishable by fine with the possibility of imprisonment for its non-payment in those circumstances where the legislation provides that the imposition and collection of any fine is subject to a means test.

This issue has been addressed, however, by a few provincial courts of appeal. For example, the Saskatchewan Court of Appeal held, in *Burt* (1987) that section 7 of the *Charter* is infringed where conviction of an absolute liability offence could lead to imprisonment, if only as a consequence of non-payment of a fine. As Justice Wakeling said in the *Burt* case,

With reference to the application of s. 7, is there a basis to distinguish a sentence which is restricted to payment of a fine, with imprisonment for non-payment, from one where the sentence is for imprisonment in the first instance? To the person in prison, it is of little consequence to have it said the original sentence only required payment of a fine and he is in jail because of his failure to do so. The prisoner will surely be convinced he is in jail because he was found guilty of the original offence and will be inclined to accuse judges and lawyers who say otherwise of exercising their legal skills to distinguish where no real difference exists.

The Appeal Division of the Nova Scotia Supreme Court expressly adopted this approach in the case of *Williams* (1992). Furthermore, in *Nickel City Transport (Sudbury) Ltd.* (1993), one of the members of the Ontario Court of Appeal, Justice Arbour, expressed the view that "the combination of an absolute liability regime, *together with a scheme of imprisonment for default of payment of a fine that does not address ability to pay,*" would infringe section 7 of the *Charter*. (Significantly, Justice Arbour's analysis was subsequently endorsed by Justice Fish of the Québec Court of Appeal in *Québec (Procureur Général) v. Enterprises M.G. de Guy Ltée* (1996).) All of this would definitely appear to suggest that imprisonment for non-payment of a fine imposed upon conviction of an absolute liability offence will only infringe section 7 if there is no procedure in place that operates to ensure that the offender's ability to pay is taken into account. Hopefully, the Supreme Court of Canada will provide a definitive ruling on this important issue in the near future. Until it does so, the law relating to regulatory offences will continue to be cast in an aura of uncertainty.

It was argued, in *Reference Re Section 94(2) of the Motor Vehicle Act* (1985), that even if section 94(2) did infringe section 7 of the *Charter*, it was nevertheless "saved" by section 1 of the *Charter*, which permits the imposition of reasonable limits upon the rights and freedoms set out in it, provided these were such limits "as can be demonstrably justified in a free and democratic society."

The B.C. government contended that section 94(2) constituted a reasonable limit on individual freedom because it was designed to keep bad drivers off the road and to punish severely bad drivers who contemptuously ignore prohibitions against their driving. Justice Lamer totally rejected this line of reasoning and pointed out that the B.C. statute could have accomplished these goals by creating an offence of strict (rather than absolute) liability:

> The bottom line of the question to be addressed here is: whether the Government of British Columbia has demonstrated as justifiable that the risk of imprisonment of a few innocent is, given the desirability of ridding the roads of British Columbia of bad drivers, a reasonable limit in a free and democratic society. That result is to be measured against the offence being one of strict liability open to a defence of due diligence, the success of which does nothing more than let those few who did nothing wrong remain free.
>
> As did the Court of Appeal, I find that this demonstration has not been satisfied, indeed, not in the least.

The decision by the Supreme Court of Canada in *Reference Re Section 94(2) of the Motor Vehicle Act* (1985) dramatically illustrates the profound impact that the *Charter* may have on the substantive criminal law. In the specific case of absolute liability offences, it is clear that the Supreme Court has greatly reduced the sting of such offences by se-

verely circumscribing the range of punishments that may be imposed. Indeed, the Court has unequivocally stated that, if the legislature wishes to give the courts the option to impose a term of imprisonment upon conviction of a regulatory offence, it must ensure that it makes a due diligence defence available to those persons accused of such an offence.

The Supreme Court of Canada revisited this issue in the *Wholesale Travel Group Inc.* case (1991), in which the accused corporation had been charged with the offence of false or misleading advertising, under the provisions of the *Competition Act*, R.S.C. 1970, c. C-23. We have already seen that, under (what was then) section 37.3(2) of the Act, Parliament made available a defence of due diligence to those charged with false or misleading advertising. The relevant statutory provisions are as follows:

> No person shall be convicted of an offence under section 36 or 36.1, if he establishes that,
>
> (a) the act or omission giving rise to the offence with which he was charged was the result of error;
>
> (b) he took reasonable precautions and exercised due diligence to prevent the occurrence of such error;
>
> (c) he, or another person, took reasonable precautions to bring the error to the attention of the class of persons likely to have been reached by the representations or testimonial; and
>
> (d) the measures referred to in paragraph (c), except where the representation or testimonial related to a security, were taken forthwith after the representation was made or the testimonial was published.

The Ontario Court of Appeal noted that, in effect, paragraphs (c) and (d) of section 37.3(2) imposed a positive obligation on the accused to make an *immediate* retraction before he or she could claim the benefit of the defence of due diligence. This could lead to the result that an individual who did not make such an immediate retraction could be prevented from raising the defence *even if he or she acted with due diligence.* For example, an accused person might not discover that he or she has made a false or misleading statement in an advertisement until some time after it has has been published. Even if the accused person issues a retraction as soon he or she becomes aware of the error, the defence of due diligence would not apply because the retraction had not been taken place *immediately after the advertisement was originally published.* In effect, this means that absolute liability could be imposed on a blameless defendant who had, through no fault of his or her own, failed to make an *immediate* retraction and, since imprisonment was a potential penalty under the *Competition Act,* the Supreme Court of Canada ruled that paragaphs (c) and (d) of section 37.3(2) of the act were invalid in light of section 7 of the *Charter.*

Chief Justice Lamer pointed out that the offence of false or misleading advertising carries a penalty of up to five years' imprisonment and that "it is clear from the developing jurisprudence of this court that the offence must not be one of absolute liability." On the contrary, there must be a "miminimum fault requirement of negligence, in that *at least* a defence of due diligence must always be open to the accused to comply with the requirements of s. 7 of the *Charter.*"

According to Chief Justice Lamer, paragraphs (a) and (b) of section 37.3 (2) of the *Competition Act* unquestionably provide the accused with a defence of due diligence as that defence had been delineated in the *Sault Ste. Marie* case (1978):

> paras. (a) and (b) operate so as to provide a defence to an accused who has taken reasonable precautions to prevent false/misleading advertising and who has been duly diligent in ensuring that advertising is not false or misleading in nature.

However, paragraphs (c) and (d) of section 37.3(2) added an additional requirement to the defence, namely, that there must be a retraction "forthwith" after the false or misleading advertisement has been published. This requirement of "timely retraction" means, according to Chief Justice Lamer, that the defence embodied in section 37.3 of the *Competition Act* "is considerably more narrow than the common law defence of due diligence." He stated that he agreed with the majority of the Ontario Court of Appeal that

> paras. (c) and (d) of s. 37.3(2) could have the effect of depriving an accused of the defence of due diligence and could therefore require the conviction of an accused who was not negligent. Paragraphs (c) and (d) make the failure to undertake corrective advertising (a component of false/misleading advertising) an "offence" of absolute liability. Consequently, the constitutionally required fault level is not present in the false/misleading advertising provisions.

In addition to ruling that paragraphs (c) and (d) of section 37.3(2) of the *Competition Act* infringed an accused person's rights under section 7 of the *Charter* because they combined absolute liability with the possibility of imprisonment, Chief Justice Lamer also held that these paragraphs could not be justified under section 1 of the *Charter.* As a consequence, these two paragraphs were declared to be of "no force and effect." However, the due diligence defence, articulated in paragraphs (a) and (b) of section 37.3(2), remains in effect; all that the ruling in the *Wholesale Travel Group Inc.* case (1991) has done is to remove the restrictive "timely retraction" requirement from the defence.

However, it is important to bear in mind that the Supreme Court of Canada did not rule that *all* absolute liability offences are presumed to be invalid under the *Charter.* In fact, in the later case of *Pontes* (1995), the Supreme Court re-emphasized the point that absolute liability will only infringe section 7 of the *Charter* if it is coupled with the possibility of imprisonment. As was the case in *Reference Re Section 94(2) of the Motor Vehicle Act* (1985), *Pontes* concerned the offence of driving while prohibited under the provisions of the B.C. *Motor Vehicle Act*, R.S.B.C. 1979, c. 288. Section 92 of the amended Act provided that a person who was convicted of one of a number of serious *Criminal Code* or provincial motoring offences "is automatically and without notice prohibited from driving a motor vehicle for 12 months from the date of sentencing." Section 94 of the Act made it an offence to drive while prohibited under section 92.

Having determined that the offence of prohibited driving under section 94 of the *Motor Vehicle Act* was an offence of absolute liability, the critical issue for the Supreme Court of Canada to decide was whether the offence was invalid under the *Charter*. The majority of the Court held that it was not invalid *because there was no potential for imprisonment upon conviction*. This situation was brought about by section 4.1 of the *Offence Act*, R.S.B.C. 1979, c. 305 (amended in 1990), which stated that "no person is liable to imprisonment with respect to an absolute liability offence" under any British Columbia legislation, and by section 72(1) of the *Offence Act*, that stipulated that no person shall be imprisoned for nonpayment of a fine. As a consequence of these provisions of the *Offence Act*, Justice Cory stated that the absolute liability offence of prohibited driving did not infringe the *Charter*:

> an accused convicted under ss. 92 and 94 of the B.C. *Motor Vehicle Act* faces no risk of imprisonment and there is, accordingly, no violation of the right to life, liberty and security of the person under s. 7 of the *Charter*.

It is also crucial to remember that it is possible for a court to rule that, while a combination of absolute liability and potential imprisonment clearly infringes an accused person's rights under section 7 of the *Charter*, this combination may nevertheless be considered a "reasonable limit" on those

rights by virtue of the application of section 1 of the *Charter*. Take, for example, the case of *Gray* (1988). The accused had been charged with a number of motoring offences under the Manitoba *Highway Traffic Act*, R.S.M. 1985 – 86, c. 3. However, he was not charged as the driver of the vehicle involved in the incidents that led to his prosecution. The actual driver was apparently "unknown," but the accused was the "registered owner" of the vehicle. Section 229(1) of the *Highway Traffic Act* provided that an owner may be charged with the commission of any offence involving his or her vehicle unless he or she can prove that the vehicle was being driven by another person without the owner's consent. The issue arose as to whether section 229(1) of the Act violated the accused's rights under section 7 of the *Charter*.

Ultimately, the Manitoba Court of Appeal ruled that section 229(1) did infringe section 7 of the *Charter*. Justice Huband, in delivering the judgment of the court, noted that section 229(1) imposed a regime of absolute liability insofar as it did not allow the accused to raise a defence of due diligence. Indeed, even an extremely careful accused might still be convicted of an offence as a consequence of the operation of section 229(1). In Justice Huband's view,

> In theory at least, *even if the owner of a vehicle exercised consummate care in loaning it to another*, and was entirely forthcoming about the circumstances, he would still stand liable to a charge under s. 229(1). The proper identification of the driver is no defence to a charge, though I understand that it is not the practice to lay a charge against an owner if the identity of the driver is known. It makes no difference if the driver is a person of impeccable character and saintly habits. If a charge is laid under s. 229(1), once proof of ownership is established, and that the vehicle was involved in a violation of the driving code such as speeding, then the accused has no defence other than that specified in s. 229(1), namely, that the vehicle was in the possession of a person without the owner's

consent. *Reasonable care or due diligence in the lending of the vehicle are pertinent only in terms of sentencing.* [emphasis added]

Justice Huband also went on to find that this regime of absolute liability was coupled with the potential for imprisonment because, although a trial judge could only impose a fine for the offence in question, provincial legislation permitted imprisonment for non-payment of such a fine.

However, having found that the accused's rights under section 7 of the *Charter* were violated by section 229(1), the Court of Appeal ruled that this provision nevertheless constituted a reasonable limitation under section 1 of the *Charter*. Therefore, the Court of Appeal held that section 229(1) was not invalid under the *Charter*. Justice Huband pointed out that the objective of section 229(1) was to render the owner of a vehicle liable for the commission of motoring offences in those circumstances where the vehicle can be postively identified but the operator cannot. For example, the operator may try to flee from the police, and it may be more prudent for the latter to take the licence number of the vehicle rather than engage in a potentially dangerous high-speed chase. Similarly, the operator may avoid arrest by escaping on foot and the police are unable to identify him or her. In such cases, there is a chance that the owner was in fact the driver of the vehicle but the police lack the evidence to prove it. Section 229(1) furnishes a solution to this problem by making the owner liable for all of the infractions committed in the course of operating his or her vehicle, no matter whether the owner or some other party was actually at the wheel. Justice Huband went on to point out that, in the examples given above, it is also possible that the vehicle was being operated by someone other than the registered owner:

If that person obtained the vehicle without the owner's consent, then the owner has a defence. But the statute holds the owner responsible if he entrusts his vehicle, or allows it to fall under the con-

Making the owner of a motor vehicle absolutely liable for the traffic infractions committed by an individual who drives the vehicle with the owner's consent: Gray *(1988).*

trol of those who are irresponsible in the use of it. All nine common law provinces have enacted similar legislation. It makes considerable good sense.

An important component in the Court of Appeal's decision to "save" section 229(1) by declaring it a "reasonable limitation" under section 1 of the *Charter* was the court's view that the possibility of imprisonment was very remote indeed. In Justice Huband's view,

the specific charges against this accused could result in a term of imprisonment only in default of fines levied upon the accused, and then only if the accused sleeps on his rights under the fine-option programme [a programme allowing an accused to perform community service instead of paying a fine].

Finally, it should be pointed out that the courts are generally somewhat loath to declare legislation invalid under the *Charter* if they can avoid doing so. Since absolute liability offences that carry a potential penalty of imprisonment will almost always be struck down as being invalid under the *Charter*, there is a tendency on the part of the courts to designate a regulatory offence as being one of strict, rather than absolute, liability. After all, the Supreme Court of Canada has ruled, in the *Wholesale Travel Group Inc.* case (1991), that strict liablity is perfectly valid under the *Charter*.

The case of *Rube* (1991) neatly demonstrates this tendency to avoid interpreting regulatory offences in such a manner as to impose absolute liability. In this case, the accused was charged, under section 5(1) of the *Food and Drugs Act*, R.S.C. 1970, c. F-27, with misleading labelling of food (in this case, sides of beef). The Act did not explicitly provide a defence of due diligence for those who, like the accused, packaged food items themselves and used a "false, misleading, or deceptive" label. However, section 29(1) of the *Food and Drugs Act* did provide such a defence where the accused had purchased food items in prepackaged form from another person and sold them in their orginal packaging. The trial judge ruled that section 5(1) imposed a regime of abolute liability and that, since it was combined with the potential penalty of imprisonment, it was invalid under the *Charter*. However, the Crown appealed to the B.C. Court of Appeal, which ruled that section 5(1) was an offence of strict, not absolute, liability and that, therefore, it was valid under the *Charter*.

In delivering the judgment of the court, Justice Toy held that, even though Parliament had not explicitly included a defence of due diligence when enacting section 5(1), there was no indication that it intended to impose absolute liability in relation to the offence of misleading labelling of food items. Justice Toy suggested that section 5(1) was directed at "saving the pocketbooks or members of the public" rather than at "the health, welfare or safety of the general public" and that the range of penalties under the Act could be "severe when viewed in the context of a lack of harm to the general public." In other words, the severity of the penalties prescribed by the Act suggested that the legislature did not intend to impose absolute liability. However, it is highly significant that, in the case of *Grottoli* (1978), which was decided before the enactment of the *Charter*, the Ontario Court of Appeal had ruled that exactly the same offence under section 5(1) was an offence of absolute liability! Perhaps the B.C. Court of Appeal was influenced by the fact that declaring the offence to be one of absolute liability would result in it being struck down under the *Charter*.

In *Rube* (1992), the Supreme Court of Canada affirmed the decision made by the B.C. Court of Appeal. In delivering the judgment of the Supreme Court, Chief Justice Lamer explicitly acknowledged the significance of *Charter* considerations in drawing the distinction between offences of strict and absolute liability:

> We agree that given the penalties, this is not an offence that could, without offending the *Canadian Charter of Rights and Freedoms*, be one of absolute liability.
>
> *On the presumption that Parliament intends its legislation to conform to the exigencies of the* Charter, we are of the view that the section is one of strict liability and that a defence of due diligence is available to the accused. [emphasis added]

STUDY QUESTION

Assume that a provincial legislature enacts the following provision in its *Retail Sales Act*:

(1) No retailer shall sell packaged bread without indicating the date of baking on the package.
(2) Every person who violates subsection (1) is guilty of an offence under this act and is liable to a maximum fine of five thousand dollars.

The *Offence Act* of the province provides that a person may be imprisoned in default of payment of a fine but also stipulates that this penalty should only be used for a person who wilfully refuses to pay even though he or she has the means to do so.

Marmaduke purchases a loaf of packaged bread from the corner grocery store, which is owned by Donald. Marmaduke notices that the package does not bear a stamp indicating when the loaf was baked and he complains to the provincial authorities, who charge Donald under the provisions set out above. Donald claims that he purchased the loaf from the Crusty Bakery, which has always stamped its packaged loaves whenever he has obtained bread from it in the past. A spokesman from Crusty states that an inexperienced employee had forgotten to replenish the ink in the date stamp and had not noticed that the stamp was failing to made any impression on the packaging paper. What principles would the court apply in determining whether Donald is guilty of the charge?

FURTHER READING

Archibald, B.P. 1991. Liability for Provincial Offences: Fault, Penalty and the Principles of Fundamental Justice in Canada (A Review of Law Reform Proposals from Ontario, Saskatchewan and Alberta). 14 *Dalhousie Law Journal:* 65.

Brudner, A. 1990. Imprisonment and Strict Liability. 40 *University of Toronto Law Journal:* 738.

Healy, P. 1991. Regulatory Offences: The Case for a Purposive Test of Proportionality in Public Liability. *W.C.J. Meredith Personal Lectures.* Montreal: McGill University Faculty of Law. 195 – 231.

Hughes, E.L. 1991. Environmental Prosecutions: Characterizing the Offence. 1 *Journal of Environmental Law and Practice:* 323.

Keefe, J. 1993. The Due Diligence Defence: A Wholesale Review. 35 *Criminal Law Quarterly:* 480.

Kehoe, J. 1991. *Ellis Don* and Strict Liability for Provincial Offences: Where has *Sault Ste. Marie* Gone? 36 *McGill Law Journal:* 1089.

Law Reform Commission of Canada. 1974. Working Paper No. 2: *The Meaning of Guilt: Strict Liability.* Ottawa: Information Canada.

———. 1974. *Studies in Strict Liability.* Ottawa: Information Canada.

McNaughton, W.K. 1992. Case Comment. *R. v. The Wholesale Travel Group Inc.*: The Ends Justify the Means. 50 *The Advocate:* 77.

Mewett, A.W. 1992. Editorial: Regulatory Offences. 34 *Criminal Law Quarterly:* 257.

Mewett, A.W. and M. Manning. 1994. *Mewett & Manning on Criminal Law.* 3d ed. Toronto: Butterworths. Chap. 7.

Ontario Law Reform Commission. 1990. *Report on the Basis of Liability for Provincial Offences.* Toronto: The Ontario Law Reform Commission.

Pearson, J. 1998. Delegating Away Responsibility?: A Case Comment on *Regina v. Safety-Kleen Canada Inc.* 16 *Criminal Reports (5th):* 99.

Perry, S.R. 1988. The Impossibility of General Strict Liability. 1 *Canadian Journal of Law and Jurisprudence:* 147.

Presser, J.R. 1995. Absolute Liability and Mistakes of Law in the Regulatory Context: *Pontes* Disappoints and Confuses. 41 *Criminal Reports (4th):* 249.

Requadt, S. 1993. Regulatory Offences since *Wholesale Travel*: The Need to Re-evaluate Sections 1, 7, and 11(d) of the *Charter.* 22 *Canadian Business Law Journal:* 407.

Roach, K. 1996. *Criminal Law.* Concord, Ont.: Irwin Law. 112 – 122.

Ruby, C. and K. Jull. 1992. The *Charter* and Regulatory Offences: A Wholesale Revision. 14 *Criminal Reports (4th):* 226.

Saxe, D. 1990. *Environmental Offences: Corporate Responsibility and Executive Liability.* Aurora, Ont.: Canada Law Book.

Simons, K.W. 1997. When is Strict Liability Just? 87 *Journal of Criminal Law & Criminology:* 1075.

Stuart, D. 1992. *Wholesale Travel:* Presuming Guilt for Regulatory Offences is Constitutional but Wrong. 8 *Criminal Reports (4th):* 225.

———. 1995. *Canadian Criminal Law.* 3d ed. Toronto: Carswell. 149 – 181.

———. Annotation: *R. v. Smillie.* 20 *Criminal Reports (5th):* 180.

Stuart, D. and R.J. Delisle. 1997. *Learning Canadian Criminal Law.* 6th ed. Toronto: Carswell. 302 – 370.

Stuesser, L. 1989. Convicting the Innocent Owner: Vicarious Liability Under Highway Traffic Legislation. 67 *Criminal Reports (3d):* 316.

Swaigen, J. 1992. Negligence, Reverse Onuses and Environmental Offences: Some Practical Considerations. 2 *Journal of Environmental Law and Practice:* 149.

———. 1992. *Regulatory Offences in Canada: Liability and Defences.* Toronto: Carswell.

Tilleman, W.A. 1991. Due Diligence Defence in Canada for Hazardous Clean Up and Related Problems: Comparison with the American Superfund Law. 1 *Journal of Environmental Law and Practice:* 179.

Tuck-Jackson, A. 1990. The Defence of Due Diligence and the Presumption of Innocence. 33 *Criminal Law Quarterly:* 11.

Verdun-Jones, S.N. 1999. *Canadian Criminal Cases: Selected Highlights.* Toronto: Harcourt Brace. 130–152.

Modes of Participation in Crime and Inchoate Crimes

OVERVIEW

This chapter examines the following:

1. The various ways in which an accused person may become a party to a criminal offence;
2. the liability under the *Criminal Code* of the person who actually commits a criminal offence (the principal), and the liability of those who become parties to criminal offences by aiding and/or abetting the offences committed by others (section 21(1));
3. the *actus reus* and *mens rea* elements of aiding and abetting and the general principle that mere passive acquiescence cannot found the basis for liability as an aider and/or abettor;
4. the manner in which accused persons may become parties to criminal offences that are committed by others whom they have "counselled" to do so (section 22);
5. the manner in which a person may become a party to a criminal offence by virtue of sharing a common intent to carry out an unlawful purpose with an individual who commits the offence in pursuit of that unlawful purpose (section 21(2));
6. the liability that may imposed where a party is considered to be an accessory after the fact (section 23(1));
7. the various *inchoate offences* defined in the *Criminal Code* (counselling (section 464), attempt (section 24), conspiracy (section 465));

8. the liability that may be imposed for counselling an offence that is not ultimately committed and for attempts to commit criminal offences;
9. the *mens rea* and *actus reus* requirements of attempts, as defined by the courts;
10. the particular problem of articulating a suitable test to determine whether an accused person has gone beyond mere preparation and has committed an act that is sufficiently "proximate" to the complete offence as to justify the imposition of liability for a criminal attempt;
11. the three central elements of the offence of conspiracy:

    (a) that there was an agreement for a common purpose,
    (b) that this was an agreement between two or more parties, and
    (c) that the common purpose of the agreement was to commit a criminal offence.

INTRODUCTION

This chapter examines a number of miscellaneous (but, nevertheless, critical) issues concerning the various modes of participation in criminal offences as well as the so-called *inchoate* offences. Specifically, it explores the following ways in which one can become a party to a criminal offence or commit an inchoate crime, such as counselling, attempt, or conspiracy:

1. Actually committing an offence.
2. Aiding and abetting the commission of an offence.
3. Counselling an offence that is later committed.
4. Becoming a party to an offence by virtue of common **intention.**
5. Incurring criminal liability as an **accessory** after the fact.
6. Counselling an offence that is not committed.
7. Attempting to commit a criminal offence.
8. Becoming part of a conspiracy to commit an offence.

ACTUALLY COMMITTING AN OFFENCE

Section 21(1) of the *Criminal Code* provides that

Every one is a party to an offence who

(a) actually commits it,
(b) does or omits to do anything for the purpose of aiding any person to commit it, or
(c) abets any person in committing it.

It is clear that this provision of the Code places the person who aids and/or abets an offence upon exactly the same basis (as far as criminal responsibility is concerned) as the person who actually commits it. The latter person is sometimes referred to as the "**principal**" and is, for example, in the case of **murder** by shooting, the individual who "actually pulls the trigger." There may be more than one principal when an offence is committed. For example, if the assassins, Brutus and Cassius, simultaneously inflict fatal stab wounds on the unfortunate Julius Caesar, they will both be considered to have "*actually committed*" the crime of murder. On the other hand, if Brutus merely supplies a knife to Cassius and maintains a "lookout," while Cassius stabs Caesar to death, then it is probable that Brutus will be considered to have been a party to the murder on the basis that he *aided and/or abetted* Cassius. As the Ontario Court of Appeal stated in the *Suzack* case

(2000), "it is beyond question that where two persons, each with the requisite intent, act in concert in the commission of a crime, they are both guilty of that crime." However, whether they are principals or aiders or abettors depends on "what each did in the course of the common design." Principals are, of course, always *present* when the crime is perpetrated. However, there are some rare situations in which their presence may be "constructive" (or "inferred") rather than "actual." Suppose, for example, that Desmond decides to liquidate his aged aunt, Moneybags, since he is her sole heir and he owes a considerable amount of money to his various bookies. Desmond decides to dispatch his aunt with poison. He summons his fourteen-year-old daughter, Faith, and tells her to take a cup of hot milk, laced with cyanide, to Moneybags. Faith takes the fatal cup to the bedroom of the doomed Moneybags, who dutifully follows the script by drinking the milk; two minutes later she is dead. It is clear that Desmond was not actually present when Moneybags was killed. However, he will still be considered to be the person who "actually committed" the offence on the basis that he was "constructively" present (in other words, his presence, at the scene of the heinous crime, may be legitimately "inferred"). Faith is considered to be "an innocent agent" of Desmond since she clearly did not know what she was doing when she delivered the poison to her great aunt. In this sense, Desmond is considered to have committed the act himself through the *innocent agency* of his daughter.

Similarly, in the case of *Berryman* (1990), the **accused** was working as a passport application officer in a passport office. On two occasions, she accepted passport applications knowing that the person from whom they were received was not, in fact, the applicant. She dishonestly stated, in writing, on the front of each application, that the applicant had produced evidence of citizenship and other identification. When the passport documents were completed, the accused forged the signatures of the purported applicants so as to indicate that the documents had been picked up personally by the persons to whom they had seemingly been issued. She was charged with two counts of forgery of a passport (contrary to section 57(1)(a) of the *Criminal Code*). However, the Crown was faced with the difficulty that the accused did not "make" the passport documents herself; they were actually made by another employee who had no knowledge that the information contained in the applications was completely false. Could the accused be convicted of forgery in these circumstances? She was acquitted at trial, but the Crown **appealed**. The B.C. Court of Appeal allowed the appeal and entered convictions against the accused. The Court of Appeal basically held that the accused could be convicted of forgery under section 21(1)(a) even though the *actus reus* of the offence (the actual making of the passports) was carried out by an innocent agent. As Justice Wood pointed out, "a person who commits an offence by means of an instrument 'whose movements are regulated' by him, actually commits the offences himself."

However, the doctrine of *innocent agency* understandably has a somewhat limited scope. For example, in the case of *Verma* (1996), the accused, a physician, was charged with three counts of trafficking in a narcotic (namely, codeine), contrary to the provisions of section 4 of the (now-repealed) *Narcotic Control Act*, R.S.C. 1985, c. N-1. The allegation was that Verma had sold three prescriptions to an undercover police officer, "for the use and in the name of the officer's fictitious girlfriend." In order to convict Verma of drug trafficking, the Crown would have to prove that any pharmacist, who later filled Verma's prescriptions, could legitimately be considered to have acted as Verma's "innocent agent." Ultimately, the Crown could not establish this critical element of the *actus reus* of the crime of trafficking and Verma was acquitted at his trial. The Crown's subsequent appeal to the Ontario Court of Appeal was firmly rejected.

In delivering the judgment of the Court of Appeal, Justice Finlayson emphasized that "the actions of the innocent agent must be controlled by or directly attributable to the acts of the principal." However, in this particular case, Verma clearly had no *control* over the pharmacist. Indeed, it was the patient who would have to make the decision whether to present the pre-

scriptions to a pharmacist and, if he did so, he would have to pay the pharmacist for the drugs concerned. In Justice Finlayson's words,

> *The doctor does not "act through" the pharmacist*; the doctor provides the means through which a purchaser may, in his or her discretion, obtain drugs from a pharmacist. *The doctor is not the "primary author" of the ultimate exchange of drugs for money between purchaser and pharmacist*; indeed, after writing the prescription the doctor has no control over whether such an exchange will even take place. [emphasis added]

Another reason for the Court of Appeal's refusal to apply the doctrine of innocent agency in the *Verma* case is that the pharmacist would not have committed the *actus reus* of any crime. Indeed, as Justice Finlayson noted, the doctrine of innocent agency only applies "where the *actus reus* of an offence is committed at the instigation of an accused by an innocent agent who has some exemption from liability that is personal to the agent." However, a pharmacist would not commit any crime where he or she merely supplies a narcotic pursuant to the presentation of a legitimate prescription. This situation is quite distinct from that suggested by our earlier hypothetical example of a young person unwittingly giving her great-aunt a fatal dose of cyanide at the instigation of her father. Here, the father clearly acted through his daughter to poison his aunt, and his offspring did commit the *actus reus* of culpable homicide (but, of course, she lacked any *mens rea* for murder or **manslaughter** and would be declared innocent of any culpable involvement in her relative's tragic death).

AIDING AND ABETTING THE COMMISSION OF AN OFFENCE

Definition of the Concepts

Having examined some of the problems that arise in relation to the person who actually commits an offence, we must now focus our attention upon the principles that determine the liability of those who "aid" and "abet" the principal. In their book *Mewett and Manning on Criminal Law* (1994), the authors state that "abetting is defined as instigating, promoting or procuring a crime to be committed, while aiding means assisting or helping without necessarily encouraging or instigating the actor."

Generally, in order to obtain a conviction, the Crown must prove that the alleged aider and/or abettor *actively* rendered assistance to, and/or encouraged, the principal in the commission of the offence (*actus reus*). Equally, it must be established that the accused *intended* to render such assistance or to provide such encouragement, as the case may be (*mens rea*).

The *Actus Reus* Elements of Aiding and Abetting

In general, mere passive acquiescence in the commission of an offence or mere presence at the scene of a crime are *not* sufficient for the purpose of establishing that the accused aided and/or abetted the principal. However, drawing the line between passive acquiescence or mere physical presence, on the one hand, and acts or omissions that actually assist or encourage the principal, on the other, is an extremely difficult task in practice. This task was attempted, however, by the Supreme Court of Canada in *Dunlop and Sylvester* (1979). In this case, the accused were charged with the offence of rape (today, the charge would be sexual assault). The evidence was that there had been a brutal "gang rape," in which some eighteen members of a motorcycle club had forced sexual intercourse with a sixteen-year-old girl. The accused were members of this club. Dunlop and Sylvester, along with other members of the gang, had been present at a bar where the victim and a friend were drinking together; the latter were then taken to a dump site by two other gang members. The victim was, apparently, left alone for a few minutes. She was subsequently attacked and raped by other gang members. Dunlop and Sylvester testified that they had been requested to bring some beer to the dump site for a party and that they did

so. Although the victim claimed that the two accused had participated in the gang rape, Dunlop and Sylvester denied this. In fact, they claimed that, although they saw a woman having intercourse with gang members, they merely delivered the beer and left after a few minutes. At their trial, the accused were convicted and they launched an appeal.

The issue, which eventually came before the Supreme Court of Canada, concerned the liability of Dunlop and Sylvester as aiders and/or abettors under section 21(1)(b) and (c) of the *Criminal Code*—in other words, was their admitted presence at the scene of the crime sufficient to convict them of rape?

In delivering the majority judgment of the Supreme Court, Justice Dickson said:

> Mere presence at the scene of a crime is not sufficient to ground culpability. Something more is needed: encouragement of the principal offender; an act which facilitates the commission of the offence, such as keeping watch or enticing the victim away, or an act which tends to prevent or hinder interference with accomplishment of the criminal act, such as preventing the intended victim from escaping or being ready to assist the prime culprit. ...

Justice Dickson then turned his attention to the particular set of circumstances that were alleged to exist in the *Dunlop and Sylvester* case:

> In the case at bar I have great difficulty in finding any evidence of anything more than mere presence and passive acquiescence. *Presence at the commission of an offence can be evidence of aiding and abetting if accompanied by other factors, such as prior knowledge of the principal offender's intention to commit the offence or attendance for the purpose of encouragement.* There was no evidence that while the crime was being committed either of the accused rendered aid, assistance or encouragement to the rape of [the victim]. ... There was no evidence of any positive act or omission to facilitate the unlawful purpose. One can infer that the

accused knew that a party was to be held, and that their presence at the dump was not accidental or in the nature of causal passers-by, but that is not sufficient. *A person cannot properly be convicted of aiding or abetting in the commission of acts which he does not know may be or are intended. …*

One must be able to infer that the accused had prior knowledge that an offence of the type committed was planned, *i.e.,* that their presence was with knowledge of the intended rape. On this issue, the Crown elicited no evidence. …

A person is not guilty merely because he is present at the scene of a crime and does nothing to prevent it. … If there is no evidence of encouragement by him, a man's presence at the scene of the crime will not suffice to render him liable as aider and abettor. A person who, aware of a rape taking place in his presence, looks on and does nothing is not, as a matter of law, an accomplice. The classic case is the hardened urbanite who stands around in a subway station when an individual is murdered. [emphasis added]

The Supreme Court of Canada, in applying these principles, ultimately allowed the appeals of both Dunlop and Sylvester and directed a verdict of **acquittal** in respect of each **appellant**.

Similarly, it has been held that an accused person's *mere passive acquiescence* in the transportation of illegal drugs into Canada does not render the accused a party to the offence of importation, by virtue of aiding and/or abetting. For example, in *Williams* (1998), the accused had been a passenger in a car that was driven by Snieg and that was owned by Snieg's girlfriend. When the car was searched as it crossed into Canada via Niagara Falls, New York, Canada Customs officers discovered seven bags of cocaine that had been hidden inside the vehicle. The accused was charged with, and subsequently convicted of, the serious offence of importing a narcotic, contrary to section 5(1) of the (now-repealed) *Narcotic Control Act*, R.S.C. 1985, c. N-1. However, the Ontario Court of Appeal later set aside the conviction and ordered a new trial on the basis that, *even if the Crown could prove that*

Williams knew of the presence of the drugs, his "mere passive acquiescence" in their transportation by Snieg would not be sufficient to justify a conviction of importing a narcotic. In order to be successful, the Crown would have to prove that Williams actually provided some *assistance or encouragement* to Snieg (e.g., by helping Snieg to conceal the drugs in the car).

However, there are certain, exceptional circumstances in which a mere failure to act may well constitute aiding and/or abetting within the meaning of section 21(b) and (c) of the *Criminal Code*. If, for example, the accused is *under a legal duty to act and fails to do so*, then — *provided the failure to act is accompanied by the intent to provide assistance or encouragement* to the person(s) actually committing an offence — the accused will become a party to

The person who aids and/or abets another to commit an assault is also guilty of assault: section 21(1)(b) and (c).

that offence as an aider and/or abettor. This was the principle that was articulated by the B.C. Court of Appeal in the case of *Nixon* (1990).

The accused was the officer in charge of the lock-up or jail where a citizen was brutally assaulted by one or more police officers. The victim's knee cap was completely broken as a consequence of the attack. Nixon was charged with aggravated assault, but the trial judge was not satisfied that he had actually committed the assault himself. However, the B.C. Court of Appeal ruled that the trial judge had been correct to convict the accused on the basis that he aided or abetted the officers who did commit the assault. Under the provisions of the B.C. *Police Act*, the accused was clearly under a duty to enforce the criminal law (by, for example, preventing the commission of an assault). Furthermore, by virtue of the **common law**, Nixon was, as a person in charge of a jail, under a *clear duty to safeguard the lives and safety of his prisoners*. Nixon's failure to perform these duties constituted aiding or abetting the assault, assuming, of course, that his failure to act was prompted by the intention to assist or encourage the other officers in their criminal activities. Speaking on behalf of the Court of Appeal, Justice Legg stated that

> the fact which highly relevant to this case is that the accused has been found to have been present when the assault was committed and had a duty to prevent the offence and did not perform that duty. *Where an accused has such a duty and fails to act to discharge it, his failure to act may be held to have encouraged the offence.* [emphasis added]

The *Mens Rea* Elements of Aiding and Abetting

It was pointed out earlier that in order to establish the *mens rea* of aiding and/or abetting, the Crown must provide that the accused *intended* to render assistance and/or encouragement to the principal when the offence was actually committed. This requirement is clearly illustrated by the macabre case of *Curran* (1977). The accused was charged with the murder of one Armand. Curran was accompanying a man, called Defoe, in a shopping plaza. Defoe decided to rob Armand and, in the course of the robbery, he flung the victim down a flight of concrete steps. There was, apparently, no evidence to suggest that Curran was a party to this robbery. Defoe later gouged Armand's eyes out and choked him to death. Curran was convicted of murder at his trial. It was not entirely clear whether the jury convicted him because he was a direct participant in the murder or because he abetted the murders, since the Crown advanced both theories. Curran's appeal to the Alberta Supreme Court, Appellate Division, was successful and a new trial was ordered. One of the critical issues in the appeal was Curran's potential liability, under section 21(1)(c), as an abettor of the murder perpetrated by Defoe. The theory of the Crown was that Curran was present at the scene of the murder and encouraged the dastardly act by the words he uttered at the time. In a statement to the police, Curran stated, " ... so I went back with him, he took the guy's eyes out. He said that wasn't good enough because *I said a blind man can still talk.*" [emphasis added] The theory of the Crown was that Curran had abetted the murder by uttering these words. The defence, on the other hand, contended that Curran's statement, far from being intended to encourage Defoe, was actually an expression of utter "disgust." In delivering the judgment of the court, Justice Moir stated that, in his opinion,

> although s. 21(1)(c) does not expressly say that the words or actions must be for the purpose of abetting the person, it is clear that the acts or words of abetting must be accompanied by a state of mind. The accused must intend that the words or acts will encourage the principal. The criminal law is concerned with acts or words that are done or uttered with the intent or for the purpose of counselling, encouraging, instigating or promoting the commission of the acts by the principal actor. Accordingly, before an accused person can be convicted *the Crown must prove, beyond a reasonable doubt, both the words of*

encouragement and the intention of the appellant to so encourage. [emphasis added]

The court ruled that the trial judge had not instructed the jury correctly as to the critical element of the *mens rea* required for the conviction of abetting and ordered a new trial.

A tragic case that clearly illustrates the requisite *mens rea* for aiding and abetting the crime of murder is that of *Kent, Sinclair and Gode* (1986). In the course of a prison riot, two guards had been killed. There was evidence that Sinclair had stabbed the guards with a pair of scissors. A critical issue in the case was what the "respective intents" of Kent and Gode were when they participated in the riot. The Crown had argued that these two men assisted in killing the guards. In the Manitoba Court of Appeal, Justice Twaddle presented a lucid definition of the *mens rea* that must be proved in relation to a charge of aiding and abetting:

> *In the case of one who aids or abets the commission of a murder, the intent necessary for a conviction of murder is the same as that required of the person who actually does the act causing death.* The person aiding or abetting the commission of the crime must intend that death ensue or that bodily harm of a kind likely to cause death be caused, he being reckless whether death ensues or not. If the intent of the aider and abetter is insufficient to support a conviction of murder, he still might be convicted of manslaughter if the unlawful act he aids or abets is one he knows likely will cause some harm short of death. [emphasis added]

In this particular case, the majority of the Court of Appeal ruled that the trial judge had been in error in not instructing the jury that they might convict Kent and Gode of manslaughter, regardless of the offence for which it convicted Sinclair (**first degree murder**).

This issue was later addressed by the Supreme Court of Canada in the case of *Davy* (1993), in which the Court added an important gloss to Jus-

tice Twaddle's statement concerning the *mens rea* requirements that must be proved in order to convict an accused of aiding or abetting manslaughter. As the reader will no doubt remember from Chapter 5, the Supreme Court ruled in the *Creighton* case (1993) that the *mens rea* that must be proved in relation to unlawful act manslaughter is that of *objective foreseeability* of the risk of bodily harm that is neither trivial nor transitory. In *Davy*, the Supreme Court ruled that this objective test equally applies to a person charged with manslaughter on the basis of having aided and/or abetted someone to kill another person. As was the case in *Kent, Sinclair and Gode*, Davy had assisted someone who was ultimately convicted of murder. Nevertheless, the Supreme Court of Canada ruled that, if Davy lacked the necessary *mens rea* for conviction of murder, he could still be convicted of manslaughter on the basis that he aided and/or abetted that other person in the situation where a *reasonable person would have foreseen the risk of bodily harm to the victim*. As Justice McLachlin, as she then was, (with whom seven other Justices of the Supreme Court concurred) stated in her judgment in *Davy*,

> I conclude that a person may be convicted of manslaughter who aids and abets another person in the offence of murder, where a reasonable person in all the circumstances would have appreciated that bodily harm was the foreseeable consequence of the dangerous act which was being undertaken.

Aiding and Abetting in the Context of the Purchase of Illegal Drugs

A significant issue facing the courts is the extent to which those persons who provide incidental assistance to those who purchase illegal drugs should be held criminally responsible for their actions. This question was addressed by the Supreme Court of Canada in the case of *Greyeyes* (1997). The accused had been charged with the very serious offence of trafficking in cocaine, on the basis that he was a party to the crime by virtue of aiding and/or abetting.

An undercover police officer, Morgan, had asked Greyeyes if he knew where he (Morgan) could obtain some cocaine. Greyeyes indicated that he knew where a source could be found, and he and Morgan went to an apartment building together. Greyeyes identified himself at the door of a particular apartment. An individual inside asked what Greyeyes and his companion wanted: Greyeyes responded with the word, "cocaine." When asked how much cocaine was required, Greyeyes looked at Morgan, who indicated "one." Greyeyes relayed this information to the supplier and told Morgan that he would have to pay $40. The person inside the apartment instructed Greyeyes to slide the money under the door. He did so and a small pink flap, containing two-tenths of a gram of cocaine, was passed under the door to him. Greyeyes then gave the drug to Morgan.

The trial judge acquitted Greyeyes on the basis that he had only acted as an agent for Morgan, who was the *purchaser*— not the *seller*— of the cocaine. In effect, the trial judge ruled that Greyeyes had only acted as the mouthpiece for the undercover police officer and had not done anything to assist the vendor in the making of the sale. However, the Saskatchewan Court of Appeal subsequently allowed an appeal by the Crown and convicted Greyeyes of trafficking in cocaine. The Supreme Court of Canada then rejected Greyeyes's ensuing appeal.

It is significant that Justice L'Heureux-Dubé, speaking on behalf of the majority of the Supreme Court, ruled that, in normal circumstances, the purchaser of an illegal drug is not found guilty of *trafficking*, but rather of *possession*. This is a critical difference because the severity of the penalty for trafficking is much greater than for mere possession (a maximum term of imprisonment of life as opposed to one of seven years). Clearly, this logic should be extended to cover those individuals who have provided "no more than incidental assistance of the sale through rendering aid to the purchaser." Such individuals should be treated as parties to the offence of *possession*, rather than *trafficking*. As Justice L'Heureux-Dubé noted in her judgment, an individual whose conduct was primarily designed to assist a *purchaser* of illegal drugs should "share the culpability and stigma of the purchaser rather than that of the vendor."

In the particular circumstances of the *Greyeyes* case, however, the Supreme Court ruled that the accused had gone far beyond providing assistance to the purchaser, Morgan. Indeed, Justice L'Heureux-Dubé stated that the "facts demonstrate a concerted effort on his part to effect the transfer of narcotics." In her view,

The appellant located the seller, brought the buyer to the site and introduced the parties. It is clear that without this assistance, the purchase would never have taken place. Moreover, he acted as a spokesperson, negotiated the price of the drugs, and passed the money over to the seller. He also accepted money for having facilitated the deal ... without the appellant's assistance, the buyer would never have been able to enter the apartment building to contact the seller. *These are not the acts of a mere purchaser, and as a result it is clear that the appellant aided the traffic of narcotics.* [emphasis added]

Greyeyes, therefore, was found to be a party to the crime of *trafficking* (as an aider or abettor), because his actions were designed to provide a significant degree of assistance to the *seller* of the cocaine.

To What Extent Must the Aider or Abettor Know the Principal's Plans?

One significant problem that arises in relation to the proof of the necessary *mens rea* for aiding and/or abetting an offence concerns the situation where the accused renders only *incidental assistance* to the principal. The problem revolves around the issue of the precise extent to which the accused must have knowledge of the principal's plans at the time he or she provides such assistance. It is clear that the accused must know the principal's "general" purpose but, in many cases, the thorny issue arises as to exactly how far this knowledge must extend in order to render them liable to conviction as aiders and/or abettors.

This problem is well illustrated by the case of *Yanover and Gerol* (1985). Gerol was charged with the offence of placing dynamite with intent to cause an explosion at a restaurant and disco in Toronto (contrary to what is now section 81(1)(a) of the *Criminal Code*). Gerol had provided the dynamite that was ultimately used by a man called Moon in the creation of the explosion. Gerol asked Moon what the dynamite was for and was told that, "my friend asked me to do the job." Apparently, Gerol did not ask Moon what the job was nor did he inquire as to the identity of the friend. The accused was convicted at trial, but the Ontario Court of Appeal allowed his appeal and ordered a new trial.

The new trial was ordered because of matters relating to the admission of fresh evidence. However, the Ontario Court of Appeal did take the opportunity to articulate the general principles that should be applied when a trial court has to determine whether an individual in Gerol's circumstances possessed the requisite degree of *mens rea* for conviction of an offence on the basis of aiding or abetting. Clearly, Gerol himself had not been present at the time of the explosion. He was plainly ignorant of the identity of the specific building that was going to be blown up; nor did he know anything about its location. Furthermore, he did not have any knowledge as to when the explosion would take place. However, it does appear that he was fully aware that the dynamite was to be used for the criminal purpose of causing an explosion. In these circumstances, the Ontario Court of Appeal ruled that it would be open to a jury to conclude that the accused was a party to the offence on the basis of aiding and/or abetting (under section 21(1)(b) or (c) of the *Criminal Code*). As Justice Martin stated, in delivering the judgment of the court,

> For liability to attach under s. 21(1)(b) or (c) it is unnecessary that the person supplying the instrument for the commission of the intended crime know the precise details of the crime intended to be committed such as the particular premises intended to be blown up or the precise time when the offence is intended to be committed, *provided that the accused is aware of the type of crime intended to be committed.* [emphasis added]

Similarly, suppose that Titus assists and/or encourages Quintus to perpetrate an attack against Demetrius. As a consequence of the assault, Demetrius suffers bodily injuries that are primarily caused by a stab wound inflicted by Quintus. Is it open to Titus to deny that he was a party to the offence of assault causing bodily harm by claiming that he did not know that Quintus had a knife? The answer would be in the negative because Titus intended to assist or encourage Quintus in the commission of an act that clearly created a very real risk of non-trivial bodily injury. It does not matter exactly how the bodily harm was inflicted on Demetrius — whether by fist blows or by use of a weapon. Titus undoubtedly knew that Quintus intended to inflict bodily harm. He therefore knew the *general nature* of the offence that was to be committed and he would be convicted as a party to assault causing bodily harm, even though he might not have known exactly how Quintus would ultimately inflict the injuries in question.

This type of scenario unfolded in the *Cuadra* case (1998), in which the accused was charged with aggravated assault. Armed with a baseball bat, Cuadra had participated in an attack on a man called Hatchard. One of the other assailants, Arbuto, stabbed Hatchard, thereby inflicting serious injuries. There was no evidence to suggest that Cuadra had stuck the victim with the baseball bat, and he claimed that he only intended to assist in a fist fight. At his trial, the accused was nevertheless convicted of *aggravated assault* (section 268 of the Code), and his subsequent appeal to the B.C. Court of Appeal was dismissed. The Court of Appeal rejected the argument of Cuadra's **counsel** that the Crown had to establish that Cuadra was aware that Arbuto had a knife and that it was objectively foreseeable that the victim would be stabbed. As Justice Cumming said, in delivering the judgment of the Court of Appeal,

> ... it is clear to me that an objective foresight of the specific wounds resulting from an assault is not

the threshold test; the test is simply an objective foresight of bodily *harm*. Thus specific wounds do not have to be foreseeable ...

When Cuadra entered the fray he did so with a weapon, his weapon of choice was a baseball bat, he was assisting Arbuto in a fight that went beyond a mere "fist fight." The harm that resulted from the escalation of the fight may not have been specifically foreseeable but it is undeniable that bodily harm was objectively foreseeable and that ... is the *mens rea* requirement for the offence of aggravated assault.

However, it is important to bear in mind that the courts will not convict an accused person as a party to *murder*, on the basis of aiding and/or abetting, unless he or she *intended to help or encourage the principal either to kill the victim or to inflict grievous bodily harm that the accused knows is likely to cause death.* This critical principle was applied, for example, in the case of *Hartford and Frigon* (1980), in which the accused were both charged with the murder of a man called Pollock, who had been drowned in a creek.

The evidence indicated that a third man, Rattray, had actually killed Pollock, perhaps with the assistance of one or both of the **defendants**. The latter claimed that Rattray "held the deceased underwater and pummeled him to get the air out of his lungs." It was clear that both Hartford and Frigon had "participated under Rattray's leadership in kicking the deceased and throwing him in the water from time to time." However, there was considerable dispute as to the precise nature of the accused's involvement in the act of drowning Pollock. The accused were convicted at trial, but their appeal to the B.C. Court of Appeal was successful. A new trial was ordered because the trial judge, in his instruction to the jury, had left unclear the necessary *mens rea* for conviction as an aider and/or abettor. In delivering the judgment of the court, Justice Seaton said

The jury was left with the impression that the intention to be found in an aider and abettor under s. 21(1)(b) and (c) was the intention to aid or abet, without the qualification that the aider know what he was aiding. That I think to be wrong. If one of the appellants aided Rattray, thinking that what they were going to do was rough the deceased up and not cause him any bodily harm that would be likely to cause death, then I think that that appellant might be guilty of manslaughter, notwithstanding that Rattray be guilty of murder.

The intention that the jury ought to have been directed to consider as an essential ingredient for a finding of murder on the basis of aiding and abetting would be the intention to help Rattray, knowing that he was going to kill or cause bodily harm that was likely to cause death, or the intention to help Rattray no matter which of a number of crimes he chose to commit. ...

Before leaving the topic of aiding and abetting, it is instructive to consider the well-publicized case of *Thatcher* (1987). This case resulted in the conviction of a former Saskatchewan Minister of Energy and Mines for the brutal murder of his ex-wife. The Crown contended that Colin Thatcher had either killed the victim himself or arranged for someone else to do so and had aided or abetted them to achieve that result. However, the Crown was unable to identify any other party who may have committed the murder on Thatcher's behalf, if indeed that was the way in which the unfortunate victim met her terrible end. The trial judge instructed the jury that they could convict the accused of murder on the basis either that he actually killed the victim himself or, alternatively, that he was a party to the offence, having aided and abetted another person to carry out the fatal deed. The jury convicted the accused of first degree murder. His appeal against conviction ultimately went to the Supreme Court of Canada, which ruled that the trial judge's instruction to the jury had been perfectly correct. The Supreme Court, therefore, rejected Thatcher's appeal. The Court also held that it was not necessary for the jury to be unanimous in its verdict as to the question of whether the accused was the actual murderer or whether he aided and/or abetted another person to kill the victim. Indeed,

Chief Justice Dickson asserted that this conclusion was implicit in the very wording of section 21 of the *Criminal Code*:

> ... s. 21 has been designed to alleviate the necessity for the Crown choosing between two different forms of participation in a criminal offence. The law stipulates that both forms of participation are not only equally culpable, but should be treated as one single mode of incurring criminal liability. The Crown is not under a duty to separate the different forms of participation in a criminal offence into different counts. Obviously, if the charge against Thatcher had been separated into different counts, he might well have been acquitted on each count notwithstanding that each and every juror was certain beyond a reasonable doubt that Thatcher personally killed his ex-wife or that he aided and abetted someone else who killed his ex-wife. That is precisely what s. 21 is designed to prevent.

Clearly, the ruling in the *Thatcher* case represents a significant advantage to the prosecution where it is not obvious on what basis the accused was involved in the commission of an alleged offence.

COUNSELLING AN OFFENCE

An individual may also become a party to a criminal offence as a consequence of "counselling" a criminal act. Indeed, section 22 of the *Criminal Code* establishes a broad basis for the imposition of criminal liability:

21(1) where a person counsels another person to be a party to an offence and that other person is afterwards a party to that offence, the person who counselled is a party to that offence, notwithstanding that the offence was committed in a way different from that which was counselled.

(2) Every one who counsels another person to be a party to an offence is a party to every offence that the other commits in consequence of the counselling that the person

who counselled or procured knew or *ought to have known* was likely to be committed in consequence of the counselling. [emphasis added]

(3) For the purposes of this Act, "counsel" includes procure, solicit or incite.

As a reading of section 22(1) readily indicates, if accused persons counsel or procure an offence and that offence is ultimately committed, they will be convicted of that offence in exactly the same manner as "aiders" and/or "abettors" may be convicted under section 21. Section 22(2) also saddles accused persons who counsel or procure a crime with the responsibility for every other offence that the principal commits as a direct consequence of the counselling or procuring. The only limitation placed upon their liability is the requirement that the Crown establish that the accused knew, or *ought to have known*, that such an offence was likely to be committed as a consequence of the counselling or procuring. The use of the words "ought to have known" clearly imposes an *objective standard of liability* based upon what the "reasonable" person would have known in the same circumstances as the accused. The only exception to this principle of objective liability would arise where the principal commits the offences of murder or attempted murder. In this situation, the Supreme Court of Canada's decision in *Martineau* (1990) (see Chapter 4) dictates that, in order to safeguard the rights of accused persons under sections 7 and 11(d) of the *Charter*, they cannot become parties to these offences unless they had subjective foresight of the death of the victim.

It should be noted that section 22(3) states that the word "counsel" includes "procure, solicit or incite." What is the difference between these terms? In their textbook, *Mewett and Manning on Criminal Law* (1994), the authors suggest that "counselling would seem to connote the act of recommending to someone else that he commit an offence; procuring the act of going out to find someone to commit an offence; soliciting the act of importuning someone to commit an offence; and incitement, the act of urging someone to commit an offence."

An interesting case involving the counselling of an offence is that of *Soloway* (1975). In this case, the accused was convicted by a provincial court judge of a charge that he " … did unlawfully steal a driver's licence, registration and Alberta Health Care Card of a value not exceeding $200. … " It appears that the victim was invited to Soloway's home by a Mrs. Daniels, who was a friend of the accused. The victim felt tired and went to sleep, face-down, on a couch in Soloway's living room. The victim woke up when he felt Mrs. Daniels removing his wallet from his back pocket. He pretended he was still sleeping, because he feared that he might be attacked if he did not do so. There was no money in the wallet. In his evidence at trial, the victim said

When [Mrs. Daniels] … decided that there was nothing in the wallet, she was going to return it … like I figured common sense would tell them to; and Mr. Soloway says, "No, keep it," … "It's worth good money, I can sell it at any bar." He says, "You know, there's good money in that sort of thing. You can take strangers around, bop them over the head, and get their wallets. If there is no money you can always make money on the other things that are in the wallets."

The trial judge convicted Soloway as a party to theft on the basis that he counselled Mrs. Daniels to steal the *contents* of the victim's wallet. Soloway appealed to the Appellate Division of the Alberta Supreme Court, but his conviction was affirmed. Justice Allen crystallized the central issue by stating that

the whole point involved in this case is whether the appellant's presence when the wallet was extracted from [the victim's] … hip pocket and the advice he gave to the woman with respect to keeping the credentials made him a party to the offence of stealing those credentials and thus guilty of the offence of theft. …

Defence counsel had contended that Soloway could not be convicted of being a party to theft,

because that crime was already complete when Mrs. Daniels removed the wallet from the victim's pocket. Justice Allen rejected this contention:

The evidence seems clearly to establish that after the woman discovered no money in the wallet she intended to put it back in [the victim's] … pocket (which she eventually did) and that it was the counselling and advice she received from the appellant that persuaded her to extract and retain the credentials found to be in it. Soloway was charged with theft of its contents. In my view, the theft of these contents was not completed until they were extracted from the wallet with the intention to deprive [the victim] … of them and to turn them some way into account … during the course of the offence and before its completion the appellant counselled the woman who had lifted the wallet to retain its contents, in respect of which the charge was laid and, consequently, was properly convicted as a party to the offence.

BECOMING A PARTY TO AN OFFENCE BY VIRTUE OF COMMON INTENTION

The Basic Principles of Liability Under Section 21(2)

Section 21(2) of the *Criminal Code* provides that:

Where two or more persons form an intention in common to carry out an unlawful purpose and to assist each other therein and any one of them, in carrying out the common purpose, commits an offence, each of them who knew or *ought to have known* that the commission of the offence would be a probable consequence of carrying out the common purpose is a party to that offence. [emphasis added]

This provision basically codifies the ancient English common law doctrine of "common intent," whereby, if two or more persons set out to execute an unlawful purpose, each of them is equally liable for the consequences of the other's (or others') criminal acts that are committed in pursuit of that common objective. As in other, similar situations, the Code imposes an unequivocally *objective* test: once the Crown has established the "common purpose," accused persons are liable to conviction for any offence that they either knew or "ought to have known" would be a probable consequence of carrying it out.

Let us suppose, by way of example, that Toby and Malvolio agree to rob Orsino's corner store. Toby hopes that Orsino will hand over the cash from his till in response to threats rather than actual violence. However, Orsino refuses to hand over the money and Malvolio strikes Orsino on the head with a club. Malvolio and Toby run off with the cash and are soon apprehended by members of the local constabulary. There is no doubt that Malvolio and Toby are both guilty of *robbery*. However, Toby claims that he is not guilty of the offence of *aggravated assault* (section 268 of the Code), because not only was it Malvolio who actually struck Orsino but it was also the case that he (Toby) only intended to scare Orsino by threats. In spite of his claims, Toby would nevertheless be convicted of the crime of aggravated assault by virtue of the application of the principle of "common intention," encapsulated in section 21(2) of the *Criminal Code*. Toby and Malvolio formed a *common intention to commit the crime of robbery "and to assist each other therein."* The Crown would undoubtedly find it relatively easy to prove either that Toby *actually knew*, or that he that he "*ought to have known*" that the infliction of non-trivial bodily harm would be a "probable consequence of carrying out the common purpose." After all, the very nature of a robbery is that the victim is exposed to the risk of non-trivial bodily harm.

In the case of *Vang* (1999), the accused had acted in concert with two other men to attack one Rampersaud. One of Vang's companions, Nguyen, stabbed Rampersaud in the back, puncturing his lung and lacerating his kidney—injuries that might have led to potentially fatal internal bleeding.

Vang was charged with *aggravated assault* on the basis that he had formed a common intention with his companions to assault Rampersaud and that he either knew or ought to have known that a probable consequence of carrying out this common intention was the infliction of non-trivial bodily harm. There was no evidence that Vang knew that Nguyen had a knife, although it appeared that Vang had used a beer bottle as part of the assault on the victim. Vang was convicted of the charge and his subsequent appeal to the Ontario Court of Appeal was dismissed. In delivering the judgment of the court, Associate Chief Justice Morden stated that

> ... the question is whether the appellants, in engaging in the common unlawful purpose of assaulting Rampersaud, foresaw, or ought to have foreseen, that bodily harm was a probable consequence of carrying out the common purpose. If the answer is yes, then, provided Rampersaud's injuries did, in fact, endanger his life, the appellants are guilty of aggravated assault.
>
> ... *The specific harm that resulted may not have been foreseeable, but it is clear that, as the trial judge found, bodily harm was objectively foreseeable as a probable consequence of engaging in the fight.* [emphasis added]

The application of section 21(2) was considered by the Supreme Court of Canada in the case of *Jackson* (1993). In this case, Jackson and Davy were charged with first degree murder. The theory of the Crown was that Davy drove Jackson to the house of the victim where they both participated in his killing. The Crown also suggested that the **motive** for the killing was robbery and that both Davy and Jackson intended to kill the victim during the robbery. However, there was evidence that Davy did not actually participate in the slaughter of the victim, and he testified that he did not form any plan to rob and kill him. Jackson was convicted of first degree murder and the question arose as to whether Davy could be convicted of murder or manslaughter on the basis of having formed an intention in common to rob the victim. He was actually convicted of

second degree murder, but the Ontario Court of Appeal granted him a new trial. This decision was later affirmed by the Supreme Court of Canada.

In delivering her judgment (in which seven other justices of the Supreme Court concurred), Justice McLachlin set out the circumstances in which Davy might be convicted of manslaughter by virtue of the operation of section 21(2):

> On the evidence presented, one of the scenarios available to the jury was that Jackson and Davy had formed a common intention to rob Rae [the victim] and that, in the course of the robbery, Jackson murdered Rae. Even if he did not participate in the murder, Davy could be liable under s. 21(2) in this scenario. If he foresaw that murder was a probable consequence of carrying out the common purpose—in this case the robbery—he would be guilty of second degree murder. On the other hand, *if Davy did not foresee the probability of murder but a reasonable person in the circumstances would have foreseen at least a risk of harm to another as a result of carrying out the common intention, Davy could be found guilty of manslaughter* under s. 21(2). [emphasis added]

The Requirement of Subjective Foreseeability of Death in Murder and Attempted Murder Cases

We have seen that section 21(2) imposes *objective* liability insofar as accused persons can be convicted of an offence that they "ought to have known" would be a probable consequence of carrying out the common unlawful purpose that they have formed with the principal offender(s). However, in the *Martineau* case (1990), the Supreme Court of Canada ruled that, in light of the guarantees provided by the *Charter*, accused persons may not be convicted of murder unless they *subjectively* foresaw the likelihood of death ensuing from their conduct. What impact does this principle have in the context of section 21(2)?

In the cases of *Logan* (1990) and *Rodney* (1990), the Supreme Court of Canada ruled that section 7

of the *Charter* renders inoperative the words "ought to have known" in section 21(2), whenever the charge is murder or attempted murder. In other words, where the Crown seeks to obtain a murder (or attempted murder) conviction on the basis of common intention under section 21(2), it must be shown that the accused actually foresaw that the death of the victim was a probable consequence of carrying out the common purpose in question.

In *Logan*, a case involving attempted murder, Chief Justice Lamer (with whom four other justices concurred) indicated that the Court should:

> declare inoperative the words "or ought to have known" when considering under s. 21(2) whether a person is a party to any offence where it is a constitutional requirement for a conviction that foresight of the consequences be subjective, which is the case for attempted murder. Once these words are deleted, the remaining section requires, in the context of attempted murder, that the party to the common venture know that it is probable that his accomplice would do something with the intent to kill in carrying out the common purpose.

The Ontario Court of Appeal applied these principles in *Laliberty* (1997). In this case, three women had been charged with second degree murder. The theory of the Crown was that the three accused had formed a plan to rob the victim and that one of them stabbed him with a butcher knife in the course of carrying out the robbery. All three of the accused were convicted at trial, but the Ontario Court of Appeal subsequently allowed their appeals and ordered a new trial because the trial judge had not given the jury a correct instruction in relation to the application of section 21(2) of the *Criminal Code* to the facts of the specific case. Section 21(2) would, of course, apply to the two accused who did not actually stab the victim, and the Court of Appeal ruled, at a new trial, that the trial judge must make it clear to the jury that "guilt could only be found if each of the appellants, considered separately for the purposes of s. 21(2), had actual foresight or actual knowledge that another appellant would stab the deceased with the intent to kill him in carrying out the robbery of the deceased."

How Broad Is the Scope of the "Common Purpose" Under Section 21(2)?

It will be remembered that section 21(2) refers to the "common purpose" of the accused and his or her accomplice(s). This phrase would appear to lay the basis for a potential defence based upon the contention that the accomplices committed an act that fell outside the scope of the so-called common purpose. However, the courts have emphasized that such a defence, if it is applicable, has a very limited scope.

For example, the issue was raised before the Manitoba Court of Appeal in the case of *Puffer, McFall and Kizyma* (1977). In this case, the co-accused were charged with murder. The body of the victim was discovered in a badly beaten state. However, it was established that the actual cause of death was asphyxiation due to a pillow being tied around his face. In the words of Chief Justice Freedman,

> So here is a man helplessly and hopelessly trussed up—his feet crossed and securely tied, his hands no less securely tied behind his back, and, covering his face, a pillow held firmly in place by a sweater, the arms of which were knotted at the back of his neck. Effectively immobilized as he was, he could not have survived very long.

The theory advanced by the Crown was that the accused had formed a plan to rob the deceased and that they killed him in order to facilitate the robbery or their subsequent escape. Statements given to the police by the accused indicated that they had indeed intended to rob the victim (or, as one accused put it, their plan was to "roll some fags"—meaning the robbery of some homosexuals). However, McFall and Puffer strenuously claimed that the

tying of the pillow over the victim's face was executed by Kizyma at a time when they were not present. However, evidence presented at the trial indicated that all three co-accused participated, to some extent, in beating the victim and tying his arms and legs. The co-accused were all convicted of noncapital murder, and they appealed to the Manitoba Court of Appeal.

Counsel for McFall and Puffer contended, in effect, that the tying of the pillow by Kizyma went beyond the scope of the common purpose formed between the three co-accused. Counsel, therefore, claimed that the trial judge should have instructed the jury that the bodily harm, which actually caused death, can only render the co-accused liable to conviction of murder if "it was of a nature or type falling within the scope of the plan or conspiracy." Since McFall and Puffer asserted that Kizyma's use of the pillow as a gag went beyond the scope of their plan, their counsel contended that they should not have been convicted of murder. This contention was firmly rejected by the Court of Appeal, which affirmed the convictions of all three co-accused.

In rejecting the point made by counsel for McFall and Puffer, Chief Justice Freedman said

> In any event the present case is not one in which, either expressly or tacitly, the accused had agreed upon or defined just how far they would go or just what they would do. The enterprise was described merely as one to roll a fag. I find it completely unrealistic to say that blows to the face or body, the pinioning of hands, the tying of feet could be regarded as within the plan, but that the use of the pillow as a gag must be looked upon as falling outside the plan. Distinctions of this kind could lead to findings that a blow above the belt was within a scheme to rob, while a blow below the belt was not. The violence involved in the carrying out of a robbery ought not later to be measured or tested by Marquis of Queensbury rules or anything of that nature.

The facts in the *Puffer, McFall and Kizyma* case were such that it was highly unlikely that the

iments would be treated with even
e tinge of sympathy by the courts.
ire no doubt other circumstances in
which the defence of "going beyond the scope of the
common intention" is much more likely to be successful. Suppose, for example, that Caliban and
Trinculo agree to break and enter Prospero's residence in order to steal a valuable painting. Caliban
insists that they carry out their plan without any
violence and expressly warns Trinculo against bringing any sort of weapon with him. The two burglars
break into Prospero's house and are about to remove
the painting. However, at this point, Prospero dis-
turbs them and says that he has called the police.
Caliban wishes to surrender peacefully, but Trinculo
takes out a knife that he has concealed in his boot
and stabs Prospero, causing him severe injuries.
Here, Caliban could legitimately assert that Trinculo's vicious assault on Prospero fell outside the
scope of the common intent. While Caliban would
certainly be guilty of committing the offence of
breaking and entering with intent to commit theft
(section 348(1)(a) of the *Criminal Code*), it is highly
unlikely that he would be convicted of aggravated
assault under section 21(2) of the Code.

Withdrawal from the "Common Purpose"

In what circumstances may an accomplice *withdraw* from a common intention to carry out an
unlawful purpose and thereby absolve him- or herself from liability for all acts subsequently committed by his or her co-conspirators? The parameters of
the so-called defence of "abandonment" were outlined by Justice Sloan in the B.C. case of *Whitehouse
(Savage)* (1940):

> I would not attempt to define too closely what
> must be done in criminal matters involving partic-
> ipation in a common unlawful purpose to break
> the chain of causation and responsibility. That
> must depend upon the circumstances of each case
> but it seems to me that one essential element
> ought to be established in a case of this kind: *where
> practical and reasonable there must be timely com-*

> *munication of the intention to abandon the common
> purpose from those who desire to continue in it.* What
> is "timely communication" must be determined by
> the facts of each case but where practicable and
> reasonable it ought to be such communication,
> verbal or otherwise, that will serve unequivocal
> notice upon the other party to the common un-
> lawful cause that if he proceeds upon it he does so
> without the further aid and assistance of those
> who withdraw. [emphasis added]

As Justice Sloan indicates, the application of the
defence of abandonment will depend upon the precise set of facts in each case. An illustration of the
approach taken by the courts is furnished by *Joyce*
(1978). In this case, the three co-accused were
charged with murder as the consequence of the killing
of an employee of a lumber yard during a robbery. It
appears that the three co-accused (Richard, Gordon,
and Peter Joyce) agreed with one Michael Coleman to
rob two stores simultaneously so as to "confuse the
police." Coleman testified that he and Peter Joyce
were supposed to rob a Lumberland store in Vancouver while Gordon and Richard Joyce would rob a
Lumberland store in Burnaby. It turned out that
Coleman and Peter Joyce decided to abandon the
Vancouver robbery after lurking in the vicinity for a
while. Meanwhile, the Burnaby robbery proceeded
according to plan. Some $27 283 was taken from the
store. However, an employee was tragically killed
when one of the robber's guns discharged accidentally
as he was taping the employee. The three accused
were all convicted of murder, and their appeals to the
B.C. Court of Appeal were ultimately dismissed.
However, for the present purposes, it is important to
emphasize one of the issues raised by counsel for Peter
Joyce, who had been convicted on the basis of section
21(2) of the *Criminal Code*. It was contested, on his
behalf, that he had withdrawn from the common purpose when he and Coleman abandoned the proposed
Vancouver robbery, and that he, therefore, could not
be rendered liable for the shooting that took place at
the Burnaby Lumberland store.

The force of this argument was considerably
diminished by evidence that, on the day *after* the

Burnaby robbery, "the four conspirators met to split the proceeds from the robbery." However, the reasons given by Justice Hinkson for rejecting Peter Joyce's appeal, on this point, are nevertheless most instructive in terms of the application of the defence of abandonment:

> In my view, there are two answers to that proposition. The scheme propounded by Richard Joyce was a plan of robbery. The robbery involved stores at two separate locations. They were to be robbed simultaneously but throughout the planning stage it was recognized by the conspirators that it might not be possible to complete the robbery successfully at one or other of the locations. Thus, when Peter Joyce proposed that the robbery of [the Vancouver store] ... be abandoned he was not withdrawing from the over-all scheme. In my view, this fact is confirmed by the evidence which disclosed that he was present when the division of the proceeds from the Burnaby store robbery was discussed and it was indicated that he was to participate in a share of the proceeds. Secondly, as a matter of law, Peter Joyce did not withdraw from the common purpose, because he failed to communicate his withdrawal to Richard Joyce and Gordon Joyce. I note parenthetically that such a communication might have had a significant result: the purpose of committing the two robberies simultaneously was to confuse the police; if Richard and Gordon Joyce had known that Peter Joyce and Coleman weren't going ahead with their part of the scheme, they might have abandoned their own part. ... On the evidence here the appellant Peter Joyce did not abandon the common purpose.

The case of *Kirkness* (1990), however, provides an illustration of circumstances in which the defence of "abandoning the common intent" was raised successfully. In this case, the accused had formed an intention in common with his co-accused to carry out the unlawful purpose of breaking and entering. The two men broke into the deceased person's house. The accused put a chair at the front door to prevent anyone from entering the premises and ransacked the house while the co-accused sexually assaulted and then killed the deceased by suffocation. There was no evidence to establish that the accused knew beforehand that the co-accused would commit sexual assault or kill the victim. Following the sexual assault and at the point when the co-accused was strangling the deceased, the accused told his co-accused not to do so because he might kill her. Was the accused a party to the killing by virtue of common intention under section 21(2)? Justice Cory, in delivering the majority judgment of the Supreme Court of Canada, dealt with the contention that the accused had abandoned the common intention prior to the killing and held that

> There is no evidence that the appellant was a party to the suffocation of Elizabeth Johnson. Rather, he told Snowbird not to strangle the victim as he was going to kill her. His statement makes it clear that he was not aiding or abetting Snowbird in the strangulation or suffocation of Mrs. Johnson. *These words of the appellant constituted "timely notice" to Snowbird that he was not a party to the strangulation and suffocation....* Thus in those misdeeds Snowbird was acting on his own. It is therefore apparent that even if the appellant could be considered a party to the sexual assault, by the time of the attempted strangulation he had clearly resiled from any agreement or arrangement with Snowbird and was not a party to the suffocation of the victim. [emphasis added]

LIABILITY AS AN ACCESSORY AFTER THE FACT

Section 23(1) of the *Criminal Code* provides:

> An accessory after the fact to an offence is one who, knowing that a person has been party to the offence, receives, comforts or assists him for the purpose of enabling him to escape.

The *mens rea* and *actus reus* elements, defined by section 23(1), are relatively straightforward. For example, in the case of *Young* (1950), Justice Bissonnette said:

> This section obviously admits three constituent elements of the offence: knowledge that a crime had been committed, the desire to help the delinquent to escape and finally a positive act or omission intended to aid him in making his escape.

In the *Young* case, it appears that a man named Douglas Perreault killed a police constable in Montréal. Perreault's sister, Young, and two other men set out from Montréal to Sheenboro, Ontario, to inform Douglas Perreault's mother of the killing. Not long before reaching their destination, they met a car containing Douglas and Donald Perreault. Both cars stopped and the Perreault brothers were informed that the police were looking for them in connection with the murder. They also learned that the police knew their names and the licence number of their car. Young offered to hide the Perreault brothers but his offer was refused. Young was convicted as an accessory after the fact to murder and appealed his conviction to the Québec Court of Appeal. His appeal was dismissed. Justice Bissonnette addressed the critical issues in the following manner:

> In the present case, there is no doubt that Young knew that a crime had been committed by Douglas and Donald Perreault ... the information that he furnished ... meant efficacious assistance to the delinquents' escape. To tell them that the police are on their trail is to tell them that they have been identified, when they were still able, at that moment, to entertain the hope that they were not suspected of being the authors of this crime. It was giving them, by this information, immediate and efficacious assistance. The fact that the accused chose, after this information, a method of escape different from that suggested by appellant, does not dispel the efficacy of appellant's intervention.

The requirement that the accused person "know" that an offence has been committed, by the individual to whom he or she gives assistance, is clearly of pivotal importance. However, the courts have emphasized that *wilful blindness* on the part of the accused will be treated as being equivalent to actual knowledge in the context of section 23(1) of the *Criminal Code*. For example, in *Duong* (1998), the accused was charged with being an accessory after the fact to a murder allegedly committed by one Lam. Both television and newspaper reports had linked Lam to two homicides. Lam told Duong that he was "in trouble for murder" and needed shelter. Duong allowed Lam to hide in his apartment for about two weeks before the latter was discovered by the police. Duong knew of the media reports but did not ask Lam any questions about them. He told the police that Lam "just came to me and told me he was in trouble for it but I didn't want to know anything because I knew I would be in trouble for helping him hide, so I didn't want to know anymore." The Ontario Court of Appeal ruled that wilful blindness on the part of the accused would be sufficient *mens rea* for conviction of the offence of being an accessory after the fact. As Justice Doherty noted,

> Wilful blindness refers to a state of mind which is aptly described as "deliberate ignorance" ... *Actual suspicion, combined with a conscious decision not to make inquiries which could confirm that suspicion, is equated in the eyes of the criminal law with actual knowledge.* Both are subjective and both are sufficiently blameworthy to justify the imposition of criminal liability. [emphasis added]

The punishment for being an accessory after the fact is set out in section 463 of the Code; it is the same as the punishment for an *attempt* to commit an offence.

Section 23(2) recognizes that it would be extremely unjust, given the nature of marital relationships, to punish married persons for assisting their spouses:

> No married person whose spouse has been a party to an offence is an accessory after the fact to that offence

by receiving, comforting or assisting the spouse for the purpose of enabling the spouse to escape.

THE IMPACT OF SECTION 23.1 OF THE *CRIMINAL CODE*

After the *Young Offenders Act* came into force in April 1984, considerable concern was expressed as to the potential impact of the provision of the Act that raised the age of criminal responsibility to twelve years. Since children under this age could no longer be found criminally responsible, it was suggested that it might be possible for older individuals to use children under the age of twelve to commit crimes for which the latter could not be prosecuted and thereby operate with impunity. In other words, there was an understandable fear that the Act would encourage the emergence of figures such as Fagin, who stalked the pages of Dickens's novel *Oliver Twist*. Section 23.1 of the Code (which came into force in 1985) now ensures, beyond a shadow of a doubt, that such Fagin-like figures will be criminally liable even if they employ children under the age of twelve to carry out their nefarious activities:

> For greater certainty, sections 21 to 23 apply in respect of an accused notwithstanding the fact that the person whom the accused aids, abets, counsels or procures or receives, comforts or assists cannot be convicted of the offence.

However, section 23.1 is general in its application and is not limited to the case where the principal offender is underage. In *Camponi* (1993), for example, the accused was charged with being an accessory after the fact to murder. A charge of murder against the principal offender was stayed by the Crown after the trial judge ruled that incriminating statements that the principal offender had made to the police were not admissible in evidence against him. Camponi argued that she could not be convicted of being an accessory after the fact to an offence if the principal offender had not been convicted. The B.C. Court of Appeal, however, upheld

her conviction. Justice Wood, in delivering the judgment of the court, stated that section 23.1 "has put to rest any notion that an accessory after the fact can only be tried and convicted after the principal, or another party to the alleged offence, has been convicted."

Significantly, this generous interpretation of section 23.1 has been expanded to include those situations where the principal has actually been *acquitted* of the offence concerned. For example, in the case of *S. (F.J.)* (1997), the accused had been charged with being an accessory after the fact to murder. Her brother was tried separately in Youth Court for having committed the murder but was acquitted. It was argued on behalf of the accused that she could not be convicted as an accessory after the fact if the alleged principal had been acquitted. However, the Nova Scotia Court of Appeal ruled that, in light of section 23.1 of the Code, the accused should nevertheless be convicted of the offence. It is important to bear in mind that the trial judge in the accused's case had found, strictly on the basis of the evidence presented *at the accused's trial*, that the accused's brother had, in fact, committed murder and that the accused had deliberately tried to cover it up.

In delivering the judgment of the Court of Appeal, Justice Jones noted that section 23.1 had made a significant change to the old common law concerning the liability of accessories:

> It would appear that the provisions of the *Code* were intended to treat parties to offences in the same manner, i.e. that accessories before the fact, aiders and abettors and accessories after the fact would be treated as principals. This is confirmed by s. 23.1 of the *Code*. It is clear from that section and s. 592 of the *Code* it is not necessary to convict a principal in order to convict an accessory. While the language does not refer to the acquittal of the principal, in my view the words "whether or not the principal" is convicted, are broad enough to encompass the acquittal of the principal. Those provisions have changed the common law.

This remarkably expansive interpretation of section 23.1 was later endorsed by the Supreme Court of Canada (*S. (F.J.)* (1998)).

INCHOATE OFFENCES

The final section of this chapter concerns an extremely important topic, namely, the various *inchoate* (incomplete or preventive) offences that are defined in the *Criminal Code*. The rationale for such offences is fairly obvious in that they permit the police to intervene and prevent the commission of more serious crimes. This is well illustrated, for example, by the popular phrase "to nip a conspiracy in the bud." The inchoate offences to be considered are (a) counselling, (b) attempts, and (c) conspiracy.

Counselling an Offence That Is Not Committed

Earlier in this chapter, we discussed the criminal liability of individuals who counsel the commission of offences that are ultimately perpetrated; this liability is governed by section 22 of the Code. However, section 464 deals with the situation where an individual "counsels" another person to commit an offence which is *not* ultimately perpetrated:

> Except where otherwise expressly provided by law, the following provisions apply in respect of persons who counsel, procure or incite other persons to commit offences, namely,
>
> (a) everyone who counsels another person to commit an indictable offence is, if the offence is not completed, guilty of an indictable offence and is liable to the same punishment to which a person who attempts to commit that offence is liable; and
>
> (b) everyone who counsels another person to commit an offence punishable on summary conviction is, if the offence is not committed, guilty of an offence punishable on summary conviction.

It should be remembered that section 22(3) states that, for the purposes of the *Criminal Code*, the word counsel includes "procure, solicit or incite."

Since, of its very nature, counselling is an inchoate offence, the courts have noted that it is not necessary for the Crown to prove that anyone was actually influenced by the accused's counselling. This proposition is well illustrated by the case of *McLeod and Georgia Straight Publishing Co.* (1970). In this case, the publishing company and its editor-in-chief were charged with counselling the commission of an **indictable** offence that was not committed, namely, the cultivation of marijuana (contrary to the provisions of section 6 of the (now repealed) *Narcotic Control Act*). Under the heading "Plant Your Seeds," an issue of the *Georgia Straight* magazine contained an article that furnished detailed instructions concerning the planting, fertilization, cultivation, and harvesting of the marijuana plant. A woman who had purchased a copy of the magazine appeared as a witness at the trial and admitted she was not influenced by the counselling contained in the article concerned. However, the provincial court judge convicted both McLeod and the publishing company, stating that "if the person bought the paper and the only fair inference is that it was on public sale at the corner of Georgia and Granville street and if the person bought the paper and read it, they were in fact being counselled to grow marijuana." The defendants appealed to the B.C. Court of Appeal, which affirmed the company's conviction but set aside McLeod's conviction on the basis that there was "insufficient evidence" to convict him. Justice Maclean made the following significant observations:

> Defence counsel has suggested that "counselling" is not complete unless the person to whom the communication is directed has been influenced by the communication. I cannot accept this submission as in my view there is no justification for assigning such a limited meaning to the word "counselling." … In my view, the purchaser of this newspaper was counselled to cultivate marijuana.

In the somewhat bizarre case of *Glubisz* (1979), the B.C. Court of Appeal applied an extremely broad definition of the term "procure." Glubisz was charged with unlawfully procuring another person to commit first degree murder. The West Vancouver police had heard that the accused wished to "do away" with his wife and that he had engaged in conversations about killing her with a man named "Larry." The police arranged for a detective, Catlin, to pose as a "contract killer" and to communicate with Glubisz. Catlin called the accused a number of times in an attempt to make a deal to kill Glubisz's wife. After several calls, Catlin and the accused met. At this point, Catlin offered to kill the accused's wife for $2000. Glubisz finally agreed, gave Catlin some materials that identified his wife and suggested a time and place for the killing so that he could arrange an alibi. Glubisz was convicted at trial and appealed to the B.C. Court of Appeal, which dismissed his appeal. A central issue in the appeal was whether Glubisz could be found guilty of "procuring" when it was Catlin who had first approached the accused and persuaded the latter to engage him (Catlin) as a hired killer. The Court of Appeal held that these circumstances did not prevent Glubisz's actions from constituting procuring within the meaning of section 464 of the Code. Justice Aikins, who delivered one of the three concurring judgments stated that

> Counsel for the appellant gave us the third definition of "procure" from the Shorter Oxford English Dictionary—"to prevail upon, induce, persuade [a person] to do something." In my view, the crucial question is, what was the act on which the Crown relied as being procurement? It is true that in many cases of procuring, the procuring by an accused may involve a longer course of persuasion and bargaining with respect to the inducement, or otherwise, but, in my view, *procurement may consist of no more than the brief acceptance of an offer to commit a crime with the promise of reward for doing it.* What the Crown relies on as procurement in the present case appears to me to be the acceptance

by the appellant of Catlin's offer to kill his wife and the promise to pay $2000 if he did so. In my judgment, this amounts to procuring in the generally understood sense of that word and is within the dictionary definition because the promise to pay was (using the words of the definition) the inducing or persuading factor which completed the illegal bargain. [emphasis added]

Significantly, the Court of Appeal also ruled that it was immaterial that Catlin never had any intention of committing the offence "procured" by Glubisz.

An important principle was established in the *Gonzague* case (1983), which involved a charge of procuring the commission of the offence of first degree murder (which was, fortunately, not committed). The accused was convicted, but the Ontario Court of Appeal ordered a new trial on procedural and evidentiary grounds. However, the court also dealt with the issue of whether an accused person could renounce a previous act of incitement and, thereby, acquire a defence to a charge of procuring. The response of the court was both forthright and clear. In the words of Justice Martin,

> The offence of procuring under s. [464] is complete when the solicitation or incitement occurs even though it is immediately rejected by the person solicited, or even though the person solicited merely pretends assent and has no intention of committing the offence. There is no authority in either the Canadian or Commonwealth decision(s) in support of the view that renunciation of the criminal purpose constitutes a defence to a charge of "counselling, procuring or inciting" under s. [464]. ...

Attempts

SECTION 24 OF THE CODE AND ATTEMPTS
The crime of *attempting* to commit an offence, is, like all inchoate offences, somewhat unusual in that the criminal law is here concerned primarily with

the punishment of individuals for their criminal *intentions*. The rationale underlying the criminal law relating to attempts is clearly *preventive*. As Professor Stuart has remarked in his book, *Canadian Criminal Law: A Treatise* (1995),

> It would be preposterous if the police were powerless to intervene until a burglar had broken a window or a robber had robbed a bank. The law of attempts exists because there is usually just as much need to stop and punish a person who has unsuccessfully attempted, or is in the process of attempting, a crime as one who has already committed it.

The general provision concerning criminal attempts is set out in section 24 of the *Criminal Code*:

(1) Every one who, having an intent to commit an offence, does or omits to do anything for the purpose of carrying out his intention is guilty of an attempt to commit the offence whether or not it was possible under the circumstances to commit the offence.

(2) The question whether an act or omission by a person who has an intent to commit an offence is or is not mere preparation to commit the offence, and too remote to constitute an attempt to commit the offence, is a question of law.

The various punishments for criminal attempts are prescribed by section 463 of the Code:

Except where otherwise expressly provided by law, the following provisions apply in respect of persons who attempt to commit or any accessories after the fact to the commission of offences, namely,

(a) every one who attempts to commit or is an accessory after the fact to the commission of an indictable offence for which, upon conviction, an accused is liable to be sentenced to death or to imprisonment for life, is guilty of an indictable offence and is liable to imprisonment for fourteen years;

(b) every one who attempts to commit or is an accessory after the fact to the commission of an indictable offence for which, upon conviction, an accused is liable to imprisonment for fourteen years or less, is guilty of an indictable offence and is liable to imprisonment for a term that is one-half of the longest term to which a person who is guilty of that offence is liable; and

(c) every one who attempts to commit or is an accessory after the fact to the commission of an offence punishable on summary conviction is guilty of an offence punishable on summary conviction.

(d) every one who attempts to commit or is an accessory after the fact to the commission of an offence for which the offender may be prosecuted by indictment or for which he is punishable on summary conviction

    (i) is guilty of an indictable offence and is liable to imprisonment for a term not exceeding a term that is one-half of the longest term to which a person who is guilty of that offence is liable, or

    (ii) is guilty of an offence punishable on summary conviction.

The Code also contains special provisions relating to attempted high treason (section 46(1)(a)) and attempted murder (section 239).

THE *MENS REA* RELATING TO CRIMINAL ATTEMPTS

Since the major objective of the criminal law relating to attempts is unequivocally preventive in nature, it is scarcely surprising that the courts have emphasized the *mens rea* requirements of criminal attempts. As Justice Laidlaw commented in the *Cline* case (1956),

Criminal intention alone is insufficient to establish a criminal attempt. There must be *mens rea* and also an *actus reus*. But it is to be observed that whereas in most crimes it is the *actus reus* which the law endeavours to prevent, and the *mens rea* is only a necessary element of the offence, *in a criminal attempt the* mens rea *is of primary importance and the* actus reus *is the necessary element.* [emphasis added]

Significantly, section 24(1) of the Code clearly requires proof of "an intent to commit an offence" as a prerequisite for conviction of any criminal attempt. This requirement of an actual intent to commit an offence undoubtedly implies that the *mens rea* for an attempt may be quite different from that required for conviction of the completed offence. This situation would arise where the *mens rea* for the completed offence falls short of an intention to commit it.

Take, for example, the offence of unlawfully causing bodily harm, contrary to section 269 of the Code. In the *DeSousa* case (1992), the Supreme Court of Canada ruled that the accused may be convicted of the complete offence of unlawfully causing bodily harm without having the actual intention to cause bodily harm. However, in the case of a charge of *attempt* to unlawfully cause bodily harm, the Crown would be required to prove the intention to cause bodily harm before it could obtain a conviction against the accused. Indeed, this was precisely the conclusion of the Québec Court of Appeal when it considered this situation in the case of *Colburne* (1991). As Justice Lebel pointed out,

Even if in certain respects one may find it illogical that the incomplete offence [or attempt] requires a degree of *mens rea* greater than that required for the completed offence, to do otherwise is to transform the attempt into a purely relational offence whose constituent elements would strictly depend on the underlying offence. It exists by itself, although it requires the identification of the underlying offence that the author of the attempt was pursuing. Its distinctive element, in respect of the identification of its mental element, is found precisely in this desire to commit the underlying offence, which corresponds to the notion of specific intent. Section 24(1) makes an attempt a question of intent, of desire of a result and not only, for example, of negligence or gross imprudence, even if that would be sufficient to find the presence of the guilty mind required for the completed offence.

One of the implications of requiring proof of an actual intent to commit an offence is that all attempts will be treated by the courts as being crimes of **specific intent**; this, of course, means that the defence of intoxication may be raised in relation to attempts.

For many years, the courts have rigorously enforced the requirement that the Crown must prove *actual intent* in relation to a charge of an attempt to commit a crime. However, until relatively recently, a different approach was taken with respect to the specific offence of attempted murder (which is dealt with separately, in the *Criminal Code*, under section 239). It will be remembered that section 229(a) of the *Criminal Code* provides that culpable homicide is murder

(a) where the person who causes the death of a human being

(i) means to cause his death, or
(ii) means to cause him bodily harm that he knows is likely to cause his death, and is *reckless* whether death ensues or not. ... [emphasis added]

Undoubtedly, section 229(a)(ii) provides that the completed offence of murder may be committed by "reckless" defendants who deliberately inflict injuries that they know are likely to cause death. The issue was, therefore, raised as to whether accused persons may also be convicted of an *attempted* murder where they lack the intent to kill when inflicting serious injuries but are, nevertheless, "reckless" as to the likelihood of death (within the definition of section 229(a)(ii)). The Supreme Court of Canada answered this question in the affirmative in the case of *Lajoie* (1973). This meant that accused persons could be convicted of attempted murder even when they did not have the intention to kill their victims.

However, the Supreme Court of Canada subsequently overruled its own decision in the *Lajoie* case and re-established the principle that, for all types of attempts (including murder), the Crown must establish a genuine intent to commit the offence in question. The restoration of this critical principle occurred in the important case of *Ancio* (1984), in which the Crown had argued that an accused person should be convicted of attempted murder in any circumstance in which he or she would have been guilty of murder had the victim actually died. In *Ancio*, the contention was that the accused would have been convicted of murder under the provisions of section 230(d) of the *Criminal Code* (since repealed), if his victim had died from the gunshot wound inflicted by the accused during the course of a breaking and entering offence. Ancio stated that the gun had discharged accidentally. However, under section 230(d), the fact that the gunshot wound occurred accidentally would have been totally irrelevant had the victim died because, under this provision of the Code, the accused could have been convicted of murder whether or not he had the intention to kill. In the Crown's view, therefore, Ancio could properly be convicted of attempted murder in the circumstance where the victim fortuitously survived such a wound. Although the trial judge acccepted this argument and Ancio was convicted of attempted murder, the Supreme Court of Canada ultimately disagreed and ordered a new trial. In order to accomplish this result, the Supreme Court of Canada was obliged to overrule its own decision in the *Lajoie* case (which it did, by a majority of seven to one).

The judgment of Justice McIntyre in the *Ancio* case unequivocally places the offence of attempted

murder on the same footing as all other attempted crimes:

A reading of s. 24 of the Code and its predecessors since the enactment of the first Code in 1892 confirms that the intent to commit the desired offence is a basic element of the offence of attempt. Indeed, because the crime of attempt may be complete without the commission of any other offence and even without the performance of any act unlawful in itself, it is abundantly clear that the criminal element of the offence of attempt may lie solely in the intent. ...

The completed offence of murder involves a killing. The intention to commit the complete offence of murder must therefore include an intention to kill. I find it impossible to conclude that a person may intend to commit the unintentional killings described in ss. [229 and 230] of the Code. I am then of the view that the *mens rea* for an attempted murder cannot be less than the specific intent to kill.

Justice McIntyre also addressed the issue of whether it is illogical to require a higher degree of *mens rea* for the offence of attempted murder than for the completed offence of murder. He stated that

The intent to kill is the highest intent in murder and there is no reason in logic why an attempt to murder, aimed at the completion of the full crime of murder, should have any lesser intent. If there is any illogic in this matter, it is in the statutory characterization of unintentional killing as murder.

Clearly, the decision of the Supreme Court in the *Ancio* case represented a categorical return to an "orthodox" interpretation of the law relating to criminal attempts. To some extent, this approach was further solidified in the subsequent case of *Logan* (1990), which addressed the impact of the *Charter* on the offence of attempted murder. In *Logan*, the Supreme Court of Canada ruled that, in light of section 7 of the *Charter*, there can be no conviction of attempted murder unless the accused had subjective foresight of death.

The case of *Coleville* (1988) illustrates the proposition that the *mens rea* for an attempt may be *inferred* from the surrounding circumstances. The accused was charged with the attempted theft of a car. He was observed attempting to break into the car on the passenger's door side. He and his companion fled when they saw that they had been spotted. They were later apprehended by the police and were found to be in possession of a number of items that are frequently used to break into cars as well as to remove and replace starting mechanisms. The trial judge acquitted the accused on the basis that the evidence did not permit him to ascertain with certainty whether it was the victim's vehicle or its contents that the accused intended to steal. The Crown appealed, and the Québec Court of Appeal ultimately allowed the appeal and entered a conviction against the accused. Justice Chevalier said that

> The specific intent of a person found attempting to open a vehicle, while he has in his possession a "slim Jim" or a clothes-hanger is perhaps not totally certain. However, if one finds that in addition he has a tool which can be used to rip out the starting mechanism for the motor ("puller"), for which the intruder does not have the key, and a complete replacement mechanism for the one removed, I consider that one can logically conclude that the purpose of the operation was not to carry out some little search inside the area commonly called the glove compartment. It is only normal to think that it is the automobile and not its hypothetical contents that the intruder was attempting to steal. Even more so, when there is nothing in the evidence indicating that there were some suitable objects within the respondent's view which might have attracted his attention and stimulated his covetous desire.

THE *ACTUS REUS* REQUIREMENTS RELATING TO CRIMINAL ATTEMPTS

Providing a general definition of the *actus reus* requirements of criminal attempts is an extraordi-

narily difficult task since such requirements must necessarily vary in relation to the different types of criminal offences that may be attempted. Historically, the courts have discussed the issue of the *actus reus* of an attempt in terms of whether the accused's conduct was too "remote" from the completed offence to justify the imposition of criminal liability. The notorious and intractable problem underlying the law of criminal attempts is that of where to draw the line between acts that are sufficiently "proximate" to the completed offence so as to deserve the imposition of criminal liability upon the accused and acts that are too "remote" from the completed offence to justify any form of punishment. The dilemma was succinctly summarized by Baron Parke in the old English case of *Eagleton* (1855):

> The mere intention to commit a misdemeanour is not criminal. Some act is required, and we do not think that all acts towards committing a misdemeanour are indictable. Acts remotely leading towards the commission of the offence are not to be considered as attempts to commit it, but acts immediately connected with it are. ...

Significantly, section 24(2) of the Code provides that the question of whether an act or omission is to be considered "mere preparation to commit an offence, and [therefore] too remote to constitute an attempt to commit the offence," is to be treated as a "question of law" rather than fact; in other words, in a jury trial, this question must be answered by the trial judge as a matter of legal interpretation rather than by the jury as an issue of fact.

How have the courts actually dealt with the thorny issue of specifying the *actus reus* requirements of criminal attempts? In the past, they vainly attempted to devise a general test that could be applicable to all cases of criminal attempts. The history of the law of attempts is littered with the remains of such unsuccessful tests. Fortunately, the courts gradually came to realize that the judicial approach to the task of determining whether the *actus reus* requirements of the attempt have been established by the Crown must necessarily vary according to both the nature of the crime attempted and a number of circumstances peculiar to each individual case. Therefore, it now appears to be generally accepted that there can be no universal test that will determine the *actus reus* requirements of all criminal attempts.

An example of this more "flexible" approach to the determination of the *actus reus* requirements of criminal attempts is the leading Canadian case of *Cline* (1956). Justice Laidlaw delivered the judgment of the Ontario Court of Appeal and articulated a number of principles that have been widely applied by Canadian courts ever since:

> It is my respectful opinion that there is no theory or test applicable in all cases, and I doubt whether a satisfactory one can be formulated. Each case must be determined on its own facts, having due regard to the nature of the offence and the particular acts in question. ...
>
> The consummation of a crime usually comprises a set of acts which have their genesis in an idea to do a criminal act; the idea develops to a decision to do that act; a plan may be made for putting that decision into effect; the next step may be preparation only for carrying out the intention and plan; but when that preparation is in fact fully completed, the next step in the series of acts done by the accused for the purpose and with the intention of committing the crime as planned cannot, in my opinion, be regarded as remote in its connection with that crime. The connection is in fact proximate.

Justice Laidlaw then proceeded to specify a number of basic principles, including the following:

> (1) There must be *mens rea* and also an *actus reus* to constitute a criminal attempt, but the criminality of misconduct lies mainly in the intention of the accused. ... (4) It is not essential that the *actus reus* be a crime or a tort or even a moral wrong or social mischief. (5) The *actus reus* must be more

than mere preparation to commit a crime. But (6) *when the preparation to commit a crime is in fact fully complete and ended, the next step done by the accused for the purpose and with the intention of committing a specific crime constitutes an* actus reus *sufficient in law to establish a criminal attempt to commit that crime.* ... (emphasis added)

The factors in the *Cline* case illustrate the inherent difficulties involved in the task of determining whether the *actus reus* of attempt has been proved. Cline was charged with indecent assault on a twelve-year-old boy, Peter C. He was convicted at trial and appealed to the Ontario Court of Appeal, which set aside the conviction of indecent assault and, instead, substituted one for attempt (see section 660 of the Code). Cline had approached Peter C., asking him to carry his suitcases for a "couple of dollars." In fact, Cline had no suitcases with him. Peter C. said "no" and went on his way. The boy testified that Cline had been wearing dark sunglasses that "almost covered his whole face," even though the encounter took place at night. If Cline's conduct had been an isolated act, it is doubtful that the Crown would have been able to establish that an attempt to commit an indecent assault had been committed.

However, evidence was introduced that clearly established that Cline had previously approached a number of other boys in similar circumstances; in at least one of these cases, Cline had actually performed an indecent act without the victim's consent. The Court of Appeal ruled that this evidence was sufficient to establish the *mens rea* of the attempt to commit an indecent assault upon Peter C.: "evidence of similar acts done by the accused before the offence with which he is charged, and also afterwards if such acts are not too remote in time, is admissible to establish a pattern of conduct from which the Court may properly find *mens rea*." The remaining question to be resolved was whether Cline's approach to Peter C. constituted "mere preparation" or whether it could be considered sufficiently "proximate" to the completed offence so as to justify conviction of an attempt; in other words, had the Crown established the *actus reus* of the attempt? In dealing with this issue, Justice Laidlaw stated

> The appellant intended to commit the crime of indecent assault. He made a plan in detail to carry out his intention. The plan comprised a series of acts which form a clear-cut pattern of conduct, and the accused followed that pattern of conduct on all occasions or the occasion in question, and in precise accordance with that pattern of conduct, he chose a time and place where he might procure a victim necessary for the consummation of the crime. He went to that place at the chosen time. Before or after doing so he put on large sunglasses to disguise his identity. He then waited for the opportunity to pursue his planned conduct to the end. His preparation to commit the intended crime was fully complete. He was ready to embark on the course of committing the intended crime. It was necessary only to lure a victim to a secluded place. ... The acts of the appellant from the first moment he approached Peter C. were not preparation. They were not too remote to constitute an attempt to commit the offence of indecent assault. ...

A more recent example of the application of the flexible test articulated in the *Cline* case is furnished by the decision of the Supreme Court of Canada in *Deutsch* (1986). Deutsch was charged with attempting to procure women to have illicit sexual intercourse with other persons, contrary to the provisions of section 212(1)(a) of the Code. He interviewed three applicants for a secretary/sales assistant position with a franchise marketing business. During the course of the interviews, he indicated that a successful applicant would be expected to have sexual intercourse with clients if that was necessary to secure a contract for his company. He also suggested that a secretary/sales assistant could earn up to $100 000 per year from commission or bonuses in relation to the sale of franchises. Deutsch did not actually make an offer of employment during the interviews. After they had heard what the job entailed, all three of the women said that they were not interested. A police officer also posed as an applicant. When she indicated that she was interested in the position despite the unusual requirements, Deutsch did not make an offer of employment to her but, rather, told her to think it over and let him know.

The critical issue in the *Deutsch* case was whether the acts and statements of the accused were sufficient to constitute the *actus reus* of an attempt to procure women to have illicit sexual intercourse. In short, had he gone beyone mere preparation? The trial judge ruled that the accused's actions were too remote from the commission of the full offence of procuring and that, therefore, they did not amount to an attempt. The judge apparently believed that, if the accused had actually made an offer of employment, he would have crossed the line between preparation and attempt. Deutsch was, therefore, acquitted at his trial. However, the Crown launched a successful appeal to the Ontario Court of Appeal, which ordered a new trial on the basis that the accused had indeed committed an attempt to procure. The Supreme Court of Canada upheld the Court of Appeal's decision in this respect. Justice Le Dain agreed with the proposition that it was not possible to formulate a "satisfactory general criterion" for drawing the line between mere preparation and attempt. Indeed, he suggested that this distinction should be left to "common sense judgment" in the context of individual cases and that, in his opinion,

> the distinction between preparation and attempt is essentially a qualitative one, involving the relationship between the nature and quality of the act in question and the nature of the complete offence, although consideration must necessarily be given, in making that qualitative distinction, to the relative proximity of the act in question to what would have been the completed offence, in terms of time, location and acts under the control of the accused remaining to be accomplished.

Justice Le Dain also stated that the accused's actions could constitute the *actus reus* of an attempt

"When the preparation to commit a crime is in fact fully complete and ended, the next step done by the accused for the purpose and with the intention of committing a specific crime constitutes an actus reus *sufficient in law to establish a criminal attempt to commit that crime."* Cline *(1956).*

even if further acts were required on the part of the accused or a significant period of time might elapse before the offence could finally be completed. In the *Deutsch* case, Justice Le Dain believed that holding out the prospect of large rewards in the course of the interviews, during which the requirement of sexual intercourse with clients was mentioned, could indeed constitute the *actus reus* of an attempt to procure the women involved. It could be considered "an important step" in the commission of the offence:

> Before an offer of employment could be made in such circumstances an applicant would have to seek the position, despite its special requirement. Thus such inducement or persuasion would be the decisive act in the procuring. There would be little else that the appellant would be required to do towards the completion of the offence other than to make the formal offer of employment.

Similarly, in *Gladstone* (1996), the two accused were charged with attempting to sell herring spawn on kelp that had not been not caught under the authority of the licence required by the terms of the *Pacific Herring Regulations,* SOR/84-324. The accused were members of the Heiltsuk Band, and they shipped 4 200 pounds of herring spawn on kelp from Bella Bella to Richmond, a suburb of Vancouver. The accused entered a fish store in Vancouver and asked the owner if he was "interested" in herring spawn on kelp. The owner declined and the accused, who had been under surveillance, were arrested by fisheries officers. Their entire supply of herring spawn on kelp was later seized. The accused claimed that the requirement for a licence to sell herring spawn on kelp infringed their aboriginal right to fish. The case proceeded all the way to the Supreme Court of Canada, which ordered a new trial on the question of whether the fisheries regulations were valid. However, the Court did advert to the important issue of whether the Crown had established the necessary *actus reus* requirement for the charge of attempting to sell the herring spawn on kelp.

Chief Justice Lamer, in delivering the judgment of the majority of the Supreme Court, held that the accused had gone beyond mere preparation and had, in fact, attempted to sell the herring spawn on kelp:

> In this case the facts as found by the trial judge clearly demonstrate the appellants attempted to sell herring spawn on kelp to Mr. Hirose. The appellants arranged for the shipment of the herring spawn on kelp to Vancouver, they took a sample of the herring spawn on kelp to Mr. Hirose's store and they specifically asked Mr. Hirose if he was "interested" in herring spawn on kelp. *The appellants' actions have sufficient proximity to the acts necessary to complete the offence of selling herring spawn on kelp to move those actions beyond mere preparation to actual attempt.* [emphasis added]

ATTEMPTING THE IMPOSSIBLE

It will be remembered that section 24(1) of the Code provides that an accused person may be convicted of an attempt to commit an offence "whether or not it was possible under the circumstances to commit the offence." This provision may seem to be a little strange at first sight. However, Canadian courts have generally encountered few difficulties in applying it in practice. The judicial approach, in this matter, is well-illustrated by the leading case of *Scott* (1964). In this case, the accused was charged with attempting to steal "cash valued at less than $50." The facts were that Scott put his hand in the back pocket of a man called Dodd. Scott was apprehended by Dodd and turned over to the police. There was a wallet in Dodd's pocket but it contained no cash. The accused was convicted of attempted theft, and his subsequent appeal to the Alberta Court of Appeal was dismissed. Justice Macdonald, in delivering the majority judgment, stated that

> There can be no doubt about the appellant's attempt to steal from the pocket of Dodd. The difficulty arises from the fact that he was charged with attempting to steal money, while there is nothing in the evidence to show that Dodd had any money in his pocket.
>
> In the present case, the appellant pickpocket could not know what was in the pocket of Dodd. I think, however, it is a self-evident fact that a pickpocket is desirous of stealing money. A pickpocket could not be convicted of stealing money unless the money was there, but it does seem that an attempt to steal money stands on an entirely different footing.
>
> It seems to me that the proper and reasonable inference to be made under the circumstances that existed was that the appellant had the intent to steal money from the pocket of Dodd. The evidence established that the appellant did an act towards the accomplishment of that objective.

In *Dynar* (1997), the Supreme Court of Canada undertook an extensive analysis of the so-called question of "impossibility" in the law of criminal attempts and re-affirmed the view that section 24(1) of the Code must be given a literal interpretation insofar as it clearly precludes an accused per-

son from raising impossibility as a defence to a charge of attempt. *Dynar* involved an extradition request by the United States of America. Dynar had been the subject of a failed "sting" operation conducted by the Federal Bureau of Investigation in the United States, and the United States government now sought to extradite Dynar from Canada on charges of attempting to launder money and conspiracy to launder money. Dynar could not be extradited unless it could be established that his conduct would have amounted to a criminal attempt or criminal conspiracy if it had taken place entirely in Canada.

The two relevant money-laundering offences under Canadian criminal law arose under section 462.31(1) of the *Criminal Code* and section 19.2(1) of the (now repealed) *Narcotic Control Act*. At the time that the case first arose, the offences of money laundering under these two statutes required that the Crown prove that the accused laundered money "*knowing*" that it had been obtained by the commission of a designated offence. In fact, the moneys involved in the Dynar sting operation were not the proceeds of crime at all, but rather moneys belonging to the United States government. This meant that Dynar could not have committed the (completed) money laundering offences because one cannot *know* something that is not true. However, the critical question was whether he could instead be convicted of *attempting* and/or *conspiring* to commit these offences.

The Supreme Court of Canada ultimately rejected Dynar's argument that, since it would have been impossible for him to have committed the completed money-laundering offences, he had, therefore, not committed any offences known to Canadian law. Since the Court ruled that Dynar could potentially have been convicted of both an attempt and a conspiracy to commit the money-laundering offences, he was ordered to be extradited to stand trial in the United States.

On behalf of the majority of the Supreme Court, Justices Cory and Iacobucci stated that "sufficient evidence was produced to show that Mr. Dynar intended to commit the money-laundering offences, and that he took steps more than merely preparatory in order to realize his intention" and they pointed out that this was "enough to establish that he attempted to launder money contrary to s. 24(1) of the *Criminal Code.*" The Supreme Court essentially held that the issue of impossibility was, by virtue of the wording of section 24(1), totally irrelevant to the determination of whether an accused person is guilty of a criminal attempt. Indeed, Justices Cory and Iacobucci firmly noted that so-called "impossible" attempts "are no less menacing than other attempts":

> After all, the only difference between an attempt to do the possible and an attempt to do the impossible is chance. A person who enters a bedroom and stabs a corpse thinking he is stabbing a living person has the same intention as a person who enters a bedroom and stabs someone who is alive. In the former instance, by some chance, the intended victim expired in his sleep perhaps only moments before the would-be assassin acted. It is difficult to see why this circumstance, of which the tardy killer has no knowledge and over which he has no control, should in any way mitigate his culpability. Next time, the victim might be alive. Similarly, even if Mr. Dynar could not actually have laundered the proceeds of crime this time around, there is hardly any guarantee that his next customer might not be someone other than an agent of the United States Government.

It was clear that Dynar had attempted to engage in activities that, if they had been completed, would have fallen within the definition of crimes that were duly established under the *Criminal Code* and the (now repealed) *Narcotic Control Act.* However, it is noteworthy that the Supreme Court took the opportunity to make it clear that an accused person who attempts to do *something that does not, in fact, amount to a crime* cannot be found guilty of an attempt under section 24(1) — even if the accused fervently believes that he or she is involved in activity that is criminal. Putting it more simply, there

can be no criminal liability for attempting to commit an "*imaginary crime.*" As Justices Cory and Iacobucci noted in their judgment, there is a critical distinction between "a failed attempt to do something that is a crime and an imaginary crime":

> It is one thing to attempt to steal a wallet, believing such thievery to be a crime, and quite another to bring sugar into Canada, believing the importation of sugar to be a crime. In the former case, the would-be thief has the *mens rea* associated with thievery. In the latter case, the would-be smuggler has no *mens rea* known to law. Because s. 24(1) clearly provides that it is an element of the offence of attempt to have "an intent to commit an offence," the latter sort of attempt is not a crime.

The Supreme Court emphasized that the major purpose of the law of criminal attempts is to discourage individuals from committing subsequent offences. However, this purpose would not be served by punishing attempts to commit so-called "imaginary crimes." As Justices Cory and Iacobucci aptly pointed out,

> … one who attempts something that is not a crime or even one who actually does something that is not a crime, believing that what he has done or has attempted to do is a crime, has not displayed any propensity to commit crimes in the future, unless perhaps he has betrayed a vague willingness to break the law. Probably all he has shown is that he might be inclined to do the same sort of thing in the future; and from a societal point of view, that is not a very worrisome prospect, because by hypothesis what he attempted to do is perfectly legal.

REFORM OF THE LAW OF CRIMINAL ATTEMPTS

There is no doubt that the law relating to criminal attempts is riddled with vagueness and uncertainties—particularly insofar as the *actus reus* requirements of attempts are concerned. Some authorities have contended that the whole doctrine of criminal attempts should be abandoned, and that, instead, the definitions of the various substantive criminal offences should be redrafted so as to cover specifically all those acts that the legislature wishes to punish. In contrast, there are commentators who point out that such an approach would lead to hopelessly complicated definitions of substantive criminal offences and would also make it difficult for the police to perform a preventive role in battling crime. In their view, it is vital to retain the general offence of criminal attempts as a residual device to punish those who set in motion a train of events that, if it is not halted, will lead to the commission of a substantive criminal offence. However, even those authorities who would retain the doctrine of criminal attempts generally admit that the present law could be greatly improved.

For example, Professor Don Stuart has suggested, in his *Canadian Criminal Law: A Treatise* (1995), that there is much to commend the approach of the American Law Institute in its *Model Penal Code* (1962). The *Model Penal Code* not only retains a general offence of criminal attempt but also provides concrete guidance to courts that have to decide whether the accused's conduct in a particular case amounts to "mere preparation," on the one hand, or the *actus reus* of a criminal attempt, on the other. Provided the necessary *mens rea* requirements are satisfied, then, under the *Model Penal Code* provisions, an individual will be considered to have committed a criminal attempt when he or she performs an act or omission that constitutes "*a substantial step* in a course of conduct planned to culminate" in the commission of a crime. What is particularly useful in the approach adopted by the *Model Penal Code* is the articulation of concrete examples of situations in which the courts should hold that the accused has taken the "substantial step" that constitutes the *actus reus* of criminal attempt. For example, the following situations are considered to fall within the definition of a "substantial step": "lying in wait, searching for or following the contemplated victim of the crime"; "reconnoitering the place contem-

plated for the commission of the crime"; and "unlawful entry of a structure, vehicle or enclosure in which it is contemplated that the crime will be committed." Undoubtedly, this approach provides much greater certainty to the criminal law, while simultaneously preserving the flexibility necessary to the effective performance of the preventive functions of the police. However, to date, Parliament has not undertaken any reform of section 24 of the *Criminal Code* and, accordingly, Canadian courts are left to cope with a vague provision that offers little guidance as to how the inchoate crime of attempt should be defined. In the long run, the pervasive uncertainty generated by the existing law constitutes a very real threat to the civil liberties of all Canadians.

CONSPIRACY

The General Principles and Section 423

The criminal law relating to the inchoate offence of conspiracy is extraordinarily complex and probably deserves to be analyzed in a separate treatise. However, given the constraints of time and space in this book, we can only scratch the surface and offer a brief summary of some of the major issues raised by the crime of conspiracy.

Police authorities generally regard the offence of conspiracy as an absolutely vital weapon for fighting organized crime, and certainly a considerable number of convictions of individuals involved in organized crime are obtained primarily as a result of proving conspiracies through "wiretap" evidence. However, conspiracy is an offence that is viewed with extreme suspicion by civil libertarians, owing to its vague parameters. Furthermore, the power to charge an accused person with conspiracy is believed to place an unfair advantage in the hands of the Crown; indeed, the offence is sometimes referred to as "the darling in the prosecutor's nursery." Some of the trepidation experienced by civil libertarians when analyzing the nature of conspiracy is reflected in the following passage from Justice

Dickson's judgment, in the Supreme Court of Canada's decision in the case of *Cotroni and Papalia* (1979):

> Conspiracy is an inchoate or preliminary crime, dating from the time of Edward I, but much refined in the Court of Star Chamber in the 17th Century. Notwithstanding its antiquity, the law of conspiracy is still uncertain. It can, however, be said that the indictment for conspiracy is a formidable weapon in the armory of the prosecutor. According to the cases, it permits a vague definition of the offence, broader standards of admissibility of evidence apply; it may provide the solution to prosecutorial problems as to situs and jurisdiction. ... But the very looseness generally allowed for specifying the offence, for receiving proof, and generally in the conduct of the trial, imposes upon a trial Judge an added duty to ensure against the possibility of improper transference of guilt from one accused to another. There is, I have no doubt, a subconscious tendency upon the part of jurors in a conspiracy case to regard all co-conspirators alike and ignore the fact that guilt is something individual and personal.

The *Criminal Code* provision dealing with conspiracy is section 465, which states, in part, that

465(1) Except where otherwise expressly provided by law, the following provisions apply in respect of conspiracy, namely,

(a) every one who conspires with any one to commit murder or to cause another person to be murdered, whether in Canada or not, is guilty of an indictable offence and is liable to a maximum term of imprisonment for life.

(b) every one who conspires with any one to prosecute a person for an alleged offence, knowing that he did not commit that offence, is guilty of an indictable offence and is liable

(i) to imprisonment for a term not exceeding ten years, if the alleged offence is one for which, on conviction, that person would be liable to be sentenced to death or to imprisonment for life or for a term not exceeding fourteen years, or

(ii) to imprisonment for a term not exceeding five years, if the alleged offence is one for which, on conviction, that person would be liable to imprisonment for less than fourteen years;

(c) every one who conspires with any one to commit an indictable offence not provided for in paragraph (a) or (b) is guilty of an indictable offence and is liable to the same punishment as that to which an accused who is guilty of that offence would, on conviction, be liable; and

(d) every one who conspires with anyone to commit an offence punishable on summary conviction is guilty of an offence punishable on summary conviction.

It will be noted that, in general, the penalties for conspiracy are considerably more harsh than is the case for criminal attempts. Indeed, the penalties for conspiracy in relation to an indictable offence are normally identical to those imposed where the complete offence has actually been committed; however, in the case of criminal attempts, the penalties for attempting to commit indictable offences are (normally) only one half of those that may be imposed for committing the complete offence (section 463 of the Code). In the *Dynar* case (1997), the Supreme Court of Canada indicated why Parliament has treated conspiracy as constituting such a serious threat to social order. Indeed, Justices Cory and Iacobucci stated that

The crime has a long and malevolent history. Conspirators have plotted to overthrow monarchs from biblical times through the time of the Plantaganets and Tudors. Guy Fawkes conspired with others to blow up the parliament buildings. Today conspirators plot with others to carry out terrorist acts, to commit murders or to import forbidden drugs. *Society is properly concerned with conspiracies since two or more persons working together can achieve evil results that would be impossible for an individual working alone.* For example, it usually takes two or more conspirators to manufacture and secrete explosives or to arrange for the purchase, importation and sale of heroin. *The very fact that several persons in combination agree to do something has for many years been considered to constitute "a menace to society" ... In fact, the scale of injury that might be caused to the fabric of society can be far greater when two or more persons conspire to commit a crime than when an individual sets out alone to do an unlawful act.* [emphasis added]

The function of the *Criminal Code* provisions relating to conspiracy is, therefore, to prevent the conspirators from putting their unlawful plans into execution, i.e., to intervene and punish those involved *before* any serious harm is caused to society. Furthermore, according to Justices Cory and Iacobucci, the severe penalties are necessary to deter the accused from repeating their conduct in the future.

Curiously, the Code does not provide any statutory definition of the elements of conspiracy. As a consequence, Canadian courts have adopted the traditional common law requirements formulated by the English courts. For example, Justice Tachereau, in delivering the judgment of the majority of the Supreme Court of Canada in the case of *O'Brien* (1954) adopted the following definition of conspiracy, which had been fashioned by Justice Willes in the old English case of *Mulcahy* (1868):

> A conspiracy consists not merely in the intention of two or more, but in the agreement of two or

more to do an unlawful act, or to do a lawful act by unlawful means. So long as such a design rests in intention only, it is not indictable. When two agree to carry it into effect, the very plot is an action itself, and the act of each of the parties ... punishable if for a criminal object.

The *actus reus* of conspiracy is the agreement; the requisite *mens rea* is to be found in the *objective* of the agreement. The *actus reus* is complete as soon as agreement is reached between the parties. It, therefore, does not matter that no steps are subsequently taken in order to carry out the objective of the agreement; the parties are guilty of conspiracy just as soon as the agreement is reached with the necessary *mens rea*.

For the purpose of analysis, it may be useful to refer to the view of Justice Turgeon, expressed in the case of *McNaughton* (1976), that the offence of conspiracy may be analyzed in terms of three, separate elements:

> In order for there to be a conspiracy, the prosecution must prove 1. an agreement among the parties for a common purpose; 2. that this agreement existed between at least two persons; 3. that the common object was unlawful or, if the common object was lawful, that the planned means to accomplish it were unlawful.

Element 1: Agreement for a Common Purpose

The necessity of establishing the element of an agreement for a common purpose is well illustrated by the leading Canadian case of *Cotroni and Papalia* (1979). As Justice Dickson of the Supreme Court of Canada suggested, "the facts of the case are bizarre." Cotroni and Papalia were tried in Toronto on a charge that they, together with two men named Swartz and Violi, "unlawfully did conspire together each with the other and with persons unknown to have possession of $300 000, more or less, knowing that the said $300 000 was obtained by the commission in Canada of the indictable offence of extortion." The Crown contended that Swartz and Papalia extracted some $300 000 from one Bader and from one Rosen (a friend of Bader in Toronto). The money was paid in response to Swartz's story that Bader would be killed if he did not come up with the cash. Swartz indicated that the threats to Bader's life emanated from Montréal. Both Bader and Rosen believed Swartz's story implicitly. Approximately one year later, two residents of Montréal, Cotroni and Violi, came to believe that their names had been used in order to extort the $300 000 from Bader. They, therefore, telephoned Papalia and demanded the **extortion** money for themselves. Papalia indicated that he had only received $40 000 and suggested that they "beat up" Swartz to obtain the rest. Violi told Papalia that this information "[is] gonna save your life."

It was eventually agreed that Violi would come to Toronto to relieve Swartz of the money. The planned meeting in Toronto never took place. Cotroni, Papalia, Swartz, and Violi were all convicted of conspiracy. They appealed to the Ontario Court of Appeal. The appeals of Swartz and Papalia were dismissed, but the appeals of Cotroni and Violi were allowed. The Crown appealed Cotroni's acquittal (Violi having died in the interim period) to the Supreme Court of Canada, and Papalia appealed against the dismissal of his appeal.

The Supreme Court of Canada upheld the judgment of the Court of Appeal and dismissed the appeals of both the Crown and Papalia. Justice Dickson pointed out that there was no evidence of any "common agreement" or "common object" among Cotroni, Violi, Papalia, and Swartz. In his view, the evidence established the existence of two separate conspiracies. The first conspiracy involved Papalia and Swartz; its purpose was to have possession of the extorted money. The second conspiracy involved Cotroni and Violi and, possibly, Papalia; its purpose was to obtain, and subsequently to have possession of, a portion of the same money. Justice Dickson also pointed out that the second conspiracy took place solely within Québec, and therefore the Province of Ontario had no jurisdiction in rela-

tion to it. The learned justice proceeded to conclude that "this is not the conspiracy described in the indictment." Justice Dickson ruled that Papalia was properly convicted of the conspiracy with Swartz. However, he determined that "the only evidence against Cotroni is in respect of a conspiracy not covered by the indictment."

Justice Dickson's judgment casts considerable light on the requirement that there be an agreement for a common purpose:

The word "conspire" derives from two Latin words, "con" and "spirare," meaning "to breathe together." To conspire is to agree. *The essence of criminal conspiracy is proof of agreement.* On a charge of conspiracy the agreement itself is the gist of the offence. ... The *actus reus* is the fact of agreement. ... The agreement reached by the co-conspirators may contemplate a number of acts or offences. Any number of persons may be privy to it. Additional persons may join the ongoing scheme while others may drop out. So long as there is a continuing overall, dominant plan there may be changes in methods of operation, personnel, or victims, without bringing the conspiracy to an end. *The important inquiry is not as to the acts done in pursuance of the agreement, but whether there was, in fact, a common agreement to which the acts are referable and to which all of the alleged offenders were privy.* ... There must be evidence that the alleged conspirators acted in concert in pursuit of a common goal. ... Some improbable groupings of individuals have been held to be single conspiracies by the simple technique of positing a very general "object," and in the case at bar that technique was attempted. The Crown contends that the "object" was the indictable offence of having possession of funds knowing they were obtained by extortion, that there existed only one conspiracy to achieve one object and hence that all four accused may be convicted of conspiracy. This view overlooks the essential point that, in order to have a conspiracy, one must have agreement between the co-conspirators. There was simply *no* evidence of agreement between the four alleged conspirators. There was not the common purpose of a single enterprise, but rather the several purposes of two separate adventures. It is true that, in the most general of terms, it might be said that each of these adventures had a common object, money, with Swartz and Papalia in possession of extorted funds, and Cotroni and Violi desirous of relieving them of those funds, but there was no general agreement. A common desire to have money cannot create a conspiracy in the absence of a meeting of minds. The facts here show two competing and mutually exclusive objects. Counsel suggested the analogy of four hungry dogs, fighting over a bone. ... [emphasis added]

The courts have held that, although there must be a "common object" or "common agreement" in order to establish a conspiracy, it is not necessary for the Crown to establish that there is any *direct* communication between the co-conspirators (as the Newfoundland Court of Appeal decided in *Lawrence* (1987)). For this reason, it is possible to impose criminal liability for participation in so-called "chain" and "wheel" conspiracies. In a "chain" conspiracy, defendant A is in contact with defendant B, B with C, C with D, and so on. In a "wheel" conspiracy, one or more defendants communicate with each of the other conspirators, thus serving as the "hub" of the conspiracy. However, Canadian courts have been vigilant to ensure that the Crown does not roll up what are, in fact, several *separate* conspiracies into one overall conspiracy. For example, in *Longworth, Freeman, Newton and Wolfe* (1982), the Ontario Court of Appeal ruled that a drug dealer who purchases a relatively small quantity of drugs for the purpose of resale to his own customers does not, as a consequence of this simple purchase, thereby become a party to an overall conspiracy that has the distribution of drugs as its object and to which the distributor, his supplier, and all the distributor's customers are parties. In this particular case, the Crown had, inappropriately, attempted to establish the existence of a wheel conspiracy with the distributor allegedly being the hub of the conspir-

acy. In delivering the judgment of the Court of Appeal, Justice Martin said

I agree that it is not necessary to show that parties to a conspiracy were in direct communication with each other, or even that they were aware of the identity of the alleged co-conspirators. Moreover, it is not necessary to show that each conspirator was aware of all the details of the common scheme, but it must be shown that each of the conspirators were aware of the general nature of the common design and intended to adhere to it. ...

I cannot think that a retailer who purchases from a distributor a relatively small quantity of marijuana for resale to his customers *thereby* becomes a party to an overall conspiracy having for its object the distribution of marijuana (which might involve millions of dollars worth) and to which the distributor, his supplier and all the distributor's customers are parties. It seems to me that if the mere purchaser thereby becomes a party to such an over-all conspiracy, there is no logical reason why he does not equally become a party to a conspiracy to import where he knows that the marijuana is of foreign origin. ... I do not think that because the evidence permits an inference that the "retailer" (Newton) must have known that he was not the only customer of the distributor (Wolfe), and that the distributor in all likelihood had a supplier, without more, that fact makes him a party to an over-all conspiracy such as is here alleged. ... *There must be evidence beyond reasonable doubt that the alleged conspirators acted in concert in pursuit of a common goal.* [emphasis added]

In the *Longman, Freeman, Newton and Wolfe* case, the court evidently entertained a reasonable doubt as to whether the various accused parties had agreed to a common objective that involved the widespread distribution of illegal drugs. Therefore, it was not possible to find them guilty of participating in a broad conspiracy to traffic in drugs. However, where large quantities of drugs are sold, the court may well conclude that the parties involved in such large-scale transactions do indeed intend to participate in a broad conspiracy to distribute drugs; in other words, they form a common objective that goes far beyond the confines of the simple sale of the drugs by one party to another.

Take, for example, the case of *Chaulk and DiCristo* (1991), in which the accused had been charged with conspiracy to traffic in a narcotic drug (namely, cannabis resin). Chaulk had picked up at least one package containing cannabis resin from an Air Cargo Depot in the Wabush-Labrador city area. He had also sent at least two packages containing $9000 each to DiCristo in Montréal. Defence counsel raised the argument that a single transaction, involving the sale of a drug, could not support the conclusion that Chaulk and DiCristo formed the mutual objective to traffic in that drug. However, this contention was rejected at their trial and they were convicted. Their appeal to the Newfoundland Court of Appeal was subsequently dismissed. As Justice Marshall noted,

> Whether or not a single transaction forms the basis of a common design to traffic will depend upon whether the compact pursuant to which the transaction was undertaken is found to transcend beyond a mere agreement of purchase and sale between the dealer and buyer to one establishing an intention by both parties for resale. The scope to be attributed to such an agreement depends upon the individual circumstances.

Clearly, a critically important circumstance in this respect is the quantity of drugs involved. In the case of *Chaulk and DiCristo*, the amount of drugs contained in the package was quite inconsistent with the possession for the purpose of purely personal use, and therefore the inference could be drawn that it was intended for resale. On this basis, the Court of Appeal concluded that "the scope of the agreement of sale and purchase extends beyond transaction between the appellants and extends it to a conspiracy to traffic in the prohibited substance."

Where accused persons are alleged to have joined a *pre-existing conspiracy*, they may not be convicted of the crime of conspiracy unless the Crown can prove that they *adopted the criminal plan as their own and consented to participate in carrying it out.* Merely knowing about the existence of a conspiracy does not render one criminally liable. Take, for example, the case of *Lamontagne* (1999). It appeared that a criminal gang in Québec City possessed two stolen trailers and sought to sell them to a criminal gang in Montréal. The accused was an independent trucker who was contacted by an intermediary to bring his truck to a restaurant. The truck was driven away and was shortly thereafter returned to Lamontagne with a stolen trailer attached to it. Lamontagne was then arrested as he started to put gas into his vehicle. The accused was convicted of possession of the trailer (section 354(1) of the *Criminal Code*) on the basis that he was, at the very least, "wilfully blind" to the fact that it had been stolen. He was also convicted of conspiracy to commit theft and possession of stolen property. On his appeal to the Québec Court of Appeal, the conviction for possession of stolen property was upheld but, significantly, the conviction for conspiracy was quashed.

In acquitting Lamontagne of conspiracy, the Court of Appeal emphasized that the accused only learned of the existence of the stolen trailer several days after the members of the two criminal gangs had formed their plan to transfer the trailer from one gang to the other. This, in itself, would not prevent Lamontagne from becoming party to the conspiracy, but he could only do so by adopting the unlawful object (dealing in stolen property) as his own and by consenting to take part in its implementation. In the view of the Court of Appeal, the Crown could not prove these essential elements of the offence of conspiracy in the particular circumstances of this case. As Justice Dussault pointed out,

> It was not sufficient for the Crown to prove that the appellant was wilfully blind as to the unlawful provenance of his load, in order to prove that the appellant voluntarily participated in the conspiracy. *The Crown had to prove beyond a reasonable doubt that the appellant agreed with the other conspirators to commit the crime of possession of property*

MODES OF PARTICIPATION IN CRIME AND INCHOATE CRIMES

obtained by crime and to participate in achieving it. In my view, the Crown did not prove this. . . . [emphasis added]

In *O'Brien* (1954), the Supreme Court of Canada ruled that, in addition to a common agreement or common intention, the Crown must prove that there was "an intention to put the common design into effect." In other words, if a party to an alleged agreement does not intend to carry out the common object, that party cannot be convicted of conspiracy. In the *O'Brien* case, the accused was charged with having unlawfully conspired with one Tulley to commit the indictable offence of kidnapping. Tulley was not charged and was called as a Crown witness at O'Brien's trial. Tulley testified that he had met with the accused on a number of occasions and that, for the sum of $500, he had agreed to assist O'Brien in the kidnapping of a Mrs. Pritchard. Tulley also testified that he received $240 from O'Brien and that the accused had pointed out both the target and her residence to him. However, Tulley insisted that he "never had any intention of going through with this plan, but was just fooling the respondent, or hoaxing him." Tulley then indicated that he had both informed Pritchard of O'Brien's intentions and denounced the scheme to the police. O'Brien was convicted at his trial, but his appeal to the B.C. Court of Appeal was successful and a new trial was ordered. The Crown appealed this ruling to the Supreme Court of Canada, which affirmed the decision of the Court of Appeal.

O'Brien's counsel contended that, if Tulley never intended to carry out the agreement to kidnap Pritchard, he could not have been a party to a conspiracy. Since there were no other parties involved, O'Brien must be acquitted because he could not conspire with himself. The Supreme Court of Canada essentially accepted this contention. In the words of Justice Tachereau, who delivered the judgment of the majority of the Court,

It is, of course, essential that the conspirators have the *intention to agree*, and this agreement must be complete. There must also be a common

design to do something unlawful, or something lawful by illegal means. Although it is not necessary that there should be an overt action in furtherance of the conspiracy, to complete the crime, I have no doubt that *there must exist an intention to put the common design in to effect.* A common design necessarily involves an intention. Both are synonymous. The intention cannot be anything else but the will to attain the object of the agreement. I cannot imagine several conspirators agreeing to defraud, to restrain trade, or to commit any indictable offence, without having the intention to reach the common goal. . . .

This is not the case of the conspirator, who after having completed the crime, withdraws from the conspiracy. If a person, with one or several others, agrees to commit an unlawful act, and later, after having had the intention to carry it through, refuses to put the plan into effect, that person is nevertheless guilty, because all the ingredients of conspiracy can be found in the accused's conduct. But, when the conspiracy has never existed, there can be no withdrawal. [emphasis added]

In O'Brien's case, there was only one other potential co-conspirator (namely, Tulley), and once it was established that he did not have the intention to put the agreement into effect, it was clear that the accused could not be convicted of the offence charged because it takes at least two parties to hatch a conspiracy. However, as long as at least two parties to an alleged conspiracy do have the intention to carry out the agreement, it does not matter that various other alleged co-conspirators lack such intent. As Justice Lambert of the B.C. Court of Appeal said in the case of *Miller* (1984),

the lack of intent of two of the co-conspirators, even if established, does not afford any defence to the other conspirators who have the requisite intent, unless the number of conspirators who have the requisite intent is reduced to one person. At that stage he cannot agree with himself and would be acquitted.

On the other hand, it is important to bear in mind that the courts will normally assume that an accused person who has entered into an agreement to commit an offence does, in fact, intend to carry it out. As the Supreme Court of Canada noted in the *Nova Scotia Pharmaceutical Society* case (1992),

> the Crown must prove that the accused had the intention to enter into the agreement and had knowledge of the terms of that agreement. Once that is established, *it would ordinarily be reasonable to draw the inference that the accused intended to carry out the terms in the agreement,* unless there was evidence that the accused did not intend to carry out the terms of the agreement. [emphasis added]

It should be mentioned that it is possible to become a party to a conspiracy on the basis of *aiding and/or abetting* members of a conspiracy (section 21(1)(b) and (c) of the Code) or *counselling* other persons to join a conspiracy (section 22(1) of the Code). For example, in *Vucetic* (1998), the Ontario Court of Appeal ruled that an accused person may be convicted of conspiracy if he or she provides assistance or encouragement to members of an existing conspiracy—provided the Crown could prove that the accused "knew the object of the conspiracy" and that the assistance "was intended to assist the conspirators in attaining their unlawful criminal object." Similarly, in *Bérubé* (1999), the Québec Court of Appeal held that it is "well-established in jurisprudence that one can be found guilty of conspiracy to commit an indictable offence by encouraging someone to become a member of the conspiracy."

Element 2: An Agreement Between at Least Two Persons—It Takes Two to Tango?

It is a common sense proposition that, since an agreement constitutes the essence of a conspiracy, there must be at least two parties. As the Supreme

Court ruled in *O'Brien* (1954), an accused person cannot be convicted of conspiring with him- or herself.

In Canadian criminal law, one of the consequences of this requirement is that a husband cannot be convicted of conspiracy with his wife and *vice versa*. In the case of *Kowbel* (1953), the Supreme Court of Canada justified this rule on the basis that, historically, spouses have been treated, for the purpose of the law, as "one person." The apparent policy underlying the rule was the perceived need to maintain the stability of the marriage institution. However, it is important to remember that this rule only applies in the situation where the husband and wife are the only alleged co-conspirators. As the Ontario Court of Appeal stated in *Rowbotham* (1988) case, "although a husband and wife cannot be convicted of conspiring with one another, they can severally or jointly conspire with other persons." In this particular case, which involved an alleged conspiracy to import and traffic in narcotics, the court set out the applicable principles in the following fashion:

> It was incumbent on the Crown to prove that Laura Konow was aware of the general scheme to traffic in hashish in which others, in addition to her husband, were involved. It was not, of course, necessary for the Crown to prove that she knew the identities of the other parties to the common design or the precise details of the agreement. If the jury found the requisite knowledge was brought home to Laura Konow, it was open to them to draw the inference that she was a participant in the over-all conspiracy alleged.

Similarly, in *Barbeau* (1996), the accused and her husband were charged, along with three other men, of the offence of conspiracy to import cocaine. Barbeau stated that all she had done was to give and transcribe messages by phone and fax because her husband's grasp of English was poor. She said that she had no knowledge of any conspiracy and that she thought the messages related to contraband cigarettes, not cocaine. Although there was no evidence that the accused had met or conspired with the other alleged co-conspirators or that she had agreed with anyone to join a conspiracy, the Crown took the position that she "knew that her husband was involved with others in a conspiracy to import cocaine and that she participated in it by her own acts in furtherance of the object of the conspiracy." Barbeau was convicted at her trial, but the Québec Court of Appeal subsequently set aside the conviction and ordered a new trial. The trial judge had instructed the members of the jury that they could find the accused guilty of conspiracy if she had been "wilfully blind" as to the existence and nature of the conspiracy that allegedly involved her husband. In so doing, the trial judge left the impression that the test for *wilful blindness* is an *objective* one — namely, would a *reasonable* person have asked questions in the particular set of circumstances facing the accused? In delivering the judgment of the Court of Appeal, Justice Rothman emphasized that wilful blindness is a form of *subjective*, not *objective*, *mens rea* and that, therefore, it was a serious error for the trial judge to have instructed the jury to consider what a "normal" person would have done in light of the knowledge that Barbeau had of the whole situation:

> The test was not whether the appellant "should" have known or should "normally" have known from the suspicious circumstances that her husband was probably involved in a conspiracy to import cocaine. *The question was whether the circumstances were such that she, herself, was in fact, suspicious that this was the case but deliberately refrained from making inquiries so that she could remain in ignorance as to the truth.* [emphasis added]

Another implication of the "two parties" requirement is that, where an undercover police officer or **agent provocateur** makes an agreement with *only one other party*, there can be no conspiracy since, as the *O'Brien* case illustrates, the officer or *agent provocateur* will not have the intention to put the common design into effect. (It is possible that the other party could be convicted, instead, of counselling an offence.) Of course, if there is an agree-

ment with more than one other party, there can be a conspiracy even through the office or *agent provocateur* is not personally guilty of the offence.

Element 3: Unlawful Object or Means

Until 1985, the *Criminal Code* (section 423(2)) stated that

> Every one who conspires with any one
>
> (a) to effect an unlawful purpose, or
> (b) to effect a lawful purpose by unlawful means,
>
> is guilty of an indictable offence and is liable to imprisonment for two years.

This provision, which was derived from the old English common law, was extremely vague and it created the situation in which an individual who conspired to commit an offence punishable on summary conviction (such an offence would constitute an "unlawful purpose") could be prosecuted for the offence of conspiracy, which was triable only on indictment. Clearly, the prosecution of an accused person by an indictment (the most serious form of criminal proceeding) for conspiring to commit a mere summary conviction offence raised some major questions concerning the fairness of the criminal law. Fortunately, in 1985, the *Criminal Code* was amended and section 423(2) was repealed. Section 423(1)(d) now states that it is an indictable offence to conspire to commit an indictable offence, and section 423(1)(e) states that it is a summary conviction offence to conspire to commit a summary conviction offence.

This amendment indubitably represents a much more satisfactory approach to the offence of conspiracy and clearly enhances the rationality of the relevant *Criminal Code* provisions. However, as Professor Stuart aptly points out in *Canadian Criminal Law: A Treatise* (1995), it is not entirely clear whether there is any limitation on the type of summary conviction offences that might be the subject of a conspiracy. Since 1985, there have not been any decided cases that have addressed the question of whether section 423(1)(e) covers all summary conviction offences, regardless of their seriousness, or whether there should be some criteria that restrict the operation of the section to those offences in relation to which a conspiracy would pose a significant threat to the public.

However, it is clear that a conspiracy must involve an intent to commit a crime that is known to Canadian criminal law. Just as one cannot *attempt* to commit an "imaginary crime," so one cannot *conspire* to commit an "imaginary" crime. The Supreme Court of Canada firmly underscored this point in the *Dynar* case (1997). As Justices Cory and Iacobucci stated in their majority judgment, planning to commit "imaginary crimes" falls outside the scope of the law: "conspiracy to commit such fanciful offences cannot give rise to criminal liability."

On the other hand, it is important to bear in mind that, provided the accused conspire to commit an offence known to the law, then it is irrelevant that, for some reason, it would have been impossible for the accused to complete the offence. In this respect, the law of conspiracy is identical to the law of criminal attempts (see the earlier discussion of *Dynar* in the section on attempts). As the Supreme Court of Canada ruled in the *Dynar* case (1997), the rationale for punishing those who conspire to commit a crime is to punish them *before* their combined efforts cause harm to society. Furthermore, according to Justices Cory and Iacobucci,

> ... *since the offence of conspiracy only requires an intention to commit the substantive offence, and not the commission of the offence itself, it does not matter that, from an objective point of view, commission of the offence may be impossible.* It is the subjective point of view that is important, and from a subjective perspective, conspirators who intend to commit an indictable offence intend to do everything necessary to satisfy the conditions of the offence. The fact that they cannot do so because an objective circumstance is not as they believe it to

be does not in any way affect this intention. The intention of the conspirators remains the same, regardless of the absence of the circumstance that would make the realization of that intention possible. It is only in retrospect that the impossibility of accomplishing the design becomes apparent. [emphasis added]

It will be remembered that, in the *Dynar* case (1997), the accused would not have been able to complete the offence of money laundering because the funds that he believed were the fruits of crime were actually moneys belonging to the United States government. Since the offence, at that time, required proof of *knowledge* that the funds were the proceeds of crime, Dynar could not be convicted of the completed offence of money laundering because he could not "know" something that was, in fact, false. However, as we have already seen, the Supreme Court of Canada had no difficulty in stating that Dynar could have been convicted of *attempting* to launder illicitly obtained money, and the very same logic was robustly applied to the offence of *conspiracy* to carry out this criminal intention.

STUDY QUESTIONS

1. Arthur and Desmond are sitting on a bench in the Paradise Shopping Mall. They suddenly notice that one of their friends, Fred, has without any warning attacked Goliath, a security guard. Arthur and Desmond get up and walk over to see what is happening at close quarters. Although Fred's attack is quite vicious, neither Desmond nor Arthur do anything to help the unfortunate Goliath. Desmond laughs loudly and Arthur yells, "Great stuff, Fred." Goliath is saved by the intervention of a passing law and security student. Fred is later convicted of assault causing bodily harm. Are Desmond and Arthur guilty of the same offence? Would it make any difference to your answer if you were told that

Desmond is a plainclothes police officer, taking a break for his lunch?

2. Tom, Dick, and Harry make an agreement to kidnap Ludwig (who is the heir to a vast fortune). The three men watch Ludwig's movements for a couple of days and Tom (the ring leader) then pays Dick and Harry $50 each "for services rendered." Harry then exposes the kidnapping plot to the police. He claims that he never really meant to take part in this plan, but went along with it only as a means of "learning enough to protect Ludwig." Tom, Dick, and Harry are charged with conspiracy to kidnap Ludwig. Are any (or all) of the co-accused guilty of the offence charged?

3. Egbert and Marmaduke decide to rob a store, owned by Horace. Marmaduke is known to be a very violent person. Egbert acts as the lookout while Marmaduke is in the store. However, Egbert, who is becoming very fearful, decides to abandon the robbery and runs away before Marmaduke has completed his task in the store. Meanwhile, Marmaduke discovers that Horace is surprisingly unwilling to part with the money in his cash register. Marmaduke eventually strangles him and flees the scene, taking some $500 in cash with him. Marmaduke is subsequently killed in a car accident as he tries to make good his escape. However, Egbert is later arrested by the police and Crown counsel is wondering whether charges should be laid against him. What charges (if any) could reasonably be laid against Egbert?

4. Cecil and Eustace decide to rob the Tight Fist Bank. They make elaborate plans and purchase some firearms to assist them in their venture. On the appointed day, they drive to a street corner just one block away from the bank; they intend to observe the bank for a while and then undertake the robbery at the most appropriate moment. However, a police cruiser passes by and the two officers notice that Cecil and Eustace look suspicious. The officers arrest the would-be bandits when they

find two sawn-off shot guns and two masks on the back seat of the car. Cecil and Eustace are subsequently charged with attempted robbery. Are they guilty of this offence?

5. Lancelot decides to steal a valuable diamond ring from Arthur. He goes to Arthur's house and tries to obtain entry by inserting a credit card into the lock on the front door. He is unable to open the door and returns to a bar, where he drowns his sorrows in whiskey. Guinevere, Lancelot's close friend, is disappointed when she discovers that he has failed to fulfill his criminal mission. She, therefore, travels to Arthur's house, where she manages to obtain entrance by using a set of skeleton keys. However, when she looks in the box in which Arthur usually keeps the ring, she discovers that it is empty. Arthur has taken the ring to a local jeweller for repairs. Merlin, who lives in the basement of Arthur's house, tells the police that he saw exactly what Lancelot and Guinevere had done and that he had heard them talk, on previous occasions, about stealing Arthur's ring. What charges (if any) could reasonably be laid against Lancelot and Guinevere?

6. Buccaneer believes that it is an offence to bring a certain type of computer chip into Canada without declaring it (and paying any duty). He arrives at an international airport in Canada, having concealed a large number of the tiny computer chips at the bottom of his suitcase. He attempts to pass through Canada Customs without declaring his hidden cargo. When his luggage is searched, the chips are discovered by a vigilant customs officer. However, the officer informs Buccaneer that, owing to the recent signing of a free-trade agreement, this particular type of computer chip can now be imported into Canada without the need to pay any duty. Is Buccaneer guilty of a criminal offence? Would it make any difference to your answer if Buccaneer had agreed with his partner, Swallow, to smuggle the computer chips on a joint basis?

FURTHER READING

Alexander, L. and K.D. Kessler. 1997. *Mens Rea* and Inchoate Crimes. 87 *Journal of Criminal Law & Criminology:* 1138.

Ashworth, A. 1995. *Principles of Criminal Law.* 2d ed. Oxford: Oxford University Press. Chaps. 10, 11.

Crampton, S. and J.T. Kissick. 1993. Recent Developments in Conspiracy Law and Enforcement: New Risks and Opportunities. 38 *McGill Law Journal:* 569.

Davis, M. 1986. Why Attempts Deserve Less Punishment Than Complete Crimes. 5 *Law and Philosophy:* 1.

Delisle, R.J. 1987. Annotation: *R. v. Thatcher.* 57 *Criminal Reports (3d):* 98.

Department of Justice Canada. 1994. *Towards a New General Part of the* Criminal Code *of Canada.* Ottawa: Department of Justice (December 5, 1994). 28–30.

Goode, M.R. 1975. *Criminal Conspiracy in Canada.* Toronto: Carswell.

Hoeber, P.R. 1986. The Abandonment Defense to Criminal Attempt and Other Problems of Temporal Individuation. 74 *California Law Review:* 377.

Katz, L. 2000. Why the Successful Assassin Is More Wicked than the Unsuccessful One. 88 *California Law Review:* 791.

Law Reform Commission of Canada. 1985. Working Paper No. 45: *Criminal Law; Secondary Liability: Participation in Crime and Inchoate Offences.* Ottawa: L.R.C.C.

———. 1987. Report No. 31: *Recodifying Criminal Law.* 2d ed. Ottawa: L.R.C.C. 45–49.

Mackinnon, P. 1977. Conspiracy and Sedition as Canadian Political Crimes. 23 *McGill Law Journal:* 622.

———. 1981. Developments in the Law of Criminal Conspiracy. 59 *Canadian Bar Review:* 301.

———. 1982. Making Sense of Attempts. 7 *Queen's Law Journal:* 253.

———. 1986. Attempting Murder Recklessly: The Significance of *R. v. Ancio.* 28 *Criminal Law Quarterly:* 121.

McWilliams, P.K. 2000. *Canadian Criminal Evidence.* 3d ed. Aurora, Ont.: Canada Law Book. Chap. 22.

Manson, A. 1989. Recodifying Attempts, Parties and Abandoned Intentions. 14 *Queen's Law Journal:* 85.

Meehan, E. 1984. *The Law of Criminal Attempt—A Treatise.* Calgary: Carswell.

Meehan, E.R. 1979. The Trying Problem of Criminal Attempt—Historical Perspectives, 14 *U.B.C. Law Review:* 137.

Mewett, A.W. and M. Manning. 1994. *Mewett & Manning on Criminal Law.* 3d ed. Toronto: Butterworths. 268–93, 303–46.

Minister of Justice of Canada. 1993. *White Paper: Proposals to Amend the Criminal Code (General Principles).* Ottawa: Minister of Justice of Canada (June 28, 1993).

Smith, J.C. 1997. Criminal Liability of Accessories: Law and Law Reform. 113 *Law Quarterly Review:* 453.

Stuart, D. 1995. *Canadian Criminal Law: A Treatise.* 3d ed. Toronto: Carswell. 547–652.

———. 1999. A Case for a General Part. In R.J. Delisle and A. Manson, eds. *Towards a Clear and Just Criminal Law: A Criminal Reports Forum.* 95. Toronto: Carswell.

Stuart, D. and R.J. Delisle. 1997. *Learning Canadian Criminal Law.* 6th ed. Toronto: Carswell. Chaps. 8, 9.

Verdun-Jones, S.N. 1999. *Canadian Criminal Cases: Selected Highlights.* Toronto: Harcourt Brace. Chap. 6.

CHAPTER

8

Mental Disorder as a Defence: The Verdict of Not Criminally Responsible on Account of Mental Disorder (NCRMD)

OVERVIEW

This chapter examines the following:

1. The way in which the criminal law deals with defendants who are suffering from mental disorder;
2. the defence of "not criminally responsible on account of mental disorder" (NCRMD), which is set out in section 16 of the *Criminal Code*;
3. the evolution of (what used to be known as) the insanity defence from the articulation of the so-called *M'Naghten* Rules in 1843 and the original *Criminal Code* formulation of the defence in 1892 right up to the present day;
4. the interpretation of section 16 by the Canadian courts (in particular by the Supreme Court of Canada) in a series of recent decisions;
5. the special verdict that, in most cases, results in the NCRMD acquittee being subject to restraints on his or her freedom (in some cases, such restraints may include detention in a secure mental health facility);
6. a number of important procedural issues that arise in the specific context of the NCRMD defence, including the presumption that a defendant is not suffering from a mental disorder so as to be exempt from criminal responsibility (section 16(2) of the *Criminal Code*) and the power of the Crown to raise the NCRMD defence contrary to the wishes of the accused.

INTRODUCTION

As Justice McLachlin, as she then was, said in the Supreme Court of Canada's recent decision in the *Winko* case (1999),

> In every society, there are those who commit criminal acts because of mental illness. The criminal law must find a way to deal with these people fairly, while protecting the public against further harms. The task is not an easy one.

In Canada, this difficult task is undertaken through the application by the courts of the special defence of *not criminally responsible on account of mental disorder* (**NCRMD**). Since our system of criminal law is constructed on the premise that individuals should not be convicted of an offence unless they deliberately chose to do something wrong, the case of the mentally disordered offender clearly raises some fundamental questions about the appropriateness of applying the criminal law to persons who may not be capable of making real choices because of their mental illness. As Chief Justice Lamer of the Supreme Court of Canada said in the *Chaulk* case (1990),

> The rationale underlying the [NCRMD] defence in Canada ... rests on the belief that persons suffering from insanity should not be subject to standard criminal culpability with its resulting pun-

ishment and stigmatization. This belief, in turn, flows from the *principle that individuals are held responsible for the commission of criminal offences because they possess the capacity to distinguish between what is right and what is wrong.* [emphasis added]

However, as we shall soon see, the mere fact that an **accused** person was mentally disordered at the time of the alleged offence does not automatically excuse him or her from criminal responsibility. Indeed, only a relatively few mentally disordered persons meet the strict criteria for the successful application of the NCRMD defence.

The NCRMD defence is concerned with the state of mind of the accused person *at the time that the alleged offence was actually committed*. If the accused person concerned could not appreciate the nature or quality of the act or omission in question or did not realize it was wrong (in the sense that it would be morally condemned by reasonable members of society), he or she will be duly acquitted. Nevertheless, it is critical to bear in mind that the NCRMD defence is something of a misnomer. Indeed, it is not really a defence in the true sense of the word because, as section 672.1 of the *Criminal Code* clearly states, a verdict of NCRMD is not a finding that the accused "didn't do it" but rather a ruling that "the accused committed the act or made the omission that formed the basis of the offence with which the accused is charged but is not criminally responsible on account of mental disorder." Furthermore, although the **defendant** is found "not criminally responsible," he or she is not automatically entitled to walk out of the courtroom as a free man or woman; instead, the accused may well be subjected to restraints on his or her liberty (including the very real possibility of detention in a secure mental health facility).

The modern foundations for the Canadian NCRMD defence were laid in two notorious nineteenth-century cases decided in England. In the *Hadfield* case (1800), the accused was charged with high treason after having fired a pistol shot over the head of King George III. Hadfield was acquitted of the charge because of his mental disorder (or "insanity") at the time of the shooting. However, the court was most concerned with the question of what should be done with Hadfield. The jury was asked to bring in a verdict that specified that the accused was being acquitted because he had been "under the influence of insanity at the time the act was committed"; the jurors duly obliged the court, and the Chief Justice remanded Hadfield to Newgate Prison from where he had come for his trial. Hadfield was never released from custody again (although he did escape for a brief period during 1802); indeed, he was incarcerated until his death in 1841, and of the 41 years that he suffered in confinement, twelve of them were spent in prison. Hadfield's case is significant because it established the principle that a person acquitted of a criminal charge because of a mental disorder would not automatically be set free "to walk the streets."

As a direct consequence of the *Hadfield* acquittal, the English Parliament passed The *Criminal Lunatics Act* of 1800. This Act created the special verdict of insanity (which had been foreshadowed in the *Hadfield* case) and empowered the court to order the strict confinement of an insanity acquittee until "His Majesty's pleasure be known" (that is, indefinitely). Interestingly enough, Parliament took the somewhat unusual step of declaring the Act to be retroactive so as to apply to Hadfield himself. As we shall see, these particular stipulations of the 1800 Act were later adopted in Canada and, to some extent, are still reflected in the present day provisions of the *Criminal Code* (namely, the requirement that a *special verdict* be delivered in such cases, and the specification of a procedure that permits the imposition of post-trial restraints on the liberty of a person found "not criminally responsible" on the basis of the NCRMD defence).

The other nineteenth-century case, which has had a major impact on the shape of the so-called insanity defence in the English-speaking world, was the case of Daniel M'Naghten (also spelled McNaughtan), the namesake of the celebrated *M'Naghten* Rules. In 1843, M'Naghten shot and killed Edward Drummond (the Secretary to Sir

Robert Peel, the Prime Minister of the day). M'Naghten shot at Drummond under the mistaken impression that he was Sir Robert Peel. M'Naghten believed that Peel and the Tories were responsible for a systematic campaign of persecution against him. M'Naghten was duly tried for **murder** and had the excellent fortune to be defended by the brilliant Queen's Counsel, Alexander Cockburn. At his trial, evidence was presented that M'Naghten was insane at the time of the shooting, and he was acquitted by the jury, who brought in a special verdict of insanity. It was generally felt that the test of insanity that had apparently been applied by the jury went considerably beyond the scope of the existing law. It had been argued that, even though M'Naghten's conduct had to a large extent appeared rational and even though he clearly knew what he was doing and was capable of telling right from wrong, he nevertheless was suffering from a form of insanity that deprived him of all "power of self-control." The jury's verdict seemed to imply that, even though M'Naghten knew what he was doing and that it was wrong, he should be acquitted because his delusions of persecution caused him to lose his ability to control his actions.

M'Naghten was subsequently confined in hospital until his death in 1865. Although M'Naghten was kept in strict custody, there was a public outcry against his acquittal. Even Queen Victoria herself indicated that she definitely was "not amused." As a consequence of this negative public reaction, the House of Lords was asked a series of questions concerning the appropriate test of "insanity" that should be presented to a jury in future cases. Their Lordships' answers to the questions constitute what have become known as the *M'Naghten* Rules. The most important statement was as follows:

> We have to submit our opinion that the jurors ought to be told in all cases that every man is presumed to be sane and to possess a sufficient degree of reason to be responsible for his crimes until the contrary be proved to their satisfaction, and that to establish a defence on the ground of insanity it must be clearly proved that, *at the time of the com-*

> *mitting of the act the party accused was labouring under such a defect of reason, from disease of the mind, as not to know the nature and quality of the act he was doing, or, if he did know it, that he did not know he was doing what was wrong.* [emphasis added]

It may well be conjectured that their Lordships felt that M'Naghten should really have been convicted of murder. After all, the somewhat narrow test of insanity they articulated would almost certainly not have been applicable to the specific facts of M'Naghten's case because M'Naghten did appear to have known what he was doing and that it was wrong to kill another human being. It is, therefore, one of the supreme ironies of legal history that the test of insanity, which is still applicable in England, Wales, and (in a modified version) Canada, bears M'Naghten's name.

The debate over the precise meaning of the *M'Naghten* Rules has raged for more than 150 years. The major criticism levelled against the rules is that they focus almost exclusively on *cognitive* factors (that is, the accused's reasoning abilities) to the apparent exclusion of *emotional* and *volitional* factors. In particular, the rules have been criticized for not taking into account the proposition that individuals may be perfectly aware of what they are doing and know that it is "morally wrong," but may, nevertheless, be utterly incapable of controlling their conduct.

THE NCRMD DEFENCE IN CANADA

The basic elements of the *M'Naghten* Rules were incorporated into Canada's *Criminal Code* in 1892, although there were a number of significant modifications, as we shall see shortly. The present version of the rules, defining the circumstances in which a mentally disordered accused must be acquitted of a criminal charge, is set out in section 16 of the Code:

> 16(1) No person is criminally responsible for an act committed or an omission made while

suffering from a mental disorder that rendered the person incapable of appreciating the nature and quality of the act or omission or of knowing that it was wrong.

As the reader will immediately notice, this provision of the modern *Criminal Code* bears a close resemblance to the *M'Naghten* Rules of 1843. However, some significant differences must be taken into account. Perhaps the most significant variation between the *M'Naghten* Rules and the version of section 16 originally enacted by the Canadian Parliament in 1892 is the use of the word "appreciate" as a substitute for the word "know" in the original phrase "know the nature and quality of the act." In addition, the Canadian Parliament referred to the issue of the accused's "capacity" to appreciate the nature and quality of an act or omission or to know that it was "wrong," whereas the *M'Naghten* Rules were concerned only with the accused's actual "knowledge" of these matters. These particular modifications to the *M'Naghten* Rules are still enshrined in today's version of section 16. It is reasonably clear that the Canadian Parliament, by making these modifications in 1892, sought to maintain the basic substance of the *M'Naghten* Rules while expanding their scope in certain critical respects. In 1991, Parliament amended section 16(1) by replacing the stigmatizing word "insane" with the term "mental disorder"; hence, it is now necessary to refer to the NCRMD defence rather than the insanity defence.

How have the Canadian courts interpreted the wording of the NCRMD defence, that is now contained in section 16(1) of the Code?

The Meaning of "Mental Disorder" in Section 16(1) of the Code

Before defendants can successfully assert the NCRMD defence, they must first establish that, at the time of the alleged offence, they were suffering from a "mental disorder." Section 2 of the Code states that mental disorder means "a disease of the mind." We have already encountered some of the

issues surrounding the definition of disease of the mind. Indeed, it will no doubt be remembered from the discussion in Chapter 2, dealing with **automatism**, that it is important to draw a distinction between automatism caused by a disease of the mind and automatism stemming from other causes. Where automatism is caused by a disease of the mind, the appropriate defence is that of NCRMD, under the provisions of section 16 of the Code.

In the case of *Cooper* (1980), the Supreme Court of Canada adopted a broad definition of "disease of the mind." Justice Dickson emphasized that this term is a *legal* concept, not a medical concept, and that, although medical evidence is critical in order to determine the accused's mental condition, it is a matter for the court to decide whether the condition described by psychiatric evidence does, from the *legal* point of view, constitute a disease of the mind. Justice Dickson then formulated the following definition of the term:

> In summary, one might say that in a legal sense "disease of the mind" embraces any illness, disorder or abnormal condition which impairs the human mind and its functioning, excluding however, self-induced states caused by alcohol or drugs, as well as transitory mental states such as hysteria or concussion. In order to support a defence of insanity the disease must, of course, be of such intensity as to render the accused incapable of appreciating the nature and quality of the violent act or of knowing that it is wrong.

In the *Stone* case (1999), the Supreme Court of Canada re-affirmed the general principles that were articulated in *Cooper*. In particular, Justice Bastarache emphasized that the question of "what mental conditions are included in the term disease of the mind" is a *legal one for the trial judge to decide*. In essence, the trial judge is entrusted with the task of deciding "whether the condition the accused claims to have suffered from satisfies the legal test for disease of the mind." However, once the trial judge has made this legal determination, the question of "whether the accused actually suffered from a disease of the mind is a question of fact" to be determined by the **trier of fact** (the jury, if there is a jury trial, or the trial judge in all other cases). In other words, whether a particular condition, such as "cocaine-induced **psychosis**," should be considered to be a disease of mind for the purpose of section 16 of the *Criminal Code* is a legal question that is determined exclusively by the trial judge; however, the issue of whether the accused actually suffered from this condition at the time of the alleged offence is a question of fact that is left firmly in the hands of the trier of fact.

Furthermore, as we saw in Chapter 2, Justice Bastarache articulated a remarkably expansive definition of "disease of the mind," in the *Stone* case. Indeed, he recommended that Canadian courts adopt an "holistic approach" that involves an examination of not only the "internal cause" and "continuing danger" elements of the mental condition in question but also various policy factors (such as whether the alleged condition can be easily feigned). This definitional approach is even broader in its scope than that which was adopted by the Supreme Court of Canada in the earlier *Cooper* (1980) case.

It is most significant that the Supreme Court of Canada has unequivocally adopted a broad definition of the phrase "disease of the mind." Perhaps the most interesting consequence to follow from this broad definition is that **personality disorders** and psychopathy may be considered diseases of the mind. Individuals who suffer from a psychotic disorder (such as **schizophrenia**) are considered to be subject to a "gross impairment in reality testing" or, in other words, their perception of reality is grossly distorted. One frequent symptom of their illness may well be that they experience delusions. Such individuals, therefore, tend to have established an impressive record of mental abnormalities indicating that they have problems coping with reality well before they become involved in behaviour that is alleged to be criminal. This is not the case with those who are suffering only from personality disorders or who have been designated **psychopaths**.

Perhaps the most well-known personality disorder is "**antisocial personality disorder**." In defining this particular type of personality disorder, the *Diagnostic and Statistical Manual of Mental Disorders* (1994) states that "the essential feature" is a "pervasive pattern of disregard for, and violation of, the rights of others that begins in childhood or early adolescence and continues into adulthood." The *Manual* goes on to indicate that individuals with this disorder

> fail to conform to social norms with respect to lawful behavior ... they may repeatedly perform acts that are grounds for arrest ... disregard the wishes, rights, or feelings of others ... are frequently deceitful and manipulative in order to gain personal profit or pleasure ... may repeatedly lie. ... A pattern of impulsivity may be manifested by a failure to plan ahead. ... [they] tend to be irritable and aggressive and may repeatedly get into physical fights or commit acts of physical assault. ... these individuals also display a reckless disregard for the safety of themselves or others. ...

In addition to anti-social personality disorder, another condition associated with repeated criminal conduct is that of *psychopathy*. There is some degree of overlap between these conditions, but they are nevertheless distinct from each other. American authors, Schopp and Slain (2000), have described psychopaths as being

> ... callous, remorseless individuals who demonstrate no major impairment of cognition, perception, or reality testing. Yet, they engage in repetitive criminal behavior with no evidence of empathy or remorse, and sometimes with apparent disregard for the consequences ... The criminal justice system frequently encounters psychopaths, and these individuals raise unique concerns for that institution because they do not respond to punishment in a manner similar to ordinary adults.

In posing the question of whether mentally disordered persons should be excused from criminal responsibility, we immediately encounter a major problem of principle when we consider the cases of individuals with an antisocial personality disorder or psychopaths. The problem lies in the fact such individuals do not have a noteworthy record of symptoms other than those of social irresponsibility and the commission of antisocial conduct. How, therefore, can we distinguish such individuals from "real criminals"? Although acutely psychotic patients may commit antisocial acts, and even crimes, they have usually established a dramatic record of bizarre symptoms that indicate that they have broken with reality. Individuals with a personality disorder or psychopaths may only be able to point to a long record of social irresponsibility and crime to substantiate a claim that they were NCRMD at the time of the offence. If too many individuals with personality disorders or psychopaths are permitted to raise the NCRMD defence successfully, it could justifiably be argued that the basic concept of criminal responsibility starts to disintegrate. If individuals are considered to be NCRMD simply because they commit crimes, every major criminal in Canada is NCRMD! Obviously, no system of criminal law could function on this basis.

The Supreme Court of Canada has ruled, on more than one occasion, that a personality disorder is *capable* of being a "disease of the mind" under section 16(1) of the Code. However, it has also emphasized that such a condition does not *per se* cause the accused to fall within the criteria for the NCRMD defence. Indeed, this was precisely the approach taken by the Supreme Court in the *Cooper* case (1980), in which Justice Dickson emphasized the principle that it is *not* enough for accused persons to demonstrate that they were suffering from a disease of the mind at the time of the alleged offence. In order to establish that they were "mentally disordered" within the meaning of section 16(1), such persons must *also* prove that their disease of the mind was "of such intensity as to render them incapable of appreciating the nature and quality of the violent act or of knowing that it is wrong." In light of this strict interpretation of the Code, it is clear

that it would be most difficult for a person suffering only from a personality disorder to raise the NCRMD defence with any degree of success. Such individuals would nearly always be capable of appreciating the nature and quality of their act and of knowing that it was wrong.

In short, although the Supreme Court has indicated that personality disorders may qualify as diseases of the mind, the harsh reality appears to be that it is next to impossible for persons suffering from such a disorder to establish that it produced the precise state of mind that must be proved under the provisions of section 16.

The Meaning of "Appreciate" in Section 16(1)

The Code's substitution of the word "appreciate" for "know" in the "first leg" of the mental disorder defence is most telling. This significant departure from the *M'Naghten* Rules was underscored in the case of *Barnier* (1980). In this case, the accused had shot and killed a woman in an office building and had subsequently taken his gun on the roof and demanded to speak to the prime minister of Canada. It was contended that the accused was suffering from severe delusions. However, at his trial for noncapital murder, there was a highly unusual development. All the psychiatrists were agreed that Barnier was incapable of *appreciating* the nature and quality of his act, but the Crown argued that, in law, the word "appreciate" means "know." The two Crown psychiatrists then changed their opinions. They testified that, if "appreciate" means no more than "know," then the accused knew what he was doing and that it was wrong.

The trial judge accepted the Crown's interpretation and Barnier was convicted of murder. The B.C. Court of Appeal allowed his **appeal** and substituted a verdict of not guilty by reason of insanity. In the view of the court, the trial judge had made a serious error in treating the word "appreciate" as being a mere synonym of the word "know." Although the Crown appealed this ruling, it was ultimately upheld by the Supreme Court of Canada. In delivering the unanimous decision of the Supreme Court, Justice Estey emphasized that Parliament had deliberately employed two different words in the critical portion of section 16(2), namely "appreciating" (the nature and quality of the act) and "knowing" (that the act is wrong). Therefore, it was obvious that Parliament intended these two words to be given different meanings; otherwise, the "Legislature would have employed one or the other only." In discussing the distinction between the two words, Justice Estey went on to say that

> The verb "know" has a positive connotation requiring a bare awareness, the act of receiving information without more. The act of appreciating, on the other hand, is a second stage in a mental process requiring the analysis of knowledge or experience in one manner or another. It is therefore clear on the plain meaning of the section that Parliament intended that for a person to be insane within the statutory definition, he must be incapable first of appreciating in the analytical sense the nature and quality of the act or of knowing in the positive sense that his act was wrong. ...

The Supreme Court of Canada also had occasion to deal with the distinction between the words "know" and "appreciate" in *Cooper* (1980). In this case, the accused, a man with a long history of hospitalization for mental disorder, had strangled a female patient after a dance. There was medical evidence that, although Cooper may have been capable of intending bodily harm and of choking the young woman, he was not capable of intending to kill her. Nevertheless, he was convicted of murder at his trial and the Ontario Court of Appeal subsequently affirmed his conviction. However, the Supreme Court of Canada ultimately allowed his appeal and ordered a new trial. In delivering the judgment of the majority of the Supreme Court, Justice Dickson stated that the person who had drafted the original Code had made a deliberate change in language from the *M'Naghten* Rules by

replacing "know" with "appreciate" in the first part of section 16(1). This change was made in order to "broaden the legal and medical considerations bearing upon the mental state of the accused and to make it clear that cognition was not to be the sole criterion." Indeed, Justice Dickson suggested that "emotional, as well as intellectual awareness of the significance of the conduct, is in issue." He went on to declare that

> With respect, I accept the view that the first branch of the test, in employing the word "appreciates," imports an additional requirement to mere knowledge of the physical quality of the act. *The requirement, unique to Canada, is that of perception, an ability to perceive the consequences, impact, and results of a physical act.* An accused may be aware of the physical character of his action (i.e. in choking) without necessarily having the capacity to appreciate that, in nature and quality, that act will result in the death of a human being. This is simply a restatement, specific to the defence of insanity, of the principle that *mens rea*, or intention as to the consequences of an act, is a requisite element in the commission of a crime. [emphasis added]

The Supreme Court of Canada decisions in *Barnier* and *Cooper* are extremely important since they establish, beyond any shadow of a doubt, that the word "appreciate," in section 16(1) of the Code, is much broader in scope than the word "know," which appears in the *M'Naghten* Rules. In effect, the cases underscore the fact that the Canadian Parliament made a deliberate effort, in 1892, to expand the scope of the insanity defence beyond the narrow limitations set by the English *M'Naghten* Rules.

The Meaning of "Nature and Quality of the Act" in Section 16(1)

The Supreme Court of Canada has clearly stated that the phrase "nature and quality" of an act refers exclusively to the *physical* nature and quality of the act concerned. In other words, as Chief Justice Lamer said in the *Landry* case (1991), the "first branch of the s. 16(1) test protects an accused who, because of a disease of the mind, was incapable of appreciating the *physical* consequences of his act."

The Supreme Court's approach to this issues is perhaps best illustrated by the highly disturbing case of *Kjeldsen* (1981). The accused, who was apparently suffering from a psychopathic disorder, was convicted of the brutal murder of a taxi-driver. Kjeldsen had previously been found not guilty by reason of "insanity" on charges involving rape and attempted murder. He was on a day pass from a mental hospital when he killed the taxi-driver by shattering her skull with a large rock. All the medical witnesses agreed that Kjeldsen was "a dangerous psychopath with sexually deviant tendencies." The accused, however, was unsuccessful in his attempt to raise (what is now known as) the NCRMD defence. He was convicted at trial, and his subsequent appeals to both the Alberta Court of Appeal and the Supreme Court of Canada were rejected.

Although it was accepted that Kjeldsen was suffering from a disease of the mind (in this case, a psychopathic personality), there was considerable disagreement, among the psychiatric witnesses, as to whether it was of such intensity as to render him "incapable of appreciating the nature and quality of the violent act or of knowing that it is wrong." Justice McIntyre addressed this issue, in delivering the unanimous judgment of the Supreme Court of Canada:

> [Those witnesses] called for the defence applied a wide definition of "appreciating," which involved not only an ability to foresee the physical consequences of one's acts but, as well, a capacity to foresee and understand the subjective or emotional reactions of those affected. They were of the opinion that a psychopath, such as the appellant, could not be said to have the capacity to appreciate the nature and quality of his acts. Those called for the Crown, applying a definition which was

limited to a capacity to understand and foresee the physical consequences of conduct, were of the view that a psychopath, such as the appellant, would be fully capable of appreciating the nature and quality of his acts though indifferent to such consequences. ... *To be capable of "appreciating" the nature and quality of his acts, an accused person must have the capacity to know what he is doing;* in the case at bar, for example, to know that he was hitting the woman on the head with the rock, with great force, *and in addition he must have the capacity to estimate and to understand the physical consequences which would flow from his act*, in this case that he was causing physical injury which could result in death. [emphasis added]

Justice McIntyre also expressly approved the following passage from the judgment of Justice Martin of the Ontario Court of Appeal in *Simpson* (1977):

> I do not think the exemption provided by ... [section 16(1)] extends to one who has the necessary understanding of the nature, character and consequences of the act, but merely lacks appropriate feelings for the victim or lacks feelings of remorse or guilt for what he has done, even though such lack of feeling stems from "disease of the mind." *Appreciation of the nature and quality of the act does not import a requirement that the act be accompanied by appropriate feeling about the effect of the act on other people.* ... No doubt the absence of such feelings is a common characteristic of many persons who engage in repeated and serious criminal conduct. [emphasis added]

In rejecting Kjeldsen's appeal, the Supreme Court of Canada reached an eminently reasonable result. After all, the Canadian public would scarcely tolerate a system of criminal justice that acquitted individuals of violent crimes merely because they lacked the appropriate feelings for their victims or did not experience the appropriate pangs of remorse or guilt. Since Kjeldsen knew what he was doing and that it was wrong, the Court was fully justified in holding him accountable for his actions. In essence, the *Kjeldsen* case reflects the Court's view that those who are suffering only from a personality disorder do not meet the criteria for an NCRMD acquittal under section 16(1).

Clearly, the narrow interpretation of the first arm of the NCRMD defence in the *Landry* and *Kjeldsen* cases renders it more difficult for some accused persons to obtain an acquittal on this basis. However, it should be remembered that, in light of the Supreme Court of Canada's broad interpretation of the word "appreciate" in section 16(1), accused persons must be acquitted as NCRMD if they did not have a full appreciation of the physical consequences of their actions. For example, in the case of *Swain* (1986), the accused was charged with both assault and aggravated assault, the victims being members of his own family. Swain had come home at midnight, closed the door and put a sheet over the windows. He took his sixteen-month-old son, removed all his clothes and twirled him around his head upside down. He then held his wife down and scratched an "X" on her chest with a meat cleaver. Fortunately, the scratch was only superficial in nature. The accused also splashed or spit out water on his family, broke furniture, and threw a number of objects out of the window. His wife testified that Swain appeared to be "fighting with the air and talking about spirits." It appeared that Swain was engaging in some type of ritualistic activity and was trying to clear the family of evil spirits. The accused himself testified that he thought that he was protecting his family from devils who were attacking them. When the police arrived, they found Swain holding his two-month-old baby by her ankles and swinging her over his head. There was little doubt that Swain had been suffering from a severe form of psychosis at the time of these events.

The Crown raised the issue of insanity over the accused's objections. In order to avoid a finding of insanity, Swain's **counsel** argued that her client appreciated the physical character and consequences of his conduct, and therefore, in light of the *Kjeldsen* case, he did not fall within the scope of section

16(1) of the Code. The trial judge rejected this contention and found the accused not guilty by reason of insanity. Swain appealed, but the trial judge's finding was upheld by the Court of Appeal. After quoting from the judgment of Justice McIntyre, in the *Kjeldsen* case, Justice Thorson said

> By that definition, in our case, the appellant (Swain) did not have the capacity to appreciate the nature and quality of his act for, although he knew he was moving a knife or a sharp instrument on the skin and that it could produce a scratch, he did not estimate or understand the physical consequences of his act. He did not think he was causing injuries; he believed he was protecting his family from evil spirits. ...
>
> According to *Kjeldsen*, one who understands the physical character of an act but lacks the normal emotional response, like a psychopath, appreciates the nature and quality of the act. *Kjeldsen* does not hold that, whenever a person knows he is cutting someone with a knife and knows that bleeding might follow, he therefore appreciates the nature and quality of his act.

As we shall see shortly, the *Swain* case later went to the Supreme Court of Canada. However, the Supreme Court's decision did not address the question of the correct interpretation of the first arm of section 16(1) and, therefore, the Ontario Court of Appeal's approach to this difficult issue remains a valuable **precedent** in Canada.

The Meaning of "Wrong" in Section 16(1)

The *M'Naghten* Rules themselves did not make clear whether the word "wrong," in the phrase "know he was doing what was wrong," meant *morally* wrong or *legally* wrong. It is clear that the distinction may well have eminently practical consequences insosfar as the application of the insanity defence is concerned. Let us suppose that Arthur kills Bernard, fully appreciating that he is killing the latter and realizing that it is a crime to do so. However, Arthur believes that he has been ordered by God to sacrifice Bernard in order to save the whole human race from imminent destruction. Here Arthur appreciates the nature and quality of his act, so the first arm of the insanity defence is not applicable. However, does the second arm of the defence apply? If wrong means *legally* wrong, section 16(1) cannot apply to Arthur's case. However, if wrong means *morally* wrong, section 16(1) would be applicable because Arthur believed that he was acting on the direct orders of the Almighty and was therefore acting in a morally correct manner. How have the courts resolved this conundrum?

In England and Wales, the courts have traditionally adopted the approach that the word wrong in the *M'Naghten* Rules means *legally* wrong. In this jurisdiction, if the accused knew that he or she was committing a crime, mental disorder does not excuse him or her from criminal responsibility. In contrast, in Australia, the High Court of Australia has taken a distinctively different view. In *Stapleton* (1952), for example, it was stated that, in interpreting the word wrong, the following question should be posed:

> Could this man be said to know in this sense whether his act was wrong if through a disease or defect or disorder of the mind *he could not think rationally of the reasons which to ordinary people make that act right or wrong*? If through the disordered condition of the mind he could not reason about the matter with a moderate degree of sense and composure it may be said that he could not know that what he was doing was wrong. What is meant by "wrong"? *What is meant by wrong is wrong having regard to the everyday standards of reasonable people.* [emphasis added]

In Canada, the Supreme Court of Canada initially followed the narrow interpretation of the word wrong that was favoured by the courts in England and Wales. Indeed, in the case of *Schwartz* (1976), the Supreme Court, by a razor-thin majority of five to four, unequivocally rejected the Australian approach articulated in the *Stapleton* case. Speaking for the majority, Justice Martland contended that,

> In my opinion, the test provided in s. 16(1) is not as to whether the accused, by reason of mental disease, could or could not calmly consider whether or not the crime which he committed was morally wrong. *He is not to be considered as insane within s. 16(1) if he knew what he was doing and also knew that he was committing a criminal act.* [emphasis added]

This decision was somewhat surprising in light of the fact that the draftsman of the 1892 *Criminal Code* had deliberately altered the *M'Naghten* Rules so as to focus upon the issue of the defendant's *capacity* to know that an act or omission is wrong rather than upon his or her mere "knowledge" of its wrongfulness. The approach in the Australian case of *Stapleton* emphasizes the critical importance of examining the question of whether the accused has the *capacity* to think rationally of the reasons that make an act "right" or "wrong" by the standards of reasonable people. Therefore, it seems to be more in tune with the apparent **intention** of the Canadian Parliament than with the approach taken in England and Wales, where the courts seem to have been concerned only with the accused's knowledge of the criminality of his or her conduct. This is an important point because the Australian approach focuses on the accused's capacity to think rationally of those reasons that to an ordinary person would make an act morally right or wrong. This requires an examination of whether the thought processes of the accused have been so affected by mental disorder that he or she is not capable of making the moral decisions that are made by their fellow citizens who do not share the misfortune of suffering from such an affliction. It really makes no sense to investigate whether the accused had the capacity to apply the principles of criminal law to the situation confronting him or her!

In his vigorous dissenting judgment in the *Schwartz* case, Justice Dickson pointed out, on behalf of the minority of the Court, that Justice Martland's narrow interpretation of the word wrong effectively precludes investigation of the very issue that Parliament had apparently intended to be central to any consideration of the insanity defence, namely, whether mental illness or natural imbecility has rendered the defendant *incapable* of "knowing that an act or omission is wrong":

Section 16(1) must be read *in toto*. One looks at capacity to reach rational decisions as to whether the act is morally wrong. *If wrong simply means "illegal," this virtually forecloses any inquiry as to capacity.* The question for the jury is whether mental illness so obstructed the thought processes of the accused as to make him incapable of knowing that his acts were morally wrong. [emphasis added]

It is quite remarkable that, only fifteen years later, the Supreme Court of Canada revisited this issue and decided that it had, after all, made an error in the *Schwartz* case. Indeed, it accepted the view that the dissenting judgment of Justice Dickson better represented the intention of Parliament as expressed in section 16(1) of the Code and ruled that the word wrong in this provision means *morally* wrong or, more specifically, *"wrong according to the ordinary moral standards of reasonable members of society."* Chief Justice Lamer, in delivering the majority judgment in the case of *Chaulk* (1990), stated that it would be unjust for the courts to find a mentally disordered accused person criminally responsible merely because he or she knew that his or her conduct was contrary to the law of the land. In his view,

A person may well be aware that an act is contrary to law but, by reason of ... disease of the mind, is at the same time incapable of knowing that the act is morally wrong in the circumstances according

to the moral standards of society. This would be the case, for example, if the person suffered from a disease of the mind to such a degree as to know that it is legally wrong to kill but ... kills "in the belief that it is in response to a divine order and therefore not morally wrong."...

Does the Supreme Court's ruling mean that those offenders who lack basic moral principles will now be acquitted as NCRMD? The answer is clearly in the negative. As the Chief Justice emphasized in his judgment, the Court's judgment provided absolutely no comfort to amoral offenders because, in order for an NCRMD defence to be successful, *the accused's incapacity to make moral distinctions must be causally related to his or her mental disorder.* Furthermore, the appropriate test is not whether the individual accused person believes his or her actions are morally justified but rather it is *whether he or she is capable of knowing that society at large regards the conduct as being morally wrong*; in other words, "the accused will not benefit from substituting his own moral code for that of society."

A straightforward illustration of the application of the Supreme Court's revised interpretation of the word "wrong" may be seen in the case of *Landry* (1991). The accused was charged with **first degree murder** and admitted that he had killed the victim. However, he advanced a defence of (what is now known as) NCRMD. It was accepted that Landry suffered from a severe psychosis that caused him to form the belief that he was God and that he had a mission to annihilate all the forces of evil in the world. He also suffered from a delusion that the victim was really Satan and that he had to kill him if the world was to be rid of the forces of evil. Landry realized that murder was a crime and that he would almost certainly be arrested if he killed another human being, but he nevertheless believed that he had to proceed with his divine mission.

Landry was tried prior to the Supreme Court of Canada's decision in *Chaulk,* and the trial judge (following the decision of the Supreme Court in the

Schwartz case) ruled that Landry could only be acquitted if he was incapable of knowing that he was committing a killing or of knowing that such an act is a crime under the laws of Canada. The accused was convicted of murder. The case eventually reached the Supreme Court of Canada, where it was ruled that the accused did not meet the criteria for the first arm of the test in section 16(1) (because he undoubtedly appreciated the physical consequence of his actions). However, the Supreme Court also held that, in light of its own change of heart as expressed in the *Chaulk* case, Landry should have been found NCRMD under the second arm of the test because his mental disorder had rendered him incapable of knowing that his conduct was morally wrong in the circumstances. In the circumstances, the Supreme Court substituted a verdict of (what would now be known as) NCRMD.

There is absolutely no doubt that the reinterpretation of the word wrong by the Supreme Court in the *Chaulk* case has significantly expanded the scope of the NCRMD defence in Canada. In cases such as *Chaulk* and *Landry*, it was argued that the accused either thought they had some type of divine status or that God had ordered them to do something that would be considered a crime under Canadian law. These are all situations in which it is clear that, if these delusions existed, the accused would automatically assume that their actions were morally right. However, the impact of the *Chaulk* decision extends considerably beyond situations where the accused believes he or she has divine status or is acting on divine commands. This is dramatically illustrated by the case of *Oommen* (1994).

Oommen had killed a young woman by shooting her as she lay sleeping on a mattress in his apartment, and he was charged with **second degree murder**. It was generally agreed that there was no rational **motive** for the killing. The accused had suffered for many years from "paranoid delusional psychosis." He came to believe that the members of a local union were involved in a conspiracy to kill him. Tragically, he formed the opinion that the

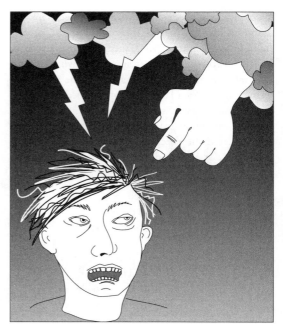

Mentally disordered persons, who are under the delusion that they are following a divine command, are entitled to be found not criminally responsible because they are incapable of knowing that their conduct would be considered "morally wrong" by the average member of Canadian society.

young woman had been commissioned by his enemies to murder him in his own apartment and he became convinced that he had to destroy her before she had the opportunity to kill him. He, therefore, fired nine to thirteen shots at her from a semi-automatic weapon and she subsequently died. A psychiatrist testified that Oommen's mental disorder would not cause him to lose the intellectual capacity to distinguish between right and wrong in the abstract and to know that, in general, killing was wrong. However, his mental disorder would cause him to form an honest belief that the shooting of the young woman was justified under the particular circumstances (namely, that he honestly believed that she was going to kill him if he did not act first). The trial judge found that the killing was "caused, and indeed, compelled" by Oommen's mental condition and that "subjectively the accused did not believe his act to be wrong." However, the trial judge concluded that Oommen did have the "general capacity to know right from wrong" and ruled that he was not relieved from criminal responsibility under section 16(1).

Oommen appealed his conviction to the Alberta Court of Appeal, which ordered a new trial on the grounds that the trial judge had misapplied the *Chaulk* decision. The Crown then appealed to the Supreme Court of Canada, which agreed with the decision made by the Court of Appeal. In delivering the judgment of the Supreme Court, Justice McLachlin stated that, in the *Chaulk* case, the Court had held that "the focus must be on capacity to know that the act committed was wrong, and not merely on a general capacity to distinguish right from wrong." In Justice McLachlin's view, "*the issue is whether the accused possessed the capacity present in the ordinary person to know that the act in question was wrong according to the everyday standards of the reasonable person.*" She added that "the real question is whether the accused should be exempted from criminal responsibility because a mental disorder at the time of the act deprived him of the capacity for rational perception and hence rational choice about the rightness or wrongness of the act." In this sense, the trial judge had made a significant error in focusing on Oommen's general ability to distinguish right from wrong instead of concentrating on his capacity to know that the killing of the young woman was right or wrong in the circumstances as he honestly believed them to be. As Justice McLachlin commented, "s. 16(1) of the *Criminal Code* embraces not only the intellectual ability to know right from wrong, but the capacity to apply that knowledge to the situation at hand."

The Supreme Court of Canada dealt with the same issue some six years later. In the *Molodowic* case (2000), the accused was charged with second

degree murder following the shooting death of his grandfather. There was no doubt that Molodowic suffered from a serious mental disorder—paranoid schizophrenia—and was affected by visual and auditory hallucinations and delusions of persecution. In short, his mental disorder severely impaired his grasp of reality. The psychiatrists who were called to testify by the defence were agreed that Molodowic did appreciate the nature and quality of his act (namely, that he was killing his grandfather) and that he knew that this was a crime. However, they also expressed the opinion that Molodowic *did not know that his act was morally wrong.* Both of these psychiatrists testified to the effect that Molodowic's "act of shooting was consistent with his mental disorder having caused him to believe that only in so doing could he save himself from further torment." Significantly, the Crown did not call its own psychiatric experts to contradict this evidence.

Molodowic was convicted of murder by a jury, and his subsequent appeal to the Manitoba Court of Appeal was dismissed. However, on a further appeal to the Supreme Court of Canada, the conviction was set aside and a verdict of NCRMD was substituted. The Supreme Court ruled that the jury's verdict was unreasonable in light of the psychiatric testimony presented at the trial. In delivering the judgment of the Court, Justice Arbour stated that the evidence just did not support the conclusion that, at the time of the shooting, Molodowic was sufficiently lucid to know that his acts were morally wrong. She went on to state that

> ... the totality of the psychiatric evidence did not give rise to the reasonable possibility that the appellant, who laboured under the effects of a severe mental disorder at the time he committed a homicide, and whose moral judgment was impaired as a result, would have had a momentary reprieve from the effects of his disorder, at the critical time, sufficient to provide him with the moral insight necessary to engage his criminal responsibility ...

... It is not necessarily easy for a jury to accept that, in lay person's terms, an accused who knows what he is doing and knows that it is a crime, could still genuinely believe that he would not be morally condemned by reasonable members of society for his conduct. In my view, the defence proved this to be the case and, on the evidence tendered at his trial, it was unreasonable to conclude otherwise.

However, it is important to remember that the mere fact that the accused was suffering from a severe mental disorder does not automatically lead to the conclusion that the accused lacked the capacity to know that his or her conduct would be considered morally wrong by ordinary members of society. In this respect, it is useful to compare *Oommen* (1994) and *Molodowic* (2000) with the decision of the B.C. Court of Appeal in *W. (J.M.)* (1998). Here, the two accused were young persons who had been charged with hostage taking, kidnapping, and various weapons charges. They had hijacked a school bus that was transporting students from their school. Fortunately, the accused eventually surrendered to the police without anyone suffering physical injuries. Both of the youths were diagnosed as suffering from a serious psychotic disorder — schizophrenia — and they laboured under a number of delusions that were generated by that mental condition. The hostage-taking scheme was originally conceived as a means of coercing the government into allocating the accused a portion of Baffin Island to establish their own state. This enclave was then to be used to accumulate a large cache of nuclear weapons with which they could threaten the rest of the world into implementing a new social order. The accused agreed that, if this ambitious plan failed, then they would use their hostages to negotiate a situation in which they would be held together in solitary confinement, "where they could meditate, expand their spirituality and power, as well as learning greater 'magic' and practice their music." The accused were convicted at their trial in Youth Court and appealed to the B.C. Court of Appeal.

The central issue was whether the accused fell within the second prong of the NCRMD test, articulated in section 16(1) of the *Criminal Code*— namely, did their mental disorder render them incapable of knowing that their plans and actions were wrong? The majority of the Court of Appeal affirmed the convictions, even though it was accepted that both of the accused suffered from a serious mental disorder. Chief Justice McEachern, speaking for the majority, took the view that this was not a case in which the accused lacked the capacity to understand society's values. They knew that the ordinary person would regard their actions as being morally wrong:

> The evidence ... does not establish that the accused were so driven by their delusions that they did not have the capacity to rationally choose which course to follow. *Rather the evidence supports the view that these young men believed that society's rules did not or should not apply to them.* The fact that they chose to proceed with their plan does not establish that they did not have the capacity rationally to assess their acts. [emphasis added]

The Problem of Irresistible Impulse

In a (recently decreasing!) number of jurisdictions in the United States, defendants who do not meet the criteria of either of the two arms of the NCRMD defence discussed above, may nevertheless be entitled to raise the "insanity defence" (as it is known in the United States) if they can establish that, because of mental illness, they lacked "substantial capacity" to "conform their conduct to the requirements of the law." In other words, in these American jurisdictions, an accused person can say "I appreciated what I was doing and knew that I was doing something that was wrong; however, an irresistible impulse came over me and I couldn't help myself."

In Canada, it is perfectly clear that the irresistible impulse defence is not recognized by the courts. If the accused does not meet the criteria of either of the two arms of the insanity test set out in section 16(1), the question of irresistible impulse is absolutely irrelevant. Of course, as the Supreme Court of Canada noted in the *Borg* (1969) and *Abbey* (1982) cases, an irresistible impulse may be a "symptom or manifestation of a disease of the mind," but such a mental condition will not excuse the defendant under section 16(1) unless the other requirements of that provision are met.

Why have the courts taken such a firm stand on the issue of irresistible impulse as the basis for a defence of NCRMD? Perhaps they are understandably reluctant to open the door of the insanity defence to individuals who suffer only from a personality disorder and claim that they cannot help themselves. This attitude certainly seems to underlie the Supreme Court of Canada's leading decision in *Chartrand* (1976). In this case, the accused had been convicted of killing a police officer. His appeal to the Supreme Court was ultimately rejected. However, the Court's approach to the issue of irresistible impulse is most interesting. It had been contended that the defendant suffered from a psychopathic personality. The medical director of Montréal's Institut Pinel, Dr. Béliveau, stated that Chartrand was

> Capable of distinguishing between right and wrong—he understands the nature of his actions, and so forth—but that does not mean that there is not an inner pathological process at work that can prompt him to exhibit a form of behaviour that is unacceptable, dangerous, violent and so on, as well as a psychotic process that would be clearly, if you will, obvious in another person.

However, the Supreme Court totally rejected this as a basis for a successful defence under section 16(1) of the Code. Indeed, Justice De Grandpré held that

Chartrand was…able to distinguish between right and wrong, and although he was ill, he was technically sane. What the witness adds on the subject of the inner pathological process cannot be taken into consideration under our criminal legislation, which does not recognize the diminished responsibility theory.

This decision has clearly shut the door to the irresistible impulse claim as an independent basis for raising the insanity defence in Canada. The Supreme Court's approach clearly underlines the fact that section 16(1) has been interpreted in such a way as to focus upon *cognitive*, rather than *volitional*, factors in determining the issue of insanity. No doubt, the approach stems from an understandable reluctance to acquit personality disordered offenders (particularly those identified as "psychopaths") who simply claim that they could not control themselves. It is always difficult to assess the validity of such claims. On the other hand, it may well be argued that there should be some kind of defence open to defendants who can make a plausible claim that they could not control their conduct because of their mental illness. In England and Wales, for example, such individuals may raise the defence of diminished responsibility in such circumstances. This defence operates only in relation to a charge of murder, however, and, if successful, leads to a conviction of **manslaughter** rather than an acquittal; in other words, it is only a **partial defence**. Whether some form of diminished responsibility defence should be made available in Canada is a matter that has been hotly debated for a number of years and, to date, Parliament has not been willing to introduce it into the *Criminal Code*.

Before leaving the matter of irresistible impulse it might be useful to consider the possibility that the decision in the *Chaulk* case might open the door to some defendants claiming that they suffered an irresistible impulse that caused them to lack the capacity to know that their conduct was wrong according to the ordinary standards of reasonable people. If a mentally disordered accused person can demonstrate that he or she was so overwhelmed by an irresistible impulse that he or she could not, with a reasonable degree of composure, think of the reasons that ordinary persons make their conduct right or wrong, such an accused person should be acquitted as being NCRMD. It remains to be seen whether the courts will be willing to view such a scenario as one in which the irresistible impulse is a symptom of a mental disorder that excuses the accused under the second arm of section 16(1).

MISCELLANEOUS PROCEDURAL ISSUES

The Power of the Crown to Raise the Mental Disorder Defence

Most people assume that the NCRMD defence is an issue raised exclusively by accused persons themselves (or by their counsel on their behalf). In Canada, however, the Crown has traditionally been granted considerable latitude in raising the NCRMD defence—even over the clear objections of the accused. Such latitude was granted by the courts in the absence of any legislative guidance and is, therefore, considered to be the creature of **common law**. In Canada, as a consequence of the common law rule adopted by the courts until 1991, the question of the NCRMD defence could be raised by either the defence or the Crown (or even by the court itself) *regardless of whether the accused had put the state of his or her mind in issue* (for example, by raising the defence of automatism).

Clearly, such a cavalier approach raised serious questions concerning the potential injustice of "forcing an accused person to be acquitted by reason of mental disorder" even where the offence involved was relatively minor. The potential injustice lies in the fact that an NCRMD acquittee may be subjected to prolonged custody or close supervision in the community, whereas a person convicted of the same offence may be sentenced to a relatively brief period of imprisonment or some lesser sen-

tence. Furthermore, there are certain dangers inherent in permitting the Crown to raise the issue of the accused's mental disorder during the course of a criminal trial. Indeed, the Crown may very well prejudice the outcome of a case by introducing evidence of mental disorder. By way of illustration, one might consider the possibility that a jury may reason that, if the accused is mentally disordered, he or she is "just the sort of person" who would have committed the offence in question. Given the prejudice often shown against the mentally disordered, whom many members of the public automatically presume are "dangerous," it is important to ensure that the evidence of the accused's mental disorder does not taint the fact-finding process at the time that the jury is considering the question of innocence or guilt.

In the *Swain* case (1991), the Supreme Court re-examined the validity of the existing common law rule that permitted the Crown to raise the NCRMD defence on its own initiative. As we saw earlier, *Swain* was a case in which the Crown raised the issue of mental disorder in spite of the strong objections of the accused's counsel. These objections were made primarily because Swain had fully recovered from his mental disorder by the time he came to trial. However, under the provisions of the *Criminal Code* then in force, the Court had no option but to order that he be kept in indefinite custody in a psychiatric facility should he be acquitted "by reason of insanity." The accused considered that this outcome was grossly unfair in light of his excellent recovery.

The Supreme Court of Canada ultimately concluded that the then-existing common law rule must be jettisoned on the basis that it infringed the accused's rights to liberty and security of the person (rights that are guaranteed by section 7 of the *Charter*). Chief Justice Lamer suggested a new common law rule that would govern the question of when the prosecution may raise the question of the accused's mental disorder. Under this new rule, there would only be two situations in which this could occur:

First, the Crown may raise evidence of [mental disorder] after the trier of fact has concluded that the accused is otherwise guilty of the offence charged. In these circumstances the Crown's ability to do so will not be triggered until after the accused has concluded his or her defence. Secondly the Crown may raise evidence of [mental disorder] if the accused's own defence has (in the view of the trial judge) put the accused's capacity for criminal intent in issue. In these circumstances the Crown's ability to raise evidence of [mental disorder] is not inconsistent with the accused's right to control the conduct of his or her defence because the very issue has been raised by the accused's conduct of his or her defence. ...

In essence, the Supreme Court of Canada not only re-affirmed the traditional principle that permitted the Crown to raise the mental disorder defence when the accused person had put his or her state of mind in issue, but has also taken a further step, which is quite novel in Canadian criminal jurisprudence. This additional step involves considering the insanity issue *after the accused has concluded his or her defence.* The new rule unquestionably prevents the Crown from prejudicing the judge or jury's determination of guilt or innocence by requiring that evidence of the accused's mental disorder not be considered by the court until after he or she has been found guilty of the offence charged (except, of course, in the situation where the accused has put his or her state of mind in issue). Likewise, the common law rule fashioned by the Supreme Court would clearly circumvent the potential danger of the Crown raising the defence as a convenient means of ensuring the continued detention or supervision of the accused without having to proceed with a full trial on the facts. However, the new rule still leaves open the possibility that those accused persons who have not put their state of mind in issue may be found NCRMD contrary to their own wishes—albeit after the determination of guilt has been made—and it is quite possible that such

persons could be kept in some form of psychiatric detention or supervision for a longer period than they would, in fact, serve if convicted and sentenced to prison.

It is interesting that the *Criminal Code* amendments that were introduced after the Supreme Court of Canada's decision in the *Swain* case contain a potential source of conflict with the new common law rule concerning the Crown's ability to raise the mental disorder defence. More specifically, the amendments (sections 672.11 to 672.21 of the Code) include a comprehensive set of rules governing the ordering of mental health assessments of the accused and permit the Crown to request such an assessment where there is a question whether the accused was NCRMD at the time of the alleged offence. The prosecutor may request the assessment *without the consent of the accused* not only where the latter has put the state of his or her mind in issue but also where "the prosecutor satisfies the court that there are reasonable grounds to doubt that the accused is criminally responsible for the alleged offence, on account of mental disorder" (section 672.12). The question naturally arises as to how this provision should be applied in light of the new common law rule articulated in *Swain*. The only course of action that would appear to meet the requirements of the new common law rule, *in the situation where the accused has not put the state of his or her mind in issue,* would be for the court to prevent the Crown from referring to the results of such an assessment until after the accused has presented his or her defence. Therefore, it is possible that, although an assessment requested by the Crown may be conducted prior to the trial or in the early stages of the trial process, consideration of the results of such an assessment may be postponed until the end of the trial. It remains to be seen whether this is the practice that will ultimately emerge in the future. Arguably, however, any departure from such a course of action would infringe the *Charter* rights of the accused as defined in the *Swain* case.

The Burden and Standard of Proof When the Defence of NCRMD is Raised

Other critical procedural issues that arise in connection with the NCRMD defence are the question of who must shoulder the *burden of proof* in a case in which the NCRMD defence is raised and the matter of the *standard of proof* that must be met (that is, "beyond a reasonable doubt" or "on the balance of probabilities"). In this respect, section 16(3) of the *Criminal Code* states that the "burden of proof that an accused was suffering from a mental disorder so as to be exempt from criminal responsibility is on the party that raises that issue." Furthermore, section 16(2) of the Code states that "every one person is presumed not to suffer from a mental disorder so as to be exempt from criminal responsibility by virtue of subsection (1), until the contrary is proved on the balance of probabilities."

These provisions mean that the party raising the issue of the NCRMD defence (whether that is the Crown or the defendant) must *prove* it and that the standard of proof is "on the balance of probabilities." Therefore, if accused persons wish to raise the NCRMD defence, they must establish that it was more likely that they were NCRMD at the time of the alleged offence than that they were not; it is not up to the Crown to prove that the defence does not apply in the particular circumstances of the case concerned. However, if the Crown raises the NCRMD defence, it must prove that the accused in question was NCRMD and must do so on the balance of probabilities.

The requirement that accused persons must prove their mental disorder within the meaning of section 16(1), if they raise the issue of the NCRMD defence, is quite unusual in that the Crown is normally required to prove all the elements of the *actus reus* and *mens rea* of an offence (and do so *beyond a reasonable doubt*) before a conviction may be obtained; indeed, the accused is normally given the benefit of the doubt in our system of criminal justice. However, in the case of the NCRMD defence, the onus of establishing the defence rests squarely on the shoulders of the party who raises it and, where the defence decides to do so, it could be considered somewhat harsh to require that the accused must establish the absence of criminal responsibility on his or her part.

Does the apparent harshness of placing the burden of proving the NCRMD defence on the accused, where he or she raises it, amount to an infringement of the *Charter*? This question was examined in depth by the Supreme Court of Canada in the *Chaulk* case (1990), where it was contended that placing the burden of proving the NCRMD defence on the accused infringed section 11(d) of the *Charter*, which enshrines the right of a person accused of a criminal offence "to be presumed innocent until proven guilty according to law in a fair and public hearing by an independent and impartial tribunal." Speaking for the majority of the Court, Chief Justice Lamer held that (what is now) section 16(2) and (3) do, indeed, limit the presumption of innocence protected by the *Charter*; however, he also ruled that this limitation was justified in the light of section 1 of the *Charter*, which states that the rights and freedoms contained are "subject only to such reasonable limits prescribed by law as can be demonstrably justified in a free and democratic society." In his view, the objective of Parliament—to avoid placing an impossible burden of proof on the prosecution (namely, disproving mental disorder) and thereby to secure the conviction of the guilty (who are not "sick")—was "sufficiently important to warrant limiting constitutionally protected rights." Furthermore, the means Parliament used to achieve this objective (namely, section 16(2) and (3)) passed the requisite test of proportionality. More specifically, there was a "rational connection" between the objective of these provisions of the Code and the particular means chosen to achieve that objective, since placing the burden of proving his or her mental disorder on the accused clearly furthers the objective of avoiding placing a burden on the prosecution "which is virtually impossible to meet." Furthermore, section 16(2) and (3) violated the presumption of innocence "as little as is reasonably possible." Finally, there was a "proportionality between the effects" of section 16(4) and its legitimate objective:

> The presumption [that the accused is not mentally disordered within the meaning of section 16(1)] and the reversal of onus embodied in [subsections (2) and (3) of section 16] exist in order to avoid placing a virtually impossible burden on the Crown. The burden on the accused is not the full criminal burden; rather, the accused is required to prove his or her [mental disorder] on the balance of probabilities. If an accused were able to rebut the presumption ... merely by raising a reasonable doubt as to his or her [mental disorder within the meaning of section 16(1)], the very purpose of the presumption ... would be defeated and the objective would not be achieved. Any other means of achieving the objective could also give rise to violation of *Charter* rights.

Of particular importance to the Court was the fact that the Crown has no means of compelling an accused person to submit to an examination by a psychiatrist who will testify for the prosecution even if he or she does decide to co-operate fully with a psychiatrist who is called by the defence. If an accused person refuses to co-operate with a "Crown" psychiatrist, the prosecution could be placed in an impossible position if it were required to disprove that the accused was NCRMD at the time of the alleged offence. The defence may present testimony from a psychiatrist who has examined the accused firsthand, but the Crown would not be able to so so and this would place it at a considerable disadvantage before a judge and/or jury. Since the state of the accused's mind at the time of the alleged offence is something that is peculiarly within his or her knowledge, it is reasonable, in the view of the Supreme Court, to require him or her to present evidence on this matter and to prove that the requirements of section 16(1) are met before entering an acquittal.

THE DISPOSITION OF NCRMD ACQUITTEES

The Situation Prior to 1992

As we noted earlier, a successful NCRMD defence leads only to a "qualified" acquittal. Prior to 1992, section 614(2) of the *Criminal Code* provided that, where an accused person was found not guilty of a criminal offence by reason of insanity, the trial judge had no discretion but to order that the accused be kept "in strict custody" until the "pleasure of the lieutenant governor of the province (was) known" (that is, indefinitely). Such individuals could only be released by a decision of the provincial government. Although each province had a **review board** that periodically examined the cases of all those held under such warrants, the role of such boards was purely *advisory* and their advice might be ignored by the government of the day. Section 614(2) provided absolutely no procedural safeguards for such "insanity acquittees"; in particular, there was no provision for a judicial determination of their current mental condition and whether they continued to be dangerous. The section unequivocally provided for the *automatic* commitment of such acquittees regardless of their particular circumstances.

The Impact of the *Swain* Case

The rather dismal status of those acquitted by virtue of (what was then known as) the insanity defence was finally ameliorated by the ruling of the Supreme Court of Canada in the *Swain* case (1991). Swain, as we saw earlier in this chapter, had been acquitted of charges of assault and aggravated assault at his trial, even though he did not wish such a defence to be presented to the jury. Following his arrest, he had been treated with antipsychotic drugs in a mental health centre and recovered to such an extent that he was released pending his trial. The Crown introduced evidence relevant to (what would now be known as) the NCRMD defence over the accused's objections, and he was ultimately acquitted "by reason of insanity." Upon the rendering of this verdict, the accused was detained in strict custody at the pleasure of the lieutenant governor of Ontario. However, within one year of the trial, the warrant detaining the accused was vacated and Swain was absolutely discharged. Nevertheless, Swain's *Charter* challenge to section 614(2) of the Code was subsequently heard by the Supreme Court of Canada, which took the bold step of declaring that the existing system of automatic, and indefinite, detention of those acquitted by reason of insanity offended the provisions of the *Canadian Charter of Rights and Freedoms* by invalidating section 614(2) of the Code. The invalidation of such a critical statutory provision on the basis that it infringed the rights enshrined in sections 7 and 9 of the *Charter* represented a clear statement by the Court of the need to safeguard the rights of the mentally disordered in the criminal justice process.

On behalf of the majority of the Court, Chief Justice Lamer ruled that section 614(2) undoubtedly infringed rights that were protected by sections 7 and 9 of the *Charter*. Section 7 safeguards "the right to life, liberty and security of the person and the right not to be deprived thereof except in accordance with the principles of fundamental justice"; section 9 enshrines "the right not to be arbitrarily detained or imprisoned." Furthermore, the Court held that section 614(2) could not be saved by section 1 of the *Charter* on the basis that it could be viewed as a reasonable limitation on the rights of an accused person in a free and democratic society. Although it was a legitimate objective of Parliament to protect the public from those mentally disordered acquittees who continue to be dangerous, the Chief Justice concluded that section 614(2) was an unreasonable limitation on the *Charter* rights of accused persons. It was not necessary for Parliament to employ such an arbitrary mechanism in order to achieve its objective; clearly less intrusive mechanisms might be used for this purpose. In particular, the indefinite nature of the detention coupled with the complete lack of any criteria for making a cus-

tody order meant that the harsh effects of section 614(2) were ultimately out of all proportion to the legitimate objective of protecting society from dangerous insanity acquittees.

Amendments to the *Criminal Code*

In July 1991, the federal Ministry of Justice released its proposals for amending the *Criminal Code* provisions relating to mentally disordered offenders. Such amendments had been in process for a considerable period; however, the ruling in the *Swain* case made their swift introduction a pressing necessity. Eventually, after passing through the tortuous legislative process, the *Criminal Code* amendments came into effect in February 1992.

The whole system by means of which decisions are made about the disposition of those who are acquitted on the basis of mental disorder was totally refashioned as a consequence of these extensive amendments to the *Criminal Code*. The new provisions of the Code required the establishment of review boards in each province (section 672.38). These tribunals took over the primary responsibility for deciding whether an NCRMD accused should be detained and, if so, for how long. According to the *Criminal Code*, the boards consist of no less than five members, of whom at least one must be licenced to practise psychiatry. The chair must be a senior judge or a person who is qualified for appointment to, or has retired from, such judicial office (section 672.4(1)). In hearing any individual case, there must be a quorum of three members, including the chair and the member who is a psychiatrist (section 672.41(1)). Presumably, the requirement that the chair of the review boards should be a senior judge or someone with equivalent qualifications is designed to ensure public confidence in the tribunals and to allay fears that dangerous persons will be released onto the streets.

These *Criminal Code* provisions empowered the trial court to make a disposition of an NCRMD accused "if it is satisfied that it can readily do so and that a disposition should be made without delay" (section 672.45(2)). The accused may be discharged absolutely or on conditions or, alternatively, may be detained in custody in a hospital (section 672.54). However, any custody order made by a court would be only temporary in nature, being limited to a maximum of 90 days (section 672.55(2)). Where the court does not make a disposition, the review board must make such a disposition normally within 45 days after the verdict is rendered—although this period may be extended to 90 days by the court (section 672.47). In essence, the review boards assume responsibility for making the initial disposition of NCR accused persons if the court does not do so and for overseeing the cases of all those individuals who have not been granted an absolute discharge. In the latter situation, the boards are the sole decision-making authorities. This situation contrasts starkly with the previous role of the boards, which was purely advisory in nature.

Furthermore, it is significant that the *Criminal Code* amendments state that the boards are required to follow the basic principles of procedural fairness, such as recognizing the right of NCRMD accuseds to call and cross-examine witnesses (section 672.5) and that NCRMD accuseds have *the right to appeal to the provincial court of appeal* against any disposition made by a court or a board of review (section 672.72). Prior to 1992, "insanity acquittees" could not challenge their continued detention in the courts; therefore, in this respect, there is no doubt that the *Criminal Code* amendments have greatly enhanced the status of such individuals.

Where a court or review board makes a disposition, it must take into consideration "the need to protect the public from dangerous persons, the mental condition of the accused, the reintegration of the accused into society, and the other needs of the accused" and, in light of these considerations, it must choose the disposition that is "the least onerous and least restrictive to the accused" (section 672.54). The possible dispositions are (i) an absolute discharge, (ii) a discharge on conditions, or (iii) an order for holding the accused person in custody

in a hospital. Incidentally, treatment can not be imposed as a condition of release or as part of a custodial order (section 672.55(1)).

How is a board or a court supposed to make the choice between these three potential dispositions? In the *Winko* case (1999), the Supreme Court of Canada held that section 672.54(a) of the *Criminal Code* stipulates that, unless a court or a board of review concludes that the not criminally responsible (NCR) accused person constitutes a *"significant threat to the safety of the public,"* then it *must* order an absolute discharge. On the other hand, if the court or review board does conclude that the accused is indeed a significant threat to the public, it has two choices: it may order the NCR accused person be "discharged subject to the conditions the court or Review Board deems necessary" or "it may direct that the NCR accused be detained in custody in a hospital, again subject to appropriate conditons."

Justice McLachlin, who delivered the judgment of the majority of the justices of the Supreme Court of Canada in *Winko*, made it very clear that the threshold for justifying the imposition of restrictions on the liberty of a person who has been found NCRMD is very high:

> A "significant threat to the safety of the public" means a real risk of physical or psychological harm to members of the public that is serious in the sense of going beyond the merely trivial or annoying. *The conduct giving rise to the harm must be criminal in nature.* [emphasis added]

According to Justice McLachlin, "a miniscule risk of grave harm will not suffice," nor will a "high risk of trivial harm meet the threshold."

The Supreme Court also emphasized that there is absolutely no presumption that an NCR person poses a serious threat to the safety of the public. This means that there is no onus on the NCR accused to prove that he or she is *not* dangerous—a task that would be extraordinarily difficult to accomplish. It is only if the evidence presented to the court or review board establishes that the accused person actually constitutes a significant threat to the safety of the public that restrictions may be placed on his or her liberty.

Section 672.54 and the *Charter*

In the *Winko* case (1999), the Supreme Court of Canada stoutly rejected a *Charter* challenge to the constitutional validity of section 672.54 of the *Criminal Code*, which constitutes the heart of the new system for determining the fate of those who have been found NCRMD. More specifically, the Court held that section 672.54 does not infringe either section 7 or section 15 of the *Charter*. Essentially, the Supreme Court took the view that the new system, introduced in 1992, provides an individualized risk assessment of each NCR accused person: *only those individuals who are shown to constitute a "significant threat to the safety of the public" will be subjected to restrictions on their liberty, following a verdict of NCRMD.* Even if such restrictions are necessary, trial courts and review boards now have the power to discharge an NCR accused person on conditions, rather than automatically placing him or her in custody in a mental health facility. This legislative reform undoubtedly represents a fundamental change from the system that existed at the time of the *Swain* case (1991). Under that ancient régime, the trial judge had no discretion but to hold every NCR accused person in strict custody, regardless of whether the accused posed any danger to society. Under the new system, there is a considerable degree of flexibility, and the imposition of any restriction on the NCR accused person's liberty must be justified by a finding that he or she constitutes a significant threat in terms of the likelihood of committing a criminal offence in the future. Furthermore, the Supreme Court took particular account of the fact that the new system provides for regular reviews of each NCR accused person's case, primarily by a review board with special expertise in this area, and grants him or her the right of appeal to the provincial or territorial appellate courts.

According to Justice McLachlin, section 672.54 does not discriminate against NCR accused persons solely on the basis of their mental disorder (a prohibited ground of discrimination under section 15(1) of the *Charter*). Unlike accused persons who are acquitted of criminal charges, NCR accused persons are individuals who have been found to have committed the offence charged, but who have nonetheless been relieved of criminal responsibility for their actions on the grounds that they suffered from severe mental disorder, in accordance with the provisions of section 16(1) of the Code. Since the NCR accused person has committed what would otherwise be deemed a criminal act, Parliament is entitled to use the criminal law power to protect public safety and to impose restrictions on that person's liberty if he or she constitutes a significant threat in terms of the likelihood of committing future crimes. Section 672.54 does not discriminate against NCR accused persons merely on the basis of their mental disorder; indeed, it only imposes restrictions on their liberty where it has been concluded that they are *not only mentally disordered but also potentially dangerous* to society at large. For similar reasons, the Supreme Court also held that section 672.54 did not infringe the "fundamental principles of justice" enshrined in section 7 of the *Charter*.

Justice McLachlin's judgment contains some important observations on the nature of the NCRMD defence in Canada and on the justification for creating a special régime for the disposition of NCR accused persons:

> ... The NCR accused is to be treated in a special way in a system tailored to meet the twin goals of protecting the public and treating the mentally ill offender fairly and appropriately. Under the new approach, the mentally ill offender occupies a special place in the criminal justice system; he or she is spared the full weight of criminal responsibility, but is subject to those restrictions necessary to protect the public.

The verdict of NCR under Part XX.I of the *Criminal Code* ... is not a verdict of guilt. Rather, it is an acknowledgement that people who commit criminal acts under the influence of mental illnesses should not be held criminally responsible for their acts or omissions in the same way that sane responsible people are ...

Nor is the verdict that a person is NCR a verdict of acquittal. *Although people may be relieved of criminal responsibility when they commit offences while suffering from mental disorders, it does not follow that they are entitled to be released absolutely.* Parliament may properly use its criminal law power to prevent further criminal conduct and protect society ...

The preventative or protective jurisdiction exercised by the criminal law over NCR offenders extends only to those who present a significant threat to society ... *Once an NCR accused is no longer a significant threat to public safety, the criminal justice system has no further application.*

... *Parliament has signalled that the NCR accused is to be treated with the utmost dignity and afforded the utmost liberty compatible with his or her situation. The NCR accused is not to be punished ... [but is to] ... receive the disposition "that is the least onerous and least restrictive" one compatible with his or her situation, be it an absolute discharge, a conditional discharge or detention ...* [emphasis added]

There is no doubt whatsoever that the implementation of the new system for the disposition of NCR accused persons has rendered the NCRMD defence a considerably more attractive option for defendants in a criminal trial. In lieu of automatic, indefinite confinement, the new régime (i) provides courts and review boards with a set of flexible, humane options in determining the disposition of NCR accused persons; (ii) ensures that only those NCR accused persons who are shown to be dangerous are subject to restrictions on their liberty; and (iii) provides access to the appellate courts for those NCR accused persons who wish to challenge any restrictions that may be placed on them by a trial court or a review board.

It is clear that, in the years ahead, the NCRMD is likely to be raised much more frequently than was the case in the past. In particular, it will certainly now become a viable option for those defendants who have been charged with less-serious crimes. Under the pre-1992 system, all those who were found "not guilty by reason of insanity" were *automatically consigned* to indefinite detention — *regardless of the severity of the offences that they had committed.* This meant that pleading the old insanity defence was a course that most defence lawyers were extremely reluctant to follow if the offence charged was relatively minor and a conviction would be unlikely to result in imprisonment. However, the new *Criminal Code* provisions stipulate that any NCR accused person is entitled to an absolute discharge, unless he or she is deemed to be dangerous, and gives the court or review board the option of conditional discharge as an alternative to an order for detention in a psychiatric facility. Hence, under the new system, there is no disincentive for accused persons, charged with relatively minor offences, to plead NCRMD. Given these circumstances, it seems inevitable that there will be an increasing number of NCRMD pleas in the years ahead. However, this should not raise any concerns given the protective measures enshrined in the new *Criminal Code* provisions and, as Justice McLachlin points out in *Winko* (1999), "no person should be convicted of a crime if he or she was legally insane at the time of the offence." Furthermore, as our analysis of section 16 has demonstrated, it is only the most severely mentally disordered defendants who will be able to meet the strict criteria that Parliament has imposed as a prerequisite for raising the NCRMD defence successfully.

MENTAL DISORDER AS A PARTIAL DEFENCE

It should be noted that a number of Canadian courts have held that there may be certain mental disorders that, although they do not meet the strict criteria of the NCRMD defence as defined by section 16(1) of the Code, may nevertheless operate to negative the defendant's ability to form the **specific intent** required for such offences as murder or robbery. In this respect, therefore, there may be circumstances in which, although the accused's mental disorder was not so severe as to warrant an NCRMD acquittal, it was nevertheless sufficient to prevent the accused from forming the necessary *mens rea* for conviction of the offence charged. However, in practice, this approach has only be adopted in relation to such "specific intent" offences as murder or robbery and the accused concerned has been convicted of the included offences of manslaughter or assault respectively.

For example, in the *Lechasseur* case (1977), the accused had been convicted of murder and he appealed to the Québec Court of Appeal. The insanity defence had been raised at trial but was rejected by the jury. On appeal, Lechasseur's counsel successfully argued that the jury should have been instructed that they had the option of acquitting the accused of murder and convicting him instead of manslaughter. As to this issue, Justice Casey said

> Appellant now argues that while the evidence may have fallen short of what is required for the [NCRMD] defence it may have been sufficiently strong to create a reasonable doubt as to his capacity to formulate the specific intent of Criminal Code, s. [229]. His conclusion is that the presiding Judge should have given the jury a third choice—manslaughter.
>
> One of the elements of the offence is the specific intent of *Criminal Code*, s. [229]. This element had to be established beyond a reasonable doubt with the result that if there was any evidence tending to establish that appellant did not have the capacity to formulate this specific intention, the jury should have been told that a third verdict—manslaughter—was possible. They were not so directed.

> ... *evidence that falls short of what is required to establish the [NCRMD] defence may still be sufficiently strong to create a reasonable doubt as to the capacity of the accused to formulate the specific intent that the law requires.* [emphasis added]

In the circumstances, the Court of Appeal ordered a new trial for Lechasseur. Of course, the "specific intent" in section 229 is the intent to kill or the intent to cause bodily harm that the accused knows is likely to cause death and the accused is reckless as to whether death ensues or not.

Mental illness may also be insufficient to justify an acquittal by reason of insanity in relation to a charge of first degree murder. However, it may be sufficient to negative the elements of planning and deliberation that are required for a conviction of first, as opposed to second, degree murder (section 231(2) of the Code). As Chief Justice Lamer stated, in delivering the judgment of the majority of the justices of the Supreme Court of Canada in *Jacquard* (1997),

> It is true that some factor, such as mental disorder, that is insufficient to negative the charge that the accused *intended* to kill, may nevertheless be sufficient to negative the elements of *planning and deliberation*. This because one can intend to kill and yet be impulsive rather than considered in doing so. It requires less mental capacity simply to intend than it does to plan and deliberate. [emphasis in the original]

However, it is important to bear in mind that being mentally ill is not *necessarily* incompatible with a finding that the accused acted with deliberation and planning. As Justice Martin said, in delivering the judgment of the Ontario Court of Appeal in *Kirkby* (1985),

> Mental disorder may, of course, negative planning and deliberation, but if the murder is, in fact, both planned and deliberate, the existence of mental disorder does not *per se* remove the murder from

the category of first degree murder. Mental disorder may or may not negative the elements of planning and deliberation, depending on the nature of the mental disorder and the effects produced by it. The fact that the offender suffers from a mental disorder is not, however, *necessarily* incompatible with the commission by him of … a "cold-blooded" murder. … I do not think that Parliament, by using the word "deliberate," imported a requirement that the offender's previous determination to kill the victim must be the result of reasonable or normal thinking or must be rationally motivated, provided the Crown has established that the killing was planned, and that the act of killing was considered and not the result of sudden impulse.

The precise relevance of mental disorder to a charge of first degree murder has been neatly encapsulated by the Québec Court of Appeal in its judgment in the case of *Allard* (1990). In delivering this judgment, Justice Fish indicated that there are three separate questions that may be considered in relation to such a charge:

1. On a charge of first degree murder, where there is evidence for the jury to consider on the issue of [the NCRMD defence], the jury ought first to decide whether that defence has been made out. If it has, the jury must acquit the accused.
2. If the defence of [NCRMD] fails, the jury must consider all of the evidence, *including any evidence tendered with respect to [the NCRMD defence]*, in order to decide whether the requisite intent for murder has been proven beyond a reasonable doubt. If not, the accused may be convicted of manslaughter, but must be acquitted of murder.
3. If the intent to murder has been established, the jury must then decide whether the murder was planned and deliberate. With respect to each of these elements, the jury must reconsider, separately, all of the relevant evidence, including any evidence as to mental state or

condition of the accused at the time the offence was committed. Only if the jury is satisfied that the murder was planned and deliberate, may it convict of first degree murder. [emphasis in the original]

The decision in *Allard* clearly indicates that, although a person charged with first degree murder may fail to establish a defence of NCRMD under section 16(1), evidence of mental disorder may still result in an acquittal of murder or a finding of second, rather than first, degree murder.

STUDY QUESTIONS

1. Archibald, a young theology professor, kills Cromwell, his departmental chair. He claims that he was ordered by God to kill Cromwell so as to rid the university community of a tyrant and to warn the wicked that "the day of judgment is at hand." Upon his arrest by the police, Archibald says, "I suppose I'll spend the rest of my life in the slammer for this." There is a considerable degree of psychiatric evidence to the effect that Archibald is suffering from paranoid schizophrenia and that he has been under the influence of numerous religious delusions. Do you think it is possible for Archibald's counsel to advance a defence of NCRMD with any degree of success?

2. Derek brutally rapes a young woman, Jane. In the course of the attack on his victim, he inflicts several severe injuries with a hunting knife that he used to force Jane to have intercourse with him. Jane, fortunately, recovers from her physical wounds, although she has been profoundly shocked by the whole appalling experience. Derek is charged with aggravated sexual assault. His counsel raises the defence of insanity. Chalmers, a psychiatrist for the defence, claims that Derek is suffering from a "psychopathic" personality disorder. Derek testifies that, because of his mental disorder, he

just could not control his violent impulses and that he could not possibly feel any sympathy for his victim. What likelihood is there that Derek will be acquitted as NCRMD?

3. Henry is suffering from a severe form of schizophrenia. He acts under the delusion that Arthur, his neighbour, has a machine that generates death rays. One day, Henry comes to believe that Arthur is about to turn the death rays in his direction and, in order to preserve his life, he must kill Arthur immediately. Henry breaks into Arthur's house and stabs him to death with a knife. When the police question Henry, it is clear that he realizes that he has killed Arthur but he insists that "it was him or me and I had to get him before he wasted me with those death rays." Henry is charged with first degree murder. Would Henry be able to raise the defence of NCRMD with any degree of success at his trial?

4. Hamlet is charged with the first degree murder of Polonius. The circumstances are that Hamlet, who is suffering from a form of schizophrenia, killed Polonius in the university laboratory where medical research was being conducted on animal subjects. Hamlet later stated that he killed Polonius because the latter was in charge of the laboratory and, as such, was responsible for the "torture of innocent animals." Hamlet also says that animals' lives are more important than those of human beings and that it was, therefore, his duty to destroy Polonius. Would Hamlet's mental disorder furnish him with any defence(s)?

FURTHER READING

American Psychiatric Association. 1994. *Diagnostic and Statistical Manual of Mental Disorders,* 4th ed. *(DSM-IV).* Washington, D.C.: American Psychiatric Association.

Berman, M.E. and L. Slaughter. 1998. Neurobiologic Correlates of Violence: Relevance to Criminal Responsibility. 17 *Behavioral Sciences & the Law:* 303.

Bloom, H. and B.T. Butler. 1995. *Defending Mentally Disordered Persons.* Toronto: Carswell.

Borum, R. and S.M. Fulero. 1999. Empirical Research on the Insanity Defense and Attempted Reforms: Evidence Toward Informed Policy. 23(3) *Law and Human Behavior:* 375.

Bredemeir, S.J. 2000. Hollow Verdict: Not Guilty by Reason of Insanity Provokes Animus-Based Discrimination in the Social Security Act. 31 *St. Mary's Law Journal:* 697.

Buchanan, A. 1994. Brain, Mind and Behaviour Revisited. 5 *Journal of Forensic Psychiatry:* 232.

Burt, L. 1993. The Mental Disorder Provisions: Community Residence and Dispositions under s. 672.54(c). 36 *Criminal Law Quarterly:* 40.

Chunn, D.E. and R. Menzies. 1998. Out of Mind, Out of Law: The Regulation of 'Criminally Insane' Women inside British Columbia's Public Mental Hospitals, 1888–1973. 10 *Canadian Journal of Women and the Law:* 306.

Côté, G. and S. Hodgins. 1992. The Prevalence of Major Mental Disorders Among Homicide Offenders. 15 *International Journal of Law and Psychiatry:* 89.

Davis, S. 1993. Changes to the *Criminal Code* Provisions for Mentally Disordered Offenders and Their Implications for Canadian Psychiatry. 38 *Canadian Journal of Psychiatry:* 122.

——. 1994. Examining the Impact of Bill C-30 in British Columbia. 5 *International Bulletin of Law and Mental Health:* 5.

Eastman, N. 1992. Psychiatric, Psychological and Legal Models of Man. 15 *International Journal of Law and Psychiatry:* 157.

Gerard, J.B. 1999. The Medical Model of Mental Illness: Its Application to the Insanity Defense. 22 *International Journal of Law and Psychiatry:* 65.

Grant, I. 1997. Canada's New Mental Disorder Disposition Provisions: A Case Study of the British Columbia *Criminal Code* Review Board. 20 *International Journal of Law and Psychiatry:* 419.

Grant, I., J.R.P. Ogloff, and K.S. Douglas. 2000. The British Columbia Review Panel: Factors Influencing Decision-Making. 23 *International Journal of Law and Psychiatry:* 173.

Harris, G.T., M.E. Rice, and C.A. Cormier. 1991. Length of Detention in Matched Groups of Insanity Acquittees and Convicted Offenders. 14 *International Journal of Law and Psychiatry:* 223.

Hodgins, S. 1993. Mental Health Treatment Services in Québec for Persons Accused or Convicted of Criminal Offences. 16 *International Journal of Law and Psychiatry:* 179.

Keith, A.L. 1996. The Hospital Detention Order (*Criminal Code* Section 672.20). 49 *Criminal Reports (4th):* 288.

Lymburner, J.A. and R. Roesch. 1999. The Insanity Defense: Five Years of Research (1993–1997). 22 *International Journal of Law and Psychiatry:* 213.

Mackay, R. 1995. Insanity and Unfitness to Stand Trial in Canada and England: A Comparative Study of Recent Developments. 6 *Journal of Forensic Psychiatry:* 121.

MacKay, R.D. 1999. The Abnormality of Mind Factor in Diminished Responsibility. [1999] *Criminal Law Review:* 117.

Martin, M. 1993. Defending the Mentally Ill Client in Criminal Matters: Ethics, Advocacy and Responsibility. 52 *University of Toronto Faculty Law Review:* 73.

McIntyre, J. 1992. Amendments to the *Criminal Code* (Mental Disorder), Bill C-30 and Review Boards. 50 *Advocate:* 575.

McSherry, B. 1993. Defining What Is a "Disease of the Mind": The Untenability of Current Legal Interpretations. 1 *Journal of Law and Medicine:* 76.

———. 1998. Getting Away with Murder? Dissociative States and Criminal Responsibility. 21 *International Journal of Law and Psychiatry:* 163.

Mewett, A.M. and M. Manning. 1994. *Mewett and Manning on Criminal Law.* 3d ed. Toronto: Butterworths. Chap. 13.

Morin, D. 1996. Les troubles mentaux dans le *Code criminel:* une extension de l'interface entre le système pénal et le système psychiatrique? 38 *Canadian Journal of Criminology:* 129.

Morse, S.J. 1999. Craziness and Criminal Responsibility. 17 *Behavioral Sciences & the Law:* 147.

Mulvany, J. 1995. Professional Conflict and the Sentencing Process: The Case of Hospital Orders. 18 *International Journal of Law and Psychiatry:* 101.

Ogloff, J.R.P., C.F. Roberts, and R. Roesch. 1993. The Insanity Defence: Legal Standards and Clinical Assessment. 2 *Applied & Preventive Psychology:* 163.

O'Marra, A.J.C. 1993. *Hadfield* to *Swain:* The *Criminal Code* Amendments Dealing with the Mentally Disordered. 36 *Criminal Law Quarterly:* 49.

Perlin, M.C. 1994. *The Jurisprudence of the Insanity Defence.* Durham, N.C.: Carolina Academic Press.

Phillips, M.S. 1991. Initital Disposition of Persons Found Not Guilty by Reason of Insanity or Unfit to Stand Trial. 12 *Health Law in Canada:* 20.

Rice, M.E. and G.T. Harris. 1993. Ontario's Maximum Security Hospital at Penatanguishene: Past, Present and Future. 16 *International Journal of Law and Psychiatry:* 195.

Schopp, R.F. and A.J. Slain. 2000. Psychopathy, Criminal Responsibility, and Civil Commitment as a Sexual Predator. 18 *Behavioral Sciences & the Law:* 247.

Slovenko, R. 1999. The Mental Disability Requirement in the Insanity Defense. 17 *Behavioral Sciences & the Law:* 165.

Spring, R.L. 1998. The Return to *Mens Rea:* Salvaging a Reasonable Perspective on Mental Disorder on Mental Disorder in Criminal Trials. 21 *International Journal of Law and Psychiatry:* 187.

Sreenivasan, S., et al. 2000. Neurospsychological and Diagnostic Differences Between Recidivistically Violent Not Criminally Responsible and Mentally Ill Prisoners. 23 *International Journal of Law and Psychiatry:* 161.

Stuart, D. 1995. *Canadian Criminal Law.* 3d ed. Toronto: Carswell. 338–383.

Stuart, D. and R.J. Delisle. 1997. *Learning Canadian Criminal Law.* 6th ed. Toronto: Carswell. 647–680.

Tollefson, A. and B. Starkman. 1993. *Mental Disorder in Criminal Proceedings*. Toronto: Carswell.

Verdun-Jones, S.N. 1979. The Evolution of the Defences of Insanity and Automatism in Canada from 1843–1979: A Saga of Judicial Reluctance to Sever the Umbilical Cord to the Mother Country? 14 *U.B.C. Law Review:* 1.

———. 1989. Sentencing the Partly Mad and the Partly Bad: The Case of the Hospital Order in England and Wales. 12 *International Journal of Law and Psychiatry:* 1.

———. 1994. The Insanity Defence in Canada: Setting a New Course. 17 *International Journal of Law and Psychiatry:* 175.

———. 1999. *Canadian Criminal Cases: Selected Highlights.* Toronto: Harcourt Brace. Chap. 7.

———. 2000. Making the Mental Disorder Defence a More Attractive Option for Defendants in a Criminal Trial: Recent Legal Developments in Canada. In D. Eaves, J.R.P. Ogloff, and R. Roesch, eds. *Mental Disorder and the Criminal Code: Legal, Clinical and Research Perspectives,* Burnaby, B.C.: Mental Health, Law and Policy Institute. 39–75

Walsh, J.J. 1991. The Concepts of Diminished Responsibility and Cumulative Intent: A Practical Perspective. 33 *Criminal Law Quarterly:* 229.

Weiler, B.L. and C.S. Widom. 1996. Psychopathy and Violent Behaviour in Abused and Neglected Young Adults. 6 *Criminal Behaviour and Mental Health:* 253.

CHAPTER

9

Defences to a Criminal Charge: Part I

OVERVIEW

This chapter examines the following:

1. The defences of mistake of fact, mistake of law, intoxication, necessity, and duress;
2. the view that the defence of mistake of fact is primarily an assertion that the accused did not have the necessary *mens rea* for conviction of the offence charged;
3. the principle that a mistake as to a material element of the *actus reus* of the offence charged need only be honest in order to lay the basis for a successful defence—that is, that there is no separate requirement that the mistake also be reasonable;
4. the problems of dealing with the assertion of an honest mistake as to consent in the specific context of sexual assault;
5. the general principle that a mistake of law does not give rise to a valid defence to a criminal charge, and the exceptions to this principle (including officially induced error and acting "under colour of right");
6. the extent to which self-induced intoxication may be a partial defence to a criminal charge and the differential application of the defence to specific and basic intent offences;
7. the three "*Beard* Rules" that have traditionally been applied by the courts in determining the nature and scope of the defence in Canada;
8. the recognition by the Supreme Court of Canada in the *Daviault* case (1994) that intox-

ication that produces a mental state akin to automatism or mental disorder should be considered a defence even in the case of a basic intent offence such as sexual assault;

9. the enactment by Parliament of section 33.1 of the *Criminal Code* in response to the *Daviault* case;
10. the situations in which the defence of necessity may be raised as a defence to a criminal charge in Canada;
11. the difficulties associated with applying the defence of necessity in relation to the more serious criminal offences in the *Criminal Code*;
12. the nature and scope of the defence of duress both under section 17 of the Code and under the principles of the common law;
13. the rationale underlying the defences of duress and necessity.

INTRODUCTION

Both Chapters 9 and 10 explore the nature of the major defences that may be raised in a criminal trial. It is not possible to consider all of the various defences that may be brought up in a trial, and those defences that are primarily procedural or technical in nature (such as **entrapment** or **double jeopardy**) have been omitted; these latter defences are usually considered in books on criminal procedure. Of course, it should also be remembered that **accused** persons may now choose to assert their rights under the *Charter* as a means of defending themselves against a criminal charge; indeed, we have already discussed a number of cases in which criminal charges have been dismissed on constitutional grounds (for example, the *Morgentaler, Smolig and Scott* decision in 1988, which resulted in a declaration that section 251 of the Code, dealing with therapeutic abortions, was unconstitutional).

The particular defences we shall consider in Chapter 9 are the following: (i) mistake of fact; (ii) mistake of law; (iii) intoxication; (iv) necessity; and (v) duress.

MISTAKE OF FACT

General Nature of the Defence

The lawyer for a **defendant** in a criminal trial may well say, "it's true that my client committed the *actus reus* of the offence but she was nevertheless operating under a serious mistake as to the real facts of the situation. In light of the facts, *as she honestly believed them to be*, she had absolutely no reason to believe that she was committing a crime and, therefore, lacked the *mens rea* the Crown must prove in order to obtain a conviction." Such an assertion may well lead to the **acquittal** of the client because, as the Québec Court of Appeal stated in *Charbonneau* (1992), "in offences requiring *mens rea*, honest mistake of fact on an essential factual element is, as a general rule, a defence to the charge."

For example, take the English case of *Tolson* (1889). Tolson *honestly* believed that her first husband had perished in a mishap at sea. Acting on this belief, she participated in a marriage ceremony with another man. To her great consternation, however, her first husband subsequently resurfaced very much alive and well. Tolson was charged with **bigamy**. The Crown easily proved that Tolson had committed the *actus reus* of bigamy in that, being married, she had entered into a marriage ceremony with another party. However, Tolson's defence was that she lacked the necessary *mens rea* in relation to a central element of the *actus reus*—namely, knowledge of the fact that she was still a married person at the time of the alleged offence. In other words, *on*

the facts as she honestly believed them to be, her conduct was entirely innocent. Although Tolson was convicted at trial, her conviction was subsequently set aside by the appellate court on the basis that she had a valid defence of honest mistake of fact.

Although mistake of fact is traditionally considered as a specific defence to a criminal charge, the justices of the Supreme Court of Canada have emphasized that it really amounts to an assertion that the Crown has failed to prove the necessary *mens rea* requirements of the offence charged. As Justice Dickson of the Supreme Court of Canada said in the *Pappajohn* case (1980),

> Mistake is a defence, then, where it prevents an accused from having the *mens rea* which the law requires for the very crime with which he is charged. Mistake of fact is more accurately seen as a negation of guilty intention than as the affirmation of a positive defence. It avails an accused who acts innocently, pursuant to a flawed perception of the facts, and none the less commits the *actus reus* of an offence.

Take, for example, the defendant who has been charged with sexual assault and who asserts the defence of honest, but mistaken, belief in consent. As Chief Justice Lamer stated, in delivering the judgment of the Supreme Court of Canada in the *Davis* case (1999), "the defence of honest belief in consent is simply a denial of the *mens rea* of sexual assault":

> The *actus reus* of sexual assault requires a touching, of a sexual nature, without the consent of the complainant. *The mens rea requires the accused to intend the touching and to know of, or to be reckless or wilfully blind as to the complainant's lack of consent* ... In some circumstances, it is possible for the complainant not to consent to the sexual touching but for the accused to honestly but mistakenly believe that the complainant consented. In these circumstances, the *actus reus* of the offence is established, but the *mens rea* is not. [emphasis added]

A leading Canadian case dealing with mistake of fact is that of *Rees* (1956), in which the accused was charged under section 33(1) of the *Juvenile Delinquents Act* (replaced by the *Young Offenders Act*), which made it an offence to "knowingly or wilfully" do any act contributing to the delinquency of a child (defined at that time, in British Columbia where the alleged offence occurred, as a person "apparently or actually under the age of 18"). The "act" in question was sexual intercourse with a young girl of sixteen years and five months. The intercourse took place with the consent of the girl, who informed Rees that she was eighteen years of age. Rees claimed that he honestly believed that the girl was eighteen or older. Rees was, nevertheless, convicted of the offence by the Juvenile Court judge and sentenced to six months' imprisonment. An **appeal** to the B.C. Supreme Court was dismissed on the basis that Rees's mistake as to the age of the young girl failed to constitute a valid defence in law because section 33(1) did not require actual knowledge of a child's age. Nevertheless, Rees's subsequent appeal to the B.C. Court of Appeal was allowed and his conviction quashed. The Chief Justice set out the reasons why Rees's mistake as to the girl's age was a valid defence in the circumstances:

> In my view of the matter we must start out with the proposition that sexual intercourse with a woman, not under the age of 18 years and with her consent, is not a crime, except under exceptional and irrelevant circumstances. It follows that if the appellant had sexual intercourse with a girl not under 18 years of age he could not be convicted of contributing to her becoming a juvenile delinquent for the simple reason she is not a child within the meaning of the Act.
>
> *It is the age factor alone that in these circumstances moves the act from a non-criminal to a criminal category.*
>
> It follows, it seems to me, that when a man is charged with knowingly and wilfully doing an act that is unlawful only if some factor exists which makes it unlawful (in this instance the age of the girl) he cannot be convicted unless he knows of, or

is wilfully blind to, the existence of that factor, and then with that knowledge commits the act intentionally and without any justifiable excuse. [emphasis added]

The Crown appealed the Court of Appeal's decision, but this appeal was ultimately rejected by the Supreme Court of Canada.

Rees, therefore, represents an important **precedent** in the recognition of mistake of fact as a state of mind that can negative the *mens rea* requirements of the offence charged, provided, of course, that the mistake is in relation to a *material element* of the *actus reus* (in the *Rees* case, it is beyond question that age was an absolutely critical element in the definition of the *actus reus*).

Must the Mistake of Fact Be Not Only Honest but Also Reasonable?

Both the *Tolson* and *Rees* cases emphasize that a mistake of fact cannot operate as a valid defence unless the mistake is *honest*. However, a significant question is whether a mistake of fact must not only be honest but also *reasonable*. In other words, must an alleged mistake of fact be one that a *reasonable* person might have made in the circumstances if it is to be considered a valid defence? In the *Rees* case, Justice Cartwright of the Supreme Court of Canada answered this question with an emphatic "no." In his view, "the essential question is whether the belief entertained by the accused is an honest one and ... the existence or non-existence of reasonable grounds for such a belief is merely relevant evidence to be weighed by the tribunal of fact in determining such essential question."

Justice Cartwright's answer is, of course, entirely consistent with the doctrine of *mens rea* in that a person who operates under a serious mistake of fact, in relation to an essential element of an offence, cannot be considered to have made a "*choice* to do something wrong"; clearly, it cannot be asserted that Tolson and Rees *chose* to break the law when, because of a mistake, they were completely unaware of the critical elements that rendered their conduct criminal. Furthermore, even if such a mistake is *unreasonable*, it will still place accused persons in a position where they cannot make a conscious choice to do something wrong and, therefore, they obviously lack the *mens rea*, which is a prerequisite to conviction under our system of criminal law.

However, as the Supreme Court of Canada noted in the *Sansregret* case (1985), it is important to remember that defendants are excluded from receiving the benefit of the defence of mistake of fact if they were either *reckless* or *wilfully blind* as to a material element of the *actus reus* of the offence charged. In other words, if Rees had realized that there was a risk that the young woman was under age and if he had gone ahead regardless of that risk, he would not have been able to raise a successful defence of mistake of fact; after all, he would have been reckless as to the issue of age. If he had consciously taken that risk, indubitably he would have deliberately chosen to do something wrong. Similarly, if Tolson had deliberately closed her eyes as to the continuing existence of her husband when she knew there were good reasons to make further inquiries, she also would have lost the benefit of the defence of mistake. This important **common law** principle has frequently been incorporated into Parliament's definitions of the offences contained in the *Criminal Code*. For example, it is a defence to a charge of criminal harassment (section 264 of the *Criminal Code*) that the accused honestly, but mistakenly, believed that the **complainant** was not being harassed by the accused's conduct (for example, if the accused honestly believed that the complainant did not realize that the accused was repeatedly following the complainant). However, Parliament clearly indicated that this defence must fail if the accused acted "*recklessly* as to whether the other person is harassed." Furthermore, the courts have added the gloss that the defence will also be lost to the accused where there has been *wilful blindness* as to whether the complainant has been harassed; indeed, this was precisely the approach adopted,

for example, by the Alberta Court of Appeal in *Sillipp* (1997) and the Ontario Court of Appeal in *Krushel* (2000).

The disturbing case of *Sansregret* (1985) dramatically illustrates the manner in which wilful blindness may prevent the accused from raising a successful defence of mistake of fact. The accused was charged with the rape of a woman with whom he had previously been living (today, the charge would be one of sexual assault). The background facts were that, in September 1982, Sansregret had broken into the victim's house during the very early hours of the morning. He was "raging" and terrorized the victim with a file-like weapon that he was carrying. The victim was terrified by Sansregret's conduct and, in order to calm him down, she held open the prospect of reconciliation and, eventually, they had sexual intercourse. She later reported the incident to the police, claiming that she had been raped; however, no action was taken, largely because the accused's probation officer intervened and asked her not to proceed with her complaint.

In October 1982, Sansregret once again broke into the victim's house in the very early hours of the morning. He was "furious and violent" and threatened her with a butcher knife. He struck the victim and threatened to kill her if the police came. At one point, he tied her hands behind her back. After an hour of enduring this sheer terror, the victim tried to calm the accused down by holding out some hope of reconciliation. After some conversation, they engaged in sexual intercourse. The victim once again complained to the police and, on this occasion, a number of charges, including rape, were laid against the accused. Sansregret claimed that he had been operating under an honest mistake of fact as to the consent of the victim. The trial judge acquitted the accused of rape on the basis of this defence, even though she considered that the mistake was totally unreasonable:

no rational person could have been under any honest mistake of fact. However, people have an uncanny ability to blind themselves to much that they don't want to see, and to believe in the existence of facts as they would wish them to be.

The learned judge also stated that

> I do not like the conclusion which this leads me to. There was no real consent. There was submission as the result of a very real and justifiable fear. No one in his right mind could have believed that the complainant's dramatic about-face stemmed from anything other than fear. But the accused did. He saw what he wanted to see, heard what he wanted to hear, believed what he wanted to believe.

The Crown appealed the acquittal and the Manitoba Court of Appeal allowed the appeal, entering a conviction. The accused appealed to the Supreme Court of Canada, which affirmed the judgment of the Court of Appeal, on the basis that Sansregret had been wilfully blind as to the issue of consent and was, therefore, not entitled to rely on the defence of honest mistake of fact. In delivering the judgment of the Court, Justice McIntyre stated that,

> Having wilfully blinded himself to the facts before him the fact that an accused may be enabled to preserve what could be called an honest belief, in the sense that he has no specific knowledge to the contrary, will not afford a defence because, where the accused becomes deliberately blind to the existing facts, he is fixed by law with actual knowledge and his belief in another state of facts is irrelevant.

It is clear that the Supreme Court's ruling was heavily influenced by the fact that the accused had engaged in similar conduct on one previous occasion and that he was aware of the complaint made to the police. In these particular circumstances, he clearly should have been alerted to the likelihood that the victim would not give a true consent to having intercourse with him. In other words, he deliberately closed his eyes to the obvious.

In the later case of *Esau* (1997), Justice McLachlin, of the Supreme Court of Canada, further elaborated on the concept of wilful blindness and the circumstances in which such a state of mind will preclude the accused from raising the defence of mistake of fact in the context of a sexual assault. In a passage subsequently approved by a unanimous Supreme Court of Canada in the *Davis* case (1999), Justice McLachlin, as she then was, asserted that

> The term wilful blindness connotes a deliberate avoidance of the facts and circumstances. It is the legal equivalent of turning a blind eye, of not seeing or hearing what is there to see or hear. It is the making of an *assumption* that the complainant consents without determining whether, *as a matter of fact*, the complainant consents. Blindness as to the need to obtain consent can never be raised by an accused as a defence ... [emphasis in original]

In sum, an honest mistake of fact as to a material element of the *actus reus* of the crime charged will constitute an effective defence even if the mistake was not one that would have been entertained by a reasonable person. On the other hand, if a defendant is either reckless or wilfully blind as to the element of the *actus reus* concerned, he or she will lose the benefit of the defence. Finally, as we shall see in a subsequent section of this chapter, Parliament has amended the *Criminal Code* so that defendants who claim, in response to a charge of sexual assault, that they had an honest but mistaken belief in the consent of the complainant, will not be able to advance the defence of mistake of fact unless they acted *reasonably* in the circumstances. The defence of mistaken belief in consent in relation to a charge of sexual assault is, therefore, a specific, and notable, exception to the general rule that an honest, albeit unreasonable, mistake will suffice as a defence.

When Can the Defence of Mistake of Fact Be Placed Before the Jury?

As we saw in our discussion of the defence of **automatism** in Chapter 2, the accused in a criminal trial is not entitled to have any defence placed before the **trier of fact** (whether that be a jury or the trial judge sitting alone) unless the accused first satisfies the *evidentiary* **burden of proof**; the defence of mistake of fact is certainly no exception to this general principle. As the Supreme Court of Canada ruled in the *Esau* case (1997), "before a court should consider honest but mistaken belief or instruct a jury on it *there must be some plausible evidence in support so as to give an air of reality to the defence*." [emphasis added] Of course, once the accused satisfies this *evidentiary* burden of proof, the defence must be considered by the trier of fact. At the end of the trial, the onus shifts to the Crown to prove *beyond a reasonable doubt* that the accused was *not* acting under an honest, but mistaken, belief as to one or more of the essential *actus reus* elements of the offence charged; after all, the Crown is nearly always placed under the *persuasional* **burden of proof** in Canadian criminal trials. Conversely, if the trial judge rules that the accused has failed to satisfy the *evidentiary* burden of proof, then the trier of fact will not even consider the defence of honest mistake of fact when the time comes to determine the accused's guilt or innocence.

In recent years, the application of this principle to the defence of mistake of fact has occurred primarily in the context of cases in which the accused has raised the defence of "honest mistake as to consent" in response to a charge of sexual assault. However, the general principles articulated by the courts in this respect are applicable to all situations in which the defendant raises a defence of mistake of fact. Ironically, the specific defence of honest belief in consent, where the accused has been charged with sexual assault, has now been modified by Parliament so that special considerations now apply when this defence is raised. We shall discuss these modifications in the next section, but in the mean-time, the fact remains that much of the current law concerning the defence of mistake of fact has emerged from the context of the crime of sexual assault. What, then, are the general principles that pertain when the accused wishes to raise the defence of mistake of fact?

An excellent starting point for any contemporary discussion of the nature of the *evidentiary* burden of proof is the Supreme Court of Canada's recent decision in the *Davis* case (1999). This case involved a consideration of a number of different charges against the accused. However, for present purposes, we shall focus on a specific charge of sexual assault and the Supreme Court's ruling as to whether the accused had satisfied the evidentiary burden of proof in relation to his purported defence of honest, but mistaken, belief in consent. In delivering the judgment of the Court, Chief Justice Lamer emphasized that it is clearly not sufficient for an accused person merely to assert that there was an honest mistake of fact. Undoubtedly, there must be *adequate evidence* to support any such contention. It was the view of the Chief Justice that, in order for the accused to satisfy the evidentiary burden of proof, "it must be *possible* for a reasonable trier of fact to conclude that the *actus reus* is made out but the *mens rea* is not." The accused may accomplish this task by demonstrating that there is sufficient evidence for a reasonable trier of fact to conclude that, although the complainant did not consent to the sexual touching, the accused nevertheless honestly—but mistakenly—believed that the complainant had done so. Only in these circumstances does the defence have "an air of reality" and, as Chief Justice Lamer put it, "where there is no air of reality to the defence, it should not be considered, as no reasonable trier of fact could acquit on that basis."

In the *Davis* case (1999), the Supreme Court of Canada explicitly approved Justice McLachlin's characterization (in the *Esau* case (1997)) of the type of evidence to which the accused must point in order to satisfy the trial judge that there is an "air of reality" to the assertion of the defence of honest, but mistaken, belief in consent:

There must be evidence not only of non-consent and belief in consent, but in addition evidence capable of explaining how the accused could honestly have mistaken the complainant's lack of consent as consent. Otherwise, the defence cannot reasonably arise. *There must, in short, be evidence of a situation of ambiguity in which the accused could honestly have misapprehended that the complainant was consenting to the sexual activity in question.* [emphasis added]

In *Davis*, the accused had persuaded the complainant to pose for some nude photographs by claiming that he had connections with a modelling agency and that such snapshots would be necessary if the complainant wished to pursue a career as a model. When the complainant was posing for this purpose, the accused, without asking permission, started to touch the complainant in a sexual manner. The Supreme Court of Canada unanimously held that the trial judge had been correct to refuse to consider the defence of honest, but mistaken, belief in consent because there could be no "air of reality" to the defence when the evidence clearly indicated that the accused had been *wilfully blind* as to consent. As Chief Justice Lamer noted in the judgment of the Court,

> There is no suggestion by the appellant that the complainant posed nude for any reason other than to further her modelling career. Nor was there any evidence that she invited him to touch her prior to his fondling of her breasts and vagina. Nevertheless, the appellant approached the complainant when she was in an extremely vulnerable position and began fondling her breasts …

Davis himself had admitted, on cross-examination during his trial, that he had commenced by touching the complainant's shoulders and that she had remained silent. Apparently, taking the complainant's silence to be consent to this form of touching, he then proceeded, without permission, to touch the complainant's breasts. However, the

Supreme Court held that the complainant's silence, in these particular circumstances, could not possibly have led Davis to believe that she was giving her consent to more intimate sexual contact with him. As Chief Justice Lamer stated,

> Moreover, after he pinched her nipples, the appellant admits that the complainant said, "What are you doing?" Undeterred, he fondled her vagina. She then said, "Do you have to do that?" The appellant stopped. This is clear evidence that he understood she was not consenting to further contact. Notwithstanding these statements, he tied her to a chair and again fondled her breasts and vagina. The appellant provided no evidence to suggest that the complainant had a change of heart … *there can be no air of reality in these circumstances.* [emphasis added]

The same issue arose in the *Park* case (1995), in which the Supreme Court of Canada articulated a number of important principles concerning the so-called "air of reality test" in the context of a charge of sexual assault. Justice L'Heureux-Dubé (with whom a majority of the Court agreed) stated that

> Essentially, for there to be an "air of reality" to the defence of honest but mistaken belief in consent, the totality of the evidence for the accused must be reasonably and realistically capable of supporting that defence. Although there is not, strictly speaking, a requirement that the evidence be corroborated, that evidence must amount to something more than a bare assertion. There must be some support for it in the circumstances. The search for support in the whole body of evidence or circumstances can complement any insufficiency in legal terms of the accused's testimony. The presence of "independent" evidence supporting the accused's testimony will only have the effect of improving the chances of the defence.

In the view of Justice L'Heureux-Dubé, there are two circumstances in which there is no air of reality to a defence raised by the accused. The first is where "the totality of the evidence for the accused is incapable of amounting to the defence being sought." This might arise where, for example, a defendant claims a mistaken belief in consent, but the evidence points to wilful blindness on the defendant's part (as in the *Davis* case); here, there is no air of reality to the defence. The second circumstance is where "the totality of the evidence for the accused is clearly logically inconsistent with the totality of evidence which is not materially in dispute." This might arise where, for example, the accused asserts the defence of mistaken belief in consent, but there is incontrovertible evidence of severe bodily injury. Here, the accused's claim is totally inconsistent with "evidence which is not materially in dispute" and, therefore, once again there is no air of reality to the defence.

In general, it will be very difficult for an accused person to convince a judge that there is an "air of reality" to the defence of honest, but mistaken, belief in consent. Indeed, in the *Ewanchuk* case (1999), the Supreme Court of Canada noted that "cases involving a true misunderstanding between parties to a sexual encounter" arose only "infrequently." In that case, Justice Major stated that, in the context of sexual assault, "consent" means that "the complainant had *affirmatively communicated by words or conduct her agreement to engage in sexual activity with the accused.*" Therefore, in order to satisfy the evidentiary burden of proof, the accused must be able to point to some credible evidence that would support his view that *he honestly believed that the complainant was affirmatively communicating her consent to the sexual activity in question.* An honest belief that silence may be equated with consent would not suffice.

Furthermore, in the *Davis* case (1999), Chief Justice Lamer made the point that "sexual assault is not a crime that is generally committed by accident." In most cases of this type, the real question will be whether the complainant in fact consented to sexual touching. If the answer to this question is in the affirmative, then the Crown has not estab-

lished the *actus reus* of the offence and the accused must be acquitted. On the other hand, if the Crown proves that the complainant did not consent, and that the accused had subjective knowledge of this circumstance, then both the *actus reus* and *mens rea* of elements of the offence have been established and the accused will be convicted. Chief Justice offered the following example to illustrate this point:

> ... suppose the complainant and the accused relay diametrically opposed stories. The complainant alleges a brutal sexual assault and vigorous resistance, where the accused claims consensual intercourse. Suppose further that it is impossible to splice together the evidence to create a third version of events in which the accused honestly but mistakenly believed the complainant consented. In such circumstances, the trial becomes, essentially, a pure question of credibility. If the complainant is believed, the *actus reus* is made out and the *mens rea* follows straightforwardly. If the accused is believed, or if there is a reasonable doubt as to the complainant's version of events, there is no *actus reus*. There is no third possibility of an honest but mistaken belief in consent, notwithstanding the accused's assertion that the complainant consented ...

For example, in the *Ewanchuk* case (1999), the Supreme Court of Canada made it clear that the defence of honest, but mistaken, belief in consent does not apply to an accused person who refuses to take "no" for an answer. Ewanchuk had repeatedly attempted to initiate intimate sexual activity with the complainant. The complainant, who was afraid of the accused, had said "no" to intimate contact with him but, after ceasing his touching for a while, the accused recommenced his sexual touching. After being asked to "stop," the accused did so but, after another short lapse in time, he continued to engage in sexual touching of the complainant, who again asked him to "stop."

Eventually, the accused abandoned his efforts, saying "See, I'm a nice guy, I stopped."

The accused was acquitted at his trial but ultimately the Supreme Court of Canada set aside the acquittal and convicted him of sexual assault. One of the issues raised was that of honest, but mistaken, belief in consent. The Supreme Court ruled that there was no air of reality to the suggestion that Ewanchuk either believed that the complainant was consenting to the sexual touching or that he had, in some way, re-established consent before he recommenced his physical contact. As Justice Major indicated,

> Common sense should dictate that, once the complainant has expressed her unwillingness to engage in sexual contact, the accused should make certain that she has truly changed her mind before proceeding with further intimacies. The accused cannot rely on the mere lapse of time or the complainant's silence or equivocal conduct to indicate that there has been a change of heart and that consent now exists, nor can he engage in further sexual touching to "test the waters." Continuing sexual contact after someone has said "No" is, at a minimum, reckless conduct which is not excusable …
>
> … the accused relied on the fact that he momentarily stopped his advances each time the complainant said "No" as evidence of his good intentions. This demonstrates that he understood the complainant's "No's" to mean precisely that. Therefore, there is nothing on the record to support the accused's claim that he continued to believe her to be consenting, or that he re-established consent before resuming physical contact.

Undoubtedly, Ewanchuk could not point to any evidence whatsoever that would support the view that he honestly believed that the complainant had done something that might cause him to believe that she was *affirmatively communicating her consent* to his sexual advances. Indeed, it would be impossible for someone to interpret her repeated utterance of the word "no" as an affirmative communication of consent.

The *Esau* case (1997), by way of contrast, furnishes a rare example of a case in which the Supreme Court of Canada held (by a somewhat controversial majority vote) that the trial judge should have put the defence of honest, but mistaken, belief in consent to the jury. The accused had been convicted of sexual assault at his trial, but he successfully appealed to the Northwest Territories Court of Appeal, which ordered a new trial. The Crown's subsequent appeal to the Supreme Court of Canada was dismissed. The evidence was that the accused had been at a party at the home of the complainant, who was his second cousin. A considerable amount of alcohol had been consumed. The complainant testified that she was drunk, but the accused testified that she was "able to control what she was doing." The gist of Esau's evidence was that he and the complainant had kissed each other and that she then invited him to her bedroom, where they engaged in sexual intercourse. The complainant denied both that she had kissed the accused and that she had invited him to her bedroom. However, she stated that she could not remember anything that had happened from the time she went to her bedroom until the moment she woke up the next morning and discovered that she had slept with the accused. She testified that she would not have consented to sexual intercourse with Esau because they were related.

The majority of the justices of the Supreme Court of Canada believed that there was an "air of reality" to the accused's assertion of honest — but mistaken — belief in consent and that, therefore, since he had satisfied the *evidentiary* burden of proof, the defence should have been placed before the jury:

> Here, the plausible evidence comes from the testimony of the complainant and the respondent and the surrounding circumstances of the alleged sexual assault. The respondent's evidence amounted to more than a bare assertion of belief in consent.

He described specific words and actions on the part of the complainant that led him to believe that she was consenting. This may be enough to raise the defence. However, there was more. The complainant's evidence did not contradict that of the respondent, as she cannot remember what occurred after she went to her bedroom. In addition, there was no evidence of violence, no evidence of a struggle and no evidence of force ...

... The absence of memory by the complainant as to what happened in the bedroom makes it easier to "cobble together" parts of both the accused and complainant's evidence to reach a reasonable conclusion of honest but mistaken belief. Any number of things might have happened during the period in which she had no memory ...

... The jury could have believed the accused's testimony that the complainant appeared to consent, but also believed that the complainant was intoxicated to the point of legal incapability. [emphasis added]

Criminal Code Amendments Concerning the Assertion of Honest Belief in Consent as a Defence to Charges of Sexual Assault

We have seen that, as a matter of general principle, even an unreasonable mistake of fact may constitute a valid defence to a criminal charge, provided the mistake is honest and not the result of **recklessness** or wilful blindness on the part of the accused. However, this principle becomes highly controversial when its implications are fully considered in relation to the crime of sexual assault.

In the *Park* case (1995), Justice L'Heureux-Dubé presents a convincing analysis of exactly why the defence of mistake of fact raises major problems in the context of a charge of sexual assault. She points out that, normally, accused persons raise the defence of mistake of fact where they can claim that they were under a fundamental misapprehension as to an element of the *actus reus* that is generally not

in dispute. She gives the example of a defendant who shoots a man believing the latter is a deer. There would be no dispute as to the fact that the victim was killed by the accused's gunshot. The critical issue would then be whether the accused honestly believed that the victim was a deer. However, in those cases of sexual assault where the accused claims a mistaken belief relating to consent (clearly, an essential component of the *actus reus*), there usually is a dispute as to whether that element exists. As Justice L'Heureux-Dubé suggested,

> Assault differs importantly from most other Code offences in its interaction with the mistake of fact defence. Under most other offences, mistake of fact will primarily arise in contexts in which the *actus reus* of the offence is beyond dispute. Assaults raise a unique problem that the mental state of another person (i.e., consent or lack thereof) is an essential element that is relevant to both the *actus reus and* the *mens rea* of the offence—an element which almost invariably *is* materially in dispute.

Furthermore, Justice L'Heureux-Dubé made the critical point that, in trials involving charges of sexual assault, the courts face the difficulty that such assaults are not usually witnessed by anyone other than the accused and the complainant and that a conviction may be obtained without the need to prove "visible physical injury to the complainant." These factors render it more likely that there will be a dispute as to the issue of consent.

Speaking for herself, Justice L'Heureux-Dubé identified another critical reason why the defence of mistaken belief in consent is so deeply problematic in relation to charges of sexual assault. In her view, there is a "clear communication gap between how most women *experience* consent, and how many men *perceive* consent." She notes that part of this gap is caused by "genuine, often gender-based, miscommunication between the parties" and another part is attributable to "the myths and stereotypes that many men hold about consent." Among these myths and stereotypes is the view that "coercive sexuality" is "normal." In light of the inherent danger of reinforcing such myths and stereotypes, the acquittal of defendants who assert a totally unreasonable belief in consent represents a serious threat to the security of all women.

How have the courts dealt with the issue of honest belief in consent and how has Parliament intervened to modify the law that applies to such a defence?

Some twenty years ago, the Supreme Court of Canada was faced with the following question: Should a man who has been charged with rape be entitled to an acquittal when he claims that, despite the fact that his belief was totally unreasonable, he nevertheless acted under an honest mistake as to consent? In the *Pappajohn* case (1980), the Court answered this question in the affirmative. However, it is important to bear in mind that the defendant in the *Pappajohn* case was convicted of rape because it was held that, in the particular circumstances, the evidence of an honest mistake as to consent was insufficient to place it before a jury. In *Pappajohn*, the defendant claimed unambiguous consent on the part of the victim, whereas the latter claimed unambiguous refusal of consent to intercourse. In these circumstances, it was held that the accused was not really claiming that he was mistaken as to consent but rather that the victim was a liar. In other words, the issue was one of credibility, and the jury had made it abundantly clear that they preferred the victim's version of the events in question. Therefore, the defence of honest mistake was not applicable. (Of course, the offence of rape has now been abolished. In January 1983, three entirely new categories of sexual assault were added to the *Criminal Code*.)

In spite of the conviction of the accused, the *Pappajohn* case provoked a veritable storm of criticism from a variety of quarters, including (not surprisingly) a number of women's groups. Parliament responded, to some extent at least, by enacting section 265(4) of the *Criminal Code*. This provision, which came into effect in January 1983, applies to

all forms of assault (including the three categories of sexual assault established by sections 271, 272, and 273 of the Code):

> (4) Where an accused alleges that he believed that the complainant consented to the conduct that is the subject-matter of the charge, a judge, if satisfied that there is sufficient evidence and that, if believed by the jury, the evidence would constitute a defence, shall instruct the jury, when reviewing all the evidence relating to the determination of the honesty of the accused's belief, to consider the presence or absence of reasonable grounds for that belief.

The enactment of section 265(4) was, no doubt, based upon the assumption that the more unreasonable the accused's belief as to consent, the less likely it is that the jury will believe that the accused held that belief honestly. However, this provision does not stipulate that a defence of mistaken belief in consent will only be successful if the belief was reasonable. It merely requires the trial judge to instruct the members of the jury to take into account the reasonableness of the accused's belief as a means of determining whether it was honestly held. If the jury has a reasonable doubt as to whether the accused's mistaken belief in consent was honest, they must acquit him or her even if that belief would never have been entertained by a reasonable person.

In the *Osolin* case (1993), the Supreme Court of Canada held that section 265(4) did not violate an accused person's rights under the *Charter*. Justice Cory suggested that the section merely "codified" the common law defence of mistake of fact. In his view, "it is trite law that a trial judge must instruct the jury only upon those defences for which there is a real factual foundation" and section 265(4) merely states that the defence of mistaken belief in consent should not be put to a jury unless there is an evidentiary basis for it. In response to a claim that section 265(4) violated section 11(d) of the *Charter* (the presumption of innocence), Justice Cory noted that section 265(4) only places an evidentiary burden on the accused. In his view,

> all criminal defences must meet a threshold requirement of sufficient evidence, or in other words, an air of reality, before the trial judge should leave them with a jury. In my view, this does not violate the presumption of innocence.

The presumption of innocence would only be violated if, at the end of the trial, the persuasional burden of proof is placed on the accused. Section 265(4) does not alter the fact that the Crown has to prove, beyond a reasonable doubt, all the *actus reus* and *mens rea* elements of an assault. If accused persons satisfy the evidentiary burden of proof in relation to the defence of mistaken belief in consent, they are entitled to be acquitted if, at the end of the trial, there is a reasonable doubt about their belief.

The Supreme Court also rejected the argument that section 265(4) violates an accused person's right to a jury trial under section 11(f) of the *Charter*. The Court took the view that there is a legitimate division of functions between judge and jury insofar as the trial judge decides questions of law (such as the admissibility of evidence) while the members of the jury are required to make determinations on questions of fact. The trial judge is required, as a matter of law, to determine whether there is adequate evidence to place a defence before the jury and this role does not impinge upon the jury's duty to determine the facts of the case. Furthermore, as Justice Cory stated, "in considering the evidence giving rise to the air of reality, it must be remembered that the trial judge is not weighing the evidence, but is simply examining it to determine what defences are available."

The 1983 amendments to the *Criminal Code* that included the enactment of section 265(4) did not dispel the criticism that originated with the *Morgan* and *Pappajohn* rulings, and the Canadian Parliament subsequently introduced sweeping changes to the Code provisions concerning sexual assaults.

The vehicle for these changes was Bill C-49, enacted in 1992. For the first time, the *Criminal Code* now defines the concept of consent within the specific context of a charge of sexual assault. Indeed, section 273.1(1) of the Code states that consent is "the voluntary agreement of the complainant to engage in the sexual activity in question." The 1992 amendments also added to the existing section 265(3) of the Code by setting out a series of additional circumstances in which consent will be deemed not to have been given: namely, where (a) the agreement is given by someone other than the complainant; (b) the complainant is incapable of consenting due to intoxication or some other condition; (c) the agreement is obtained through the accused's abuse of a position of trust or authority; (d) the complainant expresses by words or conduct a lack of agreement to engage in the sexual activity; or (e) the complainant expresses a revocation of an agreement to engage in sexual activity. This list is not exhaustive since section 273.1(3) clearly states that there may be other circumstances that may have the effect of nullifying consent. A detailed discussion of this aspect of the amendments follows in Chapter 10 of this book.

For present purposes, the most important result of the enactment of Bill C-49 is the fact that the *Criminal Code* now makes explicit provision for dealing with the defence of mistaken belief in consent when a defendant is charged with the crime of sexual assault. Specifically, section 273.2 states that the accused's mistaken belief that the complainant consented will not be a defence where (a) the accused's belief arose from self-induced intoxication, recklessness, or wilful blindness; or (b) *the accused did not take all reasonable steps, in the circumstances known to the accused at the time, to ascertain whether the complainant was consenting.*

The first part of section 273.2 basically codifies the criminal law that already existed. However, the second component of the new section represents a significant departure from the pre-existing law. As we have seen, prior to 1992, if a defendant entertained an honest (but mistaken) belief in consent, he or she was entitled to be acquitted of a charge of sexual assault even though no reasonable person would have formed such a belief. Section 273.2(b) reverses this principle and imposes the requirement that the accused take reasonable steps to ascertain that the complainant was consenting (in light of the circumstances known to him or her). In other words, in order for a defence of mistaken belief in consent to be successful, that belief must be based on reasonable grounds. In this sense, Parliament has decided that everyone who enters into sexual activity with others is bound to observe a reasonable standard of care in determining whether consent has been given to such activity.

It is significant that the Ontario Court of Appeal ruled in the *Darrach* case (1998) that section 273.2(b) of the *Criminal Code* does not infringe the fundamental principles of justice that are guaranteed by section 7 of the *Charter*. As Associate Chief Justice Morden stated, on behalf of the court, section 273.2(b) does not remove all of the elements of subjective fault that must generally be proved by the Crown in relation to "real crimes" and, in particular, those that carry a considerable degree of social stigma where the accused is convicted. Indeed, the court held that, while section 273.2(b) undoubtedly introduced an "objective component in the mental element of the offence," Parliament has modified this component by personalizing it "according to the subjective awareness of the accused at the time":

> ... The accused is to "take reasonable steps, *in the circumstances known to the accused at the time*, to ascertain that the complainant was consenting." In other words, the accused is not under an obligation to determine all the relevant circumstances — the issue is what he actually knew, not what he ought to have known ... [emphasis in original]
>
> ... having regard to the basic rationale underlying constitutionally mandated fault requirements that it is wrong to punish a person who is "morally innocent" ..., *it is difficult to contemplate that a man who has sexual intercourse with a woman who has not consented is morally innocent if he has not taken reasonable steps to ascertain that she was consenting*. [emphasis added]

The Ontario Court of Appeal also held that section 273.2(b) does not place the **primary burden of proof** on the accused. In other words, the Crown must prove beyond a reasonable doubt that the accused did *not* take reasonable steps to ascertain whether the complainant gave consent in the circumstances known to the accused at the time of the alleged offence.

Canadians will have to wait to see how the courts interpret the phrase "reasonable steps." For example, will they rule that every individual who wishes to initiate some form of sexual contact with another person must first seek explicit permission to proceed? Perhaps such a requirement would be necessary where the accused and the complainant have not previously engaged in such contact. However, seeking advance permission might not be a practical requirement where the parties cohabit and have established a long-standing sexual relationship. In the latter situation, it might be considered reasonable for the accused merely to repeat the steps that the accused knows led to consensual sexual activity in the past. However, that certainly does not mean that the accused is entitled to proceed in any circumstance in which a reasonable person would draw the conclusion that there is a chance that the other partner may not be willing to consent. For example, in *S. (A.W.)* (1998), the accused and the complainant had been involved in a lengthy common law relationship with each other. The complainant had just undergone abdominal surgery and refused the accused's request for sexual intercourse because she was sore. Five minutes later, without seeking her permission, the accused removed the complainant's clothes and engaged in sexual intercourse with her. The complainant testified that she did not physically resist the accused because she was frightened of him. The accused was acquitted of sexual assault at his trial but, on the Crown's appeal, the Manitoba Court of Appeal substituted a conviction. As Justice Helper stated, in delivering the judgment of the court,

> The law cannot ignore the reality of normal human behaviour. Just as it would be wrong to

conclude that a person involved in an ongoing intimate relationship must secure the express consent of his or her partner prior to initiating any sexual act, it would be wrong to conclude that because the complainant and accused are involved in an ongoing intimate relationship passivity in all circumstances indicates consent ...

... The law cannot allow a person to take refuge in an intimate relationship and be wilfully blind to the condition of his or her sexual partner simply because that relationship exists.

The Court of Appeal concluded that there was no "air of reality" to the accused's defence of honest, but mistaken, belief in consent and that the trial judge should not have considered it at all. The complainant had expressly refused the accused's request for sexual intercourse and made it clear that she was physically unable to do so because of the effects of the surgery. The fact that five minutes elapsed from the express refusal to the moment that the accused commenced the act of intercourse was irrelevant in these particular circumstances. Section 273.2(b) was not applied in *S. (A.W.)*, but the case clearly emphasizes that even an accused person who is involved in a long-standing sexual relationship with another person is not entitled to take advantage of passivity where there is reason to believe that a genuine consent is not forthcoming. The complainant, in this particular case, clearly did not take "reasonable steps" to ascertain consent after the five-minute period had elapsed.

Intoxication and the Defence of Honest Mistake of Fact

May an accused person charged with sexual assault say, "I admit that my belief in consent was unreasonable but I was so drunk that I nevertheless honestly believed that the complainant consented to sexual relations"? The answer is definitely in the negative, since section 273.1(a) clearly states that a mistaken belief in consent that is the result of "self-induced intoxication" is not a valid defence.

The enactment of this provision in 1992 basically reflects the existing case law on the subject. For example, in *Moreau* (1986), the Ontario Court of Appeal had already ruled that, as a matter of sound legal policy, intoxication should only be a valid defence to a charge of an offence requiring proof of *specific* (as opposed to *general* or *basic*) intent. The offence of sexual assault requires proof only of *general* or *basic* intent and, for this reason, intoxication cannot be raised as a defence. Therefore, in the view of the court, a drunken (albeit honest) mistake as to the victim's consent cannot be considered a valid defence.

Section 273.1(a) only applies to sexual assaults, but the general principles articulated in the *Moreau* case still apply to other offences. An honest mistake of fact in relation to a crime of **specific intent** may be a defence even if the mistake was caused by intoxication, but a mistake of fact in relation to a crime of basic intent (such as damage to property under section 430) is not a valid defence.

The general rules pertaining to intoxication as a defence are discussed in detail later in this chapter.

Excluding the Defence of Honest Mistake of Fact: Implications of the *Charter*

Although the defence of mistake of fact may well serve as an effective shield against conviction of a criminal offence, it is important to bear in mind that legislators nevertheless have the power to deny a defendant the benefit of the defence of mistake of fact by writing legislation in a manner that relieves the Crown of the need to establish actual knowledge of one or more material elements of the *actus reus* of the offence charged. We have seen (in Chapter 6) that, in Canada, such a practice is common where **regulatory offences** are concerned.

In cases where it is determined that the legislators intended to impose a régime of **strict liability**, accused persons may escape conviction if they establish that they acted with "due diligence." What this means is that, as far as strict liability offences are concerned, honest mistake of fact as to a material element of the *actus reus* is not a sufficient defence. However, the accused may raise a successful defence of honest, but mistaken, belief if he or she can prove, on the balance of probabilities, that any such mistake was also *reasonable* in all of the circumstances. Significantly, in the *Wholesale Travel Group Inc.* case (1991), a majority of the members of the Supreme Court of Canada took the view that placing the onus on the accused to establish his or her innocence did not, as far as the *Charter* is concerned, invalidate legislation that imposes strict liability provided the offences concerned are *regulatory* in nature.

We also saw in Chapter 6 that, if a legislature imposes **absolute liability** in relation to a regulatory offence, then, as the Supreme Court of Canada ruled in *Reference Re Section 94(2) of the Motor Vehicle Act* (1985), such an offence will be considered invalid under the *Charter* if conviction has the potential to result in imprisonment of the accused (the only exception would be where it is successfully argued that the violation of the accused's rights under the *Charter* are justified under section 1). In other words, a legislature may generally not deny a defendant the benefit of the defence of honest mistake of fact by creating an offence of absolute liability if conviction of that offence could lead to his or her imprisonment.

The question now arises as to whether Parliament may exclude defendants from the benefit of the defence of honest mistake of fact where the offence charged is a ***true crime*** rather than a mere *regulatory offence*. Clearly, if Parliament imposes absolute liability in relation to a true crime, there is an extremely strong likelihood that a court will declare that the offence is invalid on the basis that it violates section 7 of the *Charter* and cannot be saved by section 1. This is precisely what happened in the cases of *Nguyen and Hess* (1990), in which the Supreme Court of Canada ruled that (what was then) section 146(1) of the *Criminal Code* was invalid under the *Charter of Rights and Freedoms*.

Section 146(1) of the Code (prior to 1987) provided that

Every male person who has sexual intercourse with a female person who

(a) is not his wife, and
(b) is under the age of fourteen years,

whether or not he believes that she is fourteen years of age or more, is guilty of an indictable offence and is liable to imprisonment for life. [emphasis added]

Essentially, section 146(1) denied an accused person the benefit of the defence of mistake of fact in relation to the critical element of age. In this sense, it imposed absolute liability and, since imprisonment was clearly a potential sentence, the Supreme Court of Canada ruled that it was, therefore, an infringement of the accused's rights under section 7 of the *Charter*. The Court also held that section 146(1) was not saved by section 1 of the *Charter*. Although Parliament's objective of protecting young children from premature sexual activity was sufficiently "pressing and substantial" as to justify overriding a *Charter* right, section 146(1) of the Code was not saved by section 1 of the *Charter* because it failed the test of proportionality. In particular, section 146(1) did not impair the accused's rights under section 7 of the *Charter* "as little as possible." As Justice Wilson stated,

The potential benefits flowing from the retention of absolute liability are far too speculative to be able to justify a provision that envisages the possibility of life imprisonment for one who is mentally innocent. At a minimum the provision must provide for a defence of due diligence.

The ruling in *Nguyen and Hess* turned out to be somewhat academic since, in 1987, Parliament had already repealed section 146(1), and had introduced a due diligence defence that could be raised by a defendant charged with a number of sexual offences contained in the *Criminal Code* (which is exactly the course of action that was to be suggested by the Supreme Court of Canada in the *Nguyen and Hess* case some four years later). The "new" section 150.1(4) of the Code states that

It is not a defence to a charge under section 151 or 152, subsection 160(3) or 173(2), or section 271, 272, or 273 that the accused believed that the complainant was 14 years of age or more at the time the offence is alleged to have been committed *unless the accused took all reasonable steps to ascertain the age of the complainant.* [emphasis added]

However, it is critical to remember that due diligence defences, such as that contained in section 150.1(4) of the Code, do not appear to place the onus on the accused to prove that he or she acted reasonably. Indeed, as the B.C. Court of Appeal held in *P. (L.T.)* (1997), it will be enough for accused persons in such circumstances to raise a reasonable doubt as to whether they took all reasonable steps to ascertain the age of the child concerned. In other words, although it may be deemed appropriate to impose strict liability in relation to regulatory offences (and to require the accused to prove that he or she was not negligent), it is certainly not just to place such a burden on the shoulders of a person charged with a *true crime.*

How "Honest" Must a Mistake of Fact Be?

Suppose that an accused person makes the following response to a criminal charge: "Owing to an honest mistake, I had no intention to commit the particular offence with which I am charged. It is true that, as a consequence of this mistake, I actually intended to commit a *different* offence. However, I should nevertheless be acquitted since I lacked the necessary *mens rea* in relation to the specific offence with which I am charged." Can such a defendant escape criminal liability?

The Yukon Court of Appeal addressed this issue in the somewhat bizarre case of *Ladue* (1965), in which the accused was charged with "indecently interfering with a dead human body" contrary to (what is now) section 178(b) of the *Criminal Code.* The accused either copulated or attempted to copulate with a dead woman. However, he claimed that because of intoxication, he did not realize that the woman was dead, and instead believed that she was only unconscious. In effect, Ladue claimed that he honestly believed that the woman was alive and, therefore, he clearly lacked the *mens rea* to commit the offence charged—namely, indecent interference with a dead human body. However, if the facts were as Ladue had actually believed them to be, it was clear that he possessed the *mens rea* for *rape* (an intent to have intercourse without consent). Ladue, therefore, committed the *actus reus* of the offence of indecent interference but had the *mens rea* for the offence of rape. In these circumstances, the court understandably rejected the defence of mistake of fact. Justice Davey asserted that,

> it would be only in the most exceptional case where the offender might have any doubt whether a body was quick or dead, and in such a case he might defend himself by showing that he did not know the body was dead and that according to his understanding he was acting lawfully and innocently.
>
> That is what the appellant cannot show in this case, because if the woman was alive he was raping her.

Although the *Ladue* decision represents something of a departure from the principle that the Crown must prove that accused persons possessed the specific *mens rea* for the offence with which they are actually charged, the outcome of the case is not objectionable in terms of the principles of justice: after all, Ladue intended to commit a *more serious* offence than the one with which he was actually charged. What is the legal situation where an accused person commits the *actus reus* of a *serious* offence but, because of a mistake, only possesses the *mens rea* appropriate to a *lesser* offence? Does the reasoning in *Ladue* also apply here? The Canadian courts have dealt with this issue in the context of legislation relating to the illegal sale of drugs and they have apparently expanded the reasoning employed in *Ladue.*

In *Kundeus* (1976), the accused had sold (what he allegedly believed to be) mescaline to an undercover police officer; in fact, the drug was LSD. Kundeus was charged with trafficking in LSD, which was a restricted drug under (what was then) the *Food and Drugs Act*. The penalty for this offence was a maximum of eighteen months' imprisonment (upon summary conviction) and ten years' imprisonment (upon conviction on indictment). In contrast, mescaline was not a controlled or restricted drug under the provisions of the *Food and Drugs Act*. However, it was an offence to sell mescaline under the *Food and Drugs Act* regulations. The penalty for this offence was a maximum of three months' imprisonment (for a first summary conviction), five months' imprisonment (for a secondary summary conviction), and a maximum of three years' imprisonment (for a conviction upon indictment). It is clear that the penalty for the sale of LSD considerably exceeded that which ought to have been imposed for the sale of mescaline. In essence, therefore, Kundeus alleged (in a statement that he gave to the police) that he believed he was committing the *actus reus* of the less serious offence (selling mescaline) but he actually committed the *actus reus* of the more serious offence (trafficking in LSD). Nevertheless, Kundeus was convicted of trafficking in LSD despite his alleged mistake of fact and the Supreme Court of Canada ultimately upheld his conviction.

A similar case is that of *Futa* (1976), in which the accused was charged with being in possession of a narcotic (phencyclidine) for the purpose of trafficking contrary to the provisions of the (now repealed) *Narcotic Control Act*. The maximum penalty for such an offence was life imprisonment. Futa, however, believed that he had MDA in his possession. MDA was a restricted drug under the provisions of the *Food and Drugs Act*, and the maximum penalties for conviction of the offence of possessing a restricted drug for the purpose of trafficking were eighteen months' imprisonment (upon summary conviction) or ten years (upon conviction by indictment). As in *Kundeus*, there was a considerable difference in the maximum penalties that could be imposed for illicit use of the two drugs in question. Futa believed that he was committing the lesser offence under the *Food and Drugs Act*, but he was, in fact, committing the *actus reus* of the more serious offence under the *Narcotic Control Act*. Unfortunately for Futa, the B.C. Court of Appeal entered a conviction against him on the basis that his knowledge that he was dealing in a drug that was forbidden by the *Food and Drugs Act* was sufficient proof of the *mens rea* that must accompany the commission of the offence under the *Narcotic Control Act*. In other words, his mistake was not "innocent" in nature, and his general **intention** to deal in "forbidden drugs" was sufficient to deprive him of the benefit of the defence of honest mistake of fact.

It is questionable whether the approach adopted by the courts in *Kundeus* and *Futa* is either consistent with the doctrine of *mens rea* or desirable in terms of its results.

It does seem somewhat harsh to convict defendants of a more serious offence than the offence they were actually contemplating. Furthermore, there is absolutely no doubt that such an approach flouts the basic principles of the doctrine of *mens rea* in that the Crown is normally required to establish that the accused has the appropriate *mens rea* for the *specific offence(s) charged* before a conviction can be entered. In contrast, some people would argue that those who *knowingly* deal in illegal drugs should take the risk that the consequences of being caught are more unpleasant than they had previously imagined; after all, their "honest" mistake of fact is tainted by their conscious involvement in an outlawed activity. Similarly, it might be contended that to permit a defence of honest mistake in such circumstances would "open the floodgates" to conveniently concocted defences; any individuals charged with the sale of a drug that attracts a high criminal penalty for its illicit use would automatically claim that they believed it was a drug that attracted a lesser penalty. It might well be difficult for the Crown to disprove that they really had such a belief.

MISTAKE OF LAW

The General Principles

Section 19 of the *Criminal Code* enshrines one of the most widely known principles of the criminal law, namely, that "ignorance of the law is no defence." Indeed, as Chief Justice Lamer, of the Supreme Court of Canada, noted in the *Jorgensen* case (1995), "while mistakes of fact relevant to the commission of a criminal offence excuse an accused from criminal responsibility, mistakes regarding the law do not."

Take, for example the case of *Jones and Pamajewon* (1991), in which the accused were charged with operating an unlawful bingo, contrary to the provisions of section 206 of the *Criminal Code.* Section 207 of the Code provides that a charitable or religious organization may operate a legal lottery scheme if they first obtain a provincial licence; the accused did not obtain such a licence. The accused were members of a Native band and they conducted the bingo on a Native reserve. They contended, *inter alia*, that they were under the mistaken belief that the *Criminal Code* did not apply to bingo activities conducted on a reserve. Clearly, their mistake was one of law — that the *Criminal Code* provisions concerning bingo were not in operation on the reserve. Therefore, since their mistake was one of law rather than fact, section 19 of the Code applied and they could not put forward a defence based on their mistaken belief.

Similarly, in the case of *Forster* (1992), the accused was a commissioned officer in the Canadian Armed Forces who was ordered to report to a new posting. This would have involved moving to Ottawa from Edmonton, where her husband was also stationed. Instead of obeying the order to report to her new posting in Ottawa, she attempted to submit her resignation from the Armed Forces. Such an attempt was ineffective, since she did not follow the prescribed procedures under *Queen's Regulations*, for accomplishing this end. She was later charged with being absent without leave, contrary to section 90 of the *National Defence Act*, and

was convicted by a General Court Martial in spite of her defence that she honestly believed that she had effectively resigned from the Armed Forces (i.e., an honest *mistake of law*). The Supreme Court of Canada later ordered a new trial on the basis that the General Court Martial did not meet the requirements of section 11(d) of the *Charter* (namely, that it be "an independent and impartial tribunal"). However, Chief Justice Lamer pointed out that Foster

> was mistaken about the legal consequences of her actions, because of her failure to understand that she was under a continuing legal obligation to report for duty notwithstanding her purported resignation by letter from the forces. Thus, while she may not have intended to commit an offence under military law, this lack of intention flowed from her mistake as to the continuing legal obligation to report for duty which that regime imposed upon her until properly released from service in accordance with [Queen's Regulations and Orders].
>
> It is a principle of our criminal law that an honest but mistaken belief in respect of the legal consequences of one's deliberate actions does not furnish a defence to a criminal charge, even when the mistake cannot be attributed to the negligence of the accused. ... This court recently reaffirmed *... the principle that knowledge that one's actions are contrary to the law is not a component of the* mens rea *for an offence, and consequently does not operate as a defence.* [emphasis added]

Perhaps the most frequent justification advanced in support of this principle is that it is a practical necessity; indeed, it is contended that the Crown could never successfully shoulder the burden of proving, in every case, that defendants had *actual* knowledge of the particular law under which they are charged. Furthermore, it has been suggested that, if ignorance of the law were to be considered a legitimate defence, this would in effect place a premium on ignorance of the law — a situation that would scarcely be conducive to law-abiding behaviour. However, whatever the justification for section 19 may be, it is incontrovertible that its application may well prove to be extremely harsh in those circumstances where an individual is genuinely ignorant of the law.

The harshness inherent in the application of section 19 is well demonstrated in the case of *Molis* (1981). In this case, Molis was charged with trafficking in a restricted drug (MDMA) contrary to the provisions of section 48(1) of the *Food and Drugs Act*. Molis operated a laboratory in which he manufactured a chemical substance known as MDMA. At the time that he started manufacturing this substance (in August 1975), it was not illegal for him to do so. Unfortunately for Molis, MDMA was later added to Schedule H of the Act and, at that time (June 1976) it became a restricted drug. This amendment to the schedule was brought into effect by a regulation that was duly published in the *Canada Gazette*. Molis, who was unaware of the regulation, continued to manufacture MDMA and was subsequently arrested and charged. The accused was convicted and his appeals were dismissed by both the Ontario Court of Appeal and the Supreme Court of Canada. Molis contended that there was a significant distinction to be drawn between a mistake of law (that is to say, the *wrong interpretation* of the law) and *ignorance of the existence* of a particular penal provision. In the defendant's view, the provisions of section 19 of the *Criminal Code* applied only to ignorance of law in the sense of a mistake of law and not to the ignorance of the very existence of the law. However, Justice Lamer, in delivering the judgment of the Supreme Court of Canada, rejected Molis's contention:

> Whatever may be the merit of such a distinction ... Parliament has by the clear and unequivocal language of s. 19 chosen not to make any distinction between ignorance of the existence of the law and that as to its meaning, scope or application.

In practice, it is sometimes difficult to distinguish between a mistake of *fact* and a mistake of *law*. Indeed, it occasionally appears that the courts will "bend the rules" slightly in order to achieve a "just" result. For example, it might well be argued that, in the cases of *Prue and Baril* (1979), the majority of the justices of the Supreme Court of Canada "bent over backwards" to hold that the defendants were operating under a mistake of *fact*, as opposed to a mistake of *law*. By so doing, of course, the Court furnished the defendants with a valid defence. Prue and Baril had been convicted, in British Columbia, of the offence of driving with more than 80 mg of alcohol in their blood (contrary to what is now section 253 of the *Criminal Code*). Section 86D of the B.C. *Motor-Vehicle Act* provided that the defendants' driving licences were *automatically suspended* upon conviction of such an offence. However, no one bothered to inform the defendants of the suspension of their licences and they continued to drive, were apprehended by the police, and charged with driving while disqualified (contrary to what is now section 259(4) of the *Criminal Code*). By a majority of four to three, the Supreme Court ruled that the defendants' ignorance of their suspension was a *mistake of fact* and, therefore, constituted a valid defence. Chief Justice Laskin said that

> So far as the operation of s. [259(4)] is concerned, the existence of a suspension from driving is a question of fact underlying the invocation of that provision and so too is proof that an accused charged thereunder drove while his licence to do so was under suspension.

However, it is interesting to note that three of the seven Supreme Court justices disagreed and contended that Prue and Baril's ignorance of their suspension amounted to a mistake of law. For example, Justice Ritchie stated that

> I am satisfied that the mistake made by the accused in the present cases is nothing more than a mistake as to the legal consequences of a conviction under s. [253] of the *Criminal Code* involving as they do automatic suspension of the

operator's licence under s. 86D of the *Motor-Vehicle Act*.

In short, the cases of *Prue and Baril* clearly illustrate that there is sometimes a somewhat fuzzy line between a mistake of fact and a mistake of law; consequently, the ultimate decision as to how to categorize a mistake in a difficult case may well hinge on the Court's perception of whether justice demands the accused be accorded a valid defence.

In addition, the courts have shown considerable inventiveness in devising exceptions to the general rule articulated in section 19 of the Code. For example, in *Docherty* (1989), the Supreme Court of Canada ruled that, where the *mens rea* necessary for the conviction of an offence includes *knowledge on the part of the accused that he or she is breaking the law*, then, in this context, a mistake of law amounts to a lack of *mens rea* and the accused must be acquitted. The facts in *Docherty* were that the accused was charged with wilfully failing to comply with the terms of a probation order, contrary to (what was then) section 740(1) of the Code. The probation order in question required him, *inter alia*, to "keep the peace and be of good behaviour." Docherty later pleaded guilty to a charge of being in care and control of a motor vehicle while being "over 80." The Crown contended that the conviction of the accused on the motor vehicle offence constituted a breach of the requirement of the probation order set out above. The accused stated that he had no intention of breaking the law. He had been found intoxicated in a parked vehicle and was convicted of being "in care and control" of the car even though he had no intent to drive it. Docherty testified that it never entered his mind that he might be breaking the law since he did not realize that a person can be considered to be in "care and control" of a motor vehicle even if it was impossible to start the engine (as to this principle, see the discussion in Chapter 2). Therefore, Docherty contended that he had not wilfully breached the terms of his probation.

The Supreme Court of Canada held that the accused's honest, but mistaken, belief that he was not breaking the law was a defence. His mistake—albeit a mistake of law—meant that he did not *wilfully* breach the terms of his probation order. In effect, the Court held that section 19 was not applicable because it was an essential element of the *mens rea* requirement of the charge, under section 740(1), that the accused actually *know* that his act was contrary to the law. Of course, the situation in the *Docherty* case was decidedly unusual, but the determination of the Supreme Court of Canada to avoid the imposition of a considerable injustice is most significant.*

Perhaps of more general importance, in terms of modifying the strict application of section 19 of the Code, is the decision of the Ontario Court of Appeal in the case of *Ilczyszyn* (1988), in which the court ruled that a mistake as to the legal effect of the *civil*, as opposed to the *criminal*, law could constitute a defence to a criminal charge. The accused was charged with abduction of a child in contravention of the terms of a custody order (contrary to what is now section 282 of the Code). The accused knew of the existence of the custody order but believed, on the basis of legal advice, that it was no longer valid after she recommended habitation with the child's father. The accused's mistake was one of law; she knew the order existed but was mistaken as to its legal effect. The Ontario Court of Appeal nevertheless ruled that the accused had been correctly acquitted at trial. The court stated that

> In most cases, the fact that an accused knew the terms of a custody order and in fact acted in contravention of its terms would be sufficient to persuade a trier of fact beyond a reasonable doubt that he or she *intended* to do so. However, in an unusual case such as the one before us, where the accused, although knowing of the terms of the order, truly believed on reasonable grounds that it was no longer in existence, there could be no intent to contravene a valid and subsisting order.

---

*In 1995, the *Criminal Code* was amended, and the offence became that of failing to comply with a probation order "*without reasonable excuse*," rather than "wilfully": see section 733.1.

It is interesting that the B.C. Court of Appeal made a similar decision in the case of *Hammerbeck* (1991). This would appear to suggest that Canadian courts are likely to recognize a general principle that a mistake as to the effect of the *civil* law will provide an effective defence to a criminal charge. The distinction between a mistake as to a matter of criminal law and a mistake as to a matter of civil law is, therefore, an important one to draw before applying section 19 of the Code.

The Evolution of a New Defence or "Excuse": Officially Induced Error

There is little doubt that application of the rule that ignorance of the law is no excuse is becoming increasingly problematic in an age when Canadians are faced with a rapidly burgeoning mass of regulatory laws. We have already seen, in Chapter 6, that legislation at both the federal and provincial/territorial levels has created a vast body of regulatory offences. What is particularly disturbing is that many of these offences are not contained in the provisions of a statute that is passed in Parliament or the (provincial/territorial) legislature and readily available to members of the public. Instead, they are incorporated into sets of detailed regulations that may be difficult to locate and their existence may, indeed, be completely unknown to many of those persons affected by them.

Many statutes contain provisions that permit the appropriate minister(s) of the Crown to pass regulations into the law and infringement of them may result in the accused being convicted of an offence. If we take a statute of the Province of British Columbia as a typical example, we may see that a significant number of regulations passed under the authority of the B.C. *Motor-Vehicle Act* deal with a host of detailed matters that it would be inappropriate to include within the *Motor-Vehicle Act* itself (for example, the detailed dimensions of permissible motor-vehicle equipment).*

---

*See *Interpretation Act*, R.S.B.C. 1996, c. 238, section 41.

It is clear that such regulations are considerably more inaccessible to the public than acts of Parliament or the provincial/territorial legislatures. Therefore, it may well be contended that it is unfair to apply the principle that ignorance of the law is no defence when the defendant is charged with an offence arising out of the alleged contravention of such a regulation. However, both the (federal) *Statutory Instruments Act*, R.S.C. 1985, c. S-22, section 11 and, for example, the (provincial) *Regulations Act*, R.S.B.C. 1996, c. 402, section 7, provide that, if a regulation is duly published in the *Canada Gazette* or the *British Columbia Gazette*, as the case may be, an accused person may be convicted for contravention of such a regulation in spite of the accused's complete ignorance of it. The only weakening of the general rule that precludes ignorance of the law as a defence arises when the regulation has not been published in the appropriate *Gazette*. In such a circumstance, both the *Statutory Instruments Act* and the *Regulations Act* provide that the accused person may not be convicted unless it is proved that, at the time of the alleged offence, reasonable steps were taken to bring the substance of the regulation to the attention of the public in general or, at least, of the persons most likely to be affected by it.

Given the fact that Canadians are faced with a vast array of offences, many of which are "buried" in hard-to-find regulations, should there be any general exceptions to the principle that igorance of the law is no excuse? It appears that Canadian courts are, indeed, prepared to recognize such an exception, although it is very circumscribed in its nature and application.

In *MacDougall* (1982), the Supreme Court of Canada expressly "left open" the possibility that accused persons might have a defence where they commit an offence under a mistake of law that has been induced by *"official error."* In other words, where accused persons rely on an interpretation of the law, made by a public official whose duty it is to provide citizens with advice, it has been argued that they should be absolved from criminal responsibility if the official's advice proves to be incorrect and prompts the accused to commit an offence while operating under a mistake of law. For example, if accused persons are charged with a motor vehicle offence that has been prompted by a mistake of law induced by advice received from the Provincial Registrar of Motor Vehicles, it is possible that they will be granted a valid defence. The Supreme Court of Canada did not expressly recognize the existence of the defence in the *MacDougall* case. However, its decision "to leave the question open" has resulted in the defence being espoused by a number of the lower courts, such as the Ontario Court of Appeal.

Indeed, the Ontario Court of Appeal unequivocally recognized the existence of the defence of "officially induced error" in the case of *Cancoil Thermal Corp. and Parkinson* (1986), in which there had been an accident at a factory that produced heat transfer coils. An employee had lost the tips of six of his fingers when both of his hands came into contact with a moving blade that was part of the machine with which he was working. The machine in question had originally been equipped with a guard that would have prevented this type of accident, had it been in place. Unfortunately for the employee, the guard had been removed on the initiative of both the supervisor and the general manager of the factory. These individuals believed the guard created a hazard since its presence made it more difficult for the operator of the machine to clear away pieces of scrap metal. In addition, it was felt that there was an alternative safety device, namely a foot pedal that had to be depressed before the blade could be started. As it turned out, while the employee was removing pieces of scrap metal from the machine, he accidentally hit the pedal and, as a consequence, was injured. The accused were charged with a number of offences arising under the Ontario *Occupational Health and Safety Act*, R.S.O. 1980, c. 321.

The trial judge acquitted the accused on the basis of a technical interpretation of the statute. The Crown appealed the acquittal and the Ontario Court of Appeal agreed that the trial judge's interpretation of the statute was in error. However, the accused raised the defence of "officially induced error" (for the first time) before the Court of Appeal. It was suggested that, two months before the accident, an inspector from the Occupational Health and Safety Division had been informed that the guard had been removed from the machine in question and that he had commented that "it was safe to remove the particular piece of metal in question and that with the machine being operated according to instructions that it was safe to do so." The Court of Appeal ordered that a new trial be held to deal with this issue. Most significantly, the court ruled that Canadian criminal law did, indeed, recognize the existence of the defence of "officially induced error." Justice Lacourcière held that it

> is available as a defence to an alleged violation of a regulatory statute where an accused has reasonably relied upon the erroneous legal opinion or advice of an official who is responsible for the administration or enforcement of the particular law. In order for the accused to successfully raise this defence, he must show that he relied on the erroneous legal opinion of the official and that his reliance was reasonable. The reasonableness will depend upon several factors including the efforts he made to ascertain the proper law, the complexity or obscurity of the law, the position of the official who gave the advice, and the clarity, definitiveness and reasonableness of the advice given.

Similarly, in the case of *Dubeau* (1993), a trial judge of the General Division of the Ontario Court acquitted an accused person on the basis of the defence of officially induced error. Dubeau was charged with the offence of carrying on a firearms business without a permit, contrary to the provisions of section 105 of the *Criminal Code*. He was a gun collector who had sold a considerable number of firearms at a series of garage sales. Before commencing these garage sales, Dubeau approached the local firearms officer (an employee of the local police force) who told him that there was "no limit" on the number of firearms that he could sell in this way without a "dealer's permit." The accused also wrote, at the suggestion of the firearms officer, to officials at the headquarters of the Ontario Provincial Police and requested information concerning a number of issues, including information about obtaining a dealer's permit and opening a shooting range. The request for information concerning the dealer's permit was overlooked and the letter that Dubeau received in reply dealt only with the matter of the shooting range. In the circumstances, it is clear that Dubeau should have obtained a business permit before holding the garage sales. However, could he rely on the defence of officially induced error, since he was undoubtedly operating under a mistake of law as a consequence of the advice he had, in good faith, sought and received from the firearms officer? Judge Ferguson, in acquitting the accused, ruled that Dubeau did, indeed, have the right to assert this defence:

> I am satisfied that Mr. Dubeau relied on the advice he received form the local firearms officer and in all the circumstances I think his reliance was reasonable, taking into account that this particular law is very complex and that it was the duty of local firearms officer to respond to general inquiries from the public. She did not tell him he should ask any other official.

It will be most interesting to see exactly how the defence of "officially induced error" will evolve in the years ahead. It has still not been officially endorsed by the Supreme Court of Canada. However, it is significant that, in the case of *Jorgensen* (1995), Chief Justice Lamer of the Supreme Court of Canada expressed his personal view that the defence does exist. He noted that "the complexity of contemporary regulation makes the assumption that a responsible citizen will have a comprehensive knowledge of the law unreasonable." In his opinion, the very phenomenon of extensive regulation "is one motive for creating a limited exception to the rule" that ignorance of the law is no excuse.

Although Chief Justice Lamer stated his belief that the defence of officially induced error would arise most frequently in the context of regulatory offences, he also indicated that the defence could equally well apply to the realm of "true crimes." For example, in the *Jorgensen* case, the accused had been charged with a number of counts of knowingly selling obscene material (contrary to section 163(2)(a) of the *Criminal Code*). The accused operated a video store and was charged after undercover police officers purchased eight videotapes. All of these tapes had been approved by the Ontario Film Review Board. Nevertheless, the trial court ruled that three of the tapes were obscene and the accused was convicted. The Supreme Court of Canada entered acquittals on behalf of the accused on the ground that he had not "knowingly" sold obscene material. The Crown had not established that the accused "knew of the presence of the ingredients of the subject-matter which as a matter of law rendered the exploitation of sex undue" and, therefore, obscene.

Chief Justice Lamer, speaking for himself alone, took the view that the accused could have been acquitted on the basis of the officially induced error that arose from the board's approval of the films in question. The Chief Justice's summary of the nature and scope of the defence is of considerable value since it may well reflect the approach that will be taken by the Supreme Court of Canada in the future, should that Court be called upon to decide definitively whether the defence exists and, if so, what principles should guide the courts in its application. According to Chief Justice Lamer,

> In summary, officially induced error functions as an excuse rather than a full defence. It can only be raised after the Crown has proven all the elements of the offence. *In order for an accused to rely on this excuse, she must show, after establishing she made an error of law, that she considered her legal position, consulted an appropriate official, obtained reasonable advice and relied on that advice in her actions....* [emphasis added]

Chief Justice Lamer went on to state that, since officially induced error should be seen as an "excuse" rather than a "justification," it should not lead to a conventional acquittal, but rather to a stay of proceedings by the trial court:

the accused has done nothing to entitle him to an acquittal, but the state has done something which disentitles it to a conviction ... the successful application of an officially induced error of law argument will lead to a judicial stay of proceedings rather than an acquittal. Consequently, as a stay can only be entered in the clearest of cases, *an officially induced error of law argument will only be successful in the clearest of cases.* [emphasis added]

Mistake of Law and "Colour of Right"

Officially induced error may provide a defence to a criminal charge in a limited number of circumstances. However, there is one general exception to the legal doctrine that ignorance of the law is no excuse. This exception is encompassed by the important principle that a mistake of law may constitute a valid defence where it operates to negative the specific intent required by the definition of an offence. For example, in defining theft, section 322(1) provides that the offence is committed only when the accused take or convert property to their own use "fraudulently and without *colour of right.*" The latter phrase refers to the legal principle that accused persons may not be convicted of theft if they *honestly* believe that they have a legal right to the property in question. In other words, accused persons may be acquitted where they act under an *honest* mistake of law as to whether or not they have a legal right to such property. Similar provisions exist in relation to forcible detainer of real property (section 72(2)) and damage to property, contrary to the provisions of Part XI of the *Criminal Code* (section 429(2)). In essence, a person who is operating "under colour of right" is under a mistake as to a matter of his or her private property rights, and the relevant provisions of the Code reflect the view that it would be unduly harsh to convict such a person of a criminal offence.

A typical example of the "colour of right" defence is provided by the English case of *Skivington* (1967), in which the defendant demanded wages that he believed were owing to him and his wife. He compelled his employer's agent to hand over two wage packets at knife-point. Skivington was acquitted of robbery because he had an honest belief that he had a legal right to the wage packets. Since robbery basically involves theft with violence, Skivington had to be acquitted of this charge once it was established that the specific intent required for theft (namely, that the accused acted without "colour of right") was negatived by his honest mistake of law.

This case may usefully be compared with the Canadian decision in *Hemmerly* (1976), in which the accused was charged with robbery after taking some money from his victim at gun-point. Hemmerly contended that he had acted under "colour of right" because he claimed that the victim owed him money as a result of a prior transaction for the sale of illegal drugs. Hemmerly's conviction of robbery was upheld by the Ontario Court of Appeal because he knew very well that he would have no claim in *law* to funds arising from the illicit sale of drugs. Justice Martin went on to say that "even if the appellant believed that he had a moral claim to the money (which I am far from holding), a belief in a moral claim could not constitute a colour of right." In other words, Hemmerly was not operating under an honest mistake as to his *legal* rights at the time he committed the robbery.

It is important to bear in mind that the defence of acting "under colour of right" applies despite the fact that a court may subsequently find that the accused persons concerned did not have the legal right they thought they did. This principle is clearly demonstrated by the case of *Lilly* (1983), in which the accused was a real estate broker who had been charged with the theft of some $26 000 that had been deposited in trust with his company in connection with various real estate transactions. It was alleged that the accused had misappropriated the funds in question because he took them out of the trust account *before* the various transactions had been completed. Lilly contended, *inter alia*, that he honestly believed that he had a right to take out his commission from the trust account just as soon as the offers to purchase the various properties had been accepted by the vendors. Despite this contention, the accused was convicted at his trial. The judge directed the jury that, insofar as the issue of "colour of right" was concerned, the real question was when did the commission become payable to the accused's company. He also told the jury that it was "up to you to determine if the company, through the accused, had the right to transfer the commission from the trust account" at the time that such transfer was, in fact, made. In effect, the judge was inviting the jury to decide the validity of Lilly's legal claim rather than the question of whether he honestly believed that he had such a right. Ultimately, the Supreme Court of Canada allowed the accused's appeal and ordered a new trial. Justice Lamer, speaking for the Court, held that

> The fate of the accused's defence of colour of right was not dependent upon the jury determining when the commissions were payable. That question was indeed important as relevant to whether the moneys were his or those of his clients. The fact that they still be the property of the client was a prerequisite to his having to raise a defence to the taking or conversion. Rather, the accused's defence was dependent upon whether they, the jury, were satisfied beyond a reasonable doubt that he, the accused, had not, at the time of the transfers, an honest belief that he had the right to that money, and not, as they were told, dependent on what they, the jurors thought his rights were.

The defence of "colour of right" is not limited to mistakes about ownership of private property. Indeed, section 429(2) of the *Criminal Code* expressly furnishes a defence of acting "with colour of right" in the context of Part XI of the Code, which deals with such offences as *mischief* (destroying, damaging, obstructing, or interfering with the use of property) and *arson*. In *Watson* (1999), the accused, an environmental activist, was charged with two counts of mischief causing

actual danger to life and one count of mischief (section 430). By various methods, the accused attempted to prevent a Cuban trawler from fishing for (what he believed was) cod. Watson contended that he honestly believed that he had the right to intervene in light of the provisions of the *World Charter for Nature* (an international convention originally signed in 1982). The trial judge ruled that Watson did not, in fact, have the legal right to intervene as he did. However, the judge did instruct the jury that the defence of "colour of right" was available to the accused:

> … there can be "colour of right" where an accused honestly, but incorrectly believes that he had a legal right to do something that would otherwise be a crime because he was specifically legally authorized in the particular circumstances facing him to do it … Now, in this case, Mr. Watson says that, he was justified in the circumstances here, in obstructing, interrupting or interfering with the *Rio Las Casas* because he honestly believed he was authorized to do so by the *World Charter of* [*sic*] *Nature*. Now, I am telling you that, in principle, this could constitute a defence of "colour of right" …

Significantly, the Newfoundland Court of Appeal agreed with this statement of the law, indicating that "colour of right is an honest belief in a state of facts or civil law which, if it existed, would negate the *mens rea* of an offence."

INTOXICATION

Historical Overview of the Defence

Until 1996, the *Criminal Code* made no mention of the defence of intoxication. Prior to this date, the development of the defence of intoxication was exclusively a matter of *common law*; in other words, the nature of the defence was shaped by *judges* rather than by Parliament. The common law concerning intoxication has its roots in the decisions made by the judiciary in England, and it is significant that, in this particular area of the criminal law, Canadian courts have, until recently, followed the decisions of English courts very closely indeed.

Historically, intoxication was treated by the English courts as being an *aggravating* (rather than a *mitigating*) factor in a criminal prosecution. However, during the course of the nineteenth century, the English courts gradually started to relax their approach and fashioned a compromise, in which intoxication came to be regarded as a **partial defence** to most of the more serious criminal charges. It was considered a partial defence because it would operate to reduce the severity of the charge against the accused (e.g., from **murder** to **manslaughter** or from robbery to assault). Traditionally, the English courts took the view that intoxication should not be available as a *complete* defence to criminal charges. As we shall see, this approach defence was based on the fundamental legal principle that intoxication *may* be a defence to a charge in which the Crown is required to prove specific intent in order to obtain a conviction (as in murder or robbery) but is *never* available where the offence concerned is considered to be one in which the Crown only has to prove general or basic intent (as in manslaughter or assault). The distinction between specific and general (or basic) intent offences has already been discussed in Chapter 4 and will be examined in more detail later in this chapter.

Until 1994, English and Canadian courts basically applied the same principles when dealing with the defence of intoxication. These principles were generally known as the "*Beard* rules," taking their name from the case in which they were first articulated. However, in the case of *Daviault* (1994), the majority of the justices of the Supreme Court of Canada broke away from the traditional approach to intoxication by declaring that there may be circumstances in which intoxication should be considered a *complete* defence after all. More specifically, they took the view that, if a defendant is charged with an offence of general (or basic) intent such as sexual assault, intoxication may be a valid defence if it is so extreme as to produce a "state akin to

automatism or insanity." This, of course, represented a significant change in the law, because previously intoxication was considered to be an irrelevant factor whenever the accused was charged with an offence of general (or basic) intent.

In response to the *Daviault* case, the Parliament of Canada moved, for the first time, to pass legislation dealing with intoxication as a defence to a criminal charge, and section 33.1 was added to the *Criminal Code* (coming into force in 1996). Section 33.1 states that intoxication, however extreme it may be, will not be accepted as a defence to a charge of any general (or basic) intent offence that "includes as an element an assault or any other interference or threat of interference with the bodily integrity of another person."

This brief historical overview is intended to provide a framework in which to consider the rather complex legal situation that now exists in Canada in relation to the defence of intoxication. In order to simplify our discussion of this topic, the defence of intoxication will be examined in the context of three different periods: (i) the defence prior to 1994; (ii) the defence after *Daviault*; and (iii) the defence after section 33.1 of the Code came into force (in 1996).

The Intoxication Defence Prior to 1994

THE THREE RULES IN THE *BEARD* CASE

The classic authority concerning the defence of intoxication is the English case of *Beard* (1920) decided by the House of Lords. In this case, Lord Birkenhead articulated three rules that rapidly came to be regarded as the authoritative statement of the nature and limits of the intoxication defence. As modified by subsequent judicial interpretations, the three rules may be summarized in the following manner:

(1) If intoxication induces a **mental disorder** ("disease of the mind") and renders the accused "not criminally responsible" within the meaning of section 16 of the *Criminal Code*, he or she must

be acquitted as being "not criminally responsible on account of mental disorder" (**NCRMD**).

(2) If intoxication prevents a defendant from forming the intent necessary for conviction of a crime of *specific* intent, he or she must be acquitted. However, intoxication can never be a defence to a charge of a crime of *general* (or *basic*) intent.

(3) If intoxication falls short of preventing the accused from forming the intent necessary for conviction of a crime of *specific* intent, it does not constitute a valid defence (in particular, if the accused formed the necessary intent, it is irrelevant that the intoxication made it more difficult for him or her to control his or her actions).

Significantly, the authority of these rules was strongly reaffirmed by the House of Lords in the *Majewski* case (1976). The *"Beard* rules" were also enthusiastically endorsed by the Supreme Court of Canada in the case of *George* (1960) (discussed in Chapter 4) and their authority in Canada was later reaffirmed, without any qualification, in *Leary* (1977).

The various issues surrounding the NCRMD defence have already been dealt with in Chapter 8; therefore, the application of the first *Beard* rule will not be considered here. It will suffice to emphasize that the ingestion of alcohol and other drugs may, in certain circumstances, induce a serious mental disorder. For example, the Manitoba Court of Appeal ruled in *Malcolm* (1989) that *delirium tremens* constitutes a "disease of the mind" for the purposes of section 16 of the Code and, in *Mailloux* (1985), the Ontario Court of Appeal endorsed the view that a cocaine-induced "toxic psychosis" could also be considered a "disease of the mind." However, such cases are comparatively rare and we shall now turn our attention to the application of the second and third *Beard* rules.

The impact of the second and third rules is well-illustrated by the notorious English case of *Lipman* (1970). The defendant, who was in a bedroom with his female partner, voluntarily injected himself with a dose of LSD. As a consequence of taking this drug, Lipman fell into a delusional state in which he imagined that he was on a journey to the centre of the earth. In the course of this journey, Lipman believed that he was being attacked by some distinctly unfriendly snakes and he, therefore, vigorously defended himself against the attacks of these reptiles. When Lipman finally emerged from his delusional state, he discovered that he had killed his partner by strangling her and stuffing a bedsheet down her mouth and throat. The English Court of Appeal applied the second *Beard* rule to this set of facts. The court concluded that murder must be considered an offence of *specific* intent. Indeed, murder may generally be characterized as an assault committed with the specific intent to kill. Given Lipman's delusional state, it was comparatively easy for the court to conclude that his state of intoxication had prevented him from forming the specific intent to kill. Nevertheless, the court then applied the third *Beard* rule and substituted a conviction for the offence of manslaughter, since this crime requires proof only of *general* or *basic* intent.

THE CRITICAL DISTINCTION BETWEEN CRIMES OF SPECIFIC AND GENERAL INTENT

Of course, a vital issue in determining whether intoxication may be a defence is the categorization of the offence as being one of *specific* or **general intent**. This particular issue was discussed in Chapter 4 and that discussion will not be repeated here. However, it may be useful to refer to the distinction between crimes of specific and general intent drawn by Justice McIntyre of the Supreme Court of Canada in the case of *Bernard* (1988):

> The general intent offence is one in which the only intent involved relates solely to the performance of the act in question with no further ulterior intent or purpose. The minimal intent to apply force in the offence of common assault affords an example. *A specific intent offence is one which involves the performance of the* actus reus, *coupled with an intent or purpose going beyond the mere performance of the questioned act.* Striking a blow or administering

poison with the intent to kill, or assault with intent to maim or wound, are examples of such offences. [emphasis added]

It will no doubt be recalled that the courts have declared that the following offences may be considered to be crimes of *specific* intent: murder, robbery, breaking and entering with intent, theft, assault with intent to resist arrest, touching a child for a sexual purpose, and attempting to commit an offence. On the other hand, the following offences have been declared to be crimes of *general* intent: manslaughter, assault, assault causing bodily harm, sexual assault, mischief (damage to property), pointing a firearm, impaired driving, aggravated assault, and unlawfully causing bodily harm.

The distinction between offences of specific and general intent has been criticized by many. Indeed, Chief Justice Dickson, in a dissenting judgment in the case of *Bernard* decided by the Supreme Court of Canada in 1988, argued that the distinction should be abolished for the purpose of applying the defence of intoxication. In his view, the distinction serves as "an artifical device whereby evidence, otherwise relevant, is excluded form the jury's consideration." However, the call for the abolition of the distinction has been soundly rejected by the majority of the justices of the Supreme Court of Canada in both the *Bernard* (1988) and *Daviault* (1994) cases.

In *Daviault* (1994), Justice Cory, with whom a majority of the justices of the Supreme Court agreed, curtly stated that "it is now well established by this court that there are two categories of offences ... those requiring a specific intent and others which call for nothing more than general intent." However, in the earlier case of *Bernard* (1988), Justice McIntyre provided a more detailed rationale for maintaining the distinction in Canada:

The distinction is not an artificial one nor does it rest upon any legal fiction. There is a world of difference between the man who in frustration or anger strikes out at his neighbour in a public house with no particular purpose or intent in mind, other than to perform the act of striking, and the man who strikes a similar blow with intent to cause death or injury. This difference is best illustrated by a consideration of the relationship between murder and manslaughter. He who kills intending to kill or cause bodily harm is guilty of murder, whereas he who has killed by the same act without such intent is convicted of manslaughter. The proof of the specific intent, that is, to kill or to cause bodily harm, is necessary in murder because the crime of murder is incomplete without it. No such intent is required, however, for the offence of manslaughter because it forms no part of the offence, manslaughter simply being an unlawful killing without the intent required for murder. The relevance of intoxication which could deprive an accused of the capacity to form the necessary specific intent in murder and its irrelevance in the crime of manslaughter can readily be seen.

Whatever its merits and logical deficiencies may be, it seems that the pigeonholing of offences into crimes of either specific or general intent is embedded in Canadian criminal law, and its existence will continue to have critical consequences for the manner in which the courts will apply the defence of intoxication.

APPLYING THE SECOND *BEARD* RULE TO CRIMES OF SPECIFIC INTENT

Under the *Beard* rules, it is axiomatic that intoxication *may* be a valid defence to a charge of a specific intent offence but is *never* a defence to a charge of a general intent offence. The first step to be taken when an accused raises the issue of intoxication is, therefore, to determine whether the offence is one of *specific* intent. Once it has been established that the offence with which the accused has been charged, is a crime of *specific* intent, the next matter to be considered is the nature of the circumstances in which intoxication may serve as a partial defence to such a charge. In formulating the second rule in the *Beard* case, Lord Birkenhead stated that evidence of drunkenness which renders the accused incapable of forming the specific intent essential to constitute the crime should be taken into consideration with the other facts proved in order to determine whether or not he had this intent.

There is a major difficulty with the manner in which the second *Beard* rule was articulated by Lord Birkenhead. The problem stems from his use of words that focus on the accused's *capacity* to form the specific intent required, rather than the accused's *actual intent* at the time of the alleged offence. Under the second *Beard* rule, if the accused person's defence raises a reasonable doubt as to his or her capacity to form the specific intent that must be proved by the Crown, there is no question that the accused must be acquitted. However, it by no means follows that an accused person who was *capable* of forming such a specific intent, did *in fact* form such an intent. In light of all the circumstances of the case, there may very well be a reasonable doubt as to whether the accused actually formed the requisite specific intent. Unfortunately, a literal interpretation of the second *Beard* rule would lead to a conviction of the accused because the only ground for acquittal mentioned by Lord Birkenhead is the accused's *lack of capacity to form the intent.*

In the recent case of *Robinson* (1996), the Supreme Court of Canada held that the second *Beard* rule, as written by Lord Birkenhead, is invalid since it infringed both sections 7 and 11(d) of the *Charter.* As Chief Justice Lamer pointed out in delivering his judgment (with which seven other justices agreed),

> The *Beard* rules put an accused in jeopardy of being convicted despite the fact that a reasonable doubt could exist in the minds of the jurors on the issue of actual intent. Under these rules, if the jury is satisfied that the accused's voluntary intoxication did not render the accused incapable of forming the intent, then they would be compelled to convict despite the fact that the evidence of intox-

ication raised a reasonable doubt as to whether the accused possessed the requisite intent.

The Chief Justice then proceeded to indicate how trial judges should instruct juries in relation to the second *Beard* rule. In his view,

> before a trial judge is required by law to charge the jury on intoxication, he or she must be satisfied that the effect of the intoxication was such that its effect *might* have impaired the accused's foresight of consequences sufficient to raise a reasonable doubt. Once a judge is satisfied that this threshold is met, he or she must then make it clear to the jury that the issue before them is whether the Crown has satisfied them beyond a reasonable doubt that the accused had the requisite intent. In the case of murder the issue is whether the accused intended to kill or cause bodily harm with the foresight that the likely consequence was death.

In *Lemky* (1996), a case involving a murder charge, the Supreme Court of Canada emphasized that, as with any other defence, the accused must satisfy the *evidentiary* burden of proof before the defence of intoxication may be considered by the trier of fact (whether it be judge or jury). As Justice McLachlin said,

> If the real question is whether the accused was prevented by drunkenness from actually foreseeing the consequences of his or her act, it follows that the threshold for putting the defence to the jury must be evidence sufficient to permit a reasonable inference that the accused did not in fact foresee those consequences. While capacity and intent may be related, it is possible to envisage cases where evidence which falls short of establishing that the accused lacked the capacity to form intent, may still leave the jury with a reasonable doubt that, when the offence was committed, the accused in fact foresaw the likelihood of death.

A good illustration of the application of the principle that juries should consider whether an accused actually formed the specific intent required for proof of the offence charged is provided by the case of *Otis* (1978), in which the accused was charged with **second degree murder**. The evidence established that Otis and the deceased victim were good friends and that, on the day of the latter's death, they had both been consuming a considerable amount of alcohol. Medical evidence indicated that the deceased victim had expired as a result of a massive haemorrhage of the brain and it was accepted that this injury had been caused by Otis, who had struck the victim about the face and head with both a lamp and a wine bottle. Otis was convicted at trial but the Ontario Court of Appeal allowed his appeal and ordered a new trial because the trial judge had not directed the jury to consider the question of whether the accused had actually formed the intent to kill.

Justice Martin, in delivering the judgment of the Court of Appeal, stated that

> We think that there were numerous circumstances in this case that, taken in conjunction with the amount of alcohol that the appellant had consumed, lead to a reasonable doubt as to the existence of the requisite specific intent. Without attempting to refer to all those circumstances, we have in mind that the deceased and the appellant were friends, that the appellant struck the deceased with objects at hand, that is the lamp and the wine bottle; his report to the police that he thought he had killed him, and also that in his written statement he said that he thought he had hit him with his fist.

APPLICATION OF THE THIRD *BEARD* RULE

The third rule, articulated by Lord Birkenhead in the *Beard* case, reads as follows:

> evidence of drunkenness falling short of a *proved incapacity* in the accused to *form the intent* necessary to constitute the crime, and merely establishing that his mind was affected by drink so that he

more readily gave way to some violent passion, does not rebut the presumption that a man intends the natural consequences of his acts.

Basically, this rule has been interpreted in modern times to mean that, if the accused can not raise a reasonable doubt as to whether he or she formed the intent necessary for proof of the specific offence charged, intoxication is no defence. In particular, it is irrelevant that the accused claims that intoxication caused him or her to lose the power of self-control and engage in behaviour that he or she would not have committed if sober.

The original wording of the third *Beard* rule raises many difficulties. For example, the use of the words "proved incapacity" might well suggest that the accused is under the burden of proving the defence of intoxication. In the case of *Malanik* (1952), the Supreme Court of Canada ruled that the word "proved" should be dropped from the rule and it should be made clear to the jury that the accused only has to raise a reasonable doubt in order to be successful in advancing the defence. Another difficulty stems from the use of the word "incapacity." As we saw in the previous section, the Supreme Court of Canada ruled in *Robinson* (1996) that the real question is not whether the accused had the capacity to form the specific intent in question but whether he or she actually formed this intent. Finally, the third *Beard* rule contains the phrase "does not rebut the presumption that a man intends the natural consequences of his acts." This is problematic because it might suggest to a jury that they should *presume* that every sane or sober person intends the natural consequences of his or her actions and that there is some onus on the accused to prove that intoxication prevented him or her from having such an intent. In both the *Seymour* (1996) and *Robinson* (1996) cases, the Supreme Court of Canada took great pains to counter such an interpretation of this element of the third *Beard* rule. For example, in *Robinson*, Chief Justice Lamer stated on behalf of the Court that he wished to "take the opportunity ... to hold that the presumption of intent to which *Beard* refers, should only be interpreted and referred to as a common sense and logical inference that the jury can but is not compelled to make." Significantly, in the later case of *Rathwell* (1998), the Ontario Court of Appeal suggested that trial judges' charges to juries would "generally improve if the sane sober person boilerplate were eliminated, or at least adjusted to the particular circumstances." In particular, Justice Osborne emphasized that this "boilerplate" should be scrupulously avoided whenever there is credible evidence that the accused was not, in fact, "sane" or "sober." The bottom line for Justice Osborne is that the trial judge must always make it clear that the Crown has to prove beyond a reasonable doubt that the accused had the specific intent to commit the offence charged (in the *Rathwell* case, the intent required for murder under section 229 of the Code). In this sense, the *Rathwell* decision essentially recommends that intoxication should be viewed not so much as a special defence, but rather as just one of a number of factors that may shed light on the ultimate question of whether the accused had the necessary *mens rea* for an offence of specific intent. It is noteworthy that the innovative approach, that was taken in the *Rathwell* case towards the interpretation of this aspect of the third *Beard* rule, was stoutly re-affirmed by the Ontario Court of Appeal in the later case of *Edgar* (2000).

The case of *Courville* (1982) graphically illustrates the principle laid down in the third *Beard* rule that, if accused persons *do* form the necessary intent to commit a specific intent offence, they are guilty despite the fact that they were intoxicated at the time. In this particular case, the accused was charged with robbery, but he claimed that he had been suffering from delusions induced by the consumption of drugs and alcohol. The gist of the defence was that the accused's conduct had been caused by "a loss of self-control or an irresistible impulse" that resulted from his state of intoxication. However, the evidence indicated that the accused was fully aware of what he was doing and had formed the specific intent necessary for proof of the crime of robbery. In these circumstances, the Ontario Court of Appeal ruled that Courville should

be convicted of robbery despite his intoxication. The Supreme Court of Canada subsequently affirmed this decision in *Courville* (1985). The Supreme Court briefly stated that

> Loss of self-control or irresistible impulse caused by voluntarily induced intoxication is not a defence to a criminal charge in Canada.

The Intoxication Defence After the *Daviault* Case

It is significant that the ongoing and often bitter dispute about the justification of the *Beard* rules prior to 1994 did not prompt Parliament to enact provisions in the *Criminal Code* that would potentially resolve the dilemma in which the courts found themselves when dealing with individuals who lacked even the minimal intent to commit an offence of general intent. However, the advent of the *Charter* made the traditional approach to intoxication increasingly vulnerable to a challenge on constitutional grounds. In the *Bernard* case (1988), Justice Wilson (with whom Justice L'Heureux-Dubé agreed) took the view that the *Beard* rules, as they have been qualified over the years, could withstand a *Charter* challenge if modified in one important respect, namely, that, where the accused's intoxication was *so extreme as to verge on insanity or automatism,* he or she should be able to benefit from the defence of intoxication even if the offence charged was one of general intent. Without this essential modification, the *Beard* rules would, in her view, infringe both sections 7 and 11(d) of the *Charter*.

Although the view of Justice Wilson did not have the support of the majority of her colleagues in the *Bernard* case, her judgment nevertheless proved to be of immense influence in later years; indeed, in the later *Daviault* case (1994), her approach was embraced by a majority of the justices of the Supreme Court of Canada.

Before 1994, the orthodox approach to intoxication in Canadian courts was automatically to deny the benefit of the defence to *every* defendant charged with a crime of general intent. However, in the *Daviault* case (1994), the Supreme Court of Canada decisively rejected this approach.

Daviault was charged with the sexual assault of a 65-year-old woman who was partially paralyzed and confined to a wheelchair. Daviault had apparently consumed some seven or eight beers during the day and then some 35 ounces of brandy on the evening of the alleged assault. He claimed that he did not remember anything between the time that he had a glass of brandy and the point where he woke up nude in the complainant's bed. In other words, he asserted that he had no recollection whatsoever of the events that constituted the alleged assault.

A pharmacologist, appearing on behalf of the defence, stated that, if Daviault had in fact consumed the amount of alcohol that he claimed, his blood alcohol level would have been in the region of 400 to 600 mg of alcohol per 100 ml of blood. In a normal person, this would cause death or coma. However, since Daviault was an alcoholic, he was less susceptible to the effect of alcohol and, in his case, this level of alcohol in the blood might cause him to suffer a "blackout" in which he might enter into a state of dissociation; in such a condition, he would have no awareness of what he was doing and, therefore, would have no memory of the events that occurred.

The trial judge acquitted the accused on the basis that there was a reasonable doubt as to whether he possessed the minimal intent necessary for conviction of the offence of sexual assault. However, the Québec Court of Appeal substituted a conviction because, in its view, the trial judge had made a fundamental error in holding that intoxication can be a defence to a charge of a general intent offence such as sexual assault. In other words, the Québec Court of Appeal reasserted the orthodox interpretation of the *Beard* rules. However, Daviault appealed to the Supreme Court of Canada, claiming that this interpretation of the *Beard* rules violated his rights under sections 7 and 11(d) of the *Charter*. The Supreme Court agreed and ordered a new trial.

Justice Cory, who delivered judgment on behalf of the majority of the Supreme Court of Canada, indicated that the distinction between crimes of specific and general intent was so deeply entrenched in the fabric of Canadian criminal law that there was no question of abolishing it at this stage of our legal history. However, Justice Cory held that this did not mean that Canadian courts should continue to exclude the possibility of raising the defence of intoxication in *all* cases involving charges of general intent crimes; indeed, it was his view (shared by the majority of the Court) that in certain (albeit very limited) circumstances, the *Charter* dictates that the accused should have the benefit of the defence of intoxication in relation to crimes of general intent. In essence, the majority of the Court adopted the view previously expressed by Justice Wilson in the *Bernard* case (1988), namely, that a defence should be available to a person accused of an offence of general intent if, owing to an *extreme degree of intoxication*, they were in a "state akin to automatism or insanity."

Justice Cory referred to the *Leary* case (1977), in which the Supreme Court of Canada had reaffirmed the authority of the traditional *Beard* rules. He ruled that the principle that intoxication can never be a defence to a charge of a crime of general intent violated both the principles of fundamental justice guaranteed by section 7 of the *Charter* and the presumption of innocence enshrined in section 11(d) of the *Charter*. Indeed, he said that,

> In my view, the strict application of the *Leary* rule offends both ss. 7 and 11(d) of the *Charter* for a number of reasons. The mental aspect of an offence, or *mens rea,* has long been recognized as an integral part of crime. The concept is fundamental to our criminal law. The element may be minimal in general intent offences; none the less, it exists. In this case, the requisite mental element is simply an intention to commit the sexual assault or recklessness as to whether the actions constitute an assault. The necessary mental element can ordinarily be inferred from the proof that the assault was committed by the accused. However, the sub-

stituted *mens rea* of an intention to become drunk cannot establish the *mens rea* to commit the assault.

Justice Cory went on to hold that the mere consumption of alcohol cannot lead to the conclusion that the accused intended to commit a sexual assault or any other crime. What the so-called "substituted *mens rea*" rule effectively does is to eliminate the minimal mental element required for proof of sexual assault and, in the view of Justice Cory, "*mens rea* for a crime is so well-recognized that to eliminate that mental element, an integral part of the crime, would be to deprive an accused of fundamental justice."

On behalf of the majority of the Supreme Court, Justice Cory also ruled that the traditional *Beard* rules infringed section 11(d) of the *Charter* because, under their provisions, it would be possible to convict an accused person of an offence even if there was a reasonable doubt as to one of the essential elements of the offence:

> For example, an accused in an extreme state of intoxication akin to automatism or mental illness would have to be found guilty although there was a reasonable doubt as to the voluntary nature of the act committed by the accused ... In my view, the mental element of voluntariness is a fundamental aspect of the crime which cannot be taken away by a judicially developed policy. ...
>
> The presumption of innocence requires that the Crown bear the burden of establishing all elements of a crime. These elements include the mental element of voluntariness.

Justice Cory also rejected the argument that the *Charter* is not violated by the traditonal *Beard* rules because the accused's voluntary decision to become intoxicated renders him or her "blameworthy." He stated that

> Voluntary intoxication is not yet a crime. Further, it is difficult to conclude that such behaviour should always constitute a fault to which criminal

sanctions should apply. However, assuming that voluntary intoxication is reprehensible, it does not follow that its consequences in any given situation are either voluntary or predictable. Studies demonstrate that the consumption of alcohol is not the cause of the crime. A person intending to drink cannot be said to be intending to commit a sexual assault.

It is interesting that Justice Cory considered the possibility that the issue of **voluntariness** relates to the *actus reus* rather than to the *mens rea* elements of an offence and raised the question of whether this would make any difference to the Court's ruling that the traditional *Beard* rules violated the *Charter*. In fact, he held that it would make no difference whatsoever. Justice Cory noted that

> The *actus reus* requires that the prohibited criminal act be performed voluntarily as a willed act. A person in a state of automatism cannot perform a voluntary willed act since the automatism has deprived the person of the ability to carry out such an act. It follows that someone in an extreme state of intoxication akin to automatism must also be deprived of that ability. Thus, a fundamental aspect of the *actus reus* of the criminal act is absent. It would equally infringe s. 7 of the *Charter* if an accused who was not acting voluntarily could be convicted of a criminal offence.

Having ruled that the defence of intoxication should be available to those who are charged with a crime of general intent, the Supreme Court of Canada made it clear in the *Daviault* case that it would only be in very rare and limited circumstances that such a defence would ever be successful. Why should this be so? According to Justice Cory,

> It must be remembered that those who are a "little" drunk can readily form the requisite mental element to commit the offence. The alcohol-induced relaxation of both inhibitions and socially acceptable behaviour has never been accepted as a

factor or excuse in determining whether the accused possessed the requisite *mens rea*. Given the minimal nature of the mental element required for crimes of general intent, even those who are significantly drunk will usually be able to form the requisite *mens rea* and will be found to have acted voluntarily. In reality it is only those who can demonstrate that they were in such an extreme degree of intoxication that they were in a state akin to automatism or insanity that might expect to raise a reasonable doubt as to their ability to form the minimal mental element required for a general intent offence. Neither an insane person nor one in a state of automatism is capable of forming the minimal intent required for proof of a general intent offence. Similarly, as the words themselves imply, "drunkenness akin to insanity or automatism" describes a person so severely intoxicated that he is incapable of forming even the minimal intent required of a general intent offence. The phrase refers to a person so drunk that he is an automaton. As such he may be capable of voluntary acts such as moving his arms and legs but is quite incapable of forming the most basic or simple intent required to perform the act prohibited by a general intent offence.

In addition, the defence recognized in *Daviault* would be extremely difficult to establish in practice because the Supreme Court of Canada placed the primary (or persuasional) burden of proof on the shoulders of the accused. It is not enough, said Justice Cory, for the accused to raise a reasonable doubt as to whether he or she had the minimal intent required for proof of the general intent offence charged. Instead, the accused must establish *on the balance of probabilities* that he or she was in a state of extreme intoxication akin to automatism or insanity. It is, of course, most unusual for the accused to be placed under the primary burden of proof (one other example of this approach is contained in section 16(2) of the Code, which requires the accused to prove the defence of NCRMD on the balance of probabilities). No doubt, the Supreme Court of Canada took this extraordinary step

The Daviault *case (1994): extreme intoxication that produces a state akin to mental disorder or automatism should lead to an absolute acquittal.*

in order to ensure that the defence of intoxication would not be abused.

After the *Daviault* case (1994), the *Beard* rules survived, but the second rule was considerably modified by the principle, established in *Daviault*, that the defence of intoxication should be available, in very rare and limited circumstances, to a defendant charged with a crime of general intent.

Essentially, after *Daviault*, the defence of intoxication would not be available to most defendants charged with a general intent crime because their state of intoxication would not be so serious as to prevent them from forming the minimal intent required for proof of such offences. However, where the intoxication was so extreme as to produce a state akin to automatism or insanity, the accused would be entitled to an acquittal, provided he or she proved the requirements of the defence on the balance of probabilities.

The Intoxication Defence After the Introduction of Section 33.1 of the *Criminal Code*

Although the majority of the justices of the Supreme Court of Canada apparently took considerable care in *Daviault* (1994) to indicate that it would only be in the rarest of cases that a defendant would be able to escape criminal liability for the commission of such general intent offences as sexual assault, their decision was subjected to a considerable degree of popular criticism. Much of this criticism stemmed from a deep-seated concern for the plight of sexual assault victims and a belief that the *Daviault* defence would permit violent men to avoid taking responsibility for sexual assaults that they committed while intoxicated.

In response to the robust criticism of the *Daviault* decision, the Parliament of Canada amended the *Criminal Code* by adding a new section dealing explicitly with the issue of intoxication as a defence to a charge of a general intent offence. Section 33.1, which came into effect in 1996, now provides that

33.1(1) It is not a defence to an offence referred to in subsection (3) that the accused, by reason of self-induced intoxication, lacked the general intent or the voluntariness required to commit the offence, where the accused departed markedly from the standard of care as described in subsection (2).

(2) For the purposes of this section, a person markedly departs from the standard of reasonable care generally recognized in Canadian society and is thereby criminally at fault where the person, while in a state of self-induced intoxication that renders the person unaware of or incapable of consciously controlling, their behaviour, voluntarily or involuntarily interferes or threatens to interfere with the bodily integrity of another person.

(3) This section applies in respect of an offence under this Act or any other Act of Parliament that includes as an element an assault or any other interference or threat of interference by a person with the bodily integrity of another person.

Section 33.1 does not purport to be a comprehensive statutory treatment of the defence of intoxication. In fact, it deals only with *those offences of general intent that involve an element of assault or interference (or threat of interference) with the bodily integrity of another person.* This means that section 33.1 does not apply to those general intent offences that do not require proof of this element of assault, etc. For example, mischief (damage to property) under section 430 of the Code clearly falls outside the ambit of section 33.1 and will still be governed by the Supreme Court of Canada's decision in *Daviault*. It is also most significant that Parliament did not address the issue of the intoxication defence in relation to specific intent offences and it is clear that, for these offences, the courts will continue to apply the *Beard* rules.

Section 33.1 can essentially be viewed as a direct move by Parliament to overturn the Supreme Court of Canada's ruling in the *Daviault* case in those circumstances where the charge against the accused involves an offence *against the person* as opposed to an offence *against property*. However, the enactment of section 33.1 has, unfortunately, caused the law concerning intoxication to become undesirably complex. The present state of the law would appear to be as follows:

(1) For crimes of *specific intent,* the second and third *Beard* rules will continue to apply, and intoxication may be used as a defence where it prevents the accused from forming the specific

intent that must be established by the Crown (e.g., intent to kill, intent to steal).

(2) For crimes of *basic intent,* the situation is somewhat more complicated:

(a) where the offence involves an element of assault or any other interference or threat of interference with the bodily integrity of a person (e.g., assault, manslaughter, sexual assault), self-induced intoxication can never be a valid defence no matter how severe it may have been at the time (section 33.1);

(b) where the offence does not involve an element of assault or any other interference or threat of interference with the bodily integrity of a person (e.g., damage to property), then, in those very *exceptional* cases where the intoxication is so extreme as to produce a state akin to automatism or insanity, the accused will have the benefit of an absolute defence (as required by the Supreme Court of Canada's ruling in *Daviault*).

A further difficulty with this statement of the existing law is that there are serious doubts that section 33.1 is valid under the *Charter.* It could well be argued that section 33.1 flatly contradicts the Supreme Court of Canada's unequivocal view, expressed in *Daviault,* that it is a violation of sections 7 and 11(d) of the *Charter* to convict a person who lacks even a minimal degree of *mens rea* at the time that he or she commits a general intent offence such as sexual assault. Does this mean that, when the appropriate case comes before them, the Supreme Court of Canada will strike down section 33.1 of the Code as being in violation of an accused person's rights under the *Charter*?

The argument will no doubt be made that Bill C-72, which added section 33.1 to the *Criminal Code,* represents Parliament's first attempt to legislate in the area of intoxication and, insofar as Parliament represents the will of Canadians' elected representatives, the Supreme Court of Canada

should give careful consideration to this legislation before deciding to strike it down as being invalid under the *Charter.* After all, the *Daviault* decision concerned the judge-made *Beard* rules rather than legislation enacted by Parliament.

It is most likely that the real issue will be whether section 33.1 can be justified as a reasonable limitation under section 1 of the *Charter.* It would be difficult to imagine in light of what it said in *Daviault* that the Supreme Court would change its mind and hold that section 33.1 does not violate an accused's rights under sections 7 and 11(d) of the *Charter.* However, it is possible that the Court might reconsider whether section 33.1 of the Code can be saved under section 1 of the *Charter.*

In an unusal move, Parliament included in Bill C-72 a statement of the reasons why it was enacting section 33.1. This statement is contained in nine different "whereas" clauses that serve as a "preamble" to section 33.1. For example, four of these clauses read as follows:

Whereas the Parliament of Canada is concerned about the incidence of violence in Canadian society;

Whereas the Parliament of Canada recognizes that violence has a particularly disadvantaging impact on the equal participation of women and children in society and on the rights of women and children to security of the person and to the equal protection and benefit of the law as guaranteed by sections 7, 15 and 28 of the *Canadian Charter of Rights and Freedoms*;

Whereas the Parliament of Canada recognizes that there is a close association between violence and intoxication and is concerned that self-induced intoxication may be used socially and legally to excuse violence, particularly violence against women and children ...

Whereas the Parliament of Canada shares with Canadians the moral view that people who, while in a state of self-induced intoxication, violate the physical integrity of others are blameworthy in relation to their harmful conduct and should be held criminally accountable for it. ...

These clauses could well serve as the basis for the contention that Parliament's objective in enacting section 33.1 is, in the words of the test in the *Oakes* case (1986), related to "concerns which are pressing and substantial in a free and democratic society." Clearly, section 33.1 is directed toward the dangers posed to society by intoxication-related violence, and it is likely that dealing with this problem would be considered an objective that might justify overriding a defendant's *Charter* rights. However, there is a real question as to whether section 33.1 would meet the "proportionality" test. In answering this question, the Supreme Court of Canada would have to consider whether convicting an accused person who lacks even the minimal degree of *mens rea* for conviction of a general intent offence is a reasonable method of dealing with the problem of intoxicated-related violence. It interesting that, in this respect, it could be argued that Parliament should have moved to punish the act of becoming "drunk and dangerous" rather than to enact an amendment to the Code that results in convicting an accused of an offence for which he or she has no *mens rea*. Indeed, in the *Daviault* case (1994), Justice Cory stated on behalf of the majority of the Supreme Court of Canada that

> it is always open to Parliament to fashion a remedy which would make it a crime to commit a prohibited act while drunk.

Miscellaneous Issues Relating to Intoxication as a Defence

The *Beard* rules, the *Daviault* case, and section 33.1 of the Code do not address all of the issues that arise when the defence of intoxication is raised in a criminal trial. For example, they do not explicitly deal with the situation in which an accused person deliberately ingests alcohol and/or drugs in order to create a condition of mind in which it is easier for him or her to commit a crime. Suppose such a person decides to kill someone and drinks a large amount of alcohol in order to give him or her "liquid

courage." This individual then proceeds to slaughter his or her victim while under the influence of alcohol. Can this person then claim the benefit of the defence of intoxication on the basis that there is a reasonable doubt that he or she actually formed the intent to kill at the exact time when the victim was being dispatched? This precise issue was raised in *Gallagher* (1961), a case that originated in Northern Ireland and was ultimately taken to the House of Lords. On this particular matter, Lord Denning said

> if a man, whilst sane and sober, forms an intention to kill and makes preparation for it, knowing that it is a wrong thing to do, and then gets himself drunk so as to give himself ... courage to do the killing, and whilst drunk carries out his intention, he cannot rely on his self-induced drunkenness as a defence to a charge of murder, nor even as reducing it to manslaughter. He cannot say that he got himself in such a stupid state that he was incapable of an intent to kill. So, also, when he is a psychopath, he cannot by drinking rely on his self-induced defect of reason as a defence of insanity. The wickedness of his mind before he got drunk is enough to condemn him, coupled with the act which he intended to do and did do. The psychopath who goes out intending to kill, knowing it is wrong, and does kill, cannot escape the consequences by making himself drunk before doing it.

Another issue, which should be mentioned at this point, concerns the critical effect of intoxication in relation to a charge of **first degree murder**, which requires proof of "planning and deliberation" (see section 231(2) of the *Criminal Code*). Evidence of intoxication may well raise a reasonable doubt as to whether the accused "planned" the murder or committed it with due "deliberation." In other words, even though a jury may be satisfied beyond a reasonable doubt that the accused did form the requisite specific intent to commit murder (thereby rejecting the defence of intoxication), it may nevertheless entertain a reasonable doubt as to whether the accused's state of intoxication negatived the elements of "planning and deliberation" that are necessary for a conviction of first degree murder.

NECESSITY

The General Principles

Unlike the defences of mistake of fact or intoxication, the defence of necessity is not based on a claim by defendants that they lacked the appropriate *mens rea* prerequisite for conviction of the crime charged; indeed, such defendants fully recognize that they have deliberately broken the law. Nevertheless, these defendants assert that they should be excused from criminal responsibility because their choice to break the law was dictated by necessity and was, therefore, not a free choice at all.

The defence of necessity becomes relevant where the accused can only avoid some disaster or calamity by breaking the law. In advancing the defence of necessity, defendants are basically asserting that the evil that they sought to avoid was greater than the evil inherent in the breaking of the law.

The defence of necessity is not contained in the *Criminal Code*. However, as a common law defence, it has been preserved by section 8(3) of the Code. One of the earliest definitions of the common law defence, which found some favour in Canadian courts, is that offered by the English text-writer Kenny:

probably no such defence can be accepted in any case (1) where the evil averted was a lesser evil than the offence committed to avert it, or (2) where the evil could have been averted by anything short of the commission of that offence, or (3) where more harm was done than necessary for averting the evil. Hence it is scarcely safe to lay down any more definite rule than that suggested by Sir James Stephen viz. that "it is just possible to imagine cases in which the expediency of breaking the law is so overwhelmingly great that people may be justified in breaking it; but these cases cannot be defined beforehand." [emphasis added]

The Rationale for the Defence of Necessity

In the Supreme Court of Canada's decision in *Perka* (1984), Justice Dickson spoke on behalf of four of the five justices who heard the case when he drew a sharp distinction between "justifications" and "excuses." He considered that the defence of necessity constitutes an "excuse" rather than a "justification":

A "justification" challenges the wrongfulness of an action which technically constitutes a crime. The police officer who shoots the hostage taker, the innocent object of an assault who used force to defend himself against his assailant, the good Samaritan who commandeers a car and breaks the speed laws to rush an accident victim to the hospital, these are all actors whose actions we consider *rightful,* not wrongful. For such actions people are often praised, as motivated by some great or noble object. The concept of punishment often seems incompatible with the social approval bestowed on the doer.

In contrast, an "excuse" concedes the wrongfulness of the action but asserts that the circumstances under which it was done are such that it ought not to be attributed to the actor. The perpetrator who is incapable, owing to a disease of the mind, of appreciating the nature and consequences of his acts, the person who labours under a mistake of fact, the drunkard, the sleepwalker: these are all actors of whose "criminal" actions we disapprove intensely, but whom, in appropriate circumstances, our law will not punish. [emphasis added]

In Justice Dickson's view, a valid claim of necessity should serve to "excuse" defendants from responsibility on the basis that they *acted "involuntarily" from a "moral or normative" point of view:*

The lost Alpinist who, on the point of freezing to death, breaks open an isolated mountain cabin is not literally behaving in an involuntary fashion.

He has control over his actions to the extent of being physically capable of abstaining from the act. Realistically, however, his act is not a "voluntary" one. His "choice" to break the law is no true choice at all; it is remorselessly compelled by normal human instincts.

In this light, Justice Dickson asserted that the defence of necessity "rests on a realistic assessment of human weakness, recognizing that a liberal and humane criminal law cannot hold people to the strict obedience of laws in emergency situations where normal human instincts, whether of self-preservation or of altruism, overwhelmingly impel disobedience."

Applying the Defence of Necessity in Relation to Less Serious Criminal Offences

The assertion of a defence of necessity in a situation where the accused has been charged with the commission of a "less serious" offence generally does not create any formidable policy difficulties for the courts. Indeed, there have been a number of cases involving the alleged commission of various traffic offences in which the courts have been prepared to apply the defence of necessity. For example, in *Fry* (1977), the accused was acquitted of a charge of dangerous driving as the consequence of a successful assertion of the defence of necessity. The accused had been clocked at 117 km/h in a 50 km/h zone in the city of Regina, Saskatchewan. The accused claimed that he had been forced to travel at this speed because the vehicle behind him was tailgating at close quarters. According to the accused, the faster he went, the faster the vehicle behind him went. Judge Boyce acquitted the accused at his trial and stated that

> certainly, the accused here endangered the public but I do realize an extremity of circumstance can arise where a choice is made, that is, forced to be made. For example, as I mentioned possibly occurred here, to flee by speed an actual present danger thrust upon him, or to suffer its continuance with its fearsome potential. The way ahead was clear, in fact while I do not commend his judgment, his choice to my mind was not criminal. *He substituted a constructive danger to the public in place of the actual present danger to himself.* [emphasis added]

The decision in *Fry* may be usefully compared with the case of *Walker* (1979), in which the accused, who was a police officer, had been charged with failing to stop for a stop sign, contrary to the provisions of the *Highway Traffic Act, 1970*, of Ontario. The accused, who was driving a police cruiser, had been dispatched to a bank because of a possible robbery. He turned on the siren and roof lights and set off for the bank. On his way, he passed through a stop sign at approximately 15 km/h and collided with a car at the intersection. Unfortunately, the driver of the other vehicle was seriously injured and, therefore, Walker was prosecuted. At trial, he was convicted and fined $25. He subsequently appealed to the County Court of Ontario. However, Judge Zalev rejected Walker's appeal. The learned judge pointed out that the Ontario Act specifically exempted police officers from observance of the speed limits. However, no other exemptions were provided to police officers in the legislation. Therefore, the accused was required to establish the defence of necessity on the same basis as any ordinary citizen. The learned judge ruled that there was insufficient evidence to establish the defence in this particular case. Presumably, if Walker had been able to establish that he was on his way to preserve lives that were being threatened by a robbery, the outcome would probably have been very different.

Applying the Defence of Necessity in Relation to More Serious Criminal Offences

When the defence of necessity is raised in relation to "more serious" offences, such as murder, the courts are immediately faced with policy questions of extraordinary difficulty. Indeed, the courts have been extremely reluctant to permit the assertion of such a defence in relation to the most serious criminal offices.

A classic illustration of the traditional reluctance of the courts to recognize the defence of necessity in such circumstances is the somewhat macabre English case of *Dudley and Stephens* (1884). The accused were charged with the murder of a young cabin boy after they had been shipwrecked and were drifting without food or water on the open sea and without any apparent hope of immediate rescue. The defendants had killed the boy and then proceeded to eat his flesh and drink his blood. Had they not done so, it is highly unlikely that they would have survived long enough to have been rescued by a passing ship. The defendants' defence of necessity was rejected by the English court. Although the court indicated that it sympathized with the horrific situation in which the defendants found themselves, it was not prepared to acquit the accused on the basis of necessity. One of the major policy considerations that apparently influenced the court was the belief that the recognition of a defence of necessity in such circumstances would open the floodgates to wholesale misuse of the defence by unscrupulous criminals. In the words of Lord Chief Justice Coleridge,

> Who is to be the judge of this sort of necessity? By what measure is the comparative value of lives to be measured? Is it to be strength, or intellect, or what? It is plain that the principle leaves to him who is to profit by it to determine the necessity which would justify him in deliberately taking another's life to save his own. In this case the weakest, the youngest, the most unresisting, was chosen. Was it more necessary to kill him than one of the grown men? The answer must be "No."

Although the court sentenced the accused to death, it clearly anticipated that this sentence would never be carried out. In fact, the sentence was later commuted to six months' imprisonment with hard labour. The court appeared to believe that, in cases

such as *Dudley and Stephens*, the firm letter of the law should be upheld but that it was the prerogative of the Queen to grant mercy. Lord Coleridge noted in this respect,

> there is no safe path for judges to tread but to ascertain the law to the best of their ability and to declare it according to their judgements; and if in any case the law appears to be too severe on individuals, to leave it to the Sovereign to exercise that prerogative of mercy which the Constitution has entrusted to the hands fittest to dispense it.

The first authoritative court decision in Canada that involved the assertion of the defence of necessity in response to a charge of a "more serious" offence is the case of *Morgentaler* (1975), in which the accused, a physician, was charged with performing an illegal abortion. Under the provisions of section 287 of the *Criminal Code*, certain conditions had to be met and specified procedures followed before a medical practitioner could perform a therapeutic abortion. One of the provisions of this section required that such an operation had to be approved by the therapeutic abortion committee at an accredited or approved hospital. Of course, as we saw in Chapter 1, section 287 was declared unconstitutional by the Supreme Court of Canada in January 1988. However, the *Charter* had not been enacted at the time of the "first Morgentaler case" that we are now discussing. In this case, Dr. Morgentaler had performed an abortion in direct contravention of the requirements and procedures of section 287. One of the defences advanced by Dr. Morgentaler, at his trial, was that of necessity. The defendant presented evidence to the effect that he feared the pregnant woman would "do something foolish unless she was given immediate professional medical attention to relieve her condition and her anxiety." The jury acquitted Dr. Morgentaler. However, the Crown appealed to the Québec Court of Appeal on the basis of a point of law. The Crown contended that there was no evidence upon which the jury could have acquitted the accused on the basis of necessity. The Court of Appeal substituted a verdict of guilty and, thus, overturned the jury's decision to acquit Dr. Morgentaler. The decision of the Québec Court of Appeal was upheld by the Supreme Court of Canada.

It is significant that the Supreme Court of Canada appeared to recognize the existence of the common law defence of necessity. However, the Court believed that, in this case, there was no evidence of the urgent necessity that might, in certain circumstances, justify the breaking of the criminal law. In one of the two majority judgments, Justice Dickson stated

> if it (the defence of necessity) does exist it can go no further than to justify non-compliance in urgent situations of clear and imminent peril when compliance with the law is demonstrably impossible. No system of positive law can recognize any principle which would entitle a person to violate the law because in his view the law conflicted with some higher social value.

It is quite clear that the Supreme Court of Canada intended to place formidable restrictions upon the defence of necessity when it is raised in relation to a charge of a serious offence. It should be mentioned, at this point, that the federal Minister of Justice subsequently ordered a new trial of Dr. Morgentaler on the charge. Dr. Morgentaler was once again acquitted by a jury.

By an ironic twist of fate, Dr. Morgentaler swiftly proved to be, once again, an important figure in the evolution of the defence of necessity in Canada. Dr. Morgentaler was prosecuted on a second charge of illegal abortion in the province of Québec (see *Morgentaler* (1976)). Once again, he was acquitted by a jury and, once again, the Crown appealed. However, on this occasion, the Québec Court of Appeal ruled that the Supreme Court of Canada had recognized the existence of the defence of necessity in the first *Morgentaler* case (1975), and that there was some evidence upon the record that would entitle a jury to find that the defence had been proved. The court, in these circumstances, declined to interfere with the

jury's verdict. Therefore, the second *Morgentaler* case (1976) was significant because it represented the first *successful* assertion of a necessity defence in relation to a "more serious" criminal charge in Canada.

A somewhat contoversial application of the defence of necessity to a charge of a personal injury offence came in the case of *Morris* (1981), in which the accused was charged with the offence of common assault, contrary to section 265 of the *Criminal Code*. Morris was charged with the assault of his wife and, in his defence, he claimed that he had held his wife around the neck in order to prevent her from jumping from his moving vehicle. According to the defendant, his wife was in a drunken condition and, during the course of the journey, had grabbed the steering wheel and "put the front wheels in the ditch." In these circumstances, Justice Belzil of the Alberta Court of Queen's Bench ruled that the accused was justified in his application of force in order to immobilize his wife. According to the judge,

> the respondent was suddenly confronted by an emergency situation created by the complainant. He was placed in a situation where he had to choose the lesser of evils. To have allowed his wife to get out of the truck to walk on a dark road in an intoxicated condition would have shown wanton and reckless disregard for her life or safety and could have constituted criminal negligence on his part ... he had to act quickly. It was sufficient that he in good faith and on reasonable grounds believed that intervention was necessary.

The *Perka* Case and the Apparent Move Toward Restricting the Scope of the Defence of Necessity

In 1984, the Supreme Court of Canada decided the case of *Perka,* in which it became clear that the Court was most concerned to set stricter limits upon the operation of a defence that had emerged from relative obscurity to considerable prominence during the previous decade. In *Perka* (1984), the accused were charged with importing and possession of narcotics for the purpose of trafficking. They had been arrested in Canadian waters in possession of a large quantity of cannabis. The accused asserted the defence of necessity, claiming that the load of drugs was originally supposed to have been unloaded in international waters off the coast of Alaska (in other words, they were never intended for delivery in Canada). However, they contended that their vessel encountered a number of serious mechanical problems as well as poor weather and that, for the safety of the crew, they were obliged to enter Canadian waters in order to seek refuge and to make repairs. According to the accused, the vessel ran aground in a cove on the west coast of Vancouver Island and started to list; at this point, it was decided to start unloading the cannabis in order to prevent the vessel from capsizing. However, the police arrived, arrested the accused and recovered 33.49 tons of cannabis. The trial judge put the defence of necessity to the jury, who acquitted the accused. However, the B.C. Court of Appeal allowed the Crown's appeal and ordered a new trial. The Supreme Court of Canada affirmed this ruling.

In the Supreme Court, Justice Dickson conducted an exhaustive examination of the nature and scope of the defence of necessity. As noted earlier, he underscored his belief that the true rationale for the defence rested in the need to recognize that it is inappropriate to punish actions that are *"normatively involuntary."* In this light, only those actions that can genuinely be regarded as being involuntary are entitled to the benefit of the "excuse" of necessity. The learned justice repeated his statement in the (first) *Morgentaler* case (1975) that the operation of the defence is limited to those cases where the accused has broken the law in "situations of clear and imminent peril when compliance with the law is demonstrably impossible." Only in these types of situations can the accused be considered to be acting involuntarily. He went on to say that "at a minimum, the situation must be so emergent and the peril must be so pressing that normal human

The Perka *case (1984): did the accused have any "reasonable legal alternative" (such as throwing the drugs overboard before entering Canadian waters)?*

instincts cry out for action and make a counsel of patience unreasonable."

For Justice Dickson, one of the most important factors in weighing the validity of a claim of necessity is the question of whether the accused had any *reasonable legal alternative to breaking the law*:

> The question to be asked is whether the agent had any real choice: *could he have done otherwise?* If there is a reasonable legal alternative to disobeying the law, then the decision to disobey becomes a voluntary one, impelled by some consideration beyond the dictates of "necessity" and human instincts. [emphasis added]

Finally, Justice Dickson emphasized that a defendant claiming the defence of necessity should be able to show that there was some degree of "proportionality" between the offence committed and the evil that it was designed to avoid:

> No rational criminal justice system, no matter how humane or liberal, *could excuse the infliction of a greater harm to allow the actor to avert a lesser evil*. In such circumstances we expect the individual to bear the harm and refrain from acting illegally. If he cannot control himself we will not excuse him. [emphasis added]

In the *Perka* case (1984), a new trial was ordered because the original trial judge had not directed the jury's attention to the question of whether reasonable legal alternatives had been available to the accused. In the view of Justice Dickson, the trial judge had incorrectly left the jury with the impression that the only real issue was whether the accused had acted reasonably in heading for the shoreline, together with their cargo of drugs, rather than "facing death at sea." In Justice Dickson's view, this approach did not deal with the critical issue of "whether there existed any other reasonable responses to the peril that were not illegal."

It is reasonably clear that in the *Perka* case the Supreme Court was deliberately attempting to circumscribe the scope of the defence of necessity, leaving it available to a defendant only in the most extreme situations.

The Necessity Defence After the *Perka* Decision

The immediate impact of the circumscribed approach adopted by the Supreme Court of Canada in *Perka* (1984) was most evident in yet another case involving Dr. Morgentaler. In *Morgentaler, Smolig and Scott* (1985), charges were laid against Dr. Morgentaler and others in connection with his alleged performance of abortions at his Toronto clinic. The accused were not charged with actually procuring abortions but rather with conspiracy to procure a miscarriage contrary to sections 287(1) and 465(1)(c) of the Code. The accused were acquitted at trial primarily on the basis of the defence

of necessity; however, the Crown appealed to the Court of Appeal, which ruled, *inter alia*, that the trial judge had made an error in permitting the defence to go to the jury and, consequently, ordered a new trial.

The Court of Appeal placed great emphasis on the judgment of the Supreme Court in *Perka*. The court stressed that the accused were charged with conspiracy and that they were not claiming that they had acted in an individual case to deal with an overwhelming situation of urgency facing a particular patient; instead, according to the court, the accused had in fact "entered into an agreement of a global nature to procure miscarriages of all female persons who had made the decision to terminate their pregnancies." In these circumstances, as far as the court was concerned, there was no genuine emergency that rendered their conduct "involuntary" within the meaning of Justice Dickson's judgment in *Perka*. The Ontario Court of Appeal stated that there was no evidence that compliance with the law was "demonstrably impossible, and that there was *no legal way out*." [emphasis added]

> Not only did the defendants fail to make every reasonable effort to comply with the law, but they consciously agreed to violate it. Their dissatisfaction with the state of the law, although perhaps relevant to the issue of motive, afforded no basis for the defence of necessity.

Of course, the decision of the Ontario Court of Appeal was later appealed to the Supreme Court of Canada and, as we saw in Chapter 1, the Supreme Court decided the case on the basis that section 287 of the Code infringed the *Charter*. In these circumstances, the Supreme Court declined to deal with the matter of the defence of necessity. The judgment of the Ontario Court of Appeal, therefore, remains a significant authority on this issue.

In *Latimer* (1995), the Saskatchewan Court of Appeal addressed the question of whether the defence of necessity may be raised in the context of a so-called mercy killing. The facts of the case were undoubtedly tragic. Latimer was charged with the first degree murder of his twelve-year-old daughter, Tracey, whom he had killed by carbon monoxide poisoning. Tracey suffered from severe cerebral palsy and was a quadriplegic. Her disabilities were so severe that she was bedridden for most of her life. She was described as being "physically helpless and unable to care for herself" and was "in continual pain." She also suffered from a severe mental disability and was unable to communicate except to laugh or cry. Tracey had undergone surgery to correct some of her physical problems but complications had developed that caused her considerable pain. One month before further surgery had been scheduled to deal with these complications, Tracey died. Just prior to her death, her father had declined to accept an opportunity to place Tracey in a group home.

At Latimer's trial, his counsel argued that his client acted out of necessity. He stated that "medical science had done everything possible for Tracey but that it was incapable of relieving her excruciating pain" and that "the only humane option was to see her put to sleep." The trial judge refused to put the defence of necessity to the jury because, in his view, there was another option available to the accused, namely, "to persevere in the attempts to make Tracey comfortable in her life, however disagreeable and heartwrenching those attempts might have been." Latimer was ultimately convicted of second degree murder and sentenced to imprisonment for life with no eligibility for parole for ten years.

Latimer's appeal to the Saskatchewan Court of Appeal was dismissed. Justice Tallis, writing on behalf of the majority of the court, referred to the principles articulated by Justice Dickson in the *Perka* case and concluded that, in light of these principles, the trial judge had correctly withheld the defence of necessity from the jury. He stated that this was not a case where Latimer's life was in imminent peril; rather, he was in no danger himself and he was solely concerned with his daughter's "quality of life." Terminating Tracey's life could not reasonably be viewed as a matter of necessity. Although Tracey had a "bleak future" ahead of her,

there was some prospect of her pain being alleviated if she had the planned surgery. Furthermore, Tracey's situation was not unique; indeed, there are many other families who cope with a "similar type of misfortune." Therefore, there was absolutely no evidence that terminating Tracey's life was an "involuntary" decision within the meaning expressed in the *Perka* case; indeed, it was indisputable that Latimer had another option available to him in the form of placing Tracey in a group home.

At a more general level, Justice Tallis underscored the overwhelming dangers associated with performing **euthanasia** on those individuals who are unable to give their consent to such a drastic measure:

> This is not a case of withholding potentially life-prolonging treatment to a seriously disabled person. It deals with the deliberate decision to terminate another's life rather than continue with the scheduled medical treatment and care. In such circumstances it is no defence for a parent to say because of a severe handicap, a child's life has such diminished value that the child should not live any longer. It does not advance the interest of the state or society to treat such a child as a person of lesser status or dignity than others.

The Supreme Court of Canada later ordered a new trial for *Latimer* in light of certain conduct that had been engaged in by Crown counsel (*Latimer* (1997)). At the new trial, the judge refused to place the necessity defence before the jury:

> What Mr. Latimer saw as a situation that left him no other alternative but to end Tracey's life to alleviate her pain did not create a necessitous situation that the law defines as necessary to advance this defence for this particular crime. *There is no evidence that he had to do what he did to avoid a direct and immediate peril, or that there was no other reasonable course of action open to him.* [emphasis added]

The Saskatchewan Court of Appeal later ruled that the trial judge acted correctly in withholding the defence of necessity from the jury (*Latimer* (1998)). In the view of the Court of Appeal, there was absolutely no good reason to depart from its earlier (1995) ruling on the issue of whether necessity was available to Latimer as a defence. Even though defence counsel at the second trial presented a considerable amount of evidence that focused on Tracey's suffering,

> ... the defence of necessity was still left without the necessary "air of reality" in relation to its essential elements, including the element of proportionality between the harm caused in violating the law and the harm entailed in abiding (by) it.

The decision of the Court of Appeal concerning the availability of the defence of necessity in the particular circumstances of Latimer's case was later affirmed by the Supreme Court of Canada in *Latimer* (2001). The Supreme Court stated that, even if necessity were available as a defence to a charge of murder (an issue that it did not decide), there was no "air of reality" to any of the essential elements of the defence of necessity in Latimer's case. (The question of the appropriate penalty that should be imposed in cases of so-called "mercy killing" has already been discussed in Chapter 4.)

The strange case of *Hendriks* (1988) illustrates two circumstances in which a defendant may lose the benefit of the defence of necessity. First, an accused person may not claim the benefit of the defence if his or her conduct goes beyond what is reasonably necessary to deal with an emergent situation. Second, the defence may not be raised successfully if the accused *voluntarily* created the emergent situation in circumstances in which a reasonable person would have foreseen the possibility that his or her conduct might result in the need to break the law; such an accused person would not meet the requirement that his or her actions are genuinely involuntary.

Hendriks was charged with having care and control of a motor vehicle at a time when his alcohol level was over 80 mg in 100 ml of blood. He had entered a car in order to have a sleep while waiting for his wife to collect him and take him home. He was sleeping on the front seat (on the passenger's side) and, because he felt cold, he turned on the ignition in order to heat the car. Unfortunately, the car was facing downhill and it started to move because it was in gear and the parking brake was not engaged. Hendriks climbed over into the driver's seat and took control of the vehicle in order to stop it. However, the accused continued to drive the car after the point at which he could have stopped it; in fact, he drove the car back to the street where it had originally been parked.

Hendriks was convicted at his trial in the Provincial Court. He then appealed his conviction to the Saskatchewan Court of Queen's Bench. However, Justice Noble dismissed Hendriks's appeal on the basis that even if necessity dictated that he take control of the vehicle in order to bring to a halt, he had, by continuing to drive it back to the street where it had previously been parked, "gone beyond the point the necessity of the situation called for." Moreover, Justice Noble pointed out that Hendriks had "placed himself in this so-called position of necessity when he turned on the ignition." By entering a vehicle while intoxicated and by *deliberately* switching on the ignition, he was the author of his own misfortunes. Any reasonable person would have contemplated the possibility that turning on the ignition might have the effect of putting the vehicle in motion—particularly if no attempt is made to check whether the parking brake is engaged and whether the car is in gear.

Finally, it will no doubt be remembered that an important element in Justice Dickson's judgment in the (first) *Morgentaler* case (1975) was his view that "no system of positive law can recognize any principle which would entitle a person to violate the law because in his view the law conflicted with some higher social value." This principle has been used by the courts to reject defences of necessity where accused persons have defied court orders because they believed that they were acting to preserve a "greater good" of some kind.

For example, in *Macmillan Bloedel v. Simpson* (1994), the accused were part of a group of protesters who attempted to block access to logging sites in the Clayoquot Sound area of Vancouver Island. They did so in violation of a series of B.C. Supreme Court injunctions that were designed to prevent the obstruction of logging crews who wished to carry out their work in this area and the accused were, therefore, charged with **contempt of court**. One of the defences raised on behalf of the accused was that of necessity; in particular, it was asserted that clearcut logging was so damaging to the environment that the accused were entitled to break the law. The trial judge refused to accept this defence and the accused were ultimately convicted of contempt. Their appeal to the B.C. Court of Appeal was dismissed.

Speaking on behalf of the Court of Appeal, Chief Justice McEachern stated that the defence of necessity was not available for two reasons:

First, the defendants had alternatives to breaking the law, namely, they could have applied to the court to have the injunction set aside. None of them did that prior to being arrested. I do not believe this defence operates to excuse conduct which has been specifically enjoined. By granting the order, the court prohibited the very conduct which is alleged against the defendants. An application to the court, which could be heard on fairly short notice, would have determined whether the circumstances were sufficient to engage the defence of necessity.

Secondly, I do not believe the defence of necessity can ever operate to avoid a peril that is lawfully authorized by the law. M. & B. had the legal right to log in the areas in question, and the defence cannot operate in such circumstances. [emphasis added]

DURESS

The Rationale for the Defence of Duress

It has been argued that any civilized system of criminal law must take into account the frailties of human nature by recognizing that an accused person who acts under duress should not be held criminally responsible for his or her actions. In the case of *Lynch* (1975), Lord Morris of the House of Lords (U.K.) expressed this policy most eloquently:

the law must, I think take a common sense view. If someone is forced at gunpoint either to be inactive or to do something positive—must the law not remember that the instinct and perhaps the duty of self-preservation is powerful and natural? I think it must. A man who is attacked is allowed within reason to take necessary steps to defend himself. The law would be censorious and inhumane which did not recognize the appalling plight of a person who perhaps suddenly finds his life in jeopardy unless he submits and obeys.

In one sense, duress may be conceptualized as a particular application of the general defence of necessity. When asserting the defence of necessity, defendants may point to *any* circumstances that constitute a threat to life or limb; however, where the defence of duress is raised, defendants are really claiming that their power of choice was overborne by a *human* threat. In the *Hibbert* case (1995), the Supreme Court of Canada stated clearly that the rationale supporting the defence of duress was identical to that which underpins the defence of necessity, namely, that it is wrong to punish someone who has not acted in a truly *voluntary* manner. In delivering the judgment of the Court, Chief Justice Lamer said,

In my view, the similarities between the two defences are so great that consistency and logic requires that they be understood as based on the same juristic principles. Indeed, to do otherwise would be to promote incoherence and anomaly in the criminal law. In the case of the necessity, the court has already considered the various alternative theoretical positions available (in *Perka*...), and has expounded a conceptualization of the defence of necessity as an excuse, based on the idea of *normative involuntariness*. In my opinion, the need for consistency and coherence in the law dictates that the common law defence of duress also be based on this juridical foundation. [emphasis added]

Section 17 and the Defence of Duress

Although the defences of necessity and duress are based on the same rationale, there is one significant difference between them. Whereas the defence of necessity has been developed exclusively by judges, the defence of duress is specifically addressed in the *Criminal Code*.

Indeed, section 17 of the Code provides that

A person who commits an offence under compulsion by threats of immediate death or bodily harm from a person who is present when the offence is committed is excused for committing the offence if the person believes that the threats will be carried out and if the person is not a party to a conspiracy or association whereby the person is subject to compulsion, but this section does not apply where the offence that is committed is high treason or treason, murder, piracy, attempted murder, sexual assault, sexual assault with a weapon, threats to a third party or causing bodily harm, aggravated sexual assault, forcible abduction, hostage taking, robbery, assault with a weapon or causing bodily harm, aggravated assault, unlawfully causing bodily harm, arson or an offence under section 280 to 283 (abduction and detention of young persons).

It is clear that section 17 imposes a number of stringent restrictions upon the assertion of the defence of duress. First of all, the section denies the benefit of the defence to anyone charged with committing one of the approximately twenty offences identified therein. In addition, the only threats that may be considered by a court in applying the defence are those of *immediate* death or bodily harm (threats of death or bodily harm *in the future* are not sufficient). Furthermore, the person making the threats must be *physically present* when the offence is committed; therefore, the defence is not available, for example, to an accused person who is threatened with death or bodily harm by means of a telephone call from an individual who does not attend the scene of the crime committed by the accused. Finally, a defendant is precluded from raising the defence where he or she is a member of a conspiracy or association (e.g., a criminal gang) that subjects him or her to compulsion.

The severity of the impact of these restrictions is well illustrated by the case of *Carker* (1967), in which the accused was convicted, at his trial, of a charge of committing mischief by unlawfully and wilfully damaging public property. During the course of a disturbance at the Oakalla Prison Farm in British Columbia, Carker had damaged the plumbing fixtures in his cell. Carker contended that he had not been participating in the disturbance in question and had only engaged in this act of vandalism because he had been subjected to severe duress. Indeed, a considerable number of prisoners, who were in separate cells, had shouted at Carker and threatened that if he did not smash the plumbing fixtures in his cell, "he would be kicked in the head, his arm would be broken and he would get a knife in the back at the first opportunity."

The Supreme Court of Canada ultimately rejected Carker's appeal against his conviction. The Court was quite prepared to concede that Carker committed the offence in the face of threats of death and grievous bodily harm. However, Justice Ritchie, in delivering the opinion of the Supreme Court, emphasized that section 17 of the Code required that the threats in question must be "threats of *immediate* death or grievous bodily harm." [emphasis added] The learned justice stated that the threats to which Carker was exposed could not be immediately carried out because the prisoners were in separate cells. Furthermore, Justice Ritchie pointed out that section 17 required that the person who makes such threats be "present" when the offence is committed. In his view, the threats were made by persons who were not "present" within the meaning of the section, since they were locked in cells that were separate from the place where the offence was actually committed.

It is scarcely surprising that the Supreme Court's extremely literal and, in the circumstances, extraordinarily harsh interpretation of section 17 has been widely criticized. After all, the threats made to Carker could have been carried out as soon as the prisoners were released from their cells. On the other hand, it might well be contended that the Supreme Court was bound hand-and-foot by the clear language of the federal Parliament. However, if a literal interpretation of section 17 leads to potential injustice, the question arises as to whether the section should be declared invalid under the *Charter*. The Supreme Court has not yet addressed this critical issue, but both the Québec and Ontario courts of appeal have ruled that, in light of the requirements of section 7 of the *Charter*, section 17 of the *Criminal Code* is, to some extent, "of no force and effect."

Section 17 of the *Criminal Code* and the *Charter*

In the case of *Langlois* (1993), the accused was caught smuggling drugs into Archambault Penitentiary, where he worked. He was charged with various offences under the *Food and Drugs Act*. At his trial, he raised the defence of duress. He claimed that he had received several anonymous telephone calls informing him that, if he did not wish to jeopardize the safety of his wife and children, he should not complain to the police if he were "ordered to do something." He was told by an inmate to go to a certain address and pick up some drugs. He did so, on two separate occasions, and brought the drugs into the penitentiary. The drugs were apparently intended for inmates who were members of a notorious, and allegedly violent, motorcycle gang. Langlois stated in court that he did not report these incidents to the police because he feared for the safety of his wife and children and had no confidence that the police could give them adequate protection.

The problem facing Langlois was that the person who had threatened him had made threats of future (not immediate) harm to his family and was not present when Langlois smuggled the drugs. Therefore, a strict interpretation of section 17 would clearly preclude Langlois from raising the defence of duress. Under that section, the threats must, of course, be of immediate death or bodily harm and must emanate from a person who is present when the accused commits the offence. The trial judge ruled that section 17 of the Code was invalid under the *Charter* and permitted the accused to rely on the *common law* defence of duress which, as we shall see in the next section, does not contain the stringent restrictions stipulated in section 17. Langlois was acquitted and the Crown appealed to the Québec Court of Appeal.

The Court of Appeal dismissed the Crown's appeal and held that the trial judge had been correct to declare section 17 invalid under the *Charter*. Justice Fish, in delivering the judgment of the court, stated that section 17 violated the fundamental principles of justice enshrined in section 7 of the *Charter*. The court took this view because the restrictions in section 17 bring about the result that a "morally blameless" person could be convicted of a criminal offence. According to Justice Fish, "a person is morally blameless if he or she commits a wrongful act that is "normatively involuntary" within the meaning of [the *Perka* case]." Indeed, section 17

would permit the conviction of a morally blameless person charged with *any offence* to which it applies, since it affords a defence only to persons who are compelled to perform wrongful acts by threats of *immediate* death or bodily harm made by someone who is *present when the crime is committed*.

However forceful and paralyzing the threat, however fleeting and reparable the wrong, s. 17 would thus remain inaccessible to any person who is compelled to perform a prohibited act by threats of grave injury to a member of his or her family from a person who, though absent when the crime is committed, remains none the less positioned to actualize the threats soon if not immediately.

These limits imposed by s. 17 on an accused's right not to be punished for morally blameless behaviour are, in my opinion, not "demonstrably justified in a free and democratic society," within the meaning of s. 1 of the *Canadian Charter of Rights and Freedoms*. [emphasis in original]

Since the Québec Court of Appeal struck down section 17 as being constitutionally invalid, it recognized that the common law defence of duress applied and that the accused had met its requirements. The court, therefore, affirmed the accused's acquittal at trial.

The Ontario Court of Appeal subsequently adopted a similar approach in the case of *Ruzic* (1998). The accused had been charged with importing heroin, contrary to section 5(1) of the (now repealed) *Narcotic Control Act*. Ruzic admitted that she had imported the drugs; however, she nevertheless asserted that she only did so as the consequence of a threat to kill or harm her mother in Serbia if she (the accused) did not bring heroin into Canada. The accused stated that the police in Serbia could not provide any protection to her mother. The offence of importing heroin is not one of those offences (such as murder or robbery) that are specifically excluded from the scope of the defence of duress by section 17 of the Code. However, the problem for the accused was similar to that facing her counterpart in the *Langlois* case. Namely, the threats made were not of "immediate death or bodily harm" and were clearly not made by an individual who was "present" when the offence took place (indeed, the person who made the threats remained in Serbia). Therefore, if section 17 were applied to Ruzic's case, she would be denied the benefit of the defence of duress. The trial judge ruled that such an outcome would violate section 7 of the *Charter* and could not be saved by section 1 of the *Charter*. The jury acquitted the accused on the basis of the common law defence of duress and the Ontario Court of Appeal upheld the acquittal.

In delivering the judgment of the Court of Appeal, Justice Laskin stated that the "immediacy and presence" requirements in section 17 "arbitrarily and unfairly exclude many who may legitimately seek the compassion of the law for committing an offence under duress." He went on to rule that

> ... I find it is a fundamental principle of justice that the defence of duress be available to persons who act under threat of death or bodily harm to themselves or others when it would be unreasonable to have expected them to have behaved differently. By its immediacy and presence restrictions s. 17 of the *Criminal Code* denies this defence arbitrarily and unfairly and therefore infringes s. 7 of the *Charter*.

The Ontario Court of Appeal declared section 17 to be of "no force or effect" in relation only to those offences that have not been specifically excluded by Parliament from the scope of the defence. In Justice Laskin's words, the declaration of invalidity was "intended to permit an accused person charged with an offence other than the offences specifically excluded in s. 17 to rely on the common law defence of duress." The court did not wish to address the constitutionality of the list of excluded offences because it may "raise different considerations from those raised in this case"; hence, the Court of Appeal did not strike down all parts of section 17, as the Québec Court of Appeal had done in *Langlois*. In Ontario, therefore, it is not clear whether the exclusion by section 17 of offences such as murder and robbery from the benefit of the defence of duress will be declared a violation of the *Charter*.

Of course, it is to be hoped that the current uncertainty concerning the constitutionality of section 17 across Canada will be resolved by a definitive decision of the Supreme Court of Canada or by legislative action by Parliament. In the interim, in those provinces where the appellate courts have ruled, or will rule in the future, that section 17 is "of no force and effect," defendants will be entitled to rely on the much broader defence that exists at common law (as did the accused in both the *Lan-glois* and *Ruzic* cases). It is to the common law defence, therefore, that we now turn our attention.

The Common Law Defence of Duress

For some time, Canadian courts have held that the highly restrictive requirements of section 17 only apply to those defendants who "actually commit-ted" the offence charged (e.g., pulling the trigger of a firearm in a murder case). Conversely, they have ruled that those defendants who are charged as being parties to an offence on some other basis (e.g., aiding and abetting the offence charged) are not covered by the provisions of section 17 and may, instead, rely on the common law defence of duress.

It was in the case of *Paquette* (1976) that the Supreme Court of Canada ruled that Parliament had clearly confined the application of section 17 to "a person who commits an offence." The signifi-cance of this phrase only becomes apparent if one refers to section 21 of the *Criminal Code*. This sec-tion provides:

(1) every one is a party to an offence who

    (a) actually commits it,
    (b) does or omits to do anything for the pur-pose of aiding any person to commit it, or
    (c) abets any person in committing it.

(2) where two or more persons form an intention in common to carry out an unlawful purpose and to assist each other therein and any one of them, in carrying out the common pur-pose, commits an offence, each of them who knew or ought to have known that the com-mission of the offence would be a probable consequence of carrying out the common purpose is a party to that offence.

It is clear, from a reading of section 21 of the Code, that there are at least four modes of partici-pating in a criminal offence. The accused may be charged with (i) having committed the offence, (ii) having aided in the commission of the offence, (iii) having abetted the commission of the offence, or (iv) having become a party to the offence by virtue of "common intention to carry out an unlawful purpose."

In the *Paquette* case, the accused had been charged with murder. Paquette had been forced to drive two individuals, named Clermont and Simard, to the Pop Shoppe, in the city of Ottawa in March 1973. In the course of a robbery committed by Clermont and Simard at the Pop Shoppe, an innocent bystander was killed by a bullet from a rifle fired by Simard. Although Paquette had been threatened with revenge if he did not serve as the "getaway driver" for the two robbers, he refused to let them into his car after the commission of the robbery. Understandably, Paquette pleaded that he had been subjected to severe duress. The Crown contended that section 17 of the Code withheld the benefit of defence of duress to someone who was charged with the offence of murder. However, Paquette's acquittal at trial was ultimately upheld by the Supreme Court of Canada.

Justice Martland, in delivering the judgment of the Court, ruled that Paquette was not a person who had been charged with actually committing the offence himself. On the contrary, Paquette was charged with being a party to the offence of murder solely on the basis that he had allegedly formed an intention in common with Clermont and Simard to commit an offence of robbery and that he either knew or ought to have known that the commission of murder was a probable consequence of carrying out their common purpose. Therefore, the Court held that Paquette was not excluded from raising the defence of duress in relation to a charge of mur-der. Of course, if he had been charged with actually committing the offence himself, the specific word-ing of section 17 would clearly have excluded him from the benefit of the defence of duress. After all, the offence of murder is specifically identified, in section 17, as being a crime that is totally excluded from the benefit of the defence of duress when it is asserted by an individual who has "actually committed it."

Significantly, the result of the *Paquette* case is that *the courts must turn to the principles of the common law defence whenever duress is raised by an individual who did not actually commit the offence with which he or she is charged.* This is extremely important since the common law defence of duress, as it evolved in the English courts, is considerably less restrictive in its conditions than the statutory defence defined by section 17 of the *Criminal Code*.

The nature of the common law defence of duress was discussed at length in the case of *Morrison and McQueen* (1981), in which Wanda McQueen had been charged with robbery. The evidence indicated that the robbery had been extremely brutal in nature. In fact, the unfortunate victim had been beaten into unconsciousness by the application of an iron bar and dragged out into an alley where his body had been covered with snow. Miraculously, the victim managed to survive this ordeal. It appeared that Wanda had provided only incidental assistance to the individuals who actually committed the robbery. Part of this assistance involved removing the victim's body from the residence of the man with whom she was living. Wanda claimed that she had only provided this assistance because she was fearful that this man would commit serious injury to herself or her children at a later time. She, therefore, claimed the benefit of the defence of duress. Since Wanda was being charged with the offence of robbery solely on the basis that she had "aided" the persons who had actually committed it, the trial judge ruled that section 17 had no application to her particular case. Instead, Judge Kurisko ruled that the common law principles relating to the defense of duress must be applied. The learned judge quoted from the English textbook entitled *Archbold: Criminal Pleading, Evidence and Practice*:

(ii) A man acts under duress when he acts solely as a result of threats of death or serious injury

to himself or another, operating on his mind at the time of his act (under such gravity that they might well have caused a reasonable person placed in the same situation to act as he did).

(iii) The threat may be of immediate or future death or injury.

(iv) Once the judge has ruled that there is evidence of duress fit to be left to the jury, it is for the Crown to prove beyond reasonable doubt that the defendant was not acting under duress.

(v) Depending on the facts of the particular case it may be desirable to point out to the jury matters which may affect their decision on this issue, e.g. whether the defendant could have reasonably avoided acting as he did by running away, or by seeking police protection, in particular where the threat is for the future. They should be told to consider the gravity of the threat in relation to the gravity of the offence.

In light of these principles, the trial judge acquitted Wanda McQueen of the charge of robbery. In his words,

I have considered the state of her mind at the time in question and I believe that her reason for complying with the order given to her by Michael was solely as a result of her fear of Michael doing serious injury to herself or possibly at a later time to her children ... having regard to all the evidence I am unable to say that a reasonable person (let alone a person with the timid nature of Wanda) placed in the same situation and circumstances as Wanda would have acted any differently than Wanda.

It is important to bear in mind that the common law principles relating to duress contain certain critical differences from the provisions of section 17 of the Code. Under the common law principles, the threat of death or serious injury may be either to the individual defendants or to other persons, whereas under the terms of section 17, it appears that such threats can only be made in relation to the defendants themselves if the latter are to be successful in asserting the defence of duress. In this particular case, the *implicit* threats to Wanda's children were taken into account by the trial judge; presumably, under section 17, such threats could not have been considered by the court. It is also significant that, under the common law principles, the threat of death or injury may be either immediate *or* future. In contrast, as will be remembered from the *Carker* case, the provisions of section 17 provide that only threats of *immediate* death or injury are relevant to the defence of duress.

The *Morrison and McQueen* case also illustrates the proposition that, under the common law rules, the defence of duress may be claimed even if the threats against the accused are only implicit. This proposition was affirmed by the Ontario Court of Appeal in the case of *Mena* (1987). In light of the facts in that case, Justice Martin said that

> The threat required to invoke duress may be express or implied ... The appellant did not testify that Yee had expressly stated that he would shoot him unless he accompanied Yee but it would be open to the jury to find that Yee, by producing the gun, pointing it at the appellant and telling him that he was to go with him, had conveyed a threat to the appellant that if he did not go with Yee he would be shot. The appellant testified that he believed Yee was going to shoot him.

A critical consideration when the defence of duress is raised is whether or not the accused could *reasonably* have been expected to take an alternative course of action. If such an alternative were available, he or she would be expected to act on it and thereby avoid breaking the law. For example, if the opportunity to escape arises, the accused person must take it; otherwise, he or she will lose the right to claim the benefit of the defence of duress.

Indeed, in the case of *Keller* (1998), the Alberta Court of Appeal stated with manifest clarity that, where the accused has a safe avenue of escape and fails to pursue it, then the trial judge should not even allow the defence to go to the jury:

> Whether there was a safe avenue of escape is a question of fact for the jury ... However, if on the evidence most favourable to the accused, he had a safe means of escaping the threatened harm without committing the offence, no reasonable jury could possibly acquit on the basis of the defence of duress. *There would be no air of reality to the defence and a trial judge would be obliged to keep the defence from the jury.* [emphasis added]

Why should a defendant who has a "safe avenue of escape" lose the benefit of the defence of duress? In the *Hibbert* case (1995), the Supreme Court of Canada answered this question by referring to the underlying rationale of the defence. In the words of Chief Justice Lamer, who delivered the judgment of the Court,

> An accused person cannot rely on the common law defence of duress if he or she had an opportunity to safely extricate himself or herself from the situation of duress. The rationale for this rule is simply that in such circumstances the condition of "normative involuntariness" that provides the theoretical basis for both the defences of duress and necessity is absent — *if the accused had the chance to take action that would have allowed him or her to avoid committing an offence, it cannot be said that he or she had no real choice when deciding whether or not to break the law.* [emphasis added]

The Supreme Court also dealt with the critical question of whether the existence of a "safe avenue of escape" should be determined on an objective or a subjective basis. In approaching this question, Chief Justice Lamer took into account the views expressed by Justice Dickson when he was discussing the defence of necessity in the *Perka* case

(1984). The Chief Justice restated his opinion that "normative involuntariness" constitutes the theoretical foundation for both the defences of duress and necessity and came to the conclusion that courts should adopt an *objective* approach in determining whether the accused had a "safe avenue of escape." In his view,

> a degree of objectivity is inherent to excuses that are based on the notion of normative involuntariness, to the extent that this concept turns on the objective availability, or lack of availability, of true choice. Indeed, [Justice Dickson] clearly indicates that the operative standard for the defence of necessity is to be an objective one, based on whether "there is a *reasonable* legal alternative to disobeying the law."

However, Chief Justice Lamer hastened to add that, even though the "safe avenue of escape" issue was to be determined on an objective basis, nevertheless the court must "take into account the particular circumstances of the accused, including his or her ability to perceive the existence of alternative courses of action." As the Alberta Court of Appeal stated in the *Keller* case (1998), "the question is whether a reasonable person, with similar history, personal circumstances, abilities, capacities and human frailties as the accused would, in the particular circumstances, reasonably believe there was no safe avenue of escape and that he had no choice but to yield to the coercion." It is noteworthy that the Alberta Court of Appeal also suggested that the accused must take reasonable steps to "discover his or her full range of options before deciding to engage in the wrongful conduct."

Frequently, a central consideration in determining whether there was a "safe avenue of escape" is the perceived availability of police protection for the accused. The Supreme Court of Canada addressed this issue in the case of *Hébert* (1989), in which the accused had been charged with perjury and attempting to obstruct justice after he gave false evidence in a court case. He claimed that he had

been threatened with death and harassed by "the menacing acts of three or four tough-looking motorcycle gang members" who were present at the court-house when he gave his evidence. The accused did not tell the police about the death threats and did not seek their protection before he testified.

Since Hébert had been prosecuted on the basis that he had actually committed the offences charged, he was subject to the restrictions articulated in section 17 of the *Criminal Code*. The trial judge acquitted the accused of both charges on the basis that, although Hébert could have avoided "immediate" death as he was giving his evidence by seeking police protection, the reality was that such protection would only have lasted while the accused was in the court-house. However, the Québec Court of Appeal allowed the Crown's appeal against the perjury acquittal because Hébert could have avoided the "immediate" death that he feared by asking for the assistance of police officers present at the court. The Court of Appeal stated that only threats of *immediate* death, not "immediate threats of [later] death," were covered by section 17. According to Justice Paré,

> The threats, the danger of death and the offence have to be concomitant. A threat of death from which the respondent could have easily escaped and that he could have rendered unenforceable when he gave his evidence does not permit him to invoke the excuse of compulsion found in s. 17.

The Supreme Court of Canada later affirmed this aspect of the Court of Appeal's judgment.

This is clearly an extremely harsh decision, since any reasonable person, in the position of the accused, would fear the possibility of retaliation for some time after giving evidence in such circumstances. To take the view that only threats of violence in the court-house itself are relevant flies in the face of common sense. It was highly unlikely that the police would have been able to provide around-the-clock protection for Hébert after he left the court-house; indeed, the trial judge had pointed out that the police, however well-intentioned, do not have the resources to provide such protection. It may be that the undoubted severity of the decision in the *Hébert* case is a function of the specific wording of section 17 of the Code. Perhaps the Supreme Court of Canada might have been more sympathetic to the accused had it been interpreting the requirements of the common law defence of duress.

In two recent cases dealing explicitly with the common law notion of "safe avenue of escape," the facts were such that it is likely that most people would agree that the accused could reasonably have been expected to seek police protection. In the *Keller* case (1998), the accused had been charged with trafficking in LSD, contrary to section 48(2) of the *Food and Drugs Act*. The accused argued that he had been threatened with death or bodily harm by a known drug dealer if he (Keller) did not comply with the instructions of the dealer. Over a period of four months, he retrieved at least ten packages of drugs from the Calgary International Airport. Keller claimed that he had not sought the assistance of the police because he was frightened of the drug dealer and his friends, and believed that the police were not capable of furnishing him with effective protection. The trial judge ruled that there was no "air of reality" to the accused's defence of duress and refused to put it to the jury. Keller was convicted and his subsequent appeal to the Alberta Court of Appeal was dismissed. The court pointed out that the conduct for which Keller had been charged occurred four months after he was allegedly threatened and that there had been no explicit threats in the interim. Furthermore, the court emphasized that Keller was "not abnormally vulnerable to threats of physical violence" and that he had "no reason to think that the police could not give him protection if he reported the situation." Furthermore, Keller had made absolutely no attempt to consider whether he had any legal alternatives open to him:

He did not attempt to contact the police, even anonymously, to see if they could provide protective options.

The appellant did not take reasonable steps, taking into account his history, personal circumstances, abilities, capacities, and human frailties, to discover his options. [emphasis added]

Similarly, in the *Valentini* case (1999), two of the accused were charged with importing and trafficking in narcotics and possession for the purpose of trafficking. They had attempted to smuggle 34 pounds of cocaine through customs at Pearson Airport in Toronto. They claimed that they had acted under duress — specifically, threats of violence from one of their co-accused. The trial judge instructed the jury that, in considering the question of whether the two accused had a "safe avenue of escape" open to them, they were entitled to take into account the fact that they had not sought the protection of the Canadian authorities upon their arrival at the airport after their flight from Aruba. The accused were convicted and their subsequent appeals to the Ontario Court of Appeal were dismissed. On behalf of the court, Justice Rosenberg stated that

> … the appellants could have sought the assistance of the authorities immediately upon entering the airport before they physically took possession of the contraband. The importing offence was at least not complete until that point … The fact that neither appellant sought the assistance of the police or customs officials even after they had taken possession of the bags containing the drugs was compelling evidence that the reason for completing the importation was not the lack of a safe avenue of escape.

STUDY QUESTIONS

1. Desmond strikes Boris and steals his wallet. Boris is seriously injured. Desmond is charged with robbery, but he claims that he was only recovering a gambling debt that Boris owed him and refused to pay. Does Desmond have any defence(s)?

2. Daniel is intoxicated and beats up his best friend, Victor. Daniel then steals Victor's gold watch. Daniel is charged with robbery. To what extent (if any) is Daniel's drunkenness a defence?

3. Dracula takes a heavy dose of LSD and experiences "a bad trip." In this condition, he axes his friend, Fledermaus, to death. He is charged with murder but claims that he only remembers "chopping wood." Is Dracula guilty of murder or any other charge?

4. Wayne is in the habit of simultaneously consuming both alcohol and (illicitly obtained) barbiturate drugs. One night, he smashes his way through a window in the living room of an elderly woman, called Agnes. When Agnes comes to investigate the noise, she discovers Wayne standing in the middle of the room with a large stick in his hand. Wayne moves towards Agnes who is terrified by this encounter and utters a piercing scream. Wayne hops out of the window and walks slowly down the street. Agnes calls the police, who have no difficulty in arresting Wayne on a neighbouring street corner. The Crown wishes to charge Wayne with breaking and entering, mischief (damaging property), and assault with a weapon. Wayne states that he has absolutely no memory of what happened at Agnes's residence. He states that his last memory was that of being in a bar. A blood test reveals that Wayne has extraordinarily high levels of alcohol and barbiturates in his bloodstream. Does Wayne have any viable defence(s) to the potential charges that might be laid against him?

5. Jane visits her dentist, Dr. Frankenstein, because she has a toothache. Frankenstein tells Jane that he will have to fill the tooth because parts of it are decaying. While Frankenstein goes to see another patient in an adjoining room, Jane tells Emma, the dental nurse, that under no circumstances can she have an injection of novocaine because she is highly allergic to it. Emma enters this information in Jane's file but forgets to tell Frankenstein. While Emma is attending another patient, Frankenstein returns to the room in which Jane is waiting. He tells her to open her mouth and Jane does so (at the same time, she closes her eyes). Frankenstein says he is going to freeze Jane's tooth at the same time as he starts to inject her gum with novocaine. Jane makes a loud noise in protest but, by the time Frankenstein withdraws the needle, it is too late. Jane suffers a painful reaction to the anaesthetic and has to be treated in hospital. Jane is so angry about this incident that she goes to the police and asks them to consider charging Frankenstein with assault causing bodily harm. When interviewed, Frankenstein says that he honestly believed that Jane would consent to the injection and that it was not his fault that Emma had forgotten to inform him of Jane's instructions. If Frankenstein were to be charged, would he have a defence?

6. Elizabeth has an old handgun that has been in her family's possession for many years. She has always considered it to be an "antique, collector's piece" and she has been told by Judith, a friend who is an RCMP officer, that she does not need to register it and that a licence is not necessary. In fact, the gun is not an "antique firearm" within the meaning of the definition set out in section 84(1) of the *Criminal Code*; therefore, both registration and licencing are required after all. One day, Elizabeth's house is destroyed by fire. A police officer, who is investigating the possibility of arson, finds the gun among the ashes and is thinking of charging Elizabeth with the offence of unauthorized possession of a firearm contrary to section 91(3) of the *Criminal Code*. If she were charged, would Elizabeth have any defence?

7. Dan and Mary have been living together for five years in a common law relationship. On a regular basis, they have engaged in consensual sexual activity with each other. They have not been in the habit of seeking explicit permission from each other before proceeding with such

activity. On a certain night, Dan attempts to initiate a sexual encounter with Mary, but she says that she does not want to have any sexual relations with him because she is feeling sick. Dan waits for some 30 minutes and then proceeds to engage in an act of sexual intercourse with Mary, who says nothing and remains motionless. Mary wishes to have Dan charged with sexual assault. She tells the police that she had definitely not consented to the sexual activity with Dan and that she remained silent merely because she was terrified of him losing his temper and subjecting her to physical violence. Dan claims that, in light of his previous sexual relationship with his partner, he simply assumed that Mary had changed her mind and was fully consenting to the act of intercourse. If Dan were charged with sexual assault, would any defence(s) be available to him at his trial?

8. Jim visits his local bar, where he meets Viola, who was previously unknown to him. After consuming a couple of drinks with Viola, Jim invites her to come to his apartment. Viola accepts the invitation and she accompanies Jim to his building. Once inside the apartment, Jim and Viola engage in sexual activity. The next day, Viola travels to the local police station and accuses Jim of having sexually assaulted her. She states that she had been drinking for some time before Jim arrived in the bar and that she had no memory of what happened between the moment when Jim entered the bar and the moment when she woke up next to him in his bed. Viola is adamant that she would never have willingly engaged in sexual activity with Jim. Jim tells the police that, although he realized Viola had been drinking, he assumed that she knew what she was doing and that she had unequivocally told him that she wished to participate in sexual activity with him. If you were Crown counsel, would you charge Jim with sexual assault? Do you think that Jim would have any viable defence(s) to such a charge?

9. Dennis is taking part in a wilderness survival course with his friend, Marmaduke. The two men panic, lose their survival kits, and soon become lost. They wander around a forest for one day and one night without any food, except for the occasional berries that they can find on their way. Marmaduke states that he is exhausted and wants to stay where he is. Dennis presses on alone and comes to a small log cabin. There is no one in the cabin and Dennis breaks down the door. He eats some food that he finds in the refrigerator and also drinks two or three beers. He then takes a truck that is standing outside, using the keys that he has found in the kitchen. He drives off at very high speed and, within a minute or two, reaches a town, where he asks for help. Marmaduke is later rescued from the forest and soon recovers. The police are contemplating laying the following charges against Dennis: breaking and entering, theft, taking and driving a motor vehicle without the owner's consent, and speeding. Would Dennis have any defence to these charges?

10. The S.S. Lollipop sinks in a terrible storm. There are not enough lifeboats and those that are operational are severely overloaded. One lifeboat is commanded by Captain Bligh, who escaped at the last minute from his sinking ship. The lifeboat is so overloaded and so much water is being taken on board that it is obvious the boat will sink within a few minutes. Bligh orders that all male passengers over 35 must leave the lifeboat and he commands that they be "put into the water." The other crew and passengers push the unfortunate "over 35" male passengers into the turbulent sea, where they are unable to hang on to the sides of the boat and they all perish. The remaining occupants of the lifeboat are later saved by a passing ship. Everyone is agreed that, if the unfortunate "over 35" males had not left the lifeboat, it is most probable that it would have sunk and every one on board would have been killed.

The Crown is thinking of charging Bligh with murder. Does he have any defence to any charges of murder that might be laid against him?

11. David is approached by Goliath (a local gangster). He tells David that if the latter does not drive him (Goliath) to the Cheatemwell Bank, he will kill his children. David immediately drives Goliath to the bank. While David stays in the car, Goliath goes into the bank and robs it. During the robbery, Goliath fatally shoots two bank employees with a pistol that he had concealed in his pocket. The Crown alleges that David aided and abetted the murders and, therefore, charges him with two counts of second degree murder. Is he guilty of these offences?

12. Arthur witnesses a brutal killing that is perpetrated by Cecil, a local mobster. Cecil is charged with murder and Arthur is subpoenaed by the Crown to give evidence at the trial. Before the trial takes place, Arthur receives a number of telephone calls from a man identifying himself as "the Avenging Angel." The gist of these calls is that, if Arthur does not have a convenient loss of memory at Cecil's trial, his children will be killed. Arthur is too frightened to tell the police and gives false evidence at the trial. As a consequence, Cecil is acquitted. Crown counsel decides to charge Arthur with perjury under section 131 of the Code. Are there any defences available to Arthur?

13. Ruth is a surgeon who has acquired a special expertise in the separation of conjoined twins. She is asked to separate two infant twins, Bethany and Miranda. Tragically, Miranda lacks the necessary organs of her own to permit her to survive such an operation. The attending pediatricians tell Ruth that, unless she separates the twins, both of them will die because Miranda's bodily needs will eventually overwhelm Bethany's vital organs. In short, Ruth is asked to choose between separating the twins and declining to intervene. If she separates

them, Miranda will immediately die but Bethany will almost certainly enjoy a normal life span. If she does not carry out the surgery, both Bethany and Miranda will die in a matter of months. Ruth wishes to separate the twins but she is told that, if she does so, she could be charged with the murder of Miranda. If this should happen, would Ruth have any defence(s) open to her?

FURTHER READING

2000. Note: Urgent Compassion: Medical Marijuana, Prosecutorial Discretion and the Medical Necessity Defence. 41 *Boston College Law Review:* 699.

Alexander, L. 1999. A Unified Excuse of Preemptive Self-Protection. 74 *Notre Dame Law Review:* 1475.

Archard, D. 1997. *Sexual Consent.* Boulder, Colorado: Westview Press.

Ashworth, A. 1995. *Principles of Criminal Law.* 2d ed. Oxford: Oxford Univ. Press. 137–42, 144–48, 208–25, 230–37.

Backhouse, C. 1991. The Sayer Street Outrage: Gang Rape and Male Law in 19th Century Toronto. 20 *Manitoba Law Journal:* 46.

Boland, B. 1994. Battered Women Who Act Under Duress. 28 *New England Law Review:* 603.

Boxerman, A.D. 1990. The Use of the Necessity Defense by Abortion Clinic Protesters. 81 *Journal of Criminal Law and Criminology:* 677.

Boyle, C. 1994. The Judicial Construction of Sexual Assault Offences. In J.V. Roberts and R. Mohr, eds., *Confronting Sexual Assault: A Decade of Legal and Social Change.* Toronto: University of Toronto Press. 136–56.

Boyle, C. and M. MacCrimmon. 1998. The Constitutionality of Bill C-49: Analyzing Sexual Assault as if Equality Really Mattered. 41 *Criminal Law Quarterly:* 198.

Buchanan A. and G. Virgo. 1999. Duress and Mental Abnormality. [1999] *Criminal Law Review:* 517.

Carr, C.L. 1991. Duress and Criminal Responsibility. 10 *Law and Philosophy:* 161.

Carter, M. 1995. Non-Statutory Criminal Law and the *Charter:* The Application of the *Swain* Approach in *R. v. Daviault.* 59 *Saskatchewan Law Review:* 241.

Christie, G.C. 1999. The Defence of Necessity Considered from the Legal and Moral Points of View. 48 *Duke Law Journal*: 975.

Coughlan, S.G. 1999. Annotation: *R. v. Ewanchuk*. 22 *Criminal Reports (5th)*: 6.

Dickens, B. 1976. The *Morgentaler* Case: Criminal Process and Abortion Law. 14 *Osgoode Hall Law Journal*: 1.

Doré, L.K. 1995. Downward: Adjustment and the Slippery Slope: The Use of Duress in Defense of Battered Offenders. 56 *Ohio State Law Journal*: 665.

Finkelstein, C.O. 1995. Duress: A Philosophical Account of the Defense in Law. 37 *Arizona Law Review*: 251.

Fletcher, G.P. 1998. *Basic Concepts of Criminal Law*. New York: Oxford University Press. 130–32, 138–45.

Galloway, D. 1986. Necessity as a Justification: A Critique of *Perka*. 10 *Dalhousie Law Journal*: 158.

Garneau, G.S. 1983. The Law Reform Commission of Canada and the Defence of Justification. 26 *Criminal Law Quarterly*: 121.

Gold, A.D. 1996. Comment on *R. v. Jorgensen* (1995). 38 *Criminal Law Quarterly*: 412.

———. 1997. Requirement for Reasons. 39 Defences — Intoxication — Trial Judge — *Criminal Law Quarterly*: 25.

Grant, I. 1995. Second Chances: Bill C-72 and the *Charter*. 33 *Osgoode Hall Law Journal*: 379.

———. 1996. Developments in Criminal Law: the 1994–95 Term. 7 *Supreme Court Law Review (2d)*: 203. 231–44.

Hatch, D.R. 1999. Culpability and Capitulation: Sexual Assault and Consent in the Wake of *R.v. Ewanchuk*. 43 *Criminal Law Quarterly*: 51.

Healy, P. 1992. Note on *R. v. Penno*. 71 *Canadian Bar Review*: 143.

———. 1993. Innocence and Defences. 19 *Criminal Reports (4th)*: 121.

———. 1996. *Beard* Still Not Cut Off. 46 *Criminal Reports (4th)*: 65.

Hill, J.L. 1999. A Utilitarian Theory of Duress. 84 *Iowa Law Review*: 275.

Hink, S.S. and R.W. Thomas. 1999. Rape Myth Acceptance in College Students: How Far Have We Come? 40 *Sex Roles*: 815.

Holland, W.H. 1998. *The Law of Theft and Related Offences*. Toronto: Carswell. 150–70.

Horder, J. 1994. Occupying the Moral High Ground? The Law Commission on Duress. (1994) *Criminal Law Review*: 334.

———. 1998. Self-Defence, Necessity and Duress: Understanding the Relationship. 16 *Canadian Journal of Law & Jurisprudence*: 143.

Jones, O.D. 1999. Sex, Culture, and the Biology of Rape: Toward Explanation and Prevention. 87 *California Law Review*: 827.

———. 2000. Law and the Biology of Rape: Reflections on Transitions. 11 *Hastings Women's Law Journal*: 151.

Kahan, D.M and M.C. Nussbaum. 1996. Two Conceptions of Emotion in Criminal Law. 96 *Columbia Law Review*: 269.

Kastner, N.S. 1986. Mistake of Law and the Defence of Officially Induced Error. 28 *Criminal Law Quarterly*: 308.

Klimchuk, D. 1998. Moral Innocence, Normative Involuntariness and Fundamental Justice. 18 *Criminal Reports (5th)*: 96.

Law Reform Commission of Canada. 1978. Report No. 10: *Sexual Offences*. Ottawa: Information Canada.

———. 1978. Working Paper No. 22: *Sexual Offences*. Ottawa: Information Canada.

———. 1982. Working Paper No. 29: *Criminal Law: The General Part—Liability and Defences*. Ottawa: Ministry of Supply and Services Canada.

———. 1987. Report 31: *Recodifying Criminal Law*. Rev. ed. Ottawa: L.R.C.C.

Libman, R. 1991. The Defence of Drinking and Driving Offences: Too Drunk to Drive; Too Drunk for a Defence? 3 *Journal of Motor Vehicle Law*: 25.

McCauley, F. 1998. Necessity and Duress in Criminal Law: The Confluence of Two Great Tributaries. 33 *Irish Jurist*: 120.

MacMillan-Brown, H. 1995. No Longer *"Leary"* about Intoxication: In the Aftermath of *R. v. Daviault*. 59 *Saskatchewan Law Review*: 311.

Marin, A. 1995. When is an "Honest but Mistaken Belief in Consent" NOT an "Honest but Mistaken Belief in Consent." 37 *Criminal Law Quarterly*: 451.

Marlowe, D.B., J.B. Lambert, and R.G. Thompson. 1999. Voluntary Intoxication and Criminal Responsibility. 17 *Behavioral Sciences & the Law*: 195.

Martin, R. 1993. Bill C-49: A Victory for Interest Group Politics. 42 *University of New Brunswick Law Journal*: 357.

Mewett, A.W. 1995. Editorial: A Jurisprudential Analysis of Duress. 38 *Criminal Law Quarterly:* 129.

———. 1995. Editorial: Extreme Drunkenness. 37 *Criminal Law Quarterly:* 385.

Mewett, A.W. and M. Manning. 1994. *Mewett and Manning on Criminal Law.* 3d ed. Toronto: Butterworths. 363 – 440, 519 – 32.

Morgan, E.M. 1984. The Defence of Necessity: Justification or Excuse? 42 *University of Toronto Faculty Law Review:* 165.

Odem, M.E. and J. Clay-Warner, eds. 1998. *Confronting Rape and Sexual Assault.* Wilmington, Delaware: Scholarly Resources Inc.

Paciocco, D.M. 1999. *Getting Away with Murder: The Canadian Criminal Justice System.* Concord, Ont.: Irwin Law. 251–68.

Padfield, N. 1992. Duress, Necessity and the Law Commission. [1992] *Criminal Law Review:* 778.

Parry, J.T. 1999. The Virtue of Necessity: Reshaping Culpability and the Rule of Law. 36 *Houston Law Review:* 397.

Quigley, T. 1995. *R. v. Latimer:* Hard Cases Make Interesting Law. 41 *Criminal Reports (4th):* 89.

Reed, A. 1996. Duress and Provocation as Excuse to Murder: Salutary Lesson from Recent Anglo-American Jurisprudence. 6 *Journal of Transnational Law & Policy:* 51.

———. 1997. The Need for a New Anglo-American Approach to Duress. 61 *Journal of Criminal Law:* 209.

Reilly, A. 1997–98. The Heart of the Matter: Emotion in Criminal Defences. 29 *Ottawa Law Review:* 117.

Reilly, A. and R. Mikus. 1996. *R. v. Hibbert:* The Theoretical Foundations of Duress. 30 *U.B.C. Law Review:* 181.

Roach, K. 1996. *Criminal Law.* Concord, Ont.: Irwin Law. 162–91.

Rolfes, B. 1998. The Golden Thread of Criminal Law—Moral Culpability and Sexual Assault. 61 *Saskatchewan Law Review:* 87.

Rosenthal, P. 1989. Duress in the Criminal Law. 32 *Criminal Law Quarterly:* 199.

Rutkowski, D.S. 1996. A Coercion Defense for the Street Gang Criminal: Plugging the Moral Gap in the Existing Law. 10 *Notre Dame Journal of Law, Ethics & Public Policy:* 137.

Schabas, P.B. 1984. Intoxication and Culpability: Towards an Offence of Criminal Intoxication. 42 *University of Toronto Faculty Law Review:* 147.

———. 1985. Justification, Excuse and the Defence of Necessity: A Comment on *Perka v. The Queen.* 27 *Criminal Law Quarterly:* 278.

Searles, P. and R.J. Berger. 1995. *Rape and Society: Readings on the Problem of Sexual Assault.* Boulder, Colorado: Westview Press.

Shaffer, M. 1998. Coerced into Crime: Battered Women and the Defence of Duress. 4 *Canadian Criminal Law Review:* 271.

———. 1998. Scrutinizing Duress: The Constitutional Validity of Section 17 of the *Criminal Code.* 40 *Criminal Law Quarterly:* 444.

Singer, R.G. 2000. The Proposed Duty to Inquire as Affected by Recent Criminal Law Decisions in the United States Supreme Court. 3 *Buffalo Criminal Law Review:* 701.

Smith, K.J.M. 1999. Duress and Steadfastness: In Pursuit of the Unintelligible. [1999] *Criminal Law Review:* 363.

Stewart, H. 1998. Mistake of Law under the *Charter.* 40 *Criminal Law Quarterly:* 476.

———. 1999. *R. v. Darrach:* A Step Forward in the Constitutionalization of Fault. 4 *Canadian Criminal Law Review:* 9.

Stuart, D. 1993. Sexual Assault: Substantive Issues Before and After Bill C-49. 35 *Criminal Law Quarterly:* 241.

———. 1995. *Canadian Criminal Law: A Treatise.* 3d ed. Toronto: Carswell. 253 – 326, 383 – 415, 426 – 39, 473 – 88.

———. 1999. *Ewanchuk:* Asserting "No Means No" at the Expense of Fault and Proportionality Principles. 22 *Criminal Reports (5th):* 39.

Stuart, D. and R.J. Delisle. 1997. *Learning Canadian Criminal Law.* 6th ed. Toronto: Carswell. 511–646, 716–92.

Taslitz, A.E. 2000. Race and Two Concepts of the Emotions in Date Rape. 15 *Wisconsin Women's Law Journal:* 3.

Temkin, J. 2000. Prosecuting and Defending Rape: Perspectives from the Bar. 27 *Journal of Law & Society:* 219.

Verdun-Jones, S.N. 1999. *Canadian Criminal Cases: Selected Highlights.* Toronto: Harcourt Brace. Chap. 8.

Wallace, T.J. 1999. Addiction as Defect of the Will: Some Philosophical Reflections. 18 *Law and Philosophy:* 621.

Watson, G. 1999. Excusing Addiction. 18 *Law and Philosophy:* 589.

Way, M.C. 1993. Bill C-49 and the Politics of Constitutionalized Fault. 42 *University of New Brunswick Law Journal:* 327.

Wertheim, A. 2000. What is Consent? And is it Important? 3 *Buffalo Criminal Law Review:* 557.

Yeo, S.M.H. 1990. *Compulsion in the Criminal Law.* Sydney: The Law Book Company.

———. 1992. Coercing Wives into Crime. 6 *Australian Journal of Family Law:* 214.

———. 1996. Voluntariness, Free Will and Duress. 70 *Australian Law Journal:* 304.

Young, R.E. 1999. Note and Comments: *R. v. Ruzic.* 42 *Criminal Law Quarterly:* 515.

Defences to a Criminal Charge: Part II

OVERVIEW

This chapter examines the following:

1. Three of the major defences that may be raised in response to criminal charges in Canada:

   (i)   provocation,
   (ii) self-defence and defence of property, and
   (iii) consent;

2. the defence of provocation as a partial defence to a charge of murder, with particular attention to the requirements that the alleged provocation must be such as would cause the "ordinary person" to lose the power of self-control and that the accused must act on the provocation "on the sudden and before there was time for (their) passion to cool";

3. the differing roles of the judge and jury in relation to the defence of provocation, and the situations in which accused persons may lose the benefit of the defence because their victims were doing what they had a "legal right to do";

4. the situations in which private citizens may defend their persons or property against unlawful attack:

   (i)   self-defence against an unprovoked assault, where the defendant did not intend to inflict death or grievous bodily harm (section 34(1)),

   (ii) self-defence where the defendant inflicts death or grievous bodily harm,
   (iii) the use of force in order to prevent an assault (section 37),
   (iv) the use of force in self-defence by a party who was originally the aggressor in an altercation (section 35),
   (v)   the defence of property (sections 38 to 42), and
   (vi) the use of excessive defensive force that results in the death of the victim;

5. the defence of consent to a criminal charge in the circumstances where the absence of consent is a vital element in the case that must be proved by the Crown;

6. the defence of consent in relation to cases of assault (section 265) and, in particular, to charges of assault arising in the context of professional sports;

7. the defence of consent in the context of a charge of sexual assault (sections 271, 272, 273, 273.1, and 273.2).

PROVOCATION

The General Nature of the Defence and Section 232

Like the defence of **infanticide** (section 233 of the Code), provocation provides only a *partial* excuse to the **defendant** in a criminal trial. Indeed, the defence of provocation may be raised only in relation to a charge of **murder** and, if successful, its sole effect is to ensure that the **accused** is convicted of **manslaughter** rather than murder. In essence, the defence of provocation represents an attempt by the criminal law to show a little mercy to those individuals who lose their power of self-control in the face of highly stressful circumstances. Significantly, the courts have emphasized that the defence of provocation is available to accused persons despite the fact that they *intended* to kill their victim. In the *Oickle* case (1984), for example, the Appeal Division of the Nova Scotia Supreme Court ordered a new trial, in part because the trial judge had not made it clear to the jury that provocation may reduce murder to manslaughter even if it was found that the accused had an **intention** to kill.

The defence of provocation is defined, in considerable detail, by section 232 of the *Criminal Code.* Therefore, Canadian judges have been somewhat circumscribed in their attempts to develop the law relating to provocation. The provisions of section 232 are as follows:

(1) Culpable homicide that otherwise would be murder may be reduced to manslaughter if the person who committed it did so in the heat of passion caused by sudden provocation.

(2) A wrongful act or insult that is of such a nature as to be sufficient to deprive an ordinary person of the power of self-control is provocation enough for the purposes of this section if the accused acted upon it on the sudden and before there was time for his passion to cool.

(3) For the purposes of this section the questions

   (a) whether a particular wrongful act or insult amounted to provocation, and
   (b) whether the accused was deprived of the power of self-control by the provocation that he alleges he received, are questions of fact, but no one shall be deemed to have given provocation to another by doing anything that he had

a legal right to do, or by doing anything that the accused incited him to do in order to provide the accused with an excuse for causing death or bodily harm to any human being.

(4) Culpable homicide that otherwise would be murder is not necessarily manslaughter by reason only that it was committed by a person who was being arrested illegally, but the fact that the illegality of the arrest was known to the accused may be evidence of provocation for the purpose of this section.

The Rule That the Provocation Must Be Sufficient to Deprive an "Ordinary Person" of the Power of Self-Control

It is quite apparent that section 232(2) establishes a formidable precondition to any successful attempt to raise the defence of provocation. Indeed, the Code stipulates that the wrongful act or insult that purportedly caused the accused to lose his or her temper must be of such a nature as to be sufficient to deprive an *ordinary* person of the power of self-control. It appears, on the face of it, that the courts are required to apply an *objective* test, in which the personal susceptibilities and individual characteristics of the individual accused must be ignored; instead, it would seem that the focus of inquiry must be placed on the powers of self-control of the hypothetical "ordinary person." However, recent court decisions in Canada suggest that the objective test should be modified to take into account some aspects of the accused's background and characteristics after all. Unfortunately, as we shall see, it is not entirely clear exactly how far Canadian courts are willing to go in modifying the "ordinary person" test in section 232(2).

Justice Cory, in delivering the judgment of the majority of the Supreme Court of Canada in the recent case of *Thibert* (1996), aptly pointed out that

the objective aspect would at first reading appear to be contradictory for, as legal writers have noted, the "ordinary" person does not kill. *Yet, I think that the objective element should be taken as an attempt to weigh in the balance those very human frailties which sometimes lead people to act irrationally and impulsively against the need to protect society by discouraging acts of homicidal violence.* [emphasis added]

Since Justice Cory refers to the need to balance recognition of "human frailties" against the need to protect the public, it is clear that the application of the "ordinary person" test leaves a certain amount of discretion to the courts. However, it is only in relatively recent years that Canadian courts have been willing to engage in any kind of balancing exercise when interpreting the "ordinary person" test in relation to provocation. In order to understand the full implications of the modern approach to this issue, it is necessary to trace the historical development of judicial interpretations of section 232(2).

Historically, there is no doubt that the courts applied the objective test in, what would today be viewed as, an extremely harsh manner. Take, for example, the case of *Sampson* (1935). The accused was convicted of the murder of a young boy. It appeared that, while walking down a railway track, Sampson had encountered two small boys who were picking blueberries. As Sampson passed them, they called him various names, including "coon, nigger, and baboon face," and threw stones at him. Sampson eventually lost his temper and stabbed the two boys; one of them subsequently died. Medical evidence was introduced at the trial to the effect that Sampson was not an "ordinary" person in the generally accepted sense of the word. Rather, he was afflicted with a "sub-normal mentality" (roughly equivalent to a mental age of twelve or thirteen years). Furthermore, it is clear that the racist epithets hurled at the accused were clearly designed to upset him, since the law report of the case indicates that the accused was a "coloured man." Nevertheless, the trial judge refused to instruct the jury that, in determining the question of provocation, the mental age of the accused should be taken into consideration. Furthermore, the relevance of the racial

background of the accused was totally ignored even though there was evidence that he had been subjected to racist taunts of the most vile kind.

Sampson was convicted and sentenced to death. His subsequent **appeals** to the Nova Scotia Supreme Court and the Supreme Court of Canada were unsuccessful. Essentially, Sampson was not able to claim the defence of provocation because the hypothetical "ordinary" person does not labour under the disadvantage of a developmental disability. Today, it is certain that both the accused's race and mental age would be taken into account in deciding whether an "ordinary person" with these characteristics would be likely to be deprived of the power of self-control when subjected to insults.

There is little doubt that the excessively strict interpretation of the "ordinary person" test in the *Sampson* case is at total variance with everyday common sense. After all, it is fairly obvious that the force of an insult depends, to a large extent, on its success in striking a "raw nerve" of the unfortunate individual to whom it is directed. For example, it is highly unlikely that a six-foot-five linebacker, in a professional football team, would be particularly upset if someone attempted to insult him by calling him "a dwarf." However, the very same insult might well be most hurtful to an individual of extremely diminutive stature. To put it another way, the whole intent of an insult is to provoke discomfort in its victim and such discomfort is best accomplished by ridiculing an individual characteristic about which the victim may feel sensitive. Therefore, it would appear to be a reasonable assumption that an impotent man is much more likely to respond to an insult concerning his sexual prowess than a man who is not afflicted with such an infirmity. Fortunately, the harsh, literal interpretation of the "ordinary person" test, illustrated by *Sampson*, has been considerably relaxed by the courts in more recent times.

The Relaxation of the Definition of the "Ordinary Person"

In the *Hill* case, decided in 1986, the Supreme Court of Canada for the first time gave some indication that trial courts should move away from the strict, or literal, interpretation of the "ordinary person" requirement in section 232(2) of the *Criminal Code*. In *Hill*, the accused, who was only sixteen years of age, was tried on a charge of **first degree murder**. One of his defences was that he had been provoked. The accused claimed that the victim (who had become known to Hill through the Big Brother organization) had made unexpected and unwanted homosexual advances to him (Hill) immediately before the killing. The victim's death followed the infliction of wounds from a hatchet and two knives. The trial judge instructed the jury that

> Provocation may come from actual words or a series of each or a combination of both, and it must be looked at in light of the surrounding circumstances.
>
> First, the actual words must be such as would deprive an ordinary person of self-control. In considering this part of the Defence you are not to consider the particular mental make-up of the accused; rather the standard is that of the ordinary person. You will ask yourselves would the words or acts in this case have caused an ordinary person to lose his self-control.

Hill was ultimately convicted of **second degree murder** and he appealed to the Ontario Court of Appeal, which ordered a new trial on the ground that the trial judge had erred in giving his interpretation of the objective test in section 232(2). In particular, the court held that the ordinary person within the meaning of that subsection was an "ordinary person of the *same age and sex of the accused.*" [emphasis added]. Justice Brooke said that

> The effect of the charge was that an ordinary person did not include a 16-year-old or youth and may well have established as the standard an ordinary person more experienced and mature than the ordinary 16-year-old or youth.

The Court of Appeal appeared to base its decision on the view that the age and sex of an accused person could not be excluded from consideration in the application of the ordinary person test in section 232(2) because they were not "peculiar characteristics." The Crown appealed to the Supreme Court of Canada, which (by a vote of five to three) allowed the appeal and restored the conviction. The majority decision of the Supreme Court basically upholds the view that age, sex, and race are not "peculiar characteristics" and can be considered in the application of the ordinary person test. However, the majority decision also held that the trial judge did not specifically have to bring this principle to the attention of the jury. In the view of the majority, therefore, the trial judge's direction had been adequate. This ruling is predicated on the (perhaps) questionable assumption that the "good sense" of the Canadian jury will automatically lead it to ascribe to the ordinary person, referred to in section 232(2), the age, race, or sex of the particular accused before it! Chief Justice Dickson, in delivering the majority judgment, stated that

> I think that it is clear that there is widespread agreement that the ordinary or reasonable person has a normal temperament and level of self-control. It follows that *the ordinary person is not exceptionally excitable, pugnacious or in a state of drunkenness.*
>
> In terms of other characteristics of the ordinary person, it seems to me that the "collective good sense" of the jury will naturally lead it to ascribe to the ordinary person any general characteristics relevant to the provocation in question. For example, if the provocation is a racial slur, the jury will think of an ordinary person with the racial background that forms the substance of the insult. To this extent, particular characteristics will be ascribed to the ordinary person. Indeed, it would be impossible to conceptualize a sexless or ageless ordinary person. Features such as sex, age or race do not detract from a person's characterization as ordinary. ...

The central criterion is the relevance of the particular feature to the provocation in question.
[emphasis added]

The Supreme Court decision in *Hill* was not entirely satisfying insofar as it gave little concrete guidance to Canadian courts as to the extent to which they should consider the individual characteristics of an accused person in applying the ordinary person test in section 232(2). Clearly age, race, and sex must be taken into account, but it is not clear from the *Hill* case whether other more idiosyncratic factors, such as impotence, would be considered relevant. Chief Justice Dickson appears to suggest that physical disability could be taken into account, but he did not specifically identify any other such factors.

Fortunately, much of the ambiguity that surrounded the decision of the Supreme Court of Canada in *Hill* has been dissipated by the Court's more recent ruling in the *Thibert* case (1996). In *Thibert*, the Court appears to have introduced a significant dose of subjectivism into the interpretation of section 232(2). Justice Cory, speaking for the majority of the Supreme Court of Canada, ruled that the function of the objective test is "to ensure that the criminal law encourages reasonable and responsible behaviour." In his view,

if the test is to be applied sensibly and with sensitivity, then *the ordinary person must be taken to be of the same age, and sex, and must share with the accused such other factors as would give the act or insult in question a particular significance. In other words, all the relevant background circumstances should be considered.* In the context of other cases, it may properly be found that other factors should be considered. *It is how such an "ordinary" person with those characteristics would react to the situation which confronted the accused that should be used as the basis for considering the objective element.*
[emphasis added]

This statement by Justice Cory effectively expands the interpretation of the phrase "ordinary person," so that it may now be taken to include almost any particular characteristic of the accused — *provided only that such a characteristic directly affects the gravity of any taunt or insult that is relied on by the accused as the basis for a defence of provocation.* For example, it may be presumed that the impotence of the accused is now a factor that should be taken into account in applying the "ordinary person" test if the victim taunted the accused with insults relating to this particular form of infirmity.

The only particular characteristics that should *not* be considered, in applying the ordinary person test, are those that relate to "temperament" and "power of self-control." In other words, as Chief Justice Dickson pointed out in the *Hill* case, the ordinary person must be considered to possess a "normal" temperament and level of self-control; if this were not so, a bad-tempered accused would have a definite advantage over a "normal" accused insofar as the raising of the defence of provocation is concerned.

In *Thibert*, the Supreme Court of Canada recognized that the objective test should include some consideration of the "background relationship between the deceased and the accused." As Justice Cory notes,

the wrongful act or insult must be one which could, in light of the past history of the relationship between the accused and the deceased, deprive an ordinary person, of the same age, sex, and sharing with the accused such other factors as would give the act or insult in question a special significance, of the power of self-control.

For example, in the *Thibert* case itself, the accused's wife had, on a prior occasion, planned to leave him for the deceased, but he managed to dissuade her from doing so. He apparently hoped to secure a similar outcome when his wife left him on a second occasion. When Thibert was attempting to talk to his wife alone, the deceased took hold of the wife's shoulders "in a proprietary and possessive manner" and moved her around in front of him.

The deceased simultaneously taunted Thibert to shoot him and ultimately Thibert did inflict a fatal wound.

In approaching the question of whether there was some evidence capable of meeting the requirements of the objective test, the Supreme Court of Canada held that, in light of the past history that had passed between Thibert and the deceased, a jury might well find that the deceased's actions immediately before his death were "taunting and insulting." Justice Cory went on to state that

> It might be found that under the same circumstances, an ordinary person who was a married man, faced with the breakup of his marriage, would have been provoked by the actions of the deceased so as to cause him to lose his power of self-control.

Even before the *Thibert* case, Canadian courts had emphasized the need to consider the particular background in which the alleged provocation took place. In *Conway* (1985), for example, the Ontario Court of Appeal ruled that, in applying the ordinary person test, the jury should take into account the long-standing record of frequent confrontations between the accused and his victim. Chief Justice Howland, speaking for the court, held that the trial judge should have told the jury that

> present acts or insults, in themselves insufficient to cause an ordinary man [*sic*] to lose self-control, may indeed cause such loss of self-control when they are connected with past events and external pressures of insult by acts or words and accordingly in considering whether an ordinary man would have lost self-control they must consider an ordinary man who had experienced the same series of acts or insults as experienced by the appellant. ...

It is important to bear in mind that, in order to meet the requirements of the ordinary person test, the alleged provocation must have a direct relationship to the individual characteristic on which the accused relies. For example, a racist insult would only be considered to be of such a nature as to deprive an ordinary person of the power of self-control if that person in fact identifies her- or himself as a member of the racial group against which the insult is directed. Similarly, an individual of a particular racial or ethnic background cannot raise this particular characteristic in the context of the ordinary person test unless the insult or act in question was directed at this characteristic of the accused. This is illustrated by the case of *Ly* (1988), in which the accused had come to Canada from Vietnam. He grew to believe that his common law wife was being unfaithful to him. One day, the wife returned home in the early hours of the morning even though the accused had expected her to return the previous evening. When the accused asked his wife where she had been, she replied, "Don't ask me. It's none of your business." At this point, the accused strangled his wife to death.

At his trial for second degree murder, the accused raised the defence of provocation. He testified that his wife's infidelity had caused him to lose "face" and "honour" and that this consequence had a special impact on him because of his Vietnamese background. An expert witness stated that "in the Vietnamese culture it would be a great blow to the average male to have to conclude that his wife had been unfaithful to him." However, the trial judge told the jury that, in applying the ordinary person element of section 232, they must ignore "the peculiar character or personality of the accused." In other words, the jury was instructed that they should not take into account the "reaction that an average Vietnamese male would have as a result of his cultural background to infidelity on the part of his wife." The accused was convicted of murder.

The British Columbia Court of Appeal dismissed an appeal by Ly and ruled that the trial judge had been correct in his interpretation of the ordinary person test. Justice Macfarlane referred to *Hill* and noted that, in that case, Chief Justice Dickson had indicated that, where there has been a racial slur, the jury will "think of the ordinary man with the same racial background as the accused." However, in the *Ly* case, the alleged provocation was not based on a racial slur. Instead, the provocation was supposed to consist of the victim's late arrival home and her refusal to tell the accused where she had been. Justice Macfarlane concluded that

> I think it was proper for the jury to be told to consider the effect of the words ascribed to the deceased on the ordinary man who, because of a history of the relationship between the spouses, had a belief that his wife was not being faithful to him. The fact that the husband was Vietnamese and came from a certain cultural background might have been relevant if a racial slur had been involved, but that is not the case.

However, it is significant that, according to the court, the trial judge had correctly informed the jury that the issue of the accused's cultural background would be relevant to the subjective question of whether the accused had in fact acted "on the sudden" before there was time for his passion to cool (see the following section).

Recent judicial authority in Canada has made it perfectly clear that the test in section 232(2) is not whether an ordinary person would have acted in exactly the same way as the accused, but rather whether the ordinary person would have lost the power of self-control. This principle was strongly underscored by the Ontario Court of Appeal in the case of *Carpenter* (1993). As Justice Austin noted in that case, "the 'ordinary person' test is directed to loss of control, not the conduct flowing from that loss of control."

In the case of *Cameron* (1992), the Ontario Court of Appeal considered the intriguing question of whether the ordinary person test infringes the *Charter*. The accused had been convicted of second degree murder and had appealed to the Court of Appeal. On his appeal, Cameron argued that the objective test in section 232(2) infringed his *Charter* rights because, as the Supreme Court of Canada

ruled in *Martineau* (1990), liability for murder cannot be based on objective fault. The court rejected this argument because section 232 does not change the requirement that there must be subjective foresight of death before an accused may be convicted of murder. Section 232 merely serves to reduce what otherwise would be murder to manslaughter. As Justice Doherty remarked, this provision "does not impose liability where subjective fault does not exist but reduces the liability even when that fault exists."

The Rule That the Accused Must Act in the Heat of the Moment

Section 232(2) also provides that, in order for a defence of provocation to be successful, the accused must have acted upon the alleged provocation "on the sudden and before there was time for his passion to cool." In determining this issue, a *subjective* approach must be applied. In other words, the defence of provocation will not be successful merely because the accused establishes that the alleged provocation was sufficient to "deprive an ordinary person of the power of self-control." On the contrary, in order for the defence to be successful, it must also be established that *this particular defendant* was subjected to sudden provocation and acted in the heat of passion.

In relation to this element of the defence of provocation, juries must consider such subjective factors as, for example, the extent to which the accused persons' state of intoxication caused them to lose their power of self-control. In the case of *Haight* (1976), for example, Justice Martin of the Ontario Court of Appeal referred to this issue in the following manner:

> Where there is evidence of provocation proper for the consideration of the jury, the jury is required to pass upon two questions:
>
> (1) whether there is a wrongful act or insult that is of such a nature as to be sufficient to

deprive an ordinary person of the power of self-control, and

(2) whether the accused was actually deprived of his power of self-control by the provocation.

The first question is to be decided in accordance with an objective standard, with reference to the ordinary person and without reference to any characteristics or condition peculiar to the accused. *The second question imports a subjective test in which it is proper and necessary for the jury, in deciding whether or not the accused was actually deprived of his power of self-control, to consider his particular characteristics and condition, for example, his condition with respect to drunkenness.* [emphasis added]

The requirement that the accused act "in the heat of passion" and in response to *sudden* provocation is well illustrated in the celebrated case of *Salamon* (1959), in which the accused was charged with the murder of Joyce Alexander. At the time of the homicide, he had been living with Ms. Alexander, her husband, and her child and apparently enjoyed a close relationship with her. Salamon and Ms. Alexander had been drinking at the house of a friend, and testimony was given to the effect that the accused had entered into an argument and had been requested to leave. Salamon asked Ms. Alexander to accompany him and she refused. Salamon later returned in order to ask his friend to prevail upon Ms. Alexander to come home with him, but a struggle ensued between Salamon and his friend. The struggle came to an end and Salamon fired five shots in the air with his revolver before leaving for home. Approximately two to three hours passed between Salamon's arrival at home and the subsequent return of Joyce Alexander. At this latter point, Salamon came out of his room and asked Ms. Alexander for an explanation of her failure to keep an appointment during the previous afternoon. A violent argument ensued in which "blows were struck, her skirt torn off and they began throwing dishes at each other." Eventually, Mr. Alexander emerged from his room and brought the quarrel to

an end. Ms. Alexander went to the adjoining bathroom to wash the blood off her neck. Salamon subsequently entered the bathroom and it appears that he called Joyce Alexander "a dirty name"; the latter retaliated in similar fashion, and then the accused fired a shot from his revolver. Ms. Alexander later died.

Salamon claimed the benefit of the defence of provocation. The accused was convicted at his trial and his subsequent appeals, to the Ontario Court of Appeal and the Supreme Court of Canada, were unsuccessful. In the Supreme Court of Canada, Justice Fauteux emphasized that, when Salamon had left his friend's house, he "was not mad at Joyce Alexander; he merely wished her to go home with him." Clearly, the accused was not in a state of provocation at this time. Furthermore, even if he had been, the length of time that elapsed between the accused's ejection from his friend's house and the fatal shooting would clearly negative the requirement of "suddenness" that is an essential component of the defence of provocation. Justice Fauteux went on to say

Suddenness must characterize both the insult and the act of retaliation. Evidence of sudden provocation, if any, must then be found in the events taking place subsequently at the home of the deceased woman. ... the evidence shows that from the time Joyce Alexander entered her home to that of the fatal shot, the appellant (Salamon), and not she, took, and kept throughout, the initiative of the events leading to her death. He was evidently waiting for her arrival. He started the quarrel during which she retaliated. The dispute subsided with the intervention of her husband and, as instructed by the latter, she proceeded to the washroom. Appellant went to his room, then proceeded to the washroom, called her a dirty name, caused her to retaliate in a similar fashion, and then shot, or shot without anything being said.

On this evidence, appellant cannot justify or excuse his actions in saying that he was facing a situation characterized with suddenness, unexpectedness or lack of premonition. He had and kept the initiative of the situation in which he found himself. There was no sudden provocation on the part of Joyce Alexander causing sudden retaliation on his part. [emphasis added]

The *Friesen* case (1995) provides a second example of a situation in which it was determined by the courts that there had been time for the accused's passion to cool after sudden provocation. Friesen had killed a friend with a builder's nail gun after an alleged act of sexual provocation by the victim. He claimed the defence of provocation when he was charged with first degree murder. However, the evidence established that, after the alleged provocation, the accused had left the victim and went to the garage where he connected a builder's nail gun to a compressor. Obviously, this took a fair amount of time to accomplish. He then returned to the house and shot the victim with "dozens of nails" from the gun. Significantly, at the time of the shooting, the victim was asleep. Friesen was convicted of murder at his trial (the jury having rejected his defence of provocation) and his appeal was subsequently dismissed by the Alberta Court of Appeal. In the view of the court, no reasonable jury could have found that there had been provocation within the meaning of section 232. According to Justice Côté, who delivered the judgment of the court,

> The accused took some time to go upstairs and out to the garage, to rig up the nail gun and all its power sources, and then to deploy them downstairs in the family room next to the victim. So it is very hard to think that that could be "on the sudden and before there was time for his passion to cool."…
>
> the accused says that the victim was asleep when he shot him. … The victim knew all about nail guns, and that the accused had no proper use for one then and there. One cannot sneak up on a person awake, if one carries a nail gun trailing a long air hose charged by a compressor whose motor is running. Yet the accused says that he left the victim in a state of mental and physical sexual excitement. So if the accused's story about provo-

cation was true, the victim went from such excitement to sleep before the shooting. That process would surely take time as well. So "there was time for his passion to cool."

The Differing Roles of Judge and Jury in Cases Where Provocation Is Raised

Section 232(3) provides that the determination of certain issues must remain within the exclusive realm of the jury. More specifically, the Code states that "whether a particular wrongful act or insult amounted to provocation" and "whether the accused was deprived of the power of self-control by the provocation that he alleges he received" are questions of fact. As such, the trial judge must leave such issues to the jury. However, the Supreme Court of Canada has, on a number of occasions, ruled that trial judges still have a duty to determine whether there is sufficient evidence of provocation to justify submitting the issue to the jury. As Justice Cory stated in delivering the majority judgment of the Supreme Court of Canada in *Thibert* (1996),

> before the defence of provocation is left to the jury, the trial judge must be satisfied (a) that there is *some* evidence to suggest that the particular wrongful act or insult alleged by the accused would have caused an ordinary person to be deprived of self-control, and (b) that there is some evidence showing that the accused was actually deprived of his or her self-control by that act or insult. This threshold test can be readily met, so long as there is some evidence that the objective and subjective elements may be satisfied. If there is, the defence must then be left with the jury.

In other words, trial judges are under a duty not to submit the issue of provocation to the jury unless they are satisfied that there is *some* evidence capable of raising a reasonable doubt in the mind of the jurors. However, the trial judge's role is not to weigh the sufficiency of such evidence; that is a matter entirely for the jury to decide. The trial judge's function in this respect is merely to make a *threshold* determination whether there is any evidence that could justify a reasonable jury coming to the conclusion that the accused person was subject to provocation as defined in section 232.

In this respect, therefore, provocation is no different from any other criminal law defence. There is a requirement that the accused satisfy the *evidentiary burden of proof* before the defence may be considered by the **trier of fact**. What type of evidence will meet the evidentiary burden of proof in the context of a murder trial in which provocation is asserted by the accused? A useful example is provided by the case of *Edgar* (2000), in which the Ontario Court of Appeal ordered a new trial for the accused because the trial judge had incorrectly ruled that there was no "air of reality" to the defence of provocation and had withheld it from the jury. In delivering the judgment of the court, Justice Charron offered the following observations on the evidence pertaining to provocation:

> In my view, the trial judge effectively usurped the function of the jury when he determined that the defence of provocation had no "air of reality". The defence may have no air of reality if the appellant's testimony is disbelieved. However, *that is a matter for the jury to determine.*
>
> In this case, there was some evidence in support of the partial defence of provocation. Counsel for the appellant noted the following in her submissions: the appellant's evidence that he was attacked by the deceased with two knives; his evidence that he became enraged; the absence of other evidence of motive for the killing; evidence that there was one continuous transaction with no opportunity for his passion to cool; the appellant's own injuries, some of which were consistent with being defensive wounds; and the evidence of cocaine and alcohol intoxication that may be relevant to the subjective elements of the defence. [emphasis added]

The Meaning of "Legal Right" in Section 232(3)

Section 232(3) also provides that "no one shall be deemed to have given provocation to another by doing anything that he had a legal right to do, or by doing anything that the accused incited him to do in order to provide the accused with an excuse for causing death or bodily harm to any human beings." Although the basic intent of Parliament is clear in relation to this statutory provision, there is some question as to what is meant by "legal right" in this context. Canadian courts have, understandably, interpreted this phrase very restrictively. For example, in *Galgay* (1972), the accused was charged with the murder of his former girlfriend, with whom he had been living. Galgay was serving a sentence of imprisonment when his girlfriend visited him and indicated that, since the accused was institutionalized and would not be released for another year, she had gone out with another man (K) and that she would soon leave the accused because she could not wait another year for his release. Two days later, Galgay left the reformatory unlawfully and spent the night with his girlfriend. After two days, the girlfriend left Galgay and telephoned the police to tell them where he was. The accused was, somewhat naturally, most upset and, as they were walking down a laneway, an argument ensued. The girlfriend told Galgay that she was going to live with K. She added that "You are not going to be any good. You are drinking all the time. You are stealing." The accused then inflicted blows that resulted in the death of the victim. The trial judge instructed the jury that the girlfriend had a legal right to leave the accused and a legal right to tell him that she was going to leave him. Galgay was convicted of murder. However, the Ontario Court of Appeal ordered a new trial on the basis that the trial judge had misinterpreted what is now section 232(3). Justice Brooke stated that

> What is the meaning of the term "legal right" in the provision of the section? Surely, it does not

include all legal conduct not specifically prohibited by law. *The absence of a remedy against doing
or saying something or the absence of a specific legal
prohibition in that regard does not mean or imply
that there is a legal right to so act.* There may be no
legal remedy for an insult said or done in private
but that is not because of legal right. The section
distinguishes legal right from wrongful act or
insult and the proviso of the section ought not to
be interpreted to licence insult or wrongful act
done or spoken under the cloak of legal right.

One has a right to do and to say those things
which one is specifically authorized by law to say
or to do, such as a Sheriff proceeding to execute a
warrant of the court. One has a right to do and to
say those things which arise in the ordinary course
of one's affairs and relationships. *But in neither case
does the right extend to speaking or acting so as to
insult the other person.* [emphasis added]

Incidentally, it is important to note that, in the
Galgay case, the evidence was that the victim insulted the accused by denigrating his character. She
certainly had every right to leave Galgay but she
did not, within the meaning of section 232(3), have
the "legal right" to insult him. As the Nova Scotia
Court of Appeal pointed out in the *Young* case
(1993), merely terminating a relationship with
someone cannot, on its own, be considered an
"insult" or "wrongful act" that is capable of constituting provocation under section 232.

The approach adopted by the Ontario Court of
Appeal in the *Galgay* case was later endorsed by the
Supreme Court of Canada in *Thibert* (1996). As
Justice Cory noted, in delivering the majority
judgement in *Thibert*,

> the defence of provocation is open to someone
> who is "insulted." The words or act put forward as
> provocation need not be words or act [*sic*] which
> are specifically prohibited by the law.

In what situations will the courts find that the victim had a "legal right" to do what he or she did

within the meaning of section 232(3)? A good example of such a situation may be found in the case of
Louison (1975), in which the accused was charged
with the noncapital murder of a taxi driver who had
picked him up. The victim had been brutally beaten
to death with a hammer. It appears that the accused
had pulled a knife on the victim and forced him into
the trunk of the taxi. After keeping the victim in the
trunk for a couple of hours, Louison decided to give
him some air. The deceased hit the accused in the
back with a hammer. However, Louison wrested the
hammer away from the somewhat enfeebled victim
and began to rain blows upon his head. When the
body was discovered, the hammer was embedded in
the victim's skull. Perhaps he was pushing his luck a
little too far, but the accused nevertheless advanced
provocation as one of his defences at trial. The
accused was ultimately convicted, and he appealed to
the Saskatchewan Court of Appeal. One of the reasons for rejecting the accused's appeal in relation to
the defence of provocation concerned the fact that
the deceased had been acting in self-defence and,
therefore, had a legal right to do what he did within
the meaning of section 232(3). Chief Justice Culliton
stated that:

> It seems to me that in a case of self-induced provo-
> cation s. [232] must be given a reasonable inter-
> pretation; for example—in an attempted rape, if
> the victim in resisting the assault should stick her
> finger in the eye of the assailant causing him injury
> and severe pain and he thereupon killed her, I
> think her act in this respect would be construed as
> something she had a legal right to do and would
> not be a wrongful act within s. [232]. Similarly,
> where the pilot of a plane is being held at gunpoint
> by a hijacker and if he should strike the hijacker
> with a fist or a wrench whereupon the hijacker
> shot him, I would not think such action would be
> considered a wrongful act within s. [232] of the
> *Criminal Code.*

Predictably, Louison's subsequent appeal to the Supreme Court of Canada was also rejected.

SELF-DEFENCE AND DEFENCE OF PROPERTY

The Structure of the *Criminal Code* Provisions

A number of provisions in the *Criminal Code* justify the use of force in defence of the person or property. For example, sections 25 through 33 of the Code deal with the justified use of force by those individuals who are charged with the administration and enforcement of the law in Canada. Sections 34 through 42, in contrast, are concerned with delineating the circumstances in which a private citizen may defend person or property against unlawful attack. These sections are, unfortunately, quite complex in nature and it is clearly not possible to investigate all of them. This discussion will, therefore, be confined to an examination of the major sections of the Code that deal with the justifiable use of force by the private citizen.

Self-Defence Against an Unlawful and Unprovoked Assault Where the Defendant Does Not Intend to Inflict Death or Grievous Bodily Harm

Section 34(1) of the *Criminal Code* provides that

> Everyone who is unlawfully assaulted without having provoked the assault is justified in repelling force by force if the force he uses is not intended to cause death or grievous bodily harm and is no more than is necessary to enable him to defend himself.

It will be noted that this provision of the *Criminal Code* is only applicable where the assault upon the defendant is unprovoked. (Section 36 of the Code provides a partial definition of provocation for this purpose, namely, "provocation includes ... provocation by blows, words or gestures.") Section 34(1) is also limited in its application to situations in which the defendant *did not intend to cause death or grievous*

bodily harm. If the defendant did intend to inflict such a degree of injury upon an assailant, the appropriate defence would be formulated in terms of the provisions of section 34(2). Perhaps the most significant limitation to section 34(1), however, is the requirement that the force employed must be "no more than is necessary to enable [the accused] to defend himself." This latter restriction introduces the concept of the *proportionality* of force. To use an extreme example frequently quoted by academic writers, one may not "use a tank against a chariot." In other words, there must be a reasonable degree of proportionality between the force employed by the assailant and the force employed by the accused in self-defence.

In this respect, it is critical to recognize that the *Criminal Code* appears to specify an *objective* test. However, Canadian courts have tempered this requirement of objectivity by giving some limited recognition to certain subjective factors. For example, the courts have not insisted that individuals who are defending themselves against a violent attack must calculate the "necessary" degree of retaliatory force with mathematical precision. In the case of *Baxter* (1975), Justice Martin, in delivering the judgment of the Ontario Court of Appeal, stated that

> S. 34(1) does not import a purely objective test. The doctrine of mistake of fact is applicable to s. 34(1) as well as s. 34(2). *An accused's belief that he was in imminent danger from an attack may be reasonable, although he may be mistaken in his belief.* Moreover, when deciding whether the force used by the accused was more than necessary in self-defence under both s. 34(1) and (2) the jury must bear in mind that a person defending himself against an attack, reasonably apprehended, cannot be expected to weigh to a nicety, the exact measure of necessary defensive action. ... [emphasis added]

The requirement that the force used in self-defence be proportionate to the force employed by the assailant is well illustrated by the case of *Nelson*

(1953), in which the accused was charged with manslaughter following a fight with the deceased victim. It appeared that the deceased had struck the accused with an open right hand, and the latter had responded with a blow that fractured the victim's jaw in several places. The victim fell and struck his head on the pavement causing a brain haemorrhage that resulted in his death. Although the victim had been carrying an iron bar in his hand, he had not attempted to use it. The accused was convicted at his trial and appealed to the British Columbia Court of Appeal. By a majority decision, the court dismissed Nelson's appeal. Justice Sidney Smith stated the following:

> the accused was 29 years of age, 6 ft. in height and weighed 170 lbs., while the deceased was 59 years of age, 5 ft. 10 in. in height and weighed 130 lbs. …
>
> It will be observed that a slap on the face was here answered with a blow of such force as to fracture the deceased's jaw in several places. With respect, I find it impossible on the evidence to say that this force was necessary for the purpose of self-defence, or that the appellant was under reasonable apprehension of death or grievous bodily harm. …

Clearly, in the view of the Court of Appeal, the violent response of the accused was out of all proportion to the unprovoked "slap" perpetrated by the victim.

In the *Doherty* case (2000), the New Brunswick Court of Appeal emphasized that an accused person may exercise the right to self-defence under section 34(1) of the Code, *even if he or she does not act out of fear for his or her own personal safety.* Doherty was a bouncer at a strip club and had expelled the victim from the premises. The victim and a companion become belligerent and banged and kicked on the club door. When Doherty responded by coming out of the premises, the victim attempted to hit him on the head. Doherty parried the blow and then punched the victim on the jaw. The victim fell to the ground and hit his head. He died a few hours

Under section 34(1), the force used by the accused must be proportionate to the force employed by the assailant. One cannot "use a tank against a chariot."

later from a serious head injury. Doherty was convicted of manslaughter at his trial. The trial judge took the view that section 34(1) was not applicable because Doherty's blow to the jaw of the deceased was "not actuated by fear." He also ruled that Doherty's right of self-defence did not extend beyond merely "blocking" the punches thrown at him by the deceased. The Court of Appeal rejected both of these rulings by the trial judge and entered an **acquittal**. On behalf of the court, Justice Drapeau stated that,

> … In the present case, the evidence is reasonably open to the interpretation that Mr. Doherty was unlawfully assaulted by Mr. Gillan without having provoked the assault, that, as found by the trial judge, the force used by Mr. Doherty was not intended to cause death or grievous bodily harm

and, finally, that the force used by Mr. Doherty was no more than necessary to enable him to defend himself. That being the case, I conclude that the Crown has not proven that Mr. Doherty was unjustified in repelling force by force, as he did. It follows that s. 34(1) affords Mr. Doherty a complete defence to the charge.

Self-Defence Against an Unlawful Assault Where the Accused Either Intentionally or Unintentionally Inflicts Death or Grievous Bodily Harm

Section 34(2) of the *Criminal Code* provides that

Everyone who is unlawfully assaulted and who causes death or grievous bodily harm in repelling the assault is justified if

(a) he causes it under reasonable apprehension of death or grievous bodily harm from the violence with which the assault was originally made or with which the assailant pursues his purposes, and

(b) he believes, on reasonable grounds, that he cannot otherwise preserve himself from death or grievous bodily harm.

There are two fundamental differences between sections 34(1) and 34(2). First, as the Supreme Court of Canada noted in the *McIntosh* case (1995), section 34(2) applies even if the accused was the initial aggressor in the series of events that led to the use of extreme force in self-defence. Whereas section 34(1) includes the words "without having provoked the assault," section 34(2) does not. Second, section 34(2) does *not* require that the degree of force used by the defendant be "proportionate" to that inflicted by the assailant. In other words, the Code explicitly provides for the consideration of a number of *subjective* factors in the application of section 34(2). In the case of *Baxter* (1975), Justice Martin of the Ontario Court of Appeal addressed this issue in the following manner:

Under s. 34(2) of the Code the ultimate question for the jury is not whether the accused was *actually* in danger of death or grievous bodily harm, and whether the causing of death or grievous bodily harm by him was *in fact* necessary to preserve himself from death or grievous bodily harm, but whether:

(1) he caused death or grievous bodily harm under a *reasonable apprehension* of death or grievous bodily harm, and

(2) he *believed on reasonable and probable grounds* that he could not otherwise preserve himself from death or grievous bodily harm. …

The accused's subjective belief that he was in imminent danger of death or grievous bodily harm and that his action was necessary in self-defence was … required to be based on reasonable grounds. In deciding whether the accused's belief was based upon reasonable grounds the jury would of necessity draw comparisons with what a reasonable person in the accused's situation might believe with respect to the extent and imminence of the danger by which he was threatened, and the force necessary to defend himself against the apprehended danger.

The need, under section 34(2), for the court to focus on the reasonableness of the accused's beliefs rather than on the proportionality of the force used in self-defence is neatly illustrated by the tragic case of *Berrigan* (1998). Here, the accused stabbed the deceased victim and claimed that he did so under the mistaken belief that the latter had been reaching in his pocket for a gun (in fact, the object in the deceased's pocket was a cellular phone). Since the victim was unarmed, there was clearly no objective proportionality between the degree of force threatened by the victim and the violent response of the accused. However, the British Columbia Court of Appeal ruled that the accused person was nevertheless entitled to rely on the defence provided by section 34(2) in light of this mistaken belief. Justice

Donald, on behalf of the court, stated that it was "imperative" that "the jury be told that the appellant is entitled to rely on self-defence on a reasonable but mistaken belief because on his own evidence, his belief was mistaken." He went on to say that, "the danger here is that the jury may have rejected self-defence on the basis that no actual assault occurred or was about to occur."

In the case of *Siu* (1992), the accused had been confronted by a group of men, one of whom was armed with a bayonet. The men ordered him to pay some money to a prostitute and then forcibly ejected him from the latter's apartment. About an hour later, the accused returned to the scene in order to retrieve his driver's licence. He was armed with a loaded revolver. According to Siu, he found the licence and, as he was driving away, he was confronted by the deceased who appeared to have a knife. Siu said that he fired some shots into the air and tried to drive away; however, he panicked and hit a pole. The deceased then moved towards the car, reached in and cut Siu on the cheek. At this point, the accused fired several shots, one of which killed the deceased. Siu was later charged with second degree murder.

The trial judge brought section 34(2) to the attention of the jury and referred to the requirements of reasonable apprehension of death or grievous bodily harm, etc. However, he added the instruction that the defence under section 34(2) was only available "as long as the force [the accused] used was no more than necessary in the circumstances." Siu was convicted of murder and he appealed to the B.C. Court of Appeal, which allowed his appeal and ordered a new trial. The Court of Appeal took the view that the trial judge had made a serious error when he stated there must be proportionality in the degree of force used by the accused even though he had met the requirements of reasonable apprehension under section 34(2). According to the Court of Appeal, the approach espoused by the trial judge might have left the jury with the impression that, even if the accused had fired the shots because he reasonably believed this was the only way to save himself from death or

grievous bodily harm, he could not rely on self-defence if there had in fact been a less drastic alternative than using a gun. The Court of Appeal noted that, under section 34(2), if the accused uses force that he or she reasonably believes is necessary to preserve him- or herself, such force cannot be considered excessive in the circumstances:

> the accused will not be entitled to rely upon (section 34(2)) if he did not, or could not, believe on reasonable grounds that the force he used was necessary to preserve himself. If he did not have such a belief then the force he used was excessive and the sections afford no defence. *If the requirements of the sections are satisfied then no further inquiry or consideration of the nature of the force used by the accused is necessary or permissible.* [emphasis added]

The court also noted that the trial judge's approach contravened the important principle that "a person defending himself against an upraised knife cannot be expected to weigh with nicety the exact measure of force he may use to preserve himself." Here, it was certainly arguable that the accused reasonably apprehended that his life was in danger and reasonably believed that the only way to preserve his own life was to shoot the deceased. After all, Siu had been attacked only an hour earlier by a group of men that included the deceased and, at the time of the fatal shooting, the deceased was apparently armed with a knife.

Although the courts have been quite flexible in their interpretation of section 34(2), it is still important to emphasize that, if defendants claim that they were operating under a misapprehension concerning the need to inflict death or grievous bodily harm in a self-defence situation, such a misapprehension must be based on *reasonable grounds*. This principle was stongly underscored by the Supreme Court of Canada in *Reilly* (1984). One of the issues in this case concerned the relevance of intoxication to a defence based on section 34(2). More specifically, can defendants who claim that they were mistaken as to the need for deadly force successfully assert self-defence when the mistake was induced by intoxication? The Supreme Court held that, since a defence under section 34(2) must be predicated on a belief in the need to use deadly force that is based on *reasonable grounds*, the accused's intoxication is irrelevant in the determination of the validity of the defendant's claim of self-defence. More specifically, Justice Ritchie stated that

> *although intoxication can be a factor in inducing honest mistake, it cannot induce a mistake which must be based on reasonable ... grounds.* The perspective of the reasonable man which the language of s. 34(2) places in issue here is the objective standard the law commonly adopts to measure a man's conduct. A reasonable man is a man in full possession of his faculties. In contrast, a drunken man is one whose ability to reason and to perceive are diminished by the alcohol he has consumed.
>
> I should not be taken as saying that the defence under s. 34(2) can never be available to a person who is intoxicated. *An intoxicated man may hold a reasonable belief,* i.e., the same belief a sober man would form viewing the matter before him upon reasonable and probable grounds. *Where he does so, however, it is in spite of his intoxication.* [emphasis added]

Nevertheless, it significant that in, the case of *Nelson* (1992), the Ontario Court of Appeal ruled that, in applying the test of reasonableness in section 34(2), the courts should take account of any intellectual impairment that might affect the accused's capacity to make decisions. In this particular case, the accused had suffered a serious head injury when he was a child. As Associate Chief Justice Morden stated,

> where the accused has an intellectual impairment, not within his or her control, which relates to his or her ability to perceive and react to events — an impairment that clearly takes him or her out of the broad band of normal adult intellectual capacity — I think the deficit should be taken into account.

Usually, section 34(2) will be raised by a defendant who has undoubtedly *intended* to inflict death or grievous bodily harm on another person. However, there may well be some situations in which the accused will be permitted to raise self-defence under section 34(2), even though the accused did not actually intend to kill or to cause grievous bodily harm. Take, for example, the case of *Pintar* (1996), in which the accused had been charged with two counts of second degree murder after he fatally shot two unarmed men who had previously broken into his home. At the time of the altercation, one of these men threatened Pintar with death, as he had done on numerous previous occasions. After a struggle took place over possession of the accused's gun, Pintar shot both of the intruders. At trial, the accused claimed that he had not intended to kill either of the victims; instead, he asserted that he had fired the rifle as "*an instinctive reaction to preserve my life.*" The trial judge ruled that section 34(2) was only available to those defendants who intended to cause death or grievous bodily harm. Pintar was convicted of two counts of manslaughter. However, the Ontario Court of Appeal subsequently set aside the convictions and ordered a new trial on the basis, *inter alia*, that the trial judge had misdirected the jury as to the applicability of section 34(2) to the specific facts in Pintar's case. In delivering the judgment of the Court of Appeal, Justice Moldaver stated that,

> Unlike s. 34(1) which speaks to the issue of intent, s. 34(2) does not. The plain wording of s. 34(2) reveals that the provision is triggered when a person who has been unlawfully assaulted *causes death or grievous bodily harm in repelling the assault.* On its face, this wording would certainly suggest that the applicability of s. 34(2) is dependent upon a finding that the original assailant either died or suffered grievous bodily harm as a consequence of the responsive measures taken by the person assaulted. To go beyond that and hold that when the charge is murder, accused persons can only take advantage of s. 34(2) if they intend to kill or cause grievous bodily harm has the effect not only

of adding words to the section which are simply not there, but also of creating an additional hurdle which they must overcome when the charge is murder. [emphasis in original]

The Ontario Court of Appeal re-affirmed this particular interpretation of section 34(2) of the Code in the more recent case of *Trembley* (1998). Significantly, the Crown appealed the appellate court's decision to the Supreme Court of Canada. However, in *Trembley* (1999), the Supreme Court rejected the Crown's appeal and endorsed the reasons given by the majority of the Court of Appeal. Therefore, the Ontario Court of Appeal's interpretation of this particular aspect of section 34(2) now has the authority of the Supreme Court of Canada to support it.

An important issue that has been addressed by the Supreme Court of Canada in the 1990s is whether the danger that the accused apprehends must be "imminent" in nature. In many (if not most) cases, accused persons who reasonably apprehend that they are likely to be subjected to death or grievous bodily harm will be facing either an ongoing or an imminent attack. However, what is the situation where the accused reasonably apprehends such a degree of violence but believes that the attack will take place at some time in the future? In the *Pétel* case (1994), the Supreme Court of Canada rejected the suggestion that section 34(2) is only available to an accused who is under actual attack or who is under imminent danger of such an assault. As Chief Justice Lamer stated, on behalf of the majority of the Court in *Pétel*,

> There is ... *no formal requirement that the danger be imminent.* Imminence is only one of the factors which the jury should weigh in determining whether the accused had a reasonable apprehension of danger and a reasonable belief that she could not extricate herself otherwise than by killing the attacker. [emphasis added]

The facts in the *Pétel* case were that the accused was charged with the murder (by shooting) of the companion of her daughter's boyfriend (Edsell). Both Edsell and the deceased (Raymond) had been actively involved in drug trafficking. Edsell and the daughter moved into the accused's house, and Edsell started to use the premises as a base for his illicit activities. The accused stated that Edsell frequently threatened her and that he beat her daughter. Pétel was so upset by Edsell's presence in her household that she ultimately moved to another residence, but her efforts proved to be in vain since Edsell continued to come to her house to traffic in drugs. On the day of the fatal shooting (July 21, 1989), the boyfriend went to Pétel's residence with a revolver, some cocaine, and scales. He told Pétel to hide the gun and then forced her to weigh some cocaine. He then suggested that he would kill Pétel, her daughter, and her granddaughter. Soon afterward, Pétel's daughter arrived with Raymond. Pétel then consumed a small amount of drugs and went to retrieve the revolver she had hidden. Immediately, she fired the gun at Edsell, who fell down. Raymond lunged at Pétel and she shot him as well. Edsell survived his wounds, but Raymond later died.

At Pétel's trial, the judge instructed the jury that, in order for the accused to make a successful plea of self-defence under section 34(2), she must be "unlawfully assaulted" and that the act or threat that constituted the assault must have taken place on the evening of the shooting. The accused was convicted, but her appeal to the Québec Court of Appeal was successful and a new trial was ordered. The Supreme Court of Canada rejected a subsequent appeal by the Crown. As noted earlier, the Supreme Court emphasized that there was no separate requirement under section 34(2) that the attack on the accused be "imminent." In addition, the Court ruled that the trial judge had been in serious error when he told that the jury that, in applying the requirements of section 34(2), they could only consider the threats made on the same evening as the shooting. As Chief Justice Lamer stated, the various threats made by Edsell during his cohabitation with Pétel were of particular relevance in the jury's determination of whether she had a reasonable apprehension of danger and reasonable belief in the need to kill Edsell and Raymond:

> The threats prior to July 21st form an integral part of the circumstances on which the perception of the accused might have been based. The judge's answer to this question might thus have led the jury to disregard the entire atmosphere of terror which the respondent said pervaded her house. It is clear that the way in which a reasonable person would have acted cannot be assessed without taking into account these crucial circumstances.

In the important case of *Lavallee* (1990), the Supreme Court of Canada ruled that, when a woman kills an abusive partner and raises the plea of self-defence under section 34(2) of the Code, the trial court may admit expert testimony concerning the so-called "battered wife syndrome." Such testimony can assist the jury to answer the question of whether the accused believed on reasonable and probable grounds that she had to kill the accused in order to preserve herself from death or grievous bodily harm. In *Lavallee*, the accused had been in a battering relationship with a man (Rust) for several years. She had been to hospital several times with serious injuries caused by her partner's violence. She shot Rust in the back of the head as he was leaving her room after he had physically assaulted her and threatened her with death. According to the accused, Rust had given her a gun and told her that he would kill her once all the guests had left the party that was taking place in their residence. Rust then said that, if Lavallee did not kill him first, he would kill her. The accused shot him after he had made this remark and turned away to leave the room.

At Lavallee's trial for murder, she argued that she had acted in self-defence and she, therefore, relied on the provisions of section 34(2). The trial judge permitted the defence to call a psychiatrist who testified with respect to the battered wife syndrome. This evidence was introduced in order to establish that the accused reasonably apprehended death at the hands of Rust and that she reasonably believed that killing him was the only way of saving herself. The gist of the psychiatrist's opinion was that Lavallee "had been terrorized by Rust to the point of feeling trapped, vulnerable, worthless and unable to escape the relationship despite the violence." In addition, he suggested that the continuing pattern of abuse by Rust placed the accused's life in danger. In this respect, he concluded that Lavallee's shooting of Rust should be viewed as "a final desperate act by a woman who sincerely believed that she would be killed that night." Lavallee was acquitted and the Supreme Court of Canada ultimately held that the trial judge had been correct to place the evidence of battered wife syndrome before the members of the jury.

Justice Wilson, speaking for the majority of the Supreme Court, noted that the relevant research literature has suggested that battered women experience clearly defined cycles of abuse. She emphasized that, in the case of a woman who has been subjected to such cycles of battering, "the mental state of the accused at the critical moment she pulls the trigger cannot be understood except in terms of the cumulative effect of months or years of brutality." Furthermore, the cyclical nature of abuse means that it becomes possible for the battered spouse to make accurate predictions as to the moment when her partner will commence his violent behaviour. Therefore, expert testimony is particularly relevant to the application of section 34(2) because it can point to the accused's "heightened sensitivity" to her spouse's acts and, thereby, clarify the question of whether the accused had a reasonable apprehension of death or grievous bodily harm.

The critical issue, according to Justice Wilson is not "what an outsider would have reasonably perceived but what the accused reasonably perceived given her situation and experience." In this light, it is clear that defendants such as Lavallee do not have to experience an actual attack before resorting to self-defence under section 34(2). They do not have to wait "until the knife is uplifted, the gun pointed or the fist clenched before apprehension is deemed reasonable." As Justice Wilson remarked, the evidence showed that when [Lavallee] and Rust physically fought, [Lavallee] "invariably got the worst of it. I do not think it is an unwarranted generalization to say that due to their size, strength, socialization and lack of training, women are typically no match for men in hand-to-hand combat. The requirement ... that a batttered woman wait until the physical assault is "underway" before her apprehensions can be validated in law would, in the words of an American court, be tantamount to sentencing her to "murder by instalment.". . .

The *Lavallee* case is of considerable significance in the development of Canadian criminal law because it clearly recognizes that, when a woman raises the plea of self-defence in response to an attack by a male aggressor, she is not to be judged by the standards of the "reasonable man" but rather by the standards of the "reasonable woman" who finds herself in the same situation and shares the same experience as the accused. Expert testimony concerning battered wife syndrome is not introduced to establish a special defence based on the medical or psychological condition of the accused. On the contrary, it is taken into account as a means of establishing the *reasonableness*, under the terms of section 34(2), of the accused's beliefs and actions in light of her experience of chronic abuse at the hands of her partner.

In the *Malott* case (1998), the Supreme Court of Canada provided further guidance as to the relevance of expert testimony concerning the battered woman syndrome. The Court took the view that the trial judge should always inform the members of the jury exactly how this testimony may assist them in deciding whether the accused has acted in self-defence. More specifically, Justice Major suggested that the jury should be instructed that the battered woman syndrome evidence may assist them in understanding four separate questions:

1. *Why an abused woman might remain in an abusive relationship ...*
2. *The nature and extent of the violence that may exist in a battering relationship ...*

3. *The accused's ability to perceive danger from her abuser ...*
4. *Whether the accused believed on reasonable grounds that she could not otherwise preserve herself from death or grievous bodily harm.* [emphasis in original]

In the *Vaillancourt* case (1999), the Québec Court of Appeal applied these principles to a tragic case in which the accused had shot her husband, to whom she had been married for 30 years, while he was sleeping in bed in the family home. The accused was subsequently charged with second degree murder. Evidence was presented at Vaillancourt's trial to the effect that her husband was "aggressive, irascible and violent" and that he had, in effect, treated his spouse like a "slave." There was "ample evidence" of "physical acts of violence, verbal and psychological violence" and "sexual violence," all of which had been directed against the accused by her husband. Vaillancourt wanted a divorce from her husband but, since he had frequently made death threats against her, Vaillancourt was terrified that he would find her, wherever she might go, and ultimately kill her. On the day of the shooting, the accused had tried to test her husband's reaction to a potential request for a divorce by recounting a newspaper story, in which a young woman had been strangled to death by her husband after asking him for a divorce. Vaillancourt's husband merely replied, "good for him!" The accused testified that this incident caused her to believe that "my time is coming." That night, Vaillancourt could not sleep and, in a state of severe depression, loaded a rifle with a view to committing suicide. However, she started to think of her children and grandchildren, and recalled an incident in which her husband had sexually abused her grandchildren. Vaillancourt abandoned the plan to kill herself, walked into her husband's bedroom, and shot him to death.

Although evidence concerning the battered woman syndrome was presented at her trial, Vaillancourt was nevertheless convicted of murder by the jury. However, the Québec Court of Appeal allowed her appeal and entered an *acquittal* because it considered that the jury's verdict had been "unreasonable" in light of the particular circumstances of the case. Justice Mailhot, speaking for the majority of the court, indicated that it would be preferable to substitute the phrase, "syndrome of women who are victims of violence," for "battered woman syndrome." In Justice Mailhot's view, use of this new terminology would represent an unequivocal recognition by the courts of the need to consider *psychological* violence as well as *physical* violence whenever an abused woman asserts self-defence under section 34(2).

According to Justice Mailhot,

> The question to be asked is whether the accused could reasonably be considered in a position of self-defence taking into account that she was a person affected by *battered woman syndrome*. In other words, is it reasonable under the specific circumstances of the case that this person, who is suffering from this syndrome, would consider or believe herself to be in a position of self-defence. *For this analysis, it is necessary to place oneself in the situation of the accused and not in the position of a person who is suffering from the syndrome.* [emphasis added]

This statement by Justice Mailhot is important because it makes it perfectly clear that the central issue is the *reasonableness* of the defendant's fears and actions, given her particular circumstances. The "battered woman syndrome" evidence is *relevant* to the task of assisting the members of the jury to understand what the accused believed at the time that she used force; however, the accused is not required to establish that she has all of the symptoms of a "battered woman" in order to successfully raise the plea of self-defence successfully at her trial. In this respect, the *Vaillancourt* decision provides some degree of reassurance that abused women will not be "pathologized" if they seek to rely on section 34(2) of the Code in a situation where they have employed deadly force against their abusers.

As far as the unique circumstances of the *Vaillancourt* case are concerned, Justice Mailhot stated that

It was clearly while thinking of her grandchildren that she came to the conclusion that she would be punishing herself in a useless and unjust manner by committing suicide because she would be indirectly punishing the grandchildren who would no longer benefit from the possibility of being protected by her once she was gone. So, Madame Vaillancourt clearly believed that she was protecting them, but was in no way able to protect herself from the real threat she felt in her mind of being killed unless she killed her husband and therefore considered herself in the legitimate position to take such an action to avoid being murdered by him.

In the *McConnell* case (1996), the Supreme Court of Canada injected an even greater dose of "subjectivization" into the interpretation of section 34(2) of the Code. McConnell and others had killed a fellow inmate in a penitentiary. The deceased was apparently a member of a group that had threatened the life of the accused. McConnell started to stockpile weapons (knuckle-dusters and a stick). When the victim walked by, McConnell repeatedly hit him over the head with some knuckle-dusters, while another inmate stabbed the victim in the stomach. The victim died of his injuries, and McConnell was subsequently tried and convicted of manslaughter. The trial judge refused to place before the jury McConnell's plea of self-defence under section 34(2), stating that McConnell did not believe that he was in imminent danger of death or serious bodily harm at the time of the fatal assault on the victim.

The Supreme Court of Canada ultimately allowed McConnell's appeal against his conviction and ordered a new trial. Justice La Forest, in delivering the brief judgment of the Supreme Court, indicated that he and his colleagues agreed with the (*dissenting*) views expressed by Justice Conrad, in the Alberta Court of Appeal's earlier decision to reject McConnell's appeal. Justice Conrad had asserted that, for the purposes of the application of section 34(2), an analogy should be drawn between the "battered wife syndrome" and the so-called "prison environment syndrome," a concept that was raised by an expert witness at McConnell's trial:

> There was evidence from Dr. Weston about inmate behaviour and prison culture and the similarity in the environment to the battered wife syndrome. *There is evidence about the environment in which inmates had to 'kill or be killed.' Thus a person could believe he or she was being assaulted (a threat with present ability) without it being immediate.* [emphasis added]

In ordering a new trial, the Supreme Court of Canada undoubtedly accepted McConnell's argument that section 34(2) should have been left to the jury to consider as a viable defence. The implications of this decision are somewhat disturbing, since it seems to justify the use of a pre-emptive strike in a prison environment and to legitimate the stockpiling of weapons in anticipation of such an act of violence. Certainly, the *McConnell* decision prompts one to question not only whether the "law of the jungle" should rule in Canada's prisons, but also whether the state is meeting its basic duty to provide safe and humane treatment to vulnerable and powerless inmates. Unfortunately, the members of the Supreme Court did not themselves examine the concept of "prison environment syndrome" and its relationship to a plea of self-defence under the terms of section 34(2) of the Code. Indeed, they merely endorsed the judgment of Justice Conrad in the Court of Appeal. Consequently, one suspects that this issue will, at some stage, be brought back to the Supreme Court of Canada for further, and more detailed, consideration.

The Use of Force in Order to Prevent an Assault Against the Accused or Anyone Under His or Her Protection

Section 37 of the Code provides that

(1) Everyone is justified in using force to defend himself or anyone under his protection from assault, if he uses no more force than is necessary to prevent the assault or repetition of it.

(2) Nothing in this section shall be deemed to justify the wilful infliction of any hurt or mischief that is excessive, having regard to the nature of the assault that the force used was intended to prevent.

To some extent, section 37 overlaps with section 34. However, section 37 does represent a partial extension of section 34(1) in that a defence is made available, not only where accused persons use force in order to defend themselves, but also where such force is used to protect someone "under the protection" of the accused. In the case of *Webers* (1994), Justice O'Connor of the Ontario Court (General Division) held that

> the term "under his protection" is not limited to a formal guardianship relationship, such as a parent or guardian and child, or a teacher and student. In its broadest sense, it means anyone who requires protection which the accused may be able to provide.

In *Webers*, the court ruled that a patient who was unlawfully subjected to the violent administration of an injection could be considered to be "under the protection" of a friend who had accompanied her to the hospital and that the latter was, therefore, entitled under section 37 to intervene to save her from the violent assault being perpetrated against her by both nurses and police officers. As is the case with section 34(1), section 37 requires that the force employed by the accused be "proportionate" to the threat posed by the assailant.

One of the problems that arises in the application of section 37 is that, except in the case of a defendant who takes action to protect someone under his or her protection, the provision would appear to duplicate—and even contradict—certain elements of both sections 34 and 35 of the *Criminal Code*. In the *McIntosh* case (1995), Chief Justice Lamer, on behalf of the majority of the members of the Supreme Court of Canada, noted that "Parliament's intention in enacting s. 37 is unclear." The Chief Justice pointed out that section 37 makes the defence of self-defence available where the force used by the accused is both necessary and proportionate. However, if section 37 is available to the initial aggressor in a confrontation (and the Court ruled that Parliament had not explicitly excluded this possibility), it "would appear to be in conflict with s. 35," which, as we shall see shortly, places numerous restrictions on the use of self-defence by such an accused. In the words of Chief Justice Lamer,

> it is difficult to understand why Parliament would enact the specific and detailed justifications in ss. 34 and 35, yet then make available a broad justification in s. 37 which appears to render ss. 34 and 35 redundant.

The Use of Force in Self-Defence by the Aggressor

Section 35 of the *Criminal Code* provides that

> Everyone who has without justification assaulted another but did not commence the assault with intent to cause death or grievous bodily harm, or has without justification provoked an assault on himself by another, may justify the use of force subsequent to the assault if:
>
> (a) he uses the force:
>
> > (i) under reasonable apprehension of death or grievous bodily harm from the violence of the person whom he has assaulted or provoked, and
> >
> > (ii) in the belief, on reasonable grounds, that it is necessary in order to preserve himself from death or grievous bodily harm;
>
> (b) he did not, at any time before the necessity of preserving himself from death or grievous

> bodily harm arose, endeavour to cause death or grievous bodily harm; and
>
> (c) he declined further conflict and quitted or retreated from it as far as it was feasible to do so before the necessity of preserving himself from death or grievous bodily harm arose.

This section is unnecessarily complex and has received relatively little judicial attention, apparently because it is not used with any degree of frequency. Certain of the requirements contained in section 34(2) re-appear in section 35. However, as a reading of section 35 quickly demonstrates, a number of strict requirements have been added as a prerequisite to the successful assertion of the defence of self-defence in the situation where the accused may be considered "the aggressor." In particular, section 35(c) imposes a duty on the accused to retreat whenever it is feasible to do so.

However, in light of the Supreme Court of Canada's decision in *McIntosh* (1995), it is most unlikely that an accused person will ever rely on section 35 where he or she has inflicted death or grievous bodily harm in self-defence. The *McIntosh* case, as we have seen, decided that section 34(2) of the Code may be raised even where the accused was the initial aggressor. Since section 34(2) is far less restrictive for such an accused person than section 35, it is inevitable that he or she will rely on section 34(2) rather than section 35. Nevertheless, it is significant that Chief Justice Lamer recognized in the *McIntosh* case an element of "absurdity":

> One is struck ... by the fact that if s. 34(2) is available to an initial aggressor who has killed or committed grievous bodily harm, then that accused may be in a better position to raise self-defence than an initial aggressor whose assault was less serious. This is because the less serious aggressor could not take advantage of the broader defence in s. 34(2), as that provision is only available to an accused who "causes death or bodily harm." Section 34(1) would not be available since it is explicitly limited to those who have not provoked an assault. Therefore, the less serious aggressor could

only have recourse to s. 35, which imposes a retreat requirement. It is, in my opinion, anomalous that an accused who commits the most serious act has the broadest defence.

Defence of Property

Sections 38 to 42 of the *Criminal Code* make provision for the justified use of force in relation to the defence of property. It will be noted that sections 38 and 39 deal with "movable property," whereas sections 40 to 42 are concerned with the defence of "real property" and "dwelling-houses." The term "real property" essentially refers to property in buildings and land. Section 2 of the Code defines the term "dwelling-house" in a broad manner and it is clear that the statutory definition includes apartments or even, as the Alberta Court of Appeal ruled in *Clark* (1983), rooms in a boarding house. Our discussion will primarily focus on sections 40 and 41 of the Code—particularly insofar as they interact with sections 34(1) and 34(2).

Sections 40 and 41 of the Code provide that

40. Every one who is in peaceable possession of a dwelling-house, and every one lawfully assisting him or acting under his authority, is justified in using as much force as is necessary to prevent any person from forcibly breaking into or forcibly entering the dwelling-house without lawful authority.

41(1) Everyone who is in peaceable possession of a dwelling-house or real property and everyone lawfully assisting him or acting under his authority is justified in using force to prevent any person from trespassing on the dwelling-house or real property or to remove a trespasser therefrom, if he uses no more force than is necessary.

(2) A trespasser who resists an attempt by a person who is in peaceable possession of a dwelling-house or real property or a person lawfully assisting him or acting under his authority to prevent his entry or to remove

him, shall be deemed to commit an assault without justification or provocation.

In the case of *Born With a Tooth* (1992), the Alberta Court of Appeal ruled that a successful plea of self-defence under section 41(1) must reflect four separate elements: (i) the accused must be in possession of land; (ii) this possession must be peaceable in the sense that it is "not seriously challenged by others"; (iii) the victim of the assault must be a trespasser; and (iv) the force used by the accused to remove the trespasser from his or her land must be reasonable in the circumstances. Significantly, the Court of Appeal also stated that, if an accused person honestly, but *mistakenly*, believed that the victim is a trespasser, he or she would not lose the benefit of the defence. The four elements identified by the Court of Appeal would also be applicable, in general terms, to any defence raised under section 40 of the Code. The application of these criteria for the successful assertion of a plea of defence of property is well illustrated by the decision in *George* (2000). In this case, the accused was part of a group of protestors who had occupied a provincial park and an adjacent Canadian Forces base. The protestors claimed that they had an aboriginal treaty right to both the park and the military base. The accused drove a car at a group of police officers and was subsequently convicted of criminal **negligence** in the operation of a motor vehicle and assault with a weapon. On his appeal to the Ontario Court of Appeal, George asserted that the trial judge had erroneously failed to consider a potential defence under section 41(1). However, the appeal was dismissed. The court ruled that there had been no "peaceable possession" of the land in question. Indeed, the police had clearly challenged the protestors in this respect, and the fact that the protestors had stockpiled rocks and sticks "made it clear that any challenge to their occupation could result in violence." Furthermore, there was no evidence that the accused mistakenly believed that the protestors' possession of the property was peaceable. Undoubtedly, he knew that any police interference would be resisted. The court also held that the defence under section 41(1) was not available because the force that he used was *not reasonable under the circumstances*:

> The appellant drove his car out of the parking lot and onto the grass shoulder of East Parkway Drive in such a manner that he struck a number of officers, seriously injuring one of them. At this time, the police were retreating from the park area. Their actions could not be construed as trespassing. *The force used against the police was not necessary, reasonable or proportionate.* [emphasis added]

An important question that immediately arises is, What exactly is a trespasser? Essentially, a trespasser, in the context of these provisions of the Code, is someone who violates the rights of others by entering or remaining on their property without any authority to do so. The problem is that someone may be invited onto another person's property either by the property owner or by an individual who is authorized to do so. For example, an individual may be given a specific invitation to attend a party. Similarly, a person may enter a store on the basis that members of the public have an implicit invitation to do so. However, it is possible that an invitation to enter or remain on someone else's property is subsequently withdrawn. If this occurs, can the "disinvited" guest become a tresspasser and be ejected with the use of a reasonable degree of force? The answer is "yes," provided that the property owner gives the disinvited guest a reasonable amount of time in which to withdraw voluntarily.

These principles are illustrated by the case of *Keating* (1992). In this case, a youth had entered a shopping mall with a view to purchasing a jacket. However, he subsequently began to skateboard on the mall property even though there were signs that prohibited skateboarding in this area. The accused, who owned the mall, entered into a physical confrontation with the youth. The Appeal Division of the Nova Scotia Supreme Court held that the trial judge, who had convicted the accused of assault and threatening, had been wrong to ignore the accused's plea under section 41(1) that

he was entitled to remove a trespasser from his premises. The trial judge had taken the view that the youth was an "invitee" and, therefore, could not be treated as a trespasser. However, the Appeal Division ruled that the defence under section 41(1) should be considered and ordered a new trial. The fact that the youth was originally an invitee to the mall did not mean that he remained one indefinitely. In particular, he had only been "invited" to enter the mall for the purpose of shopping, not skateboarding. If the accused reasonably believed that the youth was trespassing at the time of the altercation, he was entitled to raise the defence under section 41(1).

Section 41(2) is particularly significant in that it provides that, should trespassers resist an attempt to remove them from a dwelling-house or real property (or an attempt to prevent their unlawful entry), they will be *deemed to commit an unjustified or unprovoked assault* upon the person who is in peaceable possession of the property. Section 41(2), therefore, may well have the effect of bringing section 34 of the Code into play in such circumstances (for the benefit of the person in possession of the property concerned). However, it should be pointed out that the courts have interpreted section 41(2) somewhat restrictively. For example, in *Baxter* (1975), Justice Martin of the Ontario Court of Appeal stated that

> The meaning of this subsection is not entirely clear. I am disposed to think that its effect is not to convert mere passive resistance into an assault but merely to provide that if any *force* is used by the wrongdoer in resisting an attempt to prevent his entry or to remove him, such force is unlawful, and hence an assault. The amount of force that may be used to prevent or defend against any assault actually committed by the wrongdoer depends upon the ordinary principles of self-defence as set out in s. 34 of the Code.

An excellent illustration of the application of section 41(2) is provided by the B.C. case of *Stanley* (1977), in which the accused was convicted of murder following his fatal stabbing of the victim, one Donald Blosky. The victim was one of five individuals who arrived at Stanley's home at 2:00 or 2:30 in the morning. When Stanley came to the door, all five men entered the house and Stanley retreated to his bedroom. Stanley's common-law wife screamed at the men to leave; however, only three left. It was clear that Stanley knew Blosky and that the latter had threatened him previously. The evidence also appeared to indicate that Blosky had come to Stanley's house with the expressed intention of picking a fight with him. Stanley gave evidence that he had no intent to fight with Blosky. Stanley drew a knife and stabbed Blosky in the midsection. He testified that he was not aware that he had fatally wounded Blosky. Stanley appealed his conviction to the B.C. Court of Appeal.

The Court of Appeal ultimately ordered a new trial for Stanley. Justice Branca delivered a judgment in which the interaction between sections 41(2) and 34 is clearly delineated. The judgment also indicated the degree to which the courts are prepared to extend a good deal of sympathy toward an individual whose home has been invaded by an aggressive trespasser. Justice Branca noted that it was a long-standing principle of Canadian law that "a man's [sic] house is his castle" and made the following significant remarks:

> The fundamental picture established by the evidence was that of a bunch of five drunken goons going to the private dwelling of Stanley and Debbie, seeking a fight with Stanley and acting as a bunch of degenerate characters, virtually breaking into the premises and refusing to leave when asked to and forcing a fight upon Stanley in the most disgraceful circumstances. …
>
> Section 34 applies, as here Blosky was committing a deemed unprovoked assault under the provisions of s. 41(2). So it was then justifiable for Stanley both for his self-defence and in the defence of his home to repel force by force, if the force used was not intended to cause death or grievous bodily harm and was no more than was necessary for Stanley's defence of himself and of Debbie, a per-

son under his protection, or to remove Blosky, a trespasser from his home. …

> The law provides favourably for a person such as Stanley who is assaulted if he, in the agony of the occasion, reasonably but mistakenly believes that he must kill in order to save himself from death or grievous bodily harm.
>
> The law does not expect one in such circumstances to weigh with too much nicety the force that might be necessary to repel the attack and too, the law does not expect one to wait until he is struck before he strikes back. If he does so it may well be that it will be too late for him to retaliate in order to preserve himself. …
>
> One wonders who in his reasonable senses in the circumstances related would not have armed himself with a lethal weapon like a knife if that was the only weapon available for the purpose of self protection or for the protection of his dwelling. …
>
> The real question for determination by the jury in this case was whether or not Stanley in the circumstances proven in evidence used excessive force under s. 34(1) or caused the death of Blosky by the use of excessive force without a reasonable apprehension of death and without a belief based upon reasonable or probable grounds that he could not otherwise preserve himself or Debbie from death or grievous bodily harm.
>
> If the force used was not excessive and/or if the death was caused with a justification offered in s. 34(2)(a) and (b) then he, Stanley, was justified in killing Blosky and was not criminally responsible.

Similarly, in the *Proulx* case (1998), the B.C. Court of Appeal stated that "the law is clear that flight from one's own home is not a reasonable option for self-preservation, and that the defence of self-defence will still apply even if there is another way out of the house—the rationale is that one's home is already one's last line of defence against an assailant." It is significant that the court emphasized that an attack in one's home is the *only* circumstance in which there is never any duty laid upon the accused to consider the possibility of retreating from the assailant before using deadly force. In this respect, the court asserted that

> The principle ... is simply that within one's home one need not retreat from an assailant before claiming the defence of self-defence. *But although retreat may be an irrelevant consideration when one is attacked at home, it does not follow that it is also irrelevant when one is attacked elsewhere.* [emphasis added]

CONSENT

The General Principles

Let us suppose that Arthur visits his dentist, Pullem, in order to obtain treatment for an excruciating toothache. Pullem advises Arthur that it is necessary to extract one of his teeth. The latter agrees to this proposition, and Pullem duly removes the offending tooth. One week later, Arthur seeks to have Pullem charged with assault causing bodily harm and makes explicit reference to the fact that Pullem used a good deal of force in order to extract the tooth. Most readers will instinctively exclaim that, of course, Pullem is not guilty of an assault. However, what is the reason underlying this "common sense" view?

Let us also suppose that Desmond asks Cynthia whether he can borrow the latter's expensive sports car. Cynthia answers in the affirmative and Desmond takes the car onto the highway where, within a few minutes, he loses an argument with a cement truck. The sports car is completely destroyed, although Desmond emerges relatively unscathed. However, Cynthia now charges Desmond with theft of the car. Is Desmond guilty of this offence? Once again, the "common sense" answer must be no. However, what is the rationale underlying this response?

In each of the cases hypothesized above, the accused individuals cannot be convicted of the offences charged because the *absence of consent* is a vital element in the case that must be proved by the Crown. Section 265 (assault) and section 322 (theft) clearly require that the Crown prove the absence of consent as an essential element of the

actus reus of the particular offence charged. In a sense, therefore, the plea of "consent" is not really a special defence to a criminal charge; rather, it is an assertion that the Crown has not proved the *actus reus* of the offence charged.

Consent and Assault Under Section 265

For present purposes, discussion of consent is limited to a consideration of certain aspects of the crime of assault. Section 265 of the *Criminal Code* provides, in part, as follows:

(1) A person commits an assault when

    (a) without the consent of another person, he applies force intentionally to that other person, directly or indirectly;

    (b) he attempts or threatens, by an act or gesture, to apply force to another person, if he has, or causes that other person to believe upon reasonable grounds that he has, present ability to effect his purpose; or

    (c) while openly wearing or carrying a weapon or an imitation thereof, he accosts or impedes another person or begs.

(2) This section applies to all forms of assault, including sexual assault, sexual assault with a weapon, threats to a third party or causing bodily harm and aggravated sexual assault.

(3) For the purposes of this section, no consent is obtained when the complainant submits or does not resist by reason of:

    (a) the application of force to the complainant or to a person other than the complainant;

    (b) threats or fear of the application of force to the complainant or to a person other than the complainant;

    (c) fraud; or

    (d) the exercise of authority.

It is clear from a close reading of section 265 that there are definite limitations to the defendant's plea of consent. Section 265(3) unequivocally states that consent obtained by the application of force or the threat or fear of force, fraud, or the "the exercise of authority" cannot be considered valid. Incidentally, another requirement, strictly enforced by the civil, rather than the criminal, courts, is that any consent that is purportedly given must be "informed." For example, before patients' consent to surgery may be considered valid, it must be established that they were adequately informed concerning the nature and object of the proposed operation as well as the reasonably foreseeable risks associated with it.

Special Provisions Relating to the Defence of Consent in Relation to a Charge of Sexual Assault

In 1992, the *Criminal Code* was amended in order to provide more specific directions to judges and juries who are required to determine whether the accused may raise a valid defence of consent when he or she is charged with sexual assault (under sections 271, 272, or 273). The new section 273.1 of the Code states that, in general, consent in the context of a charge of sexual assault means "*the voluntary agreement of the complainant to engage in the sexual activity in question.*" Without limiting the range of circumstances in which a judge or jury may find that consent has not in fact been obtained, section 273.1(2) states that

No consent is obtained for the purposes of sections 271, 272 and 273, where

(a) the agreement is expressed by the words or conduct of a person other than the complainant;

(b) the complainant is incapable of consenting to the activity;

(c) the accused induces the complainant to engage in the activity by abusing a position of trust, power or authority;

(d) the complainant expresses, by words or conduct, a lack of agreement to engage in the activity; or

(e) the complainant, having consented to engage in sexual activity, expresses, by words or conduct, a lack of agreement to continue to engage in the activity.

When a defence of consent is raised in relation to a charge of sexual assault, the judge or jury must consider both section 265(3), which applies to assaults generally, and section 273.1, which pertains exclusively to sexual assaults. As we have seen, section 265(3) makes it crystal clear that no consent has been obtained where the **complainant** submits or does not resist as a consequence of the actual use of force, or as a result of threats or fear of the application of force, either to the complainant or to another person. For example, an individual who submits to sexual activity only because of a threat to beat up his or her child will not be deemed to have given a valid consent to the activity in question.

In addition, section 265(3) states that an alleged consent obtained by fraud or the exercise of authority is not a real consent at all, and the accused may not rely on it as a defence. Until recently, the only type of fraud that was covered by this provision was fraud as to the actual nature of the act in question and, fraud as to the identity of the accused. For example, if physicians engage in sexual activity with patients after having informed them that they are carrying out certain medical procedures, such fraud would render any consent totally invalid. Similarly, if the accused had impersonated the complainant's spouse (in a darkened room, for example), any ensuing consent to sexual activity would be vitiated as a direct consequence of the accused's fraud. However, other types of fraud were apparently not covered by section 265(3). For example, in *Petrozzi* (1987), the B.C. Court of Appeal ruled that the accused's fraudulent behaviour in promising to pay a prostitute for her sexual services (when he had no intention of doing so) did not render her consent invalid under this provision of the Code.

However, in the somewhat controversial case of *Cuerrier* (1998), the Supreme Court of Canada recently expanded the meaning of "fraud" in section 265(3)(c). Cuerrier had been told by the public health authorities that he had tested positive for HIV. He was given explicit instructions to use a condom whenever he engaged in sexual intercourse and to inform his partner(s) that he was HIV-positive. Cuerrier angrily refused to accept this advice, complaining that he "would never be able to have a sex life" if he were to inform potential partners that he was HIV-positive. On numerous occasions, Cuerrier had unprotected sexual intercourse with two female complainants. He never informed them of his HIV-positive status. Both of the complainants testified that they would never have engaged in unprotected sexual intercourse with Cuerrier had they known that he was HIV-positive.

Cuerrier was charged with two counts of aggravated assault on the basis that his misrepresentation of his HIV status constituted fraud under section 265(3) and that, therefore, the complainants' apparent consent to intercourse with him was nullified. The trial judge ordered the jury to acquit the accused, stating that the only type of "fraud" that would operate to negative consent to sexual intercourse was fraud as to the nature and quality of the act itself or the identity of the accused. However, the trial judge stated that fraud as to one's HIV-status did not come within these parameters. The B.C. Court of Appeal upheld the trial judge's ruling, but the Supreme Court of Canada subsequently allowed an appeal by the Crown and ordered a new trial for Cuerrier.

Justice Cory, speaking for a majority of the Supreme Court, adopted the view that a person accused of concealing or failing to disclose that he or she is HIV-positive may be found to have committed a type of fraud that vitiates any apparent consent on the part of the victim to engage in sexual activity. According to Justice Cory,

> Persons knowing they are HIV-positive who engage in sexual intercourse without advising their partner of the disease may be found to fulfil the traditional requirements for fraud namely dishonesty and deprivation. That fraud may vitiate a partner's consent to engage in sexual intercourse.
>
> ... The actions of the accused must be assessed objectively to determine whether a reasonable person would find them to be dishonest. The dishonest act consists of deliberate deceit respecting HIV status or non-disclosure of that status.
>
> ... The second requirement of fraud is that the dishonesty result in deprivation, which may consist of actual harm or simply a risk of harm ... In my view, the Crown will have to establish that the dishonest act (either falsehoods or failure to disclose) had the effect of exposing the person consenting to a *significant risk of serious bodily harm*. The risk of contracting AIDS as a result of engaging in unprotected intercourse would clearly meet that test. In this case the complainants were exposed to a significant risk of serious harm to their health. Indeed their very survival was placed in jeopardy. It is difficult to imagine a more significant risk or a more grievous bodily harm. [emphasis added]

Some commentators have expressed concern about the long-term implications of expanding the meaning of "fraud" in this manner. For example, it has been suggested that the criminal law should not be the method by *means of* which society deals with the problem of HIV transmission through unprotected sexual activity, and that the decision in *Cuerrier* might actually undermine public health initiatives by deterring those individuals who are at high risk of contracting HIV from presenting themselves for testing because they might face possible criminal consequences if the test is positive. However, in this respect, Justice Cory argued that the "risk of infection and death of partners of HIV-positive individuals is a cruel and present reality" and that it is therefore necessary to protect those individuals in the most efficacious manner possible:

> If ever there was a place for the deterrence provided by criminal sanctions it is present in these

circumstances. It may well have the desired effect of ensuring that there is disclosure of risk and that appropriate precautions are taken.

... It is unlikely that individuals would be deterred from seeking testing because of the possibility of criminal sanctions arising later. Those who seek testing basically seek treatment. It is unlikely that they will forego testing because of the possibility of facing criminal sanctions should they ignore the instructions of public health workers.

Finally, section 265(3) states that no consent has been given where the complainant submits or does not resist because of the exercise of authority by the accused. For example, if an officer in the Canadian Forces were to order a subordinate to submit to sexual activity, there would be no consent since there has been an "exercise of authority." In the *Saint-Laurent* case (1994), the Québec Court of Appeal suggested that section 265(3) would operate to negative any alleged consent given by patients to sexual activity with their treating psychiatrists because of the "overwhelming imbalance of power in the relationship between the parties."

Section 273.1(2) renders it perfectly clear that no valid consent has been given where a third party purports to give consent to sexual activity on behalf of the complainant. For example, a defendant may not claim the defence of consent where the alleged consent was given by the husband of the complainant. Furthermore, this provision of the Code states that there can be no consent where the complainant "is incapable of consenting to the [sexual] activity"; for example, a complainant who is in a state of acute intoxication would be deemed incapable of giving a valid consent to sexual activity. Indeed, in the *Daigle* case (1998), the Supreme Court of Canada upheld the conviction of the accused where the complainant had been given a dose of PCP without her knowledge or consent. Justice L'Heureux-Dubé agreed with the reasoning of the Québec Court of Appeal that "the evidence shows that [the complainant], then 15 years of age, who drank in one shot a glass of alcohol in which

there was hidden the drug, was not capable of giving a valid consent."

Section 273.1(2) also provides that no consent has been obtained where the accused has induced the complainant to engage in sexual activity "by abusing a position of trust, power or authority." This provision would potentially cover, for example, such situations as those in which a teacher engages in sexual activity with a pupil or a physician becomes physically involved with a patient. However, in order to obtain a conviction, the Crown would, of course, have to establish that the teacher or physician actually *abused* their position of trust vis-à-vis the pupil and patient respectively.

Section 273.1(2) also stipulates that no consent is obtained where "the complainant expresses, by words or conduct, a lack of agreement to engage in the activity." This means that a sexual aggressor cannot raise the defence of consent merely because the complainant did not say "no"; if the complainant's *conduct* (e.g., pushing the accused away) expressed a refusal to engage in sexual activity, the accused will be disqualified from relying on the defence of consent. Finally, this provision of the Code expressly articulates the fundamental principle that individuals have the right to withdraw their consent to engage in sexual activity *at any time*, even if they initially gave a valid consent. If the accused refuses to cease such activity at any point after the complainant's consent has been withdrawn, he or she will be guilty of a sexual assault.

Can an Individual Consent to the Infliction of Bodily Harm?

Section 14 of the *Criminal Code* provides that no one can consent to have death inflicted on him or her and that any consent that may have been given does not affect the criminal responsibility of a person who does inflict death in such circumstances. For this reason, a physician who carries out an act of voluntary **euthanasia** on a terminally ill patient is guilty of murder despite the fact that the patient, while competent to do so, has given an unequivocal consent to this course of action and, indeed, has persistently requested it because he or she is suffering extreme pain.

However, the *Criminal Code* does not deal explicitly with the question of whether an individual may consent to the infliction of a degree of bodily harm that falls short of death. Should individuals be able to give their consent to the infliction of bodily harm and turn what would otherwise be criminal assaults into lawful actions? In the *Jobidon* case (1991), the Supreme Court of Canada adopted the view that, unless there is some overriding social utility that may be identified in relation to the activity in question, consent should not be accepted as a defence to a charge of assault where more than a "non-trivial" degree of bodily harm has been inflicted.

In *Jobidon*, the accused engaged in a fist fight with one Haggart. The trial judge found that Jobidon and Haggart had agreed to a fight as a result of a prior altercation between them. Haggart died as a consequence of the blows meted out by Jobidon, and the latter was charged with manslaughter. The theory of the Crown was that Jobidon had committed the unlawful act of assault and, as a consequence, the victim had died; in these circumstances, the contention was that Jobidon was, therefore, guilty of "unlawful act" manslaughter. However, the trial judge found that there had been no assault, and hence no unlawful act. In his view, the victim had agreed to enter into a "fair fist fight," and Jobidon had not intended to exceed the scope of that consent (in the sense that he had no intention to inflict death or grievous bodily harm). In light of this view, the trial judge acquitted Jobidon, but the Crown appealed and the Ontario Court of Appeal substituted a verdict of guilty of manslaughter. The Court of Appeal took the view that, where the accused intends to cause bodily harm in a fist fight, the Crown is not required to prove the absence of consent.

Jobidon appealed to the Supreme Court of Canada, which dismissed his appeal. Speaking for the majority of the Court, Justice Gonthier said that, on the grounds of public policy, *consent should not be a defence to a charge of assault whenever adults*

intentionally apply force that causes "serious hurt or nontrivial bodily harm to each other in the course of a fist fight or brawl." Although section 265(1)(a) states that a person "commits an assault when ... without the consent of another person, he applies force intentionally to that other person," the Supreme Court took the view that the Code did not specify the full range of circumstances in which the criminal courts will not recognize a consent as being valid. According to Justice Gonthier, section 8(3) of the Code had preserved the common law rules that "explain the outlines and boundaries of an existing defence or justification" and, in his view,

> Although there is certainly no crystal-clear position in the modern Canadian common law, still, when one takes into account the combined English and Canadian jurisprudence, when one keeps sight of the common law's centuries-old persistence to limit the legal effectiveness of consent to a fist fight, and when one understands that s. 265 has always incorporated that persistence, the scale tips rather heavily against the validity of a person's consent to the infliction of bodily injury in a fight.

Why has the common law refused to recognize the validity of consent to involvement in fist fights? According to Justice Gonthier, sound public policy dictates that such an approach be adopted: "Foremost among the policy considerations" is the "social uselessness of fist fights." It is just not in the public interest that adults intentionally cause harm to each other for no good reason. Such fights may lead to tragedy, as in the *Jobidon* case itself, or may result in an even greater brawl if bystanders become involved (which also happened in the *Jobidon* case when the brothers of the protagonists also become involved in a fist fight). Furthermore, if individuals are permitted to participate in consensual fist fights, they may eventually lose their inhibitions against using violence and may start to use their fists on their spouses or partners. Finally,

> Wholly apart from deterrence, it is most unseemly from a moral point of view that the law would

countenance, much less provide a backhanded sanction to the sort of interaction displayed by the facts of this appeal. *The sanctity of the human body should militate against the validity of consent to bodily harm inflicted in a fight.* [emphasis added]

The Supreme Court of Canada's decision in *Jobidon* does not mean that consent to the infliction of bodily harm will always be considered invalid. It only states that such consent will be invalid where there is no social utitility to be gained from the activity in question. Therefore, for example, consent to "bodily harm" would be a defence where medical or surgical treatment was involved or where there was some socially redeeming value to be gained (as in the case of "rough" sports or games — a topic that will be discussed in more detail later in this chapter). Similarly, if individuals agree to perform stunts in a movie and, as part of that agreement, they consent to participate in "risky sparring or daredevil activities," their consent would be considered valid to a charge of assault, should they be injured in the course of these activities; the consent would be valid because those involved in making a movie are creating a "socially useful product."

The Supreme Court of Canada limited the application of its ruling to fist fights between adults. Indeed, Justice Gonthier stated that

the phenomenon of the "ordinary" schoolyard scuffle, where boys or girls immaturely seek to resolve differences with their hands, will not come within the scope of the limitation. That has never been the policy of the law and I do not intend to disrupt the status quo. However, I would leave the question as to whether boys or girls under the age of 18 who truly intend to harm one another, and ultimately cause more than trivial bodily harm, would be afforded the protection of a defence of consent.

It is significant that, in the case of *W. (G.)* (1994), the Ontario Court of Appeal rejected the defence of consent that had been raised by the sixteen-year-old accused in relation to a charge of assault causing

bodily harm. The charge was laid as a consequence of a consensual fist fight between the accused and another sixteen-year-old boy. The victim suffered serious injuries, including a broken nose and the loss of vision in one eye for several hours. The trial judge found that the accused "intended to do serious harm to the complainant" and convicted him of the charge. Following the suggestion made by Justice Gonthier in *Jobidon*, the Ontario Court of Appeal held that, where an accused intends to cause serious harm to his or her opponent, "the adolescence of the accused provides no policy reason for recognizing consent as a 'defence' to a charge of assault causing bodily harm." In the words of Justice Doherty, speaking on behalf of the Court of Appeal, "students must realize that acts of violence intended to do serious harm, which in fact cause bodily harm, will not be countenanced."

It has been suggested that the *Jobidon* case does not imply that all consensual fist fights between *adults* necessarily constitute criminal assaults. Indeed, in the case of *Doherty* (2000), the New Brunswick Court of Appeal took the view that the critical issue in such cases is whether the adult combatants *intended* to inflict non-trivial bodily harm on each other. If there is no such intention, then the *consent* of the parties to exchange blows may be effective to absolve them of any criminal liability. On behalf of the court, Justice Drapeau stated that,

Even in circumstances where serious harm is inflicted in the course of an altercation, the injured party's consent to the application of force to his or her person will preclude a finding of unlawful assault against the combatant who stands accused, unless the Crown establishes that such serious harm was intended by the latter's application of force. [emphasis added]

In the *Doherty* case, the accused was a bouncer at a strip club. He had expelled Mr. Gillan and his friend, Mr. Boyle, because they were drunk and engaging in "intolerable conduct." Gillan and Boyle were angry with Doherty and attempted — unsuccessfully — to incite bystanders to beat him up. They then banged on, and kicked, the door of the club. Doherty emerged and asked the two men to leave peacefully. However, they became increasingly belligerent and, ultimately, Gillan attempted to punch Doherty on the head. Doherty blocked this blow and delivered one punch to Gillan's jaw. Unfortunately, Gillan later died from a head injury that occurred when he fell to the ground. The trial judge found that Doherty did not intend to cause Gillan any serious injury but nevertheless convicted him of (unlawful act) manslaughter. The New Brunswick Court of Appeal allowed Doherty's appeal and entered an acquittal because, in its view, Gillan had *consented to the infliction of force that was not intended to cause non-trivial bodily harm.* In the words of Justice Drapeau,

> There can be no serious challenge to the proposition that, once outside the club premises, Mr. Gillan was bellicose and intent on obtaining retribution for his expulsion by Mr. Doherty ... I am satisfied that Mr. Gillan's pre-altercation conduct and his physical attack on Mr. Doherty are *outward manifestations of his consent to the application of defensive force* by Mr. Doherty. [emphasis added]

According to the Court of Appeal, Gillan implicitly consented to the use of defensive force by the accused, on the understanding that the latter would not intentionally cause him serious bodily harm. If Gillan's consent was effective in law, then Doherty did not commit an unlawful assault when he punched Gillan on the jaw. Clearly, in these circumstances, Doherty could not be found guilty of *unlawful act* manslaughter. Justice Drapeau concluded by stating that

> Mr. Doherty did not intend to cause injury to Mr. Gillan when he punched him. That being so, no properly instructed trier of fact, acting judicially, could be satisfied beyond a reasonable doubt that Mr. Doherty committed an unlawful assault when he punched Mr. Gillan. As a result, the Crown failed to prove that Mr. Doherty caused Mr. Gillan's

death by means of an unlawful act within the meaning of s. 222(5)(a) of the *Criminal Code* ...

Certainly, the *Jobidon* case left many questions unanswered. For example, does the sport of boxing have "social utility" when the argument might be made (although not without considerable opposition) that it supports the values of violence and involves the deliberate infliction of blows that may be extremely dangerous? If it does not have such social utility, presumably participation in boxing amounts to assaultive behaviour. Similarly, the question arises as to what extent an individual may consent to nonessential "surgical" procedures that inflict bodily harm. Presumably, one can consent to body-piercing or tattooing because they may have some social utility in terms of giving individuals choices in the area of fashion or enhancing their psychological well being, but exactly how far may one go in terms of submitting to so-called cosmetic procedures that may conceivably involve the risk of serious injury? All of these issues must, no doubt, be dealt with by the courts on a case-by-case basis.

In the case of *Welch* (1995), the Ontario Court of Appeal adopted the view that, on grounds of public policy, an individual cannnot consent to the infliction of nontrivial bodily harm even if that individual claims that such harm occurred in the course of consensual sexual activity. In *Welch*, the accused was charged with, *inter alia*, sexual assault causing bodily harm. According to the complainant, the accused had prevented her from leaving his condominium and then had pushed her onto a bed and tied her hands and legs. She also stated that, although she protested throughout, the accused then attempted a number of acts of sexual intercourse, beat her with a belt, and inserted an object into her rectum. The complainant suffered extensive bruising to her breast, abdomen, arm, leg, and buttocks as well as bleeding from her rectum for several days.

The accused claimed that the complainant had unequivocally consented to, and had actually encouraged, what he called "rough sex." The trial judge ruled that, even if the complainant had consented to this type of injury, consent was no defence to a charge of sexual assault causing bodily harm. Welch was subsequently convicted by a jury, and the central issue in his appeal to the Ontario Court of Appeal was whether the trial judge had erred in refusing to place the defence of consent before the jury.

Speaking on behalf of the court, Justice Griffiths stated that

> In my view ... the message delivered by the majority in *Jobidon* is that the victim cannot consent to the infliction of bodily harm upon himself or herself, as defined in section 267(2) of the Code, *unless the accused is acting in the course of a generally approved social purpose when inflicting the harm.* Specifically, the majority in *Jobidon* recognized that consent may be a defence to certain activities such as rough sporting activities, medical treatment, social interventions, and "daredevil activities" performed by stuntmen, "in the creation of a socially (valuable) cultural product." Acts of sexual violence, however, were conspicuously not included among these exceptions. [emphasis added]

According to the Court of Appeal, the facts in *Welch* revealed a course of "sadistic sexual activity" involving bondage and the deliberate infliction of harm on the body and rectum of the complainant. Even if the complainant had consented to this activity, her consent could not have detracted from the "inherently degrading and dehumanizing nature of the conduct." In such circumstances, the "personal interests of the individuals involved must yield to the more compelling societal interests which are challenged by such behaviour." As Justice Griffiths put it, it is arguable that society has the right to "enforce one fundamental residual moral value," namely, that "hurting people is wrong and this is so whether the victim consents or not, or whether the purpose is to fulfil a sexual need or to satisfy some other desire."

The problem with the *Welch* case is that it raises the spectre of state interference with consensual sexual activity that takes place in private. The facts in *Welch* raise serious questions about whether the complainant ever did consent to what can only be termed brutal treatment. However, there may be some situations in which truly consenting adults, for example, may wish to engage in sexual activity that includes the deliberate infliction of some degree of bodily harm in order to enhance sexual pleasure. Take, for example, the practice of flagellation, which may well cause "nontrivial" bruising on the bodies of the recipient(s). Should the courts use the argument of public policy to invalidate the consent of such adults and turn their sexually oriented activities, which do not harm anyone else, into criminal acts?

Consent to the Infliction of Bodily Harm in the Context of Sporting Activity

The issue of consent to what would otherwise be an assault is frequently raised in the somewhat controversial arena of contact sports—particularly those of the professional variety. It is indisputable that the very nature of such games as hockey or football require the intentional application of force to one's opponents. Therefore, it may generally be said that individuals who voluntarily participate in such sports should be deemed to have given *implicit* consent to the infliction of a certain degree of force upon their bodies. However, the question will always arise as to exactly where the law should draw the line between legitimate bodily contact and the criminal application of force.

In the *Jobidon* case (1991), Justice Gonthier of the Supreme Court of Canada clearly stated that, since "sporting activities and games usually have a significant social value," individuals can consent to the infliction of some degree of bodily harm in the course of such activities, "so long as the intentional applications of force to which consents are given within the customary norms and rules of the game."

Implied consent to the application of force in contact sports.

Clearly, professional hockey players, although they may have given their implicit consent to a reasonable degree of body contact on the ice, cannot be deemed to have given an unrestricted licence to their opponents to inflict any type of awful injury that strikes their fancy. There have been a number of cases in Canada that have explored this issue in relation to the game of hockey but, of course, the broader principles expressed in these cases are also applicable to other contact sports.

In *Watson* (1975), for example, the trial judge set out the general approach of Canadian courts in relation to sports that require a degree of body contact. In the words of the judge,

Hockey is a fast, vigorous, competitive game involving much body contact. Were the kind of body contact that routinely occurs in a hockey game to occur outside the playing area or on the street, it would, in most cases, constitute an assault to which the sanctions of the criminal law would apply. Patently, when one engages in a hockey game one expects that some assaults which would otherwise be criminal will occur and consents to such assaults. It is equally patent, however, that to engage in a game of hockey is not to enter a forum to which the criminal law does not extend. To hold otherwise would be to create the hockey arena a sanctuary for unbridled violence to which the law of Parliament and the Queen's justice could not apply.

The application of these general principles is well illustrated by two contrasting cases: *Henderson* (1976) and *St. Croix* (1979). In *Henderson*, the accused was charged with assault causing bodily harm. The incident that provoked this charge arose out of a Western Canada Junior Hockey League game in which Henderson and the victim (a young man called Lestander) played on opposing sides. It appeared that, at some stage during the second period of the game, an altercation broke out between Henderson and another player on the opposing team (Robinson). The linesman broke up the fight by taking hold of the two players involved. Apparently, very few (if any) blows were struck in this altercation, but there was a good deal of "pushing, shoving and holding onto one another." Clearly, play had been stopped at this point.

As one of the linesmen was directing Henderson toward the penalty box, Henderson reached out with his left hand and in a downward motion punched Lestander on the left side of his head, immediately below the helmet. It appeared that the latter fell to the ice in an unconscious condition and was not aware of what had happened or who had struck him. Lestander had been standing at centre ice and had not been involved in the prior altercation between Henderson and Robinson. In the words of the trial judge, "there was no overt act either by gesture or word of mouth on the part of Lestander towards Henderson which immediately proceeded the attack by Henderson, or at any other time in the hockey game or preceding the hockey game." Similarly, there was no evidence that Lestander was even looking in Henderson's direction at the time of the attack, nor was there any indication that Lestander expected to become involved in any way with Henderson. At the time of the assault, Henderson had been skating toward the penalty box under the direction of the linesman while Lestander was standing stationary at centre ice, holding onto his hockey stick. As a result of the blow, Lestander suffered injuries to his left eye and was detained in hospital for some twenty hours so that the effects of his concussion could be observed.

Judge Dohm, of the B.C. County Court, noted in his judgment that altercations may occur between hockey players either during the course of play or after play has been stopped by the referee. In both cases, conduct that is considered to be "incidental to the sport" and "within the bounds of fair play" will not be considered suitable for prosecution under the criminal law. However, the judge stated that the use of force once play has been stopped by the referee will always attract a much higher degree of scrutiny in determining whether such conduct can be considered "within the bounds of fair play and incidental to the sport." Judge Dohm continued by asking

> What then is conduct which can be classed as incidental to the game of hockey and within the bounds of fair play? I have no doubt whatsoever that fighting is part of the game of hockey. By that I do not mean that it is necessary for the game to be properly played—I mean that it has become a tradition in the sport which is expected by the players and by the spectators. It is part of the image of the sport in the same way that in soccer and football and other like sports, part of the image of those sports is that no such activity takes place, or at least it is discouraged and frowned upon by all those concerned.

> It must be not concluded by these remarks that all fighting in hockey is permissible—quite the contrary. No hard and fast rules can ever be established to determine which kind of fighting is permitted, but it appears to me that when two players, either directly or by implication, consent to involve one another in combat, *provided the combat occurs within the bounds of fair play*, each player ought to be given the immunity that is accorded those who participate in the sport generally. ...

Judge Dohm then turned to the critical question of the nature and scope of the risks to which hockey players must be deemed to have given their consent:

> I think the risks which a hockey player assumes *are those which are shown to flow naturally from the kind of activity involved, which activity falls within the bounds of fair play*. ... obviously then, the players must assume only those risks which are commensurate with the ethics of fair play. Included here must be those unintentional injuries which are received as a result of one or more of the infractions which occur during the game. ... however, *where there is conduct which shows a deliberate purpose to inflict injury, then no immunity is accorded to the offending player either in criminal or civil law.* The leeway, as it were, which is afforded those who participate in bodily contact sports—particularly ice hockey—is quickly used up when players abandon their sense of fair play, and this is so in my view even if there is provocation and passions are running high. [emphasis added]

The learned judge then addressed the facts of the particular case before him. He indicated that the situation in the *Henderson* case was that the blow had been inflicted after the regular play had been stopped by the referee "for something less than a minute." This factor clearly brought Henderson's conduct within the category of cases that the trial judge had determined required "a greater scrutiny in determining whether such conduct was within the bounds of fair play and incidental to the sport." In the words of the trial judge,

> The pertinent facts in determining the kind of conduct Henderson exhibited toward Lestander are, I suggest, that time had allowed for Henderson to calm down; that Henderson was on his way to the penalty box; that it was Lestander that Henderson struck and not Robinson with whom he had been earlier fighting; that Henderson was not wearing gloves; that Henderson's size and weight are significantly greater than Lestander's; that Lestander was stationary and presumably waiting for play to resume; that Lestander was not at all expecting the blow; and, lastly, that Lestander was not looking in the direction of Henderson at the time of the blow being struck.

In light of these circumstances, the trial judge found that the accused was guilty of the charge of assault causing bodily harm. However, Henderson was given a conditional discharge—the sole condition being that he not play for one month in regular hockey league games.

The *St. Croix* case (1979) provides an interesting contrast to that of *Henderson*. *St. Croix* concerned an injury that arose in the course of a "neighbourhood" game of hockey, as opposed to a professional version of the game. The case is significant since it suggests that the scope of implicit consent to the application of force is, perhaps, considerably narrower in "neighbourhood" games as opposed to their professional counterparts. St. Croix was charged with assault causing bodily harm. The victim (Shaule) and St. Croix were participating in an informal hockey game at a neighbourhood outdoor rink. The players wore no protective equipment, and it was understood that the puck was not to be lifted off the ice. There were, of course, no referees or linesmen and no regular goal tenders.

It appeared that the accused was carrying the puck toward the opposing goal and was "poke-checked" by Shaule. Despite this intervention, St. Croix nevertheless managed to score a goal and he then advanced upon Shaule. Evidence was intro-

duced to the effect that St. Croix accused Shaule of "slashing him across the ankle" at the time of the poke-check. St. Croix, on the other hand, contended that he accused Shaule of pushing him into the net after the goal had been scored. St. Croix then began to push Shaule's chest with his stick. Despite the fact that the blade of Shaule's hockey stick was still resting on the ice, St. Croix ultimately hit Shaule across the mouth with his hockey stick. Unfortunately for Shaule, he lost four teeth as a result of this blow. The question naturally arose as to whether the injury inflicted should be considered one of the risks to which a willing participant in a hockey game may be said to consent implicitly. In the particular circumstances, the trial judge held that the nature of the assault in question went far beyond the scope of any implicit consent to the type of body contact that may reasonably be expected to occur within a neighbourhood hockey game. In the view of Judge Stortini,

> In my view, the consent referred to in s. 265 is limited qualitatively and quantitatively. Athletes in all sports do consent to the normal risks of the game and consent to a foreseeable amount and type of assaults. I would think that professionally trained and professionally employed hockey players in the National Hockey League consent to more assaultive type behaviour than in a purely amateur (in the full sense of the word) friendly neighbourhood hockey game. I do not accept that the players in a neighbourhood match, where no protective equipment is worn, no officials are present and the puck is not to be raised off the ice, consent to being struck in the mouth by a hockey stick, that is, fore-checking of the type involved in this case. There are many assaultive acts which can be consented to even in a neighbourhood rink bearing in mind that every intentional application or immediate threat of force is capable of being an assault, but for the consent of the potential victim.
>
> I find that the assault caused by the accused on James Shaule was beyond any "foreseeably consented to act" as envisaged by s. 265 of the Code. It was not administered by the accused in self-

defence. It was not instinctive in the course of a play, in that it occurred after the poke-checking and game [*sic*] scoring play.

The trial judge found the accused guilty of the offence but granted a conditional discharge. The condition imposed was that St. Croix make restitution to the victim within a period of four months. It appears that the restitution was ordered to permit the victim to recover the expenses associated with the need to obtain a partial denture plate in his mouth.

The imposition of conditional discharges in both the *Henderson* and *St. Croix* cases, perhaps suggests that the courts realize that it is difficult to draw a clear line between sporting violence that falls within the scope of the implicit consent given by the various players and violence that should be branded as criminal and suitable for punishment. As many courts have emphasized, cases involving sporting violence must be carefully considered in relation to their individual facts. What factors should be taken into account when the courts seek to determine the scope of implied consent?

In the *Cey* case (1989), for example, the Saskatchewan Court of Appeal ruled that hockey players cannot be considered to consent to bodily harm that is *intentionally* inflicted. Furthermore, Justice Gerwing, writing for the majority of the court, made the important point that "in sporting events … the mere fact that a type of assault occurs with some frequency does not necessarily mean that it is not of such a severe nature that consent thereto is precluded." Justice Gerwing also stressed the importance of applying *objective criteria* in determining whether the implied consent of sport players to the application of force has been exceeded in any given case:

> Ordinarily consent, being a state of mind, is a wholly subjective matter to be determined accordingly, but when it comes to implied consent in the context of a team sport such as hockey, there cannot be as many different consents as there are players on the ice, and so the scope of the implied

consent, having to be uniform, must be determined by reference to objective criteria.

These objective criteria include the setting of the game, the nature of the league in which it is played (e.g., is it amateur or professional?), the age of the players, the conditions under which the game is played (e.g., is protective equipment used?), the extent of the force used, the degree of risk of injury and the probability of serious harm. In the particular circumstances of the *Cey* case, Justice Gerwing focussed on the the inherent risk of injury and the degrees of injury inflicted as being the central issues to be examined in determining the scope of any implied consent:

> Some forms of bodily contact carry with them such a high risk of injury and such a distinct probability of injury as to be beyond what, in fact, the players commonly consent to, or what, in law, they are capable of consenting to.

This last principle was applied in the *Ciccarelli* case (1989). The accused player had, after the whistle was blown in a National Hockey League game, struck another player on the head with a hockey stick. No actual bodily harm was caused. However, the accused was convicted on the basis that such violent conduct went beyond the scope of the victim's implied consent. In discussing the question of the scope of implied consent, the court referred to the objective criteria articulated in the *Cey* case and noted that Ciccarelli inflicted the blows on the victim's head *after* the whistle had been blown and that they clearly had the *potential* to cause injury (although no actual injury was caused). In the court's view, deliberately hitting an oponent's head with a hockey stick "was not a reasonable practice and fell outside the ambit" of any implied consent.

Finally, the *Leclerc* case (1991) illustrates the proposition that implied consent is not invalidated merely because there has been a serious injury in the course of sporting activity. Leclerc was charged with aggravated assault after he pushed his victim into the boards by striking him in the back or near the neck with his hockey stick. Unfortunately, owing to the speed at which the accused was travelling on the ice, his actions caused the victim to collide with the boards and, as a result, the latter was permanently paralyzed from the neck down. The trial judge found that the accused's application of force to the victim resulted from his "loss of balance and was part of [his] 'instinctive reflex action,' which had the object of minimizing the risk of bodily harm created by his high speed in close proximity to the boards." Leclerc was acquitted at his trial, and the Ontario Court of Appeal subsequently rejected an appeal by the Crown. Clearly, the outcome would have been very different if the accused had deliberately pushed his victim into the boards with intent to injure him.

Although the principles surrounding the issue of implied consent to the application of force in sporting activities are relatively straightforward, there is no doubt that trial courts have considerable discretion in applying them to the facts of individual cases.

STUDY QUESTIONS

1. Fred meets his friend Charlie in a bar. They start arguing about a sum of money that Charlie owes to Fred. Suddenly, Fred loses his temper and shouts at the top of his voice, "You're nothing but a slimy jailbird." In response to this insult, Charlie rushes out of the bar and goes to his home, which is just a few blocks away. He retrieves a kitchen knife from his home and returns to the bar, where he stabs Fred to death. Charlie had once been incarcerated in a federal correctional institution, but since his release ten years ago, he has kept out of trouble with the law. With the exception of his wife and Fred, no one in the local community knew that Charlie had once been an inmate of a prison. Does Charlie have a defence to a charge of murder?

2. Oberon finds his wife, Tatania, in bed with his best friend Puck. Oberon orders Tatania out of his house. Two days later, Oberon finds Tatania in a bar, sitting on Puck's knee. Oberon calls Tatania a "common whore" and Puck responds by calling Oberon "impotent" (which, in fact, is unfortunately true). Oberon immediately shoots and kills Puck with his revolver. Can Oberon claim the benefit of the defence of provocation?

3. Bob and Ted are professional hockey players who are playing on opposing teams. As Bob is carrying the puck, Ted pushes him into the boards along the side of the hockey rink. An altercation develops between them and some punches are thrown. The referee whistles play dead, and after a brief period, the linesmen separate Bob and Ted and lead them toward their respective penalty boxes. However, Bob breaks free from his accompanying linesman and skates up to Ted and punches him in the eye—to the delight of the local fans. Bob is 6′5″ tall and weighs 280 lbs. Ted is 5′8″ tall and weighs 150 lbs. The blow inflicted by Bob opens a deep cut underneath Ted's eye and numerous stitches are required to close the wound. Bob is charged with assault causing bodily harm. Does Bob have any defence(s)?

4. Daniel invites Highball to a party, which is held in Daniel's apartment. Highball becomes quite obnoxious and insults Daniel's girlfriend, Tia Maria. Daniel tells Highball to leave the premises "forthwith," but despite repeated requests to remove himself, Highball refuses to do so. Daniel, then, attempts to throw his unwelcome guest out of the front door. Highball resists very strenuously and starts to punch Daniel in the face with a marked degree of force. Daniel grabs a metal bar and strikes Highball on the head until the latter "falls limp" and Daniel deposits the dazed Highball outside of his apartment in the corridor. Some other tenants spot Highball and take him to the Cocktail Hospital, where he is treated for concussion and lacerations of his scalp. He subsequently recovers without any permanent damage. If Daniel were to be charged for his role in this sordid affair, would he have any special defence(s) open to him?

5. Elizabeth has lived with Jim for ten years, during which he has, on various occasions, subjected her to physical assaults, some of which have caused serious injuries (such as extensive bruising to the body, a broken nose, and concussion). One day, Elizabeth returns home late from an evening meeting and Jim becomes furious with her. He yells that he is "going to fix her once and for all." However, he is so drunk that he passes out on the couch. Elizabeth goes to the kitchen and takes a large knife. She then returns to the room where Jim is sleeping and stabs him to death. Would Elizabeth be able to raise a successful plea of self-defence if she were charged with murder or manslaughter?

6. Hippocrates is a medical practitioner who believes that boxing should be banned. In his view, those who participate in boxing are subjecting themselves to an unacceptably high risk of serious brain injury or even death. After a professional boxer dies as a consequence of head injuries inflicted in a fight, Hippocrates approaches Crown counsel and asks her to lay a charge of aggravated assault against the other protagonist in the fight. What arguments might he use to persuade Crown counsel to proceed with such a charge?

7. Elbow is an inmate in a prison that has gained an unfortunate reputation for its brutal atmosphere. Most of the prisoners have been convicted of violent offences, and there is a widespread belief that, for inmates, one is only likely to survive if one acts on the maxim "kill or be killed." Pompey, a notoriously unpredictable and violent inmate, approaches Elbow and tells him that "his time is up." Elbow interprets this as a death threat and acquires a knife for self-protection. When Pompey is taking a shower, Elbow approaches him from behind and stabs him to death. When charged with first degree murder, Elbow claims that he was only acting in self-defence. Is Elbow likely to be successful in raising the defence of self-defence at his trial?

FURTHER READING

1999. Feminist Legal Analysis and Sexual Autonomy: Using Statutory Rape Laws as an Illustration. 112 *Harvard Law Review:* 1065.

Alvaro, A. 1994. Emerging Issues in the Area of *Scopelliti* Evidence. 36 *Criminal Law Quarterly:* 372.

Archibald, T.L. and P.K. Tait. 1987. A Post-Script to *R. v. Hill:* Whither Goest Provocation? 29 *Criminal Law Quarterly:* 172.

Ashworth, A. 1995. *Principles of Criminal Law.* 2d ed. Oxford: Oxford University Press. 225–29, 132–37, 318–24.

Beaman, L.G. 1998. Women's Defences: Contextualizing Dilemmas of Difference and Power. 9 *Women & Criminal Justice:* 87.

Bowland, A.L. 1994. Sexual Assault Trials and the Protection of "Bad Girls": The Battle Between the Courts and Parliament. In J.V. Roberts and R.M. Mohr, eds. *Confronting Sexual Assault: A Decade of Legal and Social Change.* Toronto: University of Toronto Press. 241–67.

Boyle, C. 1990. The Battered Wife Syndrome and Self-Defence: *Lavallee v. R.* 9 *Canadian Journal of Family Law:* 171.

———. 1994. The Judicial Construction of Sexual Assault Offences. In J.V. Roberts and R.M. Mohr, eds. *Confronting Sexual Assault: A Decade of Legal and Social Change.* Toronto: University of Toronto Press. 136–56.

———. 1996. Annotation to *R. v. McConnell* (1996). 48 *Criminal Reports (4th):* 200.

Castel, J.R. 1990. Discerning Justice for Battered Women Who Kill. 48 *University of Toronto Faculty Law Review:* 229.

Cohen, S.A. 1990. Not as Easy as it Seems: Closing the Consent Loophole. 74 *Criminal Reports (3d):* 304.

Dershowitz, A.M. 2000. Moral Judgment: Does the Abuse Excuse Threaten our Legal System? 3 *Buffalo Criminal Law Review:* 775.

Dutton, M.A. and L.A. Goodman. 1994. Posttraumatic Stress Disorder Among Battered Women: Analysis of Legal Implications. 12(3) *Behavioral Sciences & the Law:* 215.

Feinberg, J. 1986. Victims' Excuses: The Case of Fraudulently Procured Consent. 96 *Ethics:* 330.

Finkelstein, C.O. 1999. On the Obligation of the State to Extend a Right of Self-Defense to its Citizens. 147 *University of Pennsylvania Law Review:* 1361.

Ginn, D. 2000. Can Failure to Disclose HIV Positivity to Sexual Partners Vitiate Consent? *R. v. Cuerrier.* 12 *Canadian Journal of Women & the Law:* 235.

Gorman, W. 1999. Provocation: The Jealous Husband Defence. 42 *Criminal Law Quarterly:* 478.

Greene, S.D. 1998. The Unconstitutionality of Section 43 of the *Criminal Code:* Children's Right to be Protected from Physical Assault: Parts 1 & 2. 41 *Criminal Law Quarterly:* 288, 462.

Hatch, D.R. 1999. Culpability and Capitulation: Sexual Assault and Consent in the Wake of *R .v. Ewanchuk.* 43 *Criminal Law Quarterly:* 51.

Heller, K.J. 1998. Beyond the Reasonable Man? A Sympathetic but Critical Assessment of the Use of Subjective Standards of Reasonableness in Self-Defense and Provocation Cases. 26(1) *American Journal of Criminal Law:* 1.

Holland, W.H. 1998. *The Law of Theft and Related Offences.* Toronto: Carswell. 115 – 34.

Howe, A. 1998. Case Note: *Green v. The Queen:* The Provocation Defence: Finally Provoking its Own Demise? 22 *Melbourne University Law Review:* 466.

Hubble, G. 1997. Feminism and the Battered Woman: The Limits of Self-Defence in the Context of Domestic Violence. 9 *Current Issues in Criminal Justice:* 113.

Hyland, E.M. 1996 – 97. *R. v. Thibert:* Are There any Ordinary People Left? 28 *Ottawa Law Review:* 145.

Kathol, T. 1993. Defence of Property in the *Criminal Code.* 35 *Criminal Law Quarterly:* 453.

Kazan, P. 1997. Reasonableness, Gender Difference, and Self-Defense Law. 24 *Manitoba Law Journal:* 549.

Klimchuk, D. 1996. Circumstances and Objectivity. 45 *Criminal Reports (4th):* 24.

Kutz, C. 2000. Self-Defense and Political Justification. 88 *California Law Review:* 751.

Law Commission. 1994. *Criminal Law: Consent and Offences Against the Person (Consultation Paper no. 134).* London: H.M.S.O.

Law Reform Commission of Canada. 1980. Working Paper No. 26: *Medical Treatment and Criminal Law.* Ottawa: Minister of Supply and Services Canada.

————. 1984. Working Paper No. 38: *Assault.* Ottawa: L.R.C.C.

————. 1986. Report No. 28: *Some Aspects of Medical Treatment and Criminal Law.* Ottawa: L.R.C.C.

————. 1987. Report No. 31: *Recodifying Criminal Law, Rev. ed.* Ottawa: L.R.C.C.

Letourneau, G. 1981. Sports, Violence and Criminal Law in Canada. 22 *Criminal Reports (3d):* 103.

Martinson, D. 1990. *Lavallee v. R.* The Supreme Court Addresses Gender Bias in the Courts. 24 *U.B.C. Law Review:* 381.

Martinson, D., et al. 1991. A Forum on *Lavallee v. R.:* Women and Self-Defence. 25 *U.B.C. Law Review:* 23.

McLachlin, B.M. 1991. Crime and Women—Feminine Equality and the Criminal Law. 25 *U.B.C. Law Review:* 23.

McIntyre, S. 1994. Redefining Reformism: The Consulations That Shaped Bill C-49. In J.V. Roberts and R.M. Mohr, eds. *Confronting Sexual Assault: A Decade of Legal and Social Change.* Toronto: University of Toronto Press. 293 – 326.

Mewett, A.W. 1993. Editorial: The Limits of Consent. 36 *Criminal Law Quarterly:* 1.

Mewett, A.W. and M. Manning. 1994. *Mewett and Manning on Criminal Law.* 3d ed. Toronto: Butterworths. 572 – 96, 736 – 47.

Minister of Justice of Canada. 1993. White Paper: *Proposals to Amend the Criminal Code (General Principles).* Ottawa: Minister of Justice of Canada (June 28, 1993).

Morgan, J. 1997. Critique and Comment: Provocation Law and Facts: Dead Women Tell No Tales, Tales are Told About Them. 21 *Melbourne University Law Review:* 237.

Mousourakis, G. 1999. Choice and the Rationale of the Provocation Defence. 30 *The Cambrian Law Review:* 21.

Nicolson, D. and R. Sanghvi. 1993. Battered Women and Provocation: The Implications of *R. v. Ahluwalia.* (1993) *Criminal Law Review:* 728.

Nsereko, D.D.N. 1996. Witchcraft as a Criminal Defence: From Uganda to Canada and Back. 24 *Manitoba Law Journal:* 38.

Quigley, T. 1991. Battered Women and the Defence of Provocation. 55 *Saskatchewan Law Review:* 223.

Paciocco, D.M. 1995. Subjective and Objective Standards of Fault for Offences and Defences. 59 *Saskatchewan Law Review:* 271.

Reilly, A. 1997 – 98. The Heart of the Matter: Emotion in Criminal Defences. 29 *Ottawa Law Review:* 117.

Roach, K.W. 1998. Editorial: Provocation and Mandatory Life Imprisonment. 41 *Criminal Law Quarterly:* 273.

Römkens, R. 2000. Ambiguous Responsibilities: Law and Conflicting Testimony on the Abused Woman Who Shot Her Sleeping Husband. 25 *Law & Social Inquiry:* 355.

Ruby, R. 1999. Apprehending the Weapon Within: The Case for Criminalizing the Intentional Transmission of HIV. 36 *American Criminal Law Review:* 313.

Sahni, R. 1997. Crossing the Line: *R. v. Thibert* and the Defence of Provocation. 55 *University of Toronto Faculty Law Review:* 143.

Scassa, T. 1993. Sentencing Intimate Femicide — A Comment on *R. v. Doyle.* 16 *Dalhousie Law Journal:* 270.

Shaffer, M. 1997. The Battered Woman Syndrome Revisited: Some Complicating Thoughts Five Years After *R. v. Lavallee.* 47 *University of Toronto Law Journal:* 1.

Sheehy, E. 2000. Review of the Self-Defence Review. 12 *Canadian Journal of Women & the Law:* 197.

Sheppard, A.F. 1991. The Supreme Court of Canada and Criminal Evidence Reform: Recent Cases on Sexual Abuse of Children and Spousal Murder. 9 *Canadian Journal of Family Law:* 11.

Simones, A. 1999. Survive as a Society: HIV Status and the Constitutional Right of Privacy. 68 *UMKC Law Review:* 195.

Smith, K.J.M. 1999. Duress and Steadfastness: In Pursuit of the Unintelligible. [1999] *Criminal Law Review:* 363.

Somin, I. 2000. Revitalizing Consent. 23 *Harvard Journal of Law & Public Policy:* 753.

Stevens, D.J. 1999. Interviews with Women Convicted of Murder: Battered Women's Syndrome Revisited. 6 *International Review of Victimology:* 117.

Stuart, D. 1995. *Canadian Criminal Law: A Treatise.* 3d ed. Toronto: Carswell. 439 – 58, 489 – 500, 511 – 27.

Stuart, D. and R.J. Delisle. 1997. *Learning Canadian Criminal Law.* 6th ed. Toronto: Carswell. 792 – 843.

Stuesser, L. 1990. The "Defence" of "Battered Woman Syndrome" in Canada. 19 *Manitoba Law Journal:* 195.

Tyson, D. 1999. "Asking For It": An Anatomy of Provocation. *The Australian Feminist Law Journal:* 66.

Vandervort, L. 1991. Consent and the Criminal Law. 28 *Osgoode Hall Law Journal:* 485.

Verdun-Jones, S.N. 1999. *Canadian Criminal Cases: Selected Highlights.* Toronto: Harcourt Brace. Chap. 9.

Waldron, J. 2000. Self-Defense: Agent-Neutral and Agent-Relative Accounts. 88 *California Law Review:* 711.

Wong, C.M. 1999. Good Intentions, Troublesome Applications: The Cultural Defence and Other Uses of Cultural Evidence in Canada. 42 *Criminal Law Quarterly:* 367.

Yeo, S.M.H. 1990. Recent Australian Pronouncements on the Ordinary Person Test in Provocation and Automatism. 33 *Criminal Law Quarterly:* 280.

A Brief Note on the Canadian Criminal Court System

In order to assist the reader to acquire a rudimentary understanding of the role of the courts mentioned in the text, this appendix offers a brief overview of the system of criminal courts in Canada. However, it should be emphasized that, at best, this overview paints a skeletal picture and the reader should be aware that there are numerous variations on the basic model as one moves from one province or territory to another.

All criminal cases enter the judicial system in the various *provincial courts* (or, in Yukon, Northwest Territories, and Nunavut, *territorial courts*), where a provincially or territorially appointed judge sits without a jury. However, although the majority of criminal cases are completed within the provincial courts, some cases must later move on to other courts for trial. All summary conviction offences are dealt with in the provincial or territorial courts, but whether an indictable offence will be tried there depends on the seriousness of the offence and, in some cases, on the choice of the accused person. Generally, the more serious criminal cases will not be tried in the provincial or territorial courts; instead, they are tried in the superior court of criminal jurisdiction of the various provinces and territories. Provincial and territorial court judges are appointed and paid by their respective provinces and territories. (In Ontario, the name for this level of court is the *Ontario Court of Justice*; in Québec, it is known as

the *Court of Québec*). The provincial or territorial courts may be organized in different divisions such as the Criminal Division, Youth Court, Family Court, or Traffic Court.

In each province and territory, there is a *superior court of criminal jurisdiction.* The name of this court is not identical in each province. It is known as the *Supreme Court* in British Columbia, the Yukon and Northwest Territories, Nova Scotia, Prince Edward Island, and Newfoundland; as the *Court of Queen's Bench* in Manitoba, Saskatchewan, Alberta, and New Brunswick; as the *Cour Supérieure* in Québec; and as the *Nunavut Court of Justice* in Nunavut. In Ontario, this court is known as the *Superior Court of Justice*. Although the superior court has a broad jurisdiction to try criminal cases, in practice it tries only the more serious types of criminal offence. The superior court judge may try cases either sitting alone or with a jury. In certain circumstances, the superior court may hear appeals from the decisions of provincial courts in relation to summary conviction offences. Judges in the superior courts are appointed and paid by the federal government.

Above the superior court of criminal jurisdiction in the judicial hierarchy is an appeal court, known as the *Court of Appeal* (the *Appellate Division of the Supreme Court* in Nova Scotia). The courts of appeal hear appeals directly from the decisions of the courts that have tried *indictable* offences, and act as the second line of appeal in the case of *summary* conviction offences.

The highest tier in the hierarchy of courts in Canada is occupied by the *Supreme Court of Canada*, which hears appeals from the various provincial and territorial courts of appeal. The Supreme Court of Canada is the highest court in the land and is the final stage in the appeal process.

Canadian Criminal Court System

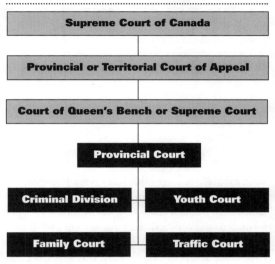

A Brief Guide to Law Reports

Each case referred to in this book is accompanied by a formal, legal citation in the Index of Cases. The citation of decided cases necessarily follows a rigid format, using standardized punctuation and abbreviations. Although most readers will probably not have ready access to a law library, this appendix will attempt to explain the system of citations for those who do wish to pursue their study of case law beyond the confines of this book.

You should note that, in Canada, criminal cases involve an issue between the Crown and the accused. Hence, in Canada, the Queen (or "Regina," abbreviated as "*R*.") will always appear as one of the parties in a case name. The case name is followed by the appropriate citation. Consider, for example, the citations below.

If the volumes of the series of law reports concerned are numbered *sequentially*, the date is given in *round* brackets (as in example (a)). However, *square* brackets are employed whenever the date itself is part of the volume reference (as in example (b)). In example (a), the reference is *adequate without the date*. If you attempted to look up the case cited in example (a), you would only need to locate volume 145 of the third series of *Canadian Criminal Cases;* the date is merely included as additional information. However, in example (b), the date is an essential component of the reference and is, in effect, part of the volume number. If you needed

to look up the case cited in example (b), you would have to locate the *third* of those volumes, of *Western Weekly Reports,* published in 1998.

Finally, it should be noted that when the date is enclosed in *round* brackets, it refers to the year when the decision was actually *rendered*. When it is enclosed in *square* brackets, it refers to the year in which the decision was *printed* in the reporting series.

In academic works, it is customary to add the abbreviated name of the court in which the reported case was decided. You will notice that *R. v. Scott* was decided in the British Columbia Court of Appeal and *R. v. Petrisor* in the Saskatchewan Court of Queen's Bench. When the deciding court is specifically referred to in an author's discussion of a case, the abbreviated name may well be omitted from the citation.

In this book, references are made primarily to Canadian criminal cases; however, references are also made to criminal cases decided in England. In both Canada and England there are numerous series of law reports. Some series are general in nature and may cover a broad range of legal issues (from criminal law to tax law), whereas others deal exclusively with a specific subject matter (such as criminal law or business law). As a consequence, some cases may actually be reported in four or five different series of law reports. Matters are somewhat complicated by the fact that there may be a number

Case Name	Date	Volume	Series	Page	Court
(a) *R. v. Scott*	(2000),	145	C.C.C. (3d)	52	(B.C.C.A.)
(b) *R. v. Petrisor,*	[1998]	3	W.W.R.	516	(Sask. Q.B.)

of different subseries within each series of law reports; for example, there are four separate subseries of *Canadian Criminal Cases*.

The following table provides information concerning the various series (and subseries) of law reports to which reference is made in this book.

Abbreviated Title	Title and Years Covered	Example of Citation
I. CANADIAN LAW REPORTS		
C.C.C.	*Canadian Criminal Cases*, 1893–1962	*Chow Bew v. The Queen* (1955), 113 C.C.C. 377
[ ] C.C.C.	*Canadian Criminal Cases*, 1963–1970	*R. v. Taylor*, [1964] 1 C.C.C. 207
C.C.C. (2d)	*Canadian Criminal Cases* (2nd series), 1971–1982	*R. v. Haight* (1976), 30 C.C.C. (2d) 168
C.C.C. (3d)	*Canadian Criminal Cases* (3rd series), 1983–	*R. v. Darrach* (2000), 148 C.C.C. (3d) 97
C.R.	*Criminal Reports*, 1950–1967	*R. v. Regan* (1954), C.R. 361
C.R.N.S.	*Criminal Reports* (new series), 1967–1978	*Peda v. The Queen* (1969), 7 C.R.N.S. 243
C.R. (3d)	*Criminal Reports* (3rd series), 1978–1990	*R. v. Conkie* (1978), 3 C.R. (3d) 317
C.R. (4th)	*Criminal Reports* (4th series), 1991–1996	*R. v. DeSousa* (1992), 15 C.R. (4th) 66
C.R. (5th)	*Criminal Reports* (5th series), 1997–	*R. v. Burk* (1999), 28 C.R. (5th) 149
D.L.R.	*Dominion Law Reports*, 1912–1922	*R. v. Dalke* (1915), 27 D.L.R. 633
[ ] D.L.R.	*Dominion Law Reports*, 1932–1955	*R v. Marchello*, [1951] 4 D.L.R. 751
D.L.R. (2d)	*Dominion Law Reports* (2nd series), 1956–1968	*R. v. Howson* (1966), 55 D.L.R. (2d) 582
D.L.R. (3d)	*Dominion Law Reports* (3rd series), 1969–1983	*R. v. Henni* (1971), 18 D.L.R. (3d) 320
D.L.R. (4th)	*Dominion Law Reports* (4th series), 1984–	*Sansregret v. The Queen* (1985), 17 D.L.R. (4th) 577
[ ] S.C.R.	*Supreme Court Reports*, 1923–1969	*R. v. George*, [1960] S.C.R. 871
[ ] S.C.R.	*Supreme Court Reports*, 1970–	*R. v. Stone*, [1999] 2 S.C.R. 270
[ ] W.W.R.	*Western Weekly Reports*, 1911–1950	*R. v. Anderson*, [1920] 1 W.W.R. 609
W.W.R.	*Western Weekly Reports* (new series), 1951–1970	*R. v. Roher* (1953), 10 W.W.R. 309
[ ] W.W.R.	*Western Weekly Reports* (current series), 1971–	*R.v. Kelly*, [1992] 4 W.W.R. 640
II. ENGLISH LAW REPORTS		
All E.R.	*All England Law Reports*, 1936–	*D.P.P. v. Morgan*, [1975] 2 All E.R. 347
Cr. App. R.	*Criminal Appeal Reports*, 1908–	*R. v. Sanderson* (1994), 98 Cr. App. R. 325
A.C.	*Law Reports, Appeal Cases*, 1891–	*R. v. R.*, [1992] 1 A.C. 599
K.B. (Q.B.)	*Law Reports, King's/Queen's Bench*, 1891–	*R. v. Quick*, [1973] Q.B. 910
W.L.R.	*Weekly Law Reports*, 1953 –	*R. v. Miller*, [1983] 2 W.L.R. 539

More detailed information may be found at <http://www.qsilver.queensu.ca/law/lrm/lawreports.htm>.

Using the Internet to Expand Your Knowledge of the Criminal Law and to Conduct Basic Legal Research

INTRODUCTION

The advent of the Internet has placed an immensely powerful research tool in the hands of those students who are able to gain access to its resources. Even if you do not have access through your own computer, you may readily obtain it through terminals in university or college computing laboratories or in your public library. By visiting relevant Web sites, you may gain further information about every legal topic discussed in this textbook, including the specific text of legislation (e.g., the *Criminal Code*) and cases decided in the courts (e.g., all recent Supreme Court of Canada decisions). This Appendix is designed to provide you with some basic navigational guides to the exploration of those Web sites that may help you to expand your knowledge of criminal law in Canada.

GENERAL CANADIAN WEB SITES THAT CONTAIN LINKS TO A VARIETY OF LEGAL RESOURCES

If you are a relative newcomer to the legal resources available on the Internet, you should probably start with Web sites that gather together automatic links to a broad range of relevant resources (you merely click on the specific resources that are highlighted and you will immediately be connected to the relevant database).

Access to Justice Network
<http://www.acjnet.org/acjeng.html>
It is suggested that one of your first visits should be to the Access to Justice Network. This extraordinarily useful Web site contains instant links to various sites providing information about Canadian law and justice resource materials. In particular, it provides direct access to the text of legislation enacted by the Parliament of Canada and by the various provincial and territorial legislatures. The Web site also makes available the text of judicial decisions made by the Supreme Court of Canada and the Federal Court of Canada, as well as to the text of judicial decisions made by certain of the courts of the various provinces and territories. This Web site also contains links to the federal and provincial/territorial Hansard (which provides information about the proceedings of the Canadian Parliament and the provincial/territorial legislatures).

The National Library of Canada – Canadian Information by Subject [34 LAW]
<http://www.nlc-bnc.ca/caninfo/ep034.htm>
This is an extraordinarily valuable Web site. It enables you to click onto a variety of specific sites that provide a cornucopia of information about law. For example, there are links to Web sites about the Constitution (342); Civil Rights (342.085); Criminal Law (345); Legislation (348); Law – Canada (349.71); Law – British Columbia (349.711), and Law – Ontario (349.713), etc.

Best Guide to Canadian Legal Research

<http://www.legalresearch.org>

This valuable site provides instant access to a broad range of legal research resources both for Canada and other jurisdictions, such as the United States, United Kingdom, Australia, European Union, and for international law. It is extremely valuable as an introduction to legal research, particularly electronic research. It also provides direct links with other research tools.

LEXUM (University of Montréal, Faculty of Law)

<http://www.lexum.umontreal.ca>

This Web site provides information about various legal resources relating to Canada (and specifically to Québec), and also furnishes access to resources that are relevant to the study of international law.

Jurist Canada: The Legal Education Network

<http://jurist.law.utoronto.ca>

This Web site provides access to on-line articles about law and links to the specific Web sites of various Canadian law journals. It also enables you to search for legal subjects that have been discussed in on-line articles, etc.

Continuing Legal Education Society of British Columbia

<http://www.cle.bc.ca/links/pages/index.html>

This Web site contains several hundred links to various Web sites dealing with law and legal resources.

Duhaime's Canadian Criminal Law Centre

<http://www.wwlia.org/cacrhome.html>

This Web site provides access to a range of "Plain Language Canadian Criminal Law Articles," "Federal Criminal Justice Laws," and "Provincial Resources." You may also explore the related World Wide Legal Information Association Home Page, which provides information about legal issues in the United States, Canada, Australia, New Zealand, and the United Kingdom: <http://www.wwlia.org/wwlia.htm>.

Canadian Legal Resources

<http://www.gahtan.com/cdnlaw>

This Web site provides a comprehensive guide to Canadian legal resources available on the Internet and contains more than 1100 links.

SPECIALIZED CANADIAN WEB SITES RELEVANT TO LAW (PARTICULARLY CRIMINAL LAW)

There is a considerable number of specialized Web sites that will provide you with immensely valuable information and research tools that address specific legal topics. This Appendix will provide you with an overview of some of these specialized sites, although it is important to remember that new sites are constantly being added, and existing sites are frequently modified (and, occasionally, eliminated).

Parliament of Canada

<http://www.parl.gc.ca>

This is an essential Web site for gaining an understanding of the contemporary functioning of the Parliament of Canada. For example, you may gain access to the text of bills that are currently being considered by the House of Commons and the Senate.

Government of Canada

<http://www.canada.gc.ca/main – e.html>

The "Government of Canada Primary Internet Site" permits direct access to general information about Canada, its government, and various programs and services provided by the government. For example, this site provides access to the text of the *Canada Gazette*, which contains official information about regulations passed under the authority of federal statutes.

Department of Justice Canada

<http://www.canada.justice.gc.ca>

The Department of Justice plays a central role in the process of federal law reform (in particular, the *Criminal Code* and other criminal law statutes). It drafts legislation and assists in the process of developing policies that guide the operation of Canada's justice system. For example, in 2000, the department played a key role in developing proposed new legislation to deal with youth criminal justice. The department is also responsible for the prosecution of offences under all federal laws other than the *Criminal Code* (including drug offences). In the territories, the department also conducts prosecutions under the *Criminal Code.*

Connecting to this Web site will provide you with access to such valuable documents as *Canada's System of Justice; Canada's Court System; Laws of Canada* (which includes access to all major federal laws); and *A Guide to the Making of Federal Acts and Regulations.* All of these documents will provide you with critical information about the criminal law and the criminal court system in Canada. In addition, as new legislation is developed and submitted to Parliament, relevant information will be available through this Web site (for example, in 2000, the Web site provided extensive information about proposed youth justice legislation under the title "Canada's Youth Criminal Justice Act").

An important component of the site is the *Consolidated Statutes of Canada*, which provides you with access to the text of all federal statutes.

The Supreme Court of Canada
<http://www.scc-csc.gc.ca>
This is the official Web site of the Supreme Court of Canada. It provides valuable background information about the Court and includes valuable links to related Web sites.

The Supreme Court of Canada Law Reports
<http://www.lexum.umontreal.ca/csc-scc/en/index.html>
This invaluable Web site gives you instant access to the complete reports of all Supreme Court of Canada decisions (starting in 1989). This is a site that you should check frequently in order to keep abreast of the very latest Supreme Court of Canada judgments.

The Federal Court of Canada
<http://www.fja.gc.ca>
This is the official Web site of the Federal Court of Canada. Although the Federal Court does not directly adjudicate issues of criminal law, it does make decisions that affect, for example, the functioning of such federal organizations as the Correctional Service of Canada.

Department of the Solicitor General of Canada
<http://www.sgc.gc.ca>
This is the official Web site of the federal Department of the Solicitor General. It provides information about issues falling within the department's range of responsibilities: corrections, Canadian Security and Intelligence Service (CSIS), policing and law enforcement, Aboriginal policing.

Law Commission of Canada
<http://www.lcc.gc.ca>
This Web site provides information about the activities of the Law Commission of Canada, which is an independent agency of law reform that is responsible to the Canadian Parliament.

Statistics Canada (Information About Justice and Crime)
<http://www.statcan.ca/english/Pgdb/State/justic.htm>
This Web site contains valuable statistical information about crimes, victims, suspects and criminals, the police, and the courts.

The Canadian Bar Association
<http://www.cba.org/home.asp>
This Web site constitutes the information service of the Canadian Bar Association. It provides valuable updates about important legal developments in Canada.

Courts of the Provinces and Territories

Many of the provincial and territorial courts in Canada have established their own Web sites. For example, you may find that the following sites contain useful information in relation to your own province or territory:

British Columbia
<http://www.courts.gov.bc.ca>
The British Columbia courts Web site is one of the most valuable, since it not only provides access to the reasons for judgment for cases decided since 1996, but also includes a "Legal Compendium" that explains many aspects of the legal system in the Province of British Columbia.

Alberta
<http://www.albertacourts.ab.ca>

Ontario
<http://www.ontariocourts.on.ca>
Court of Appeal for Ontario
<http://www.ontariocourts.on.ca/appeal.htm>
Ontario Superior Court of Justice
<http://www.ontariocourts.on.ca/scj.htm>

Québec
<http://www.gouv.qc.ca>
On entering the Government of Québec's Web site, click "Courts."

Prince Edward Island
<http://www.gov.pe.ca/courts>
Click onto specific sites for the Supreme and Provincial Courts of Prince Edward Island.

Newfoundland
Supreme Court, Trial Division
<http://www.gov.nf.ca/just/lawcourt/trial.htm>
Supreme Court, Court of Appeal
<http://www.gov.nf.ca/just/lawcourt/appeal.htm>
Provincial Court
<http://www.gov.nf.ca/just/lawcourt/prov.htm>

LEGISLATURES OF THE PROVINCES AND TERRITORIES

By visiting the Web sites of the various provinces and territories, you may gain access to information about the regulatory legislation that constitutes a

significant part of the "quasi-criminal law" discussed in the textbook.

British Columbia
<http://www.legis.gov.bc.ca>

Alberta
<http://www.assembly.ab.ca>

Saskatchewan
<http://www.legassembly.sk.ca>

Manitoba
<http://www.gov.mb.ca/leg-asmb/index.html>

Ontario
<http://www.ontla.on.ca>

Québec
<http://www.assnat.qc.ca/eng/indexne2.html>

Nova Scotia
<http://www.gov.ns.ca/legi>

New Brunswick
<http://www.gov.nb.ca/legis/index.htm>

Prince Edward Island
<http://www.gov.pe.ca/leg/index.php3>

Newfoundland
<http://www.gov.nf.ca/hoa>

Nunavut
<http://www.assembly.nu.ca/english/index.html>

Northwest Territories
<http://www.assembly.gov.nt.ca>

Yukon
<http://www.gov.yk.ca/legassem.html>

GOVERNMENTS OF THE PROVINCES AND TERRITORIES

Each province and territory in Canada maintains an official Web site. You may gain valuable information about governmental initiatives in the area of criminal justice by visiting the following sites:

British Columbia
<http://www.gov.bc.ca>

Alberta
<http://www.gov.ab.ca/index.cfm>

Saskatchewan
<http://www.gov.sk.ca/default.htm>

Manitoba
<http://www.gov.mb.ca>

Ontario
<http://www.gov.on.ca>

Québec
<http://www.gouv.qc.ca>

Nova Scotia
<http://www.gov.ns.ca>

New Brunswick
<http://www.gov.nb.ca>

Prince Edward Island
<http://www.gov.pe.ca>

Newfoundland
<http://www.gov.nf.ca>

Nunavut
<http://www.gov.nu.ca>

Northwest Territories
<http://www.gov.nt.ca>

Yukon
<http://www.gov.yk.ca>

Note that, in most provinces and territories, the Department or Ministry of the Attorney General is responsible for the administration of criminal justice and it may be worthwhile to explore whether this department or ministry has its own Web site (see, for example, <http://www.attorneygeneral.jus.gov.on.ca> (Ontario) and <http://www.gov.bc.ca/ag> (British Columbia)).

SIGNIFICANT WEB SITES RELATING TO THE LAW AND LEGAL INSTITUTIONS OF THE UNITED KINGDOM, AUSTRALIA, AND THE UNITED STATES

As you will gather from reading this textbook, the criminal law of countries such as England and Wales, Australia, and the United States has exerted a fair degree of influence on the evolution of Canadian criminal law. It is, therefore, useful to keep abreast of developments in these jurisdictions, since many of the criminal law issues that are currently being addressed in Canada are also subject to legislative and judicial intervention in other countries. Undoubtedly, the experience of other jurisdictions constitutes a valuable resource for those readers who may wish to subject Canadian criminal law to a critical analysis and evaluation. The following is a very brief list of relevant Web sites:

The United Kingdom
The United Kingdom Parliament
<http://www.parliament.uk>
Government of the United Kingdom
<http://www.open.gov.uk> and
<http://www.cabinet-office.gov.uk>

Australia
Parliament of Australia
<http://www.aph.gov.au>
The High Court of Australia
<http://www.hcourt.gov.au>

The United States of America
The United States Senate
<http://www.senate.gov>

The United States House of Representatives
<http://www.house.gov>

The White House
<http://www.whitehouse.gov>

The Supreme Court of The United States
<http://www.supremecourtus.gov>

United States Sentencing Commission
<http://www.ussc.gov>

The United States Justice Information Centre:
NCJRS
<http://www.ncjrs.org>
This impressive Web site, operated by the National Criminal Justice Reference Service (NCJRS), provides voluminous information about crime and criminal justice in the United States. There is a specific component of the site that is dedicated to the criminal courts.

INTERNATIONAL WEB SITES

The United Nations

<http://www.un.org>
This is the official site of the United Nations and provides access to information about, *inter alia*, international law and human rights.

Web Sites of International Courts

Although this textbook does not deal with the jurisdiction and functioning of international courts, you may wish to explore some of valuable Web sites that have been established by such courts. Some of the courts have no direct role in the development of international criminal law, while others clearly do. There follows a short list of the Web sites of some of the most significant international tribunals.

The (Proposed) International Criminal Court
<http://www.igc.org/icc> and
<http://www.iccnow.org>
These Web sites provide information about the future International Criminal Court, which, if established, would try individuals accused of committing genocide, war crimes, and crimes against humanity. This court will be established after 60 countries ratify the *Rome Statute of the International Criminal Court.*

International Criminal Tribunal for the Former Yugoslavia
<http://www.un.org/icty>
This Web site provides access to the decisions made by the International Criminal Court that is charged with the trial of defendants charged with having committed war crimes in the former Yugoslavia. The court is located in The Hague, Netherlands.

The International Court of Justice
<http://www.icj-cij.org>
This is the Web site for the International Court of Justice, which is located in The Hague, Netherlands. It is the principal judicial organ of the United Nations.

The European Court of Human Rights
<http://www.echr.coe.int>
This is the official Web site of the European Court of Human Rights, which is located in Strasbourg. It provides access to information about the *European Convention on Human Rights*, the nature and function of the court, and the judgments and decisions of the court.

The European Court of Justice
<http://curia.eu.int>
This is the official site of the European Court of Justice, which is the judicial organ of the European Community and is located in Luxembourg.

COMMERCIAL ELECTRONIC DATABASE SERVICES

There are a number of commercial electronic database services that provide immensely powerful legal research tools. You may research specific legal topics in these databases and obtain detailed information concerning the applicable legislation and case, as well as the relevant legal literature (law journal articles, etc.). These automated search tools are extremely effective and will save you a considerable amount of time and effort in your research endeavours. However, unless you obtain authorized access to these databases through a university or college library or similar institution, you will normally be required to establish an account with the service providers concerned, and charges will be levied for use of the relevant electronic research facilities.

The leading databases for Canada are Quicklaw, *e*Carswell and SOQUIJ (for Québec law). For the United States, the primary databases are Westlaw and LEXIS-NEXIS.

Quicklaw, for example, provides immediate access to some 1100 databases and bulletin boards of law (as of September 1999). There are seventeen databases that are exclusively devoted to the topic of criminal law.

You may obtain information about these electronic databases (including instructions on how to subscribe to their services) by visiting their Web sites. The addresses are as follows:

Quicklaw
<http://www.quicklaw.com>

***e*Carswell**
<http://www.carswell.com>

SOQUIJ
<http://www.soquij.qc.ca>

LEXIS-NEXIS
<http://lexis-nexis.com>

Westlaw
<http://www.westlaw.com>

GLOSSARY

Absolute liability: This form of liability may be imposed in relation to the less serious types of offences arising under regulatory legislation (either federal or provincial). The Crown may obtain a conviction for a violation of such legislation without having to prove *mens rea* on the part of accused persons, who are denied a defence even if they can prove that there was no negligence on their part. Absolute liability may not be imposed, as a general rule, where there is the potential penalty of imprisonment upon conviction for the regulatory offence concerned.

Accessory: An individual who is involved in the commission of a crime in a secondary capacity. An accessory after the fact is a person who, knowing that an individual has been a party to a criminal offence, gives the latter comfort or assistance with the intention of enabling him or her to escape justice.

Accused: The accused is the person against whom a criminal charge has been laid.

Acquittal: An official discharge from prosecution, usually after a verdict of not guilty.

***Actus reus*:** This term can only be understood in light of the concept of *mens rea* (see *infra*). *Mens rea* refers to the various mental elements (other than voluntariness) that are contained in the definition of a particular criminal offence. *Actus reus* refers to all the other elements of the offence that must be proved (including voluntariness) before an accused person may be convicted of the particular offence in question.

***Agent provocateur*:** An individual (usually an undercover police officer or paid informer) who, for law enforcement purposes, associates with members of a group in order to incite them to commit an offence.

Antisocial personality disorder: According to the *Diagnostic and Statistical Manual of Mental Disorders* (1994), the essential feature of this form of personality disorder is a "pervasive pattern of disregard for, and violation of, the rights of others that begins in childhood or early adolescence and continues into adulthood." Such conduct frequently brings an individual affected by this disorder into conflict with criminal justice authorities.

Appeal: A formal proceeding by means of which the Crown or the accused may request a review of a decision by a "higher court." For example, the provincial court of appeal is a higher court than the superior court of criminal jurisdiction or the provincial court, whereas the Supreme Court of Canada is, in turn, a higher court than the court of appeal.

Appellant: The party who appeals from the decision of a "lower court." In Canada, either the Crown (the prosecution) or the accused may appeal such a decision (in accordance with certain limitations defined in the *Criminal Code*).

Automatism: A state of impaired consciousness that renders a person incapable of controlling his or her behaviour while in that state. A person in such a state cannot be said to be acting voluntarily and, therefore, cannot be held criminally responsible for his or her conduct.

Bigamy: The offence of bigamy is committed when a person goes through a form of marriage while still married to another person; goes through a form of marriage with another person knowing that this other person is still married to someone else; or goes through a form of marriage with more than one other person simultaneously (section 290 of the Code).

Blackmail: See Extortion, *infra*.

Bona fide: In good faith. That is to say, a party has acted without any dishonesty or fraud.

Burden (or onus) of proof: This indicates which party is responsible for proving certain facts in a trial. Since the Crown is asserting, in a criminal trial, that the accused has committed an offence, the *primary* or *persuasional* burden of proof is normally on the Crown to establish that the accused did indeed commit the offence with which he or she has been charged. The *standard of proof* that must be met by the Crown is that of "beyond a reasonable doubt." In the rare cases where the accused is placed under the burden of proof to establish a particular fact (e.g., that he or she was not criminally responsible because of mental disorder or was in a state of automatism), the standard of proof is that of "on the balance of probabilities."

There is also an *evidentiary* or *secondary burden of proof* that refers primarily to the requirement that, before a defence (such as mistake of fact) may be put to the trier of fact, the trial judge must be satisfied that the accused has introduced sufficient evidence to give an "air of reality" to the defence. This burden of proof merely requires that the accused introduce some evidence capable of raising a reasonable doubt as to the issue in question. The burden placed on the accused in such circumstances is a light one and is primarily designed to prevent him or her from raising totally speculative defences that have no support in any of the evidence presented to the court. Once the defence is put to the trier of fact, the Crown must prove beyond a reasonable doubt that it does not apply (e.g., that the accused was not operating under a mistake of fact).

Capping: This term refers to the *Criminal Code* provision (section 672.64) that is designed to set an upper limit on the length of time that a person who

has been found to be NCRMD can be held in a mental health facility or placed under conditions once he or she has been released from custody. However, section 672.64 has not yet been proclaimed into force.

Circumstantial evidence: Evidence of a series of circumstances that may lead the trier of fact to draw an *inference* of guilt when no direct evidence is available (evidence is "direct" when a witness testifies as to what he or she actually observed by sight, hearing, etc.).

Civil law: This term must be distinguished from the concept of a civil law system (see *infra*). The term "civil law" primarily refers to the body of laws that deals with the relationships between private citizens. For example, an individual citizen may bring a legal action for compensation on the basis that his or her neighbour's negligence has caused some degree of harm. The goal of the civil law action is solely to compensate the citizen for the loss caused by the neighbour. In contrast, the *criminal* law is primarily concerned with punishing a convicted person for the wrong done to the state by the latter's misconduct. The criminal law trial is a proceeding between the Crown and the accused, whereas the civil law action initiates a proceeding between private citizens.

Civil law system: This term (distinguished from Civil law, *supra*) refers to a legal system based on the approach of Roman law and usually characterized by the existence of a comprehensive code. This system of law is predominant in continental Europe, Scotland, and (as far as the civil law is concerned) in the province of Québec.

Code: A code is a collection or system of laws. In a civil law system, a code would ideally be a complete system of law, logically arranged according to basic principles and promulgated by the appropriate legislative authority. The origins of the civil law system are to be found in the collection of laws made by the Roman Emperor Justinian, and referred to as "The Code." In France, for example, the *Code Civil* (originally promulgated in 1804 and at one time known as the *Code Napoléon*), contains the civil law of that country.

Cognitive: Relating to a person's knowledge and reasoning abilities as opposed to the emotional factors that may influence his or her behaviour.

Colour of right: Accused persons acting on an honest, albeit mistaken, belief that they have a valid legal right are considered to be a*cting under colour of right*. In certain circumstances, such persons may have a defence to a criminal charge. For example, they may have a valid defence to a charge of theft where they honestly believe that they have a valid right to the property in question, even though it subsequently turns out that this right is not recognized by a court of law.

Complainant: One who makes a complaint to the authorities that he or she has been the victim of a criminal offence.

Common law: This term refers to that body of judge-made law that has evolved in areas that are not covered by legislation. For example, necessity is a "common law defence" because it has been developed by judges and is not defined in the *Criminal Code*.

Common law system: This term refers to a system of law that is based primarily on decisions made by judges. The common law system is predominant in England and Wales, the Canadian provinces and territories (with the exception of Québec), the American states (with the exception of Louisiana), Australia, and New Zealand.

Constitutional exemption: A potential remedy under the *Charter*. Instead of declaring a provision of the *Criminal Code* invalid, a court may rule that it is only unconstitutional in its application to a particular individual in exceptional circumstances. For example, in the *Latimer* case (1998), the accused was found guilty of second degree murder as a consequence of an act of so-called "mercy killing." Section 745 of the *Criminal Code* prescribes a mandatory sentence of life imprisonment (with no eligibility for parole for at least ten years) for second degree murder. The trial judge recognized that the Supreme Court of Canada had ruled that section 745 does not constitute "cruel and unusual punishment," contrary to the requirements of section 12 of the *Charter*. However, he

ruled that life imprisonment *in Latimer's very unusual circumstances* would be "grossly disproportionate" (hence, "cruel and unusual punishment," within the meaning of section 12 of the *Charter*) and he granted Latimer a constitutional exemption from the imposition of the mandatory sentence. Instead, Latimer was sentenced to one year in prison, followed by a one-year period of probation. The Saskatchewan Court of Appeal later ruled that Latimer was not entitled to a constitutional exemption and sentenced him to life imprisonment without eligibility for parole for ten years. The Supreme Court of Canada upheld the decsion of the Court of Appeal in *Latimer* (2001).

Constructive murder: In certain circumstances (such as killing someone in the course of committing a serious offence), it was possible to convict an accused person of murder under the provisions of the *Criminal Code* even though that person did not intend to kill or even if he or she did not subjectively foresee the likelihood of death ensuing from his or her conduct. Those provisions of the Code that impose liability for constructive murder (section 230 and part of section 229(c)) have been declared invalid under the *Charter*; see the decision of the Supreme Court of Canada in the *Martineau* case (1990).

Contempt of court: Under section 9 of the Code, courts have the power to convict a person of criminal contempt of court. The term "criminal contempt" covers any wilful conduct on the part of the accused that tends to interfere with the proper administration of justice or to bring it into disrepute. It includes, but is not limited to, the deliberate defiance or disobedience of a court order in a public manner.

Counsel: A general term that was originally applied to practising barristers in the English courts. In Canada, the term refers to the lawyer representing a party in a trial. In criminal cases, Crown counsel represents the Queen (that is to say, he or she is the prosecuting lawyer), whereas defence counsel represents the accused.

De facto: In fact.

Defendant: In a criminal trial, the defendant is the person against whom a criminal charge has been laid and who is, therefore, placed in the position of defending him or herself against such a charge.

Direct intention: This concept refers to the situation where an accused person engages in conduct with the unequivocal desire to bring about the consequence(s) prohibited by the criminal law.

Double jeopardy: This refers to the ancient doctrine of the criminal law that accused persons may not be placed twice in jeopardy for the same incident. Therefore, if they are charged again in relation to this incident, they may plead their previous conviction or acquittal as a complete defence to the second charge. The special pleas in question are known as *autrefois convict* and *autrefois acquit*.

Entrapment: This occurs where law enforcement authorities (usually through the agency of undercover officers or paid informers) instigate others to commit criminal offences (primarily those offences involving the sale of illegal drugs) for the purpose of prosecuting them. Although the police are entitled to use undercover methods of investigation, they are not entitled to persuade an individual to commit an offence that he or she would not have committed but for their persistent pressure to do so. If entrapment of this type takes place, an accused person may be granted a *stay of proceedings* (a direction by the court that criminal proceedings be suspended).

Euthanasia: The deliberate use of a painless method of causing death in order to end the suffering of another person.

Evidentiary burden of proof: See Burden (or onus) of proof, *supra*.

Extortion: A person commits the offence of extortion (section 346 of the Code) where he or she, without reasonable justification or excuse and with the intent of obtaining "anything" (e.g., money or property), induces or attempts to induce another person to "do anything or cause anything to be done" by means of "threats, accusations, menaces or violence." In popular terminology, this offence may sometimes be called blackmail.

First degree murder: Section 231 of the Code indicates the circumstances in which murder will be considered first degree, as opposed to second degree, murder. In general, first degree murder is murder that is planned and deliberate. There are also certain exceptional circumstances in which a murder will automatically be classified as first degree murder, whether or not it is planned and deliberate (e.g., murder of a police officer or murder committed in the course of a sexual assault). The penalty for first degree murder is life imprisonment with no eligibility for parole for 25 years.

General (or basic) intent: According to Justice McIntyre in the *Bernard* case (1988), a general intent offence "is one in which the only intent involved relates solely to the performance of the act in question with no further ulterior intent or purpose." Examples of such offences are assault (section 265 of the Code) and mischief, such as destruction or damage of property (section 430).

Half-way house: See Strict liability, *infra*.

Inchoate offences: The criminal law does not punish individuals for thinking about committing a crime, but once they start on a course of conduct designed to achieve a criminal goal, they may, in certain circumstances, be convicted of an offence even though that goal is never achieved. These offences are known as inchoate because the accused persons concerned do not complete the crimes that they originally had in mind. The three inchoate offences recognized in Canadian criminal law are (i) attempt, (ii) conspiracy, and (iii) counselling an offence which is not committed.

Indictable: Indictable offences are, generally, the most serious criminal offences. Furthermore, those indictable offences that are considered to be particularly serious in nature may only be tried in the superior court of criminal jurisdiction. An *indictment* (from which the indictable offence takes its name) is a formal document that sets out the charge(s) against the accused and is signed by the Attorney-General or his or her agent.

Infra: Below.

Indirect intention: This concept refers to the situation in which an accused person does *not* desire to bring about the consequences prohibited by the criminal law but is nevertheless considered to have intended them.

Infanticide: According to section 233 of the *Criminal Code,* "a female person commits infanticide when by a wilful act or omission she causes the death of her newly born child, if at the time of the act or omission she is not fully recovered from the effects of giving birth to the child and by reason thereof or of the effect of lactation consequent on the birth of the child her mind is then disturbed." In section 2 of the Code, a "newly born child" is defined as "a person under the age of one year." The maximum sentence on conviction is five years' imprisonment.

Intention: According to Justice Dickson in the *Lewis* case (1979), intention means "the exercise of a free will to use particular means to produce a particular result."

Inter alia: Among others.

Intra: Within; inside.

Intra vires: Within the power of.

Manslaughter: Generally, this offence involves the commission of an unintentional homicide. The *mens rea* for the offence is generally objective in nature: either the Crown must establish that the accused's conduct amounted to a "marked and substantial departure from the standard of care expected of a reasonable person acting prudently" (manslaughter by criminal negligence) or that the accused killed the victim in the course of committing an offence (such as an assault) that a "reasonable person would have foreseen as being likely to cause bodily harm" (unlawful act manslaughter). The successful use of the defence of provocation (section 232 of the Code) may result in an accused being convicted of manslaughter rather than murder, even though he or she intended to kill the victim; this is an exception to the general rule that manslaughter involves the commission of an unintentional homicide.

Mens rea: This concept refers to those mental elements (other than voluntariness) contained in the definition of any particular criminal offence that the Crown must must prove before an accused person may be convicted of that offence.

Mental disorder: According to section 2 of the Code, this means "a disease of the mind." The Supreme Court of Canada approved the following definition in the *Rabey* case (1981): "Any malfunctioning of the mind having its source primarily in some subjective condition or weakness *internal to the accused* (whether fully understood or not) may be a "disease of the mind" if it prevents the accused from knowing what he is doing, but transient disturbances of consciousness due to specific *external factors* do not fall within the concept of disease of the mind." [emphasis added] The Supreme Court of Canada provided a more complex definition in the *Stone* case (1999): this distinction is applicable in the context of determining whether the correct defence is automatism or NCRMD. See chapter 2.

Motive: The reason for, or explanation of, a person's conduct. Generally, the *mens rea* requirements for conviction of criminal offences do not include any reference to the accused's motive. For example, a person may intend to kill another human being, and thereby commit the crime of murder, even though some people might consider that there is a laudable motive for killing the victim (e.g., "mercy killing").

Murder: This offence involves the commission of a homicide by a person who *intends* to kill his or her victim or who *subjectively* foresees that his or her conduct is likely to cause death. Section 229 of the Code indicates that murder is committed where (i) the accused intends to kill; (ii) the accused intends to inflict bodily harm that he or she knows is likely to cause death and is reckless whether death ensues or not; or (iii) the accused, for an unlawful object, does anything that he or she subjectively knows is likely to cause death and does thereby cause death notwithstanding that he or she wishes to achieve the unlawful object without causing death or bodily harm. (In this context, unlawful object refers to "the object of conduct, which, if prosecuted fully, would amount to a serious crime that is an indictable offence requiring *mens rea*.) There are two categories of this offence: first degree murder and second degree murder.

NCRMD: This is the common abbreviation of the verdict of "not criminally responsible on account of mental disorder" (section 672.34 of the Code). In order to be found NCRMD, the accused must prove that the criteria, established in section 16(1) of the Code, have been met.

Negligence: Negligence is a form of objective *mens rea*. A person is negligent when his or her conduct falls below the standard of care expected of a reasonable person acting prudently. Negligence may be a sufficient form of *mens rea* to convict an accused person of certain *Criminal Code* offences, but only if that person's conduct amounts to a marked and substantial departure from the standard of care expected of a reasonable person facing the same circumstances as the accused. Only the most serious incidents of negligence will justify the accused's conviction of a true crime; such negligence may be called criminal (or penal) negligence.

Objective *mens rea*: Offences requiring proof of objective *mens rea* impose on the Crown the burden of establishing that a reasonable person would have appreciated the risk created by the accused's conduct and would have chosen not to take that risk. Objective *mens rea* is not concerned with what actually went on in the accused's mind at the time of the alleged offence, but rather with what the reasonable person would have known if placed in exactly the same circumstances as the accused. The fault of the accused lies in the failure to direct his or her mind to a risk the reasonable person would have appreciated.

Partial defence: Some defences operate to reduce the *severity* of the charge, of which the accused is ultimately convicted, instead of absolving the accused of all criminal responsibility whatsoever. For example, a successful plea of provocation merely reduces the charge of which the accused is convicted from one of murder to one of manslaughter. By way of contrast, if the accused successfully argues self-defence under section 34(2) of the Code, he or she is entitled to be absolved of all criminal responsibility; in this sense, self-defence is a *complete defence*.

***Per se*:** In or of itself.

Personality disorder: A form of mental disorder in which the affected individual maintains a "good grip on reality" but whose behaviour and ways of thinking about his or her environment are considered as abnormal or deviant. In the context of criminal responsibility, the most relevant of these disorders is the *antisocial personality disorder*.

Persuasional burden of proof: See Burden (or onus) of proof, *supra*.

Precedent: A previous decision or judgment of a court that is referred to as an authority that should be followed by a judge in a similar factual situation.

***Prima facie*:** At first sight; on the face of it. A *prima facie* case is literally one that will suffice until contradicted and overcome by other evidence.

Primary burden of proof: See Burden (or onus) of proof, *supra*.

Principal: This refers to the person who "actually commits" a criminal offence as opposed to those individuals who become parties to the offence on some other basis (such as aiding and abetting).

Psychopath: An individual who shares many of the characteristics of those individuals who suffer from antisocial personality disorder. Although there is considerable debate as to the precise nature of psychopathy, psychopaths may be characterized by a lack of sound judgment, an inability to learn from previous experience, a lack of remorse or guilt for anything that they do in violation of the rights of others, and a lack of capacity to understand how others see them. However, a psychopath does not lose contact with reality in the sense that a person suffering from schizophrenia may do.

Psychosis: A mental disorder that is characterized by profound disturbances in a person's thoughts, emotions, and ability to perceive reality (e.g., schizophrenia).

Quasi: Seeming, not real, half-way, almost as if it were, analogous to.

Quasi-criminal law: Refers to regulatory offences as opposed to true crimes.

Rape shield law: This term refers to provisions of the *Criminal Code* that limit the extent to which accused persons in sexual assault trials can question complainants about their sexual history (sections 276–277).

Re: In the matter of; with reference to.

Recklessness: This is a form of subjective *mens rea*. It arises where the accused subjectively knows that his or her conduct creates a risk that certain prohibited consequences will occur but nevertheless persists in that course of conduct when a reasonable person would not do so.

Regulatory offence: This is an offence arising under regulatory legislation (either federal, provincial, territorial, or municipal). Such legislation deals with the regulation of *inherently legitimate activities* connected with commerce, trade, and industry or with such everyday matters as driving, hunting, fishing, etc. Regulatory offences are, generally, not considered to be serious in nature and usually result in the imposition of only a relatively minor penalty.

Respondent: Literally, this is the party who "responds" when an appeal is launched against the decision of a lower court by the other party to a criminal case (who is known, formally, as the appellant).

Review board: The board that has been established in each province (under Part XX.1 of the *Criminal Code*) in order to make or review decisions as to what should happen to those who have been found NCRMD ("not criminally responsible on account of mental disorder").

Second degree murder: Murder that is not first degree murder is *second degree murder* (section 231(7) of the Code). Where an individual is convicted of second degree murder, the automatic penalty is life imprisonment. Section 744 of the Code provides that the trial judge may set a period of noneligibility for parole ranging from a minimum of ten years to a maximum of 25 years.

Secondary burden of proof: See Burden (or onus) of proof, *supra.*

Sociopath: A person with an *antisocial personality disorder* who habitually commits crimes.

Somnambulism: Sleepwalking.

Schizophrenia: Refers to a group of severe mental disorders in which an individual may experience incoherence in thought and speech, hallucinations, delusions, and inappropriate emotional responses.

Specific (or ulterior) intent: According to Justice McIntyre in the case of *Bernard* (1988), a specific intent offence is "one which involves the performance of the *actus reus*, coupled with an intent or purpose going beyond the mere performance of the questioned act." Examples are assault *with intent to wound* (section 244 of the Code) and breaking and entering *with intent to commit an indictable offence* (section 349(1)(a)).

Standard of proof: See Burden (or onus) of proof, *supra.*

Strict liability: This form of liability may be imposed in relation to various regulatory offences arising under both federal and provincial regulatory legislation. The Crown may obtain a conviction for a violation of such legislation without having to prove *mens rea* on the part of the accused. However, the accused may avoid liability by proving that he or she acted with "due diligence" in all the circumstances. Strict liability is sometimes referred to as the "half-way house solution" to the problem of finding an efficacious, yet fair, method of prosecuting regulatory offences.

Subjective *mens rea*: Offences that require proof of subjective *mens rea* impose on the Crown the burden of establishing either that the accused *intended* the consequences of his or her conduct or that, *knowing* of the probable consequences of such conduct, the accused proceeded in *reckless* disregard of that risk. Subjective *mens rea* is concerned with what actually went on in the accused's mind.

Supra: Above.

Transferred intent: Where *A* intends to strike *B* but misses and strikes *C*, he or she may be convicted of assault on the basis of the doctrine of *transferred* *intent. A* intends to commit the *actus reus* of assault but actually commits the *actus reus* of assault in a way other than he or she intended (that is, by striking the "wrong" victim). The *mens rea* for the *actus reus* of the assault that did not happen (the assault of *B*) is transferred to the *actus reus* of the assault that did occur (the assault of *C*). The doctrine applies to a number of offences (such as murder and the various types of assault in the *Criminal Code*), but it only operates within the confines of the same offence. For example, an intention to wound an animal cannot be transferred to the *actus reus* of assault of a human being, where the accused aims to strike a dog but instead strikes a person.

Trier of fact: The party responsible for deciding the facts in a trial. In the case of a jury trial, the members of the jury are the triers of fact and the judge is responsible for making decisions about the applicable law. Where the trial judge sits without a jury, then he or she is the trier of fact as well as the ultimate arbiter of the law.

True crimes: While regulatory offences are concerned with the regulation of inherently legitimate activities, *true crimes* are offences that represent a serious breach of community values and are considered to be both "wrong" and deserving of punishment. In general, true crimes consist of those offences contained in the *Criminal Code* as well as the serious offences contained in the *Controlled Drugs and Substances Act* and *Food and Drugs Act* (which are generally concerned with the punishment of those who are involved with the use of illegal drugs). The Law Reform Commission of Canada used a similar term to describe such offences, namely, *real crimes.*

Ultra vires: Beyond the powers of.

Voluntariness: This concept refers to the basic requirement of the criminal law that an accused person's conduct be the product of his or her own free will. It is a fundamental requirement of the *actus reus* of an offence: where there is no voluntary action (e.g., because the accused is in a state of automatism), there is no *actus reus* and the accused must be acquitted. In addition, the issue of voluntariness may be particularly relevant to the establishment of certain defences. For example, the assertion that the accused was not able to make a genuinely free choice as to whether or not to break the law may constitute valid grounds for raising the defences of duress or necessity (here, the criminal law makes reference to *normative involuntariness* as the basis for recognizing these defences).

Wilful blindness: This form of subjective *mens rea* exists when an accused person is virtually certain that particular circumstances exist (for example, that goods are stolen) but *deliberately* "shuts his or her eyes" to these circumstances. The Crown must establish that the particular accused person had become subjectively aware of the need to make an inquiry as to the relevant circumstances but deliberately refrains from making the inquiry because he or she does not want to know the truth.

INDEX

READER REPLY CARD

We are interested in your reaction to *Criminal Law in Canada: Cases, Questions, and the Code,* Third Edition, by Simon Verdun-Jones. You can help us to improve this book in future editions by completing this questionnaire.

1. What was your reason for using this book?

   ☐ university course   ☐ college course   ☐ continuing education course
   ☐ professional   ☐ personal   ☐ other _____
      development   interest   _____

2. If you are a student, please identify your school and the course in which you used this book.

3. Which chapters or parts of this book did you use? Which did you omit?

4. What did you like most about this book?

5. What did you like least?

6. Please identify any topics you think should be added to future editions.

7. Please add any comments or suggestions.

8. May we contact you for further information?

   Name: _____

   Address: _____

   _____

   Phone: _____

   E-mail: _____

(fold here and tape shut)

- -

MAIL POSTE
Canada Post Corporation / Société canadienne des postes

Postage paid   **Port payé**
If mailed in Canada   si posté au Canada

Business   **Réponse**
Reply   **d'affaires**

0116870399   01

0116870399-M8Z4X6-BR01

The Publisher
HARCOURT CANADA
55 HORNER AVENUE
TORONTO, ONTARIO
M8Z 9Z9